MySQL High Availability

Charles Bell, Mats Kindahl, and Lars Thalmann

Beijing · Cambridge · Farnham · Köln · Sebastopol · Taipei · Tokyo

MySQL High Availability

by Charles Bell, Mats Kindahl, and Lars Thalmann

Copyright © 2010 Charles Bell, Mats Kindahl, and Lars Thalmann. All rights reserved.
Printed in the United States of America.

Published by O'Reilly Media, Inc., 1005 Gravenstein Highway North, Sebastopol, CA 95472.

O'Reilly books may be purchased for educational, business, or sales promotional use. Online editions
are also available for most titles (*http://my.safaribooksonline.com*). For more information, contact our
corporate/institutional sales department: 800-998-9938 or *corporate@oreilly.com*.

Editor: Andy Oram	**Indexer:** Lucie Haskins
Production Editor: Teresa Elsey	**Cover Designer:** Karen Montgomery
Copyeditor: Amy Thomson	**Interior Designer:** David Futato
Proofreader: Sada Preisch	**Illustrator:** Robert Romano

Printing History:

　　July 2010:　　　　　First Edition.

Nutshell Handbook, the Nutshell Handbook logo, and the O'Reilly logo are registered trademarks of
O'Reilly Media, Inc. *MySQL High Availability*, the image of an American robin, and related trade dress
are trademarks of O'Reilly Media, Inc.

Many of the designations used by manufacturers and sellers to distinguish their products are claimed as
trademarks. Where those designations appear in this book, and O'Reilly Media, Inc., was aware of a
trademark claim, the designations have been printed in caps or initial caps.

While every precaution has been taken in the preparation of this book, the publisher and authors assume
no responsibility for errors or omissions, or for damages resulting from the use of the information contained herein.

ISBN: 978-0-596-80730-6

[M]

1277476942

Table of Contents

Part III.   High Availability Environments

Foreword

A lot of research has been done on replication, but most of the resulting concepts are never put into production. In contrast, MySQL replication is widely deployed but has never been adequately explained. This book changes that. Things are explained here that were previously limited to people willing to read a lot of source code and spend a lot of time debugging it in production, including a few late-night sessions.

Replication enables you to provide highly available data services while enduring the inevitable failures. There are an amazing number of ways for things to fail, including the loss of a disk, server, or data center. Even when hardware is perfect or fully redundant, people are not. Database tables will be dropped by mistake. Applications will write incorrect data. Occasional failure is assured. But with reasonable preparation, recovery from failure can also be assured. The keys to survival are redundancy and backups. Replication in MySQL supports both.

But MySQL replication is not limited to supporting failure recovery. It is frequently used to support read scale-out. MySQL can efficiently replicate to a large number of servers. For applications that are read-mostly, this is a cost-effective strategy for supporting a large number of queries on commodity hardware.

And there are other interesting uses for MySQL replication. Online DDL is a very complex feature to implement in an relational database management system. MySQL does not support online DDL, but through the use of replication you can implement something that is frequently good enough. You can get a lot done with replication if you are willing to be creative.

Replication is one of the features that made MySQL wildly popular. It is also the feature that allows you to convert a popular MySQL prototype into a successful business-critical deployment. Like most of MySQL, replication favors simplicity and ease of use. As a consequence, it is occasionally less than perfect when running in production. This book explains what you need to know to successfully use MySQL replication. It will help you to understand how replication has been implemented, what can go wrong, how to prevent problems, and how to fix them when they crop up despite your best attempts at prevention.

MySQL replication is also a work in progress. Change, like failure, is also assured. MySQL is responding to that change and replication continues to get more efficient, more robust, and more interesting. For instance, row-based replication is new in MySQL 5.1.

While MySQL deployments come in all shapes and sizes, I care most about data services for Internet applications and am excited about the potential to replicate from MySQL to distributed storage systems like HBase and Hadoop. This will make MySQL better at sharing the data center.

I have been on teams that support important MySQL deployments at Facebook and Google. I have had the opportunity, problems, and time to learn much of what is covered in this book. The authors of this book are also experts on MySQL replication, and by reading this book you can share their expertise.

—Mark Callaghan

Preface

The authors of this book have been creating parts of MySQL and working with it for many years. Charles Bell is a senior developer working on replication and backup. His interests include all things MySQL, database theory, software engineering, and agile development practices. Dr. Mats Kindahl is the lead developer for replication and a member of the MySQL Backup and Replication team. He is the main architect and implementor of the MySQL row-based replication and has also developed the unit testing framework used by MySQL. Dr. Lars Thalmann is the development manager and technical lead of the MySQL Replication and Backup team and has designed many of the replication and backup features. He has worked with development of MySQL clustering, replication, and backup technologies.

We wrote this book to fill a gap we noticed among the many books on MySQL. There are many excellent books on MySQL, but few that concentrate on its advanced features and its applications, such as high availability, reliability, and maintainability. In this book, you will find all of these topics and more.

We also wanted to make the reading a bit more interesting by including a running narrative about a MySQL professional who encounters common requests made by his boss. In the narrative, you will meet Joel Thomas, who recently decided to take a job working for a company that has just started using MySQL. You will observe Joel as he learns his way around MySQL and tackles some of the toughest problems facing MySQL professionals. We hope you find this aspect of the book entertaining.

Audience

This book is for MySQL professionals. We expect you to have a basic background in SQL, administering MySQL, and the operating system you are running. We will try to fill in background information about replication, disaster recovery, system monitoring, and other key topics of high availability. See Chapter 1 for other books that offer useful background.

Organization of This Book

This book is written in three parts. Part I encompasses MySQL replication, including high availability and scale-out. Part II examines monitoring and performance concerns for building robust data centers. Part III examines some additional areas of MySQL, including cloud computing and MySQL clusters.

Part I, Replication

Chapter 1, *Introduction*, explains how this book can help you and gives you a context for reading it.

Chapter 2, *MySQL Replication Fundamentals*, discusses both manual and automated procedures for setting up basic replication.

Chapter 3, *The Binary Log*, explains the critical file that ties together replication and helps in disaster recovery, troubleshooting, and other administrative tasks.

Chapter 4, *Replication for High Availability*, shows a number of ways to recover from server failure, including the use of automated scripts.

Chapter 5, *MySQL Replication for Scale-Out*, shows a number of techniques and topologies for improving response time and handling large data sets.

Chapter 6, *Advanced Replication*, addresses a number of topics, such as secure data transfer and row-based replication.

Part II, Monitoring and Disaster Recovery

Chapter 7, *Getting Started with Monitoring*, presents the main operating system parameters you have to be aware of, and tools for monitoring them.

Chapter 8, *Monitoring MySQL*, presents several tools for monitoring database activity and performance.

Chapter 9, *Storage Engine Monitoring*, explains some of the parameters you need to monitor on a more detailed level, focusing on issues specific to MyISAM or InnoDB.

Chapter 10, *Replication Monitoring*, offers details about how to keep track of what masters and slaves are doing.

Chapter 11, *Replication Troubleshooting*, shows how to deal with failures and restarts, corruption, and other incidents.

Chapter 12, *Protecting Your Investment*, explains the use of backups and disaster recovery techniques.

Chapter 13, *MySQL Enterprise*, introduces a suite of tools that simplifies many of the tasks presented in earlier chapters.

Part III, High Availability Environments

Chapter 14, *Cloud Computing Solutions*, introduces the most popular cloud computing service, the Amazon.com AWS, and offers techniques for using MySQL in such virtualized environments.

Chapter 15, *MySQL Cluster*, shows how to use this tool to achieve high availability.

The Appendix, *Replication Tips and Tricks*, offers a grab bag of procedures that are useful in certain situations.

Conventions Used in This Book

The following typographical conventions are used in this book:

Plain text
: Indicates menu titles, options, and buttons.

Italic
: Indicates new terms, table and database names, URLs, email addresses, filenames, and Unix utilities.

`Constant width`
: Indicates command-line options, variables and other code elements, the contents of files, and the output from commands.

`Constant width bold`
: Shows commands or other text that should be typed literally by the user.

`Constant width italic`
: Shows text that should be replaced with user-supplied values.

 This icon signifies a tip, suggestion, or general note.

 This icon indicates a warning or caution.

Using Code Examples

This book is here to help you get your job done. In general, you may use the code in this book in your programs and documentation. You do not need to contact us for permission unless you're reproducing a significant portion of the code. For example, writing a program that uses several chunks of code from this book does not require permission. Selling or distributing a CD-ROM of examples from O'Reilly books *does* require permission. Answering a question by citing this book and quoting example code does not require permission. Incorporating a significant amount of example code from this book into your product's documentation *does* require permission.

We appreciate, but do not require, attribution. An attribution usually includes the title, author, publisher, and ISBN. For example: "*MySQL High Availability*, by Charles Bell, Mats Kindahl, and Lars Thalmann. Copyright 2010 Charles Bell, Mats Kindahl, and Lars Thalmann, 9780596807306."

If you feel your use of code examples falls outside fair use or the permission given above, feel free to contact us at *permissions@oreilly.com*.

We'd Like to Hear from You

Every example in this book has been tested on various platforms. The information in this book has also been verified at each step of the production process. However, mistakes and oversights can occur and we will gratefully receive details of any you find, as well as any suggestions you would like to make for future editions. You can contact the author and editors at:

> O'Reilly Media, Inc.
> 1005 Gravenstein Highway North
> Sebastopol, CA 95472
> 800-998-9938 (in the United States or Canada)
> 707-829-0515 (international or local)
> 707-829-0104 (fax)

We have a web page for this book, where we list errata, examples, and any additional information. You can access this page at:

> *http://www.oreilly.com/catalog/9780596807306*

To comment or ask technical questions about this book, send email to the following quoting the book's ISBN number (9780596807306):

> *bookquestions@oreilly.com*

For more information about our books, conferences, Resource Centers, and the O'Reilly Network, see our website at:

> *http://www.oreilly.com*

Safari® Books Online

Safari Books Online is an on-demand digital library that lets you easily search over 7,500 technology and creative reference books and videos to find the answers you need quickly.

With a subscription, you can read any page and watch any video from our library online. Read books on your cell phone and mobile devices. Access new titles before they are available for print, and get exclusive access to manuscripts in development and post feedback for the authors. Copy and paste code samples, organize your favorites, download chapters, bookmark key sections, create notes, print out pages, and benefit from tons of other time-saving features.

O'Reilly Media has uploaded this book to the Safari Books Online service. To have full digital access to this book and others on similar topics from O'Reilly and other publishers, sign up for free at *http://my.safaribooksonline.com*.

Acknowledgments

The authors would like to thank our technical reviewers, Mark Callaghan, Luis Soares, and Morgan Tocker. Your attention to detail and insightful suggestions were invaluable. We could not have delivered a quality book without your help.

We also want to thank our extremely talented colleagues on the MySQL replication team, including Alfranio Correia, Andrei Elkin, Zhen-Xing He, Serge Kozlov, Sven Sandberg, Luis Soares, Rafal Somla, Li-Bing Song, Ingo Strüwing, and Dao-Gang Qu for their tireless dedication to making MySQL replication the robust and powerful feature set it is today. We especially would like to thank our MySQL customer support professionals, who help us bridge the gap between our customers' needs and our own desires to improve the product. We would also like to thank the many community members who so selflessly devote time and effort to improve MySQL for everyone.

Finally, and most importantly, we would like to thank our editor, Andy Oram, who helped us shape this work, for putting up with our sometimes cerebral and sometimes over-the-top enthusiasm for all things MySQL.

Charles would like to thank his loving wife, Annette, for her patience and understanding when he was spending time away from family priorities to work on this book. You are the love of his life and his inspiration. Charles would also like to thank his many colleagues on the MySQL team at Oracle who contribute their wisdom freely to everyone on a daily basis. Finally, Charles would like to thank all of his brothers and sisters in Christ who both challenge and support him daily.

Mats would like to thank his wife, Lill, and two sons, Jon and Hannes, for their unconditional love and understanding in difficult times. You are the love of his life and he cannot imagine a life without you. Mats would also like to thank his MySQL colleagues inside and outside Sun/Oracle for all the interesting, amusing, and inspiring times together: you are truly some of the sharpest minds in the trade.

Lars would like to thank all his colleagues, current and past, who have made MySQL such an interesting place to work. In fact, it is not even a place. The distributed nature of the MySQL development team and the open-mindedness of its many dedicated developers are truly extraordinary. The MySQL community has a special spirit that makes working with MySQL an honorable task. What we have created together is remarkable. It is amazing that we started with such a small group of people and managed to build a product that services so many of the Fortune 500 companies today.

## PART I

Replication

Your first task in providing a robust MySQL environment is to set up replication. What you learn along the way will help you later when you configure and manage other aspects of high availability.

## CHAPTER 1

Introduction

Joel looked through the classified ads for a new job. His current job was a good one, and the company had been very good to him while he attended college. But it had been several years since he graduated, and he wanted to do more with his career.

"This looks promising," he said and circled an advertisement for a computer science specialist working with MySQL. He had experience with MySQL and certainly met the academic requirements for the job. After reading through several other ads, he decided to call about the MySQL job. After a brief set of cursory questions, the human resources manager granted him an interview in two days' time.

Two days and three interviews later, he was introduced to the company's president and chief executive officer, Robert Summerson, for his final technical interview. He waited while Mr. Summerson paused during the questions and referred to his notes. So far, they were mostly mundane questions about information technology, but Joel knew the hard questions about MySQL were coming next.

Finally, the interviewer said, "I am impressed with your answers, Mr. Thomas. May I call you Joel?"

"Yes, sir," Joel said as he endured another uncomfortable period while the interviewer read over his notes for the third time.

"Tell me what you know about MySQL," Mr. Summerson said and placed his hands on his desk, giving Joel a very penetrating stare.

Joel began explaining what he knew about MySQL, tossing in a generous amount of the material he had read the night before. After about 10 minutes he ran out of things to talk about.

Mr. Summerson waited a couple of minutes, then stood and offered Joel his hand. As Joel rose and shook Mr. Summerson's hand, Summerson said, "That's all I need to hear, Joel. The job is yours."

"Thank you, sir."

Mr. Summerson motioned for Joel to follow him out of his office. "I'll take you back to the HR people so we can get you on the payroll. Can you start two weeks from Monday?"

Joel was elated and couldn't help but smile. "Yes, sir."

"Excellent." Mr. Summerson shook Joel's hand again and said, "I want you to come prepared to evaluate the configuration of our MySQL servers. I want a complete report on their configuration and health."

Joel's elation waned as he drove out of the parking lot. He didn't go home right away. Instead, he drove to the nearest bookstore. "I'm going to need a good book on MySQL," he thought.

So, you have decided to take on a large installation and take care of its operation. Well, you are up for some very interesting—as well as rewarding—times.

Compared to running a small site, supporting a large venture requires planning, foresight, experience, and even more planning. As a database administrator for a large venture you are required to—or will be required to—do things like the following:

- Provide plans for recovery of business-essential data in the event of a disaster. It is also likely that you will have to execute the procedure at least once.
- Provide plans for handling a large customer/user base and monitoring the load of each node in the site in order to optimize it.
- Plan for rapid scale-out in the event the user base grows rapidly.

For all these cases, it is critical to plan for the events in advance and be prepared to act quickly when necessary.

Since not all applications using big sets of servers are websites, we prefer to use the term *deployment*—rather than the term *site* or *website*—to refer to the server that you are using to support some kind of application. This could be a website, but could just as well be a CRM (customer relationship management) system or an online game. The book focuses on the database layer of such a system, but there are some examples that demonstrate how the application layer and the database layer integrate.

There are two things that you need in order to keep a site responsive and available: backups of data and redundancy in the system. The backups can restore a node to the state it was in before a crash, and redundancy allows the site to continue to operate even if one or more of the nodes stops functioning.

There are many ways to do backups, and the method you choose will depend on your needs. Do you need to recover to an exact point in time? In that case, you have to ensure that you have all that is necessary for performing a point-in-time recovery (PITR). Do you want to keep the servers up while making a backup? If so, you need to ensure that you are using some form of online backup method.

Redundancy is handled by duplicating hardware, keeping several instances running in parallel, and using replication to keep multiple copies of the same data available on several machines. If one of the machines fails, it is possible to switch over to another machine that has a copy of the same data.

Together with replication, backup also plays an important role in scaling your system and adding new nodes when needed. If done right, it is even possible to automatically add new slaves at the press of a button, at least figuratively speaking.

What's This Replication Stuff Anyway?

If you're reading this book, you probably have a pretty good idea of what replication is about. It is nevertheless a good idea to introduce the concepts and ideas.

Replication is used to replicate all changes made on a server—called the *master server* or just *master*—to another server, which is called the *slave server* or just *slave*. This is normally used to create a faithful copy of the master server, but replication can be used for other purposes as well.

The two most common uses of replication are to create a backup of the main server to avoid losing any data if the master crashes and to have a copy of the main server to perform reporting and analysis work without disturbing the rest of the business.

For a small business, this makes a lot of things simpler, but it is possible to do a lot more with replication, including the following:

Supporting several offices
> It is possible to maintain servers at each location and replicate changes to the other offices so that the information is available everywhere. This may be necessary to protect the data and also to satisfy legal requirements to keep information about the business available for auditing purposes.

Ensuring the business stays operational even if one of the servers goes down
> An extra server can be used to handle all the traffic if the original server goes down.

Ensuring the business can operate even in the presence of a disaster
> Replication can be used to send changes to an alternative data center at a different geographic location.

Protecting against mistakes ("oopses")
> It is possible to create a *delayed slave* by connecting a slave to a master such that the slave is always a fixed period—for example, an hour—behind the master. If a mistake is made on the master, it is possible to find the offending statement and remove it before it is executed by the slave.

One of the two most important uses of replication in many modern applications is that of *scaling out*. Modern applications are typically very read-intensive; they have a high proportion of reads compared to writes. To reduce the load on the master, you can set up a slave with the sole purpose of answering read queries. By connecting a load balancer, it is possible to direct read queries to a suitable slave, while write queries go to the master.

When using replication in a scale-out scenario, it is important to understand that MySQL replication is *asynchronous* in the sense that transactions are committed at the master server first, then replicated to the slave and applied there. This means that the master and slave may not be consistent, and if replication is running continuously, the slave will lag behind the master.

The advantage of using asynchronous replication is that it is faster and scales better than synchronous replication, but in cases where it is important to have current data, the asynchrony must be handled to ensure the information is actually up-to-date.

Another important application of replication is ensuring high availability by adding redundancy. The most common technique is to use a *dual-master setup*, that is, using replication to keep a pair of masters available all the time, where each master mirrors the other. If one of the masters goes down, the other one is ready to take over immediately.

In addition to the dual-master setup, there are other techniques for achieving high availability that do not involve replication, such as using shared or replicated disks. Although they are not specifically tied to MySQL, these techniques are important tools for ensuring high availability.

So, Backups Are Not Needed Then?

A backup strategy is a critical component of keeping a system available. Regular backups of the servers provide safety against crashes and disasters, which, to some extent, can be handled by replication. Even when replication is used correctly and efficiently, however, there are some things that replication cannot handle. You'll need to have a working backup strategy for the following cases:

Protection against mistakes
> If a mistake is discovered, potentially a long time after it actually occurred, replication will not help. In this case, it is necessary to roll back the system to a time before the mistake was introduced and fix the problem. This requires a working backup schedule.
>
> Replication provides some protection against mistakes if you are using a time-delayed slave, but if the mistake is discovered after the delay period, the change will have already taken effect on the slave as well. So, in general, it is not possible to protect against mistakes using replication only—backups are required as well.

Creating new servers

When creating new servers—either slaves for scale-out purposes or new masters to act as standbys—it is necessary to make a backup of an existing server and restore that backup image on the new server. This requires a quick and efficient backup method to minimize the downtime and keep the load on the system at an acceptable level.

Legal reasons

In addition to pure business reasons for data preservation, you may have legal requirements to keep data safe, even in the event of a disaster. Not complying with these requirements can pose significant problems to operating the business.

In short, a backup strategy is necessary for operating the business, regardless of any other precautions you have in place to ensure that the data is safe.

What's with All the Monitoring?

Even if you have replication set up correctly, it is necessary to understand the load on your system and to keep a keen eye on any problems that surface. As business requirements change due to changed customer usage patterns, it is necessary to balance the system to use resources as efficiently as possible and to reduce the risk of losing availability due to sudden changes in resource utilization.

There are a number of different things that you can monitor, measure, and plan for to handle these types of changes. Some examples are:

- You can add indexes to tables that are frequently read.
- You can rewrite queries or change the structure of databases to speed up execution time.
- If locks are held for a long time, it is an indication that several connections are using the same table. It might pay off to switch storage engines.
- If some of your scale-out slaves are hot-processing a disproportionate number of queries, the system might require some rebalancing to ensure that all the scale-out slaves are hit evenly.
- To handle sudden changes in resource usage, it is necessary to determine the normal load of each server and understand when the system will start to respond slowly because of a sudden increase in load.

Without monitoring, you have no way of spotting problematic queries, hot slaves, or improperly utilized tables.

Is There Anything Else I Can Read?

There is plenty of literature on using MySQL for various jobs, and also a lot of literature about high-availability systems. Here is a list of books that we strongly recommend if you are going to work with MySQL:

MySQL by Paul DuBois (Addison-Wesley)
> This is *the* reference to MySQL and consists of 1,200 pages (really!) packed with everything you want to know about MySQL (and probably a lot that you don't want to know).

High Performance MySQL, Second Edition by Baron Schwartz, et al. (O'Reilly, http://oreilly.com/catalog/9780596101718/)
> This is one of the best books on using MySQL in an enterprise setting. It covers optimizing queries and ensuring your system is responsive and available.

Scalable Internet Architectures by Theo Schlossnagle (Sams Publishing).
> Written by one of the most prominent thinkers in the industry, this is a must for anybody working with systems of scale.

 The book uses a Python library developed by the authors (called the *MySQL Python Replicant*) for many of the administrative tasks. MySQL Python is available on Launchpad at *https://launchpad.net/mysql-replicant-python*.

Conclusion

In the next chapter, we will start with the basics of setting up replication, so get a comfortable chair, open your computer, and let's get started....

Joel was adjusting his chair when a knock sounded from his door.

"Settling in, Joel?" Mr. Summerson asked.

Joel didn't know what to say. He had been tasked to set up a replication slave on his first day on the job and while it took him longer than he had expected, he had yet to hear how his boss felt about the job. Joel spoke the first thing on his mind: "Yes, sir, I'm still trying to figure out this chair."

"Nice job with the documentation, Joel. I'd like you to write a report explaining what you think we should do to improve our management of the database server."

Joel nodded. "I can do that."

"Good. I'll give you another day to get your office in order. I expect the report by Wednesday, close of business."

Before Joel could reply, Mr. Summerson walked away.

Joel sat down and flipped another lever on his chair. He heard a distinct click as the back gave way, forcing him to fling his arms wide. "Whoa!" He looked toward his door as he clumsily righted his chair, thankful no one saw his impromptu gymnastics. "OK, that lever is now off limits," he said.

## CHAPTER 2

MySQL Replication Fundamentals

Joel jumped as a sharp rap on his door announced his boss's unapologetic interruption. Before Joel could say "Come in," the boss stepped into his doorway and said, "Joel, we're getting complaints that our response time is getting slow. See what you can do to speed things up. The administrator told me there are too many read operations from the applications. See what you can do to offload some of that."

Before Joel could respond, Mr. Summerson was out the door and on his way elsewhere. "I suppose he means we need a bigger server," Joel thought.

As if he had read Joel's mind, Mr. Summerson stuck his head back in the doorway and said, "Oh, and by the way, the startup we bought all the equipment from had a bunch of servers we haven't found any use for yet; can you take a look at those and see what you can do with them? OK, Joel?" Then he was gone again.

"I wonder if I'll ever get used to this," Joel thought as he pulled his favorite MySQL book off the shelf and glanced at the table of contents. He found the chapter on replication and decided that might fit the bill.

MySQL replication is a very useful tool when used correctly, but it can also be a source of considerable headaches when it experiences a failure or when it is configured or used incorrectly. This chapter will cover the fundamentals of using MySQL replication by beginning with a simple setup to get you started and then introducing some basic techniques to store in your "replication toolkit."

This chapter covers the following use cases:

Disaster avoidance through hot standby
> If a server goes down, everything will stop; it will not be possible to execute (perhaps critical) transactions, get information about customers, or retrieve other critical data. This is something that you want to avoid at (almost) any cost since it can severely disrupt your business. The easiest solution is to configure an extra server with the sole purpose of acting as a hot standby, ready to take over the job of the main server if it fails.

Report generation

Creating reports from data on a server will degrade the server's performance, in some cases significantly. If you're running lots of background jobs to generate reports, it's worth creating an extra server just for this purpose. You can get a snapshot of the database at a certain time by stopping replication on the report server and then running large queries on it without disturbing the main business server. For example, if you stop replication after the last transaction of the day, you can extract your daily reports while the rest of the business is humming along at its normal pace.

Debugging and auditing

You can also investigate queries that have been executed on the server—for example, to see whether particular queries were executed on servers with performance problems, or whether a server has gone out of sync because of a bad query.

Basic Steps in Replication

This chapter will introduce several sophisticated techniques for maximizing the efficiency and value of replication, but as a first step we will set up the simple replication shown in Figure 2-1—a single instance of replication from a master to a slave. This does not require any knowledge of the internal architecture or execution details of the replication process (we'll explore these before we take on more complicated scenarios).

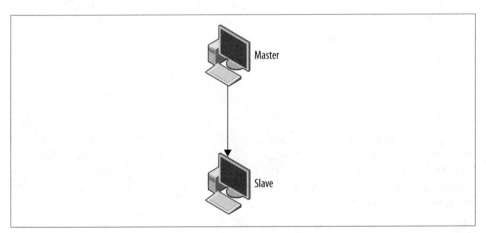

Figure 2-1. Simple replication

Setting up basic replication can be summarized in three easy steps:

1. Configure one server to be a master.
2. Configure one server to be a slave.
3. Connect the slave to the master.

Unless you plan replication from the start and include the right configuration options in the *my.cnf* files, you will have to restart each server to carry out steps 1 and 2.

 To follow the procedures in this section, it is easiest if you have a shell account on the machine with privileges to change the *my.cnf* file—which usually means mysql privileges—as well as an account on the server with ALL privileges granted.

You should be very restrictive in granting privileges in a production environment. For precise guidelines, consult "Privileges for Configuring Replication" on page 16.

Configuring the Master

To configure a server so that it can act as master, ensure the server has an active *binary log* and a unique server ID. We will examine the binary log in greater detail later, but for now it is sufficient to say that it keeps a record of all the changes the master has made so that they can be repeated on the slave. The server ID is used to distinguish two servers from each other. To set up the binary log and server ID, you have to take the server down and add the log-bin, log-bin-index, and server-id options to the *my.cnf* configuration file as shown in Example 2-1. The added options are in boldface.

Example 2-1. Options added to my.cnf to configure a master

```
[mysqld]
user            = mysql
pid-file        = /var/run/mysqld/mysqld.pid
socket          = /var/run/mysqld/mysqld.sock
port            = 3306
basedir         = /usr
datadir         = /var/lib/mysql
tmpdir          = /tmp
log-bin         = master-bin
log-bin-index   = master-bin.index
server-id       = 1
```

The log-bin option gives the base name for all the files created by the binary log (as you will see later, the binary log consists of several files). If you create a filename with an extension to log-bin, the extension will be ignored and only the file's base name will be used (that is, the name without the extension).

The log-bin-index option gives the name of the binary log index file, which keeps a list of all binlog files.

Strictly speaking, it is not necessary to give a name in the log-bin option. The default value is hostname-bin. The value for hostname is taken from the option for pid-file, which by default is the name of the host (as given by the gethostname(2) system call). If an administrator later changes the machine's hostname, the binlog files will change names as well, but they will be tracked correctly in the index file. However, it is a good idea to create a name that is unique for the server and not tied to the machine the server is running on, since it can be confusing to work with a series of binlog files that suddenly change name midstream.

If no value is provided for `log-bin-index`, the default value will be the same base name as for the binlog files (`hostname-bin` if you don't give a default for `log-bin`). This means that if you do not provide a value for `log-bin-index`, the index file is guaranteed to change its name when you change the name of the host. So, if you change the name of the host and start the server, it will not find the index file and therefore assume that it does not exist, and this will give you an empty binary log.

Each server is identified by a unique server ID, so if a slave connects to the master and has the same `server-id` as the master, an error will be generated indicating that the master and the slave have the same server ID.

Once you have added the `log-bin` and `server-id` options to the configuration file, start the server again and finish its configuration by adding a replication user.

After you make the change to the master's configuration file, restart the master for the changes to take effect.

The slave initiates a normal client connection to the master and requests the master to dump all changes to it. For the slave to connect, a user with special replication privileges is required on the master. Example 2-2 shows a standard `mysql` client session on the master server, with commands that add a new user account and give it the proper privilege.

Example 2-2. Creating a replication user on the master

```
master> CREATE USER repl_user;
Query OK, 0 rows affected (0.00 sec)
master> GRANT REPLICATION SLAVE ON *.*
    -> TO repl_user IDENTIFIED BY 'xyzzy';
Query OK, 0 rows affected (0.00 sec)
```

 There is nothing special about the REPLICATION SLAVE privilege except that the user can get a dump of the binary log from the master. It is perfectly viable to have a normal user account and grant that user the REPLICATION SLAVE privilege. It is, however, a good idea to keep the replication slave user separate from the other users. If you do that, you can remove the user if you need to disallow certain slaves from connecting later.

Configuring the Slave

After configuring the master, you must configure the slave. As with the master server, you need to assign each slave a unique server ID. You may also want to consider adding the names of the relay log and the relay log index files to the *my.cnf* file (we will discuss the relay log in more detail in "Replication Architecture Basics" on page 196) using the options `relay-log` and `relay-log-index`. The recommended configuration options are given in Example 2-3, with the added options highlighted.

Example 2-3. Options added to my.cnf to configure a slave

```
[mysqld]
user              = mysql
pid-file          = /var/run/mysqld/mysqld.pid
socket            = /var/run/mysqld/mysqld.sock
port              = 3306
basedir           = /usr
datadir           = /var/lib/mysql
tmpdir            = /tmp
server-id         = 2
relay-log-index   = slave-relay-bin.index
relay-log         = slave-relay-bin
```

Like the `log-bin` and `log-bin-index` options, the defaults for the `relay-log` and `relay-log-index` options depend on the hostname. The default for `relay-log` is *hostname-relay-bin* and the default for `relay-log-index` is *hostname*-`relay-bin.index`. Using the default introduces a problem in that if the hostname of the server changes, it will not find the relay log index file and will assume there is nothing in the relay logfiles.

After editing the *my.cnf* file, restart the slave server for the changes to take effect.

Connecting the Master and Slave

Now you can perform the final step in setting up basic replication: directing the slave to the master so that it knows where to replicate from. To do this you need four pieces of information about the master:

- A hostname
- A port number
- A user account on the master with replication slave privileges
- A password for the user account

You already created a user account with the right privileges and a password when configuring the master. The hostname is given by the operating system and can't be configured in the *my.cnf* file, but the port number can be assigned in *my.cnf* (if you do not supply a port number, the default value of 3306 will be used). The final two steps necessary to get replication up and running are to direct the slave to the master using the `CHANGE MASTER TO` command and then start replication using `START SLAVE`.

```
slave> CHANGE MASTER TO
    ->    MASTER_HOST = 'master-1',
    ->    MASTER_PORT = 3306,
    ->    MASTER_USER = 'repl_user',
    ->    MASTER_PASSWORD = 'xyzzy';
Query OK, 0 rows affected (0.00 sec)

slave> START SLAVE;
Query OK, 0 rows affected (0.15 sec)
```

Congratulations! You have now set up your first replication between a master and a slave! If you make some changes to the database on the master, such as adding new tables and filling them in, you will find that they are replicated to the slave. Try it out! Create a test database (if you do not already have one), create some tables, and add some data to the tables to see that the changes replicate over to the slave.

Observe that either a hostname or an IP address can be given to the MASTER_HOST parameter. If a hostname is given, the IP address for the hostname is retrieved by calling gethostname(3), which, depending on your configuration, could mean resolving the hostname using a DNS lookup. The steps for configuring such lookups are beyond the scope of this book.

Privileges for Configuring Replication

To connect the slave to the master for replication, it is necessary to have an account with certain privileges, in addition to a shell account with access to critical files. For security reasons, it is usually a good idea to restrict the account used for configuring the master and slave to just the necessary privileges.

- To create and drop users, the account needs to have the CREATE USER privilege.
- To grant the REPLICATION SLAVE to the replication account, it is necessary to have the REPLICATION SLAVE privilege with the GRANT OPTION.

To perform further replication-related procedures (shown later in this chapter), you need a few more options:

- To execute the FLUSH LOGS command (or any FLUSH command), you need the RELOAD privilege.
- To execute SHOW MASTER STATUS and SHOW SLAVE STATUS, you need either the SUPER or REPLICATION CLIENT privilege.
- To execute CHANGE MASTER TO, you need the SUPER privilege.

For example, to give *mats* sufficient privileges for all the procedures in this chapter, issue the following:

```
server> GRANT REPLICATION SLAVE, RELOAD, CREATE USER, SUPER
    ->    ON *.*
    ->    TO mats@'192.168.2.%'
    ->    WITH GRANT OPTION;
```

A Brief Introduction to the Binary Log

What makes replication work is the *binary log* (or just *binlog*), which is a record of all changes made to the database on a server. You need to understand how the binary log works in order to have control over replication or to fix any problems that arise, so we'll give you a bit of background in this section.

Figure 2-2 shows a schematic view of the replication architecture, containing a master with a binary log and a slave that receives changes from the master via the binary log. We will cover the replication architecture in detail in Chapter 6. When a statement is about to finish executing, it writes an entry to the end of the binary log and sends the statement parser a notification that it has completed the statement. Usually only the statement that is about to finish executing is written to the binary log, but there are some special cases where other information is written—either in addition to the statement or instead of the statement. It will soon be clear why this is so, but for the time being, you can pretend that only the statements that are being executed are being written to the binary log.

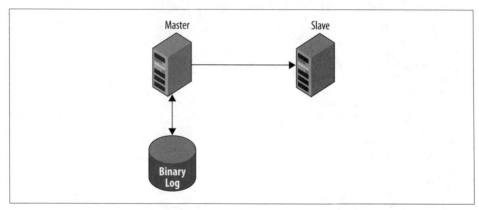

Figure 2-2. Role of the binary log in replication

What's Recorded in the Binary Log

The purpose of the binary log is to record changes made to the tables in the database. The binary log can then be used for replication, as well as for PITR (discussed in Chapter 12) and in some limited cases for auditing.

Note that the binary log contains only *changes* made to the database, so for statements that do not change any data in the database, no entry is written to the binary log.

Traditionally, MySQL replication records changes by preserving the SQL statement that made the change. This is called *statement-based replication*. Statement-based replication runs into constraints that prevent it from replicating all statements correctly, so as of version 5.1, MySQL also offers *row-based replication*. In contrast to statement-based replication, row-based replication individually records each change to a row in the binary log. In addition to being more convenient, row-based replication can offer some speed advantages in certain situations.

To imagine the difference, consider a complex update that uses a lot of joins or WHERE clauses. Instead of reexecuting all the logic on the slave in statement-based replication, all you really need to know is the state of the row after the change. On the other hand, if a single update changes 10,000 rows, you'd rather record just the statement instead of 10,000 separate changes as row-based replication does.

We will cover row-based replication in Chapter 6, explaining its implementation and its use. In the examples that follow, we'll focus on statement-based replication because it's easier to understand in respect to activities executed against the database.

Watching Replication in Action

Using the replication example from the previous section, let's take a look at the binlog events for some simple statements. Let's start by connecting a command-line client to the master and executing a few commands to get a binary log:

```
master> CREATE TABLE tbl (text TEXT);
Query OK, 0 rows affected (0.04 sec)

master> INSERT INTO tbl VALUES ("Yeah! Replication!");
Query OK, 1 row affected (0.00 sec)

master> SELECT * FROM tbl;
+--------------------+
| text               |
+--------------------+
| Yeah! Replication! |
+--------------------+
1 row in set (0.00 sec)

master> FLUSH LOGS;
Query OK, 0 rows affected (0.28 sec)
```

The FLUSH LOGS command forces the binary log to rotate, which will allow us to see a "complete" binlog file in all its glory. To take a closer look at this file, use the SHOW BINLOG EVENTS command, as shown in Example 2-4.

Example 2-4. Checking what events are in the binary log

```
master> SHOW BINLOG EVENTS\G
*************************** 1. row ***************************
   Log_name: master-bin.000001
        Pos: 4
 Event_type: Format_desc
  Server_id: 1
End_log_pos: 106
       Info: Server ver: 5.1.33, Binlog ver: 4
```

```
*************************** 2. row ***************************
  Log_name: master-bin.000001
       Pos: 106
Event_type: Query
 Server_id: 1
End_log_pos: 197
      Info: use `test`; CREATE TABLE tbl (text TEXT)
*************************** 3. row ***************************
  Log_name: master-bin.000001
       Pos: 197
Event_type: Query
 Server_id: 1
End_log_pos: 305
      Info: use `test`; INSERT INTO tbl VALUES ("Yeah! Replication!")
*************************** 4. row ***************************
  Log_name: master-bin.000001
       Pos: 305
Event_type: Rotate
 Server_id: 1
End_log_pos: 349
      Info: master-bin.000002;pos=4
4 rows in set (0.02 sec)
```

In this binary log, we can now see four events: a format description event, two query events, and a rotate event. The query event is how statements executed against the database are normally written to the binary log, whereas the format description and rotate events are used by the server internally to manage the binary log. We will discuss these events in more detail in Chapter 6, but for now, let's take a closer look at the columns given for each event:

Event_type
> This is the type of the event. We have seen three different types here, but there are many more. The type of the event is the basic way that we can transport information to the slave. Currently—in MySQL 5.1.18 to 5.1.39—there are 27 events (several of them are not used, but they are retained for backward compatibility), but this is an extensible range and new events are added if later versions require additional events.

Server_id
> This is the server ID of the server that created the event.

Log_name
> This is the name of the file that stores the event. An event is always contained in a single file and will never span two files.

Pos
> This is the position of the file where the event starts; that is, it's the first byte of the event.

End_log_pos

>   This gives the position in the file where the event ends and the next event starts. This is one higher than the last byte of the event, so the bytes in the range Pos to End_log_pos – 1 are the bytes containing the event and the length of the event can be computed as End_log_pos – Pos.

Info

>   This is human-readable text with information about the event. Different information is printed for different events, but you can at least count on the query event to print the statement that it contains.

The first two columns, Log_name and Pos, make up the *binlog position* of the event and will be used to indicate the location or position of an event. In addition to what is shown here, each event contains a lot of other information—for example, a timestamp, which is the number of seconds since the epoch (a classic Unix moment in time, such as 1970-01-01 00:00:00 UTC).

The Binary Log's Structure and Content

As we explained, the binary log is not actually a single file, but a set of files that allow for easier management (such as removing old logs without disturbing recent ones). The binary log consists of a set of binlog files with the real contents as well as a binlog index file, which keeps track of which binlog files exist. Figure 2-3 shows how a binary log is organized.

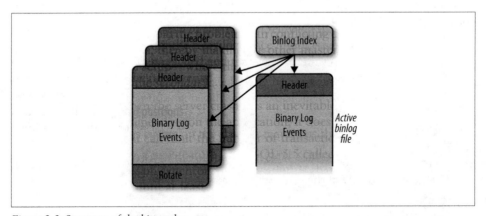

Figure 2-3. Structure of the binary log

One binlog file is the *active binlog file*. This is the file that is currently being written to (and usually read from as well).

Each binlog file starts with a *format description event* and ends with a *rotate event*. The format description log event contains, among other things, the version of the server that produced the file and general information about the server and binary log. The rotate event tells where the binary log continues by giving the filename of the next file in the sequence.

Each file is organized into binary log events, where each event makes a standalone, atomic piece of the binary log. The format description log event contains a flag that marks the file as properly closed. While a binlog file is being written, the flag is set, and when the file is closed, the flag is cleared. This way, it is possible to detect corrupt binlog files in the event of a crash and allow replication to recover.

If you try to execute additional statements at the master, you will observe something strange: no changes are seen in the binary log:

```
master> INSERT INTO tbl VALUES ("What's up?");
Query OK, 1 row affected (0.00 sec)

master> SELECT * FROM tbl;
+---------------------+
| text                |
+---------------------+
| Yeah! Replication!  |
| What's up?          |
+---------------------+
1 row in set (0.00 sec)

master> SHOW BINLOG EVENTS\G
same as before
```

What happened to the new event? Well, as you already know, the binary log consists of several files, and the SHOW BINLOG EVENTS statement shows only the contents of the *first* binlog file. This is contrary to what most users expect, which is to see the contents of the active binlog file. If the name of the first binlog file is *master-bin.000001* (containing the events shown previously), you can take a look at the events in the next binlog file, in this case named *master-bin.000002*, using the following:

```
master> SHOW BINLOG EVENTS IN 'master-bin.000002'\G
*************************** 1. row ***************************
   Log_name: master-bin.000002
        Pos: 4
 Event_type: Format_desc
  Server_id: 1
End_log_pos: 106
       Info: Server ver: 5.1.30-log, Binlog ver: 4
*************************** 2. row ***************************
   Log_name: master-bin.000002
        Pos: 106
 Event_type: Query
  Server_id: 1
End_log_pos: 205
       Info: use `test`; INSERT INTO tbl VALUES("What's up?")
2 rows in set (0.00 sec)
```

You might have noticed in Example 2-4 that the binary log ends with a rotate event and that the Info field contains the name of the next binlog file and position where the events start. To see which binlog file is currently being written, you can use the SHOW MASTER STATUS command:

```
master> SHOW MASTER STATUS\G
*************************** 1. row ***************************
            File: master-bin.000002
        Position: 205
    Binlog_Do_DB:
Binlog_Ignore_DB:
1 row in set (0.00 sec)
```

Now that you've finished taking a look at the binary log, stop and reset the slave and drop the table:

```
master> DROP TABLE tbl;
Query OK, 0 rows affected (0.00 sec)

slave> STOP SLAVE;
Query OK, 0 rows affected (0.08 sec)

slave> RESET SLAVE;
Query OK, 0 rows affected (0.00 sec)
```

After that, you can drop the table and reset the master to start fresh:

```
master> DROP TABLE tbl;
Query OK, 0 rows affected (0.00 sec)

master> RESET MASTER;
Query OK, 0 rows affected (0.04 sec)
```

The RESET MASTER command removes all the binlog files and clears the binlog index file. The RESET SLAVE statement removes all files used by replication on the slave to get a clean start.

Neither the RESET MASTER nor the RESET SLAVE command is designed to work when replication is active, so:

- When executing the RESET MASTER command (on the master), make sure that no slaves are attached.
- When executing the RESET SLAVE command (on the slave), make sure that the slave does not have replication active by issuing a STOP SLAVE command.

We will cover the most basic events in this chapter, but for the complete list with all its gory details, please refer to the MySQL Internals Manual.

Python Support for Managing Replication

The ability to automate administrative procedures is critical to handling large deployments, so you might be asking yourself, "Wouldn't it be neat if we could automate the procedures?" In this case, you'll be happy to hear that you can. Using the descriptions from the previous sections, we will start here to design a simple library for managing replication. The library will be extended with new functionality in the coming chapters.

The project is available at Launchpad (*http://launchpad.net/mysql-replicant-python*), where you can find information and download the source code and documentation.

First, you have to create a model of how your servers are connected via replication. There are innumerable ways to connect a large number of servers, but when connecting them, you set them up in a certain configuration, called the *topology*. We will cover topologies in Chapter 5, but the basic topologies are the simple one shown in Figure 2-4, a tree topology, and dual masters (used for providing high availability).

The basic idea is to have a model of how the servers are connected on a computer (any computer, such as your laptop), as in Figure 2-4, and design the library so you can manage the connections by changing the model. For example, to reconnect a slave to another master, just reconnect the slave in the model, and the library will send the appropriate commands for doing the job.

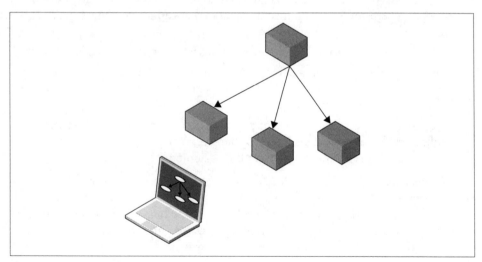

Figure 2-4. A replication topology with a model

To make the library useful on a wide variety of platforms and for a wide variety of deployments, keep the following in mind:

- The servers are likely to run on a variety of operating systems, such as Windows, Linux, and flavors of Unix such as Solaris or Mac OS X. Procedures for starting and stopping servers, as well as the names of configuration files, differ depending on the operating system. The library should therefore support different operating systems and it should be possible to extend it with new operating systems that are not in the library.

- The deployment is likely to consist of servers running different versions of MySQL. For example, while you are upgrading a deployment to use new versions of the server, it will consist of a mixture of old and new versions. The library should be able to handle such a deployment.

- A deployment consists of servers with many different roles, so it should be possible to specify different roles for the servers. In addition, it should be possible to create new roles that weren't anticipated at the beginning.

- It is necessary to be able to execute SQL queries on each server. This is needed for configuration as well as for extracting information necessary to manage the deployment.

- It is necessary to be able to execute shell commands on each machine. This is needed to perform some administrative tasks that cannot be done using the SQL interface.

- It should be possible to add and remove options from the server's configuration file.

- The library should support a deployment with multiple servers on a machine. This requires the ability to recognize different configuration files and database files used by different MySQL servers on a single machine.

- There should be a set of utilities for performing common tasks such as setting up replication, but it should also be possible to extend the library with new utility functions that were not anticipated at the beginning.

The interface hides these complexities as much as possible and presents a simple interface in Python. Python was chosen by the authors because it is concise, easy to read, available on all operating systems that run MySQL, and increasingly popular for general-purpose scripting. Example 2-5 illustrates how you can use the library, offering a short example for redirecting all slaves to use a new master.

Note that this code is just an example of how you can use the library. As the code stands, it stops replication in its tracks and is likely to lose transactions if executed on an active server. You will see how to change masters properly in Chapter 4.

Example 2-5. Using the library to redirect slaves

```
import MyDeployment

for slave in MyDeployment.slaves:
```

```
slave.stop()
change_master(slave, MyDeployment.master[1])
slave.start()
```

The following sections show the code that makes such applications possible. To avoid cluttering the code more than necessary, we have removed some error checking and other defensive measures needed to have a stable and safe library. You will find the complete code for the library at *http://launchpad.net/mysql-replicant-python*.

Basic Classes and Functions

The first things you need in order to use the library are some basic definitions for frequently used parameters.

The first classes are exceptions that will be used by functions in the library.

Error
:   This is the base class for all exceptions in the library.

EmptyRowError
:   This exception is thrown when an attempt is made to select a field from a query that did not return any rows.

NoOptionError
:   This exception is raised when ConfigManager does not find the option.

SlaveNotRunningError
:   This exception is raised when the slave is not running but was expected to run.

NotMasterError
:   This exception is raised when the server is not a master and the operation is therefore illegal.

NotSlaveError
:   This exception is raised when the server is not a slave and the operation is therefore illegal.

Position
:   This class represents a binlog position consisting of a filename and a byte offset within the file. A representation method prints out a parsable representation of the binlog positions (e.g., to store them in secondary storage or just to look at them).

    To compare and order the positions, the class defines a comparison operator that lets the library put binlog positions in order. Note that positions can be different on different servers, so it is not useful to compare positions from different servers.

User
:   This class represents a user with a name and a password. It is used for many types of accounts: a MySQL user account, a shell user account, and the replication user (which we will introduce later).

Operating System

To work with different operating systems, you can use a set of classes that abstract away the differences. The idea is to give each class methods for each of the required tasks that are implemented differently by different operating systems. At this time, all we need are methods to stop and start the server.

Machine
> This class is the base class for a machine and holds all the information that is common to this kind of machine. It is expected that a machine instance has at least the following members:
>
> Machine.defaults_file
> > The default location of the *my.cnf* file on this machine
>
> Machine.start_server(*server*)
> > Method to start the server
>
> Machine.stop_server(*server*)
> > Method to stop the server

Linux
> This class handles a server running on a Linux machine. This class uses the init(8) scripts stored under */etc/init.d* to start and stop the server.

Solaris
> This class handles servers running on a Solaris machine and uses the svadm(1M) command to start and stop the server.

Server Class

The Server class defines all the primitive functions that implement the higher-level functions we want to expose in the interface:

Server.Server(*name*, ...)
> The Server class represents a server in the system; there is one object for each running server in the entire system. Only the most important parameters are described here; for a full list, please consult the project page on Launchpad.
>
> name
> > This is the name of the server, and is used to create values for the pid-file, log-bin, and log-bin-index options. If no name parameter is provided, it will be deduced from the pid-file option, the log-bin option, the log-bin-index option, or as a last resort, using the default.
>
> host, port, *and* socket
> > The host where the server resides, the port for connecting to the server as a MySQL client, and—when on the same host—the socket through which to connect.

ssh_user

> A combination of user and password that can be used for connecting to the machine that is running the server. Use this to execute administrative commands such as starting and stopping the server and reading and writing the configuration file.

sql_user

> A combination of user and password for connecting to the server as a MySQL user account to execute SQL commands.

machine

> An object that holds operating system–specific primitives. We chose the name to avoid a name conflict with the standard library os module. This parameter lets you use different techniques for starting and stopping the server as well as other tasks and operating system–specific parameters. The parameters will be covered later.

server_id

> An optional parameter to hold the server's ID, as defined in each server's configuration file. If this option is omitted, the server ID will be read from the configuration file of the server. If there is no server ID in the configuration file either, the server is a vagabond and does not participate in replication as master or slave.

config_manager

> An optional parameter to hold a reference to a configuration manager that can be queried for information about the configuration for the server.

Server.connect() *and* Server.disconnect()

> Use the connect and disconnect methods to establish a connection to the server before executing commands in a session and disconnect from the server after finishing the session, respectively.
>
> These methods are useful because in some situations it is critical to keep the connection to the server open even after an SQL command has been executed. Otherwise, for example, when doing a FLUSH TABLES WITH READ LOCK, the lock will automatically be released when the connection is dropped.

Server.ssh(*command*) *and* Server.sql(*command, args*)

> Use these to execute a shell command or an SQL command on the server.
>
> The ssh and sql methods both return an iterable. ssh returns a list of the lines of output from the executed command, whereas sql returns a list of objects of an internal class named Row. The Row class defines the __iter__ and next methods so that you iterate over the returned lines or rows, for example:

```
for row in server.sql("SHOW DATABASES"):
    print row["Database"]
```

To handle statements that return a single row, the class also defines a _getitem_ method, which will fetch a field from the single row or raise an exception if there is no row. This means that when you know your return value has only one row (which is guaranteed for many SQL statements), you can avoid the loop shown in the previous example and write something like:

```
print server.sql("SHOW MASTER STATUS")["Position"]
```

Server.fetch_config() *and* Server.replace_config()
The methods fetch_config and replace_config fetch the configuration file into memory from the remote server to allow the user to add or remove options as well as change the values of some options. For example, to add a value to the log-bin and log-bin-index options, you can use the module as follows:

```
config = master.fetch_config()
config.set('log-bin', 'capulet-bin')
config.set('log-bin-index', 'capulet-bin.index')
master.replace_config(config)
```

Server.start() *and* Server.stop()
The methods start and stop forward information to the machine object to do their jobs, which depend on the operating system the server is using. The methods will either start the server or shut down the server, respectively.

Server Roles

Servers work slightly differently depending on their roles. For example, masters require a replication user for slaves to use when connecting, but slaves don't require that user account unless they act as a master and have other slaves connecting. To capture the configuration of the servers in a flexible manner, classes are introduced for representing different *roles*.

When you use the imbue method on a server, the appropriate commands are sent to the server to configure it correctly for that role. Note that a server might change roles in the lifetime of a deployment, so the roles given here just serve to configure the initial deployment. However, a server always has a designated role in the deployment and therefore also has an associated role.

When a server changes roles, it might be necessary to remove some of the configuration information from the server, so therefore an unimbue method is also defined for a role and used when switching roles for a server.

In this example, only three roles are defined. Later in the book you will see more roles defined.

Role
This is the base class of all the roles. Each derived class needs to define the methods imbue and (optionally) unimbue to accept a single server to imbue with the role. To

aid derived classes with some common tasks, the `Role` class defines a number of helper functions.

`Role.imbue(server)`

This method imbues the server with the new role by executing the appropriate code.

`Role.unimbue(server)`

This method allows a role to perform cleanup actions before another role is imbued.

`Role._set_server_id(server, config)`

If there is no server ID in the configuration, this method sets it to `server.server_id`. If the configuration has a server ID, it will be used to set the value of `server.server_id`.

`Role._create_repl_user(server, user)`

This method creates a replication user on the server and grants it the necessary rights to act as a replication slave.

`Role._enable_binlog(server, config)`

This method enables the binary log on the server by setting the `log-bin` and `log-bin-index` options to appropriate values. If the server already has a value for `log-bin`, this method does nothing.

`Role._disable_binlog(server, config)`

This method disables the binary log by clearing the `log-bin` and `log-bin-index` options in the configuration file.

Vagabond

This is the default role assigned to any server that does not participate in the replication deployment. As such, the server is a "vagabond" and does not have any responsibilities whatsoever.

Master

This role is for a server that acts as a master. The role will set the server ID, enable the binary log, and create a replication user for the slaves. The name and password of the replication user will be stored in the server so that when slaves are connected, the class can look up the replication username.

Final

This is the role for a (final) slave—that is, a slave that does not have a binary log of its own. When a server is imbued with this role, it will be given a server ID, the binary log will be disabled, and a `CHANGE MASTER` command will be issued to connect the slave to a master.

Note that we stop the server before we write the configuration file back to it, and restart the server after we have written the configuration file. The configuration file is read only when starting the server and closed after the reading is done, but we play it safe and stop the server before modifying the file.

One of the critical design decisions here is to not store any state information about the servers that roles apply to. It might be tempting to keep a list of all the masters by adding them to the role object, but since roles of the servers change over the lifetime of the deployment, the roles are used only to set up the system. Because we allow a role to contain parameters, you can use them to configure several servers with the same information.

```
slave_role = Final(master=MyDeployment.master)
for slave in MyDeployment.slaves:
    slave_role.imbue(slave)
```

Creating New Slaves

Now that you know a little about the binary log, we are ready to tackle one of the basic problems with the way we created a slave earlier. When we configured the slave, we provided no information about where to start replication, so the slave will start reading the binary logs on the master from the beginning. That's clearly not a very good idea if the master has been running for some time: in addition to making the slave replay quite a lot of events just to ramp up, you might not be able to obtain the necessary logs, because they might have been stored somewhere else for safekeeping and removed from the master (we'll discuss that more in Chapter 12 when we talk about backups and PITR). So we need another way to create new slaves—called *bootstrapping a slave*—without starting replication from the beginning.

The CHANGE MASTER TO command has two parameters that will help us here: MASTER_LOG_FILE and MASTER_LOG_POS. You can use these to specify the binlog position at which the master should start sending events instead of starting from the beginning.

Using these parameters to CHANGE MASTER TO, we can bootstrap a slave using the following steps:

1. Configure the new slave.
2. Make a backup of the master (or of a slave that has been replicating the master). See Chapter 12 for common backup techniques.
3. Write down the binlog position that corresponds to this backup (in other words, the position following the last event leading up to the master's current state).
4. Restore the backup on the new slave. See Chapter 12 for common restore techniques.
5. Configure the slave to start replication from this position.

Depending on whether you use the master or a slave as a baseline in step 2, the procedure differs slightly, so we will start by describing how to bootstrap a new slave when you only have a single server running that you want to use as master—this is called *cloning the master*.

Cloning a master means taking a snapshot of the server, which is usually accomplished by creating a backup. There are various techniques for backing up the server, but in this chapter, we have decided to use one of the simpler techniques: running mysql dump to create a logical backup. Other options are to create a physical backup by copying the database files, online backup techniques such as InnoDB Hot Backup, or even volume snapshots using Linux LVM (Logical Volume Manager). The various techniques will be described fully in Chapter 12, along with a discussion of their relative merits.

Cloning the Master

The mysqldump utility has options that allow you to perform all the steps in this section in a single step, but to explain the necessary operations, we will perform all the steps here individually. You will see a more compact version later in this section.

To clone the master, as shown in Figure 2-5, start by creating a backup of the master. Since the master is probably running and has a lot of tables in the cache, it is necessary to flush all tables and lock the database to prevent changes before checking the binlog position. You can do this using the FLUSH TABLES WITH READ LOCK command:

```
master> FLUSH TABLES WITH READ LOCK;
Query OK, 0 rows affected (0.02 sec)
```

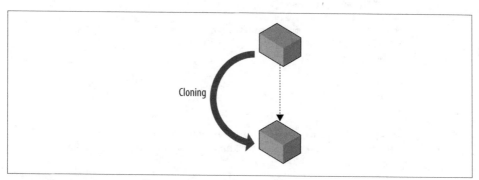

Cloning

Figure 2-5. Cloning a master to create a new slave

Once the database is locked, you are ready to create a backup and note the binlog position. Since no changes are occurring on the master, the SHOW MASTER STATUS command will correctly reveal the current file and position in the binary log. We will go through the details of the SHOW MASTER STATUS and the SHOW MASTER LOGS commands in Chapter 6.

```
master> SHOW MASTER STATUS\G
*************************** 1. row ***************************
            File: master-bin.000042
        Position: 456552
    Binlog_Do_DB:
```

```
Binlog_Ignore_DB:
1 row in set (0.00 sec)
```

The position of the next event to write is `master-bin.000042`, `456552`, which is where replication should start, since everything before this point will be in the backup. Once you have jotted down the binlog position, you can create your backup. The easiest way to create a backup of the database is to use `mysqldump`:

```
$ mysqldump --all-databases --host=master-1 >backup.sql
```

Since you now have a faithful copy of the master, you can unlock the tables of the database on the master and allow it to continue processing queries.

```
master> UNLOCK TABLES;
Query OK, 0 rows affected (0.23 sec)
```

Next, restore the backup on the slave using the `mysql` utility:

```
$ mysql --host=slave-1 <backup.sql
```

You have now restored the backup of the master on the slave and can start the slave. Recalling the binlog position of the master that you wrote down previously, configure the slave using `CHANGE MASTER TO` and start the slave:

```
slave> CHANGE MASTER TO
    ->     MASTER_HOST = 'master-1',
    ->     MASTER_PORT = 3306,
    ->     MASTER_USER = 'slave-1',
    ->     MASTER_PASSWORD = 'xyzzy',
    ->     MASTER_LOG_FILE = 'master-bin.000042',
    ->     MASTER_LOG_POS = 456552;
Query OK, 0 rows affected (0.00 sec)

slave> START SLAVE;
Query OK, 0 rows affected (0.25 sec)
```

 It is possible to have `mysqldump` perform many of the previous steps automatically. To make a logical backup of all databases on a server called *master*, enter:

```
$ mysqldump --host=master -all-databases \
> --master-data=1 >backup-source.sql
```

The `--master-data=1` option makes `mysqldump` write a `CHANGE MASTER TO` statement with the file and position in the binary log, as given by `SHOW MASTER STATUS`.

You can then restore the backup on a slave using:

```
$ mysql --host=slave-1 <backup-source.sql
```

Note that you can only use `--master-data=1` to get a `CHANGE MASTER TO` statement for the master. When cloning the slave later, it is necessary to perform all the steps given in the following section.

Congratulations! You have now cloned the master and have a new slave up and running. Depending on the load of the master, you might need to allow the slave to catch up from the position you jotted down, but that requires far less effort than starting from the beginning.

Depending on how long the backup took, there might be a lot of data to catch up to, so before bringing the slave online, you might want to read through "Managing Consistency of Data" on page 185.

Cloning the Slave

Once you have a slave connected to the master, you can use the slave instead of the master to create new slaves. That way, you can create a new slave without bringing the master offline. If you have a large or high-traffic database, the downtime could be considerable, considering both the time to create the backup and the time for the slaves to catch up.

The process of cloning a slave is illustrated in Figure 2-6 and is basically the same as for a master, but it differs in how you find the binlog position. You also need to take into consideration that the slave you are cloning from is replicating a master.

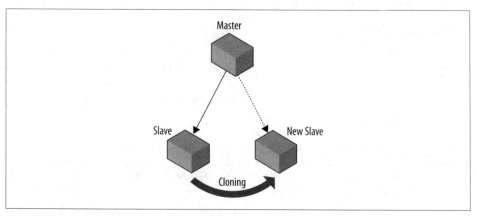

Figure 2-6. Cloning a slave to create a new slave

The first thing you have to do before starting a backup is to stop the slave so that no more changes occur on it. If replication is running while you create the backup, you will have an inconsistent backup image if changes are made to the database while it is being backed up. The exception is if you use some form of online backup method—such as InnoDB Hot Backup—in which case you do not need to stop the slave before creating the backup.

```
original-slave> STOP SLAVE;
Query OK, 0 rows affected (0.20 sec)
```

After the slave is stopped, you can flush the tables as before and create the backup. Since you created a backup of the slave (not the master), use the SHOW SLAVE STATUS command instead of SHOW MASTER STATUS to determine where to start replication. The output from this command is considerable, and it will be covered in detail in Chapter 6, but to get the position of the next event in the binary log of the master that the slave will execute, note the value of the fields Relay_Master_Log_File and Exec_Master_Log_Pos.

```
original-slave> SHOW SLAVE STATUS\G
           ...
Relay_Master_Log_File: master-bin.000042
           ...
   Exec_Master_Log_Pos: 546632
```

After creating the backup and restoring it on the new slave, configure replication to start from this position and start the new slave:

```
new-slave> CHANGE MASTER TO
        ->    MASTER_HOST = 'master-1',
        ->    MASTER_PORT = 3306,
        ->    MASTER_USER = 'slave-1',
        ->    MASTER_PASSWORD = 'xyzzy',
        ->    MASTER_LOG_FILE = 'master-bin.000042',
        ->    MASTER_LOG_POS = 546632;
Query OK, 0 rows affected (0.19 sec)

new-slave> START SLAVE;
Query OK, 0 rows affected (0.24 sec)
```

Cloning the master and cloning the slave differ only on some minor points, which means that our Python library will be able to combine the two into a single procedure for creating new slaves by creating the backup at a source server and connecting the new slave to a master.

 A common technique for making backups is to call FLUSH TABLES WITH READ LOCK and then to create an archive of the database files. This is usually much faster, but FLUSH TABLES WITH READ LOCK is *not safe for use with InnoDB!*

FLUSH TABLES WITH READ LOCK does lock the tables, preventing any new transactions from starting, but there are several activities going on in the background that FLUSH TABLES WITH READ LOCK does not prevent.

Use the following to create a backup of InnoDB tables safely:

1. Shut down the server and copy the files. This can be an advantage if the database is big, as restoring data with mysqldump can be slow.

2. Use mysqldump after performing FLUSH TABLES WITH READ LOCK (as we did earlier).

3. Use a snapshot solution such as LVM (on Linux) or ZFS (Zettabyte File System) snapshots (on Solaris) after using FLUSH TABLES WITH READ LOCK.

Scripting the Clone Operation

The Python library clones a master simply by copying the database from the master using the Server object that represents the master. To do this, it uses a clone function, which you will see in Example 2-7.

Cloning a slave is similar, but the backup is taken from one server, while the new slave connects to another server to perform replication. It is easy to support cloning both a master and a slave by using two different parameters: a source parameter that specifies where the backup should be created and a use_master parameter that indicates where the slave should connect after the backup is restored. A call to the clone method looks like:

```
clone(slave = slave[1], source = slave[0], use_master = master)
```

The next step is to write some utility functions to implement the cloning function, which will also come in handy for other activities. Example 2-6 shows the following functions:

fetch_master_pos

> Fetches the binlog position from a master (that is, the position of the next event the master will write to the binary log).

fetch_slave_pos

> Fetches the binlog position from a slave (that is, the position of the next event to read from the master).

replicate_from

> Accepts as arguments a slave, a master, and a binlog position, and directs the slave to replicate from the master starting with the given position.

The replicate_from function reads the field repl_user from the master to get the name and password of the replication user. If you look at the definition of the Server class, you'll find that there is no such field. It is added by the Master role when the server is imbued.

Example 2-6. Utility functions to fetch the master and slave positions of a server

```
_CHANGE_MASTER_TO = """CHANGE MASTER TO
    MASTER_HOST=%s, MASTER_PORT=%s,
    MASTER_USER=%s, MASTER_PASSWORD=%s,
    MASTER_LOG_FILE=%s, MASTER_LOG_POS=%s"""

def replicate_from(slave, master, position):
    slave.sql(_CHANGE_MASTER_TO, (master.host, master.port,
                                  master.repl_user.name,
                                  master.repl_user.passwd,
                                  position.file, position.pos))

def fetch_master_pos(server):
    result = server.sql("SHOW MASTER STATUS")
    return mysqlrep.Position(server.server_id, result["File"], result["Position"])
```

```
def fetch_slave_pos(server):
    result = server.sql("SHOW SLAVE STATUS")
    return mysqlrep.Position(server.server_id, result["Relay_Master_Log_File"],
                             result["Exec_Master_Log_Pos"])
```

These are all the functions needed to create the clone function. To clone a slave, the calling application passes a separate use_master argument, causing clone to direct the new slave to that master for replication. To clone a master, the calling application omits the separate use_master argument, causing the function to use the "source" server as a master.

Since there are many ways to create a backup of a server, Example 2-7 restricts the method to one choice, using mysqldump to create a logical backup of the server. Later, we will demonstrate how to generalize the backup procedure so that you can use the same basic code to bootstrap new slaves using arbitrary backup methods.

Example 2-7. Function to clone either the master or the slave

```
def clone(slave, source, use_master = None):
    from subprocess import call
    backup_file = open(server.host + "-backup.sql", "w+")
    if master is not None:
        stop_slave(source)
    lock_database(source)
    if master is None:
        position = fetch_master_position(source)
    else:
        position = fetch_slave_position(source)
    call(["mysqldump", "--all-databases", "--host='%s'" % source.host],
        stdout=backup_file)
    if master is not None:
        start_slave(source)
    backup_file.seek()                         # Rewind to beginning
    call(["mysql", "--host='%s'" % slave.host], stdin=backup_file)
    if master is None:
        replicate_from(slave, source, position)
    else:
        replicate_from(slave, master, position)
    start_slave(slave)
```

Performing Common Tasks with Replication

Each of the common scale-out strategies—hot standbys and so forth—involve their own implementation details and possible pitfalls. We'll show you how to perform some of these tasks and how to enhance the Python library to support them.

Passwords are omitted from the examples in this section. When configuring the accounts to control the servers, you can either allow access only from certain hosts that control the deployment (by creating accounts such as mats@'192.168.2.136'), or you can supply passwords to the commands.

Reporting

Most businesses need a lot of routine reports: weekly reports on the items sold, monthly reports on expenses and revenues, and various kinds of heavy data mining to spot trends or identify focus groups for the marketing department.

Running these queries on the master can prove to be troublesome. Data-mining queries can require a lot of computing resources and can slow down normal operations only to find out that, say, a focus group for left-handed scissors might not be worthwhile to conduct. In addition, these reports are typically not very urgent (compared to processing normal transactions), so there is no need to create them as quickly as possible. In other words, because these reports are not time-critical, it does not matter much if they take two hours to complete instead of one.

Reporting often needs to cover a precise interval, such as a summary of all sales for the day, so it is necessary to stop replication at the right moment so you don't get any sales for the following day in the report. Since there is no way to stop the slave when it sees an event with a certain date or time, it has to be done some other way.

A better idea is to dust off a spare server (or two, if you have enough reporting requirements) and set it up to replicate from the master. When you need to do the reporting, you can stop replication, run your reporting applications, then start replication again, all without disturbing the master.

Let's pretend that reports are needed once each day, and that all transactions from midnight to midnight shall be included. It is necessary to stop the reporting slave at midnight so that no events from after midnight are executed on the slave and all events from before midnight are executed on the slave. The intention is not to do this manually, so let's consider how we can automate the procedure. The following steps will accomplish what we want:

1. Just before midnight, perhaps five minutes before midnight, stop the reporting slave so that no events come from the master.

2. After midnight, check the binary log on the master and find the last event that was recorded before midnight. Obviously, if you do this before midnight, you might not have seen all events for the day yet.

3. Record the binlog position of this event and start the slave to run until this position.

4. Wait until the slave has reached this position and stopped.

The first issue is how to schedule the jobs correctly. There are different ways to do this, depending on the operating system. While we won't go into all the details here, you can see how to schedule tasks for Unix-like operating systems, such as Linux, in "Scheduling tasks on Unix" on page 42.

Stopping the slave is as simple as executing STOP SLAVE and noting the binlog position *after* the slave is stopped.

```
slave> STOP SLAVE;
Query OK, 0 rows affected (0.25 sec)

slave> SHOW SLAVE STATUS\G
    ...
Relay_Master_Log_File: capulet-bin.000004
    ...
  Exec_Master_Log_Pos: 2456
1 row in set (0.00 sec)
```

The remaining three steps are executed before the actual reporting starts and usually as part of the script that does the actual reporting. Before outlining the script, let's consider how to perform each step.

To read the contents of the binary log, invoke a utility called mysqlbinlog. This will be introduced in detail later, but this utility is used in the second step. The mysqlbinlog utility has the two handy options --start-datetime and --stop-datetime, which you can use to read only a portion of the binary log. So, to get all events from the time that you stopped the slave to just before midnight, use the following command:

```
$ mysqlbinlog --force --read-from-remote-server --host=reporting.bigcorp.com \
>    --start-datetime='2009-09-25 23:55:00' --stop-datetime='2009-09-25 23:59:59' \
>    binlog files
```

> The timestamp stored in each event is the timestamp when the statement started executing, not the timestamp when it was written to the binary log.
>
> Since the --stop-datetime option will stop emitting events on the *first* timestamp after the date/time supplied, it is possible that there is an event that started executing before the date/time but was written to the binary log after the date/time and is not included in the range given.

Since the master is writing to the binary logs at this time, it is necessary to supply the --force option. Otherwise, mysqlbinlog will refuse to read the open binary log. To execute this command, it is necessary to supply a set of binlog files to read. Since the names of these files are dependent on configuration options, the names of these files have to be fetched from the server. After that, it is necessary to figure out the range of binlog files that needs to be supplied to the mysqlbinlog command. Getting the list of binlog filenames is easy to do with the SHOW BINARY LOGS command:

```
master> SHOW BINARY LOGS;
+--------------------+-----------+
| Log_name           | File_size |
+--------------------+-----------+
| capulet-bin.000001 |     24316 |
| capulet-bin.000002 |      1565 |
| capulet-bin.000003 |       125 |
| capulet-bin.000004 |      2749 |
+--------------------+-----------+
4 rows in set (0.00 sec)
```

In this case, there are only four files, but there could potentially be quite a lot more. Scanning a large list of files that were written before the slave was stopped is just a waste of time, so it is a good idea to try to reduce the number of files to read in order to find the correct position to stop at. Since you recorded the binlog position in the first step, when the slave was stopped, it is an easy matter to find the name of the file where the slave stopped and then take that name and all the following names as input to the mysqlbinlog utility. Typically, this will only be one file (or two in the event that the binary log was rotated between stopping the slave and starting the reporting).

When executing the mysqlbinlog command with just a few binlog files, you will get a textual output for each with some information about the event.

```
$ mysqlbinlog --force --read-from-remote-server --host=reporting.bigcorp.com \
>     --start-datetime='2009-09-25 23:55:00' --stop-datetime='2009-09-25 23:59:59' \
>     capulet-bin.000004
/*!40019 SET @@session.max_insert_delayed_threads=0*/;
/*!50003 SET @OLD_COMPLETION_TYPE=@@COMPLETION_TYPE,COMPLETION_TYPE=0*/;
DELIMITER /*!*/;
# at 4
#090909 22:16:25 server id 1  end_log_pos 106   Start: binlog v 4, server v...
ROLLBACK/*!*/;
    .
    .
    .
# at 2495
#090929 23:58:36 server id 1  end_log_pos 2650  Query    thread_id=27    exe...
SET TIMESTAMP=1254213690/*!*/;
SET /*!*/;
INSERT INTO message_board(user, message)
    VALUES ('mats@sun.com', 'Midnight, and I'm bored')
/*!*/;
```

The interesting part here is the end_log_pos of the last event in the sequence—in this case, 2650—since this is where the next event after midnight will be written.

If you were paying attention to the output from the previous command, you saw that there is no information about which binlog file this byte position is referring to, and it is necessary to have a file to find the event. If a single file is supplied to the mysqlbin log command, the filename is obvious, but if two files are supplied, it is necessary to figure out if the last event for the day is in the first or the second file.

If you look at the line containing the end_log_pos, you will also see that the event type is there. Since every binlog file starts with a format description event—a line for such an event appears in the previous output—you can check these events to determine the location of the event you want. If there are two format description events in the output, the event is in the second file, and if there is just one, it is in the first file.

The final step before starting the reporting work is to start replication and stop it at exactly the position where the event after midnight will be written (or has already been written, should that be the case). To do this, you can use the little-known command START SLAVE UNTIL. This command accepts a master logfile and a master log position where the slave should stop, and then starts the slave. When the slave reaches the given position, it will automatically stop.

```
report> START SLAVE UNTIL
    ->     MASTER_LOG_POS='capulet-bin.000004',
    ->     MASTER_LOG_POS=2650;
Query OK, 0 rows affected (0.18 sec)
```

Like the STOP SLAVE command (without the UNTIL), the START SLAVE UNTIL command will return immediately—not, as could be expected, when the slave has reached the position where it should stop. So, commands issued after STOP SLAVE UNTIL continue to be executed as long as the slave is running. To wait for the slave to reach the position you want it to stop at, use the MASTER_POS_WAIT function. This function will block while waiting for the slave to reach the given position.

```
report> SELECT MASTER_POS_WAIT('capulet-bin.000004', 2650);
Query OK, 0 rows affected (231.15 sec)
```

At this point, the slave has stopped at the last event for the day, and the reporting process can start analyzing the data and generating reports.

Handling reporting in Python

Automating this in Python is quite straightforward.

Example 2-8 shows the code for stopping reporting at the right time.

The fetch_remote_binlog function reads a binary log from a remote server using the mysqlbinlog command. The contents of the file(s) will be returned as an iterator over the lines of the file. To optimize the fetches, you can optionally provide a list of files to scan. You can also pass a start date/time and a stop date/time to limit the date/time range of the result. These will be passed to the mysqlbinlog program.

The find_datetime_position function does the work of scanning the binlog lines to find the last end_log_pos as well as keeping track of how many start events have been observed. It also contacts the reporting server to find out where it stopped reading the binlog file and then contacts the master to get the binlog files and find the right one to start the scan from.

Example 2-8. Python code for running replication to a datetime

```python
def fetch_remote_binlog(server, binlog_files=None,
                        start_datetime=None, stop_datetime=None):
    from subprocess import Popen, PIPE
    if not binlog_files:
        binlog_files = [
            row["Log_name"] for row in server.sql("SHOW BINARY LOGS")]

    command = ["mysqlbinlog",
               "--read-from-remote-server",
               "--force",
               "--host=%s" % (server.host),
               "--user=%s" % (server.sql_user.name)]
    if server.sql_user.passwd:
        command.append("--password=%s" % (server.sql_user.passwd))
    if start_datetime:
        command.append("--start-datetime=%s" % (start_datetime))
    if stop_datetime:
        command.append("--stop-datetime=%s" % (stop_datetime))
    return iter(Popen(command + binlog_files, stdout=PIPE).stdout)

def find_datetime_position(master, report, start_datetime, stop_datetime):
    from itertools import dropwhile
    from mysqlrep import Position
    import re

    all_files = [row["Log_name"] for row in master.sql("SHOW BINARY LOGS")]
    stop_file = report.sql("SHOW SLAVE STATUS")["Relay_Master_Log_File"]
    files = list(dropwhile(lambda file: file != stop_file, all_files))
    lines = fetch_remote_binlog(server, binlog_files=files,
                                start_datetime=start_datetime,
                                stop_datetime=stop_datetime)
    binlog_files = 0
    last_epos = None
    for line in lines:
        m = re.match(r"#\d{6}\s+\d?\d:\d\d:\d\d\s+"
                     r"server id\s+(?P<sid>\d+)\s+"
                     r"end_log_pos\s+(?P<epos>\d+)\s+"
                     r"(?P<type>\w+)", line)
        if m:
            if m.group("type") == "Start":
                binlog_files += 1
            if m.group("type") == "Query":
                last_epos = m.group("epos")
    return Position(files[binlog_files-1], last_epos)
```

You can now use these functions to synchronize the reporting server before the actual reporting job:

```python
master.connect()
report.connect()
pos = find_datetime_position(master, report,
                             start_datetime="2009-09-14 23:55:00",
                             stop_datetime="2009-09-14 23:59:59")
report.sql("START SLAVE UNTIL MASTER_LOG_FILE=%s, MASTER_LOG_POS=%s",
```

```
                    (pos.file, pos.pos))
        report.sql("DO MASTER_POS_WAIT(%s,%s)", (pos.file, pos.pos))

          .
          .
          .
    code for reporting
          .
          .
          .
```

As you can see, working with replication is pretty straightforward. This particular example introduces several of the critical concepts that we will be using later when talking about scale-out: how to start and stop the slave at the right time, how to get information about binlog positions or figure it out using the standard tools, and how to integrate it all into an automated solution for your particular needs.

Scheduling tasks on Unix

To easiest way ensure the slave is stopped just before midnight and the reporting is started after midnight is to set up a job for *cron(8)* that sends a stop slave command to the slave and starts the reporting script.

For example, the following *crontab(5)* entries would ensure that the slave is stopped before midnight, and that the reporting script to roll the slave forward is executed, say, five minutes after midnight. Here we assume that the **stop_slave** script will stop the slave, and the **daily_report** will run the daily report (starting with the synchronization described above).

```
# stop reporting slave five minutes before midnight, every day
55 23 * * * $HOME/mysql_control/stop_slave

# Run reporting script five minutes after midnight, every day
5 0 * * * $HOME/mysql_control/daily_report
```

Assuming that you put this in a crontab file, *reporttab*, you can install the crontab file using the command:

```
$ crontab reporttab
```

Scheduling tasks on Windows Vista

Scheduling tasks is much easier on Windows Vista than on previous versions of Windows. There have been several major and welcome enhancements to the Task Scheduler. The Task Scheduler is now a Microsoft Management Console snap-in and is integrated with the Event Viewer, which gives you the ability to use events as triggers for starting tasks. There are also more scheduling and triggering options.

To start the Task Scheduler in Windows Vista, open the Event Scheduler using the Control Panel, via the Administrator's Folder on the Start Menu, or by using the run feature (Windows key + R) and enter **taskschd.msc**. You will need to respond to the User Account Control (UAC) dialog box to continue.

To create a new task trigger by time, choose Create Basic Task from the Action pane. This opens the Create Basic Task Wizard, which will guide you through the steps to create a simple task.

On the first pane of the wizard, name the task and provide an optional description, then click Next.

The second pane allows you to specify the frequency of the firing of the task. There are many options here for controlling when the task runs: a single run, daily, weekly, and even when you log on or when a specific event occurs. Click Next once you've made your choice.

Depending on the frequency you chose, the third pane will allow you to specify the details (for example, date and time) of when the task fires. Click Next once you have configured the trigger timing options.

The fourth pane is where you specify the task or action to occur when the task event occurs (when the task fires). You can choose to start a program, send an email message, or display a message to the user. Make your selection and click Next to move to the next pane.

Depending on the action you chose on the previous pane, here you can specify what happens when the task fires. For example, if you chose to run an application, you enter the name of the application or script, any arguments, and which folder the task starts in.

Once you have entered all of this information, click Next to review the task on the final pane. If you're satisfied all is set correctly, click Finish to schedule the task. You can click Back to return to any of the previous screens and make changes. Finally, you have the option to open the properties page after you click Finish; this allows you to make additional changes to the task.

Conclusion

In this chapter, we have presented an introduction to MySQL replication, including a look at why replication is used and how to set it up. We also took a quick look into the binary log. In the next chapter, we examine the binary log in greater detail.

Joel finished giving Mr. Summerson his report on how he was going to balance the load across four new slaves, along with plans for how the topology could be expanded to handle future needs.

"That's fine work, Joel. Now explain to me again what this slave thing is."

Joel suppressed a sigh and said, "A slave is a copy of the data on the database server that gets its changes from the original database server called the master...."

## CHAPTER 3

The Binary Log

"Joel?"

Joel jumped, nearly banging his head as he crawled out from under his desk. "I was just rerouting a few cables," he said by way of an explanation.

Mr. Summerson merely nodded and said in a very authoritative manner, "I need you to look into a problem the marketing people are having with the new server. They need to roll back the data to a certain point."

"Well, that depends...," Joel started, worried about whether he had snapshots of old states of the system.

"I told them you'd be right down."

With that, Mr. Summerson turned and walked away. A moment later one of the developers, a woman Joel found very attractive, stopped in front of his door and said, "He's always like that. Don't take it personally. Most of us call it a drive-by tasking." She laughed and introduced herself. "My name's Amy."

Joel walked around his desk and met her at the door. "I'm Joel."

After a moment of awkward silence Joel said, "I, er, better get on that thing."

Amy smiled and said, "See you around."

"Just focus on what you have to do to succeed," Joel thought as he returned to his desk to search for that MySQL book he bought last week.

The previous chapter included a very brief introduction to the binary log. In this chapter, we will fill in more details and give a more thorough description of the binary log structure, the replication event format, and how to use the `mysqlbinlog` tool to investigate and work with the contents of binary logs.

The binary log records changes made to the database so that the same changes can be made on any of the slaves as well. Since the binary log normally keeps a record of all changes, you can also use it for auditing purposes to see what happened in the database, and for PITR by playing back the binary log to a server, repeating changes that were recorded in the binary log.

The binary log contains only statements that could change the database. Note that statements that do not change the database but that could *potentially* change the database are logged. The most notable statements are those that optionally make a change, such as DROP TABLE IF EXISTS or CREATE TABLE IF NOT EXISTS, along with statements such as DELETE and UPDATE that have WHERE conditions that don't happen to match any rows.

SELECT statements are not normally logged, since they do not make any changes to any database. There are, however, exceptions.

Transactions on a server are not normally executed in sequence, one after the other, but are rather interleaved and executed in parallel. To ensure that two transactions do not conflict and generate an inconsistent result, the server ensures the transaction execution is *serializable,* meaning the transactions are executed in such a way that the execution yields the same result as if they were executed in a *serial* order—that is, in a fixed order, one transaction after another.

The binary log records each transaction in the order that the commit took place on the master. Although transactions may be interleaved on the master, each appears as an uninterrupted sequence in the binary log, the order determined by the time of the commit.

Structure of the Binary Log

Conceptually, the binary log is a sequence of *binary log events* (also called *binlog events* or even just *events* when there is no risk of confusion). As you saw in Chapter 2, the binary log actually consists of several files, as shown in Figure 3-1, that together form the binary log.

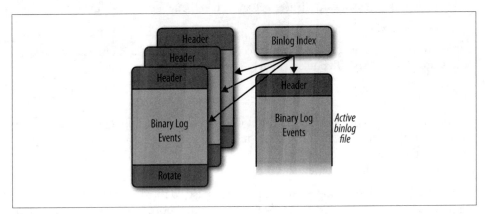

Figure 3-1. The structure of the binary log

The actual events are stored in a series of files called *binlog files* with names in the form *host-bin.000001*, accompanied by a *binlog index file* that is usually named *host-bin.index* and keeps track of the existing binlog files. The binlog file that is currently being written to by the server is called the *active* binlog file. If all the slaves have caught up with the master, this is also the file that is being read by the slaves. The names of the binlog files and the binlog index file can be controlled using the options `log-bin` and `log-bin-index`, which are covered later in the chapter.

The index file keeps track of all the binlog files used by the server so that the server can correctly create new binlog files when necessary, even after server restarts. Each line in the index file contains the full name of a binlog file that is part of the binary log. Commands that affect the binlog files, such as `PURGE BINARY LOGS`, `RESET MASTER`, and `FLUSH LOGS`, also affect the index file by adding or removing lines to match the files that were added or removed by the command.

As shown in Figure 3-2, each binlog file is made up of binlog events, with the `Format_description` event serving as the file's header and the `Rotate` event as its footer. Note that a binlog file might not end with a rotate event if the server was stopped or crashed.

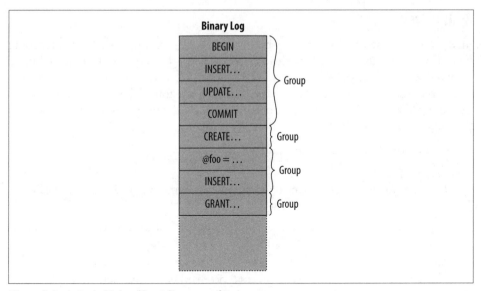

Figure 3-2. A single binlog file with groups of events

The `Format_description` event contains information about the server that wrote the binlog file as well as some critical information about the file's status. If the server is stopped and restarted, a new binlog file is created and a new `Format_description` event is written to it. This is necessary since changes can potentially occur between bringing a server down and bringing it up again. For example, the server could be upgraded, in which case a new `Format_description` event would have to be written.

When the server has finished writing a binlog file, a `Rotate` event is added to end the file. The event points to the next binlog file in sequence by giving the name of the file as well as the position to start reading from.

The `Format_description` event and the `Rotate` event will be described in detail in the next section.

With the exception of the `Format_description` and `Rotate` events, the events of a binlog file are grouped into units called *groups*. In transactional storage engines, each group is roughly equivalent to a transaction, but for nontransactional storage engines or statements that cannot be part of a transaction, such as `CREATE` or `ALTER` statements, each statement is a group by itself. In short, each group of events in the binlog file contains either a single statement not in a transaction or a transaction consisting of several statements.

Normally, each group is executed entirely or not at all. If, for some reason, the slave stops in the middle of a group, replication will start from the beginning of the group and not from the last statement executed. Chapter 6 describes in detail how the slave executes events.

Binlog Event Structure

In MySQL 5.0, a new binlog format—binlog format 4—was introduced. The preceding formats were not easy to extend with additional fields if the need should arise, so binlog format 4 was designed specifically to be extensible. This is still the event format used in every server version since 5.0, even though each version of the server has extended the binlog format with new events and some events with new fields. Binlog format 4 is the event format described in this chapter.

Each binlog event consists of three parts:

Common header
> The common header is—as the name suggests—common to all events in the binlog file.
>
> The common header contains basic information about the event, the most important fields being the event type and the size of the event.

Post header
> The post header is specific to each event type; in other words, each event type stores different information in this field. But the size of this header, just as with the common header, is the same throughout a given binlog file. The size of each event type is given by the `Format_description` event.

Event body
> Last in each event comes the event body, which is the variable-sized part of the event. The size is listed in the common header for the event. The event body stores the main data of the event, which is different for different event types. For the

`Query` event, for instance, the body stores the query, and for the `User_var` event, the body stores the name and value of a user variable that was just set by a statement.

A complete listing of the formats of all events is beyond the scope of this book, but since the `Format_description` and `Rotate` events are critical to how the other events are interpreted, we will briefly cover them here.

As already noted, the `Format_description` event starts every binlog file and contains common information about the events in the file. The result is that the `Format_description` event can be different between different files; this typically occurs when a server is upgraded and restarted.

Binlog file format version
> This is the version of the binlog file, which should not be confused with the version of the server. MySQL versions 3.23, 4.0, and 4.1 use version 3 of the binary log, while MySQL versions 5.0 and later use version 4 of the binary log.
>
> The binlog file format version changes when developers make significant changes in the overall structure of the file or the events. In version 5.0, the start event for a binlog file was changed to use a different format and the common headers for all events were also changed, which prompted the change in the binlog file format version.

Server version
> This is a version string denoting the server that created the file. This includes the version of the server as well as additional information if special builds are made. The format is normally the three-position version number, followed by a hyphen and any additional build options. For example, "5.1.40-debug-log" means debug build version 5.1.40 of the server.

Common header length
> This field stores the length of the common header. Since it's here in the `Format_description`, this length can be different for different binlog files. This holds for all events except the `Format_description` and `Rotate` events, which cannot vary. The length of `Format_description` is fixed because a server has to read the event regardless of which version of the server produced it. The reason the `Rotate` event has a fixed common header is that the event is used when the slave connects to the master, before any events from the binlog file have been seen. So for these two events, the size of the common header is fixed and will never change between server versions.

Post-header lengths
> The post-header length for each event is fixed within a binlog file, and this field stores an array of the post-header length for each event that can occur in the binlog file. Since the number of events can vary between servers, the number of events that the server can produce is stored before this field.

Since both the size of the common header and the size of the post header for each event type are given in the `Format_description` event, extending the format with new events or even increasing the size of the post headers by adding new fields will not affect the high-level format of the binlog file.

With each extension, particular care is taken to ensure that the extension does not affect interpretation of earlier-version events. For example, the common header can be extended with an additional field to indicate that the event is compressed and the type of compression used, but if this field is missing—which would be the case if a slave is reading events from an old master—the server should still be able to fall back on its old behavior.

Logging Statements

MySQL has traditionally employed statement-based replication and just recently implemented row-based replication, which we will cover in Chapter 6.

In statement-based replication, the actual executed statement is written to the binary log together with some execution information, and the statement is reexecuted on the slave. Since not all statements can be logged as statements, there are some exceptions that you should be aware of. This section will describe the process of logging statements as well as the important caveats.

Since the binary log is a common resource—all threads write statements to it—it is critical to prevent two threads from updating the binary log at the same time. To handle this, a lock for the binary log—the `LOCK_log` mutex—is acquired just before the event is written to the binary log and released just after the event has been written. Because all session threads for the server log statements to the binary log, it is quite common for several session threads to block on this lock.

Logging Data Manipulation Language Statements

Data Manipulation Language (DML) statements are usually `DELETE`, `INSERT`, and `UPDATE` statements. To support safe logging, MySQL writes the binary log while transaction-level locks are held, and releases them after the binary log has been written.

To ensure the binary log is updated consistently with the tables that the statement modifies, the statement is logged to the binary log at the same time that the statement is being committed, just before the table locks are released. If the logging were not made as part of the statement, another statement could be "injected" between the changes that the statement introduces to the database and the logging of the statement to the binary log. This would mean that the statements would be logged in a different order than the one in which they took effect in the database, which clearly could lead to inconsistencies between master and slave. For instance, an `UPDATE` statement with a

`WHERE` clause could update different rows on the slave because the values in those rows could change if the statement order changed.

Logging Data Definition Language Statements

Data Definition Language (DDL) statements affect a schema, such as `CREATE TABLE` and `ALTER TABLE` statements. These create or change objects in the filesystem—for example, table definitions are stored in *.frm* files and databases are represented as filesystem directories—so the server keeps information about these available in data structures internally. To protect the update of the internal data structure, it is necessary to acquire a lock before altering the table definition.

Since a single lock is used to protect these data structures, the creation, alteration, and destruction of database objects can be a considerable source of performance problems. This includes the creation and destruction of temporary tables, which is quite common as a technique to create an intermediate result set to perform computations on.

If you are creating and destroying a lot of temporary tables, it is often possible to boost performance by reducing the creation (and subsequent destruction) of temporary tables.

Logging Queries

For statement-based replication, the most common binlog event is the `Query` event, which is used to hold a statement executed on the master. In addition to the actual statement executed, the event contains some additional information necessary for execution of the statement.

Recall that the binary log can be used for many purposes and contains statements in a potentially different order than that in which they were executed on the master. In some cases, part of the binary log may be played back to a server to perform PITR, and in some cases, replication may start in the middle of a sequence of events because a backup has been restored on a slave before starting replication. Furthermore, a database administrator (DBA) might manually tweak the binary log to fix a problem.

In all these cases, the events are executing in different *contexts*. That is, there is information that is implicit when the server executes the statement but that has to be known to execute the statement correctly. Examples include:

Current database
> If the statement refers to a table, function, or procedure without qualifying it with the database, the current database is implicit for the statement.

Value of user-defined variable
> If a statement refers to a user-defined variable, the value of the variable is implicit for the statement.

Seed for the RAND function

The RAND function is based on a pseudorandom number function, meaning that it can generate a sequence of numbers that are reproducible but appear random in the sense that they are evenly distributed. The function is not really random, but starts from a seed number and applies a pseudorandom function to generate a deterministic sequence of numbers. This means that given the same seed, the RAND function will always return the same number. However, this makes the seed implicit for the statement.

The current time

Obviously, the time the statement started executing is implicit. Having a correct time is important when calling functions that are dependent on the current time—such as NOW and UNIX_TIMESTAMP—because otherwise they will return different results if there is a delay between the statement execution on the master and on the slave.

Value used when inserting into an AUTO_INCREMENT column

If a statement inserts a row into a table with a column defined with the AUTO_INCREMENT attribute, the value used for that row is implicit for the statement since it depends on the rows inserted before it.

Value returned by a call to LAST_INSERT_ID

If the LAST_INSERT_ID function is used in a statement, it depends on the value inserted by a previous statement, which makes this value implicit for the statement.

Thread ID

For some statements, the thread ID is implicit. For example, if the statement refers to a temporary table or uses the CURRENT_ID function, the thread ID is implicit for the statement.

Since the context for executing the statements cannot be known when they're replayed—either on a slave or on the master after a crash and restart—it is necessary to make the implicit information explicit by adding it to the binary log. This is done in slightly different ways depending on the kind of information.

In addition to the previous list, some information is implicit to the execution of triggers and stored routines, but we will cover that separately in the section "Triggers, Events, and Stored Routines" on page 61.

Let's consider each of the cases of implicit information individually, demonstrate the problem with each one, and examine how the server handles it.

Current database

The log records the current database by adding it to a special field of the Query event. This field also exists for the events used to handle the LOAD DATA INFILE statement, discussed in the section "LOAD DATA INFILE Statements" on page 57, so the description here applies to that statement as well. The current database also plays an important role in filtering on the database and is described later in this chapter.

Current time

Five functions use the current time to compute their values: NOW, CURDATE, CURTIME, UNIX_TIMESTAMP, and SYSDATE. The first four functions return a value based on the time when the statement *started* to execute. In contrast, SYSDATE will return the value of time(2). The difference can best be demonstrated by comparing the execution of NOW and SYSDATE with an intermediate sleep:

```
mysql> SELECT SYSDATE(), SLEEP(2), SYSDATE();
+---------------------+----------+---------------------+
| SYSDATE()           | SLEEP(2) | SYSDATE()           |
+---------------------+----------+---------------------+
| 2010-03-27 22:27:36 |        0 | 2010-03-27 22:27:38 |
+---------------------+----------+---------------------+
1 row in set (2.00 sec)

mysql> SELECT NOW(), SLEEP(2), NOW();
+---------------------+----------+---------------------+
| NOW()               | SLEEP(2) | NOW()               |
+---------------------+----------+---------------------+
| 2010-03-27 22:27:49 |        0 | 2010-03-27 22:27:49 |
+---------------------+----------+---------------------+
1 row in set (2.00 sec)
```

Both functions are evaluated when they are encountered, but NOW returns the time that the statement started executing and SYSDATE returns the time from time(2).

To handle these time functions correctly, the timestamp indicating when the event *started* executing is stored in the event. This value is then copied from the event to the slave execution thread and used as if it were the time the event started executing when computing the value of the time functions.

Since SYSDATE calls time(2) directly, it is not safe for replication and will return different values on the master and slave when executed. So unless you really want to have the actual time inserted into your tables, it is prudent to stay away from this function.

Context events

Some implicit information is associated with statements that meet certain conditions:

- If the statement contains a reference to a user-defined variable (as in Example 3-1), it is necessary to add the value of the user-defined variable to the binary log.
- If the statement contains a call to the RAND function, it is necessary to add the pseudorandom seed to the binary log.
- If the statement contain a call to the LAST_INSERT_ID function, it is necessary to add the last inserted ID to the binary log.
- If the statement performs an insert into a table with an AUTO_INCREMENT column, it is necessary to add the value that was used for the column (or columns) to the binary log.

Example 3-1. Statements with user-defined variables

```
SET @value = 45;
INSERT INTO t1 VALUES (@value);
```

In each of these cases, one or more *context events* are added to the binary log before the event containing the query is written. Since there can be several context events preceding a Query event, the binary log can handle multiple user-defined variables together with the RAND function, or (almost) any combination of the previously listed conditions. The binary log stores the necessary context information through the following events:

User_var

Each such event records the name and value of a single user-defined variable.

Rand

Records the random number seed used by the RAND function. The seed is fetched internally from the session's state.

Intvar

If the statement is inserting into an autoincrement column, this event records the value of the internal autoincrement counter for the table before the statement starts.

If the statement contains a call to LAST_INSERT_ID, this event records the value that this function returned in the statement.

Example 3-2 shows some statements that generate all of the context events and how the events appear when displayed using SHOW BINLOG EVENTS. Note that there can be several context events before each statement.

Example 3-2. Query events with context events

```
master> CREATE TABLE t1 (a INT AUTO_INCREMENT PRIMARY KEY, b INT, c CHAR(64));
Query OK, 0 rows affected (0.00 sec)

master> SET @foo = 12;
Query OK, 0 rows affected (0.00 sec)

master> SET @bar = 'Smoothnoodlemaps';
Query OK, 0 rows affected (0.00 sec)

master> INSERT INTO t1(b,c) VALUES (@foo,@bar), (RAND(), 'random');
Query OK, 2 rows affected (0.00 sec)
Records: 2  Duplicates: 0  Warnings: 0

master> INSERT INTO t1(b) VALUES (LAST_INSERT_ID());
Query OK, 1 row affected (0.00 sec)

master> SHOW BINLOG EVENTS FROM 238\G
*************************** 1. row ***************************
   Log_name: mysqld1-bin.000001
        Pos: 238
```

```
   Event_type: Query
    Server_id: 1
  End_log_pos: 306
         Info: BEGIN
*************************** 2. row ***************************
    Log_name: mysqld1-bin.000001
         Pos: 306
   Event_type: Intvar
    Server_id: 1
  End_log_pos: 334
         Info: INSERT_ID=1
*************************** 3. row ***************************
    Log_name: mysqld1-bin.000001
         Pos: 334
   Event_type: RAND
    Server_id: 1
  End_log_pos: 369
         Info: rand_seed1=952494611,rand_seed2=949641547
*************************** 4. row ***************************
    Log_name: mysqld1-bin.000001
         Pos: 369
   Event_type: User var
    Server_id: 1
  End_log_pos: 413
         Info: @`foo`=12
*************************** 5. row ***************************
    Log_name: mysqld1-bin.000001
         Pos: 413
   Event_type: User var
    Server_id: 1
  End_log_pos: 465
         Info: @`bar`=_latin1 0x536D6F6F74686E6F6F6... COLLATE latin1_swedish_ci
*************************** 6. row ***************************
    Log_name: mysqld1-bin.000001
         Pos: 465
   Event_type: Query
    Server_id: 1
  End_log_pos: 586
         Info: use `test`; INSERT INTO t1(b,c) VALUES (@foo,@bar), (RAND(), ...
*************************** 7. row ***************************
    Log_name: mysqld1-bin.000001
         Pos: 586
   Event_type: Xid
    Server_id: 1
  End_log_pos: 613
         Info: COMMIT /* xid=44 */
*************************** 8. row ***************************
    Log_name: mysqld1-bin.000001
         Pos: 613
   Event_type: Query
    Server_id: 1
  End_log_pos: 681
         Info: BEGIN
```

```
*************************** 9. row ***************************
  Log_name: mysqld1-bin.000001
       Pos: 681
Event_type: Intvar
 Server_id: 1
End_log_pos: 709
      Info: LAST_INSERT_ID=1
*************************** 10. row ***************************
  Log_name: mysqld1-bin.000001
       Pos: 709
Event_type: Intvar
 Server_id: 1
End_log_pos: 737
      Info: INSERT_ID=3
*************************** 11. row ***************************
  Log_name: mysqld1-bin.000001
       Pos: 737
Event_type: Query
 Server_id: 1
End_log_pos: 843
      Info: use `test`; INSERT INTO t1(b) VALUES (LAST_INSERT_ID())
*************************** 12. row ***************************
  Log_name: mysqld1-bin.000001
       Pos: 843
Event_type: Xid
 Server_id: 1
End_log_pos: 870
      Info: COMMIT /* xid=45 */
12 rows in set (0.00 sec)
```

Thread ID

The last implicit piece of information that the binary log sometimes needs is the thread ID of the MySQL session handling the statement. The thread ID is necessary when a function is dependent on the thread ID—such as when it refers to CONNECTION_ID—but most importantly for handling temporary tables.

Temporary tables are specific to each thread, meaning that two temporary tables with the same name are allowed to coexist, provided they are defined in different sessions. Temporary tables can provide an effective means to improve the performance of certain operations, but they require special handling to work with the binary log.

Internally in the server, temporary tables are handled by creating obscure names for storing the table definitions. The names are based on the process ID of the server, the thread ID that creates the table, and a thread-specific counter to distinguish between different instances of the table from the same thread. This naming scheme allows tables from different threads to be distinguished from each other, but each statement can access its proper table only if the thread ID is stored in the binary log.

Similar to how the current database is handled in the binary log, the thread ID is stored as a separate field in every Query event and can therefore be used to compute thread-specific data and handle temporary tables correctly.

When writing the Query event, the thread ID to store in the event is read from the server variable pseudo_thread_id. This means that it can be set before executing a statement, but only if you have SUPER privileges. This server variable is intended to be used by mysqlbinlog to emit statements correctly and should not normally be used.

For a statement that contains a call to the CONNECTION_ID function or that uses or creates a temporary table, the Query event is marked as thread-specific in the binary log. Since the thread ID is always present in the Query event, this flag is not necessary, but is mainly used to allow mysqlbinlog to avoid printing unnecessary assignments to the pseudo_thread_id variable.

LOAD DATA INFILE Statements

The LOAD DATA INFILE statement makes it easy to fill tables quickly from a file. Unfortunately, it is dependent on a certain kind of context that cannot be covered by the context events we have discussed: files that need to be read from the filesystem.

To handle LOAD DATA INFILE, the MySQL server uses a special set of events to handle the transfer of the file using the binary log. In addition to solving the problem for LOAD DATA INFILE, this makes the statement a very convenient tool for transferring large amounts of data from the master to the slave, as you will see soon. To correctly transfer and execute a LOAD DATA INFILE statement, several new events are introduced:

Begin_load_query
: This event starts to transfer data in the file.

Append_block
: A sequence of one or more of these events follows the Begin_load_query event to contain the rest of the file's data if the file was larger than the maximum allowed packet size on the connection.

Execute_load_query
: This event is a specialized variant of the Query event that contains the LOAD DATA INFILE statement executed on the master.

: Even though the statement contained in this event contains the name of the file that was used on the master, this file will not be sought by the slave. Instead, the contents provided by the preceding Begin_load_query and Append_block events will be used.

For each LOAD DATA INFILE statement executed on the master, the file to read is mapped to an internal file-backed buffer, which is used in the following processing. In addition, a unique file ID is assigned to the execution of the statement and is used to refer to the file read by the statement.

While the statement is executing, the file contents are written to the binary log as a sequence of events starting with a Begin_load_query event—which indicates the beginning of a new file—followed by zero or more Append_block events. Each event written to the binary log is no larger than the maximum allowed packet size, as specified by the max-allowed-packet option.

After the entire file is read and applied to the table, the execution of the statement terminates by writing the Execute_load_query event to the binary log. This event contains the statement executed together with the file ID assigned to the execution of the statement. Note that the statement is not the original statement as the user wrote it, but rather a re-created version of the statement.

 If you are reading an old binary log, you might instead find Load_log_event, Execute_log_event, and Create_file_log_event. These were the events used to replicate LOAD DATA INFILE prior to MySQL version 5.0.3 and were replaced by the implementation described above.

Example 3-3 shows the events written to the binary log by a successful execution of a LOAD DATA INFILE statement. In the Info field, you can see the assigned file ID—1 in this case—and see that it is used for all the events that are part of the execution of the statement. You can also see that the file *foo.dat* used by the statement contains more than the maximum allowed packet size of 16384, so it is split into three events.

Example 3-3. Successful execution of a LOAD DATA INFILE

```
master> SHOW BINLOG EVENTS IN 'master-bin.000042' FROM 269\G
*************************** 1. row ***************************
   Log_name: master-bin.000042
        Pos: 269
 Event_type: Begin_load_query
  Server_id: 1
End_log_pos: 16676
       Info: ;file_id=1;block_len=16384
*************************** 2. row ***************************
   Log_name: master-bin.000042
        Pos: 16676
 Event_type: Append_block
  Server_id: 1
End_log_pos: 33083
       Info: ;file_id=1;block_len=16384
*************************** 3. row ***************************
   Log_name: master-bin.000042
        Pos: 33083
 Event_type: Append_block
  Server_id: 1
End_log_pos: 33633
       Info: ;file_id=1;block_len=527
*************************** 4. row ***************************
   Log_name: master-bin.000042
        Pos: 33633
 Event_type: Execute_load_query
  Server_id: 1
End_log_pos: 33756
```

```
         Info: use `test`; LOAD DATA LOCAL INFILE 'foo.dat' INTO ... ;file_id=1
4 rows in set (0.00 sec)
```

Binary Log Filters

It is possible to filter out statements from the binary log using two options: `binlog-do-db` and `binlog-ignore-db` (which we will call `binlog-*-db` collectively). The `binlog-do-db` is used when you want to filter only statements belonging to a certain database, and the `binlog-ignore-db` is used when you want to ignore a certain database but replicate all other databases.

These options can be given multiple times, so to filter out both the database one_db and the database two_db, you must give both options in the *my.cnf* file, for example:

```
[mysqld]
binlog-ignore-db=one_db
binlog-ignore-db=two_db
```

The way MySQL filters events can be quite a surprise to unfamiliar users, so we'll explain how filtering works and make some recommendations on how to avoid some of the major headaches.

Figure 3-3 shows how MySQL determines whether the statement is filtered. The filtering is done on a statement level—either the entire statement is filtered or the entire statement is written to the binary log—and the `binlog-*-db` options use the *current* database to decide whether the statement should be filtered, not the database of the table affected by the statement.

To help you understand the behavior, Example 3-4 shows some statements that change tables in different databases. Each line uses **test** as the current database:

- Line 1 changes a table in the current database named **test** since it does not qualify the table name with a database name.
- Line 2 changes a table in a different database than the current database.
- Line 3 changes two tables in two different databases, neither of which is the current database.

Example 3-4. Statements using different databases

```
USE bad; INSERT INTO t1 VALUES (1),(2);
USE bad; INSERT INTO good.t2 VALUES (1),(2);
USE bad; UPDATE good.t1, ugly.t2 SET a = b;
```

Consider what happens if the *bad* database is filtered using `binlog-ignore-db=bad`. None of the three statements in Example 3-4 will be written to the binary log, even though the second and third statements change tables on the *good* and *ugly* database. This might seem strange at first—why not filter the statement based on the database of the table changed? But consider what would happen with the third statement if the *ugly* database was filtered instead of the *bad* database. Now one database in the

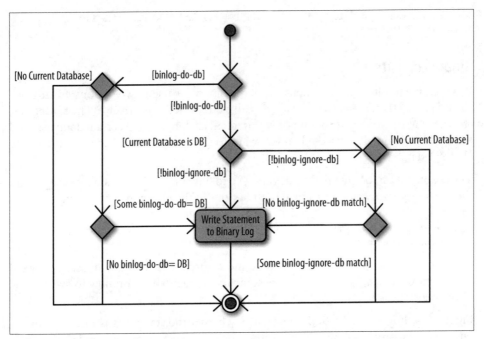

Figure 3-3. Logic for binlog-*-db filters

UPDATE is filtered out and other isn't. This puts the server in a catch-22 situation, so the problem is solved by just filtering on the current database, and this rule is used for all statements (with a few exceptions).

To avoid mistakes when executing statements that can potentially be filtered, make it a habit not to write statements so they qualify table, function, or procedure names with the database name. Instead, whenever you want to access a table in a different database, issue a USE statement to make that database the current database. In other words, instead of writing:

```
INSERT INTO other.book VALUES ('MySQL', 'Paul DuBois');
```

write:

```
USE other; INSERT INTO book VALUES ('MySQL', 'Paul DuBois');
```

This behavior does not apply when row-based replication is used. Row-based replication will be discussed in Chapter 6, but since row-based replication can work with each individual row change, it is able to filter on the actual table that the row is targeted for, and does not use the current database.

So, what happens when both binlog-do-db and binlog-ignore-db are used at the same time? For example, consider a configuration file containing the following two rules:

```
[mysqld]
binlog-do-db=good
binlog-ignore-db=bad
```

In this case, will the following statement be filtered or not?

```
USE ugly; INSERT INTO t1 VALUES (1);
```

Following the diagram in Figure 3-3, you can see that if there is at least a `binlog-do-db` rule, all `binlog-ignore-db` rules are ignored completely, and since only the *good* database is included, the statement above will be filtered.

 Because of the way that the `binlog-*-db` rules are evaluated, it is pointless to have both `binlog-do-db` and `binlog-ignore-db` rules at the same time. The recommendation is to *not* use the `binlog-*-db` options, because the binary log can be used for recovery as well as replication. If you filter out statements from the binary log, you will be unable to restore the database from the binary log in the event of a crash.

Triggers, Events, and Stored Routines

A few other constructions that are treated specially when logged are *stored programs*—that is, triggers, events, and stored routines (the last is a collective name for stored procedures and stored functions). Their treatment with respect to the binary log contains some elements in common, so they will be covered together in this section. The explanation distinguishes statements of two types: statements that define or destroy stored programs and statements that invoke them.

Statements that define or destroy stored programs

The following discussion shows triggers in the examples, but the same principles apply to definition of events and stored routines. To understand why the server needs to handle these features specially when writing them to the binary log, consider the code in Example 3-5.

In the example, a table named *employee* keeps information about all employees of an imagined system and a table named *log* keeps a log of interesting information. Note that the *log* table has a `timestamp` column that notes the time of a change and that the `name` column in the *employee* table is the primary key for the table. There is also a `status` column to tell whether the addition succeeded or failed.

To track information about employee information changes—for example, for auditing purposes—three triggers are created so that whenever an employee is added, removed, or changed, a log entry of the change is added to a log table.

Notice that the triggers are after triggers, which means that entries are added only if the executed statement is successful. Failed statements will not be logged. We will later extend the example so that unsuccessful attempts are also logged.

Example 3-5. Definitions of tables and triggers for employee administration

```sql
CREATE TABLE employee (
    name CHAR(64) NOT NULL,
    email CHAR(64),
    password CHAR(64),
    PRIMARY KEY (name)
);

CREATE TABLE log (
    id INT AUTO_INCREMENT,
    email CHAR(64),
    message TEXT,
    ts TIMESTAMP,
    PRIMARY KEY (id)
);

CREATE TRIGGER tr_employee_insert_after AFTER INSERT ON employee FOR EACH ROW
    INSERT INTO log(email, status, message)
      VALUES (NEW.email, 'OK', CONCAT('Adding employee ', NEW.name));

CREATE TRIGGER tr_employee_delete_after AFTER DELETE ON employee FOR EACH ROW
    INSERT INTO log(email, status, message)
      VALUES (OLD.email, 'OK', 'Removing employee');

delimiter $$
CREATE TRIGGER tr_employee_update_after AFTER UPDATE ON employee FOR EACH ROW
BEGIN
  IF OLD.name != NEW.name THEN
    INSERT INTO log(email, status, message)
      VALUES (OLD.email, 'OK',
              CONCAT('Name change from ', OLD.name, ' to ', NEW.name));
  END IF;
  IF OLD.password != NEW.password THEN
    INSERT INTO log(email, status, message)
      VALUES (OLD.email, 'OK', 'Password change');
  END IF;
  IF OLD.email != NEW.email THEN
    INSERT INTO log(email, status, message)
      VALUES (OLD.email, 'OK', CONCAT('E-mail change to ', NEW.email));
  END IF;
END $$
delimiter ;
```

With these trigger definitions, it is now possible to add and remove employees as shown in Example 3-6. Here an employee is added, modified, and removed, and as you can see, each of the operations is logged to the *log* table.

The operations of adding, removing, and modifying employees may be done by a user who has access to the *employee* table, but what about access to the *log* table? In this case, a user who can manipulate the *employee* table should *not* be able to make changes to the *log* table. There are many reasons for this, but they all boil down to trusting the contents of the *log* table for purposes of maintenance, auditing, disclosure to legal authorities, etc. So the DBA may choose to make access to the *employee* table available to many users while keeping access to the *log* table very restricted.

To make sure the triggers can execute successfully against a highly protected table, they are executed as the user who defined the trigger, not as the user who changed the contents of the *employee* table. So, the **CREATE TRIGGER** statements in Example 3-5 are executed by the DBA, who has privileges to make additions to the *log* table, whereas the statements altering employee information in Example 3-6 are executed through a user management account that only has privileges to change the *employee* table.

When the statements in Example 3-6 are executed, the employee management account is used for updating entries in the *employee* table, but the DBA privileges are used to make additions to the *log* table. The employee management account cannot be used to add or remove entries from the *log* table.

As an aside, Example 3-6 assigns passwords to a user variable before using them in the statement. This is done to avoid sending sensitive data in plain text to another server; more details can be found in "Security and the Binary Log" on page 64.

Example 3-6. Adding, removing, and modifying users

```
master> SET @pass = PASSWORD('xyzzy');
Query OK, 0 rows affected (0.00 sec)

master> INSERT INTO employee VALUES ('mats', 'mats@example.com', @pass);
Query OK, 1 row affected (0.00 sec)

master> UPDATE employee SET name = 'matz' WHERE email = 'mats@example.com';
Query OK, 1 row affected (0.00 sec)
Rows matched: 1  Changed: 1  Warnings: 0

master> SET @pass = PASSWORD('foobar');
Query OK, 0 rows affected (0.00 sec)

master> UPDATE employee SET password = @pass WHERE email = 'mats@example.com';
Query OK, 1 row affected (0.00 sec)
Rows matched: 1  Changed: 1  Warnings: 0

master> DELETE FROM employee WHERE email = 'mats@example.com';
Query OK, 1 row affected (0.00 sec)

master> SELECT * FROM log;
+----+------------------+------------------------------+---------------------+
| id | email            | message                      | ts                  |
+----+------------------+------------------------------+---------------------+
|  1 | mats@example.com | Adding employee mats         | 2010-01-13 18:56:08 |
|  2 | mats@example.com | Name change from mats to matz | 2010-01-13 18:56:11 |
|  3 | mats@example.com | Removing employee            | 2010-01-13 18:57:11 |
+----+------------------+------------------------------+---------------------+
3 rows in set (0.00 sec)
```

Security and the Binary Log

In general, a user with `REPLICATION SLAVE` privileges has privileges to read everything that occurs on the master and should therefore be secured so that the account cannot be compromised. Details are beyond the scope of this book, but here are some examples of precautions you can take:

- Make it impossible to log into the account from outside the firewall.
- Log all attempts to log into the account, and place the log on a separate secure server.
- Encrypt the connection between the master and the slave using, for example, MySQL's built-in SSL (Secure Sockets Layer) support.

Even if the account has been secured, there is information that does not have to be in the binary log, so it makes sense not to store it there in the first place.

One of the more common types of sensitive information is passwords. Events containing passwords can be written to the binary log when executing statements that change tables on the server and that include the password required for access to the tables.

A typical example is:

```
UPDATE employee SET pass = PASSWORD('foobar')
    WHERE email = 'mats@example.com';
```

If replication is in place, it is better to rewrite this statement without the password. This is done by computing and storing the hashed password into a user-defined variable and then using that in the expression:

```
SET @password = PASSWORD('foobar');
UPDATE employee SET pass = @password WHERE email = 'mats@example.com';
```

Since the `SET` statement is not replicated, the original password will not be stored in the binary log, only in the memory of the server while executing the statement.

As long as the *password hash*, rather than the plain-text password, is stored in the table, this technique works. If the raw password is stored directly in the table, there is no way to prevent the password from ending up in the binary log. But storing hashes for passwords is a standard good practice in any case, to prevent someone who gets his hands on the raw data from learning the passwords.

Encrypting the connection between the master and the slave offers some protection, but if the binary log itself is compromised, encrypting the connection doesn't help.

If you recall the earlier discussion about implicit information, you may already have noticed that both the user executing a line of code and the user who defines a trigger are implicit. As you will see in Chapter 6, neither the definer nor the invoker of the trigger is critical to executing the trigger on the slave, and the user information is effectively ignored when the slave executes the statement. However, the information *is* important when the binary log is played back to a server—for instance, when doing a PITR.

To play back a binary log to the server without problems in handling privileges on all the various tables, it is necessary to execute all the statements as a user with SUPER privileges. But the triggers may not have been defined using SUPER privileges, so it is important to re-create the triggers with the correct user as the trigger's definer. If a trigger is defined with SUPER privileges instead of by the user who defined the trigger originally, it might cause a privilege escalation.

To permit a DBA to specify the user under which to execute a trigger, the CREATE TRIGGER syntax includes an optional DEFINER clause. If a DEFINER is not given to the statements—as is the case in Example 3-7—the statement will be rewritten for the binary log to add a DEFINER clause and use the current user as the definer. This means that the definition of the insert trigger appears in the binary log, as shown in Example 3-7. It lists the account that created the trigger (root@localhost) as the definer, which is what we want in this case.

Example 3-7. A CREATE TRIGGER statement in the binary log

```
master> SHOW BINLOG EVENTS FROM 92236 LIMIT 1\G
*************************** 1. row ***************************
   Log_name: master-bin.000038
        Pos: 92236
 Event_type: Query
  Server_id: 1
End_log_pos: 92491
       Info: use `test`; CREATE DEFINER=`root`@`localhost` TRIGGER ...
1 row in set (0.00 sec)
```

Statements that invoke triggers and stored routines

Moving over from definitions to invocations, we can ask how the master's triggers are handled during replication. Well, actually they're not handled at all.

The statement that invokes the trigger is logged to the binary log, but it is not linked to the particular trigger. Instead, when the slave executes the statement, it automatically executes any triggers associated with the tables affected by the statement. This means that there can be different triggers on the master and the slave, and the triggers on the master will be invoked on the master while the triggers on the slave will be invoked on the slave. For example, if the trigger to add entries to the log table is not necessary on the slave, performance can be improved by eliminating the trigger from the slave.

Still, any context events necessary for replicating correctly will be written to the binary log before the statement that invokes the trigger, even if it is just the statements in the trigger that require the context events. Thus, Example 3-8 shows the binary log after executing the INSERT statement in Example 3-5. Note that the first event writes the INSERT ID for the *log* table's primary key. This reflects the use of the log table in the trigger, but it might appear to be redundant because the slave will not use the trigger.

You should, however, note that using different triggers on the master and slave—or no trigger at all on either the master or slave—is the exception and that the INSERT ID is necessary for replicating the INSERT statement correctly when the trigger is both on the master and slave.

Example 3-8. Contents of the binary log after executing INSERT

```
master> SHOW BINLOG EVENTS FROM 93340\G
*************************** 1. row ***************************
  Log_name: master-bin.000038
       Pos: 93340
Event_type: Intvar
 Server_id: 1
End_log_pos: 93368
      Info: INSERT_ID=1
*************************** 2. row ***************************
  Log_name: master-bin.000038
       Pos: 93368
Event_type: User var
 Server_id: 1
End_log_pos: 93396h
      Info: @`pass`=_latin1
0x2A3942353030333433342433532453239313131137324542353241... COLLATE
latin1_swedish_ci
*************************** 3. row ***************************
  Log_name: master-bin.000038
       Pos: 93396
Event_type: Query
 Server_id: 1
End_log_pos: 93537
      Info: use `test`; INSERT INTO employee VALUES ...
3 rows in set (0.00 sec)
```

Stored Procedures

Stored functions, stored procedures, and events are known by the common name *stored routines*. Since the server treats stored procedures and stored functions very differently, stored procedures will be covered in this section and stored functions in the next section.

The situation for stored routines is similar to triggers in some aspects, but very different in others. Like triggers, stored routines offer a DEFINER clause, and it must be explicitly added to the binary log whether or not the statement includes it. But the invocation of stored routines is handled differently from triggers.

To begin, let's extend Example 3-6, which defines tables for employees and logs, with some utility routines to work with the employees. Even though this can be handled with standard INSERT, DELETE, and UPDATE statements, we'll used stored procedures to demonstrate some issues involved in writing them to the binary log. For these purposes, let's extend the example with the functions in Example 3-9 for adding and removing employees.

Example 3-9. Stored procedure definitions for managing employees

```
delimiter $$
CREATE PROCEDURE employee_add(p_name CHAR(64), p_email CHAR(64),
                             p_password CHAR(64))
   MODIFIES SQL DATA
BEGIN
   DECLARE pass CHAR(64);
   SET pass = PASSWORD(p_pass)
   INSERT INTO employee(name, email, password)
     VALUES (p_name, p_email, pass);
END $$

CREATE PROCEDURE employee_passwd(p_email CHAR(64), p_password CHAR(64))
   MODIFIES SQL DATA
BEGIN
   DECLARE pass CHAR(64);
   SET pass = PASSWORD(p_password)
   UPDATE employee SET password = pass WHERE email = p_email;
END $$

CREATE PROCEDURE employee_del(p_name CHAR(64))
   MODIFIES SQL DATA
BEGIN
   DELETE FROM employee WHERE name = p_name;
END $$
delimiter ;
```

For the `employee_add` and `employee_passwd` procedures, we have extracted the encrypted password into a separate variable for the reasons already explained, but the `employee_del` procedure just contains a `DELETE` statement, since nothing else is needed. A binlog entry corresponding to one function is:

```
master> SHOW BINLOG EVENTS FROM 97911 LIMIT 1\G
*************************** 1. row ***************************
    Log_name: master-bin.000038
         Pos: 97911
  Event_type: Query
   Server_id: 1
 End_log_pos: 98275
        Info: use `test`; CREATE DEFINER=`root`@`localhost` PROCEDURE ...
1 row in set (0.00 sec)
```

As expected, the definition of this procedure is extended with the `DEFINER` clause before writing the definition to the binary log, but apart from that, the body of the procedure is left intact. Notice that the `CREATE PROCEDURE` statement is replicated as a `Query` event, as are all DDL statements.

In this regard, stored routines are similar to triggers in the way they are treated by the binary log. But invocation differs significantly from triggers. Example 3-10 calls the procedure that adds an employee and shows the resulting contents of the binary log.

Example 3-10. Calling a stored procedure

```
master> CALL employee_add('chuck', 'chuck@example.com', 'abrakadabra');
Query OK, 1 row affected (0.00 sec)

master> SHOW BINLOG EVENTS FROM 104033\G
*************************** 1. row ***************************
   Log_name: master-bin.000038
        Pos: 104033
 Event_type: Intvar
  Server_id: 1
End_log_pos: 104061
       Info: INSERT_ID=1
*************************** 2. row ***************************
   Log_name: master-bin.000038
        Pos: 104061
 Event_type: Query
  Server_id: 1
End_log_pos: 104416
       Info: use `test`; INSERT INTO employee(name, email, password)
             VALUES ( NAME_CONST('p_name',_latin1'chuck' COLLATE 'latin1_swedish_ci'),
             NAME_CONST('p_email',_latin1'chuck@example.com' COLLATE 'latin1_swedish_ci'),
             NAME_CONST('pass',_latin1'*FEB349C4FDAA307A...' COLLATE 'latin1_swedish_ci'))
2 rows in set (0.00 sec)
```

In Example 3-10, there are four things that you should note:

- The CALL statement is not written to the binary log. Instead, the statements executed as a *result* of the call are written to the binary log. In other words, the body of the stored procedure is unrolled into the binary log.

- The statement is rewritten to not contain any references to the parameters of the stored procedure—that is, p_name, p_email, and p_password. Instead, the NAME_CONST function is used for each parameter to create a result set with a single value.

- The locally declared variable pass is also replaced with a NAME_CONST expression, where the second parameter contains the encrypted password.

- Just as when a statement that invokes a trigger is written to the binary log, the statement that calls the stored procedure is preceded by an Intvar event holding the insert ID used when adding the employee to the *log* table.

Since neither the parameter names nor the locally declared names are available outside the stored routine, NAME_CONST is used to associate the name of the parameter or local variable with the constant value used when executing the function. This guarantees that the value can be used in the same way as the parameter or local variable. However, this change is not significant; currently it offers no advantages over using the parameters directly.

Stored Functions

Stored functions share many similarities with stored procedures and some similarities with triggers. Similar to both stored procedures and triggers, stored functions have a DEFINER clause that is normally (but not always) used when the CREATE FUNCTION statement is written to the binary log.

In contrast to stored procedures, stored routines can return values and you can therefore embed them in various places in SQL statements. For example, consider the definition of a stored routine in Example 3-11, which extracts the email address of an employee given the employee's name. The function is a little contrived—it is significantly more efficient to just execute statements directly—but it suits our purposes well.

Example 3-11. A stored function to fetch the name of an employee

```
delimiter $$
CREATE FUNCTION employee_email(p_name CHAR(64))
    RETURNS CHAR(64)
    DETERMINISTIC
BEGIN
    DECLARE l_email CHAR(64);
    SELECT email INTO l_email FROM employee WHERE name = p_name;
    RETURN l_email;
END $$
delimiter ;
```

This stored function can be used conveniently in other statements, as shown in Example 3-12. In contrast to stored procedures, stored functions have to specify a characteristic—such as DETERMINISTIC, NO SQL, or READS SQL DATA—if they are to be written to the binary log.

Example 3-12. Examples of using the stored function

```
master> INSERT INTO collected(name, email) ('mats', employee_email('mats'));
Query OK, 1 row affected (0.01 sec)

master> SELECT employee_email('mats');
+------------------------+
| employee_email('mats') |
+------------------------+
| mats@example.com       |
+------------------------+
1 row in set (0.00 sec)
```

When it comes to calls, stored functions are replicated in the same manner as triggers: as part of the statement that executes the function. For instance, the binary log doesn't need any events preceding the INSERT statement in Example 3-12, but it will contain the context events necessary to replicate the stored function inside the INSERT.

What about SELECT? Normally, SELECT statements are not written to the binary log, since they don't change any data, but a SELECT containing a stored function is an exception. When executing the stored function, the server notices that it adds a row to the *log* table and marks the statement as an "updating" statement, which means that it will be written to the binary log.

Stored Functions and Privileges

The `CREATE ROUTINE` privilege is required to define a stored procedure or stored function. Strictly speaking, no other privileges are needed to create a stored routine, but since it normally executes under the privileges of the definer, defining a stored routine would not make much sense if the definer of the procedure didn't have the necessary privileges to read to or write from tables referenced by the stored procedure.

But replication threads on the slave execute without privilege checks. This leaves a serious security hole allowing any user with the `CREATE ROUTINE` privilege to elevate her privileges and execute any statement on the slave.

In MySQL versions earlier than 5.0, this does not cause problems, since all paths of a statement are explored when the statement is executed on the master. A privilege violation on the master will prevent a statement from being written to the binary log, so users cannot access objects on the slave that were out of bounds on the master. However, with the introduction of stored routines, it is possible to create conditional execution paths, and the server does not explore all paths when executing a stored routine.

Since stored procedures are unrolled, the exact statements executed on the master are also executed on the slave, and since the statement is only logged if it was successfully executed on the master, it is not possible to get access to other objects. Not so with stored functions.

If a stored function is defined with `SQL SECURITY INVOKER`, a malicious user can craft a function that will execute differently on the master and the slave. The security breach can then be buried in the branch executed on the slave. This is demonstrated in the following example:

```
CREATE FUNCTION magic()
  RETURNS CHAR(64)
  SQL SECURITY INVOKER
BEGIN
  DECLARE result CHAR(64);
  IF @@server_id <> 1 THEN
     SELECT what INTO result FROM secret.agents LIMIT 1;
     RETURN result;
  ELSE
     RETURN 'I am magic!';
  END IF;
END $$
```

One piece of code executes on the master (the `ELSE` branch), whereas a separate piece of code (the `IF` branch) executes on the slave where the privilege checks are disabled. The effect is to elevate the user's privileges from `CREATE ROUTINE` to the equivalent of `SUPER`.

Notice that this problem doesn't occur if the function is defined with SQL SECURITY DEFINER, because the function executes with the user's privileges and will be blocked on the slave.

To prevent privilege escalation on a slave, MySQL requires SUPER privileges by default to define stored functions. But since stored functions are very useful, and some database administrators trust their users with creating proper functions, this check can be disabled with the log-bin-trust-function-creators option.

Events

The events feature is a MySQL extension, not part of standard SQL. Events, which should not be confused with binlog events, are handled by a stored program that is executed regularly by a special event scheduler.

Similar to all other stored programs, definitions of events are also logged with a DEFINER clause. Since events are invoked by the event scheduler, they are always executed as the definer and do not pose a security risk in the way that stored functions do.

When events are executed, the statements are written to the binary log directly.

Since the events will be executed on the master, they are automatically disabled on the slave and will therefore not be executed there. If the events were not disabled, they would be executed twice on the slave: once by the master executing the event and replicating the changes to the slave, and once by the slave executing the event directly.

Since the events are disabled on the slave, it is necessary to enable these events if the slave, for some reason, should lose the master.

So, for example, when promoting a slave as described in Chapter 4, don't forget to enable the events that were replicated from the master. This is easiest to do using the following statement:

```
UPDATE mysql.events
    SET Status = ENABLED
    WHERE Status = SLAVESIDE_DISABLED;
```

The purpose of the check is to enable only the events that were disabled when being replicated from the master. There might be events that are disabled for other reasons.

Special Constructions

Even though statement-based replication is normally straightforward, some special constructions have to be handled with care. Recall that for the statement to be executed correctly on the slave, the context has to be correct for the statement. Even though the context events discussed earlier handle part of the context, some constructions have additional context that is not transferred as part of the replication process.

The LOAD_FILE function

The `LOAD_FILE` function allows you to fetch a file and use it as part of an expression. Although quite convenient at times, the file has to exist on the slave server to replicate correctly since the file is *not* transferred during replication, as the file to `LOAD DATA INFILE` is. With some ingenuity, you can rewrite a statement involving the `LOAD_FILE` function either to use the `LOAD DATA INFILE` statement or to define a user-defined variable to hold the contents of the file. For example, take the following statement that inserts a document into a table:

```
master> INSERT INTO document(author, body)
    ->    VALUES ('Mats Kindahl', LOAD_FILE('go_intro.xml'));
```

You can rewrite this statement to use `LOAD DATA INFILE` instead. In this case, you have to take care to specify character strings that cannot exist in the document as field and line delimiters, since you are going to read the entire file contents as a single column.

```
master> LOAD DATA INFILE 'go_intro.xml' INTO TABLE document
    ->    FIELDS TERMINATED BY '@*@' LINES TERMINATED BY '&%&'
    ->    (author, body) SET author = 'Mats Kindahl';
```

An alternative is to store the file contents in a user-defined variable and then use it in the statement.

```
master> SET @document = LOAD_FILE('go_intro.xml');
master> INSERT INTO document(author, body) VALUES('Mats Kindahl, @document);
```

Nontransactional Changes and Error Handling

So far we have considered only transactional changes and have not looked at error handling at all. For transactional changes, error handling is pretty uncomplicated: a statement that tries to change transactional tables and fails will not have any effect at all on the table. That's the entire point of having a transactional system—so the changes that the statement attempts to introduce can be safely ignored. The same applies to transactions that are rolled back: they have no effect on the tables and can therefore simply be discarded without risking inconsistencies between the master and the slave.

A specialty of MySQL is the provisioning of nontransactional storage engines. This can offer some speed advantages, since the storage engine does not have to administer the transactional log that the transactional engines use, and it allows some optimizations on disk access. From a replication perspective, however, nontransactional engines require special considerations.

The most important aspect to note is that replication cannot handle arbitrary nontransactional engines, but has to make some assumptions about how they behave. Some of those limitations are lifted with the introduction of row-based replication in version 5.1—a subject that will be covered in Chapter 6—but even in that case, it cannot handle arbitrary storage engines.

One of the features that complicates the issue further, from a replication perspective, is that it is possible to mix transactional and nontransactional engines in the same transaction, and even in the same statement.

To continue with the example used earlier, consider Example 3-13, where the *log* table from Example 3-5 is given a nontransactional storage engine while the *employee* table is given a transactional one. We use the nontransactional MyISAM storage engine for the *log* table to improve its speed, while keeping the transactional behavior for the *employee* table.

We can further extend the example to track unsuccessful attempts to add employees by creating a pair of insert triggers: a before trigger and an after trigger. If an administrator sees an entry in the log with a **status** field of **FAIL**, it means the before trigger ran, but the after trigger did not, and therefore an attempt to add an employee failed.

Example 3-13. Definition of log and employee tables with storage engines

```
CREATE TABLE employee (
    name CHAR(64) NOT NULL,
    email CHAR(64),
    password CHAR(64),
    PRIMARY KEY (email)
) ENGINE = InnoDB;

CREATE TABLE log (
    id INT AUTO_INCREMENT,
    email CHAR(64),
    message TEXT,
    status ENUM('FAIL', 'OK') DEFAULT 'FAIL',
    ts TIMESTAMP,
    PRIMARY KEY (id)
) ENGINE = MyISAM;

delimiter $$
CREATE TRIGGER tr_employee_insert_before BEFORE INSERT ON employee FOR EACH ROW
BEGIN
  INSERT INTO log(email, message)
    VALUES (NEW.email, CONCAT('Adding employee ', NEW.name));
  SET @LAST_INSERT_ID = LAST_INSERT_ID();
END $$
delimiter ;

CREATE TRIGGER tr_employee_insert_after AFTER INSERT ON employee FOR EACH ROW
    UPDATE log SET status = 'OK' WHERE id = @LAST_INSERT_ID;
```

What are the effects of this change on the binary log?

To begin, let's consider the **INSERT** statement from Example 3-6. Assuming the statement is not inside a transaction and **AUTOCOMMIT** is 1, the statement will be a transaction by itself. If the statement executes without errors, everything will proceed as planned and the statement will be written to the binary log as a **Query** event.

Now, consider what happens if the INSERT is repeated with the same employee. Since the *email* column is the primary key, this will generate a duplicate key error when the insertion is attempted, but what will happen with the statement? Is it written to the binary log or not?

Let's have a look...

```
master> SET @pass = PASSWORD('xyzzy');
Query OK, 0 rows affected (0.00 sec)

master> INSERT INTO employee(name,email,pass)
    ->    VALUES ('mats','mats@example.com',@pass);
ERROR 1062 (23000): Duplicate entry 'mats@example.com' for key 'PRIMARY'
master> SELECT * FROM employee;
+------+------------------+--------------------------------------------+
| name | email            | password                                   |
+------+------------------+--------------------------------------------+
| mats | mats@example.com | *151AF6B8C3A6AA09CFCCBD34601F2D309ED54888  |
+------+------------------+--------------------------------------------+
1 row in set (0.00 sec)

master> SHOW BINLOG EVENTS FROM 38493\G
*************************** 1. row ***************************
   Log_name: master-bin.000038
        Pos: 38493
  Event_type: User var
   Server_id: 1
End_log_pos: 38571
       Info: @`pass`=_latin1 0x2A31353141463642384333413641413039343464434...
             COLLATE latin1_swedish_ci
*************************** 2. row ***************************
   Log_name: master-bin.000038
        Pos: 38571
  Event_type: Query
   Server_id: 1
End_log_pos: 38689
       Info: use `test`; INSERT INTO employee(name,email,pass) VALUES ...
2 rows in set (0.00 sec)
```

As you can see, the statement is written to the binary log even though the *employee* table is transactional and the statement failed. Looking at the contents of the table using the SELECT reveals that there is still a single employee, proving the statement was rolled back—so why is the statement written to the binary log?

Looking into the log table will reveal the reason.

```
master> SELECT * FROM log;
+----+-----------------+------------------------+--------+---------------------+
| id | email           | message                | status | ts                  |
+----+-----------------+------------------------+--------+---------------------+
|  1 | mats@example.com | Adding employee mats  | OK     | 2010-01-13 15:50:45 |
|  2 | mats@example.com | Name change from ...  | OK     | 2010-01-13 15:50:48 |
|  3 | mats@example.com | Password change       | OK     | 2010-01-13 15:50:50 |
|  4 | mats@example.com | Removing employee     | OK     | 2010-01-13 15:50:52 |
|  5 | mats@example.com | Adding employee mats  | OK     | 2010-01-13 16:11:45 |
|  6 | mats@example.com | Adding employee mats  | FAIL   | 2010-01-13 16:12:00 |
+----+-----------------+------------------------+--------+---------------------+
6 rows in set (0.00 sec)
```

Look at the last line, where the status is FAIL. This line was added to the table by the before trigger `tr_employee_insert_before`. For the binary log to faithfully represent the changes made to the database on the master, it is necessary to write the statement to the binary log if there are any nontransactional changes present in the statement or in triggers that are executed as a result of executing the statement. Since the statement failed, the after trigger `tr_employee_insert_after` was not executed, and therefore the status is still FAIL from the execution of the before trigger.

Since the statement failed on the master, information about the failure needs to be written to the binary log as well. The MySQL server handles this by using an error code field in the Query event to register the exact error code that caused the statement to fail. This field is then written to the binary log together with the event.

The error code is not visible when using the SHOW BINLOG EVENTS command, but you can view it using the mysqlbinlog tool, which we will cover later in the chapter.

Logging Transactions

You have now seen how individual statements are written to the binary log, along with context information. Transactions require additional treatment.

A transaction can start under several different circumstances:

- When the user issues START TRANSACTION or BEGIN.
- When AUTOCOMMIT=1 and a statement accessing a transactional table starts to execute. Note that a statement that writes only to nontransactional tables—for example, only to MyISAM tables—does not start a transaction.
- When AUTOCOMMIT=0 and the previous transaction was committed or aborted either implicitly (by executing a statement that does an implicit commit) or explicitly by using COMMIT or ROLLBACK.

Not every statement that is executed after the transaction has started is part of that transaction. The exceptions require special care from the binary log.

Nontransactional statements are by their very definition not part of the transaction. When they are executed, they take effect immediately and do not wait for the transaction to commit. This also means that it is not possible to roll them back. They don't affect an open transaction: any transactional statement executed after the non-transactional statement is still added to the currently open transaction.

In addition, several statements do an implicit commit. These can be separated into three groups based on the reason they do an implicit commit.

Statements that write files
> Most DDL statements (CREATE, ALTER, etc.), with some exceptions, do an implicit commit of any outstanding transaction before starting to execute and an implicit commit after they have finished. These statements modify files in the filesystem and are for that reason not transactional.

Statements that modify tables in the mysql database
> All statements that create, drop, or modify user accounts or privileges for users do an implicit commit and cannot be part of a transaction. Internally, these statements modify tables in the *mysql* database, which are all nontransactional.
>
> In MySQL versions earlier than 5.1.3, these statements did not cause an implicit commit, but since they were writing to nontransactional tables, they were treated as nontransactional statements. As you will soon see, this caused some inconsistencies, so implicit commits were added for these statements over the course of several versions.

Statements that require implicit commits for pragmatic reasons
> Statements that lock tables, statements that are used for administrative purposes, and LOAD DATA INFILE cause implicit commits in various situations because the implementation requires this to make them work correctly.

Statements that cause an implicit commit are clearly not part of any transaction, because any open transaction is committed before execution starts. You can find a complete list of statements that cause an implicit commit in the online MySQL Reference Manual.

Transaction Cache

The binary log can have statements in a different order from their actual execution, because it combines all the statements in each transaction to keep them together. Multiple sessions can execute simultaneous transactions on a server, and the transactional storage engines maintain their own transactional logs to make sure each transaction executes correctly. These logs are not visible to the user. In contrast, the binary log shows all transactions from all sessions in the order in which they were committed as if each executed sequentially.

To ensure each transaction is written as a unit to the binary log, the server has to separate statements that are executing in different threads. When committing a transaction, the server writes all the statements that are part of the transaction to the binary log as a single unit. For this purpose, the server keeps a *transaction cache* for each thread, as illustrated in Figure 3-4. Each statement executed for a transaction is placed in the transaction cache, and the contents of the transaction cache are then copied to the binary log and emptied when the transaction commits.

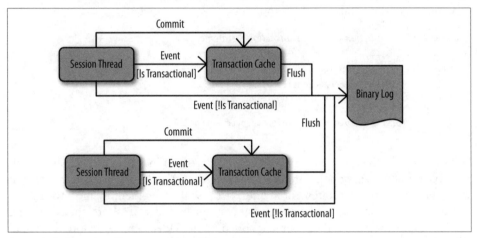

Figure 3-4. Threads with transaction caches and a binary log

Statements that contain nontransactional changes require special attention. Recall from our previous discussion that nontransactional statements do not cause the current transaction to terminate, so the changes introduced by the execution of a nontransactional statement have to be recorded somewhere without closing the currently open transaction. The situation is further complicated by statements that simultaneously affect transactional and nontransactional tables. These statements are considered transactional but include changes that are not part of the transaction.

Statement-based replication cannot handle this correctly in all situations and therefore a best-effort approach has been taken. We'll describe the measures taken by the server, followed by the issues you have to be aware of in order to avoid the replication problems that are left over.

How nontransactional statements are logged

When no transaction is open, nontransactional statements are written directly to the binary log and do not "transit" in the transaction cache before ending up in the binary log. If, however, a transaction is open, the rules for how to handle the statement are as follows:

1. If the statement is marked as transactional, it is written to the transaction cache.
2. If the statement is not marked as transactional and there are no statements in the transaction cache, the statement is written directly to the binary log.

3. If the statement is not marked as transactional, but there are statements in the transaction cache, the statement is written to the transaction cache.

The third rule might seem strange, but you can understand the reasoning if you look at Example 3-14. Returning to our *employee* and *log* tables, consider the statements in Example 3-14, where a modification of a transactional table comes before modification of a nontransactional table in the transaction.

Example 3-14. Transaction with nontransactional statement

```
1    START TRANSACTION;
2    SET @pass = PASSWORD('xyzzy');
3    INSERT INTO employee(name,email,password)
     VALUES ('mats','mats@example.com', @pass);
4    INSERT INTO log(email, message)
     VALUES ('root@example.com', 'This employee was bad');
5    COMMIT;
```

Following rule 3, the statement on line 4 is written to the transaction cache even though the table is nontransactional. If the statement were written directly to the binary log, it would end up before the statement in line 3 because the statement in line 3 would not end up in the binary log until a successful commit in line 5. In short, the slave's log would end up containing the comment added by the DBA in line 4 before the actual change to the employee in line 3, which is clearly inconsistent with the master. Rule 3 avoids such situations. The left side of Figure 3-5 shows the undesired effects if rule 3 did not apply, whereas the right side shows what actually happens thanks to rule 3.

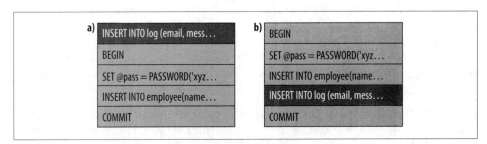

Figure 3-5. Alternative binary logs depending on rule 3

Rule 3 involves a trade-off. Since the nontransactional statement is cached while the transaction executes, there is a risk that two transactions will update a nontransactional table on the master in a different order than that in which they are written to the binary log.

This situation can arise when there is a dependency between the first transactional and the second nontransactional statement of the transaction, but this cannot generally be handled by the server because it would require parsing each statement completely, including code in all triggers invoked, and performing a dependency analysis. Although technically possible, this would add extra processing to *all* statements during an open transaction and would therefore affect performance, perhaps significantly. Since the problem can almost always be avoided by designing transactions properly and ensuring that there are no dependencies of this kind in the transaction, the overhead was not added to MySQL.

How to avoid replication problems with nontransactional statements

A strategy for avoiding the dependencies discussed in the previous section is to ensure that statements affecting nontransactional tables are written first in the transaction. In this case, the statements will be written directly to the binary log, because the transaction cache is empty (refer to rule 2 in the preceding section). The statements are known to have no dependencies.

If you need any values from these statements later in the transaction, you can assign them to temporary tables or variables. After that, the real contents of the transaction can be executed, referencing the temporary tables or variables.

Distributed Transaction Processing Using XA

MySQL version 5.0 lets you coordinate transactions involving different resources by using the X/Open Distributed Transaction Processing model XA. Although currently not very widely used, XA offers attractive opportunities for coordinating all kinds of resources with transactions.

In version 5.0, the server uses XA internally to coordinate the binary log and the storage engines.

A set of commands allows the client to take advantage of XA synchronization as well. XA allows different statements entered by different users to be treated as a single transaction. On the other hand, it imposes some overhead, so some administrators turn it off globally.

Instructions for working with the XA protocol are beyond the scope of this book, but we will give a brief introduction to XA here before describing how it affects the binary log.

XA includes a *transaction manager* that coordinates a set of *resource managers* so that they commit a global transaction as an atomic unit. Each transaction is assigned a unique XID, which is used by the transaction manager and the resource managers. When used internally in the MySQL server, the transaction manager is usually the binary log and the resource managers are the storage engines. The process of committing an XA transaction is shown in Figure 3-6 and consists of two phases.

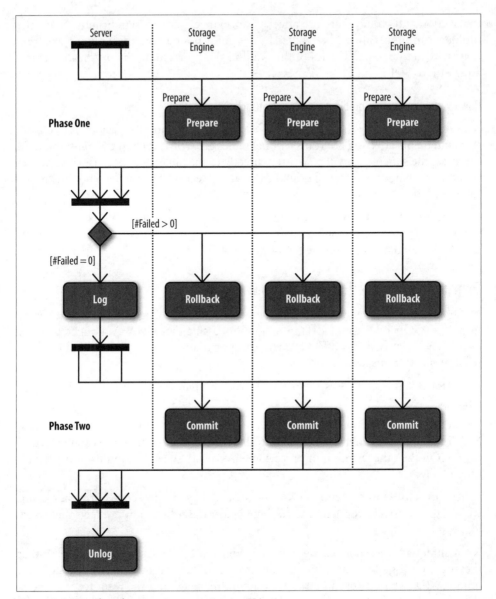

Figure 3-6. Distributed transaction commit using XA

In phase 1, each storage engine is asked to prepare for a commit. When preparing, the storage engine writes any information it needs to commit correctly to safe storage and then returns an OK message. If any storage engine replies negatively—meaning that it cannot commit the transaction—the commit is aborted and all engines are instructed to roll back the transaction.

After all storage engines have reported that they have prepared without error, and before phase 2 begins, the transaction cache is written to the binary log. In contrast to normal transactions, which are terminated with a normal `Query` event with a `COMMIT`, an XA transaction is terminated with an `Xid` event containing the XID.

In phase 2, all the storage engines that were prepared in phase 1 are asked to commit the transaction. When committing, each storage engine will report that it has committed the transaction in stable storage. It is important to understand that the commit cannot fail: once phase 1 has passed, the storage engine has guaranteed that the transaction can be committed and therefore is not allowed to report failure in phase 2. A hardware failure can, of course, cause a crash, but since the storage engines have stored the information in durable storage, they will be able to recover properly when the server restarts. The restart procedure is discussed in the section "The Binary Log and Crash Safety" on page 82.

After phase 2, the transaction manager is given a chance to discard any shared resources, should it choose to. The binary log does not need to do any such cleanup actions, so it does not do anything special with regard to XA at this step.

In the event that a crash occurs while committing an XA transaction, the recovery procedure in Figure 3-7 will take place when the server is restarted. At startup, the server will open the last binary log and check the `Format description` event. If the `binlog-in-use` flag described earlier is set, it indicates that the server crashed and XA recovery has to be executed.

The server starts by walking through the binary log that was just opened and finding the XIDs of all transactions in the binary log by reading the `Xid` events. Each storage engine loaded into the server will then be asked to commit the transactions in this list. For each XID in the list, the storage engine will determine whether a transaction with that XID is prepared but not committed, and commit it if that is the case. If the storage engine has prepared a transaction with an XID that is *not* in this list, the XID obviously did not make it to the binary log before the server crashed, so the transaction should be rolled back.

Binary Log Management

The events mentioned thus far are information carriers in the sense that they represent some real change of data that occurred on the master. There are, however, other events that can affect replication but do not represent any change of data on the master. For example, if the server is stopped, it can potentially affect replication since changes can occur on the datafiles while the server is stopped. A typical example of this is restoring a backup, or otherwise manipulating the datafiles. Such changes are not replicated because the server is not running.

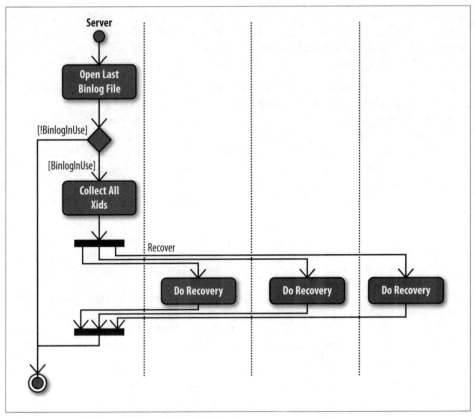

Figure 3-7. Procedure for XA recovery

Events are needed for other purposes as well. Since the binary logs consist of multiple files, it is necessary to split the groups at convenient places to form the sequence of binlog files. To handle this safely, special events are added to the log.

The Binary Log and Crash Safety

As you have seen, changes to the binary log do not correspond to changes to the master databases on a one-to-one basis. It is important to keep the databases and the binary log mutually consistent in case of a crash. In other words, there should be no changes committed to the storage engine that are not written to the binary log, and vice versa.

Nontransactional engines introduce problems right away. For example, it is not possible to guarantee consistency between the binary log and a MyISAM table because MyISAM is nontransactional and the storage engine will carry through any requested change long before any attempts at logging the statement.

But for transactional storage engines, MySQL includes measures to make sure that a crash does not cause the binary log to lose too much information.

As we described in "Logging Statements" on page 50, events are written to the binary log before releasing the locks on the table, but after all the changes have been given to the storage engine. So if there is a crash before the storage engine releases the locks, the server has to ensure that any changes recorded to the binary log are actually in the table on the disk before allowing the statement (or transaction) to commit. This requires coordination with standard filesystem synchronization.

Because disk accesses are very expensive compared to memory accesses, operating systems are designed to cache parts of the file in a dedicated part of the main memory—usually called the *page cache*—and wait to write file data to disk until necessary. Writing to disk becomes necessary when another page must be loaded from disk and the page cache is full, but it can also be requested by an application by doing an explicit call to write the pages of a file to disk.

Recall from the earlier description of XA that when the first phase is complete, all data has to be written to durable storage—that is, to disk—for the protocol to handle crashes correctly. This means that every time a transaction is committed, the page cache has to be written to disk. This can be very expensive and, depending on the application, not always necessary. To control how often the data is written to disk, you can set the `sync-binlog` option. This option takes an integer specifying how often to write the binary log to disk. If the option is set to 5, for instance, the binary log will be written to disk every fifth commit of a statement or transaction. The default value is 0, which means that the binary log is not explicitly written to disk by the server, but happens at the discretion of the operating system.

For storage engines that support XA, such as InnoDB, setting the `sync-binlog` option to 1 means that you will not lose any transactions under normal crashes. For engines that do not support XA, you might lose at most one transaction.

If, however, every group is written to disk, it means that the performance suffers, usually a lot. Disk accesses are notoriously slow and caches are used for precisely the purpose of improving the performance by not having to always write data to disk. If you are prepared to risk losing a few transactions or statements—either because you can handle the work it takes to recover this manually or because it is not important for the application—you can set `sync-binlog` to a higher value or leave it at the default.

Binlog File Rotation

MySQL starts a new file to hold binary log events at regular intervals. For practical and administrative reasons, it wouldn't work to keep writing to a single file—operating systems have limits on file sizes. As mentioned earlier, the file to which the server is currently writing is called the *active* binlog file.

Switching to a new file is called *binary log rotation* or binlog file rotation depending on the context.

There are four main activities that cause a rotation:

The server stops
Each time the server starts, it begins a new binary log. We'll discuss why shortly.

The binlog file reaches a maximum size
If the binlog file grows too large, it will be automatically rotated. You can control the size of the binlog files using the `binlog-cache-size` server variable.

The binary log is explicitly flushed
The `FLUSH LOGS` command writes all logs to disk and creates a new file to continue writing the binary log. This can be useful when administering recovery images for PITR. Reading from an open binlog file can have unexpected results, so it is advisable to force an explicit flush before trying to use binlog files for recovery.

An incident occurred on the server
In addition to stopping altogether, the server can encounter other incidents that cause the binary log to be rotated. These incidents sometimes require special manual intervention from the administrator, because they can leave a "gap" in the replication stream. It is easier for the DBA to handle the incident if the server starts on a fresh binlog file after an incident.

The first event of every binlog file is the `Format description` event, which describes the server that wrote the file along with information about the contents and status of the file.

Three items are of particular interest here:

The `binlog-in-use` flag
Because a crash can occur while the server is writing to a binlog file, it is critical to indicate when a file was closed properly. Otherwise, a DBA could replay a corrupted file on the master or slave and cause more problems. To provide assurance about the file's integrity, the `binlog-in-use` flag is set when the file is created and cleared after the final event (`Rotate`) has been written to the file. Thus, any program can see whether the binlog file was properly closed.

Binlog file format version
Over the course of MySQL development, the format for the binary log has changed several times, and it will certainly change again. Developers increment the version number for the format when significant changes—notably changes to the common headers—render new files unreadable to previous versions of the server. (The current format, starting with MySQL version 5.0, is version 4.) The binlog file format version field lists its version number; if a different server cannot handle a file with that version, it simply refuses to read the file.

Server version
This is a string denoting the version of the server that wrote the file. The server version used to run the examples in this chapter was "5.1.37-1ubuntu5-log," for

instance, and another version with the string "5.1.40-debug-log" is used to run tests. As you can see, the string is guaranteed to include the MySQL server version, but it also contains additional information related to the specific build. In some situations, this information can help you or the developers figure out and resolve subtle bugs that can occur when replicating between different versions of the server. To rotate the binary log safely even in the presence of crashes, the server uses a write-ahead strategy and records its intention in a temporary file called the *purge index file* (this name was chosen because the file is used while purging binlog files as well, as you will see). Its name is based on that of the index file, so for instance if the name of the index file is *master-bin.index*, the name of the purge index file is *master-bin.~rec~*. After creating the new binlog file and updating the index file to point to it, the server removes the purge index file.

In the event of a crash, if a purge index file is present on the server, the server can compare the purge index file and the index file when it restarts and see what was actually accomplished compared to what was intended.

In versions of MySQL earlier than 5.1.43, rotation or binlog file purging could leave orphaned files; that is, the files might exist in the filesystem without being mentioned in the index file. Because of this, old files might not be purged correctly, leaving them around and requiring manual cleaning of the files from the directory.

The orphaned files do not cause a problem for replication, but can be considered an annoyance. The procedure shown in this section ensures that no files are orphaned in the event of a crash.

Incidents

The term "incidents" refers to events that don't change data on a server but must be written to the binary log because they have the potential to affect replication. Most incidents don't require special intervention from the DBA—for instance, servers can stop and restart without changes to database files—but there will inevitably be some incidents that call for special action.

Currently, there are two incident events that you might discover in a binary log:

Stop

Indicates that the server was stopped through normal means. If the server crashed, no stop event will be written, even when the server is brought up again. This event is written in the old binlog file (restarting the server rotates to a new file) and contains only a common header; no other information is provided in the event.

When the binary log is replayed on the slave, it ignores any Stop events. Normally, the fact that the server stopped does not require special attention and replication can proceed as usual. If the server was switched to a new version while it was stopped, this will be indicated in the next binlog file, and the server reading the binlog file will then stop if it cannot handle the new version of the binlog format. In this sense, the Stop event does not represent a "gap" in the replication stream. However, the event is worth recording because someone might manually restore a backup or make other changes to files before restarting replication, and the DBA replaying the file could find this event in order to start or stop the replay at the right time.

Incident

An event type introduced in version 5.1 as a generic incident event. In contrast with the Stop event, this event contains an identifier to specify what kind of incident occurred. It is used to indicate that the server was forced to perform actions almost guaranteeing that changes are missing from the binary log.

For example, incident events in version 5.1 are written if the database was reloaded or if a nontransactional event was too big to fit in the binlog file. MySQL Cluster generates this event when one of the nodes had to reload the database and could therefore be out of sync.

When the binary log is replayed on the slave, it stops with an error if it encounters an Incident event. In the case of the MySQL Cluster reload event, it indicates a need to resynchronize the cluster and probably to search for events that are missing from the binary log.

Purging the Binlog File

Over time, the server will accumulate binlog files unless old ones are purged from the filesystem. The server can automatically purge old binary logs from the filesystem, or you can explicitly tell the server to purge the files.

To make the server automatically purge old binlog files, set the expire-logs-days option —which is available as a server variable as well—to the number of days that you want to keep binlog files. Remember that as with all server variables, this setting is not preserved between restarts of the server. So if you want the automatic purging to keep going across restarts, you have to add the setting to the *my.cnf* file for the server.

To purge the binlog files manually, use the PURGE BINARY LOGS command, which comes in two forms:

PURGE BINARY LOGS BEFORE *datetime*

This form of the command will purge all files that are before the given date. If *datetime* is in the middle of a logfile (and it usually is), all files before the one holding *datetime* will be purged.

PURGE BINARY LOGS TO '*filename*'

This form of the command will purge all files that precede the given file. In other words, all files before *filename* in the output from SHOW MASTER LOGS will be removed, leaving *filename* as the first binlog file.

Binlog files are purged when the server starts or when a binary log rotation is done. If the server discovers files that require purging, either because a file is older than `expire-logs-days` or because a `PURGE BINARY LOGS` command was executed, it will start by writing the files that the server has decided are ripe for purging to the purge index file (for example, *master-bin.~rec~*). After that, the files are removed from the filesystem, and finally the purge index file is removed.

In the event of a crash, the server can continue removing files by comparing the contents of the purge index file and the index file and removing all files that were not removed because of a crash. As you saw earlier, the purge index file is used when rotating as well, so if a crash occurs before the index file can be properly updated, the new binlog file will be removed and then re-created when the rotate is repeated.

The mysqlbinlog Utility

One of the more useful tools available to an administrator is the client program `mysql binlog`. This is a small program that can investigate the contents of binlog files as well as relay logfiles (we will cover the relay logs in Chapter 6). In addition to reading binlog files locally, `mysqlbinlog` can also fetch binlog files remotely from other servers.

In addition to being a very useful tool when investigating problems with replication, you can use this to implement PITR, as demonstrated in Chapter 2.

 The `mysqlbinlog` tool normally outputs the contents of the binary log in a form that can be executed by sending them to a running server. When statement-based replication is employed, the statements executed are emitted as SQL statements. For row-based replication, which will be introduced in Chapter 6, `mysqlbinlog` generates some additional data necessary to handle row-based replication. This chapter focuses entirely on statement-based replication, so we will use the command with options to suppress output needed to handle row-based replication.

Some options to `mysqlbinlog` will be explained in this section, but for a complete list, consult the online MySQL Reference Manual (*http://dev.mysql.com/doc/refman/5.1/en/mysqlbinlog.html*).

Basic Usage

Let's start with a simple example where we create a binlog file and then look at it using mysqlbinlog. We will start up a client connected to the master and execute the following commands to see how they end up in the binary log:

```
mysqld1> RESET MASTER;
Query OK, 0 rows affected (0.01 sec)

mysqld1> CREATE TABLE employee (
    ->     id INT AUTO_INCREMENT,
    ->     name CHAR(64) NOT NULL,
    ->     email CHAR(64),
    ->     password CHAR(64),
    ->     PRIMARY KEY (id)
    -> );
Query OK, 0 rows affected (0.00 sec)

mysqld1> SET @password = PASSWORD('xyzzy');
Query OK, 0 rows affected (0.00 sec)

mysqld1> INSERT INTO employee(name,email,password)
    ->     VALUES ('mats','mats@example.com',@password);
Query OK, 1 row affected (0.01 sec)

mysqld1> SHOW BINARY LOGS;
+--------------------+-----------+
| Log_name           | File_size |
+--------------------+-----------+
| mysqld1-bin.000038 |       670 |
+--------------------+-----------+
1 row in set (0.00 sec)
```

Let's now use mysqlbinlog to dump the contents of the binlog file *master-bin.000038*, which is where all the commands ended up. The output shown in Example 3-15 has been edited slightly to fit the page.

Example 3-15. Output from execution of mysqlbinlog

```
$ sudo mysqlbinlog                          \
>     --short-form                          \
>     --force-if-open                       \
>     --base64-output=never                 \
>     /var/lib/mysql1/mysqld1-bin.000038
1 /*!40019 SET @@session.max_insert_delayed_threads=0*/;
2 /*!50003 SET @OLD_COMPLETION_TYPE=@@COMPLETION_TYPE,COMPLETION_TYPE=0*/;
3 DELIMITER /*!*/;
4 ROLLBACK/*!*/;
5 use test/*!*/;
6 SET TIMESTAMP=1264227693/*!*/;
7 SET @@session.pseudo_thread_id=999999999/*!*/;
8 SET @@session.foreign_key_checks=1, @@session.sql_auto_is_null=1,
      @@session.unique_checks=1, @@session.autocommit=1/*!*/;
9 SET @@session.sql_mode=0/*!*/;
10 SET @@session.auto_increment_increment=1,
```

```
      @@session.auto_increment_offset=1/*!*/;
11 /*!\C latin1 *//*!*/;
12 SET @@session.character_set_client=8,@@session.collation_connection=8,
      @@session.collation_server=8/*!*/;
13 SET @@session.lc_time_names=0/*!*/;
14 SET @@session.collation_database=DEFAULT/*!*/;
15 CREATE TABLE employee (
16    id INT AUTO_INCREMENT,
17    name CHAR(64) NOT NULL,
18    email CHAR(64),
19    password CHAR(64),
20    PRIMARY KEY (id)
21 ) ENGINE=InnoDB
22 /*!*/;
23 SET TIMESTAMP=1264227693/*!*/;
24 BEGIN
25 /*!*/;
26 SET INSERT_ID=1/*!*/;
27 SET @`password`:=_latin1 0x2A31353141463... COLLATE `latin1_swedish_ci`/*!*/;
28 SET TIMESTAMP=1264227693/*!*/;
29 INSERT INTO employee(name,email,password)
30    VALUES ('mats','mats@example.com',@password)
31 /*!*/;
32 COMMIT/*!*/;
33 DELIMITER ;
34 # End of log file
35 ROLLBACK /* added by mysqlbinlog */;
36 /*!50003 SET COMPLETION_TYPE=@OLD_COMPLETION_TYPE*/;
```

To get this output, we use three options:

--short-form

> With this option, mysqlbinlog prints only information about the SQL statements issued, and leaves out comments with information about the events in the binary log. This option is useful when mysqlbinlog is used only to play back the events to a server. If you want to investigate the binary log for problems, you will need these comments and should not use this option.

--force-if-open

> If the binlog file is not closed properly, either because the binlog file is still being written to or because the server crashed, mysqlbinlog will print a warning that this binlog file was not closed properly. This option prevents the printing of that warning.

--base64-output=never

> This prevents mysqlbinlog from printing base64-encoded events. If mysqlbinlog has to print base64-encoded events, it will also print the Format description event of the binary log to show the encoding used. For statement-based replication, this is not necessary, so this option is used to suppress that event.

In Example 3-15, lines 1–4 contain the preamble printed in every output. Line 3 sets a delimiter that is unlikely to occur elsewhere in the file. The delimiter is also designed to appear as a comment in processing languages that do not recognize the setting of the delimiter.

The rollback on line 4 is issued to ensure the output is not accidentally put inside a transaction because a transaction was started on the client before the output was fed into the client.

We can skip momentarily to the end of the output—lines 33–35—to see the counterpart to lines 1–4. They restore the values set in the preamble and roll back any open transaction. This is necessary in case the binlog file was truncated in the middle of a transaction, to prevent any SQL code following this output from being included in a transaction.

The use statement on line 5 is printed whenever the database is changed. Even though the binary log specifies the current database before each SQL statement, mysqlbinlog shows only the changes to the current database. When a use statement appears, it is the first line of a new event.

The first line that is guaranteed to be in the output for each event is SET TIMESTAMP, as shown on lines 6 and 23. This statement gives the timestamp when the event started executing in seconds since the epoch.

Lines 8–14 contain general settings, but like use on line 5, they are printed only for the first event and whenever their values change.

Because the INSERT statement on lines 29–30 is inserting into a table with an auto-increment column using a user-defined variable, the INSERT_ID session variable on line 26 and the user-defined variable on line 27 are set before the statement. This is the result of the Intvar and User_var events in the binary log.

If you omit the --short-form option, each event in the output will be preceded by some comments about the event that generated the lines. You can see these comments, which start with hash marks (#) in Example 3-16.

Example 3-16. Interpreting the comments in mysqlbinlog output

```
$ sudo mysqlbinlog                          \
>      --force-if-open                       \
>      --base64-output=never                 \
>      /var/lib/mysql1/mysqld1-bin.000038
       .
       .
       .
1  # at 386
2  #100123  7:21:33 server id 1   end_log_pos 414     Intvar
3  SET INSERT_ID=1/*!*/;
4  # at 414
5  #100123  7:21:33 server id 1   end_log_pos 496     User_var
6  SET @`password`:=_latin1 0x2A313531...838 COLLATE `latin1_swedish_ci`/*!*/;
7  # at 496
8  #100123  7:21:33 server id 1   end_log_pos 643
   Query   thread_id=6    exec_time=0    error_code=0
```

```
9  SET TIMESTAMP=1264227693/*!*/;
10 INSERT INTO employee(name,email,password)
11     VALUES ('mats','mats@example.com',@password)
12 /*!*/;
13 # at 643
14 #100123  7:21:33 server id 1  end_log_pos 670    Xid = 218
15 COMMIT/*!*/;
16 DELIMITER ;
17 # End of log file
18 ROLLBACK /* added by mysqlbinlog */;
19 /*!50003 SET COMPLETION_TYPE=@OLD_COMPLETION_TYPE*/;
```

The first line of the comment gives the byte position of the event, and the second line contains other information about the event. Consider, for example, the INSERT statement line:

```
# at 496
#100123  7:21:33 server id 1  end_log_pos 643    Query    thread_id=6
    exec_time=0    error_code=0
```

The various parts of the comments have the following meanings:

at 496

> The byte position where the event starts; that is, the first byte of the event.

100123 7:21:33

> The timestamp of the event as a datetime (date plus time). This is the time when the query started executing or when the events were written to the binary log.

server_id 1

> The server ID of the server that generated the event. This server ID is used to set the pseudo_thread_id session variable, and a line setting this variable is printed if the event is thread-specific and the server ID is different from the previously printed ID.

end_log_pos 643

> The byte position of the event that follows this event. By taking the difference between this value and the position where the event starts, you can get the length of the event.

Query

> The type of event. In Example 3-16, you can see several different types of events, such as User_var, Intvar, and Xid.

The fields after these are event-specific, and hence different for each event. For the Query event, we can see two additional fields:

thread_id=6

> The ID of the thread that executed the event. This is used to handle thread-specific queries, such as queries that access temporary tables.

exec_time=0

> The execution time of the query in seconds.

Example 3-15 and Example 3-16 dump the output of a single file, but `mysqlbinlog` accepts multiple files as well. If several binlog files are given, they will be processed in order.

 The files are printed in the order you request them, and there is no checking that the `Rotate` event ending each file refers to the next file in sequence. The responsibility for ensuring that these binlog files make up part of a real binary log lies on the user.

Thanks to the way the binlog files are named, submitting multiple files to `mysqlbinlog`—such as by using * as a file-globbing wildcard—is usually not a problem. Let's look at what happens when the binlog file counter, which is used as an extension to the filename, goes from 999999 to 1000000:

```
$ ls mysqld1-bin.[0-9]*
mysqld1-bin.000007  mysqld1-bin.000011  mysqld1-bin.000039
mysqld1-bin.000008  mysqld1-bin.000035  mysqld1-bin.1000000
mysqld1-bin.000009  mysqld1-bin.000037  mysqld1-bin.999998
mysqld1-bin.000010  mysqld1-bin.000038  mysqld1-bin.999999
```

As you can see, the last binlog file to be created is listed before the two binlog files that are earlier in binary log order. So it is worth checking the names of the files before you use wildcards.

Since your binlog files are usually pretty large, you won't want to print the entire contents of the binlog files and browse them. Instead, there are a few options you can use to limit the output so that only a range of the events is printed.

start-position=*bytepos*
> The byte position of the first event to dump. Note that if several binlog files are supplied to `mysqlbinlog`, this position will be interpreted as the position in the *first* file in the sequence.
>
> If an event does not start at the position given, `mysqlbinlog` will still try to interpret the bytes starting at that position as an event, which usually leads to garbage output.

stop-position=*bytepos*
> The byte position of the last event to print. If no event ends at that position, the last event printed will be the event with a position that precedes *bytepos*. If multiple binlog files are given, the position will be the position of the *last* file in the sequence.

start-datetime=*datetime*
> Prints only events that have a timestamp at or after *datetime*. This will work correctly when multiple files are given—if all events of a file are before the *datetime*, all events will be skipped—but there is no checking that the events are printed in order according to their timestamps.

`stop-datetime=`*`datetime`*

Prints only events that have a timestamp before *datetime*. This is an exclusive range, meaning that if an event is marked 2010-01-24 07:58:32 and that exact datetime is given, the event will *not* be printed.

Note that since the timestamp of the event uses the start time of the statement but events are ordered in the binary log based on the commit time, it is possible to have events with a timestamp that comes before the timestamp of the preceding event. Since mysqlbinlog stops at the first event with a timestamp outside the range, there might be events that aren't displayed because they have timestamps before *datetime*.

Reading remote files

As well as reading files on a local filesystem, the mysqlbinlog utility can also read binlog files from a remote server. It does this by using the same mechanism that the slaves use to connect to a master and ask for events. This can be practical in some cases, since it does not require a shell account on the machine to read the binlog files, just a user on the server with REPLICATION SLAVE privileges.

To handle remote reading of binlog files, include the `--read-from-remote-server` option along with a host and user for connecting to the server, and optionally a port (if different from the default) and a password.

When reading from a remote server, give just the name of the binlog file, not the full path.

So to read the Query event from Example 3-16 remotely, the command would look something like the following (the server prompts for a password, but it is not output when you enter it):

```
$ sudo mysqlbinlog
>    --read-from-remote-server
>    --host=master.example.com
>    --base64-output=never
>    --user=repl_user --password
>    --start-position=386 --stop-position=643
>    mysqld1-bin.000038
Enter password:
/*!40019 SET @@session.max_insert_delayed_threads=0*/;
/*!50003 SET @OLD_COMPLETION_TYPE=@@COMPLETION_TYPE,COMPLETION_TYPE=0*/;
DELIMITER /*!*/;
# at 386
#100123  7:21:33 server id 1  end_log_pos 0     Start: binlog v 4,
    server v 5.1.37-1ubuntu5-log created 100123  7:21:33
# at 386
#100123  7:21:33 server id 1  end_log_pos 414   Intvar
SET INSERT_ID=1/*!*/;
# at 414
#100123  7:21:33 server id 1  end_log_pos 496   User_var
SET @`password`:=_latin1 0x2A3135314146364...38 COLLATE `latin1_swedish_ci`/*!*/;
```

```
# at 496
#100123  7:21:33 server id 1  end_log_pos 643   Query   thread_id=6
    exec_time=0      error_code=0
use test/*!*/;
SET TIMESTAMP=1264227693/*!*/;
SET @@session.pseudo_thread_id=6/*!*/;
SET @@session.foreign_key_checks=1, @@session.sql_auto_is_null=1,
    @@session.unique_checks=1, @@session.autocommit=1/*!*/;
SET @@session.sql_mode=0/*!*/;
SET @@session.auto_increment_increment=1, @@session.auto_increment_offset=1/*!*/;
/*!\C latin1 *//*!*/;
SET @@session.character_set_client=8, @@session.collation_connection=8,
    @@session.collation_server=8/*!*/;
SET @@session.lc_time_names=0/*!*/;
SET @@session.collation_database=DEFAULT/*!*/;
INSERT INTO employee(name,email,password)
  VALUES ('mats','mats@example.com',@password)
/*!*/;
DELIMITER ;
# End of log file
ROLLBACK /* added by mysqlbinlog */;
/*!50003 SET COMPLETION_TYPE=@OLD_COMPLETION_TYPE*/;
```

Interpreting Events

Sometimes, the standard information printed by mysqlbinlog is not sufficient for spotting a problem, so it is necessary to go into the details of the event and investigate its content. To handle such situations, you can pass the --hexdump option to tell mysqlbinlog to write the actual bytes of the events.

Before going into the details of the events, here are some general rules about the format of the data in the binary log:

Integer data
> Integer fields in the binary log are printed in little-endian order, so you have to read integer fields backward. This means that, for example, the 32-bit block 03 01 00 00 represents the hexadecimal number 103.

String data
> String data is usually stored both with length data and null-terminated. Sometimes, the length data appears just before the string and sometimes it is stored in the post header.

This section will cover the most common events, but an exhaustive reference concerning the format of all the events is beyond the scope of this book. Check the MySQL Internals guide (*http://forge.mysql.com/wiki/MySQL_Internals_Binary_Log*) for an exhaustive list of all the events available and their fields.

The most common of all the events is the Query event, so let's concentrate on it first. Example 3-17 shows the output for such an event.

Example 3-17. Output when using option --hexdump

```
    $ sudo mysqlbinlog                        \
    >      --force-if-open                     \
    >      --hexdump                           \
    >      --base64-output=never               \
    >      /var/lib/mysql1/mysqld1-bin.000038
           .
           .
           .
1   # at 496
2   #100123  7:21:33 server id 1  end_log_pos 643
3   # Position  Timestamp   Type    Master ID         Size       Master Pos    Flags
4   #      1f0 6d 95 5a 4b   02    01 00 00 00    93 00 00 00    83 02 00 00    10 00
5   #      203 06 00 00 00 00 00 00 00   04 00 00 1a 00 00 00 40 |................|
6   #      213 00 00 01 00 00 00 00 00   00 00 00 06 03 73 74 64 |.............std|
7   #      223 04 08 00 08 00 08 00 74   65 73 74 00 49 4e 53 45 |.......test.INSE|
8   #      233 52 54 20 49 4e 54 4f 20   75 73 65 72 28 6e 61 6d |RT.INTO.employee|
9   #      243 65 2c 65 6d 61 69 6c 2c   70 61 73 73 77 6f 72 64 |.name.email.pass|
10  #      253 29 0a 20 20 56 41 4c 55   45 53 20 28 27 6d 61 74 |word....VALUES..|
11  #      263 73 27 2c 27 6d 61 74 73   40 65 78 61 6d 70 6c 65 |.mats...mats.exa|
12  #      273 2e 63 6f 6d 27 2c 40 70   61 73 73 77 6f 72 64 29 |mple.com...passw|
13  #      283 6f 72 64 29                                        |ord.|
14  #          Query    thread_id=6       exec_time=0       error_code=0
    SET TIMESTAMP=1264227693/*!*/;
    INSERT INTO employee(name,email,password)
      VALUES ('mats','mats@example.com',@password)
```

The first two lines and line 13 are comments listing basic information that we discussed earlier. Notice that when you use the --hexdump option, the general information and the event-specific information are split into two lines, whereas they are merged in the normal output.

Lines 3 and 4 list the common header:

Timestamp
   The timestamp of the event as an integer, stored in little-endian format.

Type
   A single byte representing the type of the event. The event types in MySQL version 5.1.41 and later are given in the MySQL Internals guide (*http://forge.mysql.com/ wiki/MySQL_Internals_Binary_Log*).

Master ID
   The server ID of the server that wrote the event, written as an integer. For the event shown in Example 3-17, the server ID is 1.

Size
   The size of the event in bytes, written as an integer.

Master Pos
   The same as end_log_pos; that is, the start of the event following this event.

Flags

> This field has 16 bits reserved for general flags concerning the event. The field is mostly unused, but it stores the `binlog-in-use` flag. As you can see in Example 3-17, the `binlog-in-use` flag is set, meaning that the binary log is not closed properly (in this case, because we didn't flush the logs before calling `mysqlbinlog`).

After the common header come the post header and body for the event. As already mentioned, an exhaustive coverage of all the events is beyond the scope of this book, but we will cover the most important and commonly used events: the `Query` and `Format_description` log events.

Query event post header and body

The `Query` event is by far the most used and also the most complicated event issued by the server. Part of the reason is that it has to carry a lot of information about the context of the statement when it was executed. As already demonstrated, integer variables, user variables, and random seeds are covered using specific events, but it is also necessary to provide other information, which is part of this event.

The post header for the `Query` event consists of five fields. Recall that these fields are of fixed size and that the length of the post header is given in the `Format description` event for the binlog file, meaning that later MySQL versions may add additional fields if the need should arise.

Thread ID

> A four-byte unsigned integer representing the thread ID that executed the statement. Even though the thread ID is not always necessary to execute the statement correctly, it is always written into the event.

Execution time

> The number of seconds from the start of execution of the query to when it was written to the binary log, expressed as a four-byte unsigned integer.

Database name length

> The length of the database name, stored as an unsigned one-byte integer. The database name is stored in the event body, but the length is given here.

Error code

> The error code resulting from execution of the statement, stored as a two-byte unsigned integer. This field is included because, in some cases, statements have to be logged to the binary log even when they fail.

Status variables length

> The length of the block in the event body storing the status variables, stored as a two-byte unsigned integer. This status block is sometimes used with a `Query` event to store various status variables, such as `SQL_MODE`.

The event body consists of the following fields, which are all of variable length.

Status variables
> A sequence of status variables. Each status variable is represented by a single integer followed by the value of the status variable. The interpretation and length of each status variable value depends on which status variable it concerns. Status variables are not always present; they are added only when necessary. Some examples of status variables follow:

> `Q_SQL_MODE_CODE`
>> The value of `SQL_MODE` used when executing the statement.

> `Q_AUTO_INCREMENT`
>> This status variable contains the values of `auto_increment_increment` and `auto_increment_offset` used for the statement, assuming that they are not the default of 1.

> `Q_CHARSET`
>> This status variable contains the character set code and collation used by the connection and the server when the statement was executed.

Current database
> The name of the current database, stored as a null-terminated string. Notice that the length of the database name is given in the post header.

Statement text
> The statement that was executed. The length of the statement can be computed from the information in the common header and the post header. This statement is normally identical to the original statement written, but in some cases, the statement is rewritten before it is stored in the binary log. For instance, as you saw earlier in this chapter, triggers and stored procedures are stored with `DEFINER` clauses specified.

Format description event post header and body

The `Format_description` event records important information about the binlog file format, the event format, and the server. Since it has to remain robust between versions—it should still be possible to interpret it even if the binlog format changes—there are some restrictions on which changes are allowed.

One of the more important restrictions is that the common header of both the `Format_description` event and the `Rotate` event is fixed at 19 bytes. This means that it is not possible to extend the event with new fields in the common header.

The post header and event body for the `Format_description` event contain the following fields:

Binlog file version
> The version of the binlog file format used by this file. For MySQL versions 5.0 and later, this is 4.

Server version string
> A 50-byte string storing server version information. This is usually the three-part version number followed by information about the options used for the build, "5.1.37-1ubuntu5-log," for instance.

Creation time
> A four-byte integer holding the creation time—the number of seconds since the epoch—of the first binlog file written by the server since startup. For later binlog files written by the server, this field will be zero.

> This scheme allows a slave to determine that the server was restarted and that the slave should reset state and temporary data—for example, close any open transactions and drop any temporary tables it has created.

Common header length
> The length of the common header for all events in the binlog file *except* the `Format_description` and `Rotate` events. As described earlier, the length of the common header for the `Format_description` and `Rotate` events is fixed at 19 bytes.

Post-header lengths
> This is the only variable-length field of the `Format_description` log event. It holds an array containing the size of the post header for each event in the binlog file as a one-byte integer. The value 255 is reserved as the length for the field, so the maximum length of a post header is 254 bytes.

Binary Log Options and Variables

A set of options and variables allow you to configure a vast number of aspects of binary logging.

Several options control such properties as the name of the binlog files and the index file. Most of these options can be manipulated as server variables as well. Some have already been mentioned earlier in the chapter, but here you will find more details on each:

`expire-log-days=days`
> The number of days that binlog files should be kept. Files that are older than the specified number will be purged from the filesystem when the binary log is rotated or the server restarts.

> By default this option is 0, meaning that binlog files are never removed.

log-bin[*=basename*]
> The binary log is turned on by adding the `log-bin` option in the *my.cnf* file, as explained in Chapter 2. In addition to turning on the binary log, this option gives a base name for the binlog files; that is, the portion of the filename before the dot. If an extension is provided, it is removed when forming the base name of the binlog files.
>
> If the option is specified without a *basename*, the base name defaults to *host*-bin where *host* is the base name—that is, the filename without directory or extension—of the file given by the `pid-file` option, which is usually the hostname as given by *gethostname(2)*. For example, if `pid-file` is */usr/run/mysql/master.pid*, the default name of the binlog files will be *master-bin.000001*, *master-bin.000002*, etc.
>
> Since the default value for the `pid-file` option includes the hostname, it is strongly recommended that you give a value to the `log-bin` option. Otherwise the binlog files will change names when the hostname changes (unless `pid-file` is given an explicit value).

log-bin-index[*=filename*]
> Gives a name to the index file. This can be useful if you want to place the index file in a different place from the default.
>
> The default is the same as the base name used for `log-bin`. For example, if the base name used to create binlog files is *master-bin*, the index file will be named *master-bin.index*.
>
> Similar to the situation for the `log-bin` option, the hostname will be used for constructing the index filename, meaning that if the hostname changes, replication will break. For this reason, it is strongly recommended that you provide a value for this option.

log-bin-trust-function-creators
> When creating stored functions, it is possible to create specially crafted functions that allow arbitrary data to be read and manipulated on the slave. For this reason, creating stored functions requires the SUPER privilege. However, since stored functions are very useful in many circumstances, it might be that the DBA trusts anyone with CREATE ROUTINE privileges not to write malicious stored functions. For this reason, it is possible to disable the SUPER privilege requirement for creating stored functions (but CREATE ROUTINE is still required).

binlog-cache-size=*bytes*
> The size of the in-memory part of the transaction cache in bytes. The transaction cache is backed by disk, so whenever the size of the transaction cache exceeds this value, the remaining data will go to disk.
>
> This can potentially create a performance problem, so increasing the value of this option can improve performance if you use many large transactions.

Note that just allocating a very large buffer might not be a good idea, since that means that other parts of the server get less memory, which might cause performance degradation.

`max-binlog-cache-size=bytes`

Use this option to restrict the size of each transaction in the binary log. Since large transactions can potentially block the binary log for a long time, they will cause other threads to convoy on the binary log and can therefore create a significant performance problem. If the size of a transaction exceeds *bytes*, the statement will be aborted with an error.

`max-binlog-size=bytes`

Specifies the size of each binlog file. When writing a statement or transaction would exceed this value, the binlog file is rotated and writing proceeds in a new, empty binlog file.

Notice that if the transaction or statement exceeds `max-binlog-size`, the binary log will be rotated, but the transaction will be written to the new file in its entirety, exceeding the specified maximum. This is because transactions are never split between binlog files.

`sync-binlog=period`

Specifies how often to write the binary log to disk using *fdatasync(2)*. The value given is the number of transaction commits for each real call to *fdatasync(2)*. For instance, if a value of 1 is given, *fdatasync(2)* will be called for each transaction commit, and if a value of 10 is given, *fdatasync(2)* will be called after each 10 transaction commits.

A value of zero means that there will be no calls to *fdatasync(2)* at all and that the server trusts the operating system to write the binary log to disk as part of the normal file handling.

`read-only`

Prevents any client threads—except the slave thread and users with SUPER privileges—from updating any data on the server. This is useful on slave servers to allow replication to proceed without data being corrupted by clients that connect to the slave.

Conclusion

Clearly, there is much to the binary log—including its use, composition, and techniques. We presented these concepts and more in this chapter, including how to control the binary log behavior. The material in this chapter builds a foundation for a greater understanding of the mechanics of the binary log and its importance in logging changes to data.

Joel opened an email message from his boss that didn't have a subject. "I hate it when people do that," he thought. Mr. Summerson's email messages were like his taskings—straight and to the point. The message read, "Thanks for recovering that data for the marketing people. I'll expect a report by tomorrow morning. You can send it via email."

Joel shrugged and opened a new email message, careful to include a meaningful subject. He wondered what level of detail to include and whether he should explain what he learned about the binary log and the `mysqlbinlog` utility. After a moment of contemplation, he included as many details as he could. "He'll probably tell me to cut it back to a bulleted list," thought Joel. That seemed like a good idea, so he wrote a two-sentence summary and a few bullet points and moved them to the top of the message. When he was finished, he sent it on its way to his boss. "Maybe I should start saving these somewhere in case I have to recount something," he mused.

## CHAPTER 4

Replication for High Availability

> Joel was listening to his iPod when he noticed his boss standing directly in front of his desk. He took off his headphones and said, "Sorry, sir."
>
> Mr. Summerson smiled and said, "No problem, Joel. I need you to figure out some way to ensure we can keep our replicated servers monitored so that we don't lose data and can minimize downtime. We're starting to get some complaints from the developers that the system is too inflexible. I can deal with the developers, but the support people tell me that when we have a failure it takes too long to recover. I'd like you to make that your top priority."
>
> Joel nodded. "Sure, I'll look at load balancing and improving our recovery efforts in replication."
>
> "Excellent. Give me a report on what you think we need to do to solve this problem."
>
> Joel watched his boss leave his office. "OK, let's find out what this high availability chapter has to say," he thought, as he opened his favorite MySQL book.

Buying expensive machines known for their reliability and ensuring that you have a really good UPS in case of power failures should give you a highly available system. Right?

Well, high availability is actually not that easy to achieve. To have a system that is truly available all the time, you have to plan carefully for any contingency and ensure that you have redundancy to handle failing components. True high availability—a system that does not go down even in the most unexpected circumstances—is hard to achieve and very costly.

The principles for achieving high availability are simple enough. You need to have three things:

Redundancy
　　If a component fails, you have to have a replacement for it. The replacement can be either idly standing by or part of the existing deployment.

Contingency plans

If a component fails, you have to know what to do. This depends on which component failed and how it failed.

Procedure

If a component fails, you have to be able to detect it and then execute your plans swiftly and efficiently.

If a system has a single point of failure—a single component that, should it fail, will cause the entire system to fail—it puts a severe limit on your ability to achieve high availability. This means that one of your first goals is to locate these single points of failure and ensure you have redundancy for them.

Redundancy

To understand where redundancy might be needed, you have to identify every potential point of failure in the deployment. Even though it sounds easy—not to mention a tad tedious and boring—it requires some imagination to ensure that you really have found them all. Switches, routers, network cards, and even network cables are single points of failure. Outside of your architecture, but no less important, are power sources and physical facilities. But what about services needed to keep the deployment up? Suppose all network management is consolidated in a web-based interface? Or what if you have only one staff person who knows how to handle some types of failure?

Identifying the points of failure does not necessarily mean that you have to eliminate them all. Sometimes it is just not possible for economical, technical, or geographic reasons, but being aware of them helps you with planning.

Some things that you should consider, or at least make a conscious decision about whether to consider, are cost of duplicating components, the probability of failure for different components, the time to replace a component, and risk exposure while repairing a component. If repairing a component takes a week and you are running with the spare as the single point of failure during this time, you are taking a certain risk that the spare could be lost as well, which may or may not be acceptable.

Once you have identified where you need redundancy, you have to choose between two fundamental alternatives: you can either keep duplicates around for each component—ready to take over immediately if the original component should fail—or you can ensure you have extra capacity in the system so that if a component fails, you can still handle the load. This choice does not have to be made in an all-or-nothing fashion: you can combine the two techniques so that you duplicate some components and use extra capacity for some other parts of the system.

On the surface, the easiest approach is to duplicate components, but duplication is expensive. You have to leave a standby around and keep it up-to-date with the main component all the time. The advantages of duplicating components are that you do not lose performance when switching and that switching to the standby is usually faster than restructuring the system, which you would have to do if you approached the problem by creating spare capacity.

Creating spare capacity lets you use all the components for running the business, possibly allowing you to handle higher peaks in your load. When a component breaks, you restructure the system so that all remaining components are in use. It is, however, important to have more capacity than you normally need.

To understand why, consider a simple case where you have a master that handles the writes—actually, you should have two, since you need to have redundancy—with a set of slaves connected to the master whose only purpose is to serve read requests.

Should one of the slaves fail, the system will still be responding, but the capacity of the system will be reduced. If you have 10 slaves, each running at 50 percent capacity, the failure of one slave will increase the load on each slave to 55 percent, which is easy to handle. However, if the slaves are running at 95 percent capacity and one of the slaves fails, each server would have to handle 105 percent of the original load to handle the same load, which is clearly not possible. In this case, the read capacity of the system will be reduced and the response time will be longer.

And planning for the loss of one server is not sufficient: you have to consider the probability of losing more than one server and prepare for that situation as well. Continuing with our previous example, even if each server is running at 80 percent capacity, the system will be able to handle the loss of one server. However, the loss of two servers means that the load on each remaining server will increase to 100 percent, leaving you with no room for unexpected bursts in traffic. If this occurs once a year, it might be manageable, but you have to know how often it is likely to happen.

Table 4-1 gives example probabilities for losing 1, 2, or 3 servers in a setup of 100 servers, given different probabilities of losing a single server. As you can see, with a 1 percent probability of losing a server, you have a 16 percent risk of losing three or more servers. If you are not prepared to handle that, you're in for some problems if it actually happens.

 For a stochastic variable X representing the number of servers lost, the probabilities are calculated using the binomial tail distribution:

$$P(X \geq k) = \binom{n}{k} p^k$$

Table 4-1. Probabilities of losing servers

Probability of losing a single server	1	2	3
1.00%	100.00%	49.50%	16.17%
0.50%	50.00%	12.38%	2.02%
0.10%	10.00%	0.50%	0.02%

To avoid such a situation, you have to monitor the deployment closely to know what the load is, figure out the capacity of your system through measurements, and do your math to see where the response times will start to suffer.

Planning

Having redundancy is not sufficient; you also need to have plans for what to do when the components fail. In the previous example, it is easy to handle a failing slave, since new connections will be redirected to the working slaves, but consider the following:

- What happens with the existing connections? Just aborting and returning an error message to the user is probably not a good idea. Typically, there is an application layer between the user and the database, so in this case the application layer has to retry the query with another server.
- What happens if the master fails? In the previous example, only the slaves failed, but the master can also fail. Assuming you have added redundancy by keeping an extra master around (we will cover how to do that later in the chapter), you must also have plans for moving all the slaves over to the new master.

This chapter will cover some of the techniques and topologies that you can use to handle various situations for failing MySQL servers. There are basically three server roles to consider: master failures, slave failures, and relay failures. Slave failures are just failures of slaves that are used for read scale-out. The slaves that also act as masters are relay slaves and need special care. Master failures are the most important failures to handle quickly, since the deployment will be unavailable until the master is restored.

Slave Failures

By far, the easiest failures to handle are slave failures. Since the slaves are only used for read queries, it is sufficient to inform the load balancer that the slave is missing, which will direct new queries to the functioning slaves. There have to be enough slaves to handle the reduced capacity of the system, but apart from that, a failing slave does not normally affect the replication topology and there are no specific topologies that you need to consider to make slave failure easier to manage.

When a slave has failed, there are inevitably some queries that have been sent to the slave that are waiting for a reply. Once these connections report an error resulting from a lost server, the queries have to be repeated with a functioning slave.

Master Failures

If the master fails, it has to be replaced to keep the deployment up, and it has to be replaced quickly. The moment the master fails, all write queries will be aborted, so the first thing to do is to get a new master available and direct all clients to it.

Since the main master failed, all the slaves are now without a master as well, meaning that all the slaves have stale data, but they are still up and can reply to read queries.

However, some queries may block if they are waiting for changes to arrive at the slave. Some queries may make it into the relay log of the slave and therefore will eventually be executed by the slave. No special consideration has to be taken on the behalf of these queries.

For queries that are waiting for events that did not leave the master before it crashed, the situation is bleaker. In this case, it is necessary to ensure they are handled. This usually means they are reported as failures, so the user will have to reissue the query.

Relay Failures

For servers acting as relay servers, the situation has to be handled specially. If they fail, the remaining slaves have to be redirected to use some other relay or the master itself. Since the relay has been added to relieve the master of some load, it is likely that the master will not be able to handle the load of a batch of slaves connected to one of its relays.

Disaster Recovery

In the world of high availability, "disaster" does not have to mean earthquakes or floods; it just means that something went very bad for the computer and it is not local to the machine that failed.

Typical examples are lost power in the data center—not necessarily because the power was lost in the city; just losing power in the building is sufficient. For a real-life story, and some insight into what happened to MySQL, see the section "The mysql.com Outage" on page 110.

The nature of a disaster is that many things fail at once, making it impossible to handle redundancy by duplicating servers at a single data center. Instead, it is necessary to ensure data is kept safe at another geographic location, and it is quite common for companies to have different components at different offices, even when the company is relatively small.

Procedures

After you have eliminated all single points of failure, ensured you have sufficient redundancy for the system, and made plans for every contingency, you should be ready for the last step.

All your resources and careful planning are of no use unless you can wield them properly. You can usually manage a small site with a few servers manually with very little planning, but as the number of servers increases, automation becomes a necessity—

and if you run a successful business, the number of servers might have to increase quickly.

You're likely better off if you plan from day one to have automation—if you have to grow, you will be busy handling other matters and will probably not have time to create the necessary automation support.

Some of the basic procedures have already been discussed, but you need to consider having ready-made procedures for at least the following tasks:

Adding new slaves

> Creating new slaves when you need to scale is the basis for running a big site. There are several options for creating new slaves. They all circle around methods for taking a snapshot of an existing server, usually a slave, restoring the snapshot on a new server, and then starting replication from the correct position.

> The time for taking a snapshot will, of course, affect how quickly you can bring the new slave up; if the backup time is too long, the master may have issued a lot of changes, which means that the new slave will take longer to catch up. For this reason, the snapshot time is important. Figure 4-1 shows the snapshot time when the slave has caught up. You can see that when the slave is stopped to take a snapshot, the changes will start to accumulate, which will cause the outstanding changes to increase. Once the slave is restarted, it will start to apply the outstanding changes and the number of outstanding changes will decrease.

Some different methods of taking a snapshot include the following:

Using `mysqldump`

> Using `mysqldump` is safe but slow. It allows you to restore the data using a different storage engine than that on the original. If you use InnoDB tables, you can take a consistent snapshot, meaning you do not have to bring the server offline.

Copying the database files

> This is relatively fast, but requires you to bring the server offline before copying the files.

Using an online backup method

> There are different methods available, such as the InnoDB Hot Backup.

Using LVM to get a snapshot

> On Linux, it is possible to take a snapshot of a volume using Logical Volume Manager (LVM). It does require that you prepare beforehand, since a special LVM volume has to be created.

Using filesystem snapshot methods

> The Solaris ZFS, for example, has built-in support for taking snapshots. This is a very fast technique for creating backups, but it is similar to the other techniques above (except for `mysqldump`). This means that you cannot restore into a different engine than the one you used to take the server snapshot.

Techniques for creating new slaves are covered in Chapter 2, and the different backup methods are covered in Chapter 12.

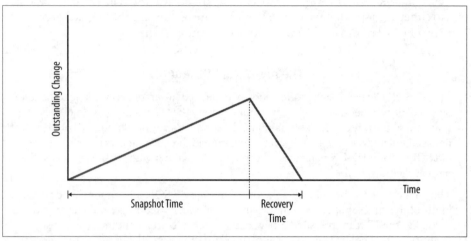

Figure 4-1. Outstanding changes when taking a snapshot

Removing slaves from the topology
Removing slaves from the setup only requires notifying the load balancer that the slave is absent. An example load balancer—with methods for adding and removing servers—can be found in Chapter 5.

Switching the master
For routine maintenance, it is common to have to switch all the slaves of a master over to a secondary master as well as notify load balancers of the master's absence. This procedure can and should be handled with no downtime at all, since it should not affect normal operations.

Using slave promotion (described later in this chapter) is one way to handle this, but it might be easier to use a hot standby instead (also covered later in this chapter).

Handling slave failures
Your slaves will fail—it is just a matter of how often. Handling slave failures must be a routine event in any deployment. It is only necessary to detect that the slave is absent and remove it from the load balancer's pool, as described in Chapter 5.

Handling master failures
When the master goes down suddenly, you have to detect the failure and move all the slaves over to a standby, or promote one of the slaves to be the new master. Techniques for this are described later in this chapter.

Upgrading slaves
Upgrading slaves to new versions of the server should usually not be a problem. However, bringing the slave out of the system for the upgrade requires removing it from the load balancer and maybe notifying other systems of the slave's absence.

Upgrading masters

To upgrade the master, it is usually necessary to upgrade all the slaves first. However, this may not always be the case. To upgrade the master, it is usually necessary to either use a standby as a master while you are performing the upgrade or promote one of the slaves to be the master for the duration of the upgrade.

The mysql.com Outage

The MySQL IT team is a versatile and very dedicated group of people, able to handle all kinds of systems and equipment. Unlike many other IT teams I have met over the years, these guys are comfortable handling the complex array of computers that MySQL has accumulated over the years—everything from high-end Windows machines to very old SGI Irix and HP-UX machines—keeping it all together with whatever means they have at their disposal.

The data center has been invaluable for testing the MySQL server on many different kinds of machines, but as MySQL began growing, it started to get quite cramped in there. So, the IT team prepared a new data center in better—and more expensive—facilities in Stockholm. The move was planned for the weekend, but events took a nasty turn in the week just before the planned move.

I usually work from home, but this particular day I needed to go to the office in Uppsala for some project meetings. I noticed that the mysql.com site was down that morning, but left for the office anyway, hoping for the best.

Arriving at the office in Uppsala, I met part of the MySQL IT team stringing power cords together, all going into the data center. Apparently, the entire building had lost all power, but the nearby buildings still had power, so the IT team had strung a long line of power cords together to get power to some critical development servers.

The power outage was quite severe and when I arrived there, the UPS had been depleted. The power grid to the building had been damaged and since the engineers from the electricity company could not say when the problem would be fixed, part of the IT team had decided to relocate the web stack immediately, basically taking whatever cars they could find and driving the machines with the web stack to the new data center in Stockholm, approximately 100 kilometers south.

After getting the web stack online in Stockholm, the mysql.com site was restored, but there was a lot of work to be done to restore the development machines using whatever power was available until the power grid was repaired. The group worked for 48 hours with almost no sleep, after which the machines were fully restored and operational—more than could be said about the IT team.

MySQL was back on track again....

Hot Standby

The easiest of the topologies for duplicating servers is the hot standby topology. This topology is shown in Figure 4-2 and consists of the master and a dedicated server called a hot standby that duplicates the main master. The hot standby server is connected to the master as a slave, and it reads and applies all changes.

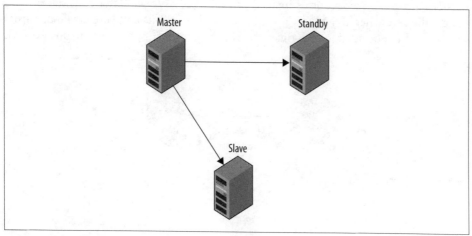

Figure 4-2. Master with a hot standby

The idea is that when the main master fails, the hot standby provides a faithful replica of the master, and all the clients and slaves can therefore be switched over to the hot standby and continue operating. As with many ideas, the reality is not always that rosy.

Failure is inevitable, at least when you run a large deployment. It is not a question of *if* servers fail, but *when* and *how often* they fail. If the master fails for any reason, it should not bring the deployment to a halt. To ensure operations proceed, it is necessary to have a hot standby server available and to redirect all slaves to the hot standby when the main master fails. This will give you a chance to check what happened with the main master, and maybe fix it or replace it. After you have repaired the master, you have to bring it back on track and either set it to be the hot standby, or redirect the slaves to the original master again.

Sounds simple, doesn't it? Ah, if only it was that easy—unfortunately, you have the following potential problems to ponder:

- When failing over to the hot standby, you are replicating from a new master, so it will be necessary to translate the binlog positions from those of the original master to those of the hot standby.

- When failing over a slave to a hot standby, the hot standby might actually not have all the changes that the slave has.

- When bringing the repaired master back into the configuration, the repaired master might have changes in the binary log that never left the server.

All these are relevant issues, but for starters, let's just consider the simpler case illustrated in Figure 4-3: that of performing a *switchover* from a running master to a standby in order to, for example, perform maintenance on the original master. In this case, the master is still running, so the situation becomes a lot simpler, since we can control the master and make it work for us instead of against us. We will later consider how to handle the case when the master just goes down because its software crashed, a frustrated coworker decided to kick the server, or the janitor tripped over the power cord.

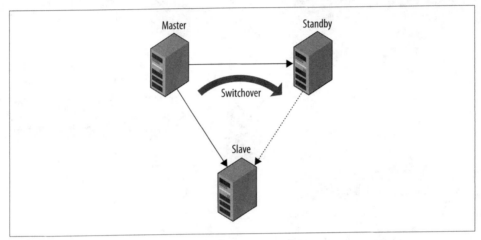

Figure 4-3. Switching over from a running master to a standby

By default, events executed by the slave thread are *not* logged to the binary log, which turns out to be a problem if the slave is a standby waiting to be used as a master. In this case, it is necessary to have all the changes sent by the master to the standby written to the binary log of the standby—if not, there will be nothing to replicate. To configure the standby server for this, add the option `log-slave-updates` to the *my.cnf* file. This option ensures that statements received from the master and executed are also written to the slave's binary log.

```
[mysqld]
user             = mysql
pid-file         = /var/run/mysqld/mysqld.pid
socket           = /var/run/mysqld/mysqld.sock
port             = 3306
basedir          = /usr
datadir          = /var/lib/mysql
tmpdir           = /tmp
log-bin          = master-bin
log-bin-index    = master-bin.index
server-id        = 1
log-slave-updates
```

After updating the options file, restart the server.

The main problem with switching over to a standby in this case is to perform the switchover in such a way that replication starts at the standby precisely where it stopped replicating on the master. If the positions were easy to translate—for example, if the positions were the same on both the master and the standby—we would not have a problem. Unfortunately, the positions may be different on the master and the standby for a number of reasons. The most common case is when the standby was not attached to the master when the master was started, but even if that is done, events cannot be guaranteed to be written the same way to the binary log on the standby as they were written to the binary log on the master.

The basic idea for performing the switchover is to stop the slave and the standby at exactly the same position and then just redirect the slave to the standby. Because the standby hasn't made any changes after the position where you stopped it, you can just check the binlog position on the standby and direct the slave to start at that position. However, just stopping the slave and the standby will not guarantee that they are synchronized, so you have to do this manually.

To do this, stop both the slave and the standby and compare the binlog positions. Since both positions refer to positions on the same master—the slave and standby are both connected to the same master—you can check the positions just by comparing the filename and the byte position lexicographically (in that order).

```
standby> SHOW SLAVE STATUS\G
    ...
  Relay_Master_Log_File: master-bin.000096
    ...
    Exec_Master_Log_Pos: 756648
1 row in set (0.00 sec)

slave> SHOW SLAVE STATUS\G
    ...
  Relay_Master_Log_File: master-bin.000096
    ...
    Exec_Master_Log_Pos: 743456
1 row in set (0.00 sec)
```

In this case, the standby is ahead of the slave, so just write down the slave position of the standby and start the slave to run until it has caught up with the standby. To have the slave catch up with the standby and stop at the right position, use the START SLAVE UNTIL command as we did when stopping the reporting slave earlier in this chapter:

```
slave> START SLAVE UNTIL
    ->    MASTER_LOG_FILE = 'master-bin.000096',
    ->    MASTER_LOG_POS = 756648;
Query OK, 0 rows affected (0.18 sec)

slave> SELECT MASTER_POS_WAIT('master-bin.000096', 756648);
Query OK, 0 rows affected (1.12 sec)
```

The slave and standby have now stopped at exactly the same position, and everything is ready to do the switchover to the standby using CHANGE MASTER TO to direct the slave to the standby and start it. But what position should you specify? Since the file and position that the master recorded for its stopping point are different from the file and position recorded by the standby for the same point, it is necessary to fetch the position that the standby recorded while recording the changes as a master. To do this, execute SHOW MASTER STATUS on the standby:

```
standby> SHOW MASTER STATUS\G
*************************** 1. row ***************************
            File: standby-bin.000019
        Position: 56447
    Binlog_Do_DB:
Binlog_Ignore_DB:
1 row in set (0.00 sec)
```

Now you can redirect the slave to the standby using the correct position:

```
slave> CHANGE MASTER TO
    ->    MASTER_HOST = 'standby-1',
    ->    MASTER_PORT = 3306,
    ->    MASTER_USER = 'repl_user',
    ->    MASTER_PASSWORD = 'xyzzy',
    ->    MASTER_LOG_FILE = '
standby-bin.000019',
    ->    MASTER_LOG_POS = 56447;
  Query OK, 0 rows affected (0.18 sec)

slave> START SLAVE;
Query OK, 0 rows affected (0.25 sec)
```

If the opposite is true—that the slave is ahead of the standby—you can just switch the roles of the standby and the slave in the previous steps. This is possible since the master is running and can provide either the slave or the standby with the missing changes. In the next section, we will consider how to handle the situation in which the master has stopped unexpectedly and hence cannot provide either the slave or the standby with the missing changes.

Handling a switchover in Python

Example 4-1 shows the Python code for switching a slave over to another master. The replicate_to_position function instructs a server to read from the master only to the given position. When the procedure returns, the slave will have stopped at exactly this position. The switch_to_master directs a slave to a new master. The procedure assumes that both the server on which it executes and the new master are connected to the same original master. If they are not, the positions are not comparable and the procedure will raise an exception.

Example 4-1. Procedure for switching to a new master

```
def replicate_to_position(server, pos):
    server.sql("START SLAVE UNTIL MASTER_LOG_FILE=%s, MASTER_LOG_POS=%s",
               (pos.file, pos.pos))
    server.sql("SELECT MASTER_POS_WAIT(%s,%s)", (pos.file, pos.pos))


def switch_to_master(server, standby):
    stop_slave(server)
    stop_slave(standby)
    server_pos = fetch_slave_position(server)
    standby_pos = fetch_slave_position(standby)
    if server_pos < standby_pos:
        replicate_to_position(server, standby_pos)
    elif server_pos > standby_pos:
        replicate_to_position(standby, server_pos)
    master_pos = fetch_master_position(standby)
    change_master(server, standby, master_pos)
    start_slave(standby)
    start_slave(server)
```

Dual Masters

One frequently mentioned setup for high availability is the dual masters topology. In this setup, two masters replicate each other to keep both current. This setup is very simple to use since it is symmetric. Failing over to the standby master does not require any reconfiguration of the main master, and failing back to the main master again when the standby master fails in turn is very easy.

Servers can be either active or passive. If a server is active it means that the server accepts writes, which are likely to be propagated elsewhere using replication. If a server is passive, it does not accept writes and is just following the active master, usually to be ready to take over when it fails.

When using dual masters, there are two different setups, each serving a different purpose:

Active-active

> In an active-active setup, writes go to both servers, which then transfer changes to the other master.

Active-passive

> In this setup, one of the masters, called the active master, handles writes while the other server, called the passive master, just keeps current with the active master.

> This is almost identical to the hot standby setup, but since it is symmetric, it is easy to switch back and forth between the masters, each taking turns being the active master.

Note that this setup does not necessarily let the passive master answer queries. For some of the solutions that you'll see in this section, the passive master is a cold standby.

These setups do not necessarily mean that replication is used to keep the servers synchronized—there are other techniques that can serve that purpose. Some techniques can support active-active masters, while other techniques can only support active-passive masters.

The most common use of an active-active dual masters setup is to have the servers geographically close to different sets of users, for example, in offices at different places in the world. The users can then work with the local server, and the changes will be replicated over to the other master so that both masters are kept in sync. Since the transactions are committed locally, the system will be perceived as more responsive. It is important to understand that the transactions are committed locally, meaning that the two masters are not consistent in the sense that they have the same information. The changes committed to one master will be propagated to the other master eventually, but until that has been done, the masters have inconsistent data.

This has two main consequences that you need to be aware of:

- If the same information is updated on the two masters—for example, a user is accidentally added to both masters—there will be a conflict between the two updates and it is likely that replication will stop.

- If a crash occurs while the two masters are inconsistent, some transactions will be lost.

To some extent, you can avoid the problem with conflicting changes by allowing writes to only one of the servers, thereby making the other master a passive master. This is called an active-passive setup—where the active server is called the *primary* and the passive server is called the *secondary*.

Losing transactions when the server crashes is an inevitable result of using asynchronous replication, but depending on the application, it does not necessarily have to be a serious problem. You can limit the number of transactions that are lost when the server crashes by using a new feature in MySQL 5.5 called *semisynchronous replication*. The idea behind semisynchronous replication is that the thread committing a transaction will block until at least one slave acknowledges that it has received the transaction. Since the events for the transaction are sent to the slave after the transaction has been committed to the storage engine, the number of lost transactions can be kept down to at most one per thread.

Similar to the active-active approach, the active-passive setup is symmetrical and therefore allows you to switch easily from the main master to the standby and back. Depending on the way you handle the mirroring, it may also be possible to use the passive master for administrative tasks such as upgrading the server and use the upgrade server as the active master once the upgrade is finished without any downtime at all.

One fundamental problem that has to be resolved when using an active-passive setup is the risk of both servers deciding that they are the primary master—this is called the *split-brain syndrome*. This can occur if network connectivity is lost for a brief period, long enough to have the secondary promote itself to primary, but then the primary is brought online again. If changes have been made to both servers while they are both in the role of primary, there may be a conflict. In the case of using a shared disk, simultaneous writes to the disks by two servers are likely to cause "interesting" problems with the database—that is, probably disastrous and difficult to pinpoint.

Shared disks

A straightforward dual masters approach is shown in Figure 4-4, where a pair of masters is connected using a shared disk architecture such as a SAN (storage area network). In this approach, both servers are connected to the same SAN and are configured to use the same files. Since one of the masters is passive, it will not write anything to the files while the active master is running as usual. If the main server fails, the standby will be ready to take over.

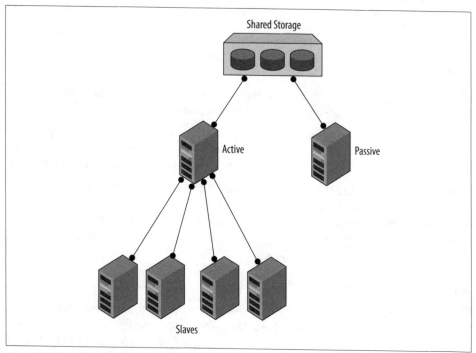

Figure 4-4. Dual masters using a shared disk

The advantage of this approach is that since the binlog files are stored on a shared disk, there is no need for translating binlog positions. The two servers are truly mirror images of each other, but they are running on two different machines. This means that switching over from the main master to the standby is very fast. There is no need for the slaves to translate positions to the new master; all that is necessary is to note the position where the slave stopped, issue a `CHANGE MASTER` command, and start replication again.

When you fail over using this technique, you have to perform recovery on the tables, since it is very likely updates were stopped midstream. Each storage engine behaves differently in this situation. For example, InnoDB has to perform a normal recovery from the transaction log, as it would in the event of a crash, whereas if you use MyISAM you probably have to repair the tables before being able to continue operation. Of these two choices, InnoDB is preferred because recovery is significantly faster than repairing a MyISAM table.

Example 4-2 shows a Python script for handling such a failover using the Replicant library. Notice that the position uses the server ID of the main server, but since both servers are using the same files, the standby server is really a mirror image of the main server. Since the position contains the server ID as well, this will also catch any mistakes made by the user, such as passing a master that is not a mirror image of the main master.

Example 4-2. Procedure to remaster a slave when using a shared disk

```
def remaster_slave(slave, master):
    position = fetch_slave_position(slave)
    change_master(slave, master, position)
```

The ability to set up dual masters using shared disks is dependent on the shared storage solution used, a discussion that is beyond the scope of this book.

The problem with using shared storage is that since the two masters are using the same files for storing data, you have to be very careful when doing any administrative tasks on the passive master. Overwriting the configuration files, even by mistake, can be fatal.

The handling of split-brain syndrome depends on which shared disk solution is used and is beyond the scope of this book. One example, however, occurs when using SCSI, which has support for reserving disks by servers. This allows a server to detect that it is really not the primary anymore by noticing that the disks are reserved by another server.

Replicated disks using DRBD

The Linux High Availability project (*http://www.linux-ha.org/*) contains a lot of useful tools for maintaining high availability systems. Most of these tools are beyond the scope of this book, but there is one tool that is interesting for our purposes: DRBD (Distributed Replicated Block Device), which is software for replicating block devices over the network.

Figure 4-5 shows a typical setup of two nodes where DRBD is used to replicate a disk to a secondary server. The setup creates two DRBD block devices, one on each node, which in turn write the data to the real disks. The two DRBD processes communicate

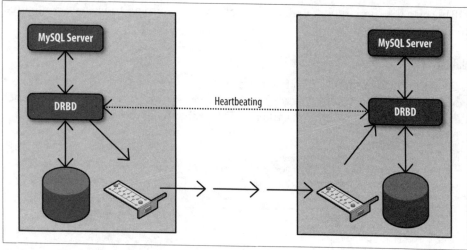

Figure 4-5. Using DRBD to replicate disks

over the network to ensure any changes made to the primary are replicated over to the secondary. To the MySQL server, the device replication is transparent. The DRBD devices look and behave like normal disks, so no special configuration is needed for the servers.

You can only use DRBD in an active-passive setup, meaning that the passive disk cannot be accessed at all. In contrast with the shared disk solution outlined earlier and the bidirectional replication implementation described later in this chapter, the passive master cannot be used—not even for pure read-only tasks.

Similar to the shared disk solution, DRBD has the advantage of not needing to translate positions between the two masters since they share the same files. However, failing over to the standby master takes longer than in the shared disk setup described earlier.

For both the shared disk and the DRBD setup, it is necessary to perform recovery of the database files before bringing the servers online. Since recovery of MyISAM tables is quite expensive, it is recommended that you use a transactional engine with good recovery performance for the database tables—InnoDB is the proven solution in this case, but other transactional engines such as PBXT are maturing quickly, so investigating the alternatives is well-invested time.

Since the *mysql* database contains strictly MyISAM tables, you should, as a general principle, avoid unnecessary changes to these tables during normal operations. It is, of course, impossible to avoid when you need to perform administrative tasks.

One advantage of DRBD over shared disks is that for the shared disk solution, the disks actually provide a single point of failure. Should the network to the shared disk array go down, it is possible that the server will not work at all. In contrast, replicating the disks means that the data is available on both servers, which reduces the risk of a total failure.

DRBD also has support built in to handle split-brain syndrome and can be configured to automatically recover from it.

Bidirectional replication

When using dual masters in an active-passive setup, there are no significant differences compared to the hot standby solution outlined earlier. However, in contrast to the other dual-masters solutions outlined earlier, it is possible to have an active-active setup (shown in Figure 4-6).

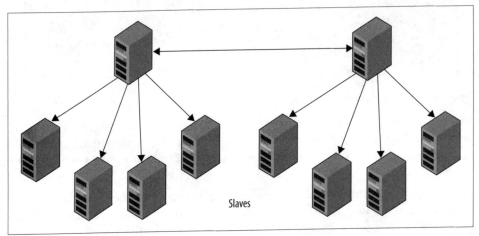

Figure 4-6. Bidirectional replication

Although controversial in some circles, an active-active setup does have its uses. A typical case is when there are two offices working with local information in the same database—for example, sales data or employee data—and want low response times when working with the database, while ensuring the data is available in both places. In this case, the data is naturally local to each office—for example, each salesperson is normally working with his own sales and rarely, if ever, makes changes to another salesperson's data.

Use the following steps to set up bidirectional replication:

1. Ensure both servers have different server IDs.
2. Ensure both servers have the same data (and that no changes are made to either system until replication has been activated).
3. Create a replication user and prepare replication (using the information in Chapter 1) on both servers.
4. Start replication on both servers.

When using bidirectional replication, be forewarned that replication includes no concept of conflict resolution. If both servers update the same piece of data, you will have a conflict that may or may not be noticed. If you are lucky, replication will stop at the offending statement, but you shouldn't count on it. If you intend to have a high availability system, you should ensure at the application level that two servers do not try to update the same data.

Even if data is naturally partitioned—as in the example given previously with two offices in separate locations—it is critical to put provisions in place to ensure data is not accidentally updated at the wrong server.

In this case the application has to connect to the server responsible for the employee and update the information there, not just update the information locally and hope for the best.

If you want to connect slaves to either of the servers, you have to ensure the `log-slave-updates` option is enabled. Since the other master is also connected as a slave, an obvious question is: what happens with events that the server sends out when they return to the server?

When replication is running, the server ID of the server that created the event is attached to each event. This server ID is then propagated further when the slave writes the event to its binary log. When a server sees an event with the same server ID as its own server ID, that event is simply skipped and replication proceeds with the next event.

Sometimes, you want to process the event anyway. This might be the case if you have removed the old server and created a new one with the same server ID and you are in the process of performing a PITR. In those cases, it is possible to disable this checking using the `replicate-same-server-id` configuration variable. However, to prevent you from shooting yourself in the foot, you cannot set this option at the same time that `log-slave-updates` is set. Otherwise, it would be possible to send events in a circle and quickly thrash all the servers. To prevent that from happening, it is not possible to forward events when using `replicate-same-server-id`.

When using an active-active setup, there is a need to handle conflicts in a safe way, and by far the easiest way—and the only recommended way to handle an active-active setup—is to ensure the different active servers write to different areas.

One possible solution is to assign different databases—or different tables—to different masters. Example 4-3 shows a setup that uses two different tables, each updated by different masters. To make it easy to view the split data, a view is created that combines the two tables.

Example 4-3. Different tables for different offices

```
CREATE TABLE Employee_Sweden (
   uid INT AUTO_INCREMENT PRIMARY KEY,
   name VARCHAR(20)
);
```

```
CREATE TABLE Employee_USA (
    uid INT AUTO_INCREMENT PRIMARY KEY,
    name VARCHAR(20)
);


-- This view is used when reading from the two tables simultaneously.
CREATE VIEW Employee AS
    SELECT 'Swe', uid, name FROM Employee_Sweden
  UNION
    SELECT 'USA', uid, name FROM Employee_USA;
```

This approach is best to use if the split is natural in that, for example, different offices have different tables for their local data and the data only needs to be combined for reporting purposes. This might seem easy enough, but the following issues can complicate usage and administration of the tables:

Reads and writes to different tables

Because of the way the view is defined, you cannot update it. Writes have to be directed at the real tables, while reads can either use the view or read directly from the tables.

It might therefore be necessary to introduce application logic to handle the split into reads and writes that go to different tables.

Accurate and current data

Since the two tables are managed by different sites, simultaneous updates to the two tables will cause the system to temporarily enter a state where both servers have information that is not available on the other server. If a snapshot of the information is taken at this time, it will not be accurate.

If accurate information is required, generate methods for ensuring the information is accurate. Since such methods are highly application-dependent, they will not be covered here.

Optimization of views

When using views, two techniques are available to construct a result set. In the first method—called MERGE—the view is expanded in place, optimized, and executed as if it was a SELECT query. In the second method—called TEMPTABLE—a temporary table is constructed and populated with the data.

If the server uses a TEMPTABLE view, it performs very poorly, whereas the MERGE view is close to the corresponding SELECT. MySQL uses TEMPTABLE whenever the view definition does not have a simple one-to-one mapping between the rows of the view and the rows of the underlying table—for example, if the view definition contains UNION, GROUP BY, subqueries, or aggregate functions—so careful design of the views is paramount for getting good performance.

In either case, you have to consider the implications of using a view for reporting, since it might affect performance.

If each server is assigned separate tables, there will be no risk of conflict at all since updates are completely separated. However, if all the sites have to update the same tables, you will have to use some other scheme.

The MySQL server has special support for handling this situation in the form of two server variables:

auto_increment_offset
> This variable controls the starting value for any AUTO_INCREMENT column in a table. This is the value that the first row inserted into the table gets for the AUTO_INCREMENT column. For subsequent rows, the value is calculated using auto_increment_increment.

auto_increment_increment
> This is the increment used to compute the next value of an AUTO_INCREMENT column.

> There are session and global versions of these two variables and they affect all tables on the server, not just the tables created. Whenever a new row is inserted into a table with an AUTO_INCREMENT column, the next value available in the sequence below is used:
>
> $value_N = auto\_increment\_offset + N*auto\_increment\_increment$
>
> Notice that the next value is *not* computed by adding the auto_increment_increment to the last value in the table.

Use auto_increment_offset and auto_increment_increment to ensure new rows added to a table are assigned numbers from different sequences of numbers depending on which server is used. The idea is that the first server uses the sequence 1, 3, 5... (odd numbers), while the second server uses the sequence 2, 4, 6... (even numbers).

Continuing with Example 4-3, Example 4-4 uses these two variables to ensure the two servers use different IDs when inserting new employees into the *Employee* table.

Example 4-4. Two servers writing to the same table

```
-- The common table can be created on either server
CREATE TABLE Employee (
   uid INT AUTO_INCREMENT PRIMARY KEY,
   name VARCHAR(20),
   office VARCHAR(20)
);

-- Setting for first master
SET GLOBAL AUTO_INCREMENT_INCREMENT = 2;
SET GLOBAL AUTO_INCREMENT_OFFSET = 1;

-- Setting for second master
SET GLOBAL AUTO_INCREMENT_INCREMENT = 2;
SET GLOBAL AUTO_INCREMENT_OFFSET = 2;
```

This scheme handles the insertion of new items in the tables, but when entries are being updated, it is still critical to ensure the update statements are sent to the correct server —the server responsible for the employee. Otherwise, data is likely to be inconsistent. If updates are not done correctly, the slaves will normally not stop—they will just replicate the information, which leads to inconsistent values on the two servers.

For example, if the first master executes the statement:

```
master-1> UPDATE Employee SET office = 'Vancouver' WHERE uid = 3;
Query OK, 1 rows affected (0.00 sec)
```

and at the same time, the same row is updated at the second server using the statement:

```
master-2> UPDATE Employee SET office = 'Paris' WHERE uid = 3;
Query OK, 1 rows affected (0.00 sec)
```

the result will be that the first master will place the employee in Paris while the second master will place the employee in Vancouver (note that the order will be swapped since each server will update the other server's statement after its own).

Detecting and preventing such inconsistencies is important because they will cascade and create more inconsistency over time. Statement-based replication executes statements based on the data in the two servers, so one inconsistency can lead to others.

If you take care to separate the changes made by the two servers as outlined previously, the row changes will be replicated and the two masters will therefore be consistent.

If users use different tables on the different servers, the easiest way to prevent such mistakes to assign privileges so that a user cannot accidentally change tables on the wrong server. This is, however, not always possible and cannot prevent the case just shown.

Semisynchronous Replication

Google has an extensive set of patches for MySQL and InnoDB to tailor the server and the storage engine. One of the patches that is available for MySQL version 5.0 is the semisynchronous replication patch. MySQL has since reworked the patch and released it with MySQL 5.5.

The idea behind semisynchronous replication is to ensure the changes are written to disk on at least one slave before allowing execution to continue. This means that for each connection, at most one transaction can be lost due to a master crash.

It is important to understand that the semisynchronous replication patch does not hold off commits of the transaction; it just avoids sending a reply back to the client until the transaction has been written to the relay log of at least one slave. Figure 4-7 shows the order of the calls when committing a transaction. As you can see, the transaction is committed to the storage engine before the transaction is sent to the slave, but the return from the client's commit call occurs after the slave has acknowledged that the transaction is in durable storage.

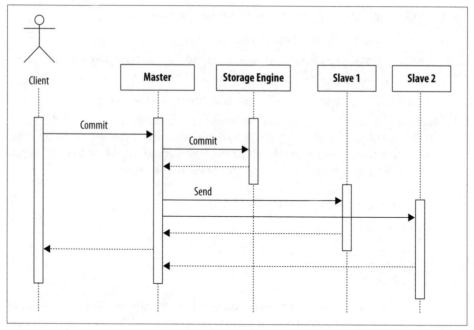

Figure 4-7. Transaction commit with semisynchronous replication

This means that for each connection, it is possible to lose a transaction if a crash occurs after the transaction has been committed to the storage engine but before the transaction has been sent to the slave. However, since the acknowledgment of the transaction goes to the client after the slave has acknowledged that it has the transaction, at most one transaction can be lost.

This usually means that, at most, one transaction can be lost per client, but if the client has multiple connections active with the master at the same time, it can lose one transaction for each connection if the client is committing multiple transactions at the same time and the server crashes.

Configuring semisynchronous replication

To use semisynchronous replication, both the master and the slave need to support it, so both the master and the slave have to be running MySQL version 5.5 or later and have semisynchronous replication enabled. If either the master or the slave does not support semisynchronous replication, it will not be used, but replication works as usual, meaning that more than one transaction can be lost unless special precautions are taken to ensure each transaction reaches the slave before a new transaction is started.

Use the following steps to enable semisynchronous replication:

1. Install the master plug-in on the master:

   ```
   master> INSTALL PLUGIN rpl_semi_sync_master SONAME 'semisync_master.so';
   ```

2. Install the slave plug-in on each slave:

   ```
   slave> INSTALL PLUGIN rpl_semi_sync_slave SONAME 'semisync_slave.so';
   ```

3. Once you have installed the plug-ins, enable them on the master and the slave. This is controlled through two server variables that are also available as options, so to ensure that the settings take effect even after restart, it is best to bring down the server and add the options to the *my.cnf* file of the master:

   ```
   [mysqld]
   rpl-semi-sync-master-enabled = 1
   ```

   and to the slave:

   ```
   [mysqld]
   rpl-semi-sync-slave-enabled = 1
   ```

4. Restart the servers.

If you followed the instructions just given, you now have a semisynchronous replication setup and can test it, but consider these cases:

- What happens if all slaves crash—which is not unlikely if you have only a single server—and therefore no slave acknowledges that it has stored the transaction to the relay log?

- What happens if all slaves disconnect gracefully? In this case, the master has no slave to which the transaction can be sent for safekeeping.

In addition to `rpl-semi-sync-master-enabled` and `rpl-semi-sync-slave-enabled`, there are two options that you can use to handle the situations given above:

`rpl-semi-sync-master-timeout=`*milliseconds*
: To prevent semisynchronous replication from blocking if it does not receive an acknowledgment, it is possible to set a timeout using the `rpl-semi-sync-master-timeout=`*milliseconds* option.

  If the master does not receive any acknowledgment before the timeout expires, it will revert to normal asynchronous replication and continue operating without semisynchronous replication.

  This option is also available as a server variable and can be set without bringing the server down. Note, however, that as with every server variable, the value will not be saved between restarts.

`rpl-semi-sync-master-wait-no-slave=`*{ON|OFF}*
: If a transaction is committed but the master does not have any slaves connected, it is not possible for the master to send the transaction anywhere for safekeeping. By default, the master will then wait for a slave to connect—as long as it is within

the timeout limit—and acknowledge that the transaction has been properly written to disk.

You can use the `rpl-semi-sync-master-wait-no-slave={ON|OFF}` option to turn off this behavior, in which case the master reverts to asynchronous replication if there are no connected slaves.

Monitoring semisynchronous replication

Both plug-ins install a number of status variables that allow you to monitor semisynchronous replication. We will cover the most interesting ones here—for a complete list, consult the online reference manual for semisynchronous replication (*http://dev .mysql.com/doc/refman/5.5/en/replication-semisync-interface.html*).

`rpl_semi_sync_master_clients`
> This status variable reports the number of connected slaves that support and have registered for semisynchronous replication.

`rpl_semi_sync_master_status`
> The status of semisynchronous replication on the master is 1 if it is active, and 0 if it is inactive—either because it has not been enabled or because it was enabled but has reverted to asynchronous replication.

`rpl_semi_sync_slave_status`
> The status of semisynchronous replication on the slave is 1 if active—that is, it has been enabled and the I/O thread is running—and 0 if it is inactive.

You can read the values of these variables either using the `SHOW STATUS` command or through the information schema table `GLOBAL_STATUS`. If you want to use the values for other purposes, the `SHOW STATUS` command is hard to use and a query as shown in Example 4-5 uses `SELECT` on the information schema to extract the value and store it in a user-defined variable.

Example 4-5. Retrieving values using the information schema

```
master> SELECT Variable_value INTO @value
    ->    FROM INFORMATION_SCHEMA.GLOBAL_STATUS
    ->   WHERE Variable_name = 'Rpl_semi_sync_master_status';
Query OK, 1 row affected (0.00 sec)
```

Slave Promotion

The procedures described so far work well when you have a master running that you can use to synchronize the standby and the slave before the switchover, but what happens if the master dies all of a sudden? Since replication has stopped in its tracks with all slaves (including the standby), it will not be possible to run replication just a little more to get all the necessary changes that would put the new master in sync.

If the standby is ahead of all the slaves that need to be reassigned, there is no problem, because you can run replication on each slave to the place where the standby stopped.

You will lose any changes that were made on the master but not yet sent to the standby. We will cover how to handle the recovery of the master in this case separately.

If the standby is behind one of the slaves, you shouldn't use the standby as the new master, since the slave knows more than the standby. As a matter of fact, it would be better if the "more knowledgeable" slave—that is, the slave that has replicated most events from the common master—were the master instead!

This is exactly the approach taken to handle master failures using slave promotion: instead of trying to keep a dedicated standby around, ensure that any one of the slaves connected to the master can be promoted to master and take over at the point where the master was lost. By selecting the "most knowledgeable" slave as the new master, you guarantee that none of the other slaves will be more knowledgeable than the new master, so they can connect to the new master and read events from it.

There is, however, a critical issue that needs to be resolved—synchronizing all slaves with the new master so that no events are lost or repeated. The problem in this situation is that all of the slaves need to read events from the new master, but the positions of the new master are not the same as the positions for the old master. So what is a poor DBA to do?

The traditional method for promoting a slave

Before delving into the final solution, let us first take a look at the recommended practice for handling slave promotion. This will work as a good introduction to the problem, and also allow us to pinpoint the tricky issues that we need to handle for the final solution.

Figure 4-8 shows a typical setup with a master and several slaves.

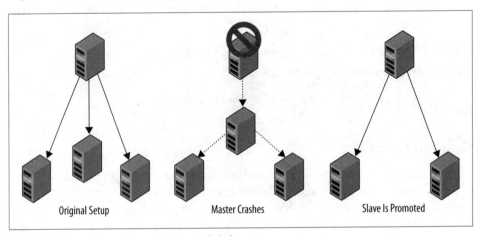

Figure 4-8. Promoting a slave to replace a failed master

For the traditional method of slave promotion, the following are required:

- Each promotable slave must have a user account for the replication user.
- Each promotable slave should run with --log-bin, that is, with the binary log enabled.
- Each promotable slave should run *without* the --log-slave-updates option (the reason will become obvious shortly).

Assume you are starting with the original setup shown in Figure 4-8 and that the master fails. You can promote a slave to be the new master by doing the following:

1. Stop the slave using STOP SLAVE.
2. Reset the slave that is going to be the new master using RESET MASTER. This will ensure the slave starts as the new master and that any connecting slave will start reading events from the time the slave was promoted.
3. Connect the other slaves to the new master using CHANGE MASTER TO. Since you reset the new master, you can start replication from the beginning of the binary log, so it is not necessary to provide any position to CHANGE MASTER TO.

Unfortunately, this approach is based on an assumption that is not generally true—that the slaves have received all changes that the master has made. In a typical setup, the slaves will lag behind the master to various degrees. It might be just a few transactions, but nevertheless, they lag behind. In the next section you will see a solution to that problem.

Regardless of that, this approach is so simple that it is useful if you can handle lost transactions or if you are operating under a low load.

A revised method for promoting a slave

The traditional approach to promoting a slave is inadequate in most cases because slaves usually lag behind the master. Figure 4-9 illustrates the typical situation when the master disappears unexpectedly. The box labeled "binary log" in the center is the master's binary log and each arrow represents how much of the binary log the slave has executed.

In the figure, each slave has stopped at a different binlog position. To resolve the issue and bring the system back online, one slave has to be selected as the new master—preferably the one that has the latest binlog position—and the other slaves have to be synchronized with the new master.

The critical problem lies in translating the positions for each slave—which are the positions in the now-defunct master—to positions on the promoted slave. Unfortunately, the history of events executed and the binlog positions they correspond to on the slaves are lost in the replication process—each time the slave executes an event that has arrived from the master, it writes a *new* event to its binary log, with a new binlog position. The slave's position bears no relation to the master's binlog position of the

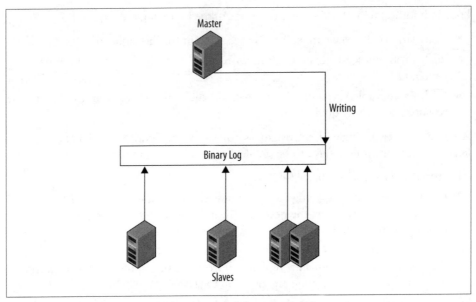

Figure 4-9. Binary log positions of the master and the connected slaves

same event. The only option that remains for us is to scan the binary log of the promoted slave. To use this technique:

- Enable the binary log; otherwise, no changes can be replicated.
- Enable log slave updates (using the `log-slave-updates` option); otherwise, no changes from the original master can be forwarded.
- Each slave needs to have a replication user to act as a master so that if it turns out to be the best candidate for a new master, other slaves can to connect to it and replicate from it.

Carry out the following steps for each of the slaves that are not promoted:

1. Figure out the last transaction it executed.
2. Find the transaction in the binary log of the promoted slave.
3. Take the binlog position for the transaction from the promoted slave.
4. Start the nonpromoted slaves to replicate from that position on the promoted slave.

To match the latest transaction on each of the slaves with the corresponding event in the binary log of the promoted slave, you need to tag each transaction. The content and structure of the tags don't matter; they just need to be uniquely identifiable no matter who executed the transaction so each transaction on the master can be found in the promoted slave's binary log. We call this kind of tag the *global transaction ID*.

The easiest way to accomplish this is to insert a statement at the end of each transaction that updates a special table and use that to keep track of where each slave is. Just before committing each transaction, a statement updates the table with a number that is unique for the transaction.

Tagging can be handled in two main ways:

- Extending the application code to perform the necessary statements
- Calling a stored procedure to perform each commit and writing the tag in the procedure

Because the first approach is easier to follow, it will be demonstrated here. If you are interested in the second approach, see "Stored Procedures to Commit Transactions" on page 141.

To implement the global transaction ID, we have created the two tables in Example 4-6: one table named *Global_Trans_ID* to generate sequence numbers and a separate table named *Last_Exec_Trans* to record the global transaction ID.

The server ID is added to the definition of *Last_Exec_Trans* to distinguish transactions committed on different servers. If, for example, the promoted slave fails before all the slaves have managed to connect, it is very important to distinguish between the transaction ID of the original master and the transaction ID of the promoted slave. Otherwise, the slaves that didn't manage to connect to the promoted slave might start to execute from a position that is wrong when being redirected to the second promoted slave. This example uses MyISAM to define the counter table, but it is possible to use InnoDB for this as well.

Example 4-6. Tables used for generating and tracking global transaction IDs

```
CREATE TABLE Global_Trans_ID (
    number INT UNSIGNED AUTO_INCREMENT PRIMARY KEY
) ENGINE = MyISAM;

CREATE TABLE Last_Exec_Trans (
    server_id INT UNSIGNED,
    trans_id INT UNSIGNED
) ENGINE = InnoDB;

-- Insert a single row with NULLs to be updated.
INSERT INTO Last_Exec_Trans() VALUES ();
```

The next step is to construct a procedure for adding a global transaction ID to the binary log so that a program promoting a slave can read the ID from the log. The following procedure is suitable for our purposes:

1. Insert an item into the transaction counter table, making sure to turn off the binary log before doing this, since the insert should not be replicated to the slaves:

   ```
   master> SET SQL_LOG_BIN = 0;
   Query OK, 0 rows affected (0.00 sec)
   ```

```
master> INSERT INTO Global_Trans_ID() VALUES ();
Query OK, 1 row affected (0.00 sec)
```

2. Fetch the global transaction ID using the function LAST_INSERT_ID. To simplify the logic, the server ID is fetched from the server variable server_id at the same time:

```
master> SELECT @@server_id as server_id, LAST_INSERT_ID() as trans_id;
+-----------+----------+
| server_id | trans_id |
+-----------+----------+
|         0 |      235 |
+-----------+----------+
1 row in set (0.00 sec)
```

3. Before inserting the global transaction ID into the *Last_Exec_Trans* tracking table, you can remove its row from the transaction counter table to save space. This optional step works only for a MyISAM table. If you use InnoDB, you have to be careful about leaving the last used global transaction ID in the table. InnoDB determines the next number from the maximum value in the autoincrement column currently in the table.

```
master> DELETE FROM Global_Trans_ID WHERE number < 235;
Query OK, 1 row affected (0.00 sec)
```

4. Turn on the binary log:

```
master> SET SQL_LOG_BIN = 1;
Query OK, 0 rows affected (0.00 sec)
```

5. Update the *Last_Exec_Trans* tracking table with the server ID and the transaction ID you got in step 2. This is the last step before committing the transaction through a COMMIT:

```
master> UPDATE Last_Exec_Trans SET server_id = 0, trans_id = 235;
Query OK, 1 row affected (0.00 sec)

master> COMMIT;
Query OK, 0 rows affected (0.00 sec)
```

Each global transaction ID represents a point where replication can be resumed. Therefore, you must carry out this procedure for every transaction. If it is not used for some transaction, the transaction will not be tagged properly and it will not be possible to start from that position.

Now, to promote a slave after the master is lost, find the slave that has the latest changes of all the slaves—that is, has the largest binlog position—and promote it to master. Then have each of the other slaves connect to it.

For a slave to connect to the promoted slave and start replication at the right position, it is necessary to find out what position on the promoted slave has the last executed transaction of the slave. Scan the binary log of the promoted slave to find the right transaction ID.

Use the following steps to carry out the recovery:

1. Stop the slave. Get the last-seen global transaction ID from its *Last_Exec_Trans* table.

2. Pick the slave with the highest global transaction ID to promote to master. If there are several, pick one.

3. Get the master position of the slave to promote and the binary logs of the slave at the same time using SHOW MASTER LOGS. Note that the last row of SHOW MASTER LOGS matches what you would see in SHOW MASTER STATUS.

4. Bring the promoted slave online and let it start accepting updates.

5. Connect to the promoted slave and scan the binary log to find the latest global transaction ID that you found in each slave's binary log. Unless you have a file position that you know is good, the only good starting position for reading a binary log is the beginning. Therefore, you have to scan the binary logs in reverse order, starting with the latest.

   This step will give you a binlog position on the promoted slave for each global transaction ID that you collected in step 1.

6. Reconnect each slave to the promoted slave, starting at the position where the slave needs to start in order to recover all information, using the information from step 5.

The first four steps are straightforward, but step 5 is tricky. To illustrate the situation, let's start with an example of some basic information gathered from the first three steps. Table 4-2 lists three sample slaves with the global transaction ID of each slave.

Table 4-2. Global transaction ID for all connected slaves

	Server ID	Trans ID
slave-1	1	245
slave-2	1	248
slave-3	1	256

As you can see in Table 4-2, slave-3 has the latest global transaction ID and is therefore the slave you will promote. It is therefore necessary to translate the global transaction ID of each slave to binlog positions on slave-3. For that, we need information about the binary log on slave-3, which we'll obtain in Example 4-7.

Example 4-7. Master positions of slave-3, which will be promoted

```
slave-3> SHOW MASTER LOGS;
+--------------------+-----------+
| Log_name           | File_size |
+--------------------+-----------+
| slave-3-bin.000001 |      3115 |
| slave-3-bin.000002 |    345217 |
| slave-3-bin.000003 |     24665 |
| slave-3-bin.000004 |    788243 |
| slave-3-bin.000005 |      1778 |
+--------------------+-----------+
5 row in set (0.00 sec)
```

The important thing to know from the output of SHOW MASTER LOGS is the names of the logs, so you can scan them for global transaction IDs. For instance, when reading the *slave-3-bin.000005* file using mysqlbinlog, part of the output will look like that shown in Example 4-8. The transaction received by slave-3 starting at position 596 (highlighted in the first line of the output) has the global transaction ID received by slave-1, as shown by an UPDATE of the Last_Exec_Trans table.

Example 4-8. Output from the mysqlbinlog command for one transaction

```
# at 596
#091018 18:35:42 server id 1  end_log_pos 664  Query    thread_id=952   ...
SET TIMESTAMP=1255883742/*!*/;
BEGIN
/*!*/;
# at 664
#091018 18:35:42 server id 1  end_log_pos 779  Query    thread_id=952   ...
SET TIMESTAMP=1255883742/*!*/;
UPDATE user SET messages = messages + 1 WHERE id = 1
/*!*/;
# at 779
#091018 18:35:42 server id 1  end_log_pos 904  Query    thread_id=952   ...
SET TIMESTAMP=1255883742/*!*/;
INSERT INTO message VALUES (1,'MySQL Python Replicant rules!')
/*!*/;
# at 904
#091018 18:35:42 server id 1  end_log_pos 1021  Query    thread_id=952   ...
SET TIMESTAMP=1255883742/*!*/;
UPDATE Last_Exec_Trans SET server_id = 1, trans_id = 245
/*!*/;
# at 1021
#091018 18:35:42 server id 1  end_log_pos 1048  Xid = 1433
COMMIT/*!*/;
```

Table 4-2 shows that the trans_id 245 is the last transaction seen by slave-1, so now you know that the start position for slave-1 is in file *slave-3-bin.000005* at byte position 1048. So to start slave-1 at the correct position, you can now execute CHANGE MASTER TO and START SLAVE:

```
slave-1> CHANGE MASTER TO
    ->     MASTER_HOST = 'slave-3',
```

```
     ->      MASTER_LOG_FILE = 'slave-3-bin.000005',
     ->      MASTER_LOG_POS = 1048;
Query OK, 0 rows affected (0.04 sec)

slave-1> START SLAVE;
Query OK, 0 rows affected (0.17 sec)
```

By going backward in this manner—locating each of the transactions that you recorded in the first step in the procedure—you can connect the slaves one by one to the new master at exactly the right position.

This technique works well if the update statement is added to every transaction commit. Unfortunately, there are statements that perform an implicit commit before and after the statement. Typical examples include CREATE TABLE, DROP TABLE, and ALTER TABLE. Since these statements do an implicit commit, they cannot be tagged properly, hence it is not possible to restart *just after* them. This means that if the sequence of statements in Example 4-9 is executed and there is a crash, you will potentially have problems.

If a slave has just executed the CREATE TABLE and then loses the master, the last seen global transaction ID is for the INSERT INTO—that is, just before the CREATE TABLE statement. Therefore, the slave will try to reconnect to the promoted slave with the transaction ID of the INSERT INTO statement. Since it will find the position in the binary log of the promoted slave, it will start by replicating the CREATE TABLE statement again, causing the slave to stop with an error.

You can avoid these problems through careful use and design of statements; for example, if CREATE TABLE is replaced with CREATE TABLE IF NOT EXISTS, the slave will notice that the table already exists and skip execution of the statement.

Example 4-9. Statements where global transaction ID cannot be assigned

```
INSERT INTO message_board VALUES ('mats@sun.com', 'Hello World!');
CREATE TABLE admin_table (a INT UNSIGNED);
INSERT INTO message_board VALUES ('', '');
```

Slave promotion in Python

You have now seen two techniques for promoting a slave: a traditional technique that suffers from a loss of transactions on some slaves, and a more complex technique that recovers all available transactions. The traditional technique is straightforward to implement in Python, so let's concentrate on the more complicated one. To handle slave promotion this way, it is necessary to:

- Configure all the slaves correctly
- Add the tables *Global_Trans_ID* and *Last_Exec_Trans* to the master
- Provide the application code to commit a transaction correctly
- Write code to automate slave promotion

You can use the `Promotable` class (shown in Example 4-10) to handle the new kind of server. As you can see, this example reuses the previously introduced `_enable_binlog` helper method, and adds a method to set the `log-slave-updates` option. Since a promotable slave requires the special tables we showed earlier for the master, the addition of a promotable slave requires the tables added to the *master*. To do this, we write a function named `_add_global_id_tables`. The function assumes that if the tables already exist, they have the correct definition, so no attempt is made to re-create them. However, the *Last_Exec_Trans* table needs to start with one row for the update to work correctly, so if no warning was produced to indicate that a table already exists, we create the table and add a row with `NULL`.

Example 4-10. The definition of a promotable slave role

```
_GLOBAL_TRANS_ID_DEF = """
CREATE TABLE IF NOT EXISTS Global_Trans_ID (
  number INT UNSIGNED NOT NULL AUTO_INCREMENT,
  PRIMARY KEY (number)
) ENGINE=MyISAM
"""

_LAST_EXEC_TRANS_DEF = """
CREATE TABLE IF NOT EXISTS Last_Exec_Trans (
  server_id INT UNSIGNED DEFAULT NULL,
  trans_id INT UNSIGNED DEFAULT NULL
) ENGINE=InnoDB
"""

class Promotable(Role):
    def __init__(self, repl_user, master):
        self.__master = master
        self.__user = repl_user

    def _add_global_id_tables(self, master):
        master.sql(_GLOBAL_TRANS_ID_DEF)
        master.sql(_LAST_EXEC_TRANS_DEF)
        if not master.sql("SELECT @@warning_count"):
            master.sql("INSERT INTO Last_Exec_Trans() VALUES ()")

    def _relay_events(self, server, config):
        config.set('mysqld', 'log-slave-updates')

    def imbue(self, server):
        # Fetch and update the configuration
        config = server.get_config()
        self._set_server_id(server, config)
        self._enable_binlog(server, config)
        self._relay_event(server, config)

        # Put the new configuration in place
        server.stop()
        server.put_config(config)
        server.start()
```

```
# Add tables to master
self._add_global_id_tables(self._master)

server.repl_user = self._master.repl_user
```

This routine configures the slaves and the master correctly for using global transaction IDs. You still have to update the *Last_Exec_Trans* table when committing each transaction. In Example 4-11 you can see an example implementation in PHP for committing transactions. The code is written using PHP, since this is part of the application code and not part of the code for managing the deployment.

Example 4-11. Code for starting, committing, and aborting transactions

```php
function start_trans($link) {
  mysql_query("START TRANSACTION", $link);
}

function commit_trans($link) {
  mysql_select_db("common", $link);
  mysql_query("SET SQL_LOG_BIN = 0", $link);
  mysql_query("INSERT INTO Global_Trans_ID() VALUES ()", $link);
  $trans_id = mysql_insert_id($link);
  $result = mysql_query("SELECT @@server_id as server_id", $link);
  $row = mysql_fetch_row($result);
  $server_id = $row[0];

  $delete_query = "DELETE FROM Global_Trans_ID WHERE number = %d";
  mysql_query(sprintf($delete_query, $trans_id),
          $link);
  mysql_query("SET SQL_LOG_BIN = 1", $link);

  $update_query = "UPDATE Last_Exec_Trans SET server_id = %d, trans_id = %d";
  mysql_query(sprintf($update_query, $server_id, $trans_id), $link);
  mysql_query("COMMIT", $link);
}

function rollback_trans($link) {
  mysql_query("ROLLBACK", $link);
}
```

We can then use this code to commit transactions by calling the functions instead of the usual `COMMIT` and `ROLLBACK`. For example, we could write a PHP function to add a message to a database and update a message counter for the user:

```php
function add_message($email, $message, $link) {
  start_trans($link);
  mysql_select_db("common", $link);
  $query = sprintf("SELECT user_id FROM user WHERE email = '%s'", $email);
  $result = mysql_query($query, $link);
  $row = mysql_fetch_row($result);
  $user_id = $row[0];

  $update_user = "UPDATE user SET messages = messages + 1 WHERE user_id = %d";
  mysql_query(sprintf($update_user, $user_id), $link);
```

```
$insert_message = "INSERT INTO message VALUES (%d,'%s')";
mysql_query(sprintf($insert_message, $user_id, $message), $link);
commit_trans($link);
}

$conn = mysql_connect(":/var/run/mysqld/mysqld1.sock", "root");
add_message('mats@example.com', "MySQL Python Replicant rules!", $conn);
```

What remains is the job of handling the actual slave promotion in the event of a failure. The procedure was already outlined above, but the implementation is more involved.

The first step is to fetch the binlog files remotely, similarly to the method used in Chapter 2. In this case, we need to fetch the entire binlog file, since we do not know where to start reading. The fetch_remote_binlog function in Example 4-12 returns an iterator to the lines of the binary log.

Example 4-12. Fetching a remote binary log

```
def fetch_remote_binlog(server, binlog_file):
    command = ["mysqlbinlog",
               "--read-from-remote-server",
               "--force",
               "--host=%s" % (server.host),
               "--user=%s" % (server.sql_user.name)]
    if server.sql_user.passwd:
        command.append("--password=%s" % (server.sql_user.passwd))
    command.append(binlog_file)
    return iter(subprocess.Popen(command, stdout=subprocess.PIPE).stdout)
```

The iterator returns the lines of the binary log one by one, so the lines have to be further separated into transactions and events to make the binary log easier to work with. In Example 4-13 you can see a function named group_by_event that groups lines belonging to the same event into a single string, and a function named group_by_trans that groups a stream of events (as returned by group_by_event) into lists, where each list represents a transaction.

Example 4-13. Parsing the mysqlbinlog output to extract transactions

```
delimiter = "/*!*/;"

def group_by_event(lines):
    event_lines = []
    for line in lines:
        if line.startswith('#'):
            if line.startswith("# End of log file"):
                del event_lines[-1]
                yield ''.join(event_lines)
                return
            if line.startswith("# at"):
                yield ''.join(event_lines)
                event_lines = []
        event_lines.append(line)
```

```
def group_by_trans(lines):
    group = []
    in_transaction = False
    for event in group_by_event(lines):
        group.append(event)
        if event.find(delimiter + "\nBEGIN\n" + delimiter) >= 0:
            in_transaction = True
        elif not in_transaction:
            yield group
            group = []
        else:
            p = event.find("\nCOMMIT")
            if p >= 0 and (event.startswith(delimiter, p+7)
                            or event.startswith(delimiter, p+8)):
                yield group
                group = []
                in_transaction = False
```

Example 4-14 shows a function named scan_logfile that scans the mysqlbinlog output for the global transaction IDs that were introduced. The function accepts a master from which to fetch the binlog file, the name of a binlog file to scan (the filename is the name of the binary log on the master), and a callback function on_gid that will be called whenever a global transaction ID is seen. The on_gid function will be called with the global transaction ID (consisting of a server_id and a trans_id) and the binlog position of the end of the transaction.

Example 4-14. Scanning a binlog file for global transaction IDs

```
_GIDCRE = re.compile(r"^UPDATE Last_Exec_Trans SET\s+"
                     r"server_id = (?P<server_id>\d+),\s+"
                     r"trans_id = (?P<trans_id>\d+)$", re.MULTILINE)
_HEADCRE = re.compile(r"#\d{6}\s+\d?\d:\d\d:\d\d\s+"
                      r"server id\s+(?P<sid>\d+)\s+"
                      r"end_log_pos\s+(?P<end_pos>\d+)\s+"
                      r"(?P<type>\w+)")

def scan_logfile(master, logfile, on_gid):
    from mysqlrep import Position
    lines = fetch_remote_binlog(master, logfile)
    # Scan the output to find global transaction ID update statements
    for trans in group_by_trans(lines):
        if len(trans) < 3:
            continue
        # Check for an update of the Last_Exec_Trans table
        m = _GIDCRE.search(trans[-2])
        if m:
            server_id = int(m.group("server_id"))
            trans_id = int(m.group("trans_id"))
            # Check for an information comment with end_log_pos. We
            # assume InnoDB tables only, so we can therefore rely on
            # the transactions to end in an Xid event.
            m = _HEADCRE.search(trans[-1])
            if m and m.group("type") == "Xid":
```

```
                pos = Position(server_id, logfile, int(m.group("end_pos")))
                on_gid(server_id, trans_id, pos)
```

The code for the last step is given in Example 4-15. The `promote_slave` function takes a list of slaves that lost their master and executes the promotion by identifying the new master from the slaves. Finally, it reconnects all the other slaves to the promoted slave by scanning the binary logs. The code uses the support function `fetch_global_trans_id` to fetch the global transaction ID from the table that we introduced.

Example 4-15. Identifying the new master and reconnecting all slaves to it

```
def fetch_global_trans_id(slave):
    result = slave.sql("SELECT server_id, trans_id FROM Last_Exec_Trans")
    return (int(result["server_id"]), int(result["trans_id"]))

def promote_slave(slaves):
    slave_info = {}

    # Collect the global transaction ID of each slave
    for slave in slaves:
        slave.connect()
        server_id, trans_id = fetch_global_trans_id(slave)
        slave_info.setdefault(trans_id, []).append((server_id, trans_id, slave))
        slave.disconnect()

    # Pick the slave to promote by taking the slave with the highest
    # global transaction id.
    new_master = slave_info[max(slave_info)].pop()[2]

    def maybe_change_master(server_id, trans_id, position):
        from mysqlrep.utility import change_master
        try:
            for sid, tid, slave in slave_info[trans_id]:
                if slave is not new_master:
                    change_master(slave, new_master, position)
        except KeyError:
            pass

    # Read the the master logfiles of the new master.
    new_master.connect()
    logs = [row["Log_name"] for row in new_master.sql("SHOW MASTER LOGS")]
    new_master.disconnect()

    # Read the master logfiles one by one in reverse order, the
    # latest binlog file first.
    logs.reverse()
    for log in logs:
        scan_logfile(new_master, log, maybe_change_master)
```

Worth noting in the code is that the slaves are collected into a dictionary using the transaction ID from the global transaction ID as a key. Since there can be several slaves associated with the same key, we used the "Associating Multiple Values with Each Key in a Dictionary" recipe in Alex Martelli et al.'s *Python Cookbook* (O'Reilly). This puts a list of servers under each key and allows quick lookup and processing in `maybe_change_master` based on only the transaction ID.

 With the code in Example 4-15, there is no guarantee that the transaction IDs will be in order, so if that is important, you will have to take additional measures. The transaction IDs could be in a nonsequential order if one transaction fetches a global transaction ID but is interrupted before it can commit another transaction, which fetches a global transaction ID and commits. To make sure the transaction IDs reflect the order in which transactions start, add a `SELECT ... FOR UPDATE` just before fetching a global transaction ID by changing the code as follows:

```
def commit_trans(cur):
    cur.execute("SELECT * FROM Last_Exec_Trans FOR UPDATE")
    cur.execute("SET SQL_LOG_BIN = 0")
        cur.execute("INSERT INTO Global_Trans_ID() VALUES ()")
        .

        .
    cur.commit()
```

This will lock the row until the transaction is committed, but will also slow down the system some, which is wasteful if the ordering is not required.

Stored Procedures to Commit Transactions

The main approach shown in this chapter to sync servers is to implement the transaction commit procedure in the application, meaning that the application code needs to know table names and the intricacies of how to produce and manipulate the global transaction ID. Once you understand them, the complexities are not as much of a barrier as they might seem at first. Often, you can handle them with relative ease by creating functions in the application code that the application writer can call without having to know the details.

Another approach is to put the transaction commit logic in the database server by using stored procedures. Depending on the situation, this can sometimes be a better alternative. For example, the commit procedure can be changed without having to change the application code.

For this technique to work, it is necessary to put the transaction ID from the *Global_Trans_ID* table and the server ID into either a user-defined variable or a local variable in the stored routine. Depending on which approach you select, the query in the binary log will look a little different.

Using local variables is less likely to interfere with surrounding code since user-defined variables "leak" out from the stored procedure.

The procedure for committing a transaction will then be:

```
CREATE PROCEDURE commit_trans ()
  SQL SECURITY DEFINER
BEGIN
  DECLARE trans_id, server_id INT UNSIGNED;
  SET SQL_LOG_BIN = 0;
  INSERT INTO global_trans_id() values ();
  SELECT LAST_INSERT_ID() INTO trans_id,
         @@server_id INTO server_id;
  SET SQL_LOG_BIN = 1;
  INSERT INTO last_exec_trans(server_id, trans_id)
      VALUES (server_id, trans_id);
  COMMIT;
END
```

Committing a transaction from the application code is then simple:

```
CALL Commit_Trans();
```

Now the task remains of changing the procedure for scanning the binary log for the global transaction ID. So, how will a call to this function appear in the binary log? Well, a quick call to `mysqlbinlog` shows:

```
# at 1724
#091129 18:35:11 server id 1  end_log_pos 1899  Query    thread_id=75
  exec_time=0      error_code=0
SET TIMESTAMP=1259516111/*!*/;
INSERT INTO last_exec_trans(server_id, trans_id)
  VALUES ( NAME_CONST('server_id',1),  NAME_CONST('trans_id',13))
/*!*/;
# at 1899
#091129 18:35:11 server id 1  end_log_pos 1926  Xid = 1444
COMMIT/*!*/;
```

As you can see, both the server ID and the transaction ID are clearly visible in the output. How to match this statement using a regular expression is left as an exercise for the reader.

Circular Replication

After reading about dual masters, you might wonder if it is possible to set up a multi-master with more than two masters replicating to each other. Since each slave can only have a single master, it is only possible to get this by setting up replication in a circular fashion.

Although this is not a recommended setup, it is certainly possible. The reason it is not recommended is because it is very hard to get it to work correctly in the presence of failure. The reasons for this will become clear in a moment.

Using a circular replication setup with three or more servers can be quite practical for reasons of locality. As a real-life example, consider the case of a mobile phone operator with subscribers all over Europe. Since the mobile phone owners travel around quite a lot, it is convenient to have the registry for the customers close to the actual phone, so by placing the data centers at some strategic places in Europe, it is possible to quickly verify call data and also register new calls locally. The changes can then be replicated to all the servers in the ring, and eventually all servers will have accurate billing information. In this case, circular replication is a perfect setup: all subscriber data is replicated to all sites, and updates of data are allowed in all data centers.

Setting up circular replication (as shown in Figure 4-10) is quite easy. Example 4-16 provides a script that sets up circular replication automatically, so where are the complications? As in every setup, you should ask yourself, "What happens when something goes wrong?"

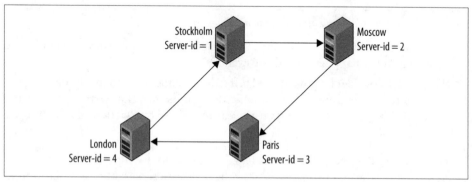

Figure 4-10. Circular replication setup

Example 4-16. Setting up circular replication

```
def circular_replication(server_list):
    count = len(server_list)
    for i in range(0, count):
        change_master(server_list[(i+1) % count], server_list[i])
```

In Figure 4-10, there are four servers named for the cities in which they are located (the names are arbitrarily picked and do not reflect a real setup). Replication goes in a circle: "Stockholm" to "Moscow" to "Paris" to "London" and back to "Stockholm." This means that "Moscow" is upstream of "Paris," but downstream of "Stockholm." Suppose that "Moscow" goes down suddenly and unexpectedly. To allow replication to continue, it is necessary to reconnect the "downstream" server "Paris" to the "upstream" server "Stockholm" to ensure the continuing operation of the system.

Figure 4-11 shows a scenario in which a single server fails and the servers reconnect to allow replication to continue. Sounds simple enough, doesn't it? Well, it's not really as simple as it looks. There are basically three issues that you have to consider:

- The downstream server—the server that was slave to the failed master—needs to connect to the upstream server and start replication from what it last saw. How is that position decided?

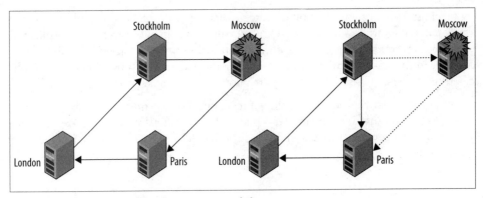

Figure 4-11. Changing topology in response to a failing server

- Suppose that the crashed server has managed to send out some events before crashing. What happens with those events?

- We need to consider how we should bring the failed server into the topology again. What if the server applied some transactions of its own that were written to the binary log but not yet sent out? It is clear that these transactions are lost, so we need to handle this.

When detecting that one of the servers failed, it is easy to use the `CHANGE MASTER` command to connect the downstream server to the upstream server, but for replication to work correctly, we must determine the right position. To find the correct position, use binary log scanning techniques similar to what we used for slave promotion. However, in this case, we have several servers to consider when deciding what position to start from. The *Last_Exec_Trans* table introduced earlier already contains the server ID and the global transaction ID seen from that server.

The second problem is more complicated. If the failing server managed to send out an event, there is nothing that can remove that event from the replication stream, so it will circle around the replication topology forever. If the statement is idempotent—it can be reapplied multiple times without causing problems—the situation could be manageable for a short period, but in general, the statement has to be removed somehow.

In MySQL version 5.5, the parameter `IGNORE_SERVER_IDS` was added to the `CHANGE MASTER` command. This parameter allows a server to remove more events from the replication stream than just the events with the same server ID as the server. So, assuming that the servers have the IDs shown in Figure 4-11, we can reconnect Paris to Stockholm using the following command:

```
paris> CHANGE MASTER TO
    ->    MASTER_HOST='stockholm.example.com',
    ->    IGNORE_SERVER_IDS = (2);
```

For versions of MySQL earlier than version 5.5, there is no such support and you may have to devise some other means of removing the offending events. The easiest method

---

is probably to bring in a server temporarily with the same ID as the crashed server for the sole purpose of removing the offending event.

The complete procedure to shrink the ring in a circular setup—assuming that you are using MySQL 5.5—is as follows:

1. Determine the global transaction IDs of the last committed transactions on the downstream server for all servers that are still up and running.

   ```
   paris> SELECT Server_ID, Trans_ID FROM Last_Exec_Trans WHERE Server_ID != 2;
   +-----------+----------+
   | Server_ID | Trans_ID |
   +-----------+----------+
   |         1 |     5768 |
   |         3 |     4563 |
   |         4 |      768 |
   +-----------+----------+
   3 rows in set (0.00 sec)
   ```

2. Scan the binary log of the upstream server for the last of the global transaction IDs seen in *Last_Exec_Trans*.

3. Connect the downstream server to this position using CHANGE MASTER.

   ```
   paris> CHANGE MASTER TO
       -> MASTER_HOST='stockholm.example.com',
       -> IGNORE_SERVER_IDS = (2);
   ```

Since the failed server can be in an alternative future compared to the other servers, the safest way to bring it into the circle again is to restore the server from one of the servers in the ring and reconnect the circle so that the new server is in the ring again. The steps to accomplish that are:

4. Restore the server from one of the existing servers—the server that will eventually be the upstream server—in the ring and attach it as a slave to that server.

   ```
   moscow> CHANGE MASTER TO MASTER_HOST='stockholm.example.com';
   Query OK, 0 rows affected (0.18 sec)

   moscow> START SLAVE;
   Query OK, 0 rows affected (0.00 sec)
   ```

5. Once the server has caught up sufficiently, break the ring by disconnecting the downstream server. This server will no longer receive any updates.

   ```
   paris> STOP SLAVE;
   Query OK, 0 rows affected (0.00 sec)
   ```

6. Since the restored server might not have all the events that the downstream server has, it is necessary to wait for the restored server to have at least all the events the downstream server has. Since the positions are for the same server, you can do this using a combination of SHOW SLAVE STATUS and MASTER_POS_WAIT.

   ```
   paris> SHOW SLAVE STATUS;
   ...
   Relay_Master_Log_File: stockholm-bin.000096
   ```

```
            ...
        Exec_Master_Log_Pos: 756648
1 row in set (0.00 sec)


moscow> SELECT MASTER_POS_WAIT('stockholm-bin.000096', 756648);
+----------------------------------------------------+
| MASTER_POS_WAIT('stockholm-bin.000096', 756648)    |
+----------------------------------------------------+
|                                            985761  |
+----------------------------------------------------+
1 row in set (156.32 sec)
```

7. Determine the position of the event on the restored server by scanning the binary log of the restored server for the global ID that was last seen by the downstream server.

8. Connect the downstream server to the restored server and start replication.

```
paris> CHANGE MASTER TO
    ->     MASTER_HOST='moscow.example.com',
    ->     MASTER_LOG_FILE='moscow-bin.000107',
    ->     MASTER_LOG_POS=196758,
Query OK, 0 rows affected (0.18 sec)

moscow> START SLAVE;
Query OK, 0 rows affected (0.00 sec)
```

Conclusion

High availability is a nontrivial concept to implement in practice. In this chapter, we presented a look into high availability and how you can achieve it with MySQL. In the next chapter, we will look more at high availability as we examine a companion topic: scaling out.

Joel's email notification chime sounded. He clicked on his email and opened the latest message. It was from Mr. Summerson, who made comments about his report. He read it through and at the bottom found what he expected. It read, "I like the redundancy ideas and especially the hot standby strategy. Make this happen."

Joel sighed as he realized his plans for getting to know some of his coworkers were going to have to wait. He had a lot of work to do.

## CHAPTER 5

MySQL Replication for Scale-Out

Joel stood and stretched and figured it was time for a soda. As he walked around his desk, headed to the break room, his boss met him at his door. "Good afternoon, sir."

"Hey, Joel. We just sold a bunch of licenses for our new applications. The marketing people tell me we can expect to see an increase in load of at least tenfold on the database server."

Joel raised his eyebrows. He had added a single slave just last week and that had improved the load problem, but not entirely.

"We need to scale out, Joel."

"Yes, sir. I'll get right on it."

Mr. Summerson tapped Joel on the shoulder and smiled, then walked down the hall to his office.

Joel stood still for a few moments as he pondered what "scale out" meant and formed a plan. "I've got to do a little more reading," he mumbled as he headed to the break room.

When the load starts to increase—and if you are running a successful deployment, it is just a matter of *when* it will start to increase—you can handle it in two ways. The first is to buy larger and more powerful servers to handle the increased load, which is called *scaling up*, whereas the second is to add more servers to handle the increased load, which is called *scaling out*. Of these two, scaling out is by far the more popular solution because it usually involves buying a batch of low-cost standard servers and is much more cost-effective.

In addition to handling an increased load, additional servers can support high availability and other business requirements. When used effectively, scaling out puts the combined resources—such as computing power—of all the servers to best use.

This chapter doesn't go into all the hardware, network, and other considerations involved in scaling out—those are beyond the scope of this book and are covered to some degree in Baron Schwartz et al.'s *High Performance MySQL* (O'Reilly, *http://oreilly.com/catalog/9780596101718/*), but we will talk about how to set up replication in MySQL to make the best use of scale-out. After some basic instructions for replication, we'll start to develop a Python library that makes it easy to administer replication over large sets of servers, and we'll examine how replication fits into your organization's business needs.

The most common uses for scaling out and replication are:

Load balancing for reads
Since the master is occupied with updating data, it can be wise to have separate servers to answer queries. Since queries only need to read data, you can use replication to send changes on the master to slaves—as many as you feel you need—so that they have current data and can process queries.

Load balancing for writes
High-traffic deployments distribute processing over many computers, sometimes several thousand. Here, replication plays a critical role in distributing the information to be processed. The information can be distributed in many different ways based on the business use of your data and the nature of the use:

- Distributed based on the information's role. Rarely updated tables can be kept on a single server, while frequently updated tables are partitioned over several servers.

- Partitioned by geographic region so that so that traffic can be directed to the closest server.

Disaster avoidance through hot standby
If the master goes down, everything will stop—it will not be possible to execute (perhaps critical) transactions, get information about customers, or retrieve other critical data. This is something that you want to avoid at (almost) any cost since it can severely disrupt your business. The easiest solution is to configure a slave with the sole purpose of acting as a hot standby, ready to take over the job of the master if it fails.

Disaster avoidance through remote replication
Every deployment runs the risk of having a data center go down due to a disaster, be it a power failure, an earthquake, or a flood. To mitigate this, use replication to transport information between geographically remote sites.

Making backups
Keeping an extra server around for making backups is very common. This allows you to make your backups without having to disturb the master at all, since you can take the backup server offline and do whatever you like with it.

Report generation
Creating reports from data on a server will degrade the server's performance, in some cases significantly. If you're running lots of background jobs to generate reports, it's worth creating a slave just for this purpose. You can get a snapshot of

the database at a certain time by stopping replication on the slave and then running large queries on it without disturbing the main business server. For example, if you stop replication after the last transaction of the day, you can extract your daily reports while the rest of the business is humming along at its normal pace.

Filtering or partitioning data

If the network connection is slow, or if some data should not be available to certain clients, you can add a server to handle data filtering. This is also useful when the data needs to be partitioned and reside on separate servers.

Scaling Out Reads, Not Writes

It is important to understand that scaling out in this manner scales out reads, not writes. Each new slave has to handle the same write load as the master. The average load of the system can be described as:

$$AverageLoad = \frac{\sum ReadLoad + \sum WriteLoad}{\sum Capacity}$$

So if you have a single server with a total capacity of 10,000 transactions per second, and there is a write load of 4,000 transactions per second on the master, while there is a read load of 6,000 transactions per second, the result will be:

$$AverageLoad = \frac{\sum ReadLoad + \sum WriteLoad}{\sum Capacity} = \frac{6000 + 4000}{10000} = 100\%$$

Now, if you add three slaves to the master, the total capacity increases to 40,000 transactions per second. Because the write queries are replicated as well, each query is executed a total of four times—once on the master and once on each of the three slaves—which means that each slave has to handle 4,000 transactions per second in write load. The total read load does not increase because it is distributed over the slaves. This means that the average load now is:

$$AverageLoad = \frac{\sum ReadLoad + \sum WriteLoad}{\sum Capacity} = \frac{6000 + 4 \times 4000}{4 \times 10000} = 55\%$$

Notice that in the formula, the capacity is increased by a factor of 4, since we now have a total of four servers, and replication causes the write load to increase by a factor of 4 as well.

It is quite common to forget that replication forwards to each slave all the write queries that the master handles. So you cannot use this simple approach to scale writes, only reads. Later in this chapter, you will see how to scale writes using a technique called *sharding*.

The Value of Asynchronous Replication

MySQL replication is *asynchronous*, a type of replication particularly suitable for modern applications such as websites.

To handle a large number of reads, sites use replication to create copies of the master and then let the slaves handle all read requests while the master handles the write requests. This replication is considered asynchronous because the master does not wait for the slaves to apply the changes, but instead just dispatches each change request to the slaves and assumes they will catch up eventually and replicate all the changes. This technique for improving performance is usually a good idea when you are scaling out.

In contrast, synchronous replication keeps the master and slaves in sync and does not allow a transaction to be committed on the master unless the slave agrees to commit it as well. That is, synchronous replication makes the master wait for all the slaves to keep up with the writes.

Asynchronous replication is a lot faster than synchronous replication, for reasons our description should make obvious. Compared to asynchronous replication, synchronous replication requires extra synchronizations to guarantee consistency. It is usually implemented through a protocol called *two-phase commit*, which guarantees consistency between the master and slaves, but requires extra messages to ping-pong between them. Typically, it works like this:

1. When a commit statement is executed, the transaction is sent to the slaves and the slave is asked to prepare for a commit.

2. Each slave prepares the transaction so that it can be committed, and then sends an OK (or ABORT) message to the master, indicating that the transaction is prepared (or that it could not be prepared).

3. The master waits for all slaves to send either an OK or an ABORT message.

    a. If the master receives an OK message from all slaves, it sends a commit message to all slaves asking them to commit the transaction.

    b. If the master receives an ABORT message from any of the slaves, it sends an abort message to all slaves asking them to abort the transaction.

4. Each slave is then waiting for either an OK or an ABORT message from the master.

    a. If the slaves receive the commit request, they commit the transaction and send an acknowledgment to the master that the transaction is committed.

    b. If the slaves receive an abort request, they abort the transaction by undoing any changes and releasing any resources they held, then send an acknowledgment to the master that the transaction was aborted.

5. When the master has received acknowledgments from all slaves, it reports the transaction as committed (or aborted) and continues with processing the next transaction.

What makes this protocol slow is that it requires a total of four messages, including the messages with the transaction and the prepare request. The major problem is not the amount of network traffic required to handle the synchronization, but the latency introduced by the network and by processing the commit on the slave, together with the fact that the commit is blocked on the master until all the slaves have acknowledged the transaction. In contrast, asynchronous replication requires only a single message to be sent with the transaction. As a bonus, the master does not have to wait for the slave, but can report the transaction as committed immediately, which improves performance significantly.

So why is it a problem that synchronous replication blocks each commit while the slaves process it? If the slaves are close to the master on the network, the extra messages needed by synchronous replication make little difference, but if the slaves are not nearby— maybe in another town or even on another continent—it makes a big difference.

Table 5-1 shows some examples for a server that can commit 10,000 transactions per second. This translates to a commit time of 0.1 ms (but note that some implementations, such as MySQL Cluster, are able to process several commits in parallel if they are independent). If the network latency is 0.01 ms (a number we've chosen as a baseline by pinging one of our own computers), the transaction commit time increases to 0.14 ms, which translates to approximately 7000 transactions per second. If the network latency is 10 ms (which we found by pinging a server in a nearby city), the transaction commit time increases to 40.1 ms, which translates to about 25 transactions per second! In contrast, asynchronous replication introduces no delay at all, because the transactions are reported as committed immediately, so the transaction commit time stays at the original 10,000 per second, just as if there were no slaves.

Table 5-1. Typical slowdowns caused by synchronous replication

Latency (ms)	Transaction commit time (ms)	Equivalent transactions per second	Example case
0.01	0.14	~7,100	Same computer
0.1	0.5	~2,000	Small LAN
1	4.1	~240	Bigger LAN
10	40.1	~25	Metropolitan network
100	400.1	~2	Satellite

The performance of asynchronous replication comes at the price of consistency. Recall that in asynchronous replication the transaction is reported as committed immediately, *without* waiting for any acknowledgment from the slave. This means the master may consider the transaction committed when the slave does not. As a matter of fact, it might not even have left the master, but is still waiting to be sent to the slave.

There are two problems with this that you need to be aware of:

- In the event of crashes on the master, transactions can "disappear."
- A query executed on the slaves might return old data.

Later in this chapter, we will talk about how to ensure you are reading current data, but for now, just remember that asynchronous replication comes with its own set of caveats that you have to handle.

Managing the Replication Topology

A deployment is scaled by creating new slaves and adding them to the collection of computers you have. The term *replication topology* refers to the ways you connect servers using replication. Figure 5-1 shows some examples of replication topologies: a simple topology, a tree topology, a dual-master topology, and a circular topology.

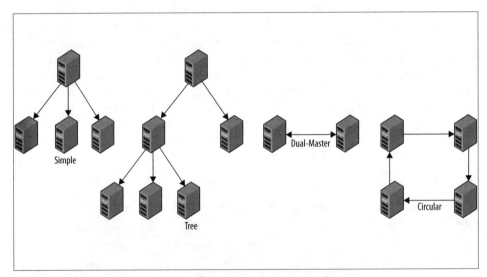

Figure 5-1. Simple, tree, dual-master, and circular replication topologies

These topologies are used for different purposes: the dual-master topology handles failovers elegantly, for example, and circular replication and dual masters allow different sites to work locally while still replicating changes over to the other sites.

The simple and tree topologies are used for scale-out. The use of replication causes the number of reads to greatly exceed the number of writes. This places special demands on the deployment in two ways:

It requires load balancing

> We're using the term *load balancing* here to describe any way of dividing queries among servers. Replication creates both reasons for load balancing and methods

for doing so. First, replication imposes a basic division of the load by specifying writes to be directed to the masters while reads go to the slaves. Furthermore, you sometimes have to send a particular query to a particular slave.

It requires you to manage the topology

Servers crash sooner or later, which makes it necessary to replace them. Replacing a crashed slave might not be urgent, but you'll have to replace a crashed master quickly.

In addition to this, if a master crashes, clients have to be redirected to the new master. If a slave crashes, it has to be taken out of the pool of load balancers so no queries are directed to it.

To handle load balancing and management, you should put tools in place to manage the replication topology, specifically tools that monitor the status and performance of servers and tools to handle the distribution of queries.

For load balancing to be effective, it is necessary to have spare capacity on the servers. There are a few reasons for ensuring you have spare capacity:

Peak load handling

You need to have margins to be able to handle peak loads. The load on a system is never even but fluctuates up and down. The spare capacity necessary to handle a large deployment depends a lot on the application, so you need to monitor it closely to know when the response times start to suffer.

Distribution cost

You need to have spare capacity for running the replication setup. Replication always causes a "waste" of some capacity on the overhead of running a distributed system. It involves extra queries to manage the distributed system, such as the extra queries necessary to figure out where to execute a read query.

One item that is easily forgotten is that each slave has to perform the same writes as the master. The queries from the master are executed in an orderly manner (that is, serially), with no risk of conflicting updates, but the slave needs extra capacity for running replication.

Administrative tasks

Restructuring the replication setup requires spare capacity so you can support temporary dual use, for example, when moving data between servers.

Load balancing works in two basic ways: either the application asks for a server based on the type of query, or an intermediate layer—usually referred to as a *proxy*—analyzes the query and sends it to the correct server.

Using an intermediate layer to analyze and distribute the queries (as shown in Figure 5-2) is by far the most flexible approach, but it has two disadvantages:

- Processing resources have to be spent on analyzing queries. This delays the query, which now has to be parsed and analyzed twice: once by the proxy and again by

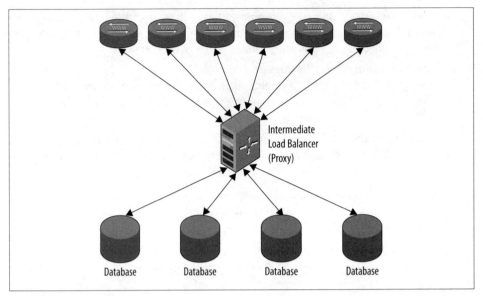

Figure 5-2. Using a proxy to distribute queries

the MySQL server. The more advanced the analysis, the more the query is delayed. Depending on the application, this may or may not be a problem.

- Correct query analysis can be hard to implement, sometimes even impossible. A proxy will often hide the internal structure of the deployment from the application programmer so that she does not have to make the hard choices. For this reason, the client may send a query that can be very hard to analyze properly and might require a significant rewrite before being sent to the servers.

One of the tools that you can use for proxy load balancing is MySQL Proxy. It contains a full implementation of the MySQL client protocol, and therefore can act as a server for the real client connecting to it and as a client when connecting to the MySQL server. This means that it can be fully transparent: a client can't distinguish between the proxy and a real server.

The MySQL Proxy is controlled using the Lua programming language. It has a built-in Lua engine that executes small—and sometimes not so small—programs to intercept and manipulate both the queries and the result sets. Since the proxy is controlled using a real programming language, it can carry out a variety of sophisticated tasks, including query analysis, query filtering, query manipulation, and query distribution.

Configuration and programming of the MySQL Proxy are beyond the scope of this book, but there are extensive publications about it online. Some of the ones we find useful are:

http://dev.mysql.com/tech-resources/articles/proxy-gettingstarted.html
> "Getting Started with MySQL Proxy" is Giuseppe Maxia's classic article introducing the MySQL Proxy.

http://forge.mysql.com/wiki/MySQL_Proxy
> The MySQL Proxy wiki page on MySQL Forge contains a lot of information about the proxy, including a lot of references and examples.

http://forge.mysql.com/wiki/MySQL_Proxy_RW_Splitting
> This is a description on MySQL Forge of how you can use MySQL Proxy for read/write splitting, that is, sending read queries to some set of servers and write queries to the master.

The precise methods for using a proxy depend entirely on the type of proxy you use, so we will not cover that information here. Instead, we'll focus on using a load balancer in the application layer. There are a number of load balancers available, including:

- Hardware
- Simple software load balancers, such as Balance (*http://www.inlab.de/balance.html*)
- Peer-based systems, such as Wackamole (*http://www.backhand.org/wackamole/*)
- Full-blown clustering solutions, such as the Linux Virtual Server (*http://www.linuxvirtualserver.org/*)

It is also possible to distribute the load on the DNS level and to handle the distribution directly in the application.

Example of an Application-Level Load Balancer

Let's tackle the task of designing and implementing a simple application-level load balancer to see how it works. In this section, we'll implement read/write splitting. We'll extend the load balancer later in the chapter to handle data partition.

The most straightforward approach to load balancing at the application level is to have the application ask the load balancer for a connection based on the type of query it is going to send. In most cases, the application already knows if the query is going to be a read or write query and also which tables will be affected. In fact, forcing the application developer to consider these issues when designing the queries may produce other benefits for the application, usually in the form of improved overall performance of the system. Based on this information, a load balancer can provide a connection to the right server, which the application then can use to execute the query.

A load balancer on the application layer needs to have a central store with information about the servers and what queries they should handle. Functions in the application layer send queries to this central store, which returns the name or IP address of the MySQL server to query.

Let's develop a simple load balancer like the one shown in Figure 5-3 for use by the application layer. We'll use PHP for the presentation logic because it's so popular on web servers. It is necessary to write functions for updating the server pool information and functions to fetch servers from the pool.

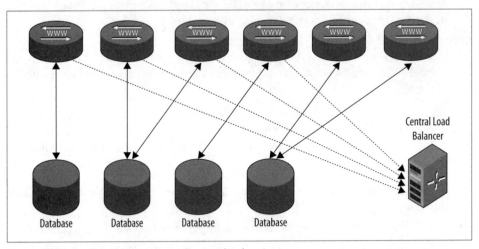

Figure 5-3. Load balancing on the application level

The pool is implemented by creating a table with all the servers in the deployment in a common database that is shared by all nodes. In this case, we just use the host and port as primary key for the table (instead of creating a host ID) and create a *common* database to contain the tables of the shared data.

> You should duplicate the central store so that it doesn't create a single point of failure. In addition, because the list of available servers does not often change, load balancing information is a perfect candidate for caching.
>
> For the sake of simplicity—and to avoid introducing dependencies on other systems—we demonstrate the application-level load balancer using a pure MySQL implementation.
>
> There are many other techniques that you can use that do not involve MySQL. The most common technique is to use round-robin DNS; another alternative is using Memcached, which is a distributed in-memory key/value store.
>
> Also note that the addition of an extra query might be a significant overhead for high-performing systems and should be avoided.

The load balancer lists servers in the load balancer pool, separated into categories based on what kind of queries they can handle. Information about the servers in the pool is stored in a central repository. The implementation consists of a table in the common database given in Example 5-1, the PHP functions in Example 5-2 for querying the load balancer from the application, and the Python functions in Example 5-3 for updating information about the servers.

Example 5-1. Database tables for the load balancer

```
CREATE TABLE nodes (
  host CHAR(28) NOT NULL,
  port INT UNSIGNED NOT NULL,
  sock CHAR(64) NOT NULL,
  type SET('READ','WRITE') NOT NULL DEFAULT '',
  PRIMARY KEY (host, port)
);
```

We store for each host regarding whether it accepts reads, writes, both, or neither. This information is stored in the **type** field. By setting it to the empty set, we can bring the server offline, which is important for maintenance.

A simple **SELECT** will suffice to find all the servers that can accept the query. Since we want just a single server, we limit the output to a single line using the **LIMIT** modifier to the **SELECT** query, and to distribute queries evenly among available servers, we use the **ORDER BY RAND()** modifier.

> Using the **ORDER BY RAND()** modifier requires the server to sort the rows in the table, which may not be the most efficient way to pick a number randomly (it's actually a very bad way to pick a number randomly), but we picked this approach for demonstration purposes only.

Example 5-2 shows the PHP function **getServerConnection**, which queries for a server and connects to it. It returns a connection to the server suitable for issuing a query, or **NULL** if no suitable server can be found. The helper function **connect_to** constructs a suitable connection string given its host, port, and a Unix socket. If the host is **local host**, it will use the socket to connect to the server for efficiency.

Example 5-2. PHP function for querying the load balancer

```
function connect_to($host, $port, $socket) {
  $db_server = $host == "localhost" ? ":{$socket}" : "{$host}:{$port}";
  return mysql_connect($db_server, 'query_user');
}

$COMMON = connect_to(host, port, socket);
mysql_select_db('common', $COMMON);

define('DB_WRITE', 'WRITE');
define('DB_READ', 'READ');
```

```
function getServerConnection($queryType)
{
  global $COMMON;
  $query = <<<END_OF_SQL
SELECT host, port, sock FROM nodes
 WHERE FIND_IN_SET('$queryType', type)
ORDER BY RAND() LIMIT 1
END_OF_SQL;
  $result = mysql_query($query, $COMMON);
  if ($row = mysql_fetch_row($result))
    return connect_to($row[0], $row[1], $row[2]);
  return NULL;
}
```

The final task is to provide utility functions for adding and removing servers and for updating the capabilities of a server. Since these are mainly to be used from the administration logic, we've implemented this function in Python using the Replicant library. The utility consists of three functions:

pool_add(common, server, type)
>   Adds a **server** to the pool. The pool is stored at the server denoted by **common**, and the **type** to use is a list—or other iterable—of values to set.

pool_del(common, server)
>   Deletes a server from the pool.

pool_set(common, server, type)
>   Changes the type of the **server**.

Example 5-3. Administrative functions for the load balancer

```
class AlreadyInPoolError(replicant.Error):
    pass

_INSERT_SERVER = """
INSERT INTO nodes(host, port, sock, type)
    VALUES (%s, %s, %s, %s)"""

_DELETE_SERVER = "DELETE FROM nodes WHERE host = %s AND port = %s"

_UPDATE_SERVER = "UPDATE nodes SET type = %s WHERE host = %s AND port = %s"

def pool_add(common, server, type=[]):
    common.use("common")
    try:
        common.sql(_INSERT_SERVER,
                   (server.host, server.port, server.socket, ','.join(type)));
    except MySQLdb.IntegrityError:
        raise AlreadyInPoolError


def pool_del(common, server):
    common.use("common")
```

```
    common.sql(_DELETE_SERVER, (server.host, server.port))

def pool_set(common, server, type):
    common.use("common")
    common.sql(_UPDATE_SERVER, (','.join(type), server.host, server.port))
```

These functions can be used as shown in the following examples:

```
pool_add(common, master, ['READ', 'WRITE'])

for slave in slaves:
    pool_add(common, slave, ['READ'])
```

Hierarchal Replication

Although the master is quite good at handling a large number of slaves, there is a limit to how many slaves it can handle before the load becomes too high for comfort (a user mentioned 70 slaves as a practical limit for his purposes, but as you probably realize, this depends a lot on the application), and an unresponsive master is always a problem. In those cases, you can add an extra slave (or several) as a *relay slave* (or simply *relay*), whose only purpose is to lighten the load of replication on the master by taking care of a bunch of slaves. Using a relay in this manner is called *hierarchal replication*. Figure 5-4 illustrates a typical setup with a master, a relay, and several slaves connected to the relay.

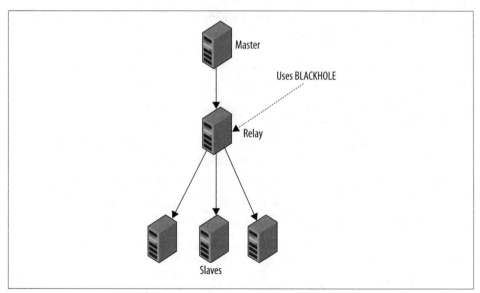

Figure 5-4. Hierarchal topology with master, relay, and slaves

By default, the changes the slave receives from its master are not written to the binary log of the slave, so if SHOW BINLOG EVENTS is executed on the slave in the previous setup, you will not see any events in the binlog. The reason for this is that there is no point in wasting disk space by recording the changes: if there is a problem and, say, the slave crashes, you can always recover by cloning the master or another slave.

On the other hand, the relay server needs to keep a binary log to record all the changes, because the relay passes them on to other slaves. Unlike typical slaves, however, the relay doesn't need to actually apply changes to a database of its own, because it doesn't answer queries.

In short, a typical slave needs to apply changes to a database, but not to a binary log. A relay server needs to keep a binary log, but does not apply changes to a database.

To avoid writing changes to the database, it is necessary to keep tables around (so the statements can be executed), but the changes should just be thrown away. A storage engine named Blackhole was created for purposes just like this one. The Blackhole engine accepts all statements and always reports success in executing them, but any changes are just thrown away. A relay introduces an extra delay that can cause its slaves to lag further behind the master than slaves that are directly connected to the master. This lag should be balanced against the benefits of removing some load from the master, since managing a hierarchal setup is significantly more difficult than managing a simple setup.

Setting Up a Relay Server

Setting up a relay slave is quite easy, but we have to consider what to do with tables that are being created on the relay as well as what to do with tables that already exist on the relay when we change its role. Not keeping data in the databases will make processing events faster and reduce the lag for the slaves at the end of the replication process, since there is no data to be updated. To set up a relay slave, we thus have to:

1. Configure the slave to forward any events executed by the slave thread by writing them to the binlog of the relay slave.

2. Change the storage engine for all tables on the relay slave to use the BLACKHOLE storage engine to preserve space and improve performance.

3. Ensure that any new tables added to the relay also use the BLACKHOLE engine.

Configuring the relay server to forward events executed by the slave thread is done by adding the log-slave-updates option to *my.cnf*, as demonstrated earlier.

To ensure all tables created on the relay slave are created with the BLACKHOLE engine, connect to the server and set the default storage engine:

```
relay> SET GLOBAL STORAGE_ENGINE = 'BLACKHOLE';
```

The final task is to change the storage engine for all tables already on the relay slave to use BLACKHOLE. Do this using the ALTER TABLE statement to change the storage engine for each table on the server. Since the ALTER TABLE statements shouldn't be written to the binary log (the last thing we want is for slaves to discard the changes they receive!), turn off the binary log temporarily while executing the `ALTER TABLE` statements. This is shown in Example 5-4.

Example 5-4. Changing the engine for all tables in database windy

```
relay> SHOW TABLES FROM windy;
+-----------------+
| Tables_in_windy |
+-----------------+
| user_data       |
    .
    .
    .
| profile         |
+-----------------+
45 row in set (0.15 sec)
relay> SET SQL_LOG_BIN = 0;
relay> ALTER TABLE user_data ENGINE = 'BLACKHOLE';
    .
    .
    .
relay> ALTER TABLE profile ENGINE = 'BLACKHOLE';
relay> SET SQL_BIN_LOG = 1;
```

This is all you need to turn a server into a relay server. The usual way you come to employ a relay is to start with a setup where all slaves attach directly to a master and discover after some time that it is necessary to introduce a relay slave. The reason is usually that the master has become too loaded, but there could be architectural reasons for making the change as well. So how do you handle that?

You can use what you learned in the previous sections and modify the existing deployment to introduce the new relay server by:

1. Connecting the relay slave to the master and configuring it to act as a relay server
2. Switching over the slaves one by one to the relay server

Adding a Relay in Python

Let's turn to the task of developing support for administering relays by extending our library. Since we have a system for creating new roles and imbuing servers with those roles, let's use that by defining a special role for the relay server. This is shown in Example 5-5.

Example 5-5. Role definition for relay

```python
class Relay(role.Base):
    def __init__(self, master):
        pass

    def imbue(self, server):
        config = server.get_config()
        self._set_server_id(server, config)
```

```
    self._enable_binlog(server, config)
    config.set('mysqld', 'log-slave-updates' '1')
    server.put_config(config)
    server.sql("SET SQL_LOG_BIN = 0")
    for db in list of databases:
        for table in server.sql("SHOW TABLES FROM %s", (db)):
            server.sql("ALTER TABLE %s.%s ENGINE=BLACKHOLE", (db,table))
    server.sql("SET SQL_LOG_BIN = 1")
```

Specialized Slaves

In the simple scale-out deployment—like the one described thus far—all slaves receive all data and can therefore handle any kind of query. It is, however, not very common to distribute requests evenly over the different parts of the data. Instead, there is usually some data that needs to be accessed very frequently and some that is rarely accessed. For example, on an e-commerce site:

- The product catalog is browsed almost all the time.
- Data about items in stock may not be requested very often.
- User data is not requested very often, since most of the critical information is recorded using session-specific information stored in the browser as cookies.
- On the other hand, if cookies are disabled, the session data will be requested from the server with almost every page request.
- Newly added items are usually accessed more frequently than old items, for example, "special offers" might be accessed more frequently than other items.

It would clearly be a waste of resources to keep the rarely accessed data on each and every slave just in case it is requested. It would be much better to use the deployment shown in Figure 5-5, where a few servers are dedicated to keeping rarely accessed data, while a different set of servers are dedicated to keeping data that is accessed frequently.

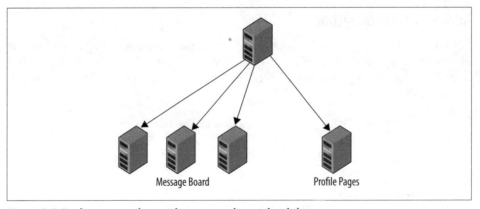

Figure 5-5. Replication topology with master and specialized slaves

To do this, it is necessary to separate tables when replicating. MySQL can do this by filtering the events that leave the master or, alternatively, filtering the events when they come to the slave.

Filtering Replication Events

The two different ways of filtering events are called *master filters* when the events are filtered on the master and *slave filters* when the events are filtered on the slave. The master filters control what goes into the binary log and therefore what is sent to the slaves, while slave filters control what is executed on the slave. For the master filters, events for filtered-out tables are not stored in the binary log at all, while for slave filters, the events are stored in the binary log and also sent to the slave and not filtered out until just before they are going to be executed.

If master filters are used, the events are not stored in the binary log at all.

This means that it is not possible to use PITR to recover these databases properly—if the databases are stored in the backup image, they will still be restored when restoring the backup, but any changes made to tables in the database since that moment will not be recovered, since the changes are not in the binary log.

If slave filters are used, all changes are sent over the network.

This clearly wastes network bandwidth, especially over long-haul network connections.

Later in this chapter, you will see a detailed discussion of the relative merits of master and slave filtering and an approach that allows the binary log to remain intact and still saves network bandwidth.

Master filters

There are two configuration options for creating master filters:

binlog-do-db=*db*
> If the current database of the statement is *db*, the statement will be written to the binary log; otherwise, the statement will be discarded.

binlog-ignore-db=*db*
> If the current database of the statement is *db*, the statement will be discarded; otherwise, the statement will be written to the binary log.

If you want to replicate everything except a few databases, use binlog-ignore-db. If you want to replicate just a few databases, use binlog-do-db. Combining them is *not* recommended, since the logic for deciding whether a database should be replicated or not is complicated (see Figure 3-3). The options do not accept lists of databases, so if you want to list several databases, you have to repeat an option multiple times.

As an example, to replicate everything except the *top* and *secret* databases, add the following options to the configuration file:

```
[mysqld]
...
binlog-ignore-db = top
binlog-ignore-db = secret
```

 Using `binlog-*-db` options to filter events means that the two databases will not be stored in the binary log at all, and hence cannot be recovered using PITR in the event of a crash. For that reason, it is strongly recommended that you use slave filters, not master filters, when you want to filter the replication stream. You should use master filters only for data that can be considered volatile and that you can afford to lose.

Slave filters

Slave filtering offers a longer list of options. In addition to being able to filter the events based on the database, slave filters can also filter individual tables and even groups of table names by using wildcards.

In the following list of rules, the `replicate-wild` rules look at the full name of the table, including both the database and table name. The pattern supplied to the option uses the same patterns as the `LIKE` string comparison function—that is, an underscore (_) matches a single character, whereas a percent sign (%) matches a string of any length. Note, however, that the pattern must contain a period to be legitimate. This means that the database name and table name are matched individually, so each wildcard applies only to the database name or table name.

replicate-do-db=*db*
> If the current database of the statement is *db*, execute the statement.

replicate-ignore-db=*db*
> If the current database of the statement is *db*, discard the statement.

replicate-do-table=*table* *and* replicate-wild-do-table=*db_pattern.tbl_pattern*
> If the name of the table being updated is *table* or matches the pattern, execute updates to the table.

replicate-ignore-table=*table* *and* replicate-wild-ignore-table=
db_pattern.tbl_pattern
> If the name of the table being updated is *table* or matches the pattern, discard updates to the table.

These filtering rules are evaluated just before the server decides whether to execute them, so all events are sent to the slave before being filtered.

Using Filtering to Partition Events to Slaves

So what are the benefits and drawbacks of filtering on the master versus filtering on the slave? At a brief glance, it might seem like a good idea to structure the databases so that it is possible to filter events on the master using the `binlog-*-db` options instead of using the `replicate-*-db` options. That way, the network is not laden with a lot of useless events that will be removed by the slave anyway. However, as mentioned earlier in the chapter, there are problems associated with filtering on the master:

- Since the events are filtered from the binary log and there is only a single binary log, it is not possible to "split" the changes and send different parts of the database to different servers.

- The binary log is also used for PITR, so if there are any problems with the server, it will not be possible to restore everything.

- If, for some reason, it becomes necessary to split the data differently, it will no longer be possible, since the binary log has already been filtered and cannot be "unfiltered."

It would be ideal if the filtering could be on the events sent from the master and not on the events written to the binary log. It would also be good if the filtering could be controlled by the slave so that the slave could decide which data to replicate. As of MySQL version 5.1, this is not possible, and instead, it is necessary to filter events using the `replicate-*` options—that is, to filter the events on the slave.

 There are ongoing discussions among the replication team about implementing an advanced filtering feature that will allow filtering of events at various points in the processing of the events, as well as complex filtering logic.

At the time of this writing, there has been no decision on which version of the server will implement this advanced filtering.

As an example, to dedicate a slave to the user data stored in the two tables *users* and *profiles* in the *app* database, shut down the server and add the following filtering options to the *my.cnf* file:

```
[mysqld]
...
replicate-wild-do-table=app.users
replicate-wild-do-table=app.profiles
```

If you are concerned about network traffic—which could be significant if you replicate over long-haul networks—you can set up a relay slave on the same machine as the master, as shown in Figure 5-6 (or on the same network segment as the master), whose only purpose is to produce a filtered version of the master's binary log.

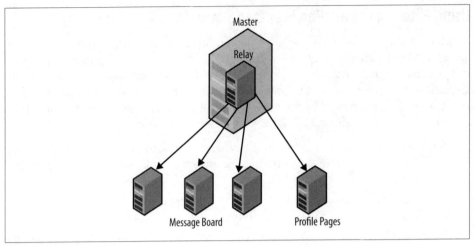

Figure 5-6. Filtering by putting master and relay on the same machine

Data Sharding

You have seen how to scale reads by attaching slaves to a master and directing reads to the slaves while writes go to the master. As the load increases, it is easy to add more slaves to the master and serve more read queries. Still, all writes go to the master, so if the number of writes increases enough, the master will become a bottleneck as the system scales up. Is there some way to scale writes as well as reads?

Before delving into the best way to scale writes, consider for a moment the setup in Figure 5-7, which consists of two masters using bidirectional replication and a set of clients that update different masters depending on which data they need to change. Although the architecture appears to double the capacity to handle writes—because there are two masters—that doesn't help you with scaling. Each statement is executed on both masters, so the number of writes doubles as well. This leaves you in no better position than before. In short, a dual-master setup doesn't help you scale writes, so it is necessary to find some other means.

The reason that the pair of masters in Figure 5-7 does not scale is because the doubling of the capacity is canceled by each statement being executed twice. Therefore, it should be possible to scale writes if the statements are not executed twice—that is, if there is no replication between the servers in Figure 5-7 and the different servers are completely separate.

With this architecture, it is possible to scale writes by partitioning the data into two completely independent sets. This way, the clients can be directed at the partition that is responsible for the data the client attempts to update, and no resources need to be devoted to processing updates for other partitions.

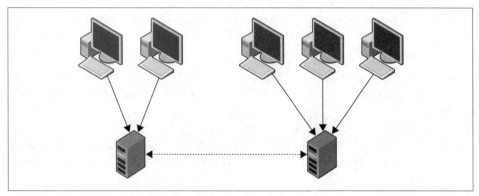

Figure 5-7. Pair of masters with bidirectional replication

Partitioning the data in this manner is usually referred to as *sharding*—other common names are *splintering* or (*horizontal*) *partitioning*—and each partition is referred to as a *shard*. It is common to shard bulky data, such as posts, comments, pictures, and videos, but to keep directories and user data in a central store, similar to the deployment shown in Figure 5-8.

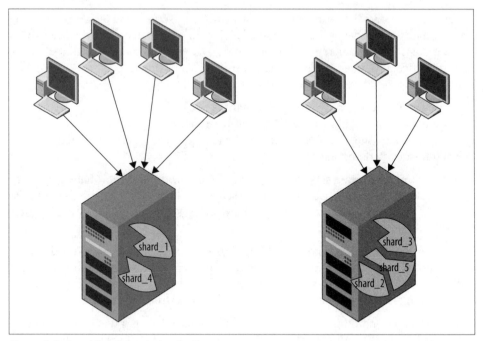

Figure 5-8. Several nodes with sharding

In addition to allowing associated data on the same node—which allows queries to be directed at a single node—placing shards geographically close to the user also improves the performance of the system, since it reduces latency. There are several reasons for sharding data:

Placing data geographically close to user
> As just mentioned, by placing bulky data close to the user, it is possible to reduce latency.

Reducing the size of the working set
> Searching through a smaller table is more efficient than searching through a larger table, and it is also possible to parallelize the search, provided that it is simple enough.
>
> This approach is efficient only when the shards are approximately the same size. So if you use this strategy, you must find a way to balance the sizes of the shards.

Balancing the load
> In addition to reducing the working set by reducing the size of each table, sharding makes it possible to balance the update load more efficiently. If some shards get a disproportionately large number of updates for their sizes, it is possible to split them into smaller shards.

When sharding data, you can place several shards on a server. The reason for keeping several shards on a server is that when rebalancing the system, it is easy to move a shard to a different server, but repartitioning the data is very difficult. In addition to the administrative advantage, making small partitions keeps down the size of each table, which improves the overall performance of the system.

With this architecture, the location of a shard is not fixed, and it is necessary to have a method for translating a shard ID to the node where the shard is stored. This is typically handled using the architecture shown in Figure 5-9, where a central repository keeps track of where the shards are.

When creating a sharding scheme for an existing application, it is probably easiest to have one shard per node, but a more general scheme will allow several shards to coexist on a node. This will allow you to reduce the working set, hopefully resulting in faster queries.

Sharding usually has to be handled in the application, or in a layer between the database and the application. Even if a database application layer is managing sharding, it is very difficult to hide the sharding structure completely without sacrificing performance. It is better to make the application aware of the sharding structure and use it efficiently.

There are several sharding implementations for MySQL. Two popular ones are Hibernate Shards by Google and HiveDB (*http://www.hivedb.org/*), which are both Java database application layers. You can also use the MySQL Proxy, but its sharding support is currently in its infancy. The MySQL development team assigns a high priority to

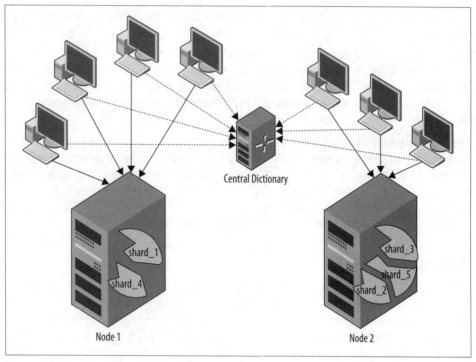

Figure 5-9. Shards with a centralized dictionary

developing efficient solutions for scaling writes, however, and the MySQL Proxy may be part of the solution.

Shard Representation

To work efficiently with a sharding structure, you need a good way to represent the shards. Consider the following:

- It has to be easy to move shards, which means that it has to be easy to make a backup of a shard and restore it in a different place.
- There may be several shards on a server, so you need to be able to distinguish between shards that coexist on the same node.
- It should be possible to replicate a single shard from a server in order to move the shard.

The only guaranteed way to satisfy the first condition is to represent each shard as a single MySQL database. Most backup methods can make backups of a single database, but may have problems with backing up individual tables. This is true, for instance, for copying a database directory directly, but also for most other backup methods. Using a single database per shard will also allow you to satisfy the last condition as well, since you can limit `replicate-do-db` to specific shards on a server (this is possible because you move shards on the masters, and the masters typically do not replicate from any-where).

Given the assignment of a single database per shard, the second condition can be sat-isfied by appending a unique number to the name of each database. This means that shards on a server are databases with names such as *shard_123* and that a partition of each table is placed in each database; for example, the *posts* table consists of *shard_1.posts, shard_2.posts, ..., shard_N.posts*.

With this approach, you can give your tables either "plain" names or names that reflect their shards. In the first scheme, you can reference the *posts* table along with the data-bases as *shard_123.posts, shard_124.posts*, and so on. In the second scheme, the names would be *shard_123.posts_123, shard_124.posts_124*, and so on. Although the shard number on the table seems redundant, it can be useful for catching problems where the application code mistakenly queries the wrong shard.

Partitioning the Data

Writing each item of data to a particular server allows you to scale writes efficiently. But that's not sufficient for scalability: efficiency is also important, and to be able to efficiently retrieve data, it is necessary to keep associated data together. For this reason, the biggest challenge in efficient sharding is to choose a good *partition key* so that data commonly requested together is on the same shard, or at least as few shards as possible.

Creating a good partition key usually requires some ingenuity together with some knowledge about the structure of the data in the database. For example, an application that allows professional photographers to store pictures safely can shard the pictures on the location of the photographer and place all pictures for a photographer on a shard geographically close to that photographer.

Once you have decided on a partition key, the question is how to use this key to shard the data. You need to decide on a *partition function* that takes a partition key and translates it to a shard number. There are two commonly used types of schemes:

Static sharding schemes

> In this case, the partition key is compared to a static assignment, typically using either a range or a hash function. For example, if your partition key is "Country," you can place all Swedes on one shard and all Americans on a different shard (for the moment, we will disregard the fact that the population of the United States is about 30 times that of Sweden).

> Other ways to assign shards in this example include basing them on the unique ID field of the user. You could use range-based assignment, such as making the first shard responsible for users 0 through 9,999, the second shard responsible for users 10,000 through 19,999, and so on. Or you could scatter users semirandomly through a hash based on the value of the last four digits of the ID.

Dynamic sharding schemes

> In this case, the partition function looks up the partition key in a dictionary that indicates which shard contains the data. This scheme is more flexible than a static scheme, but it requires a centralized store for the dictionary, which may increase query time. The centralized store is also a problem from the viewpoint of high availability, since it is a single point of failure.

As you might have realized, static sharding schemes run into problems when the distribution of the queries is not even—as in the previous example where sharding is done by country. In this case, you can expect the load on the U.S. shard to be about 30 times that of the Sweden shard. Swedes would love this because—assuming that the servers have the same capacity—they will experience very short response times. American visitors may suffer, however. For this reason, picking a good partition key is of paramount importance.

Dynamic sharding schemes are very flexible. Not only do they allow you to change the sharding, but they make it easy to move data between shards if the need arises. As always, this flexibility comes at the price of requiring extra queries to find the correct shard to retrieve data from. The use of caching systems such as Memcached offers some help, but ultimately, good performance requires a careful design that matches the patterns of user queries.

After you create a partition key and partition function, you have to map shard numbers to nodes (where each server holds one or more complete nodes). If you use a static sharding scheme, the partition function can automatically map the shard number to the node as part of the process. This bodes well for efficiency, but at the expense of flexibility, since moving a shard requires rewriting the partition function. For a dynamic sharding scheme, you can implement the mapping from shard numbers to nodes by adding a table to hold the mapping.

Balancing the Shards

To keep the system responsive even as the load on the system changes, or just for administrative reasons, you will sometimes have to move data around, either by moving entire shards to different nodes or moving data between shards. Each of these two procedures presents its own challenges in rebalancing the load with a minimum of downtime—and preferably with no downtime at all. Automated solutions should be preferred.

Moving a shard to a different node

The easiest solution is to move an entire shard to a different node. If you have followed our earlier advice and placed each shard in a separate database, moving the database is as easy as moving the directory. However, doing this while continuing to allow writes to the node is a different story.

Moving a shard from one node (the source node) to another node (the target node) without any downtime at all is not possible, but it is possible to keep the downtime to a minimum. The technique is similar to the description in Chapter 2 of creating a slave. The idea is to make a backup of the shard, restore it on the target node, and use replication to reexecute any changes that happened in between.

1. Create a backup of the database on the source node that you want to move. For the purpose of this exercise, assume that the database is named *shard_123*. Both online and offline backup methods are suitable.

2. Each backup, as we saw in earlier chapters, backs up data to a particular point in the binary log. Write this log position down.

3. Bring the target node down by stopping the server.

4. While the server is down:

   a. Set the option `replicate-do-db` in the configuration file to replicate only the shard that you want to move.

   ```
   [mysqld]
   replicate-do-db=shard_123
   ```

   b. If you have to restore the backup from the source node while the server is down, do that at this time.

5. Bring the server up again.

6. Configure replication to start reading from the position that you noted in step 2 and start replication on the target server. This will read events from the source server and apply any changes to the shard that you are moving.

   Plan to have excess capacity on the target node so that you can temporarily handle an increase in the number of writes on it.

7. When the target node is sufficiently close to the source node, lock the shard's database on the source node in order to stop changes. It is not necessary to stop changes to the shard on the target node, because no writes will go there yet.

   The easiest way to handle that is to issue `LOCK TABLES` and lock all the tables in the shard, but other schemes are possible, including just removing the tables (if the application can handle a table that disappears, for example, as outlined below, this is a possible alternative).

8. Check the log position on the source server. Since the shard is not being updated anymore, this will be the highest log position you need to restore.

9. Wait for the target server to catch up to this position, for example, by using `START SLAVE UNTIL` and `MASTER_POS_WAIT`.

10. Turn off replication on the target server by issuing `RESET SLAVE`. This will remove all replication information, including *master.info*, *relay-log.info* and all relay log-files. If you added any replication options to the *my.cnf* file to configure replication, you have to remove them, preferably in the next step.

11. Optionally bring the target server down, remove the `replicate-do-db` from the *my.cnf* file for the target server, and bring the server up again.

    This step is not strictly necessary, because the `replicate-do-db` option is used only to move shards and does not affect the functioning of the shard after the shard has been moved. When the time comes to move a shard here again, you have to change the option at that time anyway.

12. Update the shard information so that update requests are directed to the new location of the shard.

13. Unlock the database to restart writes to the shard.

14. Drop the shard database from the source server. Depending on how the shard is locked, there might still be readers of the shard at this point, so you have to take that into consideration.

Whew! That took quite a few steps. Fortunately, they can be automated using the MySQL Replicant library. The details for each individual step vary depending on how the application is implemented—you will see an example later in the chapter when we discuss the sample application.

Moving data between shards

Even though you now have a strategy for moving shards around, you will occasionally have to move data items *between* shards as well. Following up on the example of a picture storage application, a user may eventually move, or usage patterns might suggest that the deployment would be more efficient if the picture were placed in a different shard. You can imagine a photographer who lives in California but whose family in New York views the pictures most of the time. In these cases, it is necessary to automatically reshard the system and move a user to a different shard.

Methods for moving data between shards are highly dependent on the applications, so we can only offer an example. Normally, moving data between shards is expensive, since you have to bring the shard offline for longer periods of time. This is necessary to prevent changes to the user while it is being moved.

A Sharding Example

To demonstrate a method for setting up sharding, let's create a small example that initially uses a static sharding scheme and then updates it to use a dynamic sharding scheme. We'll use a simple blog site where users are registered, can create posts, and can add comments to posts.

For this example, we create an application where users can post articles and others can comment on the articles. The design of the database that we will use is shown in Figure 5-10 and, as you can see, it is very basic.

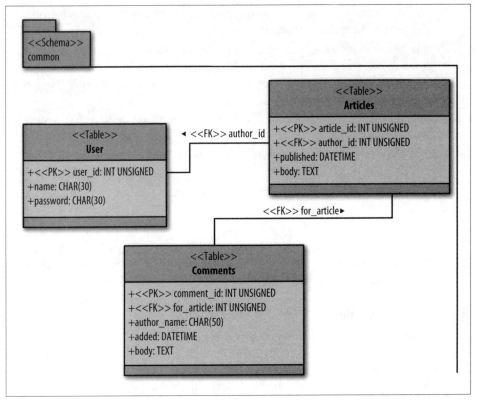

Figure 5-10. UML (Unified Modeling Language) database design schema

Example 5-6 contains the definition of the common data, which we place in the database *common* for convenience. The common data consists only of a *user* table with all of the users, but we'll add more tables later in this chapter.

Example 5-6. Tables for common data

```
CREATE TABLE user (
  user_id INT UNSIGNED AUTO_INCREMENT PRIMARY KEY,
  name CHAR(30),
  password CHAR(30)
);
```

We place the tables for the articles and the comments in another database, as shown in Example 5-7, consisting of the table *articles* for the articles and the table *comments* for the comments.

Example 5-7. Tables for articles and comments to articles

```
CREATE TABLE articles (
  article_id INT UNSIGNED AUTO_INCREMENT PRIMARY KEY,
  author_id INT,
  published DATETIME,
```

```
  body TEXT
);

CREATE TABLE comments (
  comment_id INT UNSIGNED AUTO_INCREMENT PRIMARY KEY,
  for_article INT,
  author_name CHAR(50),
  added DATETIME,
  body TEXT
);
```

As you can see, the application is very simple, but it suits our purpose of demonstrating a sharding application. To simplify the description, we have deliberately not modeled the foreign keys. For a centralized database like this, which is accessed frequently and by many clients simultaneously, the best choice of storage engine is one that has row locks, such as InnoDB.

Sharding the database

Imagine that the number of users grows a lot, and hence the number of articles posted. The user data is easiest to manage on a single node, so there is no reason to shard the user table—storing 100 million users only requires 6 GB of data, so space is not the issue here, although there are other reasons to avoid tables with 100 million entries. The articles, on the other hand, with associated comments, may indeed become very bulky, so sharding these tables is a good idea.

In this case, the articles and comments are split into different shards, with the comments on each article being in the same shard as the article itself. This will allow users to retrieve an article and its comments efficiently from the same shard using a single query. To handle this, we name each shard using a number, and place definitions of the tables given in Example 5-7 in each shard. For convenience, the base name of a shard is simply *shard*, and an example of the name with the shard number attached is *shard_123*.

Partition keys and partition functions

Someone looking up a user might find it interesting to see the titles of all the articles that user posted. When looking up an article, users often like to retrieve its comments as well.

To satisfy these usage patterns efficiently, we shard the data so that all articles from the same user are on the same shard and all comments for an article are placed on the same shard as the article. This means that there are multiple partition keys for this example:

- When a user is retrieved, the user ID is the partition key.
- When an article is retrieved, the article ID is the partition key.

Along the same lines, we create two partition functions: one going from a user ID to a shard number, and one going from an article ID to a shard number.

From user ID to shard number

> To find the shard number from the user ID, we simply take the modulus of the user ID. So, for example, if there are 100 shards and the user ID is 192, the shard number is 92.

From article ID to shard number

> Finding the shard number from the article ID is not so easy, since it is necessary to first find the author of the article. The easiest way—which unfortunately is very application-specific—is to ensure the user ID is available in the application code when an article is requested. This is easy if a user selects an article from another user's page—it can just be added to the HTML form data as a hidden field—but can be problematic in other situations.
>
> An alternative is to provide the necessary information in the common database by introducing a special table that maps each article ID to its user ID.

We won't illustrate application-specific coding, but we'll briefly explain how to add tables to the common database. This approach is more flexible than encoding the sharding scheme in the application code, even when a static sharding scheme is used, but when using the dynamic sharding scheme that we demonstrate later, it is essential to be able to dynamically update the sharding information.

The necessary changes are shown in bold in Example 5-8. Note that there is an index on the shard column, since this will be a very frequent lookup.

Example 5-8. Tables for locating shards and nodes

```
CREATE TABLE user (
  user_id INT UNSIGNED AUTO_INCREMENT,
  name CHAR(50), password CHAR(50),
  PRIMARY KEY (user_id)
);

CREATE TABLE node_for (
  shard INT UNSIGNED,
  host  CHAR(28),
  port  INT UNSIGNED,
  sock  CHAR(64),
  KEY (shard)
);

CREATE TABLE user_for (
  article_id INT UNSIGNED,
  user_id INT UNSIGNED,
  PRIMARY KEY (article_id)
);
```

Using the tables in Example 5-8, you can easily define functions for finding the shard number and node given either an article ID or a user ID. This is shown in Example 5-9. Each function makes an SQL query to the server holding the common data. If you need to retrieve a user ID followed by an article ID, you can combine the queries using a subquery to reduce the round-trip time if the server is located far away.

Notice the separate shardNumber function. This function currently implements the static sharding scheme by mapping a user ID to a shard number using simple modulus arithmetic. Later in the chapter, you will see how to change it to use a dynamic sharding scheme.

Example 5-9. PHP functions for retrieving shard number and node address

```
    function shardNumber($userId)
    {
        return $userId % 4;
    }

    $NODE = array();
    $NODE[] = array("localhost", 3307, "/var/run/mysqld/mysqld1.sock");
    $NODE[] = array("localhost", 3308, "/var/run/mysqld/mysqld2.sock");
    $NODE[] = array("localhost", 3309, "/var/run/mysqld/mysqld3.sock");
    $NODE[] = array("localhost", 3310, "/var/run/mysqld/mysqld4.sock");

    function getShardAndNodeFromUserId($userId, $common)
    {
        global $NODE;
1       $shardNo = shardNumber($userId);
2       $row = $NODE[$shardNo % count($NODE)];
        $db_server = $row[0] == "localhost" ? ":{$row[2]}" : "{$row[0]}:{$row[1]}";
        $conn = mysql_connect($db_server, 'query_user');
3       mysql_select_db("shard_$shardNo", $conn);
        return array($shardNo, $conn);
    }

    function getShardAndNodeFromArticleId($articleId, $common) {
        $query = "SELECT user_id FROM article_author WHERE article_id = %d";
        mysql_select_db("common");
        $result = mysql_query(sprintf($query, $articleId), $link);
        $row = mysql_fetch_row($result);
        return getShardAndNodeFromUserId($row[0], $common);
    }
```

Updating or reading a shard

After you have identified the shard number and the node, it is time to create the functions to retrieve information from the shards. Example 5-10 defines two such functions:

getArticlesForUser
    This function accepts a user ID and returns an array of all articles the user has written. The partition function ensures that all articles are on the same shard, so the function in line 1 computes the shard number shared by all the articles. The node for the shard is then fetched in line 2. After that, the correct database name

for the shard is computed (line 3) and a single query is sent to the node to retrieve all the articles in the shard.

getCommentsForArticle

This function accepts a user ID and an article ID and returns an array consisting of the article and all comments for the article. In this particular case, the user ID is part of the full article ID, so it is available to the caller without further searching.

The functions are pretty straightforward, and after the correct shard has been identified, it is sufficient to send the query to the correct node. Since there can be several shards on the same node, it is necessary to ensure the correct database is read. To simplify the presentation, the function does not contain any error handling at all.

Example 5-10. PHP functions for retrieving articles and comments

```php
function getArticlesForUser($userId, $common)
{
  $query = <<<END_OF_SQL
SELECT author_id, article_id, title, published, body
  FROM articles
 WHERE author_id = $userId
END_OF_SQL;

  list($shard, $node) = getShardAndNodeFromUserId($userId, $common);
  $articles = array();
  $result = mysql_query($query, $node);
  while ($obj = mysql_fetch_object($result))
    $articles[] = $obj;
  return $articles;
}

function getArticleAndComments($userId, $articleId, $common)
{
  list($shard, $node) = getShardAndNodeFromArticleId($articleId, $common);

  $article_query = <<<END_OF_SQL
SELECT author_id, article_id, title, published, body
  FROM articles
 WHERE article_id = $articleId
END_OF_SQL;

  $QUERIES[] = $article_query;
  $result = mysql_query($article_query, $node);
  $article = mysql_fetch_object($result);

  # Fetch the comments from the same shard
  $comment_query = <<<END_OF_SQL
SELECT author_name, body, published
  FROM comments
 WHERE article_ref = $articleId
END_OF_SQL;

  $result = mysql_query($comment_query, $node);
  $comments = array();
```

```
  while ($obj = mysql_fetch_object($result))
    $comments[] = $obj;
  return array($article, $comments);
}
```

In this example, we are reading from the shards directly, but if we are scaling out reads as well, read queries should be directed to the slaves instead. Implementing this is straightforward.

Implementing a dynamic sharding scheme

The disadvantage of the approach discussed so far is that the partition function is static, meaning that if certain nodes get a lot of traffic, it is not straightforward to move a shard from one node to another, since it requires a change to the application code.

An example can be found in the simple blogging application we have used so far. If a user attracts a lot of attention because she suddenly posts some very interesting articles, her shard will become very "hot." This will cause an imbalance between the shards, some shards becoming hot because their users gain fame while others become cold because of inactive users. If a lot of active users are on the same shard, the number of queries to the shard may increase to the extent that it is hard to answer all queries with an acceptable response time. The solution is to move users from hot shards to cold ones, but the current scheme offers no means to do that.

Dynamic sharding sets up your program to move shards between nodes in response to the traffic they get. To handle this, it is necessary to make some changes to the common database and add a table with information about the locations of shards. The most convenient place for this new information is the *user* table.

Example 5-11 shows the changed database with an added table named *shard_to_node* that maps each shard number to its node. The *user* table is extended with an extra column holding the shard where the user is located.

Example 5-11. Updated common database for dynamic sharding

```
CREATE TABLE user (
  user_id INT UNSIGNED AUTO_INCREMENT,
  name CHAR(50), password CHAR(50),
  shard INT UNSIGNED,
  PRIMARY KEY (user_id)
);

CREATE TABLE shard_to_node (
  shard INT UNSIGNED,
  host  CHAR(28),
  port  INT UNSIGNED,
  sock  CHAR(64),
  KEY (shard)
);
```

```
CREATE TABLE article_author (
  article_id INT UNSIGNED,
  user_id INT UNSIGNED,
  PRIMARY KEY (article_id)
);
```

To find the node location of the shard, you must change the PHP function that sends a query so it extracts the shard location from the *shard_to_node* table. The necessary changes are shown in Example 5-12. Notice that the array of nodes has disappeared and been replaced by a query to the *shard_to_node* table in the *common* database and that the function to compute the shard number now queries the *user* table to get the shard for the user.

Example 5-12. Changes to use the new dynamic sharding scheme

```
function shardNumber($userId, $common)
{
  $result = mysql_query("SELECT shard FROM user WHERE user_id = $userId", $common);
  $row = mysql_fetch_row($result);
  return $row[0];
}

function getShardAndNodeFromUserId($userId, $common)
{
  $shardNo = shardNumber($userId);
  $query = "SELECT host,port,sock FROM shard_to_node WHERE shard = %d";
  mysql_select_db("common", $common);
  $result = mysql_query(sprintf($query, $shardNo), $common);
  $row = mysql_fetch_row($result);
  $db_server = $row[0] == "localhost" ? ":{$row[2]}" : "{$row[0]}:{$row[1]}";
  $conn = mysql_connect($db_server, 'query_user');
  mysql_select_db("shard_$shardNo", $conn);
  return array($shardNo, $conn);
}
```

We've shown how to find a shard in a dynamic system, and the next step is to add code that moves shards to new nodes or uses new shards. This is the subject of the following section.

Rebalancing the shards

Moving from static to dynamic sharding gives us tools for balancing the system: namely, the ability to easily move shards between nodes and data between shards. You can use these methods as part of a resharding solution, that is, a complete rebalancing of your data across all shards.

Fortunately, moving an entire shard from one node to another is easy. The first step is to create a backup of the shard and restore it on another node. If each shard is represented as a database and you are using a storage engine that represents each database as a directory in the filesystem, there are several options for moving a shard.

Definitions of objects in a database are usually stored in the filesystem, but not all objects are stored in the directory. The exception is definitions of stored routines and events, which are stored in the *mysql* database, and depending on the storage engine, data in a database is not necessarily stored in the directory used for database information.

For that reason, check that moving a database by moving the directory really moves all objects and all data.

Various backup techniques are covered in Chapter 12, so we won't list them here. Note that when designing a solution, you don't want to tie the procedure to any specific backup method, since it might later turn out that other ways of creating the backup are more suitable.

To implement the backup procedure just described, it is necessary to have some technique to bring the shard offline, which means that it is necessary to somehow prevent updates to the shard. You can do this either by locking the shard in the application or by locking tables in the database.

Implementing locking in the application requires coordination of all requests so that there are no known conflicts, and since web applications are inherently distributed, lock management can become quite complicated very quickly.

In our case, we simplify the situation by locking a single table—the *shard_to_node* table —instead of spreading out the locks among the various tables accessed by many clients. Basically, all lookups for shard locations go through the *shard_to_node* table, so a single lock on this table ensures that no new updates to any shard will be started while we perform the move and remap the shards. It is possible that there are updates in progress that either have started to update the shard or are just about to start updating the shard. By locking the shard, any updates in progress will be allowed to finish and any updates that are about to start just wait for us to release the lock. When the lock on the shard is released, the shard will be gone, so the statements doing the update will fail and will have to be redone on the new shard.

You can use the Replicant library to automate this procedure (shown in Example 5-13).

Example 5-13. Procedure for moving a shard between nodes

```
_UPDATE_SHARD_MAP = """
UPDATE shard_to_node
   SET host = %s, port = %d, sock = %s
 WHERE shard = %d
"""

_LOCK_SHARD_MAP = """
BEGIN;
SELECT host, port, sock
  FROM shard_to_node
 WHERE shard = %d FOR UPDATE
"""
```

```
_UNLOCK_SHARD_MAP = "COMMIT"

def lock_shard(server, shard):
    server.use("common")
    server.sql(_LOCK_SHARD_MAP, (shard))

def unlock_shard(server):
    server.sql(_UNLOCK_SHARD_MAP)

def move_shard(common, shard, source, target, backup_method):
    backup_pos = backup_method.backup_to()
    config = target.fetch_config()
    config.set('replicate-do-db', shard)
    target.stop().replace_config(config).start()
    replicant.change_master(target, source, backup_pos)
    replicant.slave_start(target)

    # Wait until slave is at most 10 seconds behind master
    replicant.slave_status_wait_until(target,
                                      'Seconds_Behind_Master', lambda x: x < 10)
    lock_shard(common, shard)
    pos = replicant.fetch_master_pos(source)
    replicant.slave_wait_for_pos(target, pos)
    lock_database(target, shard_name)
    common.sql(_UPDATE_SHARD_MAP,
               (target.host, target.port, target.socket, shard))
    unlock_shard(common, shard)
    source.sql("DROP DATABASE shard_%s", (shard))
```

As described earlier, you have to keep in mind that even though the table is locked, some client sessions may be using the table because they have retrieved the node location but are not yet connected to it, or alternatively may have started updating the shard.

The application code has to take this into account. The easiest solution is to have the application recompute the node if the query to the shard fails. You can assume that a failure means the shard was recently moved and that it has to be looked up again. Example 5-14 shows the changes that are necessary to fix the getArticlesForUser function.

Example 5-14. Changes to application code to handle shard moving

```
function getArticlesForUser($userId, $common)
{
  global $QUERIES;
  $query = <<<END_OF_SQL
SELECT author_id, article_id, title, published, body
  FROM articles
 WHERE author_id = %d
END_OF_SQL;

  do {
    list($shard, $node) = getShardAndNodeFromUserId($userId, $common);
    $articles = array();
```

```
    $QUERIES[] = sprintf($query, $userId);
    $result = mysql_query(sprintf($query, $userId), $node);
  } while (!$result && mysql_errno($node) == 1146);
  while ($obj = mysql_fetch_object($result))
    $articles[] = $obj;
  return $articles;
}
```

Occasionally, as we saw in the previous section where a user suddenly became popular, it is necessary to move individual items of data between shards as well.

Moving a user is more complicated than moving a shard, because it requires extracting a user and all his associated articles and comments from a shard and reinstalling them in another shard. The technique is highly application-dependent, so the ideas we offer here are merely guidelines.

We'll present a technique for moving a user from a source shard to a target shard. The procedure is designed for a table that has row locks—such as InnoDB—so the procedure to move a user between MyISAM tables would handle locking differently. The corresponding Python code is straightforward, so we'll show only the SQL code.

If the source and target shards are located at the same node, moving the user is easily done using the following procedure. We assume that databases contain their shard numbers. We refer to the old and new shards by the placeholders *old* and *new* and to the user by *UserID*.

1. Lock the user row in the common database to block sessions that want to access that user.

   ```
   common> BEGIN;
   common> SELECT shard INTO @old_shard
        -> FROM common.user
        -> WHERE user_id = UserID FOR UPDATE;
   ```

2. Move the user articles and comments from the old shard to the new shard.

   ```
   shard> BEGIN;
   shard> INSERT INTO shard_new.articles
        ->     SELECT * FROM shard_old.articles
        ->      WHERE author_id = UserID
        ->     FOR UPDATE;
   shard> INSERT INTO shard_new.comments(comment_id, article_ref, author_name,
        ->                                 body, published)
        ->     SELECT comment_id, article_ref, author_name, body, published
        ->      FROM shard_old.comments, shard_old.articles
        ->      WHERE article_id = article_ref AND user_id = UserID;
   ```

3. Update the user information to point at the new shard.

   ```
   common> UPDATE common.user SET shard = new WHERE user_id = UserID;
   common> COMMIT;
   ```

4. Delete the user's articles and comments from the old shard.

```
shard> DELETE FROM shard_old.comments
    ->        USING shard_old.articles, shard_old.comments
    ->     WHERE article_ref = articles_id AND author_id = UserID;
shard> DELETE FROM shard_old.articles WHERE author_id = UserID;
shard> COMMIT;
```

In this case, it is necessary to keep two connections open: one for the node containing the common database and one for the node containing the shards. If the shards and the common database are on the same node, the problem is significantly simplified, but we cannot assume that.

If the shards are on different databases, the following procedure will solve the problem in a relatively straightforward way.

1. Create a backup of the articles and comments on the source node and, at the same time, get a binlog position corresponding to the backup.

   To do this, lock the rows for the user in both the *articles* and *comments* tables. Note that to do this, it is necessary to start a transaction similar to the one in which we updated the *shard_to_node* table when moving a shard, but here it is sufficient to block writes, not reads.

   ```
   shard_old> BEGIN;
   shard_old> SELECT * FROM articles, comments
           ->  WHERE article_ref = article_id AND author_id = UserID
           ->    FOR UPDATE;
   ```

2. Create a backup of the articles and comments.

   ```
   shard_old> SELECT * INTO OUTFILE 'UserID-articles.txt' FROM articles
           ->  WHERE author_id = UserID;
   shard_old> SELECT * INTO OUTFILE 'UserID-comments.txt' FROM comments
           ->  WHERE article_ref = article_id AND author_id = UserID;
   ```

3. Copy the saved articles and comments to the new node and write them to the new shard using LOAD DATA INFILE.

   ```
   shard_new> LOAD DATA INFILE 'UserID-articles.txt' INTO articles;
   shard_new> LOAD DATA INFILE 'UserID-comments.txt' INTO comments;
   ```

4. Update the shard location of the user in the common database.

   ```
   common> UPDATE user SET shard = new WHERE user_id = UserID;
   ```

5. Delete the user's articles and comments from the old shard in the same way as in the previous procedure.

   ```
   shard_old> DELETE FROM comments USING articles, comments
           ->     WHERE article_ref = articles_id AND author_id = UserID;
   shard_old> DELETE FROM articles WHERE author_id = UserID;
   shard_old> COMMIT;
   ```

Managing Consistency of Data

As discussed earlier in the chapter, one of the problems with asynchronous replication is managing consistency. To illustrate the problem, let's imagine you have an e-commerce site where customers can browse for items they want to purchase and put them in a cart. You've set up your servers so that when a user adds an item to the cart, the change request goes to the master, but when the web server requests information about the contents of the cart, the query goes to one of the slaves tasked with answering such queries. Since the master is ahead of the slave, it is possible that the change has not reached the slave yet, so a query to the slave will then find the cart empty. This will, of course, come as a big surprise to the customer, who will then promptly add the item to the cart again only to discover that the cart now contains *two* items, because this time the slave managed to catch up and replicate both changes to the cart. This situation clearly needs to be avoided or you will risk a bunch of irritated customers.

To avoid getting data that is too old, it is necessary to somehow ensure that the data provided by the slave is recent enough to be useful. As you will see, the problem becomes even trickier when a relay server is added to the mix. The basic idea of handling this is to somehow mark each transaction committed on the master, and then wait for the slave to reach that transaction (or later) before trying to execute a query on the slave.

The problem needs to be handled in different ways depending on whether there are any relay slaves between the master and the slave.

Consistency in a Nonhierarchal Deployment

When all the slaves are connected directly to the master, it is very easy to check for consistency. In this case, it is sufficient to record the binlog position after the transaction has been committed and then wait for the slave to reach this position using the previously introduced `MASTER_POS_WAIT` function. It is, however, not possible to get the exact position where a transaction was written in the binlog. Why? Because in the time between the commit of a transaction and the execution of `SHOW MASTER STATUS`, several events can be written to the binlog.

This does not matter, since in this case it is not necessary to get the exact binlog position where the transaction was written; it is sufficient to get a position that is *at or later than* the position of the transaction. Since the `SHOW MASTER STATUS` command will show the position where replication is currently writing events, executing this after the transaction has committed will be sufficient for getting a binlog position that can be used for checking consistency.

Example 5-15 shows the PHP code for processing an update to guarantee that the data presented is not stale.

Example 5-15. PHP code for avoiding read of stale data

```php
function fetch_master_pos($server) {
  $result = $server->query('SHOW MASTER STATUS');
  if ($result == NULL)
    return NULL;                          // Execution failed
  $row = $result->fetch_assoc();
  if ($row == NULL)
    return NULL;                          // No binlog enabled
  $pos = array($row['File'], $row['Position']);
  $result->close();
  return $pos;
}

function sync_with_master($master, $slave) {
  $pos = fetch_master_pos($master);
  if ($pos == NULL)
    return FALSE;
  if (!wait_for_pos($slave, $pos[0], $pos[1]))
    return FALSE;
  return TRUE;
}

function wait_for_pos($server, $file, $pos) {
  $result = $server->query("SELECT MASTER_POS_WAIT('$file', $pos)");
  if ($result == NULL)
    return FALSE;                         // Execution failed
  $row = $result->fetch_row();
  if ($row == NULL)
    return FALSE;                         // Empty result set ?!
  if ($row[0] == NULL || $row[0] < 0)
    return FALSE;                         // Sync failed
  $result->close();
  return TRUE;
}

function commit_and_sync($master, $slave) {
  if ($master->commit()) {
    if (!sync_with_master($master, $slave))
      return NULL;                        // Synchronization failed
    return TRUE;                          // Commit and sync succeeded
  }
  return FALSE;                           // Commit failed (no sync done)
}

function start_trans($server) {
  $server->autocommit(FALSE);
}
```

In Example 5-15, you see the functions commit_and_sync and start_trans together with the three support functions, fetch_master_pos, wait_for_pos, and sync_with_master. The commit_and_sync function commits a transaction and waits for it to reach a designated slave. It accepts two arguments, a connection object to a master and a connection object to the slave. The function will return TRUE if the commit and the sync succeeded,

FALSE if the commit failed, and NULL if the commit succeeded but the synchronization failed (either because there was an error in the slave or because the slave lost the master).

The function works by committing the current transaction and then, if that succeeds, fetching the current master binlog position through SHOW MASTER STATUS. Since other threads may have executed updates to the database between the commit and the call to SHOW MASTER STATUS, it is possible (even likely) that the position returned is not at the end of the transaction, but rather somewhere after where the transaction was written in the binlog. As mentioned earlier, this does not matter from an accuracy perspective, since the transaction will have been executed anyway when we reach this later position.

After fetching the binlog position from the master, the function proceeds by connecting to the slave and executing a wait for the master position using the MASTER_POS_WAIT function. If the slave is running, a call to this function will block and wait for the position to be reached, but if the slave is *not* running, NULL will be returned immediately. This is also what will happen if the slave stops while the function is waiting, for example, if an error occurs when the slave thread executes a statement. In either case, NULL indicates the transaction has not reached the slave, so it's important to check the result from the call. If MASTER_POS_WAIT returns 0, it means that the slave had already seen the transaction and therefore synchronization succeeds trivially.

To use these functions, it is sufficient to connect to the server as usual, but then use the functions to start, commit, and abort transactions. Example 5-16 shows examples of their use in context, but the error checking has been omitted since it is dependent on how errors are handled.

Example 5-16. Using the start_trans and commit_and_sync functions

```
require_once './database.inc';

start_trans($master);
$master->query('INSERT INTO t1 SELECT 2*a FROM t1');
commit_and_sync($master, $slave);
```

Consistency in a Hierarchal Deployment

Managing consistency in a hierarchal deployment is significantly different from managing consistency in a simple replication topology where each slave is connected directly to the master. Here, it is not possible to wait for a master position, since the positions are changed by every intermediate relay server. Instead, it is necessary to figure out another way to wait for the transactions. The MASTER_POS_WAIT function is quite handy when it comes to handling the wait, so if it were possible to use that function, it would solve a lot of problems. There are basically two alternatives that you can use to ensure you are not reading stale data.

The first solution is to rely on the global transaction ID introduced in Chapter 4 to handle slave promotions and to poll the slave repeatedly until it has processed the transaction.

The second solution, illustrated in Figure 5-11, connects to all the relay servers in the path from the master to the final slave to ensure the change propagates to the slave. It is necessary to connect to each relay slave between the master and the slave, since it is not possible to know which binlog position will be used on each of the relay servers.

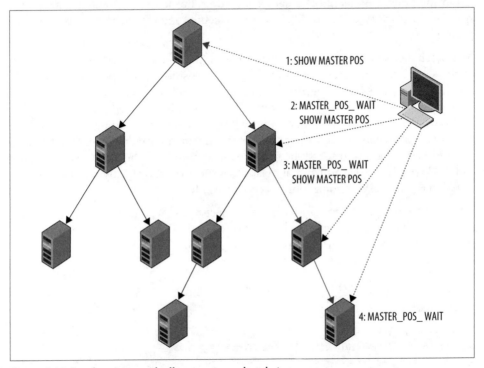

Figure 5-11. Synchronizing with all servers in a relay chain

Both solutions have their merits, so let's consider the advantages and disadvantages of each of them.

If the slaves are normally up-to-date with respect to the master, the first solution will perform a simple check of the final slave only and will usually show that the transaction has been replicated to the slave and that processing can proceed. If the transaction has not been processed yet, it is likely that it will be processed before the next check, so the second time the final slave is checked, it will show that the transaction has reached the slave. If the checking period is small enough, the delay will not be noticeable for the user, so a typical consistency check will require one or two extra messages when polling the final slave. This approach requires only the final slave to be polled, not any of the intermediate slaves. This can be an advantage from an administrative point as well, since it does not require keeping track of the intermediate slaves and how they are connected.

On the other hand, if the slaves normally lag behind, or if the replication lag varies a lot, the second approach is probably better. The first solution will repeatedly poll the slave, and most of the time will report that the transaction has *not* been committed on the slave. You can handle this by increasing the polling period, but if the polling period has to be so large that the response time is unacceptable, the first solution will not work well. In this case, it is better to use the second solution and wait for the changes to ripple down the replication tree and then execute the query.

For a tree of size N, the number of extra requests will then be proportional to $log\ N$. For instance, if you have 50 relay servers and each relay server handles 50 final slaves, you can handle all 2,500 slaves with exactly two extra requests: one to the relay slave and then one to the final slave.

The disadvantages of the second approach are:

- It requires the application code to have access to the relay slaves so that they can connect to each relay slave in turn and wait for the position to be reached.

- It requires the application code to keep track of the architecture of your replication so that the relay servers can be queried.

Querying the relay slaves will slow them down, since they have to handle more work, but in practice, this might turn out not to be a problem. By introducing a caching database connection layer, you can avoid some of the traffic. The caching layer will remember the binlog position each time a request is made and query the relay only if the binlog position is greater than the cached one. The following is a rough stub for the caching function:

```
function wait_for_pos($server, $wait_for_pos) {
  if (cached position for $server > $wait_for_pos)
    return TRUE;
  else {
    code to wait for position and update cache
  }
}
```

Since the binlog positions are always increasing—once a binlog position is passed it remains passed—there is no risk of returning an incorrect result. The only way to know for sure which technique is more efficient is to monitor and profile the deployment to make sure queries are executed fast enough for the application.

Example 5-17 shows sample code to handle the first solution—querying the slave repeatedly to see whether the transaction has been executed. This code uses the *Last_Exec_Trans* table introduced in Chapter 4 by checking it on the master, and then repeatedly reading the table on the slave until it finds the correct transaction.

Example 5-17. PHP code for avoiding read of stale data using polling

```php
function fetch_trans_id($server) {
  $result = $server->query('SELECT server_id, trans_id FROM Last_Exec_Trans');
  if ($result == NULL)
    return NULL;                          // Execution failed
  $row = $result->fetch_assoc();
  if ($row == NULL)
    return NULL;                          // Empty table !?
  $gid = array($row['server_id'], $row['trans_id']);
  $result->close();
  return $gid;
}

function wait_for_trans_id($server, $server_id, $trans_id) {
  if ($server_id == NULL || $trans_id == NULL)
    return TRUE;        // No transactions executed, trivially in sync

  $server->autocommit(TRUE);
  $gid = fetch_trans_id($server);
  if ($gid == NULL)
    return FALSE;
  list($current_server_id, $current_trans_id) = $gid;
  while ($current_server_id != $server_id || $current_trans_id < $trans_id) {
    usleep(500000);                       // Wait half a second
    $gid = fetch_trans_id($server);
    if ($gid == NULL)
      return FALSE;
    list($current_server_id, $current_trans_id) = $gid;
  }
  return TRUE;
}

function commit_and_sync($master, $slave) {
  if ($master->commit()) {
    $gid = fetch_trans_id($master);
    if ($gid == NULL)
      return NULL;
    if (!wait_for_trans_id($slave, $gid[0], $gid[1]))
      return NULL;
    return TRUE;
  }
  return FALSE;
}

function start_trans($server) {
  $server->autocommit(FALSE);
}
```

The two functions commit_and_sync and start_trans behave the same way as in Example 5-15, and can therefore be used in the same way as in Example 5-16. The difference is that the functions in 5-17 internally call fetch_trans_id and wait_for_trans_id instead of fetch_master_pos and wait_for_pos. Some points worth noting in the code:

- We turn off autocommit in `wait_for_trans_id` before starting to query the slave. This is necessary because if the isolation level is `repeatable read` or stricter, the select will find the same global transaction ID every time.

- To prevent this, we commit each `SELECT` as a separate transaction by turning on autocommit. An alternative is to use the `read committed` isolation level.

- To avoid unnecessary sleeps in `wait_for_trans_id`, we fetch the global transaction ID and check it once before entering the loop.

- This code requires access only to the master and slave, not to the intermediate relay servers.

Example 5-18 includes code for ensuring you do not read stale data. It uses the technique of querying all servers between the master and the final slave. This method proceeds by first finding the entire chain of servers between the final slave and the master, and then synchronizing each in turn all the way down the chain until the transaction reaches the final slave. The code reuses the `fetch_master_pos` and `wait_for_pos` from Example 5-13, so they are not repeated here. The code does not implement any caching layer.

Example 5-18. PHP code for avoiding reading stale data using waiting

```php
function fetch_relay_chain($master, $final) {
  $servers = array();
  $server = $final;
  while ($server !== $master) {
    $server = get_master_for($server);
    $servers[] = $server;
  }
  $servers[] = $master;
  return $servers;
}

function commit_and_sync($master, $slave) {
  if ($master->commit()) {
    $server = fetch_relay_chain($master, $slave);
    for ($i = sizeof($server) - 1; $i > 1 ; --$i) {
      if (!sync_with_master($server[$i], $server[$i-1]))
        return NULL;                          // Synchronization failed
    }
  }
}

function start_trans($server) {
  $server->autocommit(FALSE);
}
```

To find all the servers between the master and the slave, we use the function `fetch_relay_chain`. It starts from the slave and uses the function `get_master_for` to get the master for a slave. We have deliberately not included the code for this function, since it does not add anything to our current discussion. However, this function has to be defined for the code to work.

After the relay chain is fetched, the code synchronizes the master with its slave all the way down the chain. This is done with the `sync_with_master` function, which was introduced in Example 5-15.

 One way to fetch the master for a server is to use `SHOW SLAVE STATUS` and read the `Master_Host` and `Master_Port` fields. If you do this for each transaction you are about to commit, however, the system will be very slow.

Since the topology rarely changes, it is better to cache the information on the application servers, or somewhere else, to avoid excessive traffic to the database servers.

In Chapter 4, you saw how to handle the failure of a master by, for example, failing over to another master or promoting a slave to be a master. We also mentioned that once the master is repaired, you need to bring it back to the deployment. The master is a critical component of a deployment and is likely to be a more powerful machine than the slaves, so you should restore it to the master position when bringing it back. Since the master stopped unexpectedly, it is very likely to be out of sync with the rest of the deployment. This can happen in two ways:

- If the master has been offline for more than just a short time, the rest of the system will have committed many transactions that the master is not aware of. In a sense, the master is in an *alternative future* compared to the rest of the system. An illustration of this situation is shown in Figure 5-12.
- If the master committed a transaction and wrote it to the binary log, then crashed just after it acknowledged the transaction, the transaction may not have made it to the slaves. This means the master has one or more transactions that have not been seen by the slaves, nor by any other part of the system.

If the original master is not too far behind the current master, the easiest solution to the first problem is to connect the original master as a slave to the current master, and then switch over all slaves to the master once it has caught up. If, however, the original master has been offline for a significant period, it is likely to be faster to clone one of the slaves and then switch over all the slaves to the master.

If the master is in an alternative future, it is not likely that its extra transactions should be brought into the deployment. Why? Because the sudden appearance of a new transaction is likely to conflict with existing transactions in subtle ways. For example, if the transaction is a message in a message board, it is likely that a user has already recommitted the message. If a message written earlier but reported as missing—because the master crashed before the message was sent to a slave—suddenly reappears, it will befuddle the users and definitely be considered an annoyance. In a similar manner,

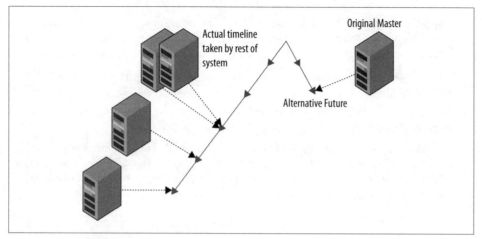

Figure 5-12. Original master in an alternative future

users will not look kindly on shopping carts suddenly having items added because the master was brought back into the system.

In short, you can solve both of the out-of-sync problems—the master in an alternative future and the master that needs to catch up—by simply cloning a slave to the original master and then switching over each of the current slaves in turn to the original master.

These problems, however, highlight how important it is to ensure consistency by checking that changes to a master are available on some other system before reporting the transaction as complete, in the event that the master should crash. The code that we have discussed in this chapter assumes that a user will try to read the data immediately, and therefore checks that it has reached the slave before a read query is carried out on the server. From a recovery perspective, this is excessive: it is sufficient to ensure the transaction is available on at least one other machine, for example on one of the slaves or relay servers connected to the master. In general, you can tolerate $n-1$ failures if you have the change available on n servers.

Conclusion

In this chapter, we looked at techniques to increase the throughput of your applications by scaling out, whereby we introduced more servers to handle more requests for data. We presented ways to set up MySQL for scaling out using replication and gave practical examples of some of the concepts. In the next chapter, we will look at some more advanced replication concepts.

A rap on Joel's door drew his attention to Mr. Summerson standing in his doorway. "I like your report on scaling out our servers, Joel. I want you to get started on that right away. Use some of those surplus servers we have down in the computer room."

Joel was happy he had decided to send his boss a proposal first. "Yes, sir. When do we need these online?"

Mr. Summerson smiled and glanced at his watch. "It's not quitting time yet," he said and walked away.

Joel wasn't sure whether he was joking or not, so he decided to get started right away. He picked up his now-well-thumbed copy of *MySQL High Availability* and his notes and headed to the computer room. "I hope I set the TiVo," he muttered, knowing this was going to be a late night.

## CHAPTER 6

Advanced Replication

A knock on his door drew Joel's attention away from reading his email. He wasn't surprised to see Mr. Summerson standing in his doorway.

"Yes, sir?"

"I am getting a little concerned about all this replication stuff we've got now. I'd like you to do some research into what we need to do to improve our knowledge of how it all works. I want you to put together a document explaining not only the current configuration, but also troubleshooting ideas with specific details on what to do when things go wrong and what makes it tick."

Joel was expecting such a task. He, too, was starting to be concerned that he needed to know more about replication. "I'll get right on it, sir."

"Great. Take your time on this one. I want to get it right."

Joel nodded as his boss walked away. He sighed and gathered his favorite MySQL books together. He needed to do some reading on the finer points of replication.

Previous chapters introduced the basics of configuring and deploying replication to keep your site up and available, but to understand replication's potential pitfalls and how to use it effectively, you should know something about its operation and the kinds of information it uses to accomplish its tasks. This is the goal of this chapter. We will cover a lot of ground, including:

- How to promote slaves to masters more robustly
- Tips for avoiding corrupted databases after a crash
- Multisource replication
- Row-based replication

Replication Architecture Basics

Chapter 3 discussed the binary log along with some of the tools that are available to investigate the events it records. But we didn't describe how events make it over to the slave and get reexecuted there. Once you understand these details, you can exert more control over replication, prevent it from causing corruption after a crash, and investigate problems by examining the logs.

Figure 6-1 shows a schematic illustration of the internal replication architecture, consisting of the clients connected to the master, the master itself, and several slaves. For each client that connects to the master, the server runs a *session* that is responsible for executing all SQL statements and sending results back to the client.

The events flow through the replication system from the master to the slaves in the following manner:

1. The session accepts a statement from the client, executes the statement, and synchronizes with other sessions to ensure each transaction is executed without conflicting with other changes made by other sessions.

2. Just before the statement finishes execution, an entry consisting of one or more events is written to the binary log. This process is covered in Chapter 2 and will not be described again in this chapter.

3. After the events have been written to the binary log, a *dump thread* in the master takes over, reads the events from the binary log, and sends them over to the slave's I/O thread.

4. When the slave I/O thread receives the event, it writes it to the end of the relay log.

5. Once in the relay log, a *slave SQL thread* reads the event from the relay log and executes the event to apply the changes to the database on the slave.

If the connection to the master is lost, the slave I/O thread will try to reconnect to the server in the same way that any MySQL client thread does. Some of the options that we'll see in this chapter deal with reconnection attempts.

The Structure of the Relay Log

As the previous section shows, the relay log is the information that ties the master and slave together—the heart of replication. It's important to be aware of how it is used and how the slave threads coordinate through it. Therefore, we'll go through the details here of how the relay log is structured and how the slave threads use the relay log to handle replication.

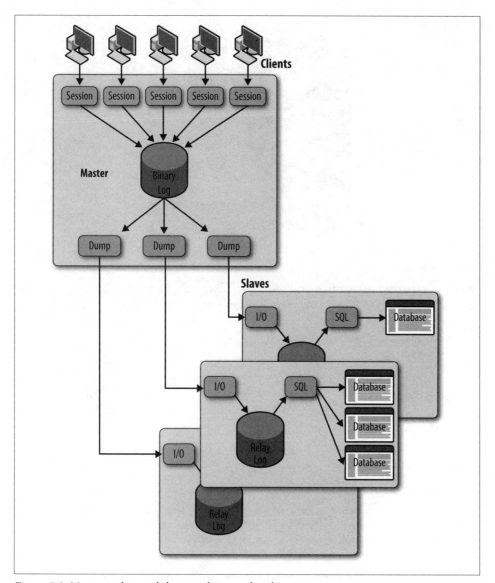

Figure 6-1. Master and several slaves with internal architecture

As described in the previous section, the events sent from the master are stored in the relay log by the I/O thread. The relay log serves as a buffer so that the master does not have to wait for the slave execution to finish before sending the next event.

Figure 6-2 shows a schematic view of the relay log. It's similar in structure to the binlog on the master but has some extra files.

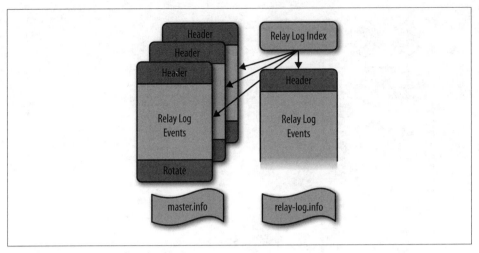

Figure 6-2. Structure of the relay log

In addition to the content files and the index files in the binary log, the relay log also maintains two files to keep track of replication progress: the *relay log information file* and the *master log information file*. The names of these two files are controlled by two options in the *my.cnf* file:

`relay-log-info-file=`*filename*
> This option sets the name of the relay log information file. It is also available as the read-only server variable `relay_log_info_file`. Unless an absolute filename is given, the filename is relative to the data directory of the server. The default filename is *relay-log.info*.

`master-info-file=`*filename*
> This option sets the name of the master log information file. The default filename is *master.info*.

 The information in the *master.info* file takes precedence over information in the *my.cnf* file. This means that if you change information in the *my.cnf* file and restart the server, the information will still be read from the *master.info* file instead of from the *my.cnf* file.

For this reason, the recommendation is *not* to put any of the options that can be specified with the `CHANGE MASTER TO` command in the *my.cnf* file, but instead to use the `CHANGE MASTER TO` command to configure replication. If, for some reason, you want to put any of the replication options in the *my.cnf* file and you want to make sure that the options are read from it when starting the slave, you have to issue `RESET SLAVE` before editing the *my.cnf* file.

Beware when executing `RESET SLAVE`! It will delete the *master.info* file, the *relay-log.info* file, and *all the relay logfiles*!

For convenience, we will use the default names of the information files in the discussion that follows.

The *master.info* file contains the master read position as well as all the information necessary to connect to the master and start replication. When the slave I/O thread starts up, it reads information from this file, if it is available.

Example 6-1 shows a short example of a *master.info* file. We've added a line number before each line and an annotation in italics at the end of each line (the file itself cannot contain comments). If the server is not compiled with SSL support, lines 9 through 15—which contain all the SSL options—will be missing. Example 6-1 shows what these options look like when SSL is compiled. The SSL fields are covered later in the chapter.

> The password is written unencrypted in the *master.info* file. For that reason, it is critical to protect the file so it can be read only by the MySQL server. The standard way to ensure this is to define a dedicated user on the server to run the server, assign all the files responsible for replication and database maintenance to this user, and remove all permissions from the files except read and write by this user.

Example 6-1. Contents of the master.info file (MySQL version 5.1.16 with SSL support)

```
1    15                            Number of lines in the file
2    master1-bin.000032            Current binlog file being read (Master_Log_File)
3    475774                        Last binlog position read (Read_Master_Log_Pos)
4    master1.example.com           Master host connected to (Master_Host)
5    repl_user                     Replication user (Master_User)
6    xyzzy                         Replication password
7    3306                          Master port used (Master_Port)
8    1                             Number of times slave will try to reconnect (Connect_Retry)
9    1                             1 if SSL is enabled, otherwise 0
10                                 SSL Certification Authority (CA)
11   /etc/ssl/certs                SSL CA Path
12   /etc/ssl/certs/slave.pem      SSL Certificate
13                                 SSL Cipher
14   /etc/ssl/private/slave.key    SSL Key
15   0                             SSL Verify Server Certificate (5.1.16 and later)
```

> If you have an old server, the format can be slightly different.
>
> In MySQL versions earlier than 4.1, the first line did not appear. Developers added a line count to the file in version 4.1.1 so they could extend the file with new fields and detect which fields are supported by just checking the line count.
>
> Version 5.1.16 introduced the last line, *SSL Verify Server Certificate*.

The *relay-log.info* file tracks the progress of replication and is updated by the SQL thread. Example 6-2 shows a sample excerpt of a *relay-log.info* file. These lines correspond to the beginning of the next event to execute.

Example 6-2. Contents of the relay-log.info file

`./slave-relay-bin.000003`	*Relay log file (Relay_Log_File)*
`380`	*Relay log position (Relay_Log_Pos)*
`master1-bin.000001`	*Master log file (Relay_Master_Log_File)*
`234`	*Master log position (Exec_Master_Log_Pos)*

If any of the files are not available, they will be created from information in the *my.cnf* file and the options given to the `CHANGE MASTER TO` command *when the slave is started.*

 It is *not* enough to just configure a slave using *my.cnf* and execute a `CHANGE MASTER TO` statement. The relay logfiles, the *master.info* file, and the *relay-log.info* file are *not* created until you issue `START SLAVE`.

The Replication Threads

As you saw earlier in the chapter, replication requires several specialized threads on both the master and the slave. The dump thread on the master handles the master's end of replication. Two slave threads—the I/O thread and the SQL thread—handle replication on the slave.

Master dump thread

This thread is created on the master when a slave I/O thread connects. The dump thread is responsible for reading entries from the binlog on the master and sending them to the slave.

There is one dump thread per connected slave.

Slave I/O thread

This thread connects to the master to request a dump of all the changes that occur and writes them to the relay log for further processing by the SQL thread.

There is one I/O thread on each slave. Once the connection is established, it is kept open so that any changes on the master are immediately received by the slave.

Slave SQL thread

This thread reads changes from the relay log and applies them to the slave database. The thread is responsible for coordinating with other MySQL threads to ensure changes do not interfere with the other activities going on in the MySQL server.

From the perspective of the master, the I/O thread is just another client thread and can execute both dump requests and SQL statements on the master. This means a client can connect to a server and pretend to be a slave to get the master to dump changes from the binary log. This is how the `mysqlbinlog` program (covered in detail in Chapter 3) operates.

The SQL thread acts as a session when working with the database. This means it maintains state information similar to that of a session, but with some differences. Since the

SQL thread has to process changes from several different threads on the master—the events from *all* threads on the master are written in commit order to the binary log— the SQL thread keeps some extra information to distinguish events properly. For example, temporary tables are session-specific, so to keep temporary tables from different sessions separated, the session ID is added to the events. The SQL thread then refers to the session ID to keep actions for different sessions on the master separate.

The details of how the SQL thread executes events are covered later in the chapter.

> The I/O thread is significantly faster than the SQL thread because the I/O thread merely writes events to a log, whereas the SQL thread has to figure out how to execute changes against the databases. Therefore, during replication, several events are usually buffered in the relay log. If the master crashes, you have to handle these before connecting to a new master.
>
> To avoid losing these events, wait for the SQL thread to catch up before trying to reconnect the slave to another master.
>
> Later in the chapter, you will see several ways of detecting whether the relay log is empty or has events left to execute.

Starting and Stopping the Slave Threads

In Chapter 2, you saw how to start the slave using the START SLAVE command, but a lot of details were glossed over. We're now ready for a more thorough description of starting and stopping the slave threads.

When the server starts, it will also start the slave threads if there is a *master.info* file. As mentioned earlier in this chapter, the *master.info* file is created if the server was set up for replication by configuring the server for replication and issuing a START SLAVE command to start the slave threads, so if the previous session had been used to replicate, replication will be resumed from the last position stored in the *master.info* and *relay-log.info* files, with slightly different behavior for the two slave threads.

Slave I/O thread
    The slave I/O thread will resume by reading from the last read position according to the *master.info* file.

    For writing the events, the I/O thread will rotate the relay logfile and start writing to a new file, updating the positions accordingly.

Slave SQL thread
    The slave SQL thread will resume reading from the relay log position given in *relay-log.info*.

You can start the slave threads explicitly using the START SLAVE command and stop them explicitly with the STOP SLAVE command. These commands control the slave threads and can be used to stop and start the I/O thread or SQL thread separately.

START SLAVE *and* STOP SLAVE
>   These will start or stop both the I/O and the slave thread.

START SLAVE IO_THREAD *and* STOP SLAVE IO_THREAD
>   These will start or stop only the I/O thread.

START SLAVE SQL_THREAD *and* STOP SLAVE SQL_THREAD
>   These will start or stop only the SQL thread.

When you stop the slave threads, the current state of replication is saved to the *master.info* and *relay-log.info* files. This information is then picked up when the slave threads are started again.

>   If you specify a master host using the master-host option (which can be either in the *my.cnf* file or passed as an option when starting mysqld), the slave will also start.
>
>   Since the recommendation is not to use this option, but instead to use the MASTER_HOST option to the CHANGE MASTER command, the master-host option will not be covered here.

Running Replication over the Internet

There are many reasons to replicate between two geographically separated data centers. One reason is to ensure you can recover from a disaster such as an earthquake or a power outage. You can also locate a site strategically close to some of your users, such as content delivery networks, to offer them faster response times. Although organizations with enough resources can lease dedicated fiber, we will assume you use the open Internet to connect.

The events sent from the master to the slave should never be considered secure in any way: as a matter of fact, it is easy to decode them to see the information that is replicated. As long as you are behind a firewall and do not replicate over the Internet—for example, replicating between two data centers—this is probably secure enough, but as soon you need to replicate to another data center in another town or on another continent, it is important to protect the information from prying eyes by encrypting it.

The standard method for encrypting data for transfer over the Internet is to use SSL. There are several options for protecting your data, all of which involve SSL in some way:

- Use the support that is built into the server to encrypt the replication from master to slave.
- Use Stunnel, a program that establishes an SSL tunnel (essentially a virtual private network) to a program that lacks SSL support.
- Use ssh in tunnel mode.

This last alternative does not appear to really offer any significant advantages over using Stunnel, but can be useful if you are not allowed to install any new programs on a machine and can enable ssh on your servers. In that case, you can use ssh to set up a tunnel. We will not cover this option further.

When using either the built-in SSL support or `stunnel` for creating a secure connection, you need:

- A certificate from a certification authority (CA)
- A (public) certificate for the server
- A (private) key for the server

The details of generating, managing, and using SSL certificates is beyond the scope of this book, but for demonstration purposes, Example 6-3 shows how to generate a self-signed public certificate and associated private key. This example assumes you use the configuration file for OpenSSL in */etc/ssl/openssl.cnf*.

Example 6-3. Generating a self-signed public certificate with a private key

```
$ sudo openssl req -new -x509 -days 365 -nodes -config /etc/ssl/openssl.cnf \
>     -out /etc/ssl/certs/master.pem -keyout /etc/ssl/private/master.key
Generating a 1024 bit RSA private key
.....++++++
.++++++
writing new private key to '/etc/ssl/private/master.key'
-----
You are about to be asked to enter information that will be incorporated
into your certificate request.
What you are about to enter is what is called a Distinguished Name or a DN.
There are quite a few fields but you can leave some blank
For some fields there will be a default value,
If you enter '.', the field will be left blank.
-----
Country Name (2 letter code) [AU]:SE
State or Province Name (full name) [Some-State]:Uppland
Locality Name (eg, city) []:Storvreta
Organization Name (eg, company) [Internet Widgits Pty Ltd]:Big Inc.
Organizational Unit Name (eg, section) []:Database Management
Common Name (eg, YOUR name) []:master-1.example.com
Email Address []:mats@example.com
```

The certificate signing procedure puts a self-signed public certificate in */etc/ssl/certs/master.pem* and the private key in */etc/ssl/private/master.key* (which is also used to sign the public certificate).

On the slave, you have to create a server key and a server certificate in a similar manner. For the sake of discussion, we'll use */etc/ssl/certs/slave.pem* as the name of the slave server's public certificate and */etc/ssl/private/slave.key* as the name of the slave server's private key.

Setting Up Secure Replication Using Built-in Support

The simplest way to encrypt the connection between the master and slave is to use a server with SSL support. Methods for compiling a server with SSL support are beyond the scope of this book: if you are interested, please consult the online reference manual.

To use the built-in SSL support, it is necessary to do the following:

- Configure the master by making the master keys available.
- Configure the slave to encrypt the replication channel.

To configure the master to use SSL support, add the following options to the *my.cnf* file:

```
[mysqld]
ssl-capath=/etc/ssl/certs
ssl-cert=/etc/ssl/certs/master.pem
ssl-key=/etc/ssl/private/master.key
```

The `ssl-capath` option contains the name of a directory that holds the certificates of trusted CAs, the `ssl-cert` option contains the name of the file that holds the server certificate, and the `ssl-key` option contains the name of the file that holds the private key for the server. As always, you need to restart the server after you have updated the *my.cnf* file.

The master is now configured to provide SSL support to any client, and since a slave uses the normal client protocol, it will allow a slave to use SSL as well.

To configure the slave to use an SSL connection, issue `CHANGE MASTER TO` with the `MASTER_SSL` option to turn on SSL for the connection, then issue `MASTER_SSL_CAPATH`, `MASTER_SSL_CERT`, and `MASTER_SSL_KEY`, which function like the `ssl-capath`, `ssl-cert`, and `ssl-key` configuration options just mentioned, but specify the slave's side of the connection to the master.

```
slave> CHANGE MASTER TO
    ->     MASTER_HOST = 'master-1',
    ->     MASTER_USER = 'repl_user',
    ->     MASTER_PASSWORD = 'xyzzy',
    ->     MASTER_SSL_CAPATH = '/etc/ssl/certs',
    ->     MASTER_SSL_CERT = '/etc/ssl/certs/slave.pem',
    ->     MASTER_SSL_KEY = '/etc/ssl/private/slave.key';
Query OK, 0 rows affected (0.00 sec)

slave> START SLAVE;
Query OK, 0 rows affected (0.15 sec)
```

Now you have a slave running with a secure channel to the master.

Setting Up Secure Replication Using Stunnel

Stunnel is an easy-to-use SSL tunneling application that you can set up either as an SSL server or as an SSL client.

Using Stunnel to set up a secure connection is almost as easy as setting up an SSL connection using the built-in support, but requires some additional configuration. This approach can be useful if the server is not compiled with SSL support or if for some reason you want to offload the extra processing required to encrypt and decrypt data from the MySQL server (which makes sense only if you have a multicore CPU).

As with the built-in support, you need to have a certificate from a CA as well as a public certificate and a private key for each server. These are then used for the `stunnel` command instead of for the server.

Figure 6-3 shows a master, a slave, and two Stunnel instances that communicate over an insecure network. One Stunnel instance on the slave server accepts data over a standard MySQL client connection from the slave server, encrypts it, and sends it over to the Stunnel instance on the master server. The Stunnel instance on the master server, in turn, listens on a dedicated SSL port to receive the encrypted data, decrypts it, and sends it over a client connection to the non-SSL port on the master server.

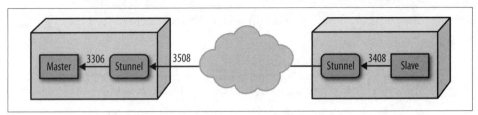

Figure 6-3. Replication over an insecure channel using Stunnel

Example 6-4 shows a configuration file that sets up Stunnel to listen on socket 3508 for an SSL connection, where the master server is listening on the default MySQL socket 3306. The example refers to the certificate and key files by the names we used earlier.

Example 6-4. Master server configuration file /etc/stunnel/master.conf

```
cert=/etc/ssl/certs/master.pem
key=/etc/ssl/private/master.key
CApath=/etc/ssl/certs
[mysqlrepl]
accept = 3508
connect = 3306
```

Example 6-5 shows the configuration file that sets up Stunnel on the client side. The example assigns port 3408 as the intermediate port—the non-SSL port that the slave will connect to locally—and Stunnel connects to the SSL port 3508 on the master server, as shown in Example 6-4.

Example 6-5. Slave server configuration file /etc/stunnel/slave.conf

```
cert=/etc/ssl/certs/slave.pem
key=/etc/ssl/private/slave.key
CApath=/etc/ssl/certs
```

```
[mysqlrepl]
accept = 3408
connect = master-1:3508
```

You can now start the Stunnel program on each server and configure the slave to connect to the Stunnel instance on the slave server. Since the Stunnel instance is on the same server as the slave, you should give localhost as the master host to connect to and the port that the Stunnel instance accepts connections on (3408). Stunnel will then take care of tunneling the connection over to the master server.

```
slave> CHANGE MASTER TO
    ->     MASTER_HOST = 'localhost',
    ->     MASTER_PORT = 3408,
    ->     MASTER_USER = 'repl_user',
    ->     MASTER_PASSWORD = 'xyzzy';
Query OK, 0 rows affected (0.00 sec)

slave> START SLAVE;
Query OK, 0 rows affected (0.15 sec)
```

You now have a secure connection set up over an insecure network.

> If you are using Debian-based Linux (for example, Debian or Ubuntu), you can start one Stunnel instance for each configuration file in the */etc/ stunnel* directory by setting ENABLED=1 in */etc/default/stunnel4*.
>
> So if you create the Stunnel configuration files as given in this section, one slave Stunnel and one master Stunnel instance will be started automatically whenever you start the machine.

Finer-Grained Control over Replication

With an understanding of replication internals and the information replication uses, you can control it more expertly and learn how to avoid some problems that can occur. We'll give you some useful background in this section.

Information About Replication Status

You can find most of the information about replication status on the slave, but there is some information available on the master as well. Most of the information on the master relates to the binlog (covered in Chapter 3), but information relating to the connected slaves is also available.

The SHOW SLAVE HOSTS command only shows information about slaves that use the report-host option, which the slave uses to give information to the master about the server that is connected. The master cannot trust the information about the connected slaves, since there are routers with NAT between the master and the slave. In addition to the hostname, there are some other options that you can use to provide information about the connecting slave:

report-host

    The name of the connecting slave. This is typically the domain name of the slave, or some other similar identifier, but can in reality be any string. In Example 6-6, we use the name "Magic Slave."

report-port

    The port on which the slave listens for connections. This default is 3306.

report-user

    This is the user for connecting to the master. The value given does not have to match the value used in CHANGE MASTER TO. This option is only shown when the show-slave-auth-info option is given to the server.

report-password

    This is the password used when connecting to the master. The password given does not have to match the password given to CHANGE MASTER TO.

show-slave-auth-info

    If this option is enabled, the master will show the additional information about the reported user and password in the output from SHOW SLAVE HOSTS.

Example 6-6 shows sample output from SHOW SLAVE HOSTS where three slaves are connected to the master.

Example 6-6. Sample output from SHOW SLAVE HOSTS

```
master> SHOW SLAVE HOSTS;
+-----------+-------------+------+--------------------+-----------+
| Server_id | Host        | Port | Rpl_recovery_rank  | Master_id |
+-----------+-------------+------+--------------------+-----------+
|         2 | slave-1     | 3306 |                  0 |         1 |
|         3 | slave-2     | 3306 |                  0 |         1 |
|         4 | Magic Slave | 3306 |                  0 |         1 |
+-----------+-------------+------+--------------------+-----------+
1 row in set (0.00 sec)
```

The output shows slaves that are connected to the master and some information about the slaves. Notice that this display also shows slaves that are indirectly connected to the master via relays. There are two additional fields shown when show-slave-auth-info is enabled (which we do not show here).

The following fields are purely informational and do not necessarily show the real slave host or port, nor the user and password used when configuring the slave in CHANGE MASTER TO:

Server_id

    This is the server ID of the connected slave.

Host

    This is the name of the host as given by **report-host**.

User

    This is the username reported by the slave by using **report-user**.

Password

    This column shows the password reported by the slave using **report-password**.

Port

    This shows the port.

Master_id

    This shows the server ID that the slave is replicating from.

Rpl_recovery_rank

    This field has never been used and is removed in MySQL version 5.5.

> The information about indirectly connected slaves cannot be entirely trusted, since it is possible for the information to be inaccurate in certain situations where slaves are being added.
>
> For this reason, there is an effort underway to remove this information and show only directly connected slaves, since this information can be trusted.

You can use the SHOW MASTER LOGS command to see which logs the master is keeping track of in the binary log. A typical output from this command can be seen in Example 6-7.

Example 6-7. Typical output from SHOW MASTER LOGS

```
master> SHOW MASTER LOGS;
+-------------------+-----------+
| Log_name          | File_size |
+-------------------+-----------+
| master-bin.000011 |    469768 |
| master-bin.000012 |   1254768 |
| master-bin.000013 |    474768 |
| master-bin.000014 |      4768 |
+-------------------+-----------+
1 row in set (0.00 sec)
```

The SHOW MASTER STATUS command (shown in Example 6-8) shows where the next event will be written in the binary log. Since a master has only a single binlog file, the table will always contain only a single line. And because of that, the last line of the output of SHOW MASTER LOGS will match the output of this command, only with different headers. This means that if you need to execute a SHOW MASTER LOGS to implement some feature, you do not need to execute a SHOW MASTER STATUS as well but can instead use the last line of SHOW MASTER LOGS.

Example 6-8. Typical output from SHOW MASTER STATUS

```
master> SHOW MASTER STATUS;
+--------------------+----------+--------------+------------------+
| File               | Position | Binlog_Do_DB | Binlog_Ignore_DB |
+--------------------+----------+--------------+------------------+
| master-bin.000014  |     4768 |              |                  |
+--------------------+----------+--------------+------------------+
1 row in set (0.00 sec)
```

To determine the status for the slave threads, use the SHOW SLAVE STATUS command. This command contains almost everything you need to know about the replication status. Let's go through the output in more detail. A typical output from SHOW SLAVE STATUS is given in Example 6-9.

Example 6-9. Sample output from SHOW SLAVE STATUS

```
              Slave_IO_State: Waiting for master to send event
                 Master_Host: master1.example.com
                 Master_User: repl_user
                 Master_Port: 3306
               Connect_Retry: 1
             Master_Log_File: master-bin.000001
         Read_Master_Log_Pos: 192
              Relay_Log_File: slave-relay-bin.000006
               Relay_Log_Pos: 252
       Relay_Master_Log_File: master-bin.000001
            Slave_IO_Running: Yes
           Slave_SQL_Running: Yes
             Replicate_Do_DB:
         Replicate_Ignore_DB:
          Replicate_Do_Table:
      Replicate_Ignore_Table:
     Replicate_Wild_Do_Table:
 Replicate_Wild_Ignore_Table:
                  Last_Errno: 0
                  Last_Error:
                Skip_Counter: 0
         Exec_Master_Log_Pos: 192
             Relay_Log_Space: 553
             Until_Condition: None
              Until_Log_File:
               Until_Log_Pos: 0
           Master_SSL_Allowed: No
           Master_SSL_CA_File:
           Master_SSL_CA_Path:
              Master_SSL_Cert:
            Master_SSL_Cipher:
               Master_SSL_Key:
        Seconds_Behind_Master: 0
Master_SSL_Verify_Server_Cert: No
               Last_IO_Errno: 0
               Last_IO_Error:
              Last_SQL_Errno: 0
              Last_SQL_Error:
```

The state of the I/O and SQL threads

The two fields `Slave_IO_Running` and `Slave_SQL_Running` indicate whether the slave I/O thread or the SQL thread, respectively, is running. If the slave threads are not running, it could be either because they have been stopped or because of an error in the replication.

If the I/O thread is not running, the fields `Last_IO_Errno` and `Last_IO_Error` will show the reason it stopped. Similarly, `Last_SQL_Errno` and `Last_SQL_Error` will show the reason why the SQL thread stopped. If either of the threads stopped without error, for example because they were explicitly stopped or reached the `until` condition, there will be no error message and the `errno` field will be 0, similar to the output in Example 6-9. The fields `Last_Errno` and `Last_Error` are synonyms for `Last_SQL_Errno` and `Last_SQL_Error`, respectively.

The `Slave_IO_State` shows a description of what the I/O thread is currently doing. Figure 6-4 shows a state diagram of how the message can change depending on the state of the I/O thread.

The messages have the following meanings:

Waiting for master update
> This message is shown briefly when the I/O thread is initialized and before it tries to establish a connection with the master.

Connecting to master
> This message is shown while the slave is trying to establish a connection with the master, but has not yet made the connection.

Checking master version
> This message is shown when the slave has managed to connect to the master and is performing a handshake with the master.

Registering slave on master
> This message is shown while the slave is trying to register itself with the master. When registering, it sends the value of the `report-host` option described earlier to the master. This usually contains the hostname or the IP number of the slave, but can contain any string. The master cannot depend simply on checking the IP address of the TCP connection, because there might be routers running network address translation (NAT) between the master and slave.

Requesting binlog dump
> This message is shown when the slave starts to request a binlog dump by sending the binlog file, binlog position, and server ID to the master.

Waiting for master to send event
> This message is printed when the slave has established a connection with the master and is waiting for the master to send an event.

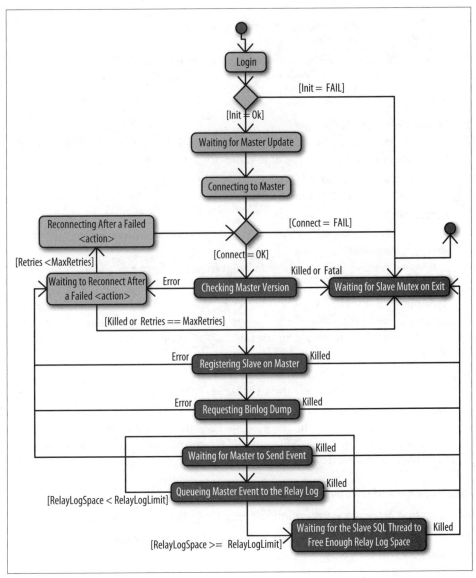

Figure 6-4. Slave I/O thread states

Queueing master event to the relay log

This message is shown when the master has sent an event and the slave I/O thread is about to write it to the relay log. This message is displayed regardless of whether the event is actually written to the relay log or skipped because of the rules outlined in "Filtering Replication Events" on page 163.

Note the spelling in the previous message ("Queueing" instead of "Queuing").

When checking for messages using scripts or other tools, it is very important to check what the message really says and not just what you think it should read.

Waiting to reconnect after `action`
This message is shown when a previous *action* failed with a transient error and the slave will try to reconnect. Possible values for *action* are:

`registration on master`
When attempting to register with the master

`binlog dump request`
When requesting a binlog dump from the master

`master event read`
When waiting for or reading an event from the master

Reconnecting after failed `action`
This message is shown when the slave is trying to reconnect to the master after trying *action* but has not yet managed to establish a connection. The possible values for *action* are the same as for the "Waiting to reconnect after *action*" message.

Waiting for slave mutex on exit
This message is shown while the I/O thread is shutting down.

Waiting for the slave SQL thread to free enough relay log space
This message is shown if the relay log space limit (as set by the `relay-log-space-limit` option) has been reached and the SQL thread needs to process some of the relay log to write the new events.

The binary log and relay log positions

As replication processes events on the slave, it maintains three positions in parallel.

These positions are shown in the output from SHOW SLAVE STATUS in Example 6-9, as the following pairs of fields.

`Master_Log_File, Read_Master_Log_Pos`
The *master read position*: the position in the master's binary log of the next event to be read by the I/O thread.

The values of these fields are taken from lines 2 and 3 of *master.info*, as shown in Example 6-1.

`Relay_Master_Log_File, Exec_Master_Log_Pos`
The *master execute position*: the position in the master's binlog of the next event to be executed by the SQL thread.

The values of these fields are taken from lines 3 and 4 of *relay-log.info*, as shown in Example 6-2.

`Relay_Log_File`, `Relay_Log_Pos`

The *relay log execute position*: the position in the slave's relay log of the next event to be executed by the SQL thread.

The values of these fields are taken from lines 1 and 2 of *relay-log.info*, as shown in Example 6-2.

You can use the positions to gain information about replication progress or to optimize some of the algorithms developed in Chapter 4.

For example, by comparing the master read position and the master execute position, it is possible to determine whether there are any events waiting to be executed. This is particularly interesting if the I/O thread has stopped, because it allows an easy way to wait for the relay log to become empty: once the positions are equal, there is nothing waiting in the relay log, and the slave can be safely stopped and redirected to another master.

Example 6-10 shows sample code that waits for an empty relay log on a slave. MySQL provides the convenient `MASTER_POS_WAIT` function to wait until a slave's relay log has processed all waiting events.

Example 6-10. Python script to wait for an empty relay log

```python
class SlaveNotRunning(Error):
    "Exception raised when slave is not running but were expected to run"
    pass

def slave_wait_for_empty_relay_log(slave):
    result = server.sql("SHOW SLAVE STATUS");
    file = result["Master_Log_File"]
    pos = result["Read_Master_Log_Pos"]
    if server.sql(_MASTER_POS_WAIT, (file, pos)) is None:
        raise SlaveNotRunning
```

Using these positions, you can also optimize the scenarios in Chapter 4. For instance, after running Example 4-15, which promotes a slave to master, you will probably have to process a lot of events in each of the other slaves' relay logs before switching the slave to the new master. In addition, ensuring that the promoted slave has executed all events before allowing any slaves to connect will allow you to lose a minimum of data.

By modifying Example 4-15 to create Example 6-11, you can make the former slaves execute all events they have in their relay logs before performing the switch.

Example 6-11. Minimizing the number of lost events when promoting a slave

```python
def fetch_global_trans_id(slave):
    result = slave.sql("SELECT server_id, trans_id FROM Last_Exec_Trans")
    return (int(result["server_id"]), int(result["trans_id"]))
```

```
def wait_for_empty_relay_log(slave):
    result = slave.sql("SHOW SLAVE STATUS")
    slave.sql("SELECT MASTER_POS_WAIT(%s,%s)",
              (result["Master_Log_File"], result["Read_Master_Log_Pos"]))

def promote_slave(slaves):
    slave_info = {}

    # Collect the global transaction ID of each slave
    for slave in slaves:
        slave.connect()
        wait_for_empty_relay_log(slave)
        server_id, trans_id = fetch_global_trans_id(slave)
        slave_info.setdefault(trans_id, []).append((server_id, trans_id, slave))
        slave.disconnect()

    # Pick the slave to promote by taking the slave with the highest
    # global transaction id.
    new_master = slave_info[max(slave_info)].pop()[2]

    def maybe_change_master(server_id, trans_id, position):
        from mysqlrep.utility import change_master
        try:
            for sid, tid, slave in slave_info[trans_id]:
                if slave is not new_master:
                    change_master(slave, new_master, position)
        except KeyError:
            pass

    # Read the the master log files of the new master.
    new_master.connect()
    logs = [row["Log_name"] for row in new_master.sql("SHOW MASTER LOGS")]
    new_master.disconnect()

    # Read the master log files one by one in reverse order, the
    # latest binlog file first.
    logs.reverse()
    for log in logs:
        scan_logfile(new_master, log, maybe_change_master)
```

In addition to the technique demonstrated here, another technique mentioned in some of the literature is to check the status of the SQL thread in the SHOW PROCESSLIST output. If the State field is "Has read all relay log; waiting for the slave I/O thread to update it," the SQL thread has read the entire relay log. This State message is generated only by the SQL thread, so you can safely search for it in all threads.

Options for Handling Broken Connections

The I/O thread has the responsibility for maintaining the connection with the master and, as you have seen in Figure 6-4, includes quite a complicated bit of logic to do so.

If the I/O thread loses the connection with the master, it will attempt to reconnect to the master a limited number of times. The period of inactivity after which the I/O thread reacts, the retry period, and the number of retries attempted are controlled by three options:

`--slave-net-timeout`

> The number of seconds of inactivity accepted before the slave decides that the connection with the master is lost and tries to reconnect. This does not apply to a situation in which a broken connection can be detected explicitly. In these cases, the slave reacts immediately, moves the I/O thread into the reconnection phase, and attempts a reconnect (possibly waiting according to the value of `master-con nect-retry` and only if the number of retries done so far does not exceed `master-retry-count`).
>
> The default is 3,600 seconds.

`--master-connect-retry`

> The number of oseconds between retries. You can specify this option as the `CONNECT_RETRY` parameter for the `CHANGE MASTER TO` command. Use of the option in *my.cnf* is deprecated.
>
> The default is 60 seconds.

`--master-retry-count`

> The number of retries before finally giving up.
>
> The default is 86,400.

These defaults are probably not what you want, so you're better off supplying your own values.

How the Slave Processes Events

Central to replication are the log events: they are the information carriers of the replication system and contain all the metadata necessary to ensure replication can execute the changes made on the master to produce a replica of the master. Because the binary log on the master is in commit order for all the transactions executed on the master, each transaction can be executed in the same order in which it appears in the binary log to produce the same result on the slave as on the master.

The slave SQL thread executes events from *all* the sessions on the master *in sequence*. This has some consequences for how the slave executes the events:

The slave reply is single-threaded, whereas the master is multithreaded

> The log events are executed in a single thread on the slave, but on multiple threads on the master. This can make it difficult for the slave to keep up with the master if the master is committing a lot of transactions.

Some statements are session-specific
> Some statements on the master are session-specific and will cause different results when executed from the single session on the slave:
> - Every user variable is session-specific.
> - Temporary tables are session-specific.
> - Some functions are session-specific—for example, `CONNECTION_ID`.

The binary log decides execution order
> Even though two transactions in the binary log appear to be independent—and in theory could be executed in parallel—they may in reality not be independent. This means that the slave is forced to execute the transactions in sequence to guarantee the master and the slave are consistent.

Housekeeping in the I/O Thread

Although the SQL thread does most of the event processing, the I/O does some house-keeping before the events even come into the SQL thread's view. So we'll look at I/O thread processing before discussing the "real execution" in the SQL thread. To keep up processing speed, the I/O thread inspects only certain bytes to determine the type of the event, then takes the necessary action to the relay log:

Stop events
> These events indicate that a slave further up in the chain has been stopped in an orderly manner. This event is ignored by the I/O thread and is not even written to the relay log.

Rotate event
> If the master binary log is rotated, so is the relay log. The relay log might be rotated more times than the master, but the relay log is rotated at least each time the master's binary log is rotated.

Format description events
> These events are saved to be written when the relay log is rotated. Recall that the format between two consecutive binlog files might change, so the I/O thread needs to remember this event to process the files correctly.

If replication is set up to replicate in a circle or through a dual-master setup (which is circular replication with only two servers), events will be forwarded in the circle until they arrive at the server that originally sent them. To avoid having events continue to replicate around in the circle indefinitely, it is necessary to remove events that have been executed before.

To implement this check, each server determines whether the event has the server's own server ID. If it does, this event was sent from this server previously, and replication on the slave has come full circle. To avoid an event that circulates infinitely (and hence is applied infinitely) this event is not written to the relay log, but just ignored. You can turn this behavior off using the `replicate-same-server-id` option on the server. If you set this option, the server will not carry out the check for an identical server ID and the event will be written to the relay log regardless of which server ID it has.

SQL Thread Processing

The slave SQL thread reads the relay log and reexecutes the master's database statements on the slave. Some of these events require special information that is not part of the SQL statement. The special handling includes:

Passing master context to the slave server
> Sometimes state information needs to be passed to the slave for the statement to execute correctly. As mentioned in Chapter 3, the master writes one or more *context events* to pass this extra information. Some of the information is thread-specific but different from the information in the next item.

Handling events from different threads
> Since the master executes transactions from several sessions, the slave SQL thread has to decide which thread generated some events. Because the master has the best knowledge about the statement, it marks any event that it considers thread-specific. For instance, the master will usually mark events that operate on temporary tables as thread-specific.

Filtering events and tables
> The SQL thread is responsible for doing filtering on the slave. MySQL provides both database filters, which are set up by `replicate-do-db` and `replicate-ignore-db`, and table filters, which are set up by `replicate-do-table`, `replicate-ignore-table`, `replicate-wild-do-table`, and `replicate-wild-ignore-table`.

Skipping events
> To recover replication after it has stopped, there are features available to skip events when restarting replication. The SQL thread handles this skipping.

Context events

On the master, some events require a context to execute correctly. The context is usually thread-specific features such as user-defined variables, but can also include state information required to execute correctly, such as autoincrement values for tables with autoincrement columns. To pass this context from the master to the slave, the master has a set of context events that it can write to the binary log.

The master writes each context event before the event that contains the actual change. Currently, context events are associated only with `Query` events and are added to the binary log before the `Query` events.

Context events fall into the following categories:

User variable event

This event holds the name and value of a user-defined variable.

This event is generated whenever the statement contains a reference to a user-defined variable.

```
SET @foo = 'SmoothNoodleMaps';
INSERT INTO my_albums(artist, album) VALUES ('Devo', @foo);
```

Integer variable event

This event holds an integer value for either the INSERT_ID session variable or LAST_INSERT_ID session variable.

The INSERT_ID integer variable event is used for statements that insert into tables with an AUTO_INCREMENT column to transfer the next value to use for the autoincrement column. This information, for example, is required by this table definition and statement:

```
CREATE TABLE Artist (id INT AUTO_INCREMENT PRIMARY KEY, artist TEXT);
INSERT INTO Artist VALUES (DEFAULT, 'The The');
```

The LAST_INSERT_ID integer variable event is generated when a statement uses the LAST_INSERT_ID function, as in this statement:

```
INSERT INTO Album VALUES (LAST_INSERT_ID(), 'Mind Bomb');
```

Rand event

If the statement contains a call to the RAND function, this event will contain the random seeds, which will allow the slave to reproduce the "random" value generated on the master.

```
INSERT INTO my_table VALUES (RAND());
```

These context events are necessary to produce correct behavior in the situations just described, but there are other situations that cannot be handled using context events. For example, the replication system cannot handle a user-defined function (UDF) unless the UDF is deterministic and also exists on the slave. In these cases, the user variable event can solve the problem.

User variable events can be very useful for avoiding problems with replicating nondeterministic functions, for improving performance, and for integrity checks.

As an example, suppose that you enter documents into a database table. Each document is automatically assigned a number using the AUTO_INCREMENT feature. To maintain the integrity of the documents, you also add an MD5 checksum of the documents in the same table. A definition of such a table is shown in Example 6-12.

Example 6-12. Definition of document table with MD5 checksum

```
CREATE TABLE document(
    id INT UNSIGNED AUTO_INCREMENT PRIMARY KEY,
    doc BLOB,
    checksum CHAR(32)
);
```

Using this table, you can now add documents to the table together with the checksum and also verify the integrity of the document, as shown in Example 6-13, to ensure it has not been corrupted. Although the MD5 checksum is currently not considered cryptographically secure, it still offers some protection against random errors such as disk and memory problems.

Example 6-13. Inserting into the table and checking document integrity

```
master> INSERT INTO document(doc) VALUES (document);
Query OK, 1 row affected (0.02 sec)

master> UPDATE document SET checksum = MD5(doc) WHERE id = LAST_INSERT_ID();
Query OK, 1 row affected (0.04 sec)

master> SELECT id,
    ->         IF(MD5(doc) = checksum, 'OK', 'CORRUPT!') AS Status
    ->     FROM document;
+-----+----------+
| id  | Status   |
+-----+----------+
|   1 | OK       |
|   2 | OK       |
|   3 | OK       |
|   4 | OK       |
|   5 | OK       |
|   6 | OK       |
|   7 | CORRUPT! |
|   8 | OK       |
|   9 | OK       |
|  10 | OK       |
|  11 | OK       |
+-----+----------+
11 row in set (5.75 sec)
```

But how well does this idea play with replication? Well, it depends on how you use it. When the INSERT statement in Example 6-13 is executed, it is written to the binary log as is, which means the MD5 checksum is recalculated on the slave. So what happens if the document is corrupted on the way to the slave? In that case, the MD5 checksum will be recalculated using the corrupt document, and the corruption will not be detected. So the statement given in Example 6-13 is not replication-safe. We can, however, do better than this.

Instead of following Example 6-13, write your code to look like Example 6-14, which stores the checksum in a user-defined variable and uses it in the INSERT statement. Since the user-defined variable contains the actual value computed by the MD5 function, it will be identical on the master and the slave even if the document is corrupted in the transfer (but, of course, not if the checksum is corrupted in the transfer). Either way, a corruption occurring when the document is replicated will be noticed.

Example 6-14. Replication-safe method of inserting a document in the table

```
master> INSERT INTO document(doc) VALUES (document);
Query OK, 1 row affected (0.02 sec)

master> SELECT MD5(doc) INTO @checksum FROM document WHERE id = LAST_INSERT_ID();
Query OK, 0 rows affected (0.00 sec)

master> UPDATE document SET checksum = @checksum WHERE id = LAST_INSERT_ID();
Query OK, 1 row affected (0.04 sec)
```

Thread-specific events

As mentioned earlier, some statements are thread-specific and will yield a different result when executed in another thread. There are several reasons for this:

Reading and writing thread-local objects
> A thread-local object can potentially clash with an identically named object in another thread. Typical examples of such objects are temporary tables or user-defined variables.

> We have already examined how replication handles user-defined variables, so this section will just concentrate on how replication handles the temporary tables.

Using variables or functions that have thread-specific results
> Some variables and functions have different values depending on which thread they are running in. A typical example of this is the server variable connection_id.

The server handles these two cases slightly differently. In addition, there are a few cases in which replication does not try to account for differences between the server and client, so results can differ in subtle ways.

To handle thread-local objects, some form of thread-local store (TLS) is required, but since the slave is executing from a single thread, it has to manage this storage and keep the TLSs separate. To handle temporary tables, the slave creates a unique (mangled) filename for the table based on the server process ID, the thread ID, and a thread-specific sequence number. This means that the two statements in Example 6-15—each runs from a different client on the master—create two different filenames on the slave to represent the temporary tables.

Example 6-15. Two threads, each creating a temporary table.

```
master-1> CREATE TEMPORARY TABLE cache (a INT, b INT);
Query OK, 0 rows affected (0.01 sec)

master-2> CREATE TEMPORARY TABLE cache (a INT, b INT);
Query OK, 0 rows affected (0.01 sec)
```

Since all the statements from all threads on the master are stored in sequence in the binary log, it is necessary to distinguish the two statements. Otherwise, they will cause an error when executed on the slave.

To distinguish the statements in the binary log so that they do not conflict, the server tags the `Query` events containing the statement as thread-specific and also adds the thread ID to the event. (Actually, the thread ID is added to all `Query` events, but is not really necessary except for thread-specific statements.)

When the slave receives a thread-specific event, it sets a variable special to the replication slave thread, called the *pseudothread ID*, to the thread ID passed with the event. The pseudothread ID will then be used when constructing the temporary tables. The process ID of the slave server—which is the same for all master threads—will be used when constructing the filename, but that does not matter as long as there is a distinction among tables from different threads.

We also mentioned that thread-specific functions and variables require special treatment to work correctly when replicated. This is not, however, handled by the server. When a server variable is referenced in a statement, the value of the server variable will be retrieved on the slave. If, for some reason, you want to replicate exactly the same value, you have to store the value in a user-defined variable as shown in Example 6-14, or use row-based replication, which we will cover later in the chapter.

Filtering and skipping events

In some cases, events may be skipped either because they are filtered out using replication filters or because the slave has been specifically instructed to skip a number of events.

The `SQL_SLAVE_SKIP_COUNTER` variable instructs the slave server to skip a specified number of events. The SQL thread should not be running when you set the variable. This condition is typically easy to satisfy, because the variable is usually used to skip some events that caused replication to stop already.

An error that stops replication should, of course, be investigated and handled, but if you fix the problem manually, it is necessary to ignore the event that stopped replication and force replication to continue after the offending event. This variable is provided as a convenience, to keep you from having to use `CHANGE MASTER TO`. Example 6-16 shows the feature in use after a bad statement has caused replication to stop.

Example 6-16. Using the SQL_SLAVE_SKIP_COUNTER

```
slave> SET GLOBAL SQL_SLAVE_SKIP_COUNTER = 3;
Query OK, 0 rows affected (0.02 sec)

slave> START SLAVE;
Query OK, 0 rows affected (0.02 sec)
```

When you start the slave, three events will be skipped before resuming replication. If skipping three events causes the slave to end up in the middle of a transaction, the slave will continue skipping events until it finds the end of the transaction.

Events can also be filtered by the slave if replication filters are set up. As we discussed in Chapter 3, the master can handle filtering, but if there are slave filters, the events are filtered in the SQL thread, which means that the events are still sent from the master and stored in the relay log.

Filtering is done differently depending on whether database filters or table filters are set up. The logic for deciding whether a statement for a certain database should be filtered out from the binary log was detailed in Chapter 3, and the same logic applies to slave filters, with the addition that here a set of table filters have to be handled as well.

One important aspect of filtering is that a filter applying to a single table causes the entire statement referring to that filter to be left out of replication. The logic for filtering statements on the slave is shown in Figure 6-5.

Filtering that involves tables can easily become difficult to understand, so we advise the following rules to avoid unwanted results:

- Do not qualify table names with the database they're a part of. Precede the statement with a USE statement instead to set a new default database.
- Do not update tables in different databases using a single statement.
- Avoid updating multiple tables in a statement, unless you know that all tables are filtered or none of the tables are filtered. Notice that from the logic in Figure 6-5, the whole statement will be filtered if even one of the tables is filtered.

Slave Safety and Recovery

Slave servers can crash too, and when they do, you need to recover them. The first step in handling a crashed slave is always to investigate why it crashed. This cannot be automated, because there are so many hard-to-anticipate reasons for crashes. A slave might be out of disk space, have read a corrupt event, or for some reason might have reexecuted a statement that resulted in a duplicate key error. However, it is possible to automate some recovery procedures and to use automation to help diagnose a problem.

Syncing, Transactions, and Problems with Database Crashes

To ensure slaves pick up replication safely after a crash on the master or slave, you need to consider two different aspects:

- Ensuring the slave stores all the necessary data needed for recovery in the event of a crash
- Executing the recovery of a slave

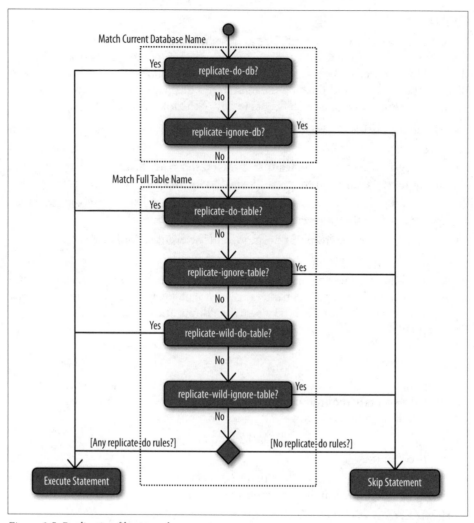

Figure 6-5. Replication filtering rules

Slaves do their best to meet the first condition by syncing to disk. To provide acceptable performance, operating systems keep files in memory while working with them, and write them to disk only periodically or when forced to. This means data written to a file is not necessarily in safe storage. If there is a crash, data left only in memory will be lost.

To force a slave to write files to disk, the database server issues an `fsync` call, which writes all data stored in memory to disk. To protect replication data, the MySQL server normally executes `fsync` calls for the relay log, the *master.info* file, and the *relay-log.info* file at regular intervals.

I/O thread syncing

For the I/O thread, two `fsync` calls are made whenever an event has been processed: one to flush the relay log to disk and one to flush the *master.info* file to disk. Doing the flushes in this order ensures that no events will be lost if the slave crashes between flushing the relay log and flushing the *master.info* file. This, however, means that an event can be duplicated if a crash occurs in any of the following cases:

- The server flushes the relay log and is about to update the master read position in *master.info*.
- The server crashes, which means that the master read position now refers to the position before the event that was flushed to the relay log.
- The server restarts and gets the master read position from *master.info*, meaning the position before the last event written to the relay log.
- Replication resumes from this position, and the event is duplicated.

If the files were flushed in the opposite order—the *master.info* file first and the relay log second—there would be potential for losing an event in the same scenario, because the slave would pick up replication after the event that it was about to write to the relay log. Losing an event is deemed to be worse than duplicating one, hence the relay log is flushed first.

SQL thread syncing

The SQL thread processes the groups in the relay log by processing each event in turn. When all the events in the group are processed, the SQL thread commits the transaction using the following process:

1. It commits the transaction to the storage engine (assuming the storage engine supports commit).
2. It updates the *relay-log.info* file with the position of the next event to process, which is also the beginning of the next group to process.
3. It writes *relay-log.info* to disk by issuing an `fsync(2)` call.

While executing inside a group, the thread increments the event position to keep track of where the SQL thread is reading in the relay log, but if there is a crash, execution will resume from the last recorded position in the *relay-log.info* file.

This behavior leaves the SQL thread with its own version of the atomic update problem mentioned for the I/O thread, so the slave database and the *relay-log.info* file can get out of sync in the following scenario:

1. The event is applied to the database and the transaction is committed. The next step is to update the *relay-log.info* file.
2. The slave crashes, which means *relay-log.info* now points to the beginning of the just-completed transaction.

3. On recovery, the SQL thread reads the information from the *relay-log.info* file and starts replication from the saved position.

4. The last executed transaction is repeated.

What all this boils down to is that committing a transaction on the slave and updating the replication information is not atomic: it is possible that *relay-log.info* does not accurately reflect what has been committed to the database.

What all this boils down to is that the replication system assumes that tables—even nontransactional tables—are crash-safe in the sense that each statement is executed atomically. This means that either the full statement is executed or the statement is not executed at all. To handle this, the storage engine must ensure that if a crash occurs in the middle of the statement, it will be rolled back when the server restarts.

Rules for Protecting Nontransactional Statements

Statements executed outside of transactions cannot be tracked and protected from reexecution after a crash. The problem is comparable on masters and slaves. If a statement against a MyISAM table is interrupted by a crash on the master, the statement is not logged at all, because logging is done after the statement has completed. Upon restart (and successful repair) the MyISAM table will contain a partial update, but the binary log will not have logged the statement at all.

The situation is similar on the slave: if a crash occurs in the middle of execution of a statement (or a transaction that modifies a nontransactional table), the changes might remain in the table, but the group position will not be changed. The nontransactional statement will be reexecuted when the slave starts up replication again.

It is not possible to automatically catch problems with crashes in the middle of updating a nontransactional table, but by obeying a few rules, it is possible to ensure you at least receive an error when this situation occurs.

INSERT *statements*

> To handle these statements, you need to have a primary key on the tables that you replicate. In this way, an INSERT that is reexecuted will generate a duplicate key error and stop the slave so that you can check why the master and the slave are not consistent.

DELETE *statements*

> To handle these, you need to stay away from LIMIT clauses. If you do this, the statement will just delete the same rows again—the rows that match the WHERE clause—which is fine since it will either pick up where the previous statement left off or do nothing if all specified rows are already deleted. However, if the statement has a LIMIT clause, only a subset of the rows matching the WHERE condition will be executed, so when the statement is executed again, another set of rows will be deleted.

UPDATE *statements*

These are the most problematic statements. To be safe, either the statement has to be *idempotent*—executing it twice should lead to the same result—or the occasional double execution of the statement should be acceptable, which could be the case if the UPDATE statement is just for maintaining statistics over, say, page accesses.

Multisource Replication

As you may have noticed, it is not possible to have a slave connect to multiple masters and receive changes from all of them. This topology is called *multisource* and should not be confused with the multimaster topology introduced in Chapter 5. In a multisource topology, changes are received from several masters, but in a multimaster topology, the servers form a group that acts as a single master by replicating changes from each master to all the other masters.

There have been plans for introducing multisource replication into MySQL for a long time, but one issue stands in the way of the design: what to do with conflicting updates. These can occur either because different sources make truly conflicting changes, or because two intermediate relays are forwarding a change made at a common master. Figure 6-6 illustrates both types of conflicts. In the first, two masters (sources) make changes to the same data and the slave cannot tell which is the final change. In the second, only a single change is made, but it looks to the slave like two changes from two different sources. In both cases, the slave will not be able to distinguish between events coming from the two relays, so an event sent from the master will be seen as two different events when arriving at the slave.

> The diamond configuration does not have to be explicitly set up: it can occur inadvertently as a result of switching from one relay to another if the replication stream is overlapping during a switchover. For this reason, it is important to ensure all events in queue—on the slave and on all the relays between the master and the slave—have been replicated to the slave before switching over to another master.

You can avoid conflicts by making sure you handle switchovers correctly and—in the case of multiple data sources—ensuring updates are done so that they never have a chance of conflicting. The typical way to accomplish this is to update different databases, but it is also possible to assign updates of different rows in the same table to different servers.

Although MySQL does not currently let you replicate from several sources simultaneously, you can come close by switching a slave among several masters, replicating periodically from each of them in turn. This is called *round-robin multisource replication*. It can be useful for certain types of applications, such as when you're aggregating

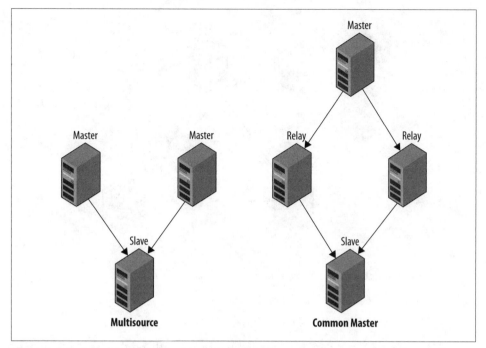

Figure 6-6. True multisource and a diamond configuration

data from different sources for reporting purposes. In these cases, you can separate data naturally by storing the writes from each master in its own database, table, or partition. There is no risk of conflict, so it should be possible to use multisource replication.

Figure 6-7 shows a slave that replicates from three masters in a round-robin fashion, running a client dedicated to handling the switches between the masters. The process for round-robin multisource replication is:

1. Set the slave up to replicate from one master. We'll call this the *current master*.

2. Let the slave replicate for a fixed period of time. The slave will the read changes from the current master and apply them while the client responsible for handling the switching just sleeps.

3. Stop the I/O thread of the slave using `STOP SLAVE IO_THREAD`.

4. Wait until the relay log is empty.

5. Stop the SQL thread using `STOP SLAVE SQL_THREAD`. `CHANGE MASTER` requires that you stop both threads.

6. Save the slave position for the current master by saving the values of the `Exec_Master_Log_Pos` and `Relay_Master_Log_File` columns from the `SHOW SLAVE STATUS` output.

7. Change the slave to replicate from the next master in sequence by taking the previously saved positions and using `CHANGE MASTER` to set up replication.

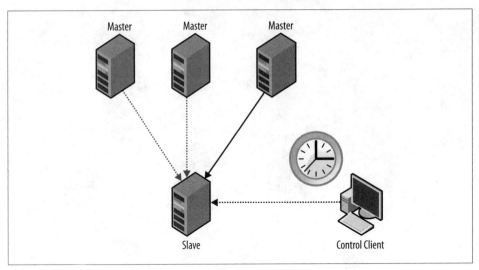

Figure 6-7. Round-robin multisource replication using a client to switch

8. Restart the slave threads using START SLAVE.

9. Repeat the sequence starting from step 2.

Note that in steps 3 through 5, we stop first the I/O thread and then the SQL thread. The reason for doing this and not just stopping replication on the slave is that the SQL thread can be lagging behind (and usually is), so if we just stop both threads, there will be a bunch of outstanding events in the relay log that will just be thrown away. If you are more concerned about executing only, say, one minute's worth of transactions from each master and don't care about throwing away those additional events, you can simply stop replication instead of performing steps 3 through 5. The procedure will still work correctly, since the events that were thrown away will be refetched from the master in the next round.

This can, of course, be automated using a separate client connection and the MySQL Replicant library as shown in Example 6-17. By using the cycle function from the itertools module, you can repeatedly read from a list of masters in turn.

Example 6-17. Round-robin multisource replication in Python

```python
import itertools

position = {}
def round_robin_multi_master(slave, masters):
    current = masters[0]
    for master in itertools.cycle(masters):
        slave.sql("STOP SLAVE IO_THREAD");
        mysqlrep.wait_for_empty_relay_log(slave)
        slave.sql("STOP SLAVE SQL_THREAD");
        position[current.name] = mysqlrep.fetch_slave_position(slave)
        slave.change_master(position[current.name])
```

```
master.sql("START SLAVE")
current = master
sleep(60)                # Sleep 1 minute
```

Row-Based Replication

The primary goal of replication is to keep the master and the slave synchronized so they have the same data. As you saw earlier, replication offers a number of special features to ensure the results are as close as possible to being identical on master and slave: context events, session-specific IDs, etc.

Despite this, there are still some situations that statement-based replication can't currently handle correctly:

- As you saw earlier in this chapter, if an UPDATE, DELETE, or INSERT statement contains a LIMIT clause, it may cause problems if a database crashes during execution.

- If there is an error during execution of a nontransactional statement, there is no guarantee that the effects are the same on the master and the slave.

- If a statement contains a call to a UDF, there is no way to ensure the same value is used on the slave.

- If the statement contains any nondeterministic function—such as USER, CURRENT_USER, CONNECTION_ID—results may differ between master and slave.

- If a statement updates two tables with autoincrement columns, it will not work correctly, because only a single last insert ID can be replicated, which will then be used for both tables on the slave, while on the master, the insert ID for each table will be used individually.

In these cases, it is better to replicate the actual data being inserted into the tables, which is what *row-based replication* does.

Instead of replicating the statement that performs the changes, row-based replication replicates each row being inserted, deleted, or updated separately, with the values that were used for the operation. Since the row that is sent to the slave is the same row that is sent to the storage engine, it contains the actual data being inserted into the table. Hence there are no UDFs to consider, no autoincrement counters to keep track of, and no partial execution of statements to take into consideration—just data, plain and simple.

Row-based replication opens up an entirely new set of scenarios that you just cannot accomplish with statement-based replication. However, you must also be aware of some differences in behavior.

When choosing between statement-based and row-based replication, consider the following:

- Do you have statements that update a lot of rows, or do the statements usually only change or insert a few rows?

If the statement changes a lot of rows, statement-based replication will have more compact statements and may execute faster. But since the statement is executed on the slave as well, this is not always true. If the statement has a complex optimization and execution plan, it might be faster to use row-based replication, because the logic for finding rows is much faster.

If the statement changes or inserts only a few rows, row-based replication is potentially faster because there is no parsing involved and all processing goes directly to the storage engine.

- Do you need to see which statements are executed? The events for handling row-based replication are hard to decode, to say the least. In statement-based replication, the statements are written into the binary log and hence can be read directly.

- Statement-based replication has a simple replication model: just execute the same statement on the slave. This has existed for quite some time and is familiar to many DBAs. Row-based replication, on the other hand, is comparably new and can potentially be harder to fix when replication fails.

- If data is different on master and slave, executing statements can yield different results on master and slave. Sometimes this is intentional—in this case, statement-based replication can and should be used—but sometimes this not intentional and can be prevented through row-based replication.

Row-based and statement-based replication offer different sets of tricks. Some ways of using statement-based replication to your advantage have been demonstrated in the earlier chapters, and you will see some ways to use row-based replication to your advantage in this chapter.

Options for Row-Based Replication

Use the following options to configure row-based replication:

binlog-format

The binlog-format option can be set to use one of the following modes:

STATEMENT

This will use the traditional statement-based replication for all statements.

ROW

This will use the shiny new row-based replication for all statements that insert or change data (data manipulation language, or DML, statements). However, statement-based replication must still be used for statements that create tables or otherwise alter the schema (data definition language, or DDL, statements).

MIXED

This is intended to be a safe version of statement-based replication and is the recommended mode to use with MySQL version 5.1. In mixed-mode replication, the server will write the statements to the binary log as statements, but switch to row-based replication if the statement is considered unsafe through one of the criteria we have discussed in this chapter.

The variable also exists as a global server variable and as a session variable. When starting a new session, the global value is copied to the session variable and then the session variable is used to decide how to write statements to the binary log.

`binlog-max-row-event-size`
Use this option to specify when to start a new event for holding the rows. Since the events are read fully into memory when being processed, this option is a rough way of controlling the size of row-holding events so that not too much memory is used when processing the rows.

Mixed-Mode Replication

Mixed-mode replication is recommended for MySQL version 5.1, but the default value for the `binlog-format` option is `STATEMENT`. This might seem odd, but that decision was made to avoid problems for users who upgrade from versions 5.0 or earlier. Because those versions had no row-based replication and users have had to use statement-based replication, the MySQL developers did not want servers to make a sudden switch. If the servers suddenly started sending out row-based replication events when they were upgraded, the deployment would likely be a mess. To reduce the number of factors that an upgrading DBA has to consider, the default for this option remains `STATEMENT`.

However, if you use one of the template files distributed with MySQL version 5.1, you will notice the `binlog-format` option has the value `MIXED`, per the recommendation.

The principles behind mixed-mode replication are simple: use statement-based replication normally and switch to row-based replication for unsafe statements. We have already examined the kinds of statements that can lead to problems and why. To summarize, mixed-mode currently switches to row-based replication if:

- The statement calls any of the following:
  - The `UUID` function
  - A user-defined function
  - The `CURRENT_USER` or `USER` function
  - The `LOAD_FILE` function
- Two or more tables with an `AUTO_INCREMENT` column are updated in the same statement.
- A server variable is used in the statement.
- The storage engine does not allow statement-based replication, for example, the MySQL Cluster engine.

This list is, by necessity, incomplete: it is being extended as new constructions are discovered unsafe. For a complete and accurate list, refer to the online MySQL Reference Manual (*http://dev.mysql.com/doc/refman/5.1/en/binary-log-mixed.html*).

Events for Handling Row-Based Replication

In statement-based replication, statements are handled by writing the statement in a single `Query` event. However, since a significant number of rows can be changed in each statement, row-based replication handles this differently and therefore requires multiple events for each statement.

To handle row-based replication, four new events have been introduced:

`Table_map` *event*
> The `Table_map` event maps a table ID to a table name (including the database name) and some basic information about the columns of the table on the master.
>
> The table information does not include the names of the columns, just the types. This is because row-based replication is positional—each column on the master goes into the same position in the table on the slave.

`Write_rows`, `Delete_rows`, *and* `Update_rows` *events*
> These events are generated whenever rows are inserted, deleted, or updated, respectively. This means that a single statement can generate multiple events.
>
> In addition to the rows, each event contains a table ID that refers to a table ID introduced by a preceding `Table_map` event and one or two *column bitmaps* specifying the columns of the table affected by the event. This allows the log to save space by including only those columns that have changed or that are necessary to locate the correct row to insert, delete, or update.
>
> Currently, only the MySQL Cluster engine uses the option of limiting the columns sent in the log.

Whenever a statement is executed, it is written into the binary log as a sequence of `Table_map` events, followed by a sequence of row events. The last row event of the statement is marked with a special flag indicating it is the last event of the statement.

Example 6-18 shows the execution of a statement and the resulting events. For the example, we have skipped the format description event, since you have seen that before.

Example 6-18. Execution of an INSERT statement and the resulting events

```
master> BEGIN;
Query OK, 0 rows affected (0.00 sec)

master> INSERT INTO t1 VALUES (1),(2),(3),(4);
Query OK, 4 rows affected (0.01 sec)
Records: 4  Duplicates: 0  Warnings: 0

master> INSERT INTO t1 VALUES (5),(6),(7),(8);
```

```
Query OK, 4 rows affected (0.01 sec)
Records: 4  Duplicates: 0  Warnings: 0

master> COMMIT;
Query OK, 0 rows affected (0.00 sec)

master> SHOW BINLOG EVENTS IN 'master-bin.000053' FROM 106\G
*************************** 1. row ***************************
   Log_name: master-bin.000054
        Pos: 106
 Event_type: Query
  Server_id: 1
End_log_pos: 174
       Info: BEGIN
*************************** 2. row ***************************
   Log_name: master-bin.000054
        Pos: 174
 Event_type: Table_map
  Server_id: 1
End_log_pos: 215
       Info: table_id: 18 (test.t1)
*************************** 3. row ***************************
   Log_name: master-bin.000054
        Pos: 215
 Event_type: Write_rows
  Server_id: 1
End_log_pos: 264
       Info: table_id: 18 flags: STMT_END_F
*************************** 4. row ***************************
   Log_name: master-bin.000054
        Pos: 264
 Event_type: Table_map
  Server_id: 1
End_log_pos: 305
       Info: table_id: 18 (test.t1)
*************************** 5. row ***************************
   Log_name: master-bin.000054
        Pos: 305
 Event_type: Write_rows
  Server_id: 1
End_log_pos: 354
       Info: table_id: 18 flags: STMT_END_F
*************************** 6. row ***************************
   Log_name: master-bin.000054
        Pos: 354
 Event_type: Xid
  Server_id: 1
End_log_pos: 381
       Info: COMMIT /* xid=23 */
6 rows in set (0.00 sec)
```

This example adds two statements to the binary log. Each statement starts with a
Table_map event followed by a single Write_rows event holding the four rows of each
statement.

You can see that each statement is terminated by setting the `statement-end flag` of the row event. Since the statements are inside a transaction, they are also wrapped with `Query` events containing `BEGIN` and `COMMIT` statements.

The size of the row events is controlled by the option `binlog-row-event-max-size`, which gives a threshold for the number of bytes in the binary log. The option does *not* give a maximum size for a row event: it is possible to have a binlog row event that has a larger size if a row contains more bytes than `binlog-row-event-max-size`.

Table map events

As already mentioned, the `Table_map` event maps a table name to an identifier so that it can be used in the row events, but that is not its only role. In addition, it contains some basic information about the fields of the table on the master. This allows the slave to check the basic structure of the table on the slave and compare it to the structure on the master to make sure they match well enough for replication to proceed.

The basic structure of the table map event is shown in Figure 6-8. The common header—the header that all replication events have—contains the basic information about the event. After the common header, the post header gives information that is special for the table map event. Most of the fields in Figure 6-8 are self-explanatory, but the representation of the field types deserves a closer look.

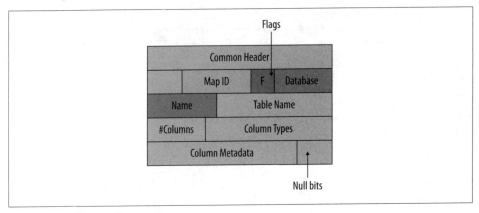

Figure 6-8. Table map event structure

The following fields together represent the column type:

Column type array
> An array listing the base types for all the columns. It indicates whether this is an integer, a string type, a decimal type, or any of the other available types, but it does not give the parameters for the column type. For example, if the type of a column is `CHAR(5)`, this array will contain 254 (the constant representing a string), but the length of the string (in this case, 5) is stored in the column metadata mentioned below.

Null bit array

An array of bits that indicate whether each field can be NULL.

Column metadata

An array of metadata for the fields, fleshing out details left out of the column type array. The piece of metadata available to each field depends on the type of the field. For example, the DECIMAL field stores the precision and decimals in the metadata, while the VARCHAR type stores the maximum length of the field.

By combining the data in these three arrays, it is possible to deduce the type of the field.

Not all type information is stored in the arrays, so in two particular cases, it is not possible for the master and the slave to distinguish between two types:

- When there is no information about whether an integer field is signed or unsigned. This means the slave will be unable to distinguish between a signed and unsigned field when checking the tables.

- When the character sets of string types are not part of the information. This means that replicating between different character sets is not supported and may lead to strange results, since the bytes will just be inserted into the column with no checking or conversion.

The structure of row events

Figure 6-9 shows the structure of a row event. This structure can vary a little depending on the type of event (write, delete, or update).

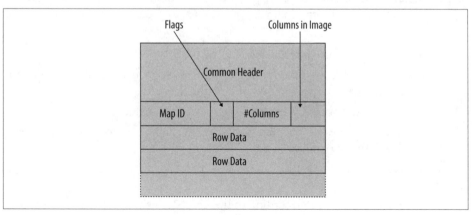

Figure 6-9. Row event header

In addition to the table ID, which refers to the table ID of a previous table map event, the event contains the following fields:

Table width
> The width of the table on the master. This width is length-encoded in the same way as for the client protocol, which is why it can be either one or two bytes. Most of the time, it will be one byte.

Columns bitmap
> The columns that are sent as part of the payload of the event. This information allows the master to send a selected set of fields with each row. There are two types of column bitmaps: one for the *before image* and one for the *after image*. The before image is needed for deletions and updates, whereas the after image is needed for writes (inserts) and updates. See Table 6-1 for more information.

Table 6-1. Row events and their images

Before image	After image	Event
None	Row to insert	Write rows
Row to delete	None	Delete rows
Column values before update	Column values after update	Update rows

Event Execution

Because multiple events can represent a single statement executed by the master, the slave has to keep state information to execute the row events correctly in the presence of concurrent threads that update the same tables. Recall that each statement in the binary log starts with one or more table map events followed by one or more row events, each of the same type. Use the following procedure to process a statement from the binary log:

1. Each event is read from the relay log.
2. If the event is a table map event, the SQL thread extracts the information about the table and saves a representation of how the master defines the table.
3. When the first row event is seen, all tables in the list are locked.
4. For each table in the list, the thread checks that the definition on the master is compatible with the definition on the slave.
5. If the tables are not compatible, the thread reports an error and stops replication on the slave.
6. Row events are processed according to the procedure shown later in this section, until the thread reads the last event of the statement—that is, an event with the statement end flag set.

This procedure is required to lock tables the correct way on the slave and is similar to how the statement was executed on the master. All tables are locked in step 3 and then checked in step 4. If the tables are not locked before checking the definitions, a thread on the slave can come between the steps and change the definition, causing the application of the row events to fail later.

Each row event consists of a set of rows that are used differently depending on the event type. For Delete_rows and Write_rows events, each row represents a change. For the Update_rows event, it is necessary to have two rows—one to locate the correct row to update and one with values to use for the update—so the event consists of an even number of rows, where each pair represents an update.

Events that have a before image require a search to locate the correct row to operate on: for a Delete_rows event, the row will be removed, whereas for the Update_rows event, it will be changed. In descending order of preference, the searches are:

Primary key lookup
> If the table on the slave has a primary key, it is used to perform a primary key lookup. This is the fastest of all the methods.

Index scan
> If there is no primary key defined for the table but there is an index defined, this will be used to locate the correct row to change. All rows in the index will be scanned and the columns compared with the row received from the master.

> If the rows match, this row will be used for the Delete_rows or Update_rows operation. If no rows match, the slave will stop replication with an error indicating that it could not locate the correct row.

Table scan
> If there is no primary key or index on the table, a full table scan is used to locate the correct row to delete or update.

> In the same way as for the index scan, each row in the scan will be compared with the row received from the master and if they match, that row will be used for the delete or update operation.

Since the index or primary key on the *slave* rather than the master is used to locate the correct row to delete or update, you should keep a few things in mind:

- If the table has a primary key on the slave, the lookup will be fast. If the table does not have a primary key, the slave has to do either a full table scan or an index scan to find the correct row to update, which is slower.
- You can have different indexes on the master and slave.

When replicating a table, it is always wise to have a primary key on the table regardless of whether row-based or statement-based replication is used.

Since statement-based replication actually executes each statement, a primary key on updates and deletes speeds up replication significantly for statement-based replication as well.

Events and Triggers

The execution of events and triggers differs in statement-based replication and row-based replication. The only difference for events is that row-based replication generates row events instead of query events.

Triggers, on the other hand, reveal a different and more interesting story.

As discussed in Chapter 3, for statement-based replication, trigger definitions are replicated to the slave so that when a statement is executed that affects a table with a trigger, the trigger will be executed on the slave as well.

For row-based replication, it doesn't matter how the rows change—whether changes come from a trigger, a stored procedure, an event, or directly from the statement. Since the rows updated by the trigger are replicated to the slave, the trigger does not need to be executed on the slave. As a matter of fact, executing it on the slave would lead to incorrect results.

Consider Example 6-19, which defines a table with a trigger.

Example 6-19. Definition of a table and triggers

```
CREATE TABLE log (
    number INT AUTO_INCREMENT PRIMARY KEY,
    user CHAR(64),
    brief TEXT
);


CREATE TABLE user (
    id INT AUTO_INCREMENT PRIMARY KEY,
    email CHAR(64),
    password CHAR(64)
);


CREATE TRIGGER tr_update_user AFTER UPDATE ON user FOR EACH ROW
    INSERT INTO log SET
        user = NEW.email,
        brief = CONCAT("Changed password from '",
                    OLD.password, "' to '",
                    NEW.password, "'");

CREATE TRIGGER tr_insert_user AFTER INSERT ON user FOR EACH ROW
```

```
INSERT INTO log SET
    user = NEW.email,
    brief = CONCAT("User '", NEW.email, "' added");
```

Given these table and trigger definitions, this sequence of statements can be executed.

```
master> INSERT INTO user(email,password) VALUES ('mats@example.com', 'xyzzy');
Query OK, 1 row affected (0.05 sec)

master> UPDATE user SET password = 'secret' WHERE email = 'mats@example.com';
Query OK, 1 row affected (0.01 sec)
Rows matched: 1  Changed: 1  Warnings: 0

master> SELECT * FROM log;
+--------+--------------+---------------------------------------------+
| number | user         | brief                                       |
+--------+--------------+---------------------------------------------+
|      1 | mats@sun.com | User 'mats@example.com' added               |
|      2 | mats@sun.com | Changed password from 'xyzzy' to 'secret'   |
+--------+--------------+---------------------------------------------+
2 rows in set (0.00 sec)
```

This is, of course, not very secure, but at least it illustrates the situation. So, how do these changes appear in the binary log when using row-based replication?

```
master> SHOW BINLOG EVENTS IN 'mysqld1-bin.000054' FROM 2180;
+------------------+------+-------------+-----------+------------+------------------------+
|Log_name          |Pos   |Event_type   |Server_id  |End_log_pos |Info                    |
+------------------+------+-------------+-----------+------------+------------------------+
|master-bin.000054 |2180  |Query        |        1  |       2248 |BEGIN                   |
|master-bin.000054 |2248  |Table_map    |        1  |       2297 |table_id: 24 (test.user)|
|master-bin.000054 |2297  |Table_map    |        1  |       2344 |table_id: 26 (test.log) |
|master-bin.000054 |2344  |Write_rows   |        1  |       2397 |table_id: 24            |
|master-bin.000054 |2397  |Write_rows   |        1  |       2471 |table_id: 26 flags:     |
|                  |      |             |           |            | STMT_END_F             |
|master-bin.000054 |2471  |Query        |        1  |       2540 |COMMIT                  |
|master-bin.000054 |2540  |Query        |        1  |       2608 |BEGIN                   |
|master-bin.000054 |2608  |Table_map    |        1  |       2657 |table_id: 24 (test.user)|
|master-bin.000054 |2657  |Table_map    |        1  |       2704 |table_id: 26 (test.log) |
|master-bin.000054 |2704  |Update_rows  |        1  |       2783 |table_id: 24            |
|master-bin.000054 |2783  |Write_rows   |        1  |       2873 |table_id: 26 flags:     |
|                  |      |             |           |            | STMT_END_F             |
|master-bin.000054 |2873  |Query        |        1  |       2942 |COMMIT                  |
+------------------+------+-------------+-----------+------------+------------------------+
12 rows in set (0.00 sec)
```

As you can see, each statement is treated as a separate transaction containing only a single statement. The statement changes two tables—the *test.user* and *test.log* tables—and therefore there are two table maps at the beginning of the statement in the binary log. When replicated to the slave, these events are executed directly and the execution goes "below the trigger radar," thereby avoiding execution of the triggers for the tables on the slave.

Filtering

Filtering also works differently in statement-based and row-based replication. Recall from Chapter 3 that statement-based replication filtering is done on the entire statement—either all of the statement is executed or the statement is not executed at all—because it is not possible to execute just part of a statement. For the database filtering options, the current database is used and not the database of the table that is being changed.

Row-based replication offers more choice. Since each row for a specific table is caught and replicated, it is possible to filter on the actual table being updated and even filter out some rows based on arbitrary conditions. For this reason, row-based replication also filters changes based on the actual table updated and is not based on the current database for the statement.

Consider what will happen with filtering on a slave that is set up to ignore the *ignore_me* database. What will be the result of executing the following statement under statement-based and row-based replication?

```
USE test; INSERT INTO ignore_me.t1 VALUES (1),(2);
```

For statement-based replication, the statement will be executed, but for row-based replication, the changes to table *t1* will be ignored since the *ignore_me* database is on the ignore list.

Continuing on this path, what will happen with the following multitable update statement?

```
USE test; UPDATE ignore_me.t1, test.t2 SET t1.a = 3, t2.a = 4 WHERE t1.a = t2.a;
```

With statement-based replication, the statement will be executed, expecting the table *ignore_me.t1* to exist—which it might not, since the database is ignored—and will update both the *ignore_me.t1* and *test.t2* tables. Row-based replication, on the other hand, will update only the *test.t2* table.

Partial Execution of Statements

As already noted, statement-based replication works pretty well unless you have to account for failures, crashes, and nondeterministic behavior. Since you can count on the failure or crash to occur at the worst possible moment, this will almost always lead to partially executed statements.

The same situation occurs when the number of rows affected by an UPDATE, DELETE, or INSERT statement is artificially limited. This may happen explicitly through a LIMIT clause or because the table is nontransactional and, say, a duplicate key error aborts execution and causes the statement to be only partially applied to the table.

In such cases, the changes that the statement describes are applied to only an initial set of rows. The master and the slave can have different opinions of how the rows are ordered, which can therefore result in the statement being applied to different sets of rows on the master and the slave.

MyISAM maintains all the rows in the order in which they were inserted. That may give you confidence that the same rows will be affected in case of partial changes. Unfortunately, however, that is not the case. If the slave has been cloned from the master using a logical backup or restored from a backup, it is possible that the insertion order changed.

Normally, you can solve this problem by adding an ORDER BY clause, but even that does not leave you entirely safe, since you are still in danger of having the statement partially executed because of a crash.

Conclusion

This chapter concludes a series of chapters about MySQL replication. We discussed advanced replication topics such as how to promote slaves to masters more robustly, looked at tips and techniques for avoiding corrupted databases after a crash, examined multisource replication configurations and considerations, and finally looked at row-based replication in detail.

In the next chapters, we examine another set of topics for building robust data centers, including monitoring, performance tuning of storage engines, and replication.

Joel met his boss in the hallway on his way back from lunch. "Hello, Mr. Summerson."

"Hello, Joel."

"Have you read my report?"

"Yes, I have, Joel. Good work. I've passed it around to some of the other departments for comment. I want to add it to our SOP manual."

Joel imagined SOP meant standard operating procedures.

"I've asked the reviewers to send you their comments. It might need some wordsmithing to fit into an SOP, but I know you're up to the task."

"Thank you, sir."

Mr. Summerson nodded, patted Joel on the shoulder, and continued on his way down the hall.

## PART II

Monitoring and Disaster Recovery

Now that you have a sophisticated, multiserver system that hopefully meets your site's needs, you must keep on top of it. This part of the book explains monitoring, with some topics in performance, and covers backups and other aspects of handling the inevitable failures that sometimes occur.

## CHAPTER 7

Getting Started with Monitoring

Joel placed his nonfat half-caf latte, fruit cup, and cheese pastry on his desk and smiled at the parody of nutrition awaiting him. Ever since he found the upscale shopping center on his walk to work, his breakfasts had gotten rather creative.

He turned on his monitor and waited for his email application to retrieve his messages while he opened the top of his latte. Scanning the message subjects and hoping there wasn't yet another message from his boss, he noticed several messages from users with subjects that hinted at performance issues.

Joel clicked through them, scanning the text. "Well, I guess something must be wrong," he mumbled, as he read complaints about how applications that queried the database system were taking too long to respond.

He unwrapped his pastry and pondered what could be causing the problems. "Things were just fine yesterday," he reasoned. After a few sips of his latte he remembered something he read about performance monitoring while working on the lab machines at college.

Joel finished his pastry and reached for his *MySQL High Availability* book. "There has got to be something in here," he said.

How do you know when your servers are performing poorly? If you wait for your users to tell you something is wrong, chances are there has been something wrong for some time. Leaving problems unaddressed for an extended period complicates the diagnosis and repair process.

In this chapter, we will begin our examination of monitoring MySQL at the operating system level, using the basic tools available on various systems. We look here first because a system service or application always relies on the performance of the operating system and its hardware. If the operating system is performing poorly, so will the database system or application.

We will first examine the reasons for monitoring systems, then we'll look at basic monitoring tasks for popular operating systems and discuss how monitoring can make your preventive maintenance tasks easier. Once you've mastered these skills, you can begin to look more closely at your database system. In the next chapter, we will look in greater detail at monitoring a MySQL server, along with some practical guides to solving common performance problems.

Ways of Monitoring

When we think of monitoring, we normally think about some form of early warning system that detects problems. However, the definition of monitor (as a verb) is "to observe, record, or detect an operation or condition with instruments that do not affect the operation or condition" (*http://www.dictionary.com*). This early warning system uses a combination of automated sampling and an alert system.

The Linux and Unix operating systems are very complex and have many parameters that affect all manner of minor and major system activities. Tuning these systems for performance can be more art than science. Unlike some desktop operating systems, Linux and Unix (and their variants) do not hide the tuning tools nor do they restrict what you can tune. Some systems, such as Mac OS X and Windows, hide many of the underlying mechanics of the system behind a very user-friendly visual interface.

The Mac OS X operating system, for example, is a very elegant and smoothly running operating system that needs little or no attention from the user under normal conditions. However, as you will see in the following sections, the Mac OS X system provides a plethora of advanced monitoring tools that can help you tune your system if you know where to look for them.

The Windows operating system has many variants, the newest at the time of this writing being Windows 7. Fortunately, most of these variants include the same set of monitoring tools, which allow the user to tune the system to meet specific needs. While not considered as suave as Mac OS X, Windows offers a greater range of user-accessible tuning options.

There are three primary categories of system monitoring: system performance, application performance, and security. You may commence monitoring for more specific reasons, but in general the task falls into one of these categories.

Each category uses a different set of tools (with some overlap) and has a different objective. For instance, you should monitor system performance to ensure the system is operating at peak efficiency. Application performance monitoring ensures a single application is performing at peak efficiency, and security monitoring helps you ensure the systems are protected in the most secure manner.

Monitoring a MySQL server is akin to monitoring an application. This is because MySQL, like most database systems, lets you measure a number of variables and status indicators that have little or nothing to do with the operating system. However, a database system is very susceptible to the performance of the host operating system, so it is important to ensure your operating system is performing well before trying to diagnose problems with the database system.

Since the goal is to monitor a MySQL system to ensure the database system is performing at peak efficiency, the following sections discuss monitoring the operating system for performance. We leave monitoring for security to other texts that specialize in the details and nuances of security monitoring.

Benefits of Monitoring

There are two approaches to monitoring. You may want to ensure nothing has changed (no degradation of performance and no security breaches) or to investigate what has changed or gone wrong. Monitoring the system to ensure nothing has changed is called *proactive monitoring*, whereas monitoring to see what went wrong is called *reactive monitoring*. Sadly, most monitoring occurs in a reactive manner. Very few IT professionals have the time or resources to conduct proactive monitoring. Reactive monitoring is therefore the only form of monitoring some professionals understand.

However, if you take the time to monitor your system proactively, you can eliminate a lot of reactive work. For example, if your users complain about poor performance (the number one trigger for reactive monitoring), you have no way of knowing how much the system has degraded unless you have previous monitoring results with which to compare. Recording such results is called *forming a baseline* of your system. That is, you monitor the performance of your system under low, normal, and high loads over a period of time. If you do the sampling frequently and consistently, you can determine the typical performance of the system under various loads. Thus, when users report performance problems, you can sample the system and compare the results to your baseline. If you include enough detail in your historical data, you can normally see, at a glance, which part of the system has changed.

System Components to Monitor

You should examine four basic parts of the system when monitoring performance:

Processor
>   Check to see how much of it is utilized and what peaks are reached by utilization.

Memory
>   Check to see how much is being used and how much is still available to run programs.

Disk
>   Check to see how much disk space is available, how disk space is used, and what demand there is for it and how fast it delivers content (response time).

Network
> Check for throughput, latency, and error rates when communicating with other systems on the network.

Processor

Monitor the system's CPU to ensure there are no runaway processes and that the CPU cycles are being shared equally among the running programs. One way to do this is to call up a list of the programs running and determine what percentage of the CPU each is using. Another method is to examine the load average of the system processes. Most operating systems provide several views of the performance of the CPU.

 A process is a unit of work in a Linux or Unix system. A program may have one or more processes running at a time. Multithreaded applications, such as MySQL, generally appear on the system as multiple processes.

When a CPU is under a performance load and contention is high, the system can exhibit very slow performance and even periods of seeming inactivity. When this occurs, you must either reduce the number of processes or reduce the CPU usage of processes that seem to be consuming more CPU time. But be sure to monitor the CPUs to make sure that high CPU utilization is really the cause of the problem—slowness is even more likely to occur because of memory contention, discussed in the next section.

Some of the common solutions to CPU overloading include:

Provision a new server to run some processes
> This is, of course, the best method, but requires money for new systems. Experienced system administrators can often find other ways to reduce CPU usage, especially when the organization is more willing to spend your time than to spend money.

Remove unnecessary processes
> An enormous number of systems run background processes that may be useful for certain occasions but just bog down the system most of the time. However, an administrator must know the system very well to identify which processes are nonessential.

Kill runaway processes
> These probably stem from buggy applications, and they are often the culprit when performance problems are intermittent or rare. In the event that you cannot stop a runaway process using a controlled or orderly method, you may need to terminate the process abruptly using a *force quit* dialog or the command line.

Optimize applications

Some applications routinely take up more CPU time or other resources than they really need. Poorly designed SQL statements are often a drag on the database system.

Lower process priorities

Some processes run as background jobs, such as report generators, and can be run more slowly to make room for interactive processes.

Reschedule processes

Maybe some of those report generators can run at night when system load is lower.

Processes that consume too much CPU time are called *CPU-bound* or *processor-bound*, meaning they do not suspend themselves for I/O and cannot be swapped out of memory.

If you find the CPU is not under contention and there are either few processes running or no processes consuming large amounts of CPU time, the problem with performance is likely to be elsewhere: waiting on disk I/O, insufficient memory, excessive page swapping, etc.

Memory

Monitor memory to ensure your applications are not requesting so much memory that they waste system time on memory management. From the very first days of limited random access memory (RAM, or main memory), operating systems have evolved to employ a sophisticated method of using disk memory to store unused portions or pages of main memory. This technique, called *paging* or *swapping*, allows a system to run more processes than main memory can load at one time, by storing the memory for suspended processes and later retrieving the memory when the process is reactivated. While the cost of moving a page of memory from memory to disk and back again is relatively high (it is time-consuming compared to accessing main memory directly), modern operating systems can do it so quickly that the penalty isn't normally an issue unless it reaches such a high level that the processor and disk cannot keep up with the demands.

However, the operating system may perform some swapping at a high level periodically to reclaim memory. Be sure to measure memory usage over a period of time to ensure you are not observing a normal cleanup operation.

When periods of high paging occur, it is likely that low memory availability may be the result of a runaway process consuming too much memory or too many processes requesting too much memory. This kind of high paging, called *thrashing*, can be treated the same way as a CPU under contention. Processes that consume too much memory are called *memory-bound*.

When treating memory performance problems, the natural tendency is to add more memory. While that may indeed solve the problem, it is also possible that the memory is not allocated correctly among the various subsystems.

There are several things you can do in this situation. You can allocate different amounts of memory to parts of the system—such as the kernel or filesystem—or to various applications that permit such tweaking, including MySQL. You can also change the priority of the paging subsystem so the operating system begins paging earlier.

 Be very careful when tweaking memory subsystems on your server. Be sure to consult your documentation or a book dedicated to improving performance for your specific operating system.

If you monitor memory and find that the system is not paging too frequently, but performance is still an issue, the problem is likely to be related to one of the other subsystems.

Disk

Monitor disk usage to ensure there is enough free disk space available, as well as sufficient I/O bandwidth to allow processes to execute without significant delay. You can measure this using either a *per-process* or *overall transfer* rate to and from disk. The per-process rate is the amount of data a single process can read or write. The overall transfer rate is the maximum bandwidth available for reading and writing data on disk. Some systems have multiple disk controllers; in these cases, overall transfer rate may be measured per disk controller.

Performance issues can arise if one or more processes are consuming too much of the maximum disk transfer rate. This can have very detrimental effects on the rest of the system in much the same way as a process that consumes too many CPU cycles: it "starves" other processes, forcing them to wait longer for disk access.

Processes that consume too much of the disk transfer rate are called *disk-bound*, meaning they are trying to access the disk at a frequency greater than the available share of the disk transfer rate. If you can reduce the pressure placed on your I/O system by a disk-bound process, you'll free up more bandwidth for other processes.

One way to meet the needs of a process performing a lot of I/O to disk is to increase the block size of the filesystem, thus making large transfers more efficient and reducing the overhead imposed by a disk-bound process. However, this may cause other processes to run more slowly.

 Be careful when tuning filesystems on servers that have only a single controller or disk. Be sure to consult your documentation or a book dedicated to improving performance for your specific operating system.

If you have the resources, one strategy for dealing with disk contention is to add another disk controller and disk array and move the data for one of the disk-bound processes to the new disk controller. Another strategy is to move a disk-bound process to another, less utilized server. Finally, in some cases it may be possible to increase the bandwidth of the disk by upgrading the disk system to a faster technology.

There are differing opinions as to where to optimize first or even which is the best choice. We believe:

- If you need to run a lot of processes, maximize the disk transfer rate or split the processes among different disk arrays or systems.
- If you need to run a few processes that access large amounts of data, maximize the per-process transfer rate by increasing the block size of the filesystem.

You may also need to strike a balance between the two solutions to meet your unique mix of processes by moving some of the processes to other systems.

Network Subsystem

Monitor network interfaces to ensure there is enough bandwidth and that the data being sent or received is of sufficient quality.

Processes that consume too much network bandwidth, because they are attempting to read or write more data than the network configuration or hardware make possible, are called *network-bound*. These processes keep other processes from accessing sufficient network bandwidth to avoid delays.

Network bandwidth issues are normally indicated by utilization of a percentage of the maximum bandwidth of the network interface. You can solve these issues with processes by assigning the processes to specific ports on a network interface.

Network data quality issues are normally indicated by a high number of errors encountered on the network interface. Luckily, the operating system and data transfer applications usually employ *checksumming* or some other algorithm to detect errors, but retransmissions place a heavy load on the network and operating system. Solving the problem may require moving some applications to other systems on the network or installing additional network cards, which normally requires a diagnosis followed by changing the network hardware, reconfiguring the network protocols, or moving the system to a different subnet on the network.

 You may hear the terms *I/O-bound* or *I/O-starved* when referring to processes. This normally means the process is consuming too much disk or network bandwidth.

Monitoring Solutions

For each of the four subsystems just discussed, a modern operating system offers its own specific tools that you can use to get information about the subsystem's status. These tools are largely standalone applications that do not correlate (at least directly) with the other tools. As you will see in the next sections, the tools are powerful in their own right, but it requires a fair amount of effort to record and analyze all of the data they produce.

Fortunately, a number of third-party monitoring solutions are available for most operating and database systems. The following are a few of the more notable offerings. It is often best to contact your systems providers for recommendations on the best solution to meet your needs and maintain compatibility with your infrastructure. Most vendors offer system monitoring tools as an option.

up.time
  http://www.uptimesoftware.com/

Cacti
  http://www.cacti.net/

KDE System Guard (KSysGuard)
  http://docs.kde.org/stable/en/kdebase-workspace/ksysguard/index.html

Gnome System Monitor
  http://library.gnome.org/users/gnome-system-monitor/

Nagios
  http://www.nagios.org/

Sun Management Center
  http://www.sun.com/software/products/sunmanagementcenter/index.xml

MySQL Enterprise Monitor
  http://www.mysql.com/products/enterprise/monitor.html

 We will discuss the MySQL Enterprise Monitor and automated monitoring and report in greater detail in Chapter 13.

The following sections describe the built-in monitoring tools for some of the major operating systems. We will study the Linux and Unix commands in a little more detail, as they are particularly suited to investigating the performance issues and strategies we've discussed. However, we will also include an examination of the monitoring tools for Mac OS X and Microsoft Windows.

Linux and Unix Monitoring

Database monitoring on Linux or Unix can involve tools for monitoring the CPU, memory, disk, network, and even security and users. In classic Unix fashion, all of the core tools run from the command line and most are located in the *bin* or *sbin* folders. Table 7-1 includes the list of tools we've found useful, with a brief description of each.

Table 7-1. System monitoring tools for Linux and Unix

Utility	Description
ps	Shows the list of processes running on the system.
top	Displays process activity sorted by CPU utilization.
vmstat	Displays information about memory, paging, block transfers, and CPU activity.
uptime	Displays how long the system has been running. It also tells you how many users are logged on and the system load average over 1, 5, and 15 minutes.
free	Displays memory usage.
iostat	Displays average disk activity and processor load.
sar	System activity report. Allows you to collect and report a wide variety of system activity.
pmap	Displays a map of how a process is using memory.
mpstat	Displays CPU usage for multiprocessor systems.
netstat	Displays information about network activity.
cron	A subsystem that allows you to schedule the execution of a process. You can schedule execution of these utilities so you can collect regular statistics over time or check statistics at specific times, such as during peak or minimal loads.

Some operating systems provide additional or alternative tools. Consult your operating system documentation for additional tools for monitoring your system performance.

As you can see from Table 7-1, a rich variety of tools is available with a host of potentially useful information. The following sections discuss some of the more popular tools and explain briefly how you can use them to identify the problems described in the previous sections.

Process Activity

Several commands provide information about processes running on your system, notably `top`, `iostat`, `mpstat`, and `ps`.

The top command

The top command provides a summary of system information and a dynamic view of the processes on your system ranked by the most CPU-intensive tasks. The display typically contains information about the process, including the process ID, the user who started the process, its priority, the percentage of CPU it is using, how much time it has consumed, and, of course, the command used to start the process. However, some operating systems have slightly different reports. This is probably the most popular utility in the set because it presents a snapshot of your system every few seconds. Figure 7-1 shows the output when running top on a Linux (Ubuntu) system under moderate load.

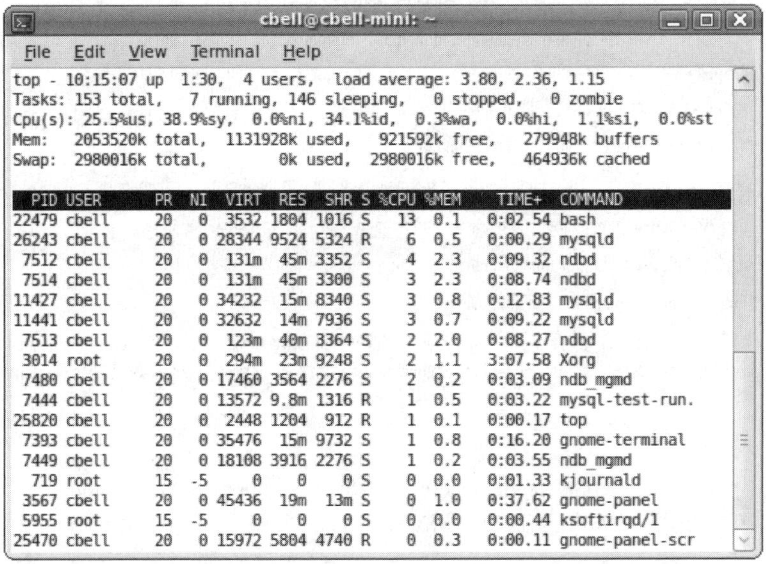

```
                            cbell@cbell-mini: ~

  File   Edit   View   Terminal   Help

top - 10:15:07 up  1:30,  4 users,  load average: 3.80, 2.36, 1.15
Tasks: 153 total,   7 running, 146 sleeping,   0 stopped,   0 zombie
Cpu(s): 25.5%us, 38.9%sy,  0.0%ni, 34.1%id,  0.3%wa,  0.0%hi,  1.1%si,  0.0%st
Mem:   2053520k total,  1131928k used,   921592k free,   279948k buffers
Swap:  2980016k total,        0k used,  2980016k free,   464936k cached

  PID USER      PR  NI  VIRT  RES  SHR S %CPU %MEM    TIME+  COMMAND
22479 cbell     20   0  3532 1804 1016 S   13  0.1  0:02.54 bash
26243 cbell     20   0 28344 9524 5324 R    6  0.5  0:00.29 mysqld
 7512 cbell     20   0  131m  45m 3352 S    4  2.3  0:09.32 ndbd
 7514 cbell     20   0  131m  45m 3300 S    3  2.3  0:08.74 ndbd
11427 cbell     20   0 34232  15m 8340 S    3  0.8  0:12.83 mysqld
11441 cbell     20   0 32632  14m 7936 S    3  0.7  0:09.22 mysqld
 7513 cbell     20   0  123m  40m 3364 S    2  2.0  0:08.27 ndbd
 3014 root      20   0  294m  23m 9248 S    2  1.1  3:07.58 Xorg
 7480 cbell     20   0 17460 3564 2276 S    2  0.2  0:03.09 ndb_mgmd
 7444 cbell     20   0 13572 9.8m 1316 R    1  0.5  0:03.22 mysql-test-run.
25820 cbell     20   0  2448 1204  912 R    1  0.1  0:00.17 top
 7393 cbell     20   0 35476  15m 9732 S    1  0.8  0:16.20 gnome-terminal
 7449 cbell     20   0 18108 3916 2276 S    1  0.2  0:03.55 ndb_mgmd
  719 root      15  -5     0    0    0 S    0  0.0  0:01.33 kjournald
 3567 cbell     20   0 45436  19m  13m S    0  1.0  0:37.62 gnome-panel
 5955 root      15  -5     0    0    0 S    0  0.0  0:00.44 ksoftirqd/1
25470 cbell     20   0 15972 5804 4740 R    0  0.3  0:00.11 gnome-panel-scr
```

Figure 7-1. The top command

The system summary is located at the top of the listing and has some interesting data. It shows the percentages of CPU time for user (%us); system (%sy); nice (%ni), which is the time spent running users' processes that have had their priorities changed; I/O wait (%wa); and even the percentage of time spent handling hardware and software interrupts. Also included are the amount of memory and swap space available, how much is being used, how much is free, and the size of the buffers.

Below the summary comes the list of processes, in descending order (which is from where the name of the command derives) based on how much CPU time is being used. In this example, a Bash shell is currently the task leader followed by one or several installations of MySQL.

Niceness

You can change the priority of a process on a Linux or Unix system. You may want to do this to lower the priorities of processes that require too much CPU power, are of lower urgency, or could run for an extended period but that you do not want to cancel or reschedule. You can use the commands nice, ionice, and renice to alter the priority of a process.

Most distributions of Linux and Unix now group processes that have had their priorities changed into a group called nice. This allows you to get statistics about these modified processes without having to remember or collate the information yourself. Having commands that report the CPU time for nice processes gives you the opportunity to see how much CPU these processes are consuming with respect to the rest of the system. For example, a high value on this parameter may indicate there is at least one process with too high of a priority.

Perhaps the best use of the top command is to allow it to run and refresh every three seconds. If you check the display at intervals over time, you will begin to see which processes are consuming the most CPU time. This can help you determine at a glance whether there is a runaway process.

> You can change the refresh rate of the command by specifying the delay on the command. For example, top -d 3 sets the delay to three seconds.

Most Linux and Unix variants have a top command that works like we have described. Some have interesting interactive hot keys that allow you to toggle information on or off, sort the list, and even change to a colored display. You should consult the manual page for the top command specific to your operating system, since the special hot keys and interactive features differ among operating systems.

The iostat command

The iostat command gives you different sets of information about your system, including statistics about CPU time, device I/O, and even partitions and network filesystems (NFS). The command is useful for monitoring processes because it gives you a picture of how the system is doing overall related to processes and the amount of time the system is waiting for I/O. Figure 7-2 shows an example of running the iostat command on a system with moderate load.

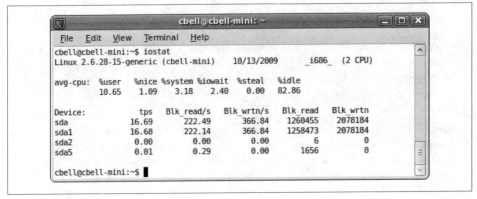

Figure 7-2. The iostat command

 The iostat, mpstat, and sar commands might not be installed on your system by default, but they can be installed as an option. For example, they are part of the sysstat package in Ubuntu distributions. Consult your operating system documentation for information about installation and setup.

Figure 7-2 shows the percentages for CPU usage from the time the system was started. These are calculated as averages among all processors. As you can see, the system is running on a dual-core CPU, but only one row of values is given. This data includes the percentage of CPU utilization:

- Executing at the user level (running applications)
- Executing at the user level with nice priority
- Executing at the system level (kernel processes)
- Waiting on I/O
- Waiting for virtual processes
- Idle time

A report like this can give you an idea of how your system has been performing since it was started. While this means that you might not notice periods of poor performance (because they are averaged over time), it does offer a unique perspective on how the processes have been consuming available processing time or waiting on I/O. For example, if %idle is very low, you can determine that the system was kept very busy. Similarly, a high value for %iowait can indicate a problem with the disk. If %system or %nice is much higher than %user, it can indicate an imbalance of system and prioritized processes that are keeping normal processes from running.

The mpstat command

The `mpstat` command presents much of the same information as `iostat` for processor time, but splits the information out by processor. If you run this command on a multi-processor system, you will see the percentage of data per processor as well as the totals for all processors. Figure 7-3 shows an example of the `mpstat` command.

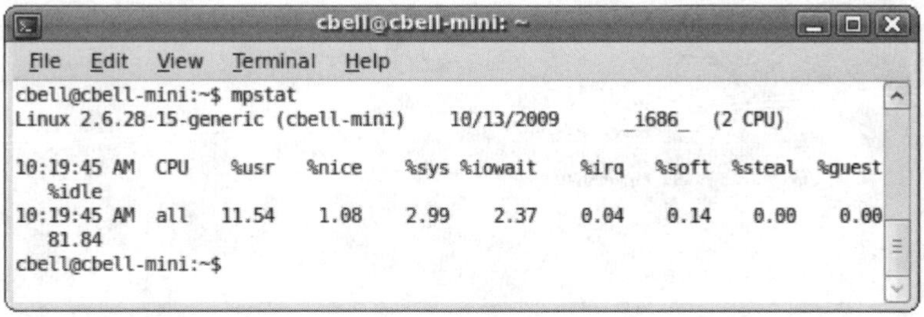

```
cbell@cbell-mini: ~
File   Edit   View   Terminal   Help
cbell@cbell-mini:~$ mpstat
Linux 2.6.28-15-generic (cbell-mini)      10/13/2009       _i686_  (2 CPU)

10:19:45 AM  CPU   %usr  %nice   %sys %iowait   %irq   %soft %steal %guest
    %idle
10:19:45 AM  all  11.54   1.08   2.99    2.37   0.04    0.14   0.00   0.00
    81.84
cbell@cbell-mini:~$
```

Figure 7-3. The mpstat command

There is an option to tell the `mpstat` command to refresh the information based on an interval passed. This can be helpful if you want to watch how your processors are performing with respect to the processes over a period of time. For instance, you can see whether your processor affinity is unbalanced (too many processes are assigned to one specific processor).

To find out more about the `mpstat` command, consult the manual page for your operating system.

The ps command

The `ps` command is one of those commands we use on a daily basis but never take the time to consider its power and utility. This command gives you a snapshot of the processes running on your system. It displays the process ID, the terminal the process is running from, the amount of time it has been running, and the command used to start the process.

What makes the `ps` command so versatile is the number of options available for displaying data. You can display the processes for a specific user, get related processes for a specific process by showing its process tree, and even change the format of the output. Consult your documentation for information about the options available on your operating system.

One of the ways you can use this output to diagnose problems is to look for processes that have been running for a long time or check process status (for instance, check those that are stuck in a suspicious state or sleeping). Unless they are known applications like MySQL, you might want to investigate why they have been running for so long.

Figure 7-4 shows an abbreviated example of the `ps` command run on a system under moderate load.

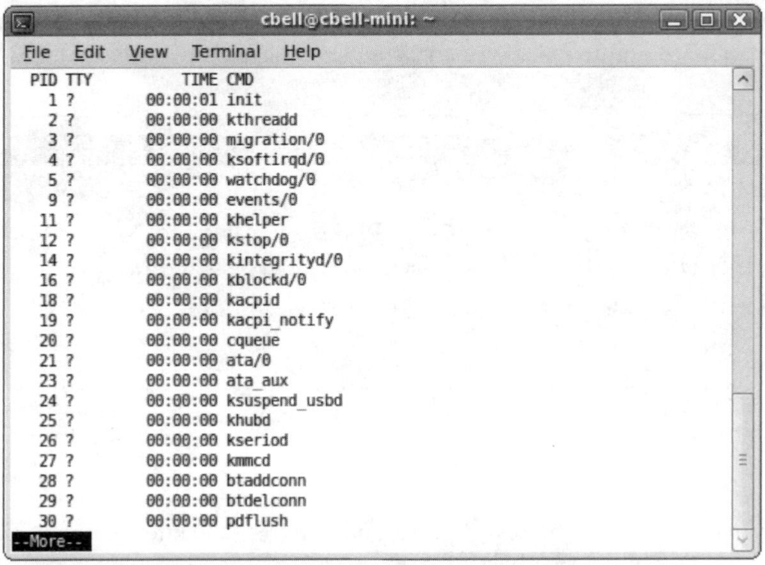

```
┌─────────────────────────────────────────────────────────────┐
│ ⊠                    cbell@cbell-mini: ~          _ □ X       │
├─────────────────────────────────────────────────────────────┤
│ File  Edit  View  Terminal  Help                             │
│  PID TTY         TIME CMD                              ∧      │
│    1 ?       00:00:01 init                                    │
│    2 ?       00:00:00 kthreadd                                │
│    3 ?       00:00:00 migration/0                             │
│    4 ?       00:00:00 ksoftirqd/0                             │
│    5 ?       00:00:00 watchdog/0                              │
│    9 ?       00:00:00 events/0                                │
│   11 ?       00:00:00 khelper                                 │
│   12 ?       00:00:00 kstop/0                                 │
│   14 ?       00:00:00 kintegrityd/0                           │
│   16 ?       00:00:00 kblockd/0                               │
│   18 ?       00:00:00 kacpid                                  │
│   19 ?       00:00:00 kacpi_notify                            │
│   20 ?       00:00:00 cqueue                                  │
│   21 ?       00:00:00 ata/0                                   │
│   23 ?       00:00:00 ata_aux                                 │
│   24 ?       00:00:00 ksuspend_usbd                           │
│   25 ?       00:00:00 khubd                                   │
│   26 ?       00:00:00 kseriod                                 │
│   27 ?       00:00:00 kmmcd                             ≡     │
│   28 ?       00:00:00 btaddconn                               │
│   29 ?       00:00:00 btdelconn                               │
│   30 ?       00:00:00 pdflush                                 │
│ --More--                                               ∨      │
└─────────────────────────────────────────────────────────────┘
```

Figure 7-4. The ps command

Another use for the output is to see whether there are processes that you do not recognize or a lot of processes run by a single user. Many times this indicates a script that is spawning processes, perhaps because it has been set up improperly, and can even indicate a dangerous security practice.

Perhaps the most common way some use the `ps` command is to determine the process IDs for a given program. For example, if you want to know the process IDs of all of the `mysqld` programs, issue the command:

```
ps -A | grep mysqld
```

This will send the list of all processes to the `grep` command, which will in turn only show those rows with "mysqld" in them. You can use this technique to find a process ID so you can get detailed information about that process using other commands.

There are many other utilities built into operating systems to display information about processes. As always, a good reference on performance tuning for your specific operating system will be the best source for more in-depth information about monitoring processes.

Memory Usage

Several commands provide information about memory usage on your system. The most popular ones include `free` and `pmap`.

The free command

The `free` command shows you the amount of physical memory available. It displays the total amount of memory, the amount used, and the amount free for physical memory, and it displays the same statistics for your swap space. It also shows the memory buffers used by the kernel and the size of the cache. Figure 7-5 shows an example of `free` run on a system with a moderate load.

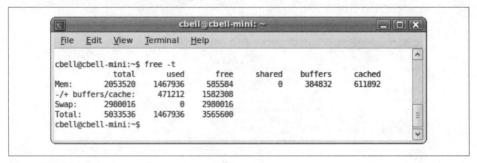

Figure 7-5. The free command

 In the output from an Ubuntu system, shown in Figure 7-5, the shared column is obsolete.

There is a switch that puts the command into a polling mode where the statistics are updated for the number of seconds provided. For example, to poll memory every five seconds, issue `free -t -s 5`.

The pmap command

The `pmap` command gives you a detailed map of the memory used for a process. To use this command, you must first find the process ID for the process you want to explore. You can get this information using the `ps` command, or even the `top` command if you are looking at a process that is consuming lots of CPU time.

You can also get the memory map of multiple processes by listing the process IDs on the command line. For example, `pmap 12578 12579` will show the memory map for process IDs 12578 and 12579.

The output shows a detailed map of all of the memory addresses and the sizes of the portions of memory used by the process at the instant the report was created. It displays the command used to launch the process, including the full path and parameters, which can be very useful for determining where the process was started and what options it is using. You'd be amazed how handy that is when trying to figure out why a process is behaving abnormally. The display also shows the mode (access rights) for the memory block. This can be useful in diagnosing interprocess issues. Figures 7-6 and 7-7 show an example of a `mysqld` process map when running on a system with moderate load.

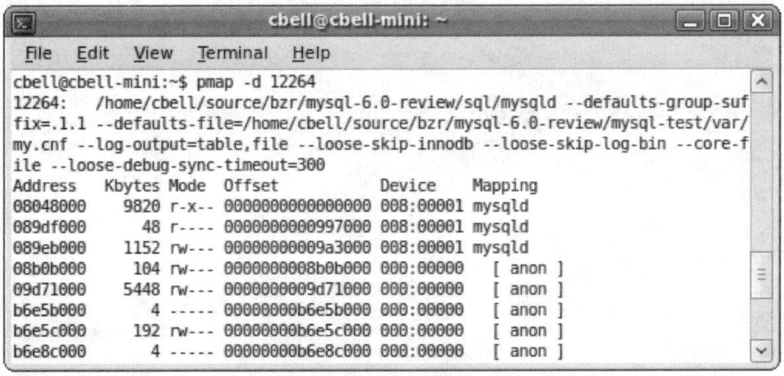

Figure 7-6. The pmap command—part 1

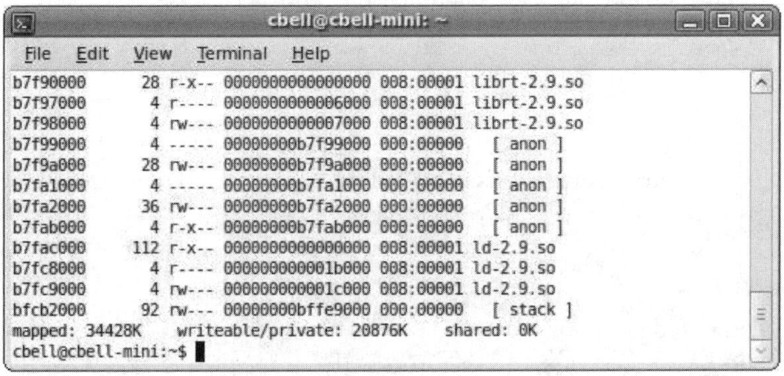

Figure 7-7. The pmap command—part 2

Notice that the listing chosen is the device output format (selected by issuing the `-d` parameter on startup) as well as where the memory is being mapped or used. This can be handy in diagnosing why a particular process is consuming lots of memory and which part (e.g., a library) is consuming the most.

Figure 7-7 shows the final line of the pmap output, which displays some useful summary information.

The final line shows how much memory is mapped to files, the amount of private memory space, and the amount shared with other processes. This information may be a key piece of data needed to solve memory allocation and sharing issues.

There are several other commands and utilities that display information about memory usage (e.g., dmesg, which can display messages from bootup); consult a good reference on performance tuning for your operating system.

Disk Usage

A number of commands can reveal the disk usage statistics on your system. This section describes and demonstrates the iostat and sar commands.

The iostat command

As you have already seen in "Process Activity" on page 253, the iostat command shows the CPU time used and a list of all of the disks and their statistics. Specifically, iostat lists each device, its transfer speed, the number of blocks read and written per second, and the total number of blocks read and written. For easy consultation, Figure 7-8 repeats Figure 7-2, which is an example of the iostat command run on a system with a moderate load.

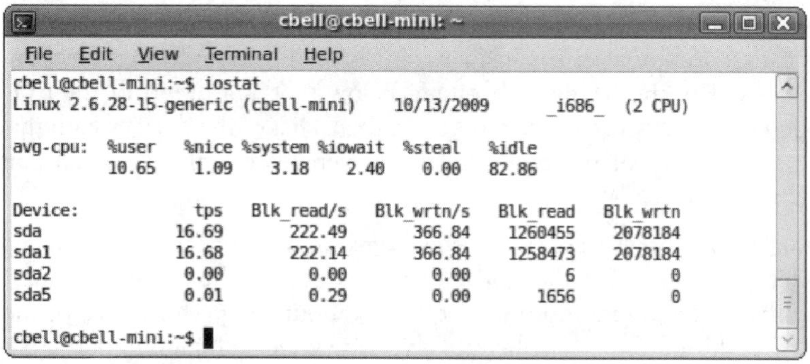

Figure 7-8. The iostat command

This report can be very important when diagnosing disk problems. At a glance, it can tell you whether some devices are being used more than others. If this is the case, you can move some processes to other devices to reduce demand for a single disk. The output can also tell you which disk is experiencing the most reads or writes—this can help you determine whether a particular device needs to be upgraded to a faster one. Conversely, you can learn which devices are underutilized. For example, if you see that your shiny new super-fast disk is not being accessed much, it is likely that you have not configured the high-volume processes to use the new disk. On the other hand, it could be that your program is using memory caches that I/O is seldom performed on.

The sar command

The sar command is a very powerful utility that displays all sorts of information about your system. It records data over time and can be configured in a variety of ways, so it can be a little tricky to set up. Consult your operating system's documentation to ensure you have it set up correctly. Like most of the system utilization commands we show, you can also configure sar to generate reports at regular intervals.

 The sar command can also display CPU usage, memory, cache, and a host of other data similar to that shown by the other commands. Some administrators set up sar to run periodically and cull the data to form a benchmark for their system. A complete tutorial on sar is beyond the scope of this book. For a more detailed examination, please see *System Performance Tuning* by Gian-Paolo D. Musumeci and Mike Loukides (O'Reilly, *http://oreilly.com/catalog/9780596002848/*).

In this section, we will look at how to use the sar command to display information about disk usage. We do this by combining displays of the I/O transfer rates, swap space and paging statistics, and block device usage. Figure 7-9 shows an example of the sar command used to display disk usage statistics.

The report displays so much information that it seems overwhelming at first glance. Notice the first section after the header. This is the paging information that displays the performance of the paging subsystem. Below that is a report of the I/O transfer rates, followed by the swap space report and then a list of the devices with their statistics. The last portion of the report displays averages calculated for all parameters sampled.

The paging report shows the rate of pages paged in or out of memory, the number of page faults per second that did not require disk access, the number of major faults requiring disk access, and additional statistics about the performance of the paging system. This information can be helpful if you are seeing a high number of page faults (major page faults are more costly), which could indicate too many processes running. Large numbers of major page faults can cause disk usage problems. That is, if this value is very high and disk usage is high, it may not be that the poor performance of the disk is just a symptom of something going wrong in the application or operating system.

The I/O transfer report shows the number of transactions per second (tps), the read and write requests, and the totals for blocks read and written. In this example, the system is not using I/O but is under heavy CPU load. This is a sign of a healthy system. If the I/O values were very high, we would suspect one or more processes of being stuck

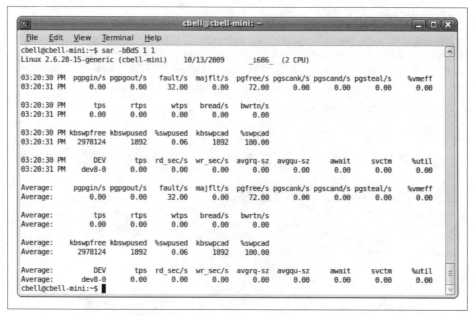

```
                              cbell@cbell-mini: ~
 File  Edit  View  Terminal  Help
 cbell@cbell-mini:~$ sar -bBdS 1 1
 Linux 2.6.28-15-generic (cbell-mini)   10/13/2009    i686   (2 CPU)

 03:20:30 PM  pgpgin/s pgpgout/s    fault/s  majflt/s  pgfree/s pgscank/s pgscand/s pgsteal/s    %vmeff
 03:20:31 PM      0.00      0.00      32.00      0.00     72.00      0.00      0.00      0.00      0.00

 03:20:30 PM        tps      rtps       wtps   bread/s   bwrtn/s
 03:20:31 PM       0.00      0.00       0.00      0.00      0.00

 03:20:30 PM kbswpfree kbswpused  %swpused  kbswpcad  %swpcad
 03:20:31 PM   2978124      1892      0.06      1892    100.00

 03:20:30 PM       DEV       tps  rd_sec/s  wr_sec/s  avgrq-sz  avgqu-sz     await     svctm     %util
 03:20:31 PM     dev8-0      0.00      0.00      0.00      0.00      0.00      0.00      0.00      0.00

 Average:     pgpgin/s pgpgout/s    fault/s  majflt/s  pgfree/s pgscank/s pgscand/s pgsteal/s    %vmeff
 Average:         0.00      0.00      32.00      0.00     72.00      0.00      0.00      0.00      0.00

 Average:          tps      rtps       wtps   bread/s   bwrtn/s
 Average:         0.00      0.00       0.00      0.00      0.00

 Average:    kbswpfree kbswpused  %swpused  kbswpcad  %swpcad
 Average:      2978124      1892      0.06      1892    100.00

 Average:          DEV       tps  rd_sec/s  wr_sec/s  avgrq-sz  avgqu-sz     await     svctm     %util
 Average:       dev8-0      0.00      0.00      0.00      0.00      0.00      0.00      0.00      0.00
 cbell@cbell-mini:~$ █
```

Figure 7-9. The sar command for disk usage

in an I/O-bound state. For MySQL, a query generating a lot of random disk accesses or tables that reside across a fragmented disk could cause such a problem.

The swap space report shows the amount of swap space available, how much is used, the percentage used, and how much cache memory is used. This can be helpful in indicating a problem with swapping out too many processes and, like the other reports, can help you determine whether the problem lies in your disks and other devices or with memory or too many processes.

The block device (any area of the system that moves data in blocks like disk, memory, etc.) report shows the transfer rate (tps), the reads and writes per second, and average wait times. This information can be helpful in diagnosing problems with your block devices. If these values are all very high (unlike this example, which shows almost no device activity), it could mean you have reached the maximum bandwidth of your devices. However, this information should be weighed against the other reports on this page to rule out a thrashing system, a system with too many processes, or a system without enough memory (or a combination of such problems).

This composite report can be helpful in determining where your disk usage problems lie. If the paging report shows an unusually high rate of faults, it's an indication you may have too many applications running or not enough memory. However, if these values are low or average, you need to look to the swap space; if that is normal, you can examine the device usage report for anomalies.

Disk Usage Analyzer

In addition to operating system utilities, the GNOME desktop project has created a graphical application called the Disk Usage Analyzer. This tool gives you an in-depth look at how your storage devices are being used. It also gives you a graphic that depicts disk usage. The utility is available in most distributions of Linux.

Figure 7-10 shows a sample report from the Disk Usage Analyzer.

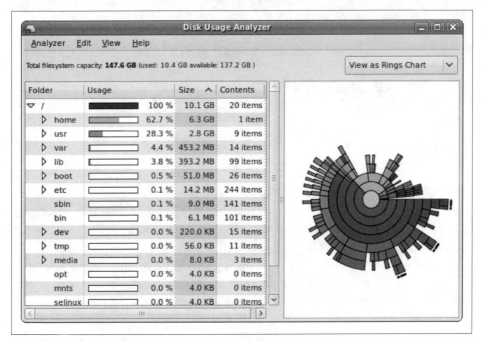

Figure 7-10. Disk Usage Analyzer

Basically, this report gives you a look at how the devices are performing alongside the paging and swap systems. Naturally, if a system is swapping a lot of processes in and out of memory, the disk usage will be unusual. This is why it is valuable to look at these items together on the same report.

Diagnosing disk problems can be challenging, and only a few commands give you the kind of detailed statistics about disk usage we've described. However, some operating systems provide more detailed and specific tools for examining disk usage. Don't forget that you can also determine available space, what is mounted, which filesystems each disk has, and much more from more general commands such as ls, df, and fdisk. Consult your operating system documentation for a list and description of all disk-related commands, as well as for disk usage and monitoring commands.

The `vmstat` command, shown later in this chapter, can also show this data. Use the `vmstat -d` command to get a text-based representation of the data.

Network Activity

Diagnosing network activity problems may require specialized knowledge of hardware and networking protocols. Detailed diagnostics are normally left to the networking specialists, but there are two commands you, as a MySQL administrator, can use to get an initial picture of the problem.

The netstat command

The `netstat` command allows you to see network connections, routing tables, interface statistics, and additional networking-related information. The command provides a lot of the information that a network specialist would use to diagnose and configure complex networking problems. However, it can be helpful to see how much traffic is passing through your network interfaces and which interfaces are being accessed the most. Figure 7-11 shows a sample report of all of the network interfaces and how much data has been transmitted over each one.

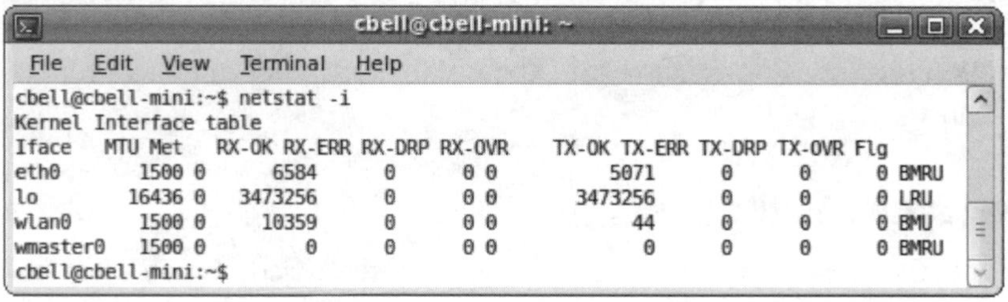

```
                         cbell@cbell-mini: ~
  File   Edit   View   Terminal   Help
cbell@cbell-mini:~$ netstat -i
Kernel Interface table
Iface    MTU Met    RX-OK RX-ERR RX-DRP RX-OVR   TX-OK TX-ERR TX-DRP TX-OVR Flg
eth0     1500 0      6584      0      0 0          5071      0      0      0 BMRU
lo      16436 0   3473256      0      0 0       3473256      0      0      0 LRU
wlan0    1500 0     10359      0      0 0            44      0      0      0 BMU
wmaster0 1500 0         0      0      0 0             0      0      0      0 BMRU
cbell@cbell-mini:~$
```

Figure 7-11. The netstat command

In systems that have multiple network interfaces, it may be helpful to determine whether any interface is being overutilized or if the wrong interfaces are active.

The ifconfig command

The `ifconfig` command, an essential tool for any network diagnostics, displays a list of the network interfaces on your system, including the status and settings for each. Figure 7-12 shows an example of the `ifconfig` command.

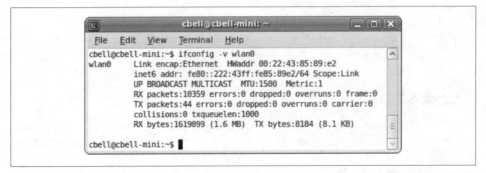

Figure 7-12. The ifconfig command

Notice how each interface, whether it is up or down, is listed, along with its configuration information. This can be very helpful in determining how an interface is configured and can tell you, for example, that instead of communicating over your super-fast Ethernet adapter, your network has failed over to a much slower interface. Many times the root of networking problems is not the traffic on the network, but rather the network interface choice or setup.

If you produce the reports shown here for your system and still need help diagnosing the problem, having this data ahead of time can help your networking specialist zero in on the problem more quickly. Once you have eliminated any processes consuming too much network bandwidth and determined where you have a viable network interface, the networking specialist can then configure the interface for optimal performance.

General System Statistics

Along with the subsystem-specific commands we've discussed, and grouped statistical reporting commands, Linux and Unix offer additional commands that give you more general information about your system. These include commands such as uptime and vmstat.

The uptime command

The uptime command displays how long a system has been running. It displays the current time; how long the system has been running; how many users have been using the system (logged on); and load averages for the past 1, 5, and 15 minutes. Figure 7-13 shows an example of the command.

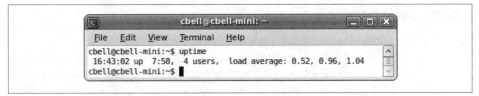

Figure 7-13. The uptime command

This information can be helpful if you want to see how the system has been performing on average in the recent past. The load averages given are for processes in an active state (not waiting on I/O or the CPU). Therefore, this information has limited use for determining performance issues, but can give you a general sense of the health of the system.

The vmstat command

The vmstat command is a general reporting tool that gives you information about processes, memory, the paging system, block I/O, disk, and CPU activity. It is sometimes used as a first stop on a quest for locating performance issues. High values in some fields may lead you to examine those areas more closely using other commands discussed in this chapter.

Figure 7-14 shows an example of the vmstat command run on a system with low load.

The data shown here includes the number of processes, where r indicates those waiting to run and b indicates those in an uninterruptible state. The next set of columns shows the swap space totals including amount of memory swapped in (si) or out (so). The next area shows the I/O reports for blocks received (bi) or sent (bo). The next area shows the number of interrupts per second (in), number of context switches per second (cs), time spent running processes in user space (us), time spent running processes in kernel space (sy), idle time (id), and time waiting for I/O (wa). These times are all in seconds.

There are more parameters and options for the vmstat command. Check your operating system manual for more details on the options available for your operating system.

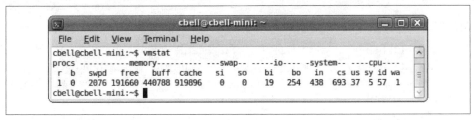

Figure 7-14. The vmstat command

Automated Monitoring with cron

Perhaps the most important tool to consider is the `cron` facility. As described in the section "Scheduling tasks on Unix" on page 42, you can use `cron` to schedule a process to run at a specific time. This allows you to run commands and save the output for later analysis. It can be a very powerful strategy, allowing you to take snapshots of the system over time. You can then use the data to form averages of the system parameters, which you can use as a benchmark to compare to when the system performs poorly in the future. This is important because it allows you to see at a glance what has changed, saving you considerable time when diagnosing performance problems.

If you run your performance monitoring tools daily, and then examine the results and compare them to your benchmark, you may be able to detect problems before your users start complaining. Indeed, this is the basic premise behind the active monitoring tools we've described.

Mac OS X Monitoring

Since the Mac OS X operating system is built on the Unix Mac kernel, you can use most of the tools described earlier to monitor your operating system. However, there are other tools specific to the Mac. These include the following graphical administration tools:

- System Profiler
- Console
- Activity Monitor

This section will present an overview of each of these tools for the purposes of monitoring a Mac OS X system. These tools form the core monitoring and reporting facilities for Mac OS X. In good Mac fashion, they are all well-written and well-behaved graphical user interfaces (GUIs). The GUIs even show the portions of the tools that report information from files. As you will see, each has a very important use and can be very helpful in diagnosing performance issues on a Mac.

System Profiler

The System Profiler gives you a snapshot of the status of your system. It provides an incredible amount of detail about just about everything in your system, including all of the hardware, the network, and the software installed. Figure 7-15 shows an example of the System Profiler.

You can find the System Profiler in the *Applications/Utilities* folder on your hard drive. You can also launch the System Profiler via Spotlight. As Figure 7-15 shows, the tool offers a tree pane on the left and a detail pane on the right. You can use the tree pane to dive into the various components of your system.

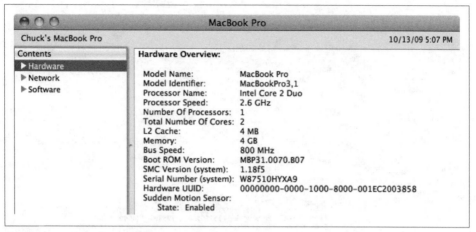

Figure 7-15. The System Profiler

If you would prefer a console-based report, the System Profiler has a command-line-equivalent application in */usr/sbin/system_profiler*. There are many parameters and options that allow you to restrict the view to certain reports. To find out more, open a terminal and type man system_profiler.

If you open the Hardware tree, you will see a listing of all of the hardware on your system. For example, if you want to see what type of memory is installed on your system, you can click the Memory item in the Hardware tree.

System Profiler provides a network report, which we have seen in another form on Linux. Click the Network tree to get a basic report of all of the network interfaces on your system. Select one of the network interfaces in the tree or in the detail pane to see all of the same (and more) information that the network information commands in Linux and Unix generate. You can also find out information about firewalls, locations you've defined, and even which volumes are shared on the network.

Another very useful report displays the applications installed on your system. Click Software→Applications report to see a list of all of the software on your system, including the name, version, when it was updated, whether it is a 64-bit application, and what kind of application it is—for instance, whether it's a universal or a native Intel binary. This last detail can be very important. For example, you can expect a universal binary to run slower than an Intel binary. It is good to know these things in advance, as they can set certain expectations for performance.

Figure 7-16 shows an example of this report.

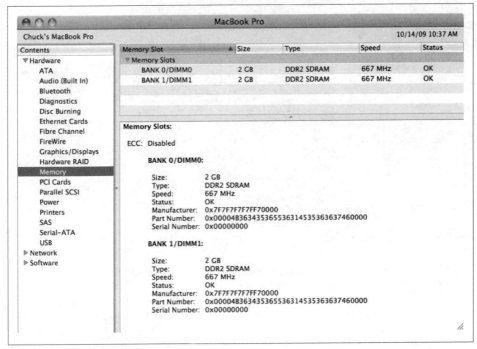

Figure 7-16. Memory report from System Profiler

As you can see, this is a lot of detail. You can see how many memory cards are installed, their speed, and even the manufacturer code and part number. Wow!

> We call each detail pane a *report* because it's essentially a detailed report for a given category. Some people may refer to all of the data as a report, which is not incorrect, but we think it's better to consider the whole thing a collection of reports.

If you are intrigued with the power of this tool, feel free to experiment and dig around in the tree for more information about your system. You will find just about any fact about it here.

The System Profiler can be very valuable during diagnostics of system problems. Many times AppleCare representatives and Apple-trained technicians will ask for a report of your system. Generate the report from the System Profiler by using the File→Save command. This saves an XML file that Apple professionals can use. You can also export the report to RTF using the File→Export command. Finally, you can print the report after saving it as a PDF file.

You can also change the level of detail reported using the View menu. It has options for *Mini*, *Basic*, and *Full*, which change the level of detail from very minimal to a complete report. Apple professionals usually ask for the full report.

A System Profiler report is the best way to determine what is on your system without opening the box. It should be your first source to determine your system configuration.

Console

The Console application displays the logfiles on your system, and is located in the */Applications/Utilities* folder or via Spotlight. Unlike the System Profiler, this tool provides you not only a data dump, but also the ability to search the logs for vital information. When diagnosing problems, it is sometimes helpful to see whether there are any messages in the logs that give more information about an event. Figure 7-17 shows an example of the Console application.

When you launch the Console application, it reads all of the system logs and categorizes them into console diagnostic messages. As you can see in Figure 7-17, the display features a log search pane on the left and a log view on the right. You can also click the individual logfiles in the Files tree to see the contents of each log. The logfiles include the following:

~/Library/Logs
> Stores all messages related to user applications. Check here for messages about applications that crash while logged in, information about iDisk activity, and other user-related tasks.

/Library/Logs
> Stores all system messages. Check here for information generated at the system level for crashes and other unusual events.

/private/var/log
> Stores all Unix BSD process-related messages. Check here for information about the system daemon or BSD utility.

 Logs are sequential text files where data is always appended, never updated in the middle, and rarely deleted.

The most powerful feature of Console is its search capability. You can create reports containing messages for a given phrase or keyword and view them later. To create a new search, select File→New Database Search in the menu. You will be presented with a generalized search builder that you can use to create your query. When you are finished, you can name and save the report for later processing. This can be a very handy way to keep an eye on troublesome applications.

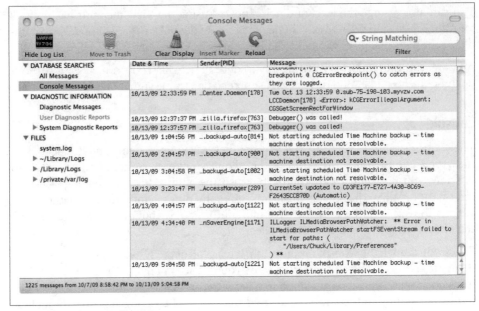

Figure 7-17. The Console application

Another really cool feature is the capability to mark a spot in a log that indicates the current date and time—you can use this to determine the last time you looked at the log. If your experience is like ours, you often find interesting messages in several places in the logs and need to review them later, but don't know where you found them or where you left off reviewing the log. Having the ability to mark a log is a real help in this case. To mark a log, highlight a location in the file and click the Mark button on the toolbar.

Although the data reported is a static snapshot of the logs upon launch and any reports you run are limited to this snapshot, you can also set up alerts for new messages in the logs. Use Console→Preferences to turn on notifications, which are delivered to you either via a bouncing icon on the Dock or by bringing the Console application to the forefront after a delay.

The Console application can be very helpful for seeing how various aspects of your system work by monitoring the events that occur and for finding errors from applications or hardware. When you are faced with a performance issue or another troublesome event, be sure to search the logs for information about the application or event. Sometimes the cure for the problem is presented to you in the form of a message generated by the application itself.

Activity Monitor

Unlike the static nature of the previously described tools, the Activity Monitor is a dynamic tool that gives you information about the system as it is running. The bulk of the data you will need to treat performance issues can be found in the Activity Monitor. Indeed, you will see information comparable to every tool presented in the Linux and Unix section as you explore the Activity Monitor: information about the CPU, system memory, disk activity, disk usage, and network interfaces.

With the Activity Monitor, for example, you can find out which processes are running and how much memory they are using as well as the percentage of CPU time each is consuming. In this case, the use is analogous to the **top** command from Linux.

The CPU display shows useful data such as the percentage of time spent executing in user space (user time), the percentage spent in system space (system time), and the percentage of time spent idle. This screen also displays the number of threads and processes running, along with a color-coded graph displaying an aggregate of the user and system time. Combined with the **top**-like display, this can be an excellent tool if you are investigating problems related to CPU-bound processes.

Figure 7-18 shows the Activity Monitor displaying a CPU report.

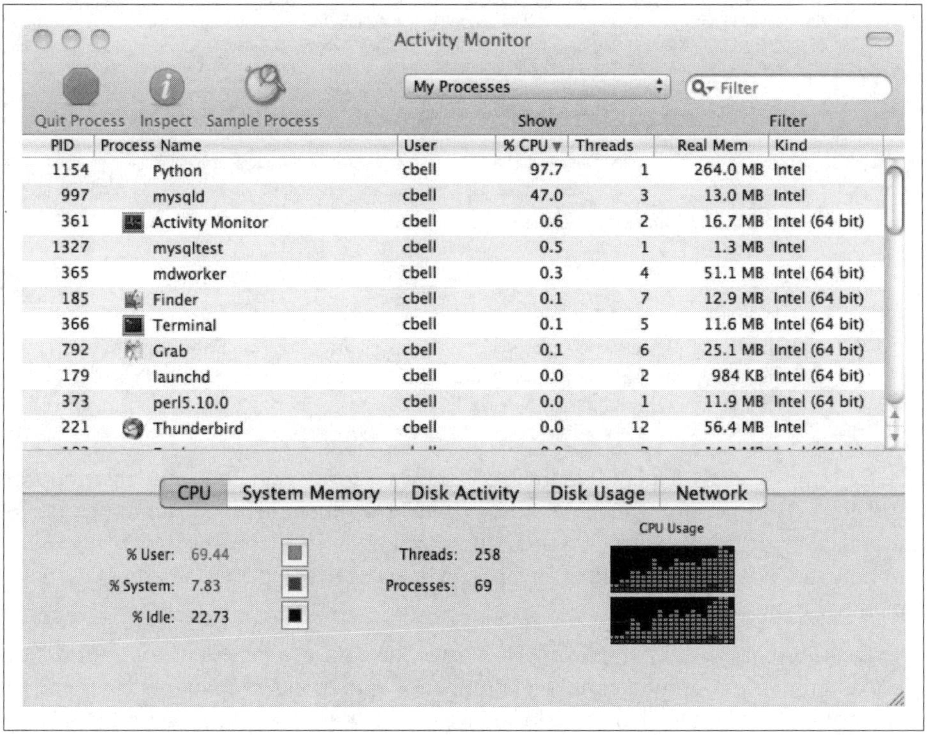

Figure 7-18. The Activity Monitor's CPU display

Notice that there is a Python script that, at the time of the sampling, was consuming a considerable portion of the CPU time. In this case, the system was running a Bazaar branch in a terminal window. The Activity Monitor shows why my system gets sluggish when branching a code tree.

You can double-click a process to get more information about it. You can also cancel a process either in a controlled manner or by forcing it to quit. Figure 7-19 shows an example of the process inspection dialog.

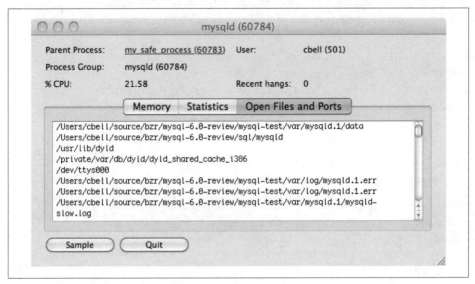

Figure 7-19. The Activity Monitor's process inspection dialog

 You can export the list of processes by selecting File→Save. You can save the list of processes either as a text file or as an XML file. Some Apple professionals may ask for the process list in addition to the System Profiler report when diagnosing problems.

The System Memory display (Figure 7-20) shows information about the distribution of memory. It shows how much memory is free, how much memory cannot be cached and must stay in RAM (in other words, the wired memory), how much is being used, and how much is inactive. With this report, you can see at a glance whether you have a memory issue.

The Disk Activity display (Figure 7-21) shows the disk activity for all of your disks. Shown in the first column are the total number of data transfers from (reads in) and to (writes out) disk along with disk performance for reads and writes per second. The next column shows the total size of the data read from and written to disk along with the

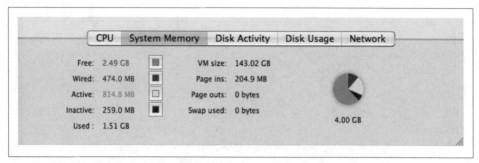

Figure 7-20. The Activity Monitor's System Memory display

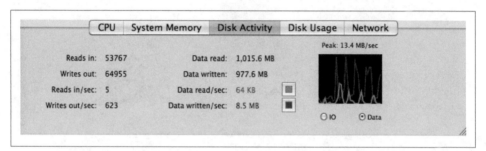

Figure 7-21. The Activity Monitor's Disk Activity display

throughput for each. Included is a graph that displays reads and writes over time in a color-coded graph.

The Disk Activity data can tell you whether you invoke a lot of disk accesses and whether the number of reads and writes (and total amount of data) is unusually high. An unusually high value could indicate you may have to run processes at different times so they do not compete for the disk or you may have to add another disk to balance the load.

The Disk Usage display (Figure 7-22) shows the used and free space for each of your drives. It also shows a color-coded pie chart to give you a quick view of the disk utilization. You can view another disk by selecting the disk in the drop-down list.

This display allows you to monitor the free space on your disk so you know when to add more disks and/or extend partitions to add more space when you run low.

The Network display (Figure 7-23) shows a lot of information about how your system is communicating with the network. Shown in the first column is how many packets were read or received (packets in) and written or sent (packets out) over the network. There are also performance statistics measured in packets per second for reads and writes. The next column shows the size of the data read and written on the network along with the transfer rate for each direction. A color-coded chart shows the relative performance of the network. Note the peak value over the chart. You can use the data

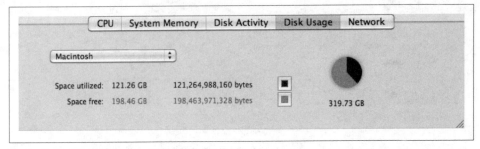

Figure 7-22. The Activity Monitor's Disk Usage display

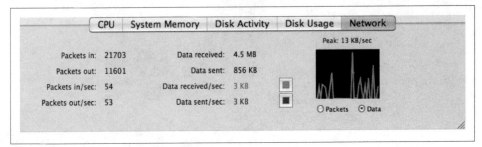

Figure 7-23. The Activity Monitor's Network display

on this display to determine whether a process is consuming the maximum bandwidth of your systems network interfaces.

This section has given you a window into the powerful monitoring tools available on Mac OS X. While not a complete tutorial, it will allow you to monitor a Mac OS X system. For complete details about each of the applications shown, be sure to consult the documentation provided by Apple on the Help menu of each application.

Microsoft Windows Monitoring

Windows is saddled with the reputation of lacking tools; some have called its monitoring counterintuitive. The good news is the barriers to monitoring a Windows system are a myth. In fact, Windows comes with some very powerful tools, including a scheduler for running tasks. You can take performance snapshots, examine errors in the Event Viewer (the Windows equivalent of logs), and monitor performance in real time.

The images shown in this section were taken from several Windows Vista machines. The tools do not differ much in Windows XP or newer versions, including Windows Server 2008 and Windows 7. However, there are differences in accessing the tools in Windows 7, and these differences are noted for each tool.

Indeed, there are a great many tools available to the Windows administrator. We won't try to cover them all here, but instead we'll focus on tools that let you monitor a Windows system in real time. Let's examine some of the basic reporting tools first.

The following are the most popular tools you can use to diagnose and monitor performance issues in Windows:

- Windows Experience Index
- System Health Report
- Event Viewer
- Task Manager
- Reliability Monitor
- Performance Monitor

An excellent source for information about Microsoft Windows performance, tools, techniques, and documentation can be found at the Microsoft Technet website (*http: //technet.microsoft.com/en-us/windows*).

The Windows Experience

If you want a quick glance at how your system is performing compared to the expectations of Microsoft's hardware performance indexes, you can run the Windows Experience report.

To launch the report, click Start, then select Control Panel→System and Maintenance→Performance Information and Tools. You will have to acknowledge the User Account Control (UAC) to continue.

You can also access the System Health Report using the search feature on the Start menu. Click Start and enter "performance" in the search box, then click Performance Information and Tools. Click Advanced Tools and then click the link "Generate a system health report" at the bottom of the dialog. You will have to acknowledge the UAC to continue.

 Microsoft has changed the Windows Experience in Windows 7. The report is very similar to that of earlier Windows versions, but it supplies more information that you can use to judge the performance of your system.

The report is run once after installation, but you can regenerate the report by clicking Update My Score.

This report rates five areas of your system's performance: processor (CPU), memory, video controller (graphics), video graphics accelerator (gaming graphics), and the primary hard drive. Figure 7-24 shows an example of the Windows Experience report.

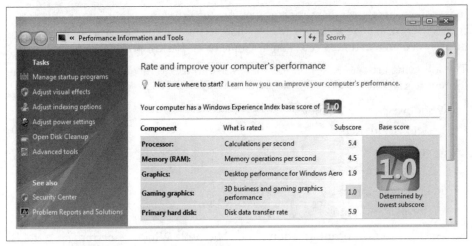

Figure 7-24. The Windows Experience report

There is a little-known feature of this report you may find valuable—click on the link "Learn how you can improve your computer's performance" to get a list of best practices for improving each of these scores.

> You should run this report and regenerate the metrics every time you change the configuration of your system. This will help you identify situations where configuration changes affect the performance of your server.

The best use for this tool is to get a general impression of how your system is performing without analyzing a ton of metrics. A low score in any of the categories can indicate a performance issue. If you examine the report in Figure 7-24, for instance, you will see that the system has a very low graphics and gaming graphics score. This is not unexpected for a Windows system running as a virtual machine or a headless server, but it might be alarming to someone who just shelled out several thousand dollars for a high-end gaming system.

The System Health Report

One of the unique features and diagnostic improvements in Windows Vista and Windows 7 is the ability to generate a report that takes a snapshot of all of the software, hardware, and performance metrics for your system. It is analogous to the System Profiler of Mac OS X, but also contains performance counters.

To launch the System Health Report, click Start, then select Control Panel→System and Maintenance→Performance Information and Tools. Next, select Advanced Tools, then click the link "Generate a system health report" at the bottom of the dialog. You will have to acknowledge the UAC to continue.

You can also access the System Health Report using the search feature on the Start menu. Click Start and enter "performance" in the search box, then click Performance Information and Tools. Click Advanced Tools and select the link "Generate a system health report" at the bottom of the dialog. Another way to access the System Health Report is to use the search feature on the Start menu. Click Start and enter "system health report" in the search box, then click the link in the Start menu. You will have to acknowledge the UAC to continue. Figure 7-25 shows an example of the System Health Report.

This report has everything—all of the hardware, software, and many other aspects of your system are documented here. Notice the report is divided into sections that you can expand or collapse for easier viewing. The following list briefly describes the information displayed by each section:

System Diagnostics Report
The system name and the date the report was generated.

Diagnostic Results
Warning messages generated while the report was being run, identifying potential problem areas on your computer. Also included is a brief overview of the performance of your system at the time the report was run.

Software Configuration
A list of all of the software installed on your system, including system security settings, system services, and startup programs.

Hardware Configuration
A list of the important metadata for disk, CPU performance counters, BIOS information, and devices.

CPU
A list of the processes running at report time and metadata about system components and services.

Network
Metadata about the network interfaces and protocols on your system.

Disk
Performance counters and metadata about all of the disk devices.

Memory
Performance counters for memory, including the process list and memory usage.

Report Statistics
General information about the system when the report was run, such as processor speed and the amount of memory installed.

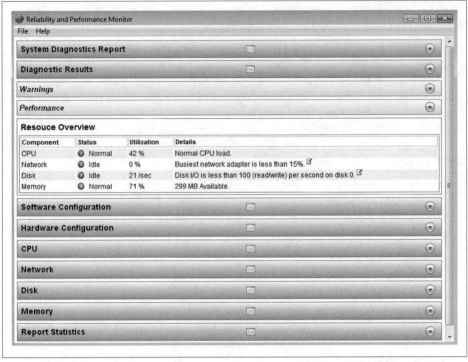

Figure 7-25. The System Health Report

The System Health Report is your key to understanding how your system is configured and is performing at a glance. It is a static report, representing a snapshot of the system.

There is a lot of detailed information in the Hardware Configuration, CPU, Network, Disk, and Memory sections. Feel free to explore those areas for greater details about your system.

The best use of this tool, beyond examining the performance counters, is to save the report for later comparison to other reports when your system is performing poorly. You can save an HTML version of the report by selecting File→Save As.

You can use the saved report as a baseline for performance of your system. If you generate the report several times over the course of low, medium, and high usage, you should be able to put together a general expectation for performance. These expectations are important because you can use them to determine whether your performance issues are within the bounds of expectations. When a system enters a period of unusually high load during a time when it is expected to have a low load, the users' experience may generate complaints. If you have these reports to compare to, you can save yourself a lot of time investigating the exact source of the slowdown.

The Event Viewer

The Windows Event Viewer shows all the messages logged for application, security, and system events. It is a great source of information about events that have occurred (or continue to occur) and should be one of the primary tools you use to diagnose and monitor your system.

You can accomplish a great deal with the Event Viewer. For example, you can generate custom views of any of the logs, save the logs for later diagnosis, and set up alerts for specific events in the future. We will concentrate on viewing the logs. For more information about the Event Viewer and how you can set up custom reports and subscribe to events, consult your Windows help files.

To launch the Event Viewer, click the Start button, then right-click Computer and choose Manage. You will have to acknowledge the UAC to continue. You can then click the Event Viewer link in the left panel. You can also launch the Event Viewer by clicking Start, typing "event viewer," and pressing Enter.

The dialog has three panes by default. The left pane is a tree view of the custom views, logfiles, and applications and services logs. The logs are displayed in the center pane, and the right pane contains the Action menu items. The log entries are sorted, by default, in descending order by date and time. This allows you to see the most recent messages first.

 You can customize the Event Viewer views however you like. You can even group and sort events by clicking on the columns in the log header.

Open the tree for the Windows logs to see the base logfiles for the applications, security, and system (among others). Figure 7-26 shows the Event Viewer open and the log tree expanded.

The logs available to view and search include:

Application
All messages generated from user applications as well as operating system services. This is a good place to look when diagnosing problems with applications.

Security
Messages related to access and privileges exercised, as well as failed attempts to access any secure object. This can be a good place to look for application failures related to username and password issues.

Setup
Messages related to application installation. This is the best place to look for information about failures to install or remove software.

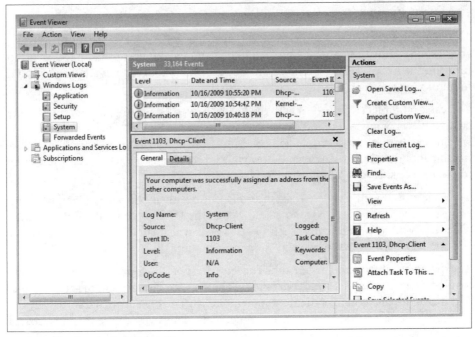

Figure 7-26. The Windows Event Viewer

System

Messages about device drivers and Windows components. This can be the most useful set of logs for diagnosing problems with devices or the system as a whole. It contains information about all manner of devices running at the system level.

Forwarded Events

Messages forwarded from other computers. Consult the Windows documentation about working with remote event logging.

Digging through these logs can be challenging, because many of them display information that is interesting to developers and not readable by mere mortals. To make things easier, you can search any of the logs by clicking the Find operation in the Actions pane and entering a text string. For example, if you are concerned about memory issues, you can enter "memory" to filter all of the log entries for ones containing the string "memory," which will then be shown in the center pane.

Each log message falls into one of the following three categories. These apply to user processes, system components, and applications alike.

Error

Indicates a failure of some magnitude, such as a failed process, out-of-memory problem, or system fault.

Warning
> Indicates a less serious condition or event of note, such as low memory or low disk space.

Information
> Conveys data about an event. This is generally not a problem, but it could provide additional information when diagnosing problems, such as when a USB drive was removed.

To view a log, open the corresponding tree in the left pane. To view the details about any message, click on the message. The message will be displayed below the log entries, as shown in Figure 7-26. In the lower part of the center pane, you can click the General tab to see general information about the message, such as the statement logged, when it occurred, what log it is in, and the user who was running the process or application. You can click the Details tab to see a report of the data logged. You can view the information as text (Friendly View) or XML (XML View). You can also save the information for later review; the XML View is useful to pass the report to tools that recognize the format.

The Reliability Monitor

The most interesting monitoring tool in Windows is the Reliability Monitor. This is a specialized tool that plots the significant performance and error events that have occurred over time in a graph.

A vertical bar represents each day over a period of time. The horizontal bar is an aggregate of the performance index for that day. If there are errors or other significant events, you will see a red X on the graph. Below the bar is a set of drop-down lists that contain the software installations and removals, any application failures, hardware failures, Windows failures, and any additional failures.

This tool is great for checking the performance of the system over a period of time. It can help diagnose situations when an application or system service has performed correctly in the past but has started performing poorly, or when a system starts generating error messages. The tool can help locate the day the event first turned up, as well as give you an idea of how the system was performing when it was running well.

Another advantage of this tool is that it gives you a set of daily baselines of your system over time. This can help you diagnose problems related to changing device drivers (one of the banes of Windows administration), which could go unnoticed until the system degrades significantly.

In short, the Reliability Monitor gives you the opportunity to go back in time and see how your system was performing. The best part of all? You don't have to turn it on— it runs automatically, gleaning much of its data from the logs, and therefore automatically knowing your system's history.

One big source of problems on Windows is connecting and configuring hardware. We will not discuss this subject here, as it can easily fill a book in its own right. If you have problems with hardware and drivers, one excellent reference is *Microsoft Windows XP Inside Out*, by Ed Bott et al. (Microsoft Press).

You can access the Reliability Monitor by clicking Start, typing "reliability," and pressing Enter or clicking on Reliability and Performance Monitor. You will have to acknowledge the UAC. Click Reliability Monitor in the tree pane on the left. Figure 7-27 shows an example of the Reliability Monitor.

In Windows 7, you can launch the Reliability Monitor by clicking Start, entering "action center" in the search box, and pressing Enter. You can then select Maintenance→View reliability report. The report differs from previous versions of Windows, but offers the same information in a tidier package. For example, instead of the drop-down lists, the new Reliability Monitor report lists known incidents in a single list.

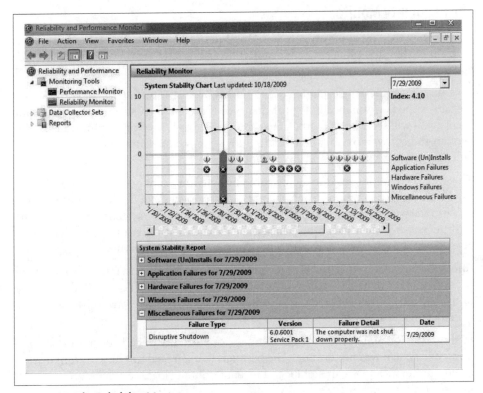

Figure 7-27. The Reliability Monitor

The Task Manager

The Windows Task Manager displays a dynamic list of running processes. It has been around for a long time and has been improved over various versions of Windows.

The Task Manager offers a tabbed dialog with displays for running applications, processes (this is most similar to the Linux **top** command), services active on the system, a CPU performance meter, a network performance meter, and a list of users. Unlike some other reports, this tool generates its data dynamically, refreshing periodically. This makes the tool a bit more useful in observing the system during periods of low performance.

The reports display the same information as the System Health Report, but in a much more compact form, and are updated continuously. You can find all of the critical metrics needed to diagnose performance issues with CPU, resource-hogging processes, memory, and the network. Conspicuously missing is a report on disk performance.

One of the interesting features of the Task Manager is that it shows a miniature performance meter in the notification area on the Start bar that gives you a chance to watch for peaks in usage.

 Running a dynamic performance monitoring tool consumes resources and can affect a system that already suffers poor performance.

You can launch the Task Manager any time by pressing Ctrl+Alt+Del and choosing Task Manager from the menu. Figure 7-28 shows an example of the Task Manager and the process list.

The Performance Monitor

The Performance Monitor is the premier tool for tracking performance in a Windows system. It allows you to select key metrics and plot their values over time. It can also store the session so you can later review it and create a baseline for your system.

The Performance Monitor has metrics for just about everything in your system. There are counters for many of the smaller details having to do with the basic areas of performance: CPU, memory, disk, and network. There are a great many other categories as well.

To launch the Performance Monitor, click Start, then select Control Panel→System and Maintenance→Performance Information and Tools. Click Advanced Tools and then click the link Open Reliability and Performance Monitor near the middle of the dialog. You will have to acknowledge the UAC to continue. Click Reliability Monitor in the tree pane on the left to access the Performance Monitor feature.

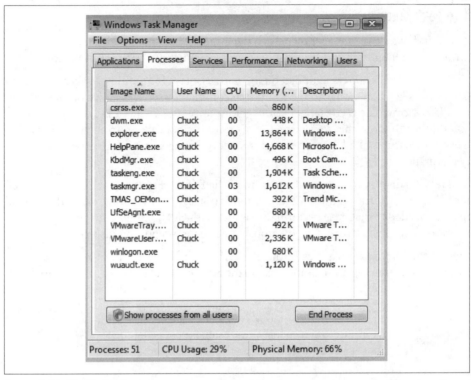

Image Name	User Name	CPU	Memory (...	Description
csrss.exe		00	860 K	
dwm.exe	Chuck	00	448 K	Desktop ...
explorer.exe	Chuck	00	13,864 K	Windows ...
HelpPane.exe	Chuck	00	4,668 K	Microsoft...
KbdMgr.exe	Chuck	00	496 K	Boot Cam...
taskeng.exe	Chuck	00	1,904 K	Task Sche...
taskmgr.exe	Chuck	03	1,612 K	Windows ...
TMAS_OEMon...	Chuck	00	392 K	Trend Mic...
UfSeAgnt.exe		00	680 K	
VMwareTray....	Chuck	00	492 K	VMware T...
VMwareUser....	Chuck	00	2,336 K	VMware T...
winlogon.exe		00	680 K	
wuaudt.exe	Chuck	00	1,120 K	Windows ...

Figure 7-28. The Task Manager

You can also launch the Performance Monitor by clicking Start, typing "reliability," and pressing Enter or clicking on Reliability and Performance Monitor. You will have to acknowledge the UAC. Click Reliability Monitor in the tree pane on the left to access the Performance Monitor feature. Figure 7-29 shows an example of the Performance Monitor.

Microsoft has two levels of metrics: objects that offer a high-level view of an area such as the processor or memory, and counters that represent a specific detail of the system. Thus, you can monitor the CPU's performance as a whole or watch the finer details, such as percentage of time idle or the number of user processes running. Add these objects or counters to the main chart by clicking the green plus sign on the toolbar. This opens a dialog that allows you to choose from a long list of items to add to the chart. Adding the items is a simple matter of selecting the object and expanding the drop-down list on the left, then dragging the desired object to the list on the right.

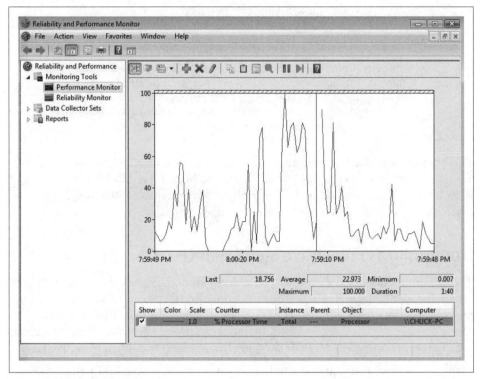

Figure 7-29. The Performance Monitor

You can add as many items as you want; the chart will change its axis accordingly. If you add too many items to track or the values are too diverse, however, the chart may become unreliable. It is best to stick to a few related items at a time (such as only memory counters) to give you the best and most meaningful chart.

A full description of the features of the Performance Monitor is well beyond the scope of this chapter. We encourage you to investigate additional features such as Data Collector Sets and changing the chart's display characteristics. There are many excellent texts that describe these features and more in great detail.

The versatility of the Performance Monitor makes it the best choice for forming baselines and recording the behavior of the system over time. You can use it as a real-time diagnostic tool.

If you have used the Reliability or Performance Monitor, you may have noticed a seldom-commented-on feature called the Resource Overview. This is the default view of the Reliability and Performance Monitor. It provides four dynamic performance graphs for CPU, disk, network, and memory. Below the graphs are drop-down detail panes containing information about these areas. This report is an expanded form of the Task Manager performance graphs and provides yet another point of reference for performance monitoring and diagnosis on Microsoft Windows.

This brief introduction to monitoring performance on Microsoft Windows should persuade you that the belief that Microsoft's Windows platform is difficult to monitor and lacks sophisticated tools is a myth. The tools are very extensive (some could argue too much so) and provide a variety of views of your system's data.

Monitoring as Preventive Maintenance

The techniques discussed so far give you a snapshot of the status of the system. However, most would agree that monitoring is normally an automated task that samples the available statistics for anomalies. When an anomaly is found, an alert is sent to an administrator (or group of administrators) to let someone know there may be a problem. This turns the reactive task of checking the system status into a proactive task.

A number of third-party utilities combine monitoring, reporting, and alerts into easy-to-use interfaces. There are even monitoring and alert systems for an entire infrastructure. For example, Nagios can monitor an entire IT infrastructure and set up alerts for anomalies.

There are also monitoring and alert systems available either as part of or an add-on for operating systems and database systems. We will examine the Enterprise Monitor for MySQL in Chapter 13.

Conclusion

There are a great many references on both performance tuning and security monitoring. This chapter provides a general introduction to system monitoring. While it is not comprehensive, the material presented is an introduction to the tools, techniques, and concepts of monitoring your operating system and server performance. In the next chapter, we will take on the task of monitoring a MySQL system and discuss some common practices to help keep your MySQL system running at peak performance.

"Joel!"

He knew that voice and that tone. Joel's boss was headed his way and about to conduct another drive-by tasking. He turned to face his office door as his boss stepped through it. "Did you read Sally's email about the slowdown?"

Joel recalled that Sally was one of the employees who sent him a message asking why her application was running slowly. He had just finished checking the low-hanging fruit—there was plenty of memory and disk space wasn't an issue.

"Yes, I was just looking into the problem now."

"Make it your top priority. Marketing has a deadline to produce their quarterly sales projections. Let me know what you find." His boss nodded once and stepped away.

Joel sighed and returned to examining the reports on CPU usage while wondering how to describe technology to the nontechnical.

## CHAPTER 8

Monitoring MySQL

Joel had a feeling today was going to be a better day. Everything was going well: the performance measurements for the servers were looking good and the user complaints were down. He had successfully reconfigured the server and improved performance greatly. There was only one application still performing poorly, but he was sure the problem wasn't hardware- or operating-system-related; more likely it was an issue with a poorly written query. Nevertheless, he had sent his boss an email message explaining his findings and that he was working on the remaining problems.

Joel heard quickened footsteps approaching his office. He instinctively looked toward his door, awaiting the now-routine appearance of his boss. He was shocked as Mr. Summerson zipped by without so much as a nod in his direction.

He shrugged his shoulders and returned to reading his email messages. Just then a new message appeared with "HIGH PRIORITY" in the subject line in capital letters. It was from his boss. Chiding himself for holding his breath, Joel relaxed and opened the message. He could hear his boss's voice in his mind as he read through the message.

"Joel, good work on those reports. I especially like the details you included about memory and disk performance. I'd like you to generate a similar report about the database server. I'd also like you to look into a problem one of the developers is having with a query. Susan will send you the details."

With a deep sigh, Joel once again opened his favorite MySQL book to learn more about monitoring the database system. "I hope it has something about drilling down into individual components," he mumbled, knowing he needed to get up to speed quickly on an advanced feature of MySQL.

Now that you understand how monitoring works and how to keep your host's operating systems at peak efficiency, how do you know if your MySQL servers are performing at their peak efficiency? Better still, how do you know when they aren't?

In this chapter, we begin with a look at monitoring MySQL, and then move on to monitoring and improving performance in your databases. We conclude with a look into best practices for improving database performance.

What Is Performance?

Before we begin discussions about database performance and general best practices for monitoring and tuning a MySQL server, it is important to define what we mean by performance. For the purposes of this chapter, good performance is defined as meeting the needs of the user such that the system performs as expediently as the user expects, whereas poor performance is defined as anything less. Typically, good performance means response time and throughput meet the users' expectations. While this may not seem very scientific, savvy administrators know the best gauge of how well things are going is the happiness of the users.

That doesn't mean we don't measure performance. On the contrary, we can and must measure performance in order to know what to fix, when, and how. Furthermore, if you measure performance regularly, you can even predict when your users will begin to be unhappy. Your users won't care if you reduce your cache hit rate by 3 percent, beating your best score to date. You may take pride in such things, but metrics and numbers are meaningless when compared to the user's experience at the keyboard.

There is a very important philosophy that you should adopt when dealing with performance. Essentially, you should never adjust the parameters of your server, database, or storage engine unless you have a deliberate plan and a full understanding of the expectations of the change as well as the consequences. More importantly, never adjust without measuring the effects of the change over time. It is entirely possible that you can improve the performance of the server in the short run but negatively impact performance in the long run. Finally, you should always consult references from several sources, including the reference manuals.

Now that we've issued that stern warning, let's turn our attention to monitoring and improving performance of the MySQL server and databases.

MySQL Server Monitoring

Managing the MySQL server falls in the category of application monitoring. This is because most of the performance parameters are generated by the MySQL software and are not part of the host operating system. As mentioned previously, you should always monitor your base operating system in tandem with monitoring MySQL because MySQL is very sensitive to performance issues of the host operating system.

There is an entire chapter in the online MySQL Reference Manual that covers all aspects of monitoring and performance improvement, intriguingly titled "Optimization." See *http://dev.mysql.com/doc/refman/5.5/en/optimization.html* for more details. Rather than repeat the facts and rhetoric of that excellent reference, we will discuss a general approach to monitoring the MySQL server and examine the various tools available.

This section is an introduction to the finer details of monitoring the MySQL server. We'll start with a short discussion of how to change and monitor the behavior of the system, then discuss monitoring primarily for the purposes of diagnosing performance issues and forming a performance benchmark. We will also discuss best practices for diagnosing performance issues and take a look at monitoring the storage engine sublayer in MySQL—an area not well understood or covered by other reference sources.

How MySQL Communicates Performance

There are two mechanisms you can use to govern and monitor behavior in the MySQL server. You use server variables to control behavior and status variables to read behavior configuration and statistical information regarding features and performance.

There are many variables you can use to configure the server. Some can be set only at startup (called startup options, which can also be set in option files). Others can be set at the global level (across all connections), the session level (for a single connection), or both the global and session levels.

 Session variable settings are not persistent beyond the current connection and are reset when the connection is closed.

You can read server variables using the following commands:

```
SHOW [GLOBAL | SESSION] VARIABLES;
```

You can change those variables that are not static (read-only) using the following commands (you can include multiple settings on a single line using a comma separator):

```
SET [GLOBAL | SESSION] <variable_name> = <value>;
SET [@@global. | @@session. | @@]<variable_name> = <value>;
```

You can read status variables using the following commands. The first two commands display the value of all local or session scope variables (the default is session). The third command displays those variables that are global in scope.

```
SHOW STATUS;
SHOW SESSION STATUS;
SHOW GLOBAL STATUS;
```

We discuss how and when to use these commands in the next section.

Performance Monitoring

Performance monitoring in MySQL is the application of the previous commands—specifically, setting and reading system variables and reading status variables. The SHOW and SET commands are only two of the possible tools you can use to accomplish the task of monitoring the MySQL server.

Indeed, there are several tools you can use to monitor your MySQL server. The tools available in the standard distributions are somewhat limited in that they are console tools and include special commands you can execute from a MySQL client (e.g., SHOW STATUS) and utilities you can run from a command line (e.g., mysqladmin).

 The MySQL client tool is sometimes called the MySQL monitor, but should not be confused with a monitoring tool.

There are also GUI tools available that make things a little easier if you prefer or require such options. You can also download the MySQL GUI tools, which include advanced tools that you can use to monitor your system, manage queries, and migrate your data from other database systems.

We begin by examining how to use the SQL commands and then discuss the MySQL Administrator GUI and Query Browser tools. We also take a look at one of the most overlooked tools available to the administrator—the server logs.

Some savvy administrators may consider the server logs the first and primary tool for administering the server. Although they are not nearly as vital for performance monitoring, they can be an important asset in diagnosing performance issues.

SQL Commands

All of the SQL monitoring commands are a variant of the SHOW command, which displays internal information about the system and its subsystems. While there are many forms of the SHOW command, the following lists the most common SQL commands you can use to monitor the MySQL server:

SHOW INDEX FROM <table>
Displays the index cardinality statistics for the specified table, which are used by the optimizer to estimate join selectivity. This command can also be very helpful when diagnosing poorly performing queries, specifically whether the query is formulated in such a way as to make use of the indexes available.

SHOW PLUGINS
Displays the list of all known plug-ins. It shows the name of the plug-in and its current status. The storage engines in newer releases of MySQL are implemented as plug-ins. Use this command to get a snapshot of the currently available plug-ins and their statuses.

SHOW [FULL] PROCESSLIST
Displays data for all threads (including connections) running on the system. This command resembles the process commands of the host operating system. The information displayed includes connection data along with the command executing, how long it has been executing, and its current state. Like the operating system

command it resembles, it can diagnose poor response (too many threads), a zombie process (long running or nonresponding), or even connection issues. When dealing with poor performance or unresponsive threads, use the KILL command to terminate them. The default behavior is to show the processes for the current user. The FULL keyword displays all processes.

 You must have the global SUPER privilege to see all processes running on the system.

SHOW [*GLOBAL* | *SESSION*] STATUS
Displays the values of all of the system variables. You will probably use this command more frequently than any other. Use this command to read all of the statistical information available on the server. Combined with the GLOBAL or SESSION keyword, you can limit the display to those statistics that are global- or session-only.

SHOW TABLE [FROM <*db*>] STATUS
Displays detailed information about the tables in a given database. This includes the storage engine, collation, creation data, index data, and row statistics. You can use this command along with the SHOW INDEX command to examine tables when diagnosing poorly performing queries.

SHOW [*GLOBAL* | *SESSION*] VARIABLES
Displays the system variables. These are typically configuration options for the server and while they do not display statistical information, viewing the variables can be very important when determining whether the current configuration has changed or if certain options are set. Some variables are read-only and can only be changed via the configuration file or the command line on startup, while others can be changed globally or set locally. You can combine this command with the GLOBAL or SESSION keyword to limit the display to those variables that are global- or session-only.

Limit the Output of SHOW Commands

The SHOW commands in MySQL are very powerful. However, they often display too much information. This is especially true for the SHOW STATUS and SHOW VARIABLES commands.

To see less information, you can use the LIKE <*pattern*> clause, which permits you to view only those rows matching the pattern specified. The most common example is using the LIKE clause to see only variables for a certain subset, such as replication or logging. You can use the standard MySQL pattern symbols and controls in the LIKE clause in the same manner as a SELECT query.

For example, the following displays the status variables that include the name "log":

```
mysql> SHOW SESSION STATUS LIKE '%log%';
+---------------------------+-------+
| Variable_name             | Value |
+---------------------------+-------+
| Binlog_cache_disk_use     | 0     |
| Binlog_cache_use          | 0     |
| Com_binlog                | 0     |
| Com_purge_bup_log         | 0     |
| Com_show_binlog_events    | 0     |
| Com_show_binlogs          | 0     |
| Com_show_engine_logs      | 0     |
| Com_show_relaylog_events  | 0     |
| Tc_log_max_pages_used     | 0     |
| Tc_log_page_size          | 0     |
| Tc_log_page_waits         | 0     |
+---------------------------+-------+
11 rows in set (0.11 sec)
```

The commands specifically related to storage engines include the following:

SHOW ENGINE <engine_name> LOGS
   Displays the log information for the specified storage engine. The information displayed is dependent on the storage engine. This can be very helpful in tuning storage engines. Some storage engines do not provide this information.

SHOW ENGINE <engine_name> STATUS
   Displays the status information for the specified storage engine. The information
   displayed depends on the storage engine. Some storage engines display more or
   less information than others. For example, the InnoDB storage engine displays
   dozens of status variables, while the NDB storage engine shows a few, and the
   MyISAM storage engine displays no information. This command is the primary
   mechanism for viewing statistical information about a given storage engine and
   can be vital for tuning certain storage engines (e.g., InnoDB).

   The older synonyms for the SHOW ENGINE commands (SHOW
   <engine> LOGS and SHOW <engine> STATUS) have been deprecated.

SHOW ENGINES
   Displays a list of all known storage engines for the MySQL release and their statuses
   (i.e., whether the storage engine is enabled). This can be helpful when deciding
   which storage engine to use for a given database or in replication to determine if
   the same storage engines exist on both the master and the slave.

The commands specifically related to MySQL replication include the following:

SHOW BINLOG EVENTS [IN '<log_file>'] [FROM <pos>] [LIMIT [<offset>,]
<row count>]

Displays the events as they were recorded to the binary log. You can specify a logfile to examine (leaving off the file tells the system to use the current logfile), and limit output to the last events from a particular position or to the first number of rows after an offset into the file. This command is the primary command used in diagnosing replication problems. It comes in very handy when an event occurs that disrupts replication or causes an error during replication.

 If you do not use a LIMIT clause and your server has been running and logging events for some time you could get a very lengthy output. If you need to examine a large number of events, you should consider using the mysqlbinlog utility instead.

SHOW BINARY LOGS

Displays the list of the binary logs on the server. Use this command to get information about past and current binlog filenames. The size of each file is also displayed. This is another useful command for diagnosing replication problems because it will permit you to specify the binlog file for the SHOW BINLOG EVENTS command, thereby reducing the amount of data you must explore to determine the problem. The SHOW MASTER LOGS command is a synonym.

SHOW RELAYLOG EVENTS [IN '<log_file>'] [FROM <pos>] [LIMIT [<offset>,]
<row count>]

Available in MySQL version 5.5.0, this command does the same thing as SHOW BINLOG EVENTS, only with relay logs on the slave. If you do not supply a filename for the log, events from the first relay log are shown. This command has no effect when run on the master.

SHOW MASTER STATUS

Displays the current configuration of the master. It shows the current binlog file, the current position in the file, and all inclusive or exclusive replication settings. Use this command when connecting or reconnecting slaves.

SHOW SLAVE HOSTS

Displays the list of slaves connected to the master that used the --report-host option. Use this information to determine which slaves are connected to your master.

SHOW SLAVE STATUS

Displays the status information for the system acting as a slave in replication. This is the primary command for tracking the performance and status of your slaves. A considerable amount of information is displayed that is vital to maintaining a healthy slave. See Chapter 2 for more information about this command.

The two most important commands in this list are SHOW VARIABLES and SHOW STATUS. There are a great many variables (over 290 status variables alone), so once you learn to master the LIKE clause, you can target the results to specific aspects of the system you want to monitor.

The variable lists are generally in alphabetical order and are often grouped by feature. However, sometimes the variables are not neatly arranged; in this case you can find them using a keyword search. For example, SHOW STATUS LIKE '%thread%' shows all of the status variables related to thread execution. Example 8-1 shows this command on a recent beta release of MySQL.

Example 8-1. Showing thread status variables

```
mysql> SHOW VARIABLES LIKE '%thread%';
+------------------------------+--------------------------+
| Variable_name                | Value                    |
+------------------------------+--------------------------+
| innodb_file_io_threads       | 4                        |
| innodb_read_io_threads       | 4                        |
| innodb_thread_concurrency    | 0                        |
| innodb_thread_sleep_delay    | 10000                    |
| innodb_write_io_threads      | 4                        |
| max_delayed_threads          | 20                       |
| max_insert_delayed_threads   | 20                       |
| myisam_repair_threads        | 1                        |
| pseudo_thread_id             | 1                        |
| thread_cache_size            | 0                        |
| thread_handling              | one-thread-per-connection |
| thread_stack                 | 262144                   |
+------------------------------+--------------------------+
12 rows in set (0.00 sec)
```

This example shows not only those status variables for thread management, but also the thread control for the InnoDB storage engine. While you sometimes get more information than you expected, a keyword-based LIKE clause is sure to help you find the specific variable you need.

Knowing which variables to change and which variables to monitor can be the most challenging part of monitoring a MySQL server. As mentioned, a great deal of valuable information on this topic is included in the online MySQL Reference Manual.

To illustrate the kinds of features you can monitor in a MySQL server, let us examine the variables that control the query cache. The query cache is one of the most important performance features in MySQL if you use the MyISAM storage engine for your application data. It allows the server to buffer frequently used queries and their results in memory. Thus, the more often a query is run, the more likely it is that the results can be read from the cache rather than reexamining the index structures and tables to retrieve the data. Clearly, reading the results from memory is much faster than reading them from disk every time. This can be a performance improvement if your data is read much more frequently than it is written (updated).

Each time you run a query, it is entered into the cache and has a lifetime governed by how recently it was used (old queries are dumped first) and how much memory there is available for the query cache. Additionally, there are a number of events that can invalidate (remove) queries from the cache. We include a partial list of these events here:

- Frequent changes (to data or indexes).
- Different forms of the query, which can cause missed cache hits. Thus, it is important to use standardized queries for commonly accessed data. You will see later in this chapter how views can help in this area.
- When a query derives data from temporary tables.
- Transaction events that can invalidate queries in the cache (e.g., COMMIT).

You can determine if the query cache is configured and available in your MySQL installation by examining the have_query_cache variable. This is a system variable with global scope, but it is read-only. You control the query cache using one of several variables. Example 8-2 shows the server variables for the query cache.

Example 8-2. Query cache server variables

```
mysql> SHOW VARIABLES LIKE '%query_cache%';
+------------------------------+----------+
| Variable_name                | Value    |
+------------------------------+----------+
| have_query_cache             | YES      |
| query_cache_limit            | 1048576  |
| query_cache_min_res_unit     | 4096     |
| query_cache_size             | 33554432 |
| query_cache_type             | ON       |
| query_cache_wlock_invalidate | OFF      |
+------------------------------+----------+
6 rows in set (0.00 sec)
```

As you can see, there are several things you can change to affect the query cache. Most notable is the ability to temporarily turn off the query cache by setting the query_cache_size variable—this sets the amount of memory available for the query cache. If you set this variable to 0, it effectively turns off the query cache. This is not related to the have_query_cache variable, which merely indicates that the feature is available. For more information about configuring the query cache, see the section titled "Query Cache Configuration" in the online MySQL Reference Manual.

You can observe the performance of the query cache by examining several status variables, as shown in Example 8-3.

Example 8-3. Query cache status variables

```
mysql> SHOW STATUS LIKE '%Qcache%';
+-------------------------+-------+
| Variable_name           | Value |
+-------------------------+-------+
| Qcache_free_blocks      | 0     |
| Qcache_free_memory      | 0     |
| Qcache_hits             | 0     |
| Qcache_inserts          | 0     |
| Qcache_lowmem_prunes    | 0     |
| Qcache_not_cached       | 0     |
| Qcache_queries_in_cache | 0     |
| Qcache_total_blocks     | 0     |
+-------------------------+-------+
8 rows in set (0.00 sec)
```

Here we see one of the more subtle inconsistencies in the MySQL server. You can control the query cache using variables that start with query_cache, but the status variables start with Qcache. While the inconsistency was intentional (to help distinguish a server variable from a status variable), oddities like this can make searching for the right items a challenge.

 You can and should periodically defragment the query cache with the FLUSH QUERY CACHE command. This does not remove results from the cache, but instead allows for internal reorganization to better utilize memory.

There are many nuances to the query cache that allow you to manage and configure it and monitor its performance. This makes the query cache an excellent example to demonstrate the complexity of monitoring the MySQL server. No single volume (or chapter in a broader work) can cover all such topics. The practices described in this chapter therefore are general and are designed to be used with any feature in the MySQL server. However, the specific details may require additional research and a good read through the online MySQL Reference Manual.

Another pair of commands that can be very useful in monitoring replication are the SHOW MASTER STATUS and SHOW SLAVE STATUS commands. We will examine these in more detail later in this chapter.

The mysqladmin Utility

The mysqladmin command-line utility is the workhorse of the suite of command-line tools. There are many options and tools (called commands) this utility can perform. The online MySQL Reference Manual discusses the mysqladmin utility briefly. In this section, we examine the options and tools for monitoring a MySQL server.

Since the utility runs from the command line, it allows administrators to script sets of operations much more easily than they can process SQL commands. Indeed, some of the third-party monitoring tools use a combination of the `mysqladmin` and SQL commands to gather information for display in other forms.

You must specify connection information (user, password, host, etc.) to connect to a running server. The following is a list of commonly used commands. As you will see, most of these have equivalent SQL commands that produce the same information.

status
: Displays a concise description of the status of the server, including uptime, number of threads (connections), number of queries, and general statistical data. This command provides a quick snapshot of the server's health.

extended-status
: Displays the entire list of system statistics and is similar to the SQL `SHOW STATUS` command.

processlist
: Displays the list of current processes and works the same way as the SQL `SHOW PROCESSLIST` command.

kill <thread id>
: Allows you to kill a specified thread. Use this in conjunction with `processlist` to help manage runaway or hung processes.

variables
: Displays the system server variables and values. This is equivalent to the SQL `SHOW VARIABLES` command.

There are many options and other commands not listed here, including commands to start and stop a slave during replication and manage the various system logs.

One of the best features of the `mysqladmin` utility is its comparison of information over time. The `--sleep` *n* option tells the utility to execute the specified command once every *n* seconds. For example, to see the process list refreshed every three seconds on the local host, use the following command:

```
mysqladmin -uroot --password --socket=<sock> processlist --sleep 3
```

This command will execute until you cancel the utility using Ctrl+C.

Perhaps the most powerful option is the comparative results for the extended status command. Use the `--relative` option to compare the previous execution values with the current values. For example, to see the previous and current values for the system status variables, use this command:

```
mysqladmin -uroot --password --socket=<sock> extended-status -relative --sleep 3
```

You can also combine commands to get several reports at the same time. For example, to see the process list and status information together, issue the following command:

```
mysqladmin --root ... processlist status
```

The `mysqladmin` tool has many other uses. You can use it to shut down the server, flush the logs, ping a server, start and stop slaves in replication, and refresh the privilege tables. For more information about the `mysqladmin` tool, see the section titled "mysqladmin—Client for Administering a MySQL Server" in the online MySQL Ref erence Manual. Figure 8-1 shows the sample output of a system with no load.

```
+----+-------------+-----------+----+---------+------+-----------------------------------+------------------+
| Id | User        | Host      | db | Command | Time | State                             | Info             |
+----+-------------+-----------+----+---------+------+-----------------------------------+------------------+
| 1  | system user |           |    | Daemon  | 0    | Waiting for event from ndbcluster |                  |
| 18 | root        | localhost |    | Query   | 0    |                                   | show processlist |
+----+-------------+-----------+----+---------+------+-----------------------------------+------------------+
Uptime: 6325  Threads: 1  Questions: 139  Slow queries: 0  Opens: 17  Flush tables: 2  Open tables: 1  Queries
per second avg: 0.21
```

Figure 8-1. Sample mysqladmin process and status report

MySQL GUI Tools

The MySQL GUI tools are currently bundled together in a single download and are available on the MySQL website. You can download the tools packaged for several popular operating systems:

- MySQL Administrator 1.2
- MySQL Query Browser 1.2
- MySQL Migration Toolkit 1.1

We will discuss the MySQL Administrator and MySQL Query Browser in more detail in the following sections. The MySQL Migration Toolkit is designed to automate the migration of database schema and data from other database systems. It can be a really handy tool to make adoption of MySQL easier and faster.

 The MySQL Migration Toolkit is not available for the Mac OS X platform.

MySQL Administrator

The MySQL Administrator is a jack of all (or most) trades. It provides facilities for viewing and changing system variables, managing configuration files, examining the server logs, monitoring status variables, and even viewing graphical representations of performance for some of the more important features. It also has a full set of adminis-tration options that allow you to manage users and view database configurations. While it was originally intended to replace the `mysqladmin` tool, popular demand ensures we will have both for the foreseeable future.

You can use MySQL Administrator on any platform and can access one or more servers connected to the client. This makes the tool much more convenient when monitoring several servers on the network.

A unique feature of the MySQL Administrator allows you to analyze a downed server. While most of the features are disabled (e.g., there are no real-time performance indicators), you can still view the configuration and examine the logs. This can be a very handy tool for diagnosing server crashes.

To connect to a downed server (called configure-service mode), open the tool and press the Ctrl key (the Apple key on Mac OS X). Notice the Connect button changes to Skip. Press Skip and the tool will switch to the configure-service mode. From here, you can start and stop the server, change startup variables, and view the server logs.

MySQL Administrator features are divided into 10 groups or tools, each represented as tabs in the application. Principally, we're interested in tools that show us the values of the status variables. The MySQL Administrator has a dynamic feature similar to the mysqladmin tool, but it takes the feature a bit further by showing a running graph of the values. These are grouped under the health tools. If you click the Connection Health tab, you will see a graph like the one shown in Figures 8-2 through 8-4.

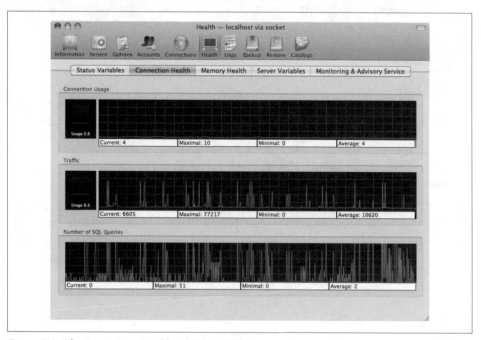

Figure 8-2. The Connection Health tab (Mac OS X)

This graph shows three sections. The first monitors the connection usage (how many connections are on the server currently); this can be very helpful in determining whether you have an overburdened server (one with too many connections) or when trouble-shooting sporadic connections.

 Figures 8-2 through 8-4 are a mixture of snapshots taken from Mac OS X, Windows 7, and Linux systems. As you'll see, each platform has a slightly different look and feel. The Mac OS X system differs in menu placement, but otherwise has the same feature set.

The Traffic graph in Figure 8-2 shows the network traffic and can be helpful in determining potential problems with your network.

The most interesting graph is the bottom graph, which shows the SQL queries that have been run over time. This can be very helpful in determining if your system is overburdened with queries.

The examples shown here depict a system running with very few connections, a minimal amount of network traffic, and a moderate load of queries that demonstrate a pattern of bursts.

The graphical representation of the status variables is one of the best features of the MySQL Administrator. While the graphs hide the underlying status variables and only present the maximum and minimum values over time, they can be very helpful in spotting potential problems pictorially.

Prolonged use of tools like this can add a small amount of overhead and skew the results slightly. However, this may not be a problem for systems with many operations.

Figure 8-3 depicts a system that is basically unused. We include it here to show you an example of the MySQL Administrator on the Windows platform. However, it is important to consider this example as something to watch out for in your replication topology. Specifically, if one of your slaves demonstrates this behavior, it is a sure sign something is seriously wrong. Similarly, it could also be an indication that your scale-out scheme is not working as you designed it to, or that your load balancing strategy has failed to distribute queries to this server.

Figure 8-4 shows MySQL Administrator on a Linux machine and demonstrates another example of a system under moderate load. Notice that the connection usage and network traffic have spike indicators that show relative percentage of usage. This gauge allows you to see spikes at a glance.

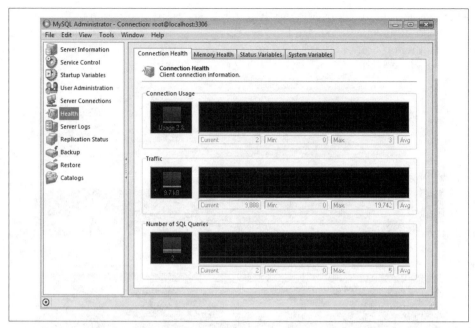

Figure 8-3. The Connection Health tab (Windows 7)

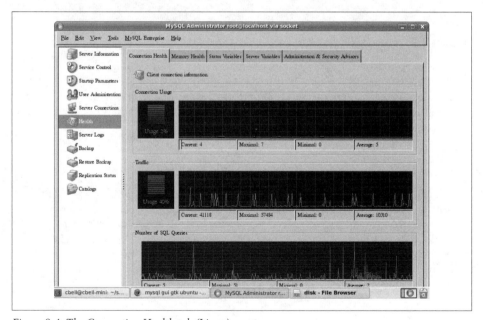

Figure 8-4. The Connection Health tab (Linux)

The MySQL Administrator Memory Health tab displays dynamic graphical charts of the health of the query cache and the key cache. Figure 8-5 shows an example of the graphical reports running on a system of moderate load. In this case, the system is running advanced diagnostic tests for the MySQL Cluster product.

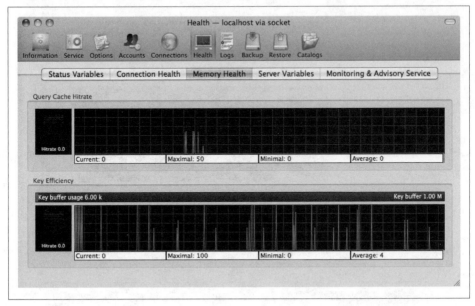

Figure 8-5. The Memory Health tab

Unlike the manual queries for the query cache status variables, this display makes it much easier to see the general trends of performance for the query cache. Like some of the other dynamic displays, this graph also has a peak indicator that can warn you of sudden peaks in the values.

Uncertainty Principle in MySQL

You may be familiar with the Heisenberg uncertainty principle, which states that the more precisely a particle's position is determined, the less precisely the momentum is known in that instant, and vice versa. Monitoring MySQL involves running queries to get the values of status variables, so each time you gather the data, you increase the value of some of the variables you're measuring. Thus, there is some overhead in monitoring MySQL, and oversampling can make the values of the metrics less meaningful. Of course, this principle applies to data probing in general.

You should consider that frequent sampling can cause the system to spend more time sampling than processing when planning your sampling frequency. This graph displays only the query cache hit rate. This is the same as the status variable with the name

`Qcache_hits`, which is a counter of the hits or successful query result retrievals from cache. Clearly, a high hit rate indicates better performance than a low rate, but the opposite is not necessarily true. A low hit rate simply means the server is not making use of the query cache, not that it is performing poorly. However, if your goal is to increase performance by using standardized queries and you see a low hit rate, it may be that you need to tune your query cache or that your database activity is causing one or more of the events that invalidate cache results.

The `Qcache_hits` is a monotonically increasing statistic that you must reset periodically to measure periods of activity. In the Query Cache Hitrate graph in Figure 8-5, the MySQL Administrator is actually issuing a `FLUSH STATUS` command to reset the value to 0 between samplings for the current session. This is a common practice for most monitoring that involves sampling.

The Key Efficiency graph shown in Figure 8-5 is a dynamic display of the key buffer usage. Specifically, this is the MyISAM key cache and it measures how much the key buffer is being used or how many requests have been made to read the key cache. The status variable used here is the `key_read_requests` variable.

The key cache is the primary mechanism the MyISAM storage engine uses to increase its performance. It caches the most frequently accessed index blocks (pointers to the data) so indexed searches (and subsequently the data) can be retrieved more quickly. We discuss the key cache in more detail in Chapter 9.

You can use this graph to determine when you need to increase the `key_cache_size` variable for better performance. That is, if the values displayed are high (a large percentage), you may want to increase the value. Basically, the higher the value, the more effective the key cache becomes. Conversely, if you see low values and you know you are executing many queries on MyISAM tables, you may want to decrease the size of the key cache.

The next tabs we will discuss present more traditional numeric data. Before we look at these, there is one feature that warrants mentioning: you can create your own custom health graphs. To add your own graph, right-click in the open space on the working area and select "New page." You will be asked to name the page. Once you enter a name, you will see the new name on the tab bar for the health tools. Click the new page, then right-click the blank form and select "New group" to name this group. You can then right-click the new group and add a new graph. Figure 8-6 shows the custom graph dialog.

From here, specify the status variable you want to monitor along with any calculations you want to perform and how to present the data. We encourage you to try this out for yourself. Notice in Figure 8-6 we chose a line graph and supplied the status variable with the notation ^ followed by the variable name inside square brackets. The dialog gives you a hint as to how you can enter a formula if you want a more complex report.

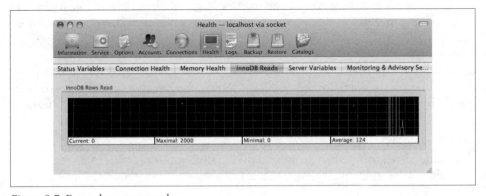

Figure 8-6. *Custom graph dialog*

You can also specify units for the value, several caption options, the minimum and maximum values, and a formula for calculating the maximum if needed. If you specify a name for the value caption, you will see the small peak indicator shown on other graphs. Figure 8-7 shows the example graph in action.

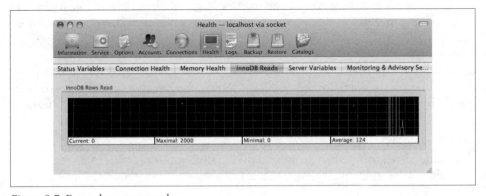

Figure 8-7. *Example custom graph*

You can right-click any of the standard graphs and edit them. Use this feature to see how some of the other graphs are calculated.

As mentioned earlier, you can also see the server variables among the health tools. Click the Server Variables tab and the display will change to a data chart similar to a spreadsheet. On the left is a tree control that groups all of the system variables into categories and subcategories.

The center pane displays the details for each of these categories. You can expand the categories by double-clicking the category name. For example, if you double-click the General category you will see several subcategories. Click once more on the Performance subcategory to see a listing of the system variables related to performance tuning.

While this is a partial list of performance tuning variables, it is indeed the most general of all of the performance variables. To see the others, click on any of the other features and those variables will be displayed with that group. Figure 8-8 shows the general performance variables for a default installation.

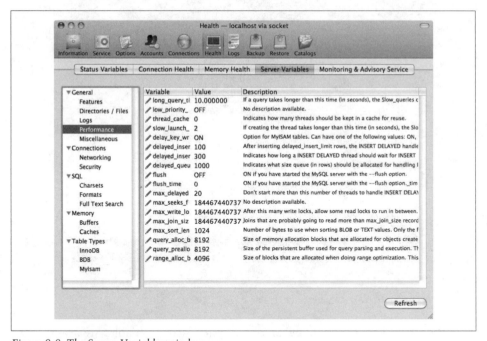

Figure 8-8. The Server Variables window

The best feature of this tool is that you can change the values dynamically. For example, if you want to increase the time the system counts slow threads, simply click the value for the `slow_launch_time` variable and enter a new value. The values are changed automatically on the server. This is a really nice feature that makes the MySQL Administrator much easier to use than a client window.

 You can tell which variables can be changed (are not read-only) by the little pencil icon next to the name. If the pencil icon is missing, the variable is read-only.

When you combine the ability to mine and edit the system variables at a glance with the ability to watch how changes affect the system under load via custom dynamic health graphs, you are using the MySQL Administrator as a professional performance tuning tool. Just remember the golden rule of tuning: change only one thing at a time and measure, measure, measure!

The Status Variables tab shows the system status variables grouped into features. For example, to see all of the status variables for network traffic, click the Networking group and then click the Traffic subgroup. Figure 8-9 shows the Status Variables window.

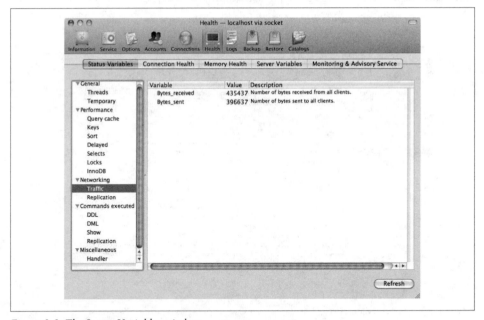

Figure 8-9. The Status Variables window

As in the Server Variables window, all of the system status variables are available for you to examine. The values shown are the values at the time the feature group was selected and they are not updated automatically. Click Refresh to retrieve new values. Unlike the dynamic health graphs, the values returned during a refresh are the values as they are read from the server with a SHOW STATUS command. Keep this in mind when using this tool—it shows only the static right-then values, not trends or historical lists.

Also included is a short description of each of the status variables. This can be really helpful when digging through the status variables looking for something to help diagnose a performance issue. It also saves a great deal of time over issuing SHOW STATUS commands and trying to guess keywords to use (see Figure 8-5).

The next tool we will discuss allows you to see snapshots of the server logs. We discuss the server logs in more detail in "Server Logs" on page 313, so we give only a minimal introduction here.

The server logs record significant events that occur while the system is running. This information can include errors incurred during an operation or connection, all of the queries run on the server, and even which queries are running the slowest.

MySQL Administrator allows you to mine these logs. While it only allows access to the error, general, and slow logs, it is still very useful.

To see the logs on the server to which you are connected, click the Logs tab in the toolbar. This will open the Logs tool (shown in Figure 8-10).

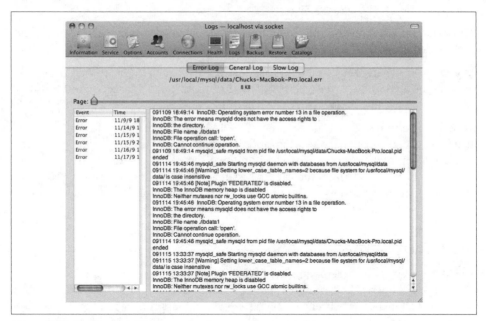

Figure 8-10. The Logs window

 On some platforms, the MySQL Administrator may require you to enter your administrator credentials to see or interact with the server logs.

Across the top of the window, under the toolbar, is a page tool that allows you to click and drag the bar to a specific page or to browse through the pages of the error log.

Figure 8-11. The MySQL Query Browser

Below that is a two-paned display that lists the significant events in the log (on the left) and the details from the log for the event (on the right).

As you can see, there are several errors listed. Click an error in the list to view its details. This can be a real time saver when you are digging through a large log to find some events that you know happened at a certain time on a certain day.

Now that you've had a look at what the MySQL Administrator provides for advanced diagnostics, performance monitoring, and tuning, we hope that you will consider this tool when you set about to practice on your own servers. The MySQL Administrator removes much of the tedium incurred by issuing the SQL commands to retrieve the same data. The new features, like the health and custom health graphs, make performance tuning a much easier and more immediate process.

MySQL Query Browser

The MySQL Query Browser is another of the optional GUI tools available for MySQL. Use it to build queries and execute them in a graphical form. Result sets are returned and displayed in a spreadsheet-like dialog. MySQL Query Browser allows for vertical scrolling through all of the results as well as changing the size of the columns and horizontally scrolling to better view the data. Many users find this tool more convenient and easier to use than the older command-line client (`mysql`).

The performance-related functionality and the value added for administrators is the graphical display of the results of the EXPLAIN command for any given query. Figure 8-11 shows a sample from the *sakila* database. We will discuss this in greater detail later in the chapter.

The MySQL Query Browser example shown here should give you an indication of the utilitarian use of the GUI. You can enter any query and see the explanation of the query execution by first executing the query, then selecting Explain Query from the Query menu.

Notice there are two parts to the results. The bottom part shows the results of the EXPLAIN command as well as the actual rows returned. You can use the scroll bars to view more data without having to reissue the query.

What makes this a performance tuning tool is the fact that it lets you write the query once; use the EXPLAIN feature; observe the results, then either rewrite the query or adjust indexes; then reissue the query and observe the changes in the GUI. And you thought query tools were for users only—not so with this tool.

But wait, there's more. The MySQL Query Browser has enhanced editing tools, such as color-coding, built into the small text box shown in Figure 8-11. To see all of the advanced features and uses for the MySQL Query Browser, see the MySQL GUI Tools documentation at *http://dev.mysql.com/doc/*.

 If you run Windows, you can install the MySQL System Tray Monitor, which displays an at-a-glance view of your server's health. A green icon means the server is running, and red means it has stopped. You can also use the MySQL System Tray Monitor to gain quick access to common functions, such as shutdown and launching the MySQL Administrator or MySQL Query Browser.

Server Logs

If you are a seasoned Linux or Unix administrator, you are familiar with the concepts and importance of logging. The MySQL server was born of this same environment. Consequently, MySQL has several logs that contain vital information about errors, events, and data changes.

This section examines the various logs in a MySQL server, including the role each log plays in monitoring and performance improvement. Logfiles can provide a lot of information about past events (that's actually the point).

There are several types of logs in the MySQL server. There are logs for recording the SQL commands executed, long-running (slow) queries, changes to data, and the results of the backup and restore commands. You can turn any of the logs on or off using startup options. Most installations have at least the error log enabled. The logs included in the MySQL server include the following:

- General query log
- Slow query log
- Error log

- Binary log
- Backup logs

The general query log, as its name implies, contains information about what the server is doing. It contains information like connections from clients, as well as a copy of the commands sent to the server. As you can imagine, this log grows very quickly. Examine the general query log whenever you are trying to diagnose client-related errors or to determine which clients are issuing certain types of commands.

 Commands in the general query log appear in the same order in which they were *received* from the clients and may not reflect the actual order of execution.

Turn on the general query log by specifying the `--log` startup option. You can also specify the name of the logfile using the `--log-output` startup option. These options have dynamic variable equivalents. For example, `SET GLOBAL log_output = FILE;` sets the log output for a running server to write to a file. Finally, you can read the values of either of these variables using the `SHOW VARIABLES` command.

The slow query log stores a copy of long-running queries. It is in the same format as the general log, and you can control it in the same manner with the `--log-slow-queries` startup option. The server variable that controls which queries go into the slow query log is `log_query_time` (in seconds). You should tune this variable to meet the expectations for your server and applications to help track times when queries perform slower than desired. You can send log entries to a file, a table, or both using the `FILE`, `TABLE`, or `BOTH` options, respectively.

The slow query log can be a very effective tool for tracking problems with queries before the users complain. The goal, of course, is to keep this log small or, better still, empty at all times. That is not to say you should set the variable very high; on the contrary, you should set it to your expectations and adjust the value as your expectations or circumstances change.

 The slave does not log slow queries. However, if you use the `--log-slow-slave-statements` option, it will write slow-running events to its slow log.

The error log contains information gathered when the MySQL server starts or stops. It also contains the errors generated while the server is running. The error log is your first stop when starting an analysis of a down or impaired MySQL server. On some operating systems, the error log can also contain a stack trace (or core dump).

You can turn the error log on or off using the `--log-error` startup option. The default name for the error log is the hostname appended by the extension *.err*. It is saved in the base directory (the same location as the host of the data directory).

> If you start your server with `--console`, errors are written to standard error output as well as to the error log.

The binary log stores all of the changes made to the data on the server as well as statistical information about the execution of the original command on the server.

> The online MySQL Reference Manual states that the binary logs are used for backup; however, practice shows that replication is a more popular use of the binary log.

The unique format of the binary log allows you to use the log for incremental backups, where you store the binlog file created between each backup. You do this by flushing and rotating the binary logs (closing the log and opening a new log); this allows you to save a set of changes since your last backup. This same technique lets you perform PITR, where you restore data from a backup and apply the binary log up to a specific point or date. For more information about the binary log, see Chapter 3. For more information about PITR, see Chapter 12.

Since the binary log makes copies of every data change, it does add a small amount of overhead to the server, but the performance penalty is well worth the benefits.

> The overhead of the binary log can be much higher depending on your disk setup. When the binary log is turned on, there is no concurrent commit when using the InnoDB storage engine. This can be a concern in high-write scenarios with binary logging and InnoDB.

You turn on the binary log using the `--log-bin` startup option, specifying the root filename of the binary log. The server appends a numeric sequence to the end of the filename, allowing for automatic and manual rotations of the log. While not normally necessary, you can also change the name of the index for the binary logs by specifying the `--log-bin-index` startup option. Perform log rotations using the `FLUSH LOGS` command.

You can also control what is logged (inclusive logging) or what is excluded (exclusive logging) using `--binlog-do-db` and `--binlog-ignore-db`, respectively.

Third-Party Tools

There are a few third-party tools that are really quite useful. Some of the more popular are MySAR, mytop, InnoTop, and MONyog. They are all text-based (command-line) tools that you can run in any console window and connect to any MySQL server reachable across the network. We discuss each of these briefly in the following sections.

MySAR

MySAR is a system activity report that resembles the output of the Linux **sar** command; thus it is a **sar** command for MySQL. In this case, MySAR accumulates the output of the SHOW STATUS, SHOW VARIABLES, and SHOW FULL PROCESSLIST commands and stores them in a database on the server named *mysar*. You can configure the data collection in a variety of ways, including limiting the data collected. You can delete older data in order to continue to run MySAR indefinitely and not worry about filling up your disk with status dumps.

MySAR is open source and licensed under the GNU Public License version 2 (GPL v2). You can download MySAR from *https://launchpad.net/mysar*.

mytop

The mytop utility monitors the thread statistics and general performance statistics of MySQL. It lists the common statistics like hostname, version of the server, how many queries have run, the average times of queries, total threads, and other key statistics. It mimics the **top** command found in Linux. It runs the SHOW PROCESSLIST and SHOW STATUS commands periodically and displays the information in a listing like the **top** command. Jeremy D. Zawodny wrote mytop, and he and the MySQL community maintain it. Figure 8-12 shows an example of the mytop utility.

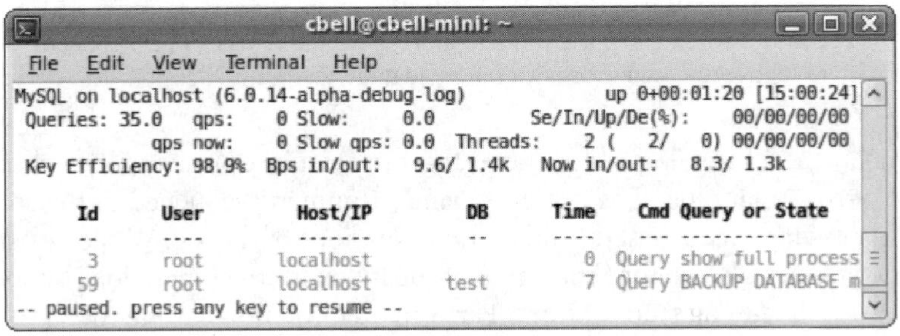

Figure 8-12. The mytop utility

The mytop utility is open source and licensed under the GNU Public License version 2 (GPL v2). You can download mytop at *http://jeremy.zawodny.com/mysql/mytop/*.

InnoTop

InnoTop is another system activity report that resembles a Linux performance tool. In this case, it mimics the **top** command and was inspired by the **mytop** utility. It has many of the same tools as **mytop**, but is specifically designed to monitor InnoDB performance as well as the MySQL server. You can monitor key statistics concerning transactions, deadlocks, foreign keys, query activity, replication activity, system variables, and a host of other details. InnoTop is widely used and considered by some to be a general performance monitoring tool. It has many features that allow you to monitor the system dynamically. If you are using InnoDB primarily as your default (or standard) storage engine and want a well-rounded monitoring tool you can run in text mode, look no further than InnoTop. Figure 8-13 shows an example of the InnoTop utility.

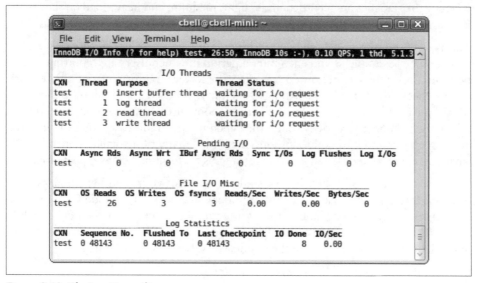

Figure 8-13. The InnoTop utility

The InnoTop utility is licensed under the GNU Public License version 2 (GPL v2). You can download InnoTop at *http://innotop.sourceforge.net/*.

MONyog

MySQL Monitor and Advisor (MONyog) is another good MySQL monitoring tool. It is a proactive monitoring solution that allows you to set parameters for key components for security and performance, and it includes tools to help tune your servers for maximum performance. You can set events to monitor specific parameters and get alerts when the system reaches the specified thresholds. The major features of MONyog are:

- Server resource monitoring
- Identification of poorly executing SQL statements

- Server log monitoring (e.g., the error log)
- Real-time query performance monitoring and identification of long-running queries
- Alerting for significant events

You can download MONyog at *http://www.webyog.com/en/*.

The MySQL Benchmark Suite

Benchmarking is the process of determining how a system performs under certain loads. The act of benchmarking varies greatly and is somewhat of an art form. The goal is to measure and record statistics about the system while running a well-defined set of tests whereby the statistics are recorded under light, medium, and heavy load on the server. In effect, benchmarking sets the expectations for the performance of the system.

This is important because it gives you a hint if your server isn't performing as well as expected. For example, if you encounter a period in which users are reporting slower performance on the server, how do you know the server is performing poorly? Let's say you've checked all of the usual things—memory, disk, etc., and all are performing within tolerance and without error or other anomalies. How, then, do you know if things are running more slowly? Enter the benchmarks. In this case, you can rerun the benchmark test and if the values produced are much larger (or smaller, depending on what you are measuring), you know the system is performing below expectations.

You can use the MySQL benchmark suite to establish your own benchmarks. The benchmark tool is located in the *sql-bench* folder and is normally included in the source code distribution. The benchmarks are written in oPerl and use the Perl DBI module for access to the server. If you do not have Perl or the Perl DBI module, see the section titled "Installing Perl on Unix" in the online MySQL Reference Manual.

Use the following command to run the benchmark suite:

```
./run-all-tests --server=mysql --cmp=mysql --user=root --socket=<socket>
```

This command will run the entire set of standard benchmark tests, recording the current results and comparing them with known results of running the tests on a MySQL server. Example 8-4 shows an excerpt of the results of running the above command on a system with limited resources.

Example 8-4. The MySQL benchmark suite results

```
cbell@cbell-mini:~/source/bzr/mysql-6.0-review/sql-bench$
Benchmark DBD suite: 2.15
Date of test:          2009-12-01 19:54:19
Running tests on:      Linux 2.6.28-16-generic i686
Arguments:             --socket=../mysql-test/var/tmp/mysqld.1.sock
Comments:
Limits from:           mysql
Server version:        MySQL 6.0.14 alpha debug log
```

```
Optimization:        None
Hardware:

alter-table: Total time: 77 wallclock secs
  ( 0.12 usr  0.05 sys +  0.00 cusr  0.00 csys =  0.17 CPU)
ATIS: Total time: 150 wallclock secs
  (20.22 usr  0.56 sys +  0.00 cusr  0.00 csys = 20.78 CPU)
big-tables: Total time: 135 wallclock secs
  (45.73 usr  1.16 sys +  0.00 cusr  0.00 csys = 46.89 CPU)
connect: Total time: 1359 wallclock secs
  (200.70 usr 30.51 sys +  0.00 cusr  0.00 csys = 231.21 CPU)
...
```

The Benchmark Function

MySQL contains a built-in function called benchmark() that you can use to execute a simple expression and obtain a benchmark result. It is best used when testing other functions or expressions to determine if they are causing delays. The function takes two parameters: a counter for looping and the expression you want to test. The following example shows the results of running 10,000,000 iterations of the concat function:

```
mysql> SELECT BENCHMARK(10000000, "SELECT CONCAT('te','s',' t')");
+-------------------------------------------------------+
| BENCHMARK(10000000, "SELECT CONCAT('te','s',' t')")   |
+-------------------------------------------------------+
|                                                   0   |
+-------------------------------------------------------+
1 row in set (0.06 sec)
```

The value of this function is the time it takes to run the benchmark function. In this example, it took 0.06 seconds to run the iterations. If you are exploring a complex query, consider testing portions of it using this command. You may find the problem is related to only one part of the query and not related to lack of indexes.

The benchmarking suite can be a very powerful tool for diagnosing your server. You should consider running the benchmarking tool on your servers to create baseline performance statistics and compare these results to the canned statistics in the suite. For more information about the benchmark suite, see the online MySQL Reference manual.

Now that we have discussed the various tools available for monitoring MySQL and have looked at some best practices, we turn our attention to one of the more advanced features of the MySQL server—storage engines.

Database Performance

Monitoring the performance of an individual database is one of the few areas in the MySQL feature set where community and third-party developers have improved the MySQL experience. There are basic tools included with MySQL that you can use to

---

improve performance, but they do not have the sophistication of some other system-tuning tools. Due to this limitation, most MySQL DBAs earn their pay through experience in relational query optimization techniques. We recognize there are several excellent references that cover database performance in great detail and many readers are likely to be well versed in basic database optimization. We list a few here for your reference:

- *Refactoring SQL Applications*, by Stephane Faroult and Pascal L'Hermite, O'Reilly Media (*http://oreilly.com/catalog/9780596514976/*)
- *SQL and Relational Theory: How to Write Accurate SQL Code*, by C.J. Date, O'Reilly Media (*http://oreilly.com/catalog/9780596523084/*)
- *SQL Cookbook*, by Anthony Mollinaro, O'Reilly Media (*http://oreilly.com/catalog/9780596009762/*)

Rather than reintroducing query optimization techniques, we will concentrate on how you can work with the tools available in MySQL to assist in optimizing databases. We will use a simple example and a known sample database to illustrate the use of the query performance command in MySQL. In the next section we list best practices for improving database performance.

Measuring Database Performance

Traditionally, database management systems have provided profiling tools and indexing tools that report statistics that you can use to fine-tune indexes. While there are some basic elements that can help you improve database performance in MySQL, there is no (free) advanced profiling tool available.

While the basic MySQL installation does not include formal tools for monitoring database improvement, the MySQL Enterprise Manager suite offers a host of performance monitoring features. We will discuss this tool in more detail in Chapter 13.

Fortunately, MySQL provides a few simple tools to help you determine if your tables and queries are optimal. They are all SQL commands and include EXPLAIN, ANALYZE TABLE, and OPTIMIZE TABLE. The following sections describe each of these commands in greater detail.

Using EXPLAIN

The EXPLAIN command provides information about how a SELECT statement (EXPLAIN works only for SELECT statements) can be executed. The syntax for the EXPLAIN command is shown below. Notice that EXPLAIN is a synonym for the DESCRIBE command found in other database systems.

```
[EXPLAIN | DESCRIBE] [EXTENDED] SELECT <select options>
```

You can also use the EXPLAIN and DESCRIBE commands to view details about the columns or partitions of a table. The syntax for this version of the command is shown below.

```
[EXPLAIN | DESCRIBE] [PARTITIONS SELECT * FROM] <table_name>
```

A synonym for EXPLAIN <table_name> is SHOW COLUMNS FROM <table_name>.

We will discuss the first use of the EXPLAIN command—examining a SELECT command to see how the MySQL optimizer executes the statement. The results of this contain a stepwise list of join operations that the optimizer predicts it would require to execute the statement.

Query processing for order-by and group-by are not shown in a stepwise format.

The best use of this command is determining if you have the correct indexes on your tables to allow for more precise targeting of candidate rows. You can also use the results to test the various optimizer override options. While this is an advanced technique and generally discouraged, under the right circumstances you may encounter a query that runs faster with certain optimizer options. We will see an example of this later in this section.

Now let's look at some examples of the EXPLAIN command in action. The following examples are queries executed on the *sakila* sample database provided for MySQL development and experimentation. You can download the *sakila* sample database from *http://downloads.mysql.com/docs/sakila-db.zip*. You can find a sample of the entity-relationship diagram on MySQL Forge at *http://forge.mysql.com/wiki/Image:SakilaSampleDB-0.8.png*.

We will use the \G or vertical display format for clarity.

Let's begin with a simple and seemingly harmless query. Let's say we want to see all of the films rated higher than a PG rating. The result set contains a single row with the following columns:

id

    Sequence number of the statement in order of execution

select_type

    The type of statement executed

table

The table operated on for this step

type

The type of join to be used

 If this column shows ALL, you are doing a full table scan. You should strive to avoid these operations by adding indexes or rewriting your query. Similarly, if this column shows INDEX, you are doing a full index scan, which is very inefficient. See the online MySQL Reference Manual for more details on the types of joins and their consequences.

possible_keys

A list of columns available if there are indexes available

key

The key selected by the optimizer

key_len

The length of the key or portion of the key used

ref

Constraints or columns to be compared

rows

An estimate of the number of rows to process

extra

Additional information from the optimizer

Example 8-5 shows how the MySQL optimizer executes this statement.

Example 8-5. A simple SELECT statement

```
mysql> EXPLAIN SELECT * FROM film WHERE rating > 'PG' \G
*************************** 1. row ***************************
           id: 1
  select_type: SIMPLE
        table: film
         type: ALL
possible_keys: NULL
          key: NULL
      key_len: NULL
          ref: NULL
         rows: 892
        Extra: Using where
1 row in set (0.01 sec)
```

You can see from this output that the optimizer has only one step to execute and it is not using any indexes. This is sensible, because we are not using any columns with indexes. Furthermore, even though there is a WHERE clause, the optimizer will still have to do a full table scan. This may be the right choice when you consider the columns used and the lack of indexes. However, if we ran this query hundreds of thousands of times, the full table scan would be a very poor use of time. In this case, we know from looking at the results that adding an index should improve execution. Let's add an index to the table and try again. Example 8-6 shows the improved query plan.

Example 8-6. Improved query plan

```
mysql> ALTER TABLE film ADD INDEX film_rating (rating);
Query OK, 0 rows affected (0.42 sec)
Records: 0  Duplicates: 0  Warnings: 0

mysql> EXPLAIN SELECT * FROM film WHERE rating >  'PG' \G
*************************** 1. row ***************************
           id: 1
  select_type: SIMPLE
        table: film
         type: ALL
possible_keys: film_rating
          key: NULL
      key_len: NULL
          ref: NULL
         rows: 892
        Extra: Using where
1 row in set (0.00 sec)
```

 For those of you with sharp eyes who have already spotted the problem, bear with us as we work through it.

Here we see the query has now identified an index (`possible_keys`) but is still not using the index, because the `key` field is `NULL`. So what can we do? For this simple example, you may note that only 892 rows are expected to be read. The actual row count is 1,000 rows and the result set would contain only 418 rows. Clearly, it would be a much faster query if it only read 42 percent of the rows!

Now let's see if we can get any additional information from the optimizer by using the `EXTENDED` keyword. This keyword allows us to see extra information via the `SHOW WARNINGS` command. You should issue the command immediately after the `EXPLAIN` command. The warning text describes how the optimizer identifies table and column names in the statement, the internal rewrite of the query, any optimizer rules applied, and any additional notes about the execution. Example 8-7 shows the results of using the `EXTENDED` keyword.

Example 8-7. Using the EXTENDED keyword for more information

```
mysql> EXPLAIN EXTENDED SELECT * FROM film WHERE rating > 'PG' \G
*************************** 1. row ***************************
           id: 1
  select_type: SIMPLE
        table: film
         type: ALL
possible_keys: film_rating
          key: NULL
      key_len: NULL
          ref: NULL
         rows: 892
     filtered: 100.00
        Extra: Using where
1 row in set, 1 warning (0.00 sec)

mysql> SHOW WARNINGS \G
*************************** 1. row ***************************
  Level: Note
   Code: 1003
Message: select `sakila`.`film`.`film_id` AS `film_id`,
`sakila`.`film`.`title` AS `title`,`sakila`.`film`.`description` AS `description`,
`sakila`.`film`.`release_year` AS `release_year`,
`sakila`.`film`.`language_id` AS `language_id`,
`sakila`.`film`.`original_language_id` AS `original_language_id`,
`sakila`.`film`.`rental_duration` AS `rental_duration`,
`sakila`.`film`.`rental_rate` AS `rental_rate`,
`sakila`.`film`.`length` AS `length`,
`sakila`.`film`.`replacement_cost` AS `replacement_cost`,
`sakila`.`film`.`rating` AS `rating`,
`sakila`.`film`.`special_features` AS `special_features`,
`sakila`.`film`.`last_update` AS `last_update`
from `sakila`.`film` where (`sakila`.`film`.`rating` > 'PG')
1 row in set (0.00 sec)
```

This time, there is one warning (used to contain the information from the optimizer) that displays a rewritten form of the query to include all columns and explicitly reference the column in the WHERE clause. Unfortunately, this simple query is in need of a bit more consideration to make it more efficient. You are likely to encounter queries like this that may force you to redesign the query, reconsider using it frequently, or (more likely) consider redesigning the table to support a better index.

Let's see what happens when we issue a query for a specific rating rather than using a range query. We will see the optimization with the index and without. Example 8-8 shows the results.

Example 8-8. Removing the range query

```
mysql> EXPLAIN SELECT * FROM film WHERE rating = 'R' \G
*************************** 1. row ***************************
           id: 1
  select_type: SIMPLE
        table: film
```

```
        type: ref
possible_keys: film_rating
          key: film_rating
      key_len: 2
          ref: const
         rows: 195
        Extra: Using where
1 row in set (0.00 sec)

mysql> ALTER TABLE film DROP INDEX film_rating;Query OK, 0 rows affected (0.37 sec)
Records: 0  Duplicates: 0  Warnings: 0

mysql> EXPLAIN SELECT * FROM film WHERE rating = 'R' \G
*************************** 1. row ***************************
           id: 1
  select_type: SIMPLE
        table: film
         type: ALL
possible_keys: NULL
          key: NULL
      key_len: NULL
          ref: NULL
         rows: 892
        Extra: Using where
1 row in set (0.00 sec)
```

Now we see a little improvement. Notice that the first query plan does indeed use the index and results in a much improved plan over not having the index at all. The question then remains, why doesn't the optimizer use the index? In this case, we've used a non-unique index on an enumerated field. What sounded like a really good idea is actually not much help at all for a range query of enumerated values. However, we could rewrite the above query differently (in several ways, actually) to produce better performance. Let's look at the query again.

We know we want all films rated higher than PG-13. We assumed that the rating is ordered and that the enumerated field reflects the order. In the *sakila* database, the rating field is defined as having values (G, PG, PG-13, R, NC-17). Thus, it appears the order is maintained if we accept the enumeration index for each value that corresponds to the order (e.g., G = 1, PG = 2, etc.). But what if the order is incorrect or if (like in this example) the list of values is incomplete?

In the example we've chosen, where we want all of the films that have a rating higher than PG-13, we know from our list of ratings that this includes films with a rating of R or NC-17. Rather than using a range query, let's examine what the optimizer would do if we listed these values.

Recall that we removed the index, so we will try the query first without the index, then add the index and see if we have an improvement. Example 8-9 shows the improved query.

Example 8-9. Improved query without range

```
mysql> EXPLAIN SELECT * FROM film WHERE rating = 'R' OR rating = 'NC-17' \G
*************************** 1. row ***************************
           id: 1
  select_type: SIMPLE
        table: film
         type: ALL
possible_keys: NULL
          key: NULL
      key_len: NULL
          ref: NULL
         rows: 892
        Extra: Using where
1 row in set (0.00 sec)

mysql> ALTER TABLE film ADD INDEX film_rating (rating);
Query OK, 0 rows affected (0.40 sec)
Records: 0  Duplicates: 0  Warnings: 0

mysql> EXPLAIN SELECT * FROM film WHERE rating = 'R' OR rating = 'NC-17' \G
*************************** 1. row ***************************
           id: 1
  select_type: SIMPLE
        table: film
         type: ALL
possible_keys: film_rating
          key: NULL
      key_len: NULL
          ref: NULL
         rows: 892
        Extra: Using where
1 row in set (0.00 sec)
```

Alas, that didn't work either. Again, we have chosen to query on a column that has an index but is not an index the optimizer can use. We know the optimizer can and will use the index for a simple equality comparison. Let's try rewriting the query as the union of two queries. Example 8-10 shows the rewritten query.

Example 8-10. Query rewritten using UNION

```
mysql> EXPLAIN SELECT * FROM film WHERE rating = 'R' UNION
SELECT * FROM film WHERE rating = 'NC-17' \G
*************************** 1. row ***************************
           id: 1
  select_type: PRIMARY
        table: film
         type: ref
possible_keys: film_rating
          key: film_rating
      key_len: 2
          ref: const
         rows: 195
        Extra: Using where
*************************** 2. row ***************************
```

```
          id: 2
  select_type: UNION
        table: film
         type: ref
possible_keys: film_rating
          key: film_rating
      key_len: 2
          ref: const
         rows: 210
        Extra: Using where
*************************** 3. row ***************************
          id: NULL
  select_type: UNION RESULT
        table: <union1,2>
         type: ALL
possible_keys: NULL
          key: NULL
      key_len: NULL
          ref: NULL
         rows: NULL
        Extra:
3 rows in set (0.00 sec)
```

Success! Now we can see we have a query plan that is using the index and processing far fewer rows. We can see from the result of the EXPLAIN command that the optimizer is running each query individually (steps execute from row 1 down to row *n*) and combines the result in the last step.

 MySQL has a session status variable named last_query_cost that stores the cost of the last query executed. Use this variable to compare two query plans for the same query. For example, after each EXPLAIN, check the value of the variable. The query with the lowest cost value is considered to be the more efficient (less time-consuming) query. A value of 0 indicates no query has been submitted for compilation.

While this exercise may seem to be a lot of work for a little gain, consider that there are many such queries being executed in applications without anyone noticing the inefficiency. Normally we encounter these types of queries only when the row count gets large enough to notice. In the *sakila* database, there are only 1,000 rows, but what if there were a million or tens of millions of rows?

Aside from EXPLAIN, there is no single tool in a standard MySQL distribution that you can use to profile a query in MySQL. The "Optimization" chapter in the online MySQL Reference Manual has a host of tips and tricks to help an experienced DBA improve the performance of various query forms.

Using ANALYZE TABLE

The MySQL optimizer, like most traditional optimizers, uses statistical information about tables to perform its analysis of the optimal query execution plan. These statistics include information about indexes, distribution of values, and table structure, among many items.

The `ANALYZE TABLE` command recalculates the key distribution for one or more tables. This information determines the table order for a join operation. The syntax for the `ANALYZE TABLE` command is shown below:

```
ANALYZE [LOCAL | NO_WRITE_TO_BINLOG] TABLE <table_list>
```

You can update the key distribution for MyISAM and InnoDB tables. This is very important to note because it is not a general tool that applies to all storage engines. However, all storage engines must report index cardinality statistics to the optimizer if they support indexes. Some storage engines, like third-party engines, have their own specific built-in statistics. A typical execution of the command is shown in Example 8-11. Running the command on a table with no indexes has no effect, but will not result in an error.

Example 8-11. Analyzing a table to update key distribution

```
mysql> ANALYZE TABLE film;
+-------------+---------+----------+----------+
| Table       | Op      | Msg_type | Msg_text |
+-------------+---------+----------+----------+
| sakila.film | analyze | status   | OK       |
+-------------+---------+----------+----------+
1 row in set (0.00 sec)
```

In this example, we see the analysis is complete and there are no unusual conditions. Should there be any unusual events during the execution of the command, the `Msg_type` field can indicate "info," "error," or "warning." In these cases, the `Msg_text` field will give you additional information about the event. You should always investigate the situation if you get any result other than "status" and "OK."

You can see the status of your indexes using the `SHOW INDEX` command. A sample of the output of the film table is shown in Example 8-12. In this case, we're interested in the cardinality of each index, which is an estimate of the number of unique values in the index. We omit the other columns from the display for brevity. For more information about `SHOW INDEX`, see the online MySQL Reference Manual.

Example 8-12. The indexes for the film table

```
mysql> SHOW INDEX FROM film \G
*************************** 1. row ***************************
       Table: film
  Non_unique: 0
    Key_name: PRIMARY
Seq_in_index: 1
```

```
 Column_name: film_id
   Collation: A
 Cardinality: 1028
...
*************************** 2. row ***************************
       Table: film
  Non_unique: 1
    Key_name: idx_title
 Seq_in_index: 1
 Column_name: title
   Collation: A
 Cardinality: 1028
...
*************************** 3. row ***************************
       Table: film
  Non_unique: 1
    Key_name: idx_fk_language_id
 Seq_in_index: 1
 Column_name: language_id
   Collation: A
 Cardinality: 2
...
*************************** 4. row ***************************
       Table: film
  Non_unique: 1
    Key_name: idx_fk_original_language_id
 Seq_in_index: 1
 Column_name: original_language_id
   Collation: A
 Cardinality: 2
...
*************************** 5. row ***************************
       Table: film
  Non_unique: 1
    Key_name: film_rating
 Seq_in_index: 1
 Column_name: rating
   Collation: A
 Cardinality: 11
    Sub_part: NULL
      Packed: NULL
        Null: YES
  Index_type: BTREE
     Comment:
5 rows in set (0.00 sec)
```

The LOCAL or NO_WRITE_TO_BINLOG keyword prevents the command from being written to the binary log (and thereby from being replicated in a replication topology). This can be very useful if you want to experiment or tune while replicating data or if you want to omit this step from your binary log and not replay it during PITR.

You should run this command whenever there have been significant updates to the table (e.g., bulk-loaded data). The system must have a read lock on the table for the duration of the operation.

Using OPTIMIZE TABLE

Tables that are updated frequently with new data and deletions can become fragmented quickly and, depending on the storage engine, can have gaps of unused space or sub-optimal storage structures. A badly fragmented table can result in slower performance, especially during table scans.

The OPTIMIZE TABLE command restructures the data structures for one or more tables. This is especially beneficial for row formats with variable length fields (rows). The syntax for the OPTIMIZE TABLE command is shown below:

```
OPTIMIZE [LOCAL | NO_WRITE_TO_BINLOG] TABLE <table_list>
```

You can use this command for MyISAM and InnoDB tables. This is very important to note because it is not a general tool that applies to all storage engines. If the table cannot be reorganized (e.g., there are no variable length records or there is no fragmentation), the command will revert to re-creating the table and updating the statistics. A sample output from this operation is shown in Example 8-13.

Example 8-13. The optimize table command

```
mysql> OPTIMIZE TABLE film \G
*************************** 1. row ***************************
   Table: sakila.film
      Op: optimize
Msg_type: note
Msg_text: Table does not support optimize, doing recreate + analyze instead
*************************** 2. row ***************************
   Table: sakila.film
      Op: optimize
Msg_type: status
Msg_text: OK
2 rows in set (0.44 sec)
```

Here we see two rows in the result set. The first row tells us the OPTIMIZE TABLE command could not be run and that the command will instead re-create the table and run the ANALYZE TABLE command. The second row is the result of the ANALYZE TABLE step.

Like the ANALYZE TABLE command above, any unusual events during the execution of the command are indicated in the Msg_type field by "info," "error," or "warning." In these cases, the Msg_text field will give you additional information about the event. You should always investigate the situation if you get any result other than "status" and "OK."

The LOCAL or NO_WRITE_TO_BINLOG keyword prevents the command from being written to the binary log (it will therefore not be replicated in a replication topology). This can be very useful if you want to experiment or tune while replicating data or if you want to omit this step from your binary log and thereby not replay it during PITR.

You should run this command whenever there have been significant updates to the table (e.g., a large number of deletes and inserts). This operation is designed to rearrange data elements into a more optimal structure and could run for longer than expected. This is one operation that is best run during times of lower loads.

 When using InnoDB, especially when there are secondary indexes (which usually get fragmented), you may not see any improvement or you may encounter long processing times for the operation unless you use the InnoDB "fast index create" option.

Database Optimization Best Practices

As mentioned earlier, there are many great examples, techniques, and practices that come highly recommended by the world's best database performance experts. Rather than passing judgment or suggesting any particular tool or technique, we will instead discuss the most common best practices for improving database performance. We encourage you to examine some of the texts referenced earlier for more detail on each of these practices.

Use indexes sparingly but effectively

Most database professionals understand the importance of indexes and how they improve performance. Using the EXPLAIN command is often the best way to determine which indexes are needed. While the problem of not having enough indexes is understood, having too much of a good thing can cause a performance issue.

As you saw when exploring the EXPLAIN command, it is possible to create too many indexes or indexes that are of little or no use. Each index adds overhead for every insert and delete against the table. In some cases, having too many indexes with wide (as in many values) distributions can slow insert and delete performance considerably. It can also lead to slower replication and restore operations.

You should periodically check your indexes to ensure they are all meaningful and utilized. You should remove any indexes that are not used, have limited use, or have wide distributions. You can often use normalization to overcome some of the problems with wide distributions.

Use normalization, but don't overdo it

Many database experts who studied computer science or a related discipline may have fond memories (or nightmares) of learning the normal forms as described by C.J. Date and others. We won't revisit the material here; rather we will discuss the impacts of taking those lessons too far.

Normalization (at least to third normal form) is a well-understood and standard practice. However, there are situations in which you may want to violate these rules.

The use of lookup tables is often a by-product of normalization. That is, you create a special table that contains a list of related information that is used frequently in other tables. However, you can impede performance when you use lookup tables with limited distributions (only a few rows or a limited number of rows with small values) that are accessed frequently. In this case, every time your users query information, they must use a join to get the complete data. Joins are expensive, and frequently accessed data can add up over time. To mitigate this potential performance problem, you can use enumerated fields to store the data rather than a lookup table. For example, rather than creating a table for hair color (despite what some subcultures may insist upon, there really are only a limited number of hair color types), you can use an enumerated field and avoid the join altogether.

Another potential issue concerns calculated fields. Typically, we do not store data that is formed from other data (such as sales tax or the sum of several columns). Rather, the calculated data is performed either during data retrieval via a view or in the application. This may not be a real issue if the calculations are simple or are seldom performed, but what if the calculations are complex and they are performed many times? In this case, you are potentially wasting a lot of time performing these calculations. One way to mitigate this problem is to use a trigger to calculate the value and store it in the table. While this technically duplicates data (a big no-no for normalization theorists), it can improve performance in situations where there are a lot of calculations being performed.

Use the right storage engine for the task

One of the most powerful features of MySQL is its support for different storage engines. Storage engines govern how data is stored and retrieved. MySQL supports a number of them, each with unique features and uses. This allows database designers to tune their database performance by selecting the storage engine that best meets their application needs. For example, if you have an environment that requires transaction control for highly active databases, choose a storage engine best suited for this task (yes, Virginia, there are some storage engines in MySQL that do not provide transactional support). You may also have identified a view or table that is often queried but almost never updated (e.g., a lookup table). In this case, you may want to use a storage engine the keeps the data in memory for faster access.

Recent changes to MySQL have permitted some storage engines to become plug-ins, and some distributions of MySQL have only certain storage engines enabled by default. To find out which storage engines are enabled, issue the SHOW ENGINES command. Example 8-14 shows the storage engines on a typical installation.

Example 8-14. Storage engines

```
mysql> SHOW ENGINES \G
*************************** 1. row ***************************
      Engine: InnoDB
     Support: YES
     Comment: Supports transactions, row-level locking, and foreign keys
Transactions: YES
```

```
        XA: YES
 Savepoints: YES
*************************** 2. row ***************************
     Engine: MyISAM
    Support: DEFAULT
    Comment: Default engine as of MySQL 3.23 with great performance
Transactions: NO
        XA: NO
 Savepoints: NO
*************************** 3. row ***************************
     Engine: BLACKHOLE
    Support: YES
    Comment: /dev/null storage engine (anything you write to it disappears)
Transactions: NO
        XA: NO
 Savepoints: NO
*************************** 4. row ***************************
     Engine: CSV
    Support: YES
    Comment: CSV storage engine
Transactions: NO
        XA: NO
 Savepoints: NO
*************************** 5. row ***************************
     Engine: MEMORY
    Support: YES
    Comment: Hash based, stored in memory, useful for temporary tables
Transactions: NO
        XA: NO
 Savepoints: NO
*************************** 6. row ***************************
     Engine: FEDERATED
    Support: NO
    Comment: Federated MySQL storage engine
Transactions: NULL
        XA: NULL
 Savepoints: NULL
*************************** 7. row ***************************
     Engine: ARCHIVE
    Support: YES
    Comment: Archive storage engine
Transactions: NO
        XA: NO
 Savepoints: NO
*************************** 8. row ***************************
     Engine: MRG_MYISAM
    Support: YES
    Comment: Collection of identical MyISAM tables
Transactions: NO
        XA: NO
 Savepoints: NO
8 rows in set (0.00 sec)
```

The result set includes all of the known storage engines; whether they are installed and configured (where Support = YES); a note about the engine's features; and whether it supports transactions, distributed transactions (XA), or *savepoints*.

 A savepoint is a named event that you can use like a transaction. You can establish a savepoint and either release (delete the savepoint) or roll back the changes since the savepoint. See the online MySQL Reference Manual for more details about savepoints.

With so many storage engines to choose from, it can be confusing when designing your database for performance. The following describes each of the storage engines briefly, including some of the uses for which they are best suited. You can choose the storage engine for a table using the `ENGINE` parameter on the `CREATE` statement, and you can change the storage engine by issuing an `ALTER TABLE` command:

```
CREATE TABLE t1 (a int) ENGINE=InnoDB;
ALTER TABLE t1 ENGINE=MEMORY;
```

The InnoDB storage engine is the premier transactional support storage engine. You should always choose this storage engine when requiring transactional support; it is currently the only transactional engine in MySQL. There are third-party storage engines in various states of production that can support transactions, but the only "out-of-the–box" option is InnoDB. Interestingly, all indexes in InnoDB are *B-trees*, in which the index records are stored in the leaf pages of the tree. InnoDB is the storage engine of choice for high reliability and transaction-processing environments.

The MyISAM storage engine is the default engine; this engine will be used if you omit the `ENGINE` option on the `CREATE` statement. MyISAM is often used for data warehousing, e-commerce, and enterprise applications. MyISAM uses advanced caching and indexing mechanisms to improve data retrieval and indexing. MyISAM is an excellent choice when you need storage in a wide variety of applications requiring fast retrieval of data without the need for transactions.

The Blackhole storage engine is very interesting. It doesn't store anything at all. In fact, it is what its name suggests—data goes in but never returns. All jocularity aside, the Blackhole storage engine fills a very special need. If binary logging is enabled, SQL statements are written to the logs, and Blackhole is used as a relay agent (or proxy) in a replication topology. In this case, the relay agent processes data from the master and passes it on to its slaves but does not actually store any data. The Blackhole storage engine can be handy in situations where you want to test an application to ensure it is writing data, but you don't want to store anything on disk.

The CSV storage engine can create, read, and write comma-separated value (CSV) files as tables. The CSV storage engine is best used to rapidly export structured business data to spreadsheets. The CSV storage engine does not provide any indexing mechanisms and has certain issues in storing and converting date/time values (they do not obey locality during queries). The CSV storage engine is best used when you want to permit other applications to share or exchange data in a common format. Given that it is not as efficient for storing data, you should use the CSV storage engine sparingly.

> The CSV storage engine is used for writing logfiles. For example, the backup logs are CSV files and can be opened by other applications that use the CSV protocol (but not while the server is running).

The Memory storage engine (sometimes called HEAP) is an in-memory storage that uses a hashing mechanism to retrieve frequently used data. This allows for much faster retrieval. Data is accessed in the same manner as with the other storage engines, but the data is stored in memory and is valid only during the MySQL session—the data is flushed and deleted on shutdown. Memory storage engines are typically good for situations in which static data is accessed frequently and rarely ever altered (e.g., lookup tables). Examples include zip code listings, state and county names, category listings, and other data that is accessed frequently and seldom updated. You can also use the Memory storage engine for databases that utilize snapshot techniques for distributed or historical data access.

The Federated storage engine creates a single table reference from multiple database systems. The Federated storage engine allows you to link tables together across database servers. This mechanism is similar in purpose to the linked data tables available in other database systems. The Federated storage engine is best suited for distributed or data mart environments. The most interesting feature of the Federated storage engine is that it does not move data, nor does it require the remote tables to use the same storage engine.

> The Federated storage engine is currently disabled in most distributions of MySQL. Consult the online MySQL Reference Manual for more details.

The Archive storage engine can store large amounts of data in a compressed format. The Archive storage engine is best suited for storing and retrieving large amounts of seldom-accessed archival or historical data. Indexes are not supported and the only access method is via a table scan. Thus, you should not use the Archive storage engine for normal database storage and retrieval.

The Merge (`MRG_MYISAM`) storage engine can encapsulate a set of MyISAM tables with the same structure (table layout or schema) and is referenced as a single table. Thus, the tables are partitioned by the location of the individual tables, but no additional partitioning mechanisms are used. All tables must reside on the same server (but not necessarily the same database).

When a `DROP` command is issued on a merged table, only the Merge specification is removed. The original tables are not altered.

The best attribute of the Merge storage engine is speed. It permits you to split a large table into several smaller tables on different disks, combine them using a merge table specification, and access them simultaneously. Searches and sorts will execute more quickly, since there is less data in each table to manipulate. Also, repairs on tables are more efficient because it is faster and easier to repair several smaller individual tables than a single large table. Unfortunately, this configuration has several disadvantages:

- You must use identical MyISAM tables to form a single merge table.
- The replace operation is not allowed.
- Indexes are less efficient than for a single table.

The Merge storage engine is best suited for very large database (VLDB) applications, like data warehousing, where data resides in more than one table in one or more databases. You can also use it to help solve partitioning problems where you want to partition horizontally but do not want to add the complexity of the partition table options.

Clearly, with so many choices of storage engines, it is possible to choose engines that can hamper performance or, in some cases, prohibit certain solutions. For example, if you never specify a storage engine when the table is created, MySQL uses the default storage engine. If not set manually, the default storage engine reverts to the platform-specific default, which may be MyISAM on some platforms. This may mean you are missing out on optimizing lookup tables or limiting features of your application by not having transactional support. It is well worth the extra time to include an analysis of storage engine choices when designing or tuning your databases.

Use views for faster results via the query cache

Views are a very handy way to encapsulate complex queries to make it easier to work with the data. You can use views to limit data both vertically (fewer columns) or horizontally (a `WHERE` clause on the underlying `SELECT` statement). Both are very handy and, of course, the more complex views use both practices to limit the result set returned to the user or to hide certain base tables or to ensure an efficient join is executed.

Using views to limit the columns returned can help you in ways you may not have considered. It not only reduces the amount of data processed, it can also help you avoid costly `SELECT *` operations that users tend to do without much thought. When many of these types of operations are run, your applications are processing far too much data and this can affect performance of not only the application, but also the server, and more importantly, can decrease available bandwidth on your network. It always a good idea to use views to limit data in this manner and hide access to the base table(s) to remove any temptation users may have to access the base table directly.

Views that limit the number of rows returned also help reduce network bandwidth and can improve the performance of your applications. These types of views also protect against proliferation of SELECT * queries. Using views in this manner requires a bit more planning, because your goal is to create meaningful subsets of the data. You will have to examine the requirements for your database and understand the queries issued to form the correct WHERE clauses for these queries.

With a little effort, you may find you can create combinations of vertically and horizontally restrictive views, thereby ensuring your applications operate on only the data that is needed. The less data moving around, the more data your applications can process in the same amount of time.

Perhaps the best way to use views is to eliminate poorly formed joins. This is especially true when you have a complex normalized schema. It may not be obvious to users how to combine the tables to form a meaningful result set. Indeed, most of the work done by DBAs when striving for better performance is focused on correcting poorly formed joins. Sometimes this can be trivial—for example, fewer rows processed during the join operation—but most of the time the improved response time is significant.

Views can also be helpful when using the query cache in MySQL. The query cache stores the results of frequently used (accessed) queries. Using views that provide a standardized result set can improve the likelihood that the results will be cached and, therefore, retrieved more efficiently.

You can improve performance with a little design work and the judicious use of views in your databases. Take the time to examine how much data is being moved around (both the number of columns and rows) and examine your application for any query that uses joins. Spend some time forming views that limit the data and identify the most efficient joins and wrap them in a view as well. Imagine how much easier you'll rest knowing your users are executing efficient joins.

Use constraints

The use of constraints provides another tool in your arsenal for combating performance problems. Rather than proselytizing about limitations on using constraints, we encourage you to consider constraints a standard practice and not an afterthought.

There are several types of constraints available in MySQL, including the following:

- Unique indexes
- Primary keys
- Foreign keys
- Enumerated values
- Sets

- Default values
- NOT NULL option

We've discussed using indexes and overusing indexes. Indexes help improve data retrieval by allowing the system to store and find data more quickly.

A *unique index* is simply an index on one field in a table that guarantees there are no duplicates in the table if used with the NOT NULL constraint to require a value. That is, only one row can have a single value in the index. Use unique indexes for fields that you want to prohibit duplicates of, such as sequence numbers, order numbers, social security numbers, etc. A table can have one or more unique indexes.

A *primary key* is also considered a unique index, but in this case it uniquely identifies each row in a table and prohibits duplication. Primary keys are created as a result of normalization and, when designed effectively, form the join columns for table joins.

One of the most common primary keys is an automatically generated sequence number (called a surrogate) that uniquely identifies a row. MySQL provides an AUTO_INCREMENT option to tell the system to generate these special unique values. The use of surrogate key values is considered a compromise by some database theorists and some discourage its use, because a primary key should be made from the existing fields and not artificially generated. While we won't go so far as to say you should never use surrogate keys, we will say that you should use them sparingly. If you find yourself using AUTO_INCREMENT on virtually every table, you are probably overusing this feature.

Foreign keys are also created as a result of the normalization process. They allow the formation of a parent/child or master/detail relationship where a row in one table is the master and one or more rows in another table contain the details of the master. A foreign key is a field identified in the detail table that refers back to the master. Foreign keys also permit cascading operations where deletion of the master row also deletes all of the detail rows.

 Currently, only InnoDB supports foreign keys.

We've discussed using *enumerated values* to replace small lookup tables. However, enumerated values can be a performance tool. This is because the text for the enumerated values is stored only once—in the table header structures. What is saved in the rows is a numeric reference value that forms an index (array index) of the enumerated value. Thus, enumerated value lists can save space and can make traversing the data a bit more efficient. An enumerated field type allows one and only one value.

The use of *sets* in MySQL is similar to using enumerated values. However, a set field type allows storage of one or more values in the set. You can use sets to store information that represents attributes of the data rather than using a master/detail relationship. This not only saves space in the table (set values are bitwise combinations), but also eliminates the need to access another table for the values.

The use of the DEFAULT option to supply default values is an excellent way to prohibit problems associated with poorly constructed data. For example, if you have a numeric field that represents values used for calculations, you may want to ensure that when the field is unknown, a default value is given instead. You can set defaults on most data types. You can also use defaults for date and time fields to avoid problems processing invalid date and time values. More importantly, default values can save your application from having to supply the values (or using the less reliable method of asking the user to provide them), thereby reducing the amount of data sent to the server during data entry.

You should also consider using the NOT NULL option when specifying fields that must have a value. If an entry is attempted where there are NOT NULL columns and no data values are provided, the INSERT statement will fail. This prevents data integrity issues by ensuring all important fields have values.

Use EXPLAIN, ANALYZE, and OPTIMIZE

We have already discussed the benefits of these commands. We list them here as a best practice to remind you that these tools are vital for diagnostic and tuning efforts. Use them often and with impunity, but follow their use carefully. Specifically, use ANALYZE and OPTIMIZE when it makes sense and not as a regular, scheduled event. We have encountered administrators who run these commands nightly, and in some cases that may be warranted, but in the general case it is not warranted and can lead to unnecessary table copies (like we saw in the earlier examples). Clearly, forcing the system to copy data regularly can be a waste of time and could lead to limited access during the operation.

Now that we've discussed how to monitor and improve database performance, let us look more closely at one of the most successful and most popular features—replication. In the next section, we will discuss how you can monitor and improve replication in MySQL. We have placed this topic last because, as you shall see, you must have a well-performing server with well-performing databases and queries before you can begin to improve replication performance.

Best Practices for Improving Performance

The details of diagnosing and improving performance of databases are covered by works devoted to the subject and indeed, the information fills many pages.

For completeness and as a general reference, we include in this section a set of best practices for combating performance anomalies; this is meant to be a checklist for you to use as a guide. We have grouped the practices by common problems.

Everything Is Slow

When the system as a whole is performing poorly, you must focus your efforts on how the system is running, starting with the operating system. You can use one or more of the following techniques to identify and improve the performance of your system:

- Check hardware for problems.
- Improve hardware (e.g., add memory).
- Consider moving data to isolated disks.
- Check the operating system for proper configuration.
- Consider moving some applications to other servers.
- Consider replication for scale-out.
- Tune the server for performance.

Slow Queries

Any query that appears in the slow query log or those identified as problematic by your users or developers can be improved using one or more of the following techniques:

- Normalize your database schema.
- Use EXPLAIN to identify missing or incorrect indexes.
- Use the benchmark() function to test parts of queries.
- Consider rewriting the query.
- Use views to standardize queries.
- Turn on the query cache.

 A replication slave does not write replicated queries to the slow query log, regardless of whether the query was written to the slow query log on the master.

Slow Applications

If you have an application that is showing signs of performance issues, you should examine the application components to determine where the problem is located. Perhaps you will find only one module is causing the problem, but sometimes it may be more serious. The following techniques can help you identify and solve application performance problems:

- Turn on the query cache.
- Consider and optimize your storage engine choices.
- Verify the problem isn't in the server or operating system.

- Define benchmarks for your applications and compare to known baselines.
- Examine internalized (written in the application) queries and maximize their performance.
- Divide and conquer—examine one part at a time.
- Use partitioning to spread out the data.
- Examine your indexes for fragmentation.

Slow Replication

The performance problems related to replication, as discussed earlier, are normally isolated to problems with the database and server performance. Use the following techniques when diagnosing performance issues for replication:

- Ensure your network is operating at peak performance.
- Ensure your servers are configured correctly.
- Optimize your databases.
- Limit updates to the master.
- Divide reads across several slaves.
- Check the slaves for replication lag.
- Perform regular maintenance on your logs (binary and relay logs).
- Use compression over your network if bandwidth is limited.
- Use inclusive and exclusive logging options to minimize what is replicated.

Conclusion

There are a lot of things to monitor on a MySQL server. We've discussed the basic SQL commands available for monitoring the server, the `mysqladmin` command-line utility, the benchmark suite, and the MySQL Administrator and MySQL Query Browser GUI tools. We have also examined some best practices for improving database performance.

Now that you know the basics of operating system monitoring, database performance, MySQL monitoring, and benchmarking, you have the tools and knowledge to successfully tune your server for optimal performance.

Joel smiled as he compiled his report about Susan's nested query problem. It had taken a few hours of digging through logfiles to find the problem, but after he explained the overhead of the query to the developers, they agreed to change the query to use a lookup table stored in a memory table. Joel felt his boss was going to be excited to learn about his ingenuity. He clicked Send just as his boss appeared in his doorframe.

"Joel!"

Joel jumped, despite knowing Mr. Summerson was there. "I've got the marketing application problem solved, sir," he said quickly.

"Great! I look forward to reading about how you solved the problem."

Joel wasn't sure his boss would understand the technical parts of his message, but he also knew his boss would keep asking if he didn't explain everything.

Mr. Summerson nodded once and went on his way. Joel opened an email message from Phil in Seattle complaining about replication problems and soon realized the problems extended much further than the server he had been working with.

Storage Engine Monitoring

Joel was enjoying his morning latte when his phone rang. It startled him because until now he had never heard it ring. He lifted the receiver and heard engine noises. Expecting the call was a wrong number, he said hesitantly, "Hello?"

"Joel! Glad I caught you." It was Mr. Summerson, calling from his car.

"Yes, sir."

"I'm on my way to the airport to meet with the sales staff in the Seattle office. I wanted to ask you to look into the new application database. The developers in Seattle tell me they think we need to figure out a better configuration for performance."

Joel had expected something like this. He knew a little about MyISAM and InnoDB, but he wasn't familiar with monitoring, much less tuning their performance. "I can look into it, sir."

"Great. Thanks, Joel. I'll email you." The connection was severed before Joel could reply. Joel finished the last of his latte and started reading about storage engines in MySQL.

Now that you know when your servers are performing well (and when they aren't), how do you know how well your storage engines are performing? If you are hosting one or more transactional databases or need your storage engine to perform at its peak for fast queries, you will need to monitor the storage engines. In this chapter, we discuss advanced monitoring, focusing on monitoring and improving storage engine performance, by examining the two most popular storage engines: MyISAM and InnoDB.

Having multiple interchangeable storage engines is a very powerful and unique feature of MySQL. While there is no built-in generic storage engine monitoring capability or even a standardized monitoring feature, you can monitor and configure (tune) the most popular storage engines for performance.

In this section, we will examine the MyISAM and InnoDB storage engines. We will discuss how to monitor each and offer some practical advice on how to improve performance.

MyISAM

There are very few things to monitor on the MyISAM storage engine. This is because the MyISAM storage engine was built for web applications with a focus on fast queries and, as such, has only one feature in the server that you can tune—the key cache. That doesn't mean there is nothing else that you can do to improve performance. On the contrary, there are many things you can do. Most fall into one of three areas—optimizing storage on disk, using memory efficiently by monitoring and tuning the key cache, and tuning your tables for maximum performance.

Rather than discussing the broader aspects of these areas, we provide a strategy organized into the following areas of performance improvement:

- Optimizing disk storage
- Tuning your tables for performance
- Using the MyISAM utilities
- Storing a table in index order
- Compressing tables
- Defragmenting tables
- Monitoring the key cache
- Preloading key caches
- Using multiple key caches
- Other parameters to consider

We will discuss each of these briefly in the sections that follow.

Optimizing Disk Storage

Optimizing disk space for MyISAM is more of a system configuration option than a MyISAM-specific tuning parameter. MyISAM stores each table as its own *.myd* (data file) and one or more *.myi* (index) files. They are stored with the *.frm* file in the folder under the name of the database in the data directory specified by the `--datadir` startup option. Thus, optimizing disk space for MyISAM is the same as optimizing disk space for the server. That is, you can see performance improvements by moving the data directory to its own disk, and you can further improve performance of the disk with RAID or other high availability storage options.

Tuning Your Tables for Performance

There are a couple of SQL commands that you can use to keep your tables in optimal condition. These include the ANALYZE TABLE, OPTIMIZE TABLE, and REPAIR TABLE commands.

The ANALYZE TABLE command examines and reorganizes the key distribution for a table. The MySQL server uses the key distribution to determine the join order when joining on a field other than a constant. Key distributions also determine which indexes to use for a query. We discuss this command in more detail in "Using ANALYZE TABLE" on page 328.

The REPAIR TABLE command is not really a performance tool—you can use it to fix a corrupted table for the MyISAM, Archive, and CSV storage engines. Use this command to try to recover tables that have become corrupt or are performing very poorly (which is usually a sign that a table has degraded and needs reorganizing or repair).

 The REPAIR TABLE command is the same as running myisamchk --recover <table name> (see the following section).

Use the OPTIMIZE TABLE command to recover deleted blocks and reorganize the table for better performance. You can use this command for MyISAM, BDB, and InnoDB tables.

While these commands are useful, there are a number of more advanced tools you can use to further manage your MyISAM tables.

Using the MyISAM Utilities

There are a number of special utilities included in the MySQL distribution that are designed for use with the MyISAM storage engine (tables).

- myisam_ftdump allows you to display information about full-text indexes.
- myisamchk allows you to perform analysis on a MyISAM table.
- myisamlog allows you to view the change logs of a MyISAM table.
- myisampack allows you to compress a table to minimize storage.

myisamchk is the workhorse utility for MyISAM. It can display information about your MyISAM tables or analyze, repair, and optimize them. You can run the command for one or more tables, but you can only use it offline (close the tables and shut down the server).

Be sure to make a backup of your tables before running this utility in case the repair or optimization steps fail. In rare cases, this has been known to leave tables corrupted and irreparable.

The options related to performance improvement are described below. See the online MySQL Reference Manual for a complete description of the available options.

analyze
> Analyzes the key distribution of indexes to improve query performance.

backup
> Makes a copy of the tables (the *.myd* file) prior to altering them.

check
> Checks the table for errors—report only.

extended-check
> Does a thorough check of the table for errors, including all indexes—report only.

force
> Performs a repair if any errors are found.

information
> Shows statistical information about the table. Use this command first to see the condition of your table before running `recover`.

medium-check
> Performs a more thorough check of the table—repair only. This does less checking than `extended-check`.

recover
> Performs a comprehensive repair of the table, repairing the data structures. Repairs everything except duplicate unique keys.

safe-recover
> Performs an older form of repair that reads through all rows in order and updates all of the indexes.

sort index
> Sorts the index tree in high-low order. This can reduce seek time to index structures and make accessing the index faster.

sort records
> Sorts the records in the order of a specified index. This can improve performance for certain index-based queries.

Example 9-1 shows the results of running the `myisamchk` command to display information about a MyISAM table.

Example 9-1. The myisamchk utility

```
MyISAM file:        /usr/local/mysql/data/employees/employees
Record format:      Packed
```

```
Character set:        latin1_swedish_ci (8)
File-version:         1
Creation time:        2009-12-03 20:52:12
Status:               changed
Data records:              297024  Deleted blocks:            3000
Datafile parts:            300024  Deleted data:             95712
Datafile pointer (bytes):       6  Keyfile pointer (bytes):      6
Datafile length:          9561268  Keyfile length:         3086336
Max datafile length: 281474976710654
Max keyfile length: 288230376151710719
Recordlength:                  44

table description:
Key Start Len Index  Type         Rec/key     Root  Blocksize
1   1     4   unique long                1  2931712       1024
```

Storing a Table in Index Order

You can improve the efficiency of large data retrieval for range queries (e.g., WHERE a > 5 AND a < 15) by storing table data in the same order as it is stored in the index. This type of ordering allows the query to access data in order, without having to search the disk pages for the data. To sort a table in index order, use the myisamchk utility sort records option (-R) and specify which index you want to use, starting with number 1 for the first index. The following command sorts table1 from the test database in the order of the second index:

```
myisamchk -R 2 /usr/local/mysql/data/test/table1
```

You can accomplish the same effect using ALTER TABLE and ORDER BY.

Sorting the table like this does not ensure the order will remain by index when new rows are added. Deletions do not disturb the order, but as new rows are added the table can become less ordered and cause your performance advantages to dwindle. If you use this technique for tables that change frequently, you may want to consider running the command periodically to ensure optimal ordering.

Compressing Tables

Compressing data saves space. While there are methods to compress data in MySQL, the MyISAM storage engine allows you to compress (*pack*) read-only tables to save space. They must be read-only because MyISAM does not have the capability to decompress, reorder, or compress additions (or deletions). To compress a table, use the myisampack utility as follows:

```
myisampack -b /usr/local/mysql/data/test/table1
```

Always use the backup (-b) option to create a backup of your table prior to compressing it. This will allow you to make the table writable without having to rerun the myisam pack command.

There are two reasons for compressing a read-only table. First and foremost, it can save a lot of space for tables that include data that is easy to compress (e.g., text). Second, when a compressed table is read and the query uses the primary key or unique index to find a row, only the single-row data is decompressed prior to additional comparisons.

There are a great many options to the myisampack command. If you are interested in compressing your read-only tables for space, see the online MySQL Reference Manual for more details about how to control the compression features.

Defragmenting Tables

When MyISAM tables have had a lot of changes in the form of deletions and insertions, the physical storage can become fragmented. Often there are small gaps in the physical store representing deleted data, or there are records stored out of the original order, or both. To optimize the table and reorganize it back to the desired order and form, use either the OPTIMIZE TABLE command or the myisamchk utility.

You should run these commands periodically for tables where you have specified a sort order to ensure they are stored in the most optimal manner. You should also run one of these commands when data has undergone many changes over a period of time.

Monitoring the Key Cache

The key cache in MySQL is a very efficient structure designed to store frequently used index data. It is used exclusively for MyISAM and stores the keys using a fast lookup mechanism (usually a B-tree). The indexes are stored internally (in memory) as linked lists and can be searched very quickly. The key cache is created automatically when the first MyISAM table is opened for reading. Each time a query is issued for a MyISAM table, the key cache is examined first. If the index is found there, it performs the index search in memory rather than reading the index from disk first. The key cache is the secret weapon that makes MyISAM so much faster for rapid queries than some other storage engines.

There are a number of variables that control the key cache, and you can monitor each using the SHOW VARIABLES and SHOW STATUS commands or the MySQL Administrator. We discussed the built-in key cache monitor in MySQL Administrator in Chapter 8 (see Figure 8-5). The variables you can monitor with the SHOW commands are shown in Example 9-2.

Example 9-2. The key cache status and system variables

```
mysql> SHOW STATUS LIKE 'Key%';
+------------------------+-------+
| Variable_name          | Value |
+------------------------+-------+
| Key_blocks_not_flushed | 0     |
| Key_blocks_unused      | 6694  |
| Key_blocks_used        | 0     |
```

```
| Key_read_requests      | 0     |
| Key_reads              | 0     |
| Key_write_requests     | 0     |
| Key_writes             | 0     |
+------------------------+-------+
7 rows in set (0.00 sec)

mysql> SHOW VARIABLES LIKE 'key%';
+--------------------------+---------+
| Variable_name            | Value   |
+--------------------------+---------+
| key_buffer_size          | 8384512 |
| key_cache_age_threshold  | 300     |
| key_cache_block_size     | 1024    |
| key_cache_division_limit | 100     |
+--------------------------+---------+
4 rows in set (0.01 sec)
```

As you can imagine, the key cache can be a very complicated mechanism. Tuning the key cache can therefore be a challenge. We recommend monitoring usage and making changes to the size of the key cache rather than changing how it performs, since it performs very well in the default configuration.

If you want to improve cache hit behavior, use one of the two techniques discussed next: preloading the cache and using multiple key caches along with adding more memory to the default key cache.

Preloading Key Caches

You can preload your indexes into the key cache. This ensures your queries will be faster, because the index is already loaded in the key cache and the index is loaded sequentially (rather than randomly, as would occur when the key cache is loaded under concurrent operation, for example). However, you must ensure there is enough room in the cache to hold the index. Preloading can be a very effective way to speed up your queries for certain applications or modes of use. For example, if you know there will be a lot of queries against a particular table during the execution of an application—for example, a typical payroll audit—you can preload the associated table indexes into the key cache, thereby improving performance during this activity. To preload the key cache for a table, use the LOAD INDEX command as shown in Example 9-3.

Example 9-3. Preloading indexes into the key cache

```
mysql> LOAD INDEX INTO CACHE salaries IGNORE LEAVES;
+--------------------+--------------+----------+----------+
| Table              | Op           | Msg_type | Msg_text |
+--------------------+--------------+----------+----------+
| employees.salaries | preload_keys | status   | OK       |
+--------------------+--------------+----------+----------+
1 row in set (1.49 sec)
```

This example loads the index for the *salary* table into the key cache. The `IGNORE LEAVES` clause preloads only the blocks for the nonleaf nodes of the index . While there is no special command to flush the key cache, you can forcibly remove an index from the key cache by modifying the table—for example, by reorganizing the index or simply dropping and re-creating the index.

Using Multiple Key Caches

One of the little-known advanced features of MySQL is the creation of multiple key caches or custom key caches to reduce contention for the default key cache. This feature allows you to load the index of one or more tables into a special cache that you configure yourself. As you can imagine, this means allocating memory to the task and as such requires careful planning. However, the performance benefits may be substantial if there are periods in which you are executing many queries against a set of tables where the indexes are frequently referenced.

To create a secondary key cache, first define it with the `SET` command by allocating memory, then issue one or more `CACHE INDEX` commands to load the indexes for one or more tables. Unlike the default key cache, you can flush or remove a secondary key cache by setting its size to 0. Example 9-4 shows how to create a secondary key cache and add the index for a table to the cache.

Example 9-4. Using secondary key caches

```
mysql> SET GLOBAL emp_cache.key_buffer_size=128*1024;
Query OK, 0 rows affected (0.00 sec)

mysql> CACHE INDEX salaries IN emp_cache;
+--------------------+--------------------+----------+----------+
| Table              | Op                 | Msg_type | Msg_text |
+--------------------+--------------------+----------+----------+
| employees.salaries | assign_to_keycache | status   | OK       |
+--------------------+--------------------+----------+----------+
1 row in set (0.00 sec)

mysql> SET GLOBAL emp_cache.key_buffer_size=0;
Query OK, 0 rows affected (0.00 sec)
```

Notice that the secondary cache involves defining a new variable named emp_cache and setting its size to 128 KB. This is a special syntax of the `SET` command and while it appears to create a new system variable, it is actually creating a new global user variable. You can discover the existence or size of a secondary key cache as follows:

```
mysql> select @@global.emp_cache.key_buffer_size;
+------------------------------------+
| @@global.emp_cache.key_buffer_size |
+------------------------------------+
|                             131072 |
+------------------------------------+
1 row in set (0.00 sec)
```

Secondary key caches are global and thus exist until you flush them by setting their size to 0 or when the server is restarted.

 You can save the configuration of multiple key caches by storing the statements in a file and using the init-file=<*path_to_file*> command in the *[mysql]* section of the MySQL option file to execute the statements on startup.

Other Parameters to Consider

There are a number of other parameters to consider. Remember, change only one thing at a time and only if you have a good reason to do so. You should never change the configuration of a complex feature like a storage engine without a good reason and reasonable expectations for the outcome.

myisam_data_pointer_size
> The default pointer size in bytes (2–7) used by CREATE TABLE if there is no value specified for MAX_ROWS (the maximum number of rows to store in the table). It has a default value of 6.

myisam_max_sort_file_size
> Maximum size of a temporary file used when sorting data. Increasing this value may make repairs and reorganization of index operations faster.

myisam_recover_options
> The recovery mode for MyISAM. You can use this for OPTIMIZE TABLE as well. The modes include default, backup, force, and quick, and can take any combination of these options. Default means recovery is performed without a backup, force, or quick checking. Backup means a backup will be created before recovery. Force means recovery continues even if data is lost (more than one row). Quick means the rows in the table are not checked if there are no blocks marked as deleted. Consider the severity of the recovery when determining which options to use.

myisam_repair_threads
> If set to a value greater than 1, repair and sorting operations are done in parallel and can make the operations a bit faster. Otherwise, they are done sequentially.

myisam_sort_buffer_size
> The size of the buffer for sorting operations. Increasing this value can help with sorting indexes. However, values greater than 4 GB work only on 64-bit machines.

myisam_stats_method
> Controls how the server counts NULL values in index value distribution for statistical operations. This can also affect the optimizer, so use with care.

`myisam_use_mmap`

    Turns the memory map option on for reading and writing MyISAM tables. Can be helpful in situations where there are a lot of small writes that contend with read queries that return large data sets.

We have discussed a number of strategies for monitoring and improving MyISAM performance. While the discussion is brief, it covers the most important aspects of using MyISAM effectively. For more information about the key cache and the MyISAM storage engine, see the online MySQL Reference Manual.

MySQL, Replication, and High Availability

There is a higher probability of corruption of MyISAM data than InnoDB data and, as a result, MyISAM requires longer recovery times. Also, since MyISAM does not support transactions, events are executed one at a time, which could lead to partial statement execution and therefore an incomplete transaction. Add to this the fact that the slave executes as a single thread, which could allow the slave to fall behind when processing long-running queries. Thus, using MyISAM on a slave in a high-availability solution with transactions can be problematic.

InnoDB

There are many tuning options for the InnoDB storage engine, and a thorough examination of all of them and the techniques that go along with each can fill an entire volume. For example, there are 50 variables that control the behavior of InnoDB and over 40 status variables to communicate metadata about performance and status. In this section, we discuss how to monitor the InnoDB storage engine and focus on some key areas for improving performance.

Rather than discussing the broader aspects of these areas, we provide a strategy organized into the following areas of performance improvement:

- Using the `SHOW ENGINE` command
- Using InnoDB monitors
- Monitoring logfiles
- Monitoring the buffer pool
- Monitoring tablespaces
- Using `INFORMATION_SCHEMA` tables
- Other parameters to consider

We will discuss each of these briefly in the sections that follow. However, before we get started, let's take a brief look at the InnoDB architectural features.

The InnoDB storage engine uses a very sophisticated architecture that is designed for high concurrency and heavy transactional activity. It has a number of advanced features that you should consider prior to attempting to improve performance. We focus on the features we can monitor and improve. These include indexes, the buffer pool, logfiles, and tablespaces.

The indexes in an InnoDB table use clustered indexes. Even if no index is specified, InnoDB assigns an internal value to each row so that it can use a clustered index. A clustered index is a data structure that stores not only the index, but also the data itself. This means once you've located the value in the index, you can retrieve the data without additional disk seeks. Naturally, the primary key index or first unique index on a table is built as a clustered index.

When you create a secondary index, the key from the clustered index (primary key, unique key, or row ID) is stored along with the value for the secondary index. This allows very fast readdressing and accessing back to the original data in the clustered index. It also means you can use the primary key columns when scanning the secondary index to allow the query to use only the secondary index to retrieve data.

The buffer pool is a caching mechanism for managing transactions and writing and reading data to or from disks and, properly configured, can boost disk access. The buffer pool is also a vital component for crash recovery, as the buffer pool is written to disk periodically (e.g., during shutdown). Since this is an in-memory component, you must monitor the effectiveness of the buffer pool to ensure it is configured correctly.

InnoDB also uses the buffer pool to store data changes and transactions. InnoDB caches changes by saving them to a page (block) of data in the buffer pool. Each time a page is referenced, it is placed in the buffer pool and when changed, it is marked as "dirty." The changes are then written to disk to update the data and a copy is written into a redo log. These logfiles are stored as files named *ib_logfile0* or *ib_logfile1*. You can see these files in the data directory of the MySQL server.

The InnoDB storage engine uses two disk-based mechanisms for storing data: logfiles and tablespaces. InnoDB also uses the logs to rebuild (or redo) data changes made prior to a shutdown or crash. On startup, InnoDB reads the logs and automatically writes the dirty pages to disk, thereby recovering buffered changes made before the crash.

Tablespaces are an organizational tool InnoDB uses as a machine-independent file that contains both data and indexes as well as a rollback mechanism (to roll back transactions). By default, all tables share one tablespace. You can also store tables in their own tablespaces. They contain both the data and the indexes for your tables. Tablespaces automatically extend across multiple files, thereby allowing you to store more data in your tables than what the operating system can handle. You can divide your tablespace into multiple files to place on different disks.

Use `innodb_file_per_table` to create a separate tablespace for each table. Any tables created prior to setting this option will remain in the shared tablespace. Using this command affects only new tables.

Using the SHOW ENGINE Command

The `SHOW ENGINE INNODB STATUS` command displays statistical and configuration information concerning the state of the InnoDB storage engine. This is the standard way to see information about InnoDB. The list of statistical data displayed is long and very comprehensive. Example 9-5 shows an excerpt of the command run on a standard installation of MySQL.

Example 9-5. The SHOW ENGINE INNODB STATUS command

```
mysql> SHOW ENGINE INNODB STATUS \G
*************************** 1. row ***************************
  Type: InnoDB
  Name:
Status:
=====================================
091205 18:31:10 INNODB MONITOR OUTPUT
=====================================
Per second averages calculated from the last 1 seconds
----------
BACKGROUND THREAD
----------
srv_master_thread loops: 233 1_second, 34 sleeps, 23 10_second,
                         3 background, 3 flush
srv_master_thread log flush and writes: 44  log writes only: 448
----------
SEMAPHORES
----------
OS WAIT ARRAY INFO: reservation count 882, signal count 901
Mutex spin waits 2501, rounds 21869, OS waits 388
RW-shared spins 165, OS waits 144; RW-excl spins 0, OS waits 335
Spin rounds per wait: 8.74 mutex, 26.70 RW-shared, 10301.00 RW-excl
------------
TRANSACTIONS
------------
Trx id counter 2969
Purge done for trx's n:o < 2519 undo n:o < 0
History list length 3
LIST OF TRANSACTIONS FOR EACH SESSION:
---TRANSACTION 0, not started, OS thread id 4491317248
MySQL thread id 4, query id 152 localhost root
SHOW ENGINE INNODB STATUS
---TRANSACTION 2968, ACTIVE 0 sec, OS thread id 4548612096 inserting
mysql tables in use 1, locked 1
7 lock struct(s), heap size 1216, 1171 row lock(s), undo log entries 11375
MySQL thread id 3, query id 151 localhost root update
INSERT INTO `salaries` VALUES (204383,71223,'1998-11-14','1999-09-07'),
...
```

```
--------
FILE I/O
--------
I/O thread 0 state: waiting for i/o request (insert buffer thread)
I/O thread 1 state: waiting for i/o request (log thread)
I/O thread 2 state: waiting for i/o request (read thread)
I/O thread 3 state: waiting for i/o request (read thread)
I/O thread 4 state: waiting for i/o request (read thread)
I/O thread 5 state: waiting for i/o request (read thread)
I/O thread 6 state: waiting for i/o request (write thread)
I/O thread 7 state: waiting for i/o request (write thread)
I/O thread 8 state: waiting for i/o request (write thread)
I/O thread 9 state: waiting for i/o request (write thread)
Pending normal aio reads: 0, aio writes: 0,
 ibuf aio reads: 0, log i/o's: 0, sync i/o's: 0
Pending flushes (fsync) log: 0; buffer pool: 1
31 OS file reads, 3979 OS file writes, 1593 OS fsyncs
0.00 reads/s, 0 avg bytes/read, 146.85 writes/s, 78.92 fsyncs/s
--------------------------------------
INSERT BUFFER AND ADAPTIVE HASH INDEX
--------------------------------------
Ibuf: size 1, free list len 0, seg size 2,
0 inserts, 0 merged recs, 0 merges
Hash table size 276707, node heap has 444 buffer(s)
92903.10 hash searches/s, 459.54 non-hash searches/s
---
LOG
---
Log sequence number 219912928
Log flushed up to   218951284
Last checkpoint at  217528539
0 pending log writes, 0 pending chkp writes
1074 log i/o's done, 46.95 log i/o's/second
----------------------
BUFFER POOL AND MEMORY
----------------------
Total memory allocated 138805248; in additional pool allocated 0
Dictionary memory allocated 70560
Buffer pool size    8192
Free buffers        760
Database pages      6988
Modified db pages   113
Pending reads 0
Pending writes: LRU 0, flush list 0, single page 0
Pages read 21, created 6968, written 10043
0.00 reads/s, 89.91 creates/s, 125.87 writes/s
Buffer pool hit rate 1000 / 1000
LRU len: 6988, unzip_LRU len: 0
I/O sum[9786]:cur[259], unzip sum[0]:cur[0]
--------------
ROW OPERATIONS
--------------
0 queries inside InnoDB, 0 queries in queue
1 read views open inside InnoDB
Main thread id 4528414720, state: sleeping
```

```
Number of rows inserted 2078594, updated 0, deleted 0, read 0
31059.94 inserts/s, 0.00 updates/s, 0.00 deletes/s, 0.00 reads/s
----------------------------
END OF INNODB MONITOR OUTPUT
============================
```

The SHOW ENGINE INNODB MUTEX command displays mutex information about InnoDB
and can be very helpful in tuning threading in the storage engine. Example 9-6 shows
an excerpt of the command run on a standard installation of MySQL.

Example 9-6. The SHOW ENGINE INNODB MUTEX command

```
mysql> SHOW ENGINE INNODB MUTEX;
+--------+--------------------+---------------+
| Type   | Name               | Status        |
+--------+--------------------+---------------+
| InnoDB | trx/trx0rseg.c:167 | os_waits=1    |
| InnoDB | trx/trx0sys.c:181  | os_waits=7    |
| InnoDB | log/log0log.c:777  | os_waits=1003 |
| InnoDB | buf/buf0buf.c:936  | os_waits=8    |
| InnoDB | fil/fil0fil.c:1487 | os_waits=2    |
| InnoDB | srv/srv0srv.c:953  | os_waits=101  |
| InnoDB | log/log0log.c:833  | os_waits=323  |
+--------+--------------------+---------------+
7 rows in set (0.00 sec)
```

The Name column displays the source file and line number where the mutex was created.
The Status column displays the number of times the mutex waited for the operating
system (e.g., os_waits=5). If the source code was compiled with the UNIV_DEBUG directive,
the column can display one of the following values:

count
    The number of times the mutex was requested

spin_waits
    The number of times a spinlock operation was run

os_waits
    The number of times the mutex waited on the operating system

os_yields
    The number of times a thread abandoned its timeslice and returned to the operating
    system

os_wait_times
    The amount of time the mutex waited for the operating system

The SHOW ENGINE INNODB STATUS command displays a lot of information directly from
the InnoDB storage engine. While it is unformatted (it isn't displayed in neat rows and
columns), there are several tools that use this information and redisplay it. For example,
the InnoTop (see "InnoTop" on page 317) command communicates data this way.

Using InnoDB Monitors

The InnoDB storage engine is the only native storage engine that supports monitoring directly. Under the hood of InnoDB is a special mechanism called a *monitor* that gathers and reports statistical information to the server and client utilities. All of the following (and most third-party tools) interact with the monitoring facility in InnoDB, hence InnoDB monitors the following items via the MySQL server:

- Table and record locks
- Lock waits
- Semaphore waits
- File I/O requests
- Buffer pool
- Purge and insert buffer merge activity

The InnoDB monitors are engaged automatically via the SHOW ENGINE INNODB STATUS command, and the information displayed is generated by the monitors. However, you can also get this information directly from the InnoDB monitors by creating a special set of tables in MySQL. The actual schema of the tables and where they reside are not important (provided you use the ENGINE = INNODB clause). Once they are created, each of the tables tells InnoDB to dump the data to stderr. You can see this information via the error log or in a console by starting MySQL with the --console option. To turn on the InnoDB monitors, create the following tables in a database of your choice:

```
mysql> SHOW TABLES LIKE 'innodb%';
+---------------------------+
| Tables_in_test (innodb%)  |
+---------------------------+
| innodb_lock_monitor       |
| innodb_monitor            |
| innodb_table_monitor      |
| innodb_tablespace_monitor |
+---------------------------+
4 rows in set (0.00 sec)
```

To turn off the monitors, simply delete the table. The monitors automatically regenerate data every 15 seconds.

Each monitor presents the following data:

innodb_monitor

> The standard monitor that prints the same information as the status SQL command. See Example 9-5 for an example of the output of this monitor. The only difference between the SQL command and the output of the innodb_monitor is that the output to stderr is formatted the same way as if you used the vertical display option in the MySQL client.

innodb_lock_monitor

> The lock monitor also displays the same information as the SQL command, but includes additional information about locks.

innodb_table_monitor

> The table monitor produces a detailed report of the internal data dictionary. Example 9-7 shows an excerpt of the report generated (formatted for readability). Notice the extensive data provided about each table, including the column definitions, indexes, approximate number of rows, foreign keys, and more. Use this report when diagnosing problems with tables or if you want to know the details of indexes.

Example 9-7. The InnoDB table monitor report

```
============================================
091208 21:10:06 INNODB TABLE MONITOR OUTPUT
============================================
-----------------------------------------
TABLE: name sakila/address, id 0 14, flags 1,
       columns 11, indexes 2, appr.rows 628
COLUMNS: address_id: DATA_INT DATA_UNSIGNED DATA_BINARY_TYPE
                     DATA_NOT_NULL len 2;
         address: type 12 DATA_NOT_NULL len 150;
         address2: type 12 len 150;
         district: type 12 DATA_NOT_NULL len 60;
         city_id: DATA_INT DATA_UNSIGNED DATA_BINARY_TYPE
                     DATA_NOT_NULL len 2;
...
   INDEX: name PRIMARY, id 0 17, fields 1/10, uniq 1, type 3
   root page 52, appr.key vals 628, leaf pages 4, size pages 5
   FIELDS:  address_id DB_TRX_ID DB_ROLL_PTR address address2
            district city_id postal_code phone last_update
   INDEX: name idx_fk_city_id, id 0 18, fields 1/2, uniq 2,
          type 0 root page 53, appr.key vals 599, leaf pages 1,
          size pages 1
   FIELDS:  city_id address_id
   FOREIGN KEY CONSTRAINT sakila/fk_address_city:
                          sakila/address ( city_id )
            REFERENCES sakila/city ( city_id )
...
-----------------------------------------
END OF INNODB TABLE MONITOR OUTPUT
==================================
```

innodb_tablespace_monitor

> Displays extended information about the shared tablespace, including a list of file segments. It also validates the tablespace allocation data structures. The report can be quite detailed and very long, as it lists all of the details about your tablespace. Example 9-8 shows an excerpt of this report.

Example 9-8. The InnoDB tablespace monitor report

```
================================================
091208 21:14:19 INNODB TABLESPACE MONITOR OUTPUT
================================================
FILE SPACE INFO: id 0
size 16000, free limit 15424, free extents 2
not full frag extents 3: used pages 144, full frag extents 41
first seg id not used 0 714
SEGMENT id 0 1 space 0; page 2; res 2 used 2; full ext 0
fragm pages 2; free extents 0; not full extents 0: pages 0

...

SEGMENT id 0 411 space 0; page 209; res 29 used 29; full ext 0
fragm pages 29; free extents 0; not full extents 0: pages 0
SEGMENT id 0 412 space 0; page 209; res 1 used 1; full ext 0
fragm pages 1; free extents 0; not full extents 0: pages 0
SEGMENT id 0 413 space 0; page 209; res 96 used 60; full ext 0
fragm pages 32; free extents 0; not full extents 1: pages 28
SEGMENT id 0 414 space 0; page 209; res 1 used 1; full ext 0
fragm pages 1; free extents 0; not full extents 0: pages 0
SEGMENT id 0 415 space 0; page 209; res 96 used 33; full ext 0
fragm pages 32; free extents 0; not full extents 1: pages 1
NUMBER of file segments: 275
Validating tablespace
Validation ok
----------------------------------------
END OF INNODB TABLESPACE MONITOR OUTPUT
========================================
```

As you can see, the InnoDB monitors report quite a lot of detail. Keeping these turned on for extended periods could add a substantial amount of data to your logfiles.

Monitoring Logfiles

Since the InnoDB logfiles buffer data between your data and the operating system, keeping these files running well will ensure good performance. You can monitor the logfiles directly by watching the following system status variables:

```
mysql> SHOW STATUS LIKE 'Innodb%log%';
+-----------------------------+-------+
| Variable_name               | Value |
+-----------------------------+-------+
| Innodb_log_waits            | 0     |
| Innodb_log_write_requests   | 0     |
| Innodb_log_writes           | 2     |
| Innodb_os_log_fsyncs        | 5     |
| Innodb_os_log_pending_fsyncs | 0    |
| Innodb_os_log_pending_writes | 0    |
| Innodb_os_log_written       | 1024  |
+-----------------------------+-------+
```

We saw some of this information presented by the InnoDB monitors, but you can also get detailed information about the logfiles using the following status variables:

Innodb_log_waits
> A count of the number of times the log was too small (i.e., did not have enough room for all of the data) and the operation had to wait for the log to be flushed. If this value begins to increase and remains higher than zero for long periods (except perhaps during bulk operations), you may want to increase the size of the logfiles.

Innodb_log_write_requests
> The number of log write requests.

Innodb_log_writes
> The number of times data was written to the log.

Innodb_os_log_fsyncs
> The number of operating system file syncs (i.e., fsync() method calls).

Innodb_os_log_pending_fsyncs
> The number of pending file sync requests. If this value begins to increase and stays higher than zero for an extended period of time, you may want to investigate possible disk access issues.

Innodb_os_log_pending_writes
> The number of pending log write requests. If this value begins to increase and stays higher than zero for an extended period of time, you may want to investigate possible disk access issues.

Innodb_os_log_written
> The total number of bytes written to the log.

Since all of these options present numerical information, you can build your own custom graphs in MySQL Administrator to display the information in graphical form.

Monitoring the Buffer Pool

The buffer pool is where InnoDB caches frequently accessed data. Any changes you make to the data in the buffer pool are also cached. The buffer pool also stores information about current transactions. Thus, the buffer pool is a critical mechanism used for performance.

You can view information about the behavior of the buffer pool using the SHOW ENGINE INNODB STATUS command, as shown in Example 9-5. We repeat the buffer pool and memory section here for your convenience.

```
----------------------
BUFFER POOL AND MEMORY
----------------------
Total memory allocated 138805248; in additional pool allocated 0
Dictionary memory allocated 70560
Buffer pool size   8192
Free buffers       760
Database pages     6988
Modified db pages  113
Pending reads 0
Pending writes: LRU 0, flush list 0, single page 0
Pages read 21, created 6968, written 10043
0.00 reads/s, 89.91 creates/s, 125.87 writes/s
Buffer pool hit rate 1000 / 1000
LRU len: 6988, unzip_LRU len: 0
I/O sum[9786]:cur[259], unzip sum[0]:cur[0]
```

The critical items to watch for in this report are listed here. We discuss more specific status variables later.

Free buffers
> The number of buffer segments that are empty and available for buffering data.

Modified pages
> The number of pages that have changes (dirty).

Pending reads
> The number of reads waiting. This value should remain low.

Pending writes
> The number of writes waiting. This value should remain low.

Hit rate
> A ratio of the number of successful buffer hits to the number of all requests. You want this value to remain as close as possible to 1:1.

There are a number of status variables you can use to see this information in greater detail. The following shows the InnoDB buffer pool status variables:

```
mysql> SHOW STATUS LIKE 'Innodb%buf%';
+-----------------------------------+-------+
| Variable_name                     | Value |
+-----------------------------------+-------+
| Innodb_buffer_pool_pages_data     | 21    |
| Innodb_buffer_pool_pages_dirty    | 0     |
| Innodb_buffer_pool_pages_flushed  | 1     |
| Innodb_buffer_pool_pages_free     | 8171  |
| Innodb_buffer_pool_pages_misc     | 0     |
| Innodb_buffer_pool_pages_total    | 8192  |
| Innodb_buffer_pool_read_ahead_rnd | 0     |
| Innodb_buffer_pool_read_ahead_seq | 0     |
| Innodb_buffer_pool_read_requests  | 558   |
| Innodb_buffer_pool_reads          | 22    |
| Innodb_buffer_pool_wait_free      | 0     |
| Innodb_buffer_pool_write_requests | 1     |
+-----------------------------------+-------+
```

There are a number of status variables for the buffer pool that display key statistical information about the performance of the buffer pool. You can monitor such detailed information as the status of the pages in the buffer pool, the reads and writes from and to the buffer pool, and how often the buffer pool causes a wait for reads or writes. The following explains each status variable in more detail:

Innodb_buffer_pool_pages_data
> The number of pages containing data, including both unchanged and changed (dirty) pages.

Innodb_buffer_pool_pages_dirty
> The number of pages that have changes (dirty).

Innodb_buffer_pool_pages_flushed
> The number of times the buffer pool pages have been flushed.

Innodb_buffer_pool_pages_free
> The number of empty (free) pages.

Innodb_buffer_pool_pages_misc
> The number of pages that are being used for administrative work by the InnoDB engine itself. This is calculated as:
>
> X = Innodb_buffer_pool_pages_total − Innodb_buffer_pool_pages_free − Innodb_buffer_pool_pages_data

Innodb_buffer_pool_pages_total
> The total number of pages in the buffer pool.

Innodb_buffer_pool_read_ahead_rnd
> The number of random read-aheads that have occurred by InnoDB scanning for a large block of data.

Innodb_buffer_pool_read_ahead_seq
> The number of sequential read-aheads that have occurred as a result of a sequential full table scan.

Innodb_buffer_pool_read_requests
> The number of logical read requests.

Innodb_buffer_pool_reads
> The number of logical reads that were not found in the buffer pool, and were read directly from the disk.

Innodb_buffer_pool_wait_free
> If the buffer pool is busy or there are no free pages, InnoDB may need to wait for pages to be flushed. This value is the number of times the wait occurred. If this value grows and stays higher than zero, you may have either an issue with the size of the buffer pool or a disk access issue.

Innodb_buffer_pool_write_requests
> The number of writes to the InnoDB buffer pool.

Since all of these options present numerical data, you can build your own custom graphs in MySQL Administrator to display the information in graphical form.

Monitoring Tablespaces

InnoDB tablespaces are basically self-sufficient, provided you have allowed InnoDB to extend them when they run low on space. You can configure tablespaces to automatically grow using the `autoextend` option for the `innodb_data_file_path` variable. For example, the default configuration of a MySQL installation sets the shared tablespace to 10 megabytes and can automatically extend to more files.

```
--innodb_data_file_path=ibdata1:10M:autoextend
```

See the "InnoDB Configuration" section in the online MySQL Reference Manual for more details.

You can see the current configuration of your tablespaces using the `SHOW ENGINE STATUS INNODB` command, and you can see the details of the tablespaces by turning on the InnoDB tablespace monitor (see the "Using Tablespace Monitors" section in the online MySQL Reference Manual for more details).

Using INFORMATION_SCHEMA Tables

If you install versions of MySQL that have the InnoDB storage engine plug-in (available in MySQL versions 5.1 and later), you also have access to seven special tables in the *INFORMATION_SCHEMA* database.

 You must install the *INFORMATION_SCHEMA* tables separately. For more details, see the InnoDB plug-in documentation (*http://www.in nodb.com/products/innodb_plugin/plugin-documentation/*).

The tables are technically not tables in the sense that the data they present is not stored on disk; rather, the data is generated when the table is queried. The tables provide another way to monitor InnoDB and provide performance information to administrators. There are tables for monitoring compression, transactions, and locks. We describe each briefly:

INNODB_CMP
> Displays details and statistics for compressed tables.

INNODB_CMP_RESET
> Displays the same information as *INNODB_CMP*, but has the unique side effect that querying the table resets the statistics. This allows you to track statistics periodically (e.g., hourly, daily, etc.).

INNODB_CMPMEM

Displays details and statistics about compression use in the buffer pool.

INNODB_CMPMEM_RESET

Displays the same information as *INNODB_CMPMEM*, but has the unique side effect that querying the table resets the statistics. This allows you to track statistics periodically (e.g., hourly, daily, etc.).

INNODB_TRX

Displays details and statistics about all transactions, including the state and query currently being processed.

INNODB_LOCKS

Displays details and statistics about all locks requested by transactions. It describes each lock, including the state, mode, type, and more.

INNODB_LOCK_WAITS

Displays details and statistics about all locks requested by transactions that are being blocked. It describes each lock, including the state, mode, type, and the blocking transaction.

 A complete description of each table, including the columns and examples of how to use each, is presented in the InnoDB plug-in documentation.

You can use the compression tables to monitor the compression of your tables, including such details as the page size, pages used, time spent in compression and decompression, and much more. This can be important information to monitor if you are using compression and want to ensure the overhead is not affecting the performance of your database server.

You can use the transaction and locking tables to monitor your transactions. This is a very valuable tool in keeping your transactional databases running smoothly. Most importantly, you can determine precisely which state each transaction is in, as well as which transactions are blocked and which are in a locked state. This information can also be critical in diagnosing complex transaction problems such as deadlock or poor performance.

Other Parameters to Consider

There are many things to monitor and tune in the InnoDB storage engine. We have discussed only a portion of those and focused mainly on monitoring the various subsystems and improving performance. However, there are a few other items you may want to consider.

Thread performance can be improved under certain circumstances by adjusting the innodb_thread_concurrency option. The default value is 0 threads, which is usually sufficient, but if you are running MySQL on a server with many processors and many independent disks (and heavy use of InnoDB), you may see a performance increase by setting this value equal to the number of processors plus independent disks. This ensures InnoDB will use enough threads to allow maximum concurrent operations. Setting this value to a value greater than what your server can support has little or no effect—if there aren't any available threads, the limit will never be reached.

If your MySQL server is part of a system that is shut down frequently or even periodically (e.g., you run MySQL at startup on your Linux laptop), you may notice when using InnoDB that shutdown can take a long time to complete. Fortunately, you can tell InnoDB to shut down quickly by setting the innodb_fast_shutdown option. This does not affect data integrity nor will it result in a loss of memory (buffer) management. It simply skips the potentially expensive operations of purging the internal caches and merging insert buffers. It still performs a controlled shutdown, storing the buffer pools on disk.

Some early releases of MySQL have issues with concurrency control and locking. For these earlier versions, you can control how InnoDB deals with deadlocks by setting the innodb_lock_wait_timeout variable. This variable has both global and session scope, and it controls how long InnoDB will allow a transaction to wait for a row lock before aborting. The default value is 50 seconds. If you are seeing a lot of lock-wait timeouts, you can increase this variable and tame some of your concurrency problems.

If you are importing lots of data, you can improve load time by making sure your incoming datafiles are sorted in primary key order. In addition, you can turn off the automatic commit by setting AUTOCOMMIT to 0. This ensures the entire load is committed only once. You can also improve bulk load by turning off foreign key and unique constraints.

 Remember, you should approach tuning InnoDB with great care. With so many things to tweak and adjust, it can be very easy for things to go wrong quickly. Be sure to follow the practice of changing one variable at a time (and only with a purpose) and measure, measure, measure.

Conclusion

This chapter examined how to monitor and improve the performance of storage engines in the MySQL server. We have discussed the specifics of two of the most popular storage engines, and in the next chapter we turn our attention to the more advanced topic of monitoring and improving the performance of replication.

> Joel paused with his mouse over the Send button. He had prepared a report on the InnoDB monitoring data he collected and had written some recommendations in an email message to his boss. But he wasn't sure he should send it without being asked. Shrugging, he figured it couldn't hurt, so he hit Send.
>
> About two minutes later, his email application popped up a box from his system tray proclaiming a new email message. Joel clicked on the message. It was from his boss.
>
> "Joel, nice work on the InnoDB stuff. I want you to call a meeting with the developers and the IT folks. Have a sit-down and get everyone on board with your recommendations. Make it happen. I'll be in the office on Monday."
>
> "OK," Joel said as he felt the burden of responsibility slip onto his shoulders. He realized this was his first meeting since being hired. He was a little nervous, so he decided to go for a walk before making an agenda and sending out an email message inviting people to attend. "Well, it can't be any worse than my thesis defense."

Replication Monitoring

Joel spent a few moments logging into the Seattle replication slave and determined that replication was still running.

A familiar voice spoke from his doorway. "What about that Seattle thing, Joel? Are you on it?"

"I'm still working on that one, sir. I need to figure out the replication configuration and monitor the problem." Joel thought to himself, "… and read more about replication monitoring."

"All right, Joel. I'll let you work. I'll check on you again after lunch."

As his boss left, Joel looked at his watch. "OK, so I've got about an hour to figure out how to monitor replication."

With a deep sigh, Joel once again opened his favorite MySQL book to learn more about monitoring MySQL. "I didn't think replication could lead to so many problems of its own," he muttered.

Now that you know when your servers are performing well (and when they aren't), how do you know how well your replication is performing? Things may be going smoothly, but how do you know that?

In this chapter, we discuss advanced monitoring, focusing on monitoring and improving replication performance.

Getting Started

There are two areas that can affect the performance of your replication topology. You must ensure both are optimized to avoid affecting replication.

First, ensure your network has the bandwidth to handle the replicated data. As we've discussed, the master makes a copy of the changes and sends it to the slaves via a network connection. If the network connection is slow or is suffering from contention, so too will your replicated data. We discuss some ways to tune your network and ways you can tune replication to make the best of certain networking environments.

Second, and most importantly, ensure the databases you are replicating are optimized. This is vital because any inefficiency in the database on the master will be compounded by the same poor database performance on the slaves. This is especially true concerning indexing and normalization. However, a well-tuned database is only half of the equation. You must also ensure your queries are optimized. For example, a poorly tuned query run on the master will run just as poorly on your slaves.

Once you have your network performing well and your databases and queries optimized, you can focus on configuring your servers for optimal performance.

Server Setup

Another very important thing you can do to create the best platform for your replication topology is make sure your servers are configured for optimal performance. A poorly performing replication topology can often be traced back to poorly performing servers. Ensure your servers are operating with enough memory and that the storage devices and storage engine choices are optimal for your databases.

Some recommend using lower-performing machines for slaves, noting that the slave does not have as much running on it (typically, slaves only process SELECT queries, while the master handles updates to data). However, this is incorrect. In a typical single master and single slave where all databases are being replicated, both machines have about the same load, but since the slave is executing the events in a single thread versus many threads on the master, even though the workload is the same, the slave may take more time to process and execute the events.

Perhaps the best way to view this issue is to consider that one of the best uses of replication is failover. If your slaves are slower than your master and if you must fail over in the event that your master suffers a failure, the expectation is that your promoted slave should have the same performance as your demoted master.

Inclusive and Exclusive Replication

You can configure your replication to replicate all data (the default); log only some data or exclude certain data on the master, thereby limiting what is written to the binary log and what is replicated; or you can configure your slave to act on only certain data. Using inclusive or exclusive replication (or both) can help resolve complex load balancing or scale-out issues, making replication more powerful and more flexible. Another name for this process is *filtering data*, where the combination of the inclusive and exclusive lists form the filter criteria.

On the master, use the `--binlog-do-db` startup option to specify that you want only events for a certain database to be written to the binary log. You can specify one or more of these options, specifying one database per option, on the command line or in your configuration file.

You can also specify that you want to exclude (ignore) events for a certain database using the `--binlog-ignore-db` startup option. You can specify one or more of these options, specifying one database per option, on the command line or in your configuration file. This option tells the master to not log any events that act on the database(s) listed.

> You can use the `--binlog-do-db` and `--binlog-ignore-db` options together, but be sure to check the values of these variables when diagnosing data replication issues (e.g., missing data on the slave).
>
> Additionally, when you use the `--binlog-do-db` or `--binlog-ignore-db` options, you are filtering what goes into the binary log. This severely limits the use of PITR, since you can only recover what was written to the binary log.

There are several options you can use to control which data is replicated on the slave. There are companion options for the binlog options on the master, options to restrict at the table level, and even a command to do a transformation (rename).

> Performing inclusive or exclusive replication on the slave may not improve performance of replication across the topology. While the slaves may store less data, the same amount of data is transmitted by the master and the overhead of doing the filter on the slave may not gain much if the inclusive and exclusive lists are complex. If you are worried about transmitting too much data over the network, it is best to perform the filtering on the master.

On the slave, you can specify that you want to include only those events for a certain database to be read and executed from the relay log with the `--replicate-do-db` startup option. You can specify one or more of these options, specifying one database per option, on the command line or in your configuration file. This option tells the slave to execute only those events that act on the database(s) listed.

You can also specify that you want to exclude (ignore) events for a certain database using the `--replicate-ignore-db` startup option. You can specify one or more of these options, specifying one database per option, on the command line or in your configuration file. This option tells the slave to not execute any events that act on the database(s) listed.

The replicate options on the slave behave differently depending on which format you use. This is especially important for statement-based replication and could lead to data loss. For example, if you are using statement-based replication and you use the `--replicate-do-db` option, the slave restricts events to only those statements following the USE *<db>* command. If you issue a statement for a different database without a change of database, the statement is ignored. See the online MySQL Reference Manual for additional details about these limitations.

You can perform inclusive and exclusive replication on the slave at the table level. Use the `--replicate-do-table` and `--replicate-ignore-table` options to execute or ignore only those events for a specific table. These commands are very handy if you have a table with sensitive data that isn't used by your application but is critical to administration or other special functions. For example, if you have an application that includes pricing information from your vendors (what you pay for something), you may want to hide that information if you employ or contract out sales services. Rather than building a special application for your contractors, you can deploy your existing application so that it uses a slave that replicates everything, excluding the tables that contain the sensitive information.

There are also forms of the last two options that permit the use of wildcard patterns. These options, `replicate-wild-do-table` and `replicate-wild-ignore-table`, perform the same functionality as their namesakes, but support the use of wildcards. For example, `--replicate-wild-do-table=tbl%` executes events for any tables that start with "tbl" (e.g., *tbl*, *tbl1*, *tbl_test*). These wildcard versions of the slave-side filtering can be another asset when solving complex replication scenarios.

There is also a transformation option you can use on the slave to rename or change the name of a database for table operations on the slave. It applies only to tables. You can do this using the `--replicate-rewrite-db="<from>-><to>"` option (you must use the quotes). This option only changes the name of the database for table events; it does not change the names for commands like CREATE DATABASE, ALTER DATABASE, etc. It only affects events for which a database is specified (or to redirect the default database for statement-based replication). You can use this option more than once for multiple database name transformations.

While not strictly an inclusive or exclusive replication option, `--replicate-same-server-id` prevents infinite loops in circular replication. If set to 0, it tells the slave to skip events that have the same `server_id`. If you set it to 1, the slave will process all events.

Replication Threads

Before we explore monitoring of the master and slave, we should reexamine the threads involved in replication. We present these again here from the perspective of monitoring and diagnosing problems.

There are three threads that control replication. Each performs a specific role. On the master, there is a single thread per connected slave called the `Binlog Dump` thread. It is responsible for sending the binlog events to the connected slaves. On the slave, there are two threads, the `Slave IO` thread and the `Slave SQL` thread. The I/O thread is responsible for reading the incoming binlog events from the master and writing them to the slave's relay log. The SQL thread is responsible for reading the events in the relay log and executing them.

You can monitor the current state of the `Binlog Dump` thread using the `SHOW PROCESS LIST` command:

```
mysql> SHOW PROCESSLIST \G
*************************** 1. row ***************************
     Id: 1
   User: rpl
   Host: localhost:54197
     db: NULL
Command: Binlog Dump
   Time: 25
  State: Master has sent all binlog to slave; waiting for binlog to be updated
   Info: NULL
```

Notice the `State` column. The data presented here is a description of what the master is doing with respect to the binary log and the slaves. The example above is a typical result for a well-running replication topology. The display shows the following columns:

Id
: Displays the connection ID.

User
: Displays the user who ran the statement.

Host
: The host where the statement originated.

db
: The default database if specified; otherwise, NULL is displayed, indicating no default database was specified.

Command
: The type of command the thread is running. See the online MySQL Reference Manual for more information.

Time
: The time (in seconds) that the thread has been in the reported state.

State

The description of the current action or state (e.g., waiting). This is normally a descriptive text message.

Info

The statement the thread is executing. NULL indicates no statement is in progress. This is the case for the replication threads when they are in waiting states.

You can also see the thread status on the slave. You can monitor the I/O and SQL threads using the SHOW PROCESSLIST command:

```
mysql> SHOW PROCESSLIST \G
*************************** 1. row ***************************
     Id: 2
   User: system user
   Host:
     db: NULL
Command: Connect
   Time: 127
  State: Waiting for master to send event
   Info: NULL
*************************** 2. row ***************************
     Id: 3
   User: system user
   Host:
     db: NULL
Command: Connect
   Time: 10
  State: Slave has read all relay log; waiting for the slave I/O thread to
         update it
   Info: NULL
```

Again, the State column contains the most important information. If you are having problems with replication on your slave, be sure to issue the SHOW PROCESSLIST command on the slave and take note of the I/O and SQL thread states. In this example, we see the normal states of a slave waiting for information from the master (I/O thread) and having executed all events in the relay log (SQL thread).

 It is always a good idea to use the SHOW PROCESSLIST command to check the status of the replication when troubleshooting.

Monitoring the Master

There are several ways to monitor your master. You can issue SHOW commands to see status information and status variables or use the MySQL Administrator. The primary SQL commands include SHOW MASTER STATUS, SHOW BINARY LOGS, and SHOW BINLOG EVENTS.

In this section, we will examine the SQL commands available for monitoring the master and provide a brief summary of the available status variables you can monitor either by using the SHOW STATUS command or by creating custom graphs with the MySQL Administrator.

Monitoring Commands for the Master

The SHOW MASTER STATUS command displays information about the master's binary log, including the name and offset position of the current binlog file. This information is vital in connecting slaves, as we have discussed in previous chapters. It also provides information about logging constraints. Example 10-1 shows the result of a typical SHOW MASTER STATUS command.

Example 10-1. The SHOW MASTER STATUS command

```
mysql> SHOW MASTER STATUS;
+------------------+-----------+--------------+------------------+
| File             | Position  | Binlog_Do_DB | Binlog_Ignore_DB |
+------------------+-----------+--------------+------------------+
| mysql-bin.000002 | 156058362 | Inventory    | Vendor_sales     |
+------------------+-----------+--------------+------------------+
1 row in set (0.00 sec)
```

The data is displayed in the following columns:

File
> This column lists the name of the current binlog file.

Position
> This column lists the current position (next write) in the binary log.

Binlog_Do_DB
> This column lists any databases specified by the --binlog-do-db startup option discussed earlier.

Binlog_Ignore_DB
> This column lists any databases specified by the --binlog-ignore-db startup option discussed earlier.

The SHOW BINARY LOGS command (also known by its alias, SHOW MASTER LOGS) displays the list of binlog files available on the master and their sizes in bytes. This command is useful for comparing the information on the slave concerning where the slave is with respect to the master, that is, which binary log the slave is currently reading from on the master. Example 10-2 shows the results of a typical SHOW BINARY LOGS command.

Example 10-2. The SHOW MASTER LOGS command on the master

```
mysql> SHOW MASTER LOGS;
+-------------------+-----------+
| Log_name          | File_size |
+-------------------+-----------+
| master-bin.000001 | 103648205 |
| master-bin.000002 |   2045693 |
| master-bin.000003 |   1022910 |
| master-bin.000004 |   3068436 |
+-------------------+-----------+
4 rows in set (0.00 sec)
```

 You can rotate the binary log on the master with the FLUSH LOGS command. This command closes and reopens all logs and opens a new log with an incremented file extension. You should periodically flush the log to help manage the growth of logs over time. It also helps with diagnosing replication problems.

You can also use the SHOW BINLOG EVENTS command to show events in the binary log. The syntax of the command is as follows:

```
SHOW BINLOG EVENTS [IN <log>] [FROM <pos>] [LIMIT [<offset>,] <rows>]
```

Take care when using this command, as it can produce a lot of data. It is best used to compare events on the master with events on the slave read from its relay log. Example 10-3 shows the binlog events from a typical replication configuration.

Example 10-3. The SHOW BINLOG EVENTS command (statement-based)

```
mysql> SHOW BINLOG EVENTS IN 'master-bin.000001' FROM 2571 LIMIT 4 \G
*************************** 1. row ***************************
   Log_name: master-bin.000001
        Pos: 2571
 Event_type: Query
  Server_id: 1
End_log_pos: 2968
       Info: use `employees`; CREATE TABLE salaries (
   emp_no      INT             NOT NULL,
   salary      INT             NOT NULL,
   from_date   DATE            NOT NULL,
   to_date     DATE            NOT NULL,
   KEY         (emp_no),
   FOREIGN KEY (emp_no) REFERENCES employees (emp_no)
   ON DELETE CASCADE,
   PRIMARY KEY (emp_no, from_date)
)
*************************** 2. row ***************************
   Log_name: master-bin.000001
        Pos: 2968
 Event_type: Query
  Server_id: 1
End_log_pos: 3041
```

```
       Info: BEGIN
*************************** 3. row ***************************
   Log_name: master-bin.000001
        Pos: 3041
 Event_type: Query
  Server_id: 1
End_log_pos: 3348
       Info: use `employees`; INSERT INTO `departments` VALUES
       ('d001','Marketing'),('d002','Finance'),('d003','Human Resources'),
       ('d004','Production'),('d005','Development'),('d006','Quality
       Management'),('d007','Sales'),('d008','Research'),('d009',
       'Customer Service')
*************************** 4. row ***************************
   Log_name: master-bin.000001
        Pos: 3348
 Event_type: Xid
  Server_id: 1
End_log_pos: 3375
       Info: COMMIT /* xid=17 */
4 rows in set (0.01 sec)
```

In this example, we are using statement-based replication. Had we used row-based replication, the binlog events would have looked very different. You can see the difference in Example 10-4.

Example 10-4. The SHOW BINLOG EVENTS command (row-based)

```
mysql> SHOW BINLOG EVENTS IN 'master-bin.000001' FROM 2571 LIMIT 4 \G
*************************** 1. row ***************************
   Log_name: master-bin.000001
        Pos: 2571
 Event_type: Query
  Server_id: 1
End_log_pos: 2968
       Info: use `employees`; CREATE TABLE salaries (
   emp_no      INT             NOT NULL,
   salary      INT             NOT NULL,
   from_date   DATE            NOT NULL,
   to_date     DATE            NOT NULL,
   KEY         (emp_no),
   FOREIGN KEY (emp_no) REFERENCES employees (emp_no) ON DELETE CASCADE,
   PRIMARY KEY (emp_no, from_date)
)
*************************** 2. row ***************************
   Log_name: master-bin.000001
        Pos: 2968
 Event_type: Query
  Server_id: 1
End_log_pos: 3041
       Info: BEGIN
*************************** 3. row ***************************
   Log_name: master-bin.000001
        Pos: 3041
 Event_type: Table_map
  Server_id: 1
```

```
End_log_pos: 3101
        Info: table_id: 15 (employees.departments)
*************************** 4. row ***************************
   Log_name: master-bin.000001
        Pos: 3101
 Event_type: Write_rows
  Server_id: 1
End_log_pos: 3292
        Info: table_id: 15 flags: STMT_END_F
4 rows in set (0.01 sec)
```

Notice there is far less information to see in the binary log of a row-based format. It can sometimes be beneficial to switch to a statement-based row format when diagnosing complex problems with data corruption or intermittent failures. For example, it may be helpful to see exactly what is written to the binary log on the master and compare that to what is read from the relay log on the slave. If there are differences, they could be easier to find in a statement-based format than in a row-based format where the data is in a machine-readable format. See Chapter 2 for more details about the formats of the binary log and the advantages and trade-offs of using one versus the other.

Master Status Variables

There are only a few status variables for monitoring the master. These are limited to counters that indicate how many times a master-related command has been issued on the master.

Com_change_master
: Shows the number of times the CHANGE MASTER command was issued. If this value changes frequently or is significantly higher than the number of your servers times the number of scheduled restarts on your slaves, you may have a situation where additional slaves are being restarted too frequently; this can be an indication of unstable connectivity.

Com_show_master_status
: Shows the number of times the SHOW MASTER STATUS command was issued. As with Com_change_master, high values of this counter can indicate an unusual number of inquiries for reconnecting slaves.

Monitoring Slaves

There are several ways to monitor your slaves. You can issue SHOW commands to see status information and status variables or use the MySQL Administrator. The primary SQL commands include SHOW SLAVE STATUS, SHOW BINARY LOGS, and SHOW BINLOG EVENTS.

In this section, we will examine the SQL commands available for monitoring a slave and give a brief summary of the available status variables that you can monitor with either the SHOW STATUS command or by creating custom graphs with the MySQL

Administrator. We will look at the MySQL Administrator in "Replication Monitoring with MySQL Administrator" on page 381.

Monitoring Commands for the Slave

The SHOW SLAVE STATUS command displays information about the slave's binary log, its connection to the server, and replication activity, including the name and offset position of the current binlog file. This information is vital in diagnosing slave performance, as we have seen in previous chapters. Example 10-5 shows the result of a typical SHOW SLAVE STATUS command executed on a server running MySQL version 5.5.

Example 10-5. The SHOW SLAVE STATUS command

```
mysql> SHOW SLAVE STATUS \G
*************************** 1. row ***************************
               Slave_IO_State: Waiting for master to send event
                  Master_Host: localhost
                  Master_User: rpl
                  Master_Port: 3306
                Connect_Retry: 60
              Master_Log_File: mysql-bin.000002
          Read_Master_Log_Pos: 39016226
               Relay_Log_File: relay-bin.000004
                Relay_Log_Pos: 9353715
        Relay_Master_Log_File: mysql-bin.000002
             Slave_IO_Running: Yes
            Slave_SQL_Running: Yes
              Replicate_Do_DB:
          Replicate_Ignore_DB:
           Replicate_Do_Table:
       Replicate_Ignore_Table:
      Replicate_Wild_Do_Table:
  Replicate_Wild_Ignore_Table:
                   Last_Errno: 0
                   Last_Error:
                 Skip_Counter: 0
          Exec_Master_Log_Pos: 25263417
              Relay_Log_Space: 39016668
              Until_Condition: None
               Until_Log_File:
                Until_Log_Pos: 0
            Master_SSL_Allowed: No
            Master_SSL_CA_File:
            Master_SSL_CA_Path:
               Master_SSL_Cert:
             Master_SSL_Cipher:
                Master_SSL_Key:
        Seconds_Behind_Master: 66
Master_SSL_Verify_Server_Cert: No
                Last_IO_Errno: 0
                Last_IO_Error:
               Last_SQL_Errno: 0
               Last_SQL_Error:
```

```
    Replicate_Ignore_Server_Ids:
              Master_Server_Id: 1
1 row in set (0.00 sec)
```

There is a lot of information here. This command is the most important command for replication. It is a good idea to study the details of each item presented. Rather than listing the information item by item, we present the information from the perspective of an administrator. That is, the information is normally inspected with a specific goal in mind. Thus, we group the information into categories for easier reference. These categories include master connection information, slave performance, log information, filtering, log performance, and error conditions.

The most important piece of information is the first column. This tells you the current status of the I/O thread. It presents one of several states: connecting to the master, waiting for events from the master, reconnecting to the master, etc.

The information displayed about the master connection includes the current hostname of the master, the user account used to connect, and the port the slave is connected to on the master. Toward the bottom of the listing is the SSL connection information (if you are using an SSL connection).

The next category includes information about the binary log on the master and the relay log on the slave. The filename and position of each are displayed. It is important to note these values whenever you diagnose replication problems. Of particular note is Relay_Master_Log_File, which shows the filename of the master binary log where the most recent event from the relay log has been executed.

Replication filtering configuration lists all of the slave-side replication filters. Check here if you are uncertain how your filters are set up.

Also included is the last error number and text for the slave and the I/O and SQL threads. Beyond the state values for the slave threads, this information is most often examined when there is an error. It can be helpful to check this information first when encountering errors on the slave, before examining the error log, as this information is the most current and normally gives you the reason for the failure.

There is also information about the configuration of the slave, including the settings for the skip counter and the until conditions. See the online MySQL Reference Manual for more information about these fields.

Near the bottom of the list is the current error information. This includes errors for the slave's I/O and SQL threads. These values should always be 0 for a properly functioning slave.

Some of the more important performance columns are discussed in more detail here:

Connect_Retry

> The number of seconds that expire between retry connect attempts. This value should always be low, but you may want to set it higher if you have a case where the slave is having issues connecting to the master.

Exec_Master_Log_Pos

> This shows the position of the last event executed from the master's binary log.

Relay_Log_Space

> The total size of all of the relay logfiles. You can use this to determine if you need to purge the relay logs in the event you are running low on disk space.

Seconds_Behind_Master

> The number of seconds between the time an event was executed and the time the event was written in the master's binary log. A high value here can indicate significant replication lag. We discuss replication lag in an upcoming section.

 The value for Seconds_Behind_Master could become stale when replication stops due to network failures, loss of heartbeat from the master, etc. It is most meaningful when replication is running.

If your slave has binary logging enabled, the SHOW BINARY LOGS command displays the list of binlog files available on the slave and their sizes in bytes. Example 10-6 shows the results of a typical SHOW BINARY LOGS command.

Example 10-6. The SHOW BINARY LOGS command on the slave

```
mysql> SHOW BINARY LOGS;
+------------------+-----------+
| Log_name         | File_size |
+------------------+-----------+
| slave-bin.000001 |   5151604 |
| slave-bin.000002 |   1030108 |
| slave-bin.000003 |   1030044 |
+------------------+-----------+
3 rows in set (0.00 sec)
```

 You can rotate the relay log on the slave with the FLUSH LOGS command.

You can also use the SHOW BINLOG EVENTS command to show events in the binary log on the slave if the slave has binary logging enabled. The difference between showing events on the slave and showing them on the master is you want to specify the binlog filename on the slave as shown in the SHOW BINARY LOGS output. Example 10-7 shows the binlog events from a typical replication configuration.

Example 10-7. The SHOW BINLOG EVENTS command (statement-based)

```
mysql> SHOW BINLOG EVENTS IN 'slave-bin.000001' FROM 2701 LIMIT 2 \G
*************************** 1. row ***************************
   Log_name: slave-bin.000001
        Pos: 2701
 Event_type: Query
  Server_id: 1
End_log_pos: 3098
       Info: use `employees`; CREATE TABLE salaries (
    emp_no      INT             NOT NULL,
    salary      INT             NOT NULL,
    from_date   DATE            NOT NULL,
    to_date     DATE            NOT NULL,
    KEY         (emp_no),
    FOREIGN KEY (emp_no) REFERENCES employees (emp_no) ON DELETE CASCADE,
    PRIMARY KEY (emp_no, from_date)
)
*************************** 2. row ***************************
   Log_name: slave-bin.000001
        Pos: 3098
 Event_type: Query
  Server_id: 1
End_log_pos: 3405
       Info: use `employees`; INSERT INTO `departments` VALUES
   ('d001','Marketing'),('d002','Finance'),
   ('d003','Human Resources'),('d004','Production'),
   ('d005','Development'),('d006','Quality Management'),
   ('d007','Sales'),('d008','Research'),
   ('d009','Customer Service')
2 rows in set (0.01 sec)
```

 In MySQL versions 5.5 and later, you can also inspect the slave's relay log with SHOW RELAYLOG EVENTS.

Slave Status Variables

There are only a few status variables for monitoring the slave. These include counters that indicate how many times a slave-related command was issued on the master and statistics for key slave operations. The first four listed here are simply counters of the various slave-related commands. The values should correspond with the frequency of the maintenance of your slaves. If they do not, you may want to investigate the possibility that there are more slaves in your topology than you expected or that a particular slave is being restarted too frequently.

Com_show_slave_hosts
:   The number of times the SHOW SLAVE HOSTS command was issued.

Com_show_slave_status
:   The number of times the SHOW SLAVE STATUS command was issued.

Com_slave_start
:   The number of times the SLAVE START command was issued.

Com_slave_stop
:   The number of times the SLAVE STOP command was issued.

Slave_heartbeat_period
:   The current configuration for the number of seconds that elapse between heartbeat checks of the master.

Slave_open_temp_tables
:   The number of temporary tables the slave's SQL thread is using. A high value can indicate the slave is overburdened.

Slave_received_heartbeats
:   The count of heartbeat replies from the master. This value should correspond roughly to the elapsed time since the slave was restarted divided by the heartbeat interval.

Slave_retried_transactions
:   The number of times the SQL thread has retried transactions since the slave was started.

Slave_running
:   Simply displays ON if the slave is connected to the master and the I/O and SQL threads are executing without error.

Replication Monitoring with MySQL Administrator

You have seen how you can use the MySQL Administrator to monitor network traffic and storage engines. It also has a simple display for monitoring the master and slave in a replication topology. You can view basic information about replication on the Replication Status tab. However, to get the most out of this information, you should start your slaves with the --report_host startup option, providing a unique name for each slave.

Figure 10-1 shows the MySQL Administrator running on a master with one connected slave. If there were slaves connected without the --report_host option, they would be omitted from the list.

If you run the MySQL Administrator on a slave, you will only see the slave's information. Figure 10-2 shows the MySQL Administrator running on the slave.

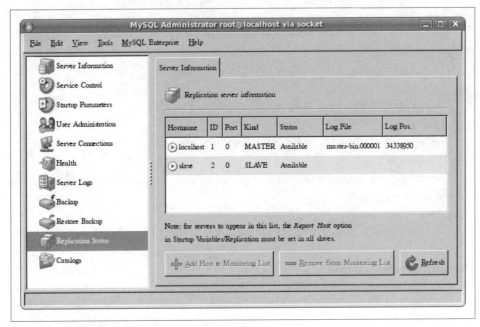

Figure 10-1. The MySQL Administrator running on the master

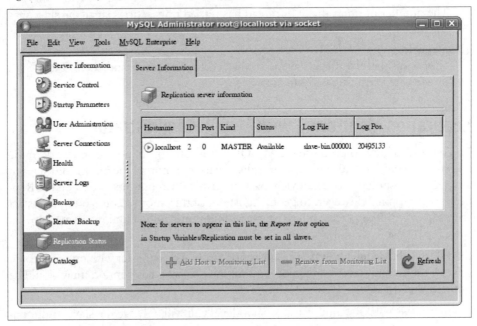

Figure 10-2. The MySQL Administrator running on the slave

In Figures 10-1 and 10-2, the information displayed includes the hostname, server ID, port, kind (master or slave), a general status, the logfile (binlog filename), and the current log position. Figure 10-1 shows the replication topology listing all of the connected slaves. This report can be handy when you want to get an at-a-glance status of your servers.

Other Items to Consider

This section discusses some additional considerations for monitoring replication. It includes special networking considerations and monitoring lag (delays in replication).

Networking

If you have limited networking bandwidth, high contention for the bandwidth, or simply a very slow connection, you can improve replication performance by using compression. You can configure compression using the `slave_compressed_protocol` variable.

In cases where network bandwidth is not a problem but you have data that you want to protect while in transit from the master to the slaves, you can use an SSL connection. You can configure the SSL connection using the `CHANGE MASTER` command. See the section titled "Setting Up Replication Using SSL" in the online MySQL Reference Manual for details on using SSL connections in replication.

Another networking configuration you may want to consider is using master heartbeats. You have seen where this information is shown on the `SHOW SLAVE STATUS` command. A heartbeat is a mechanism to automatically check connection status between a master and a slave. It can detect levels of connectivity in milliseconds. Master heartbeat is used in replication scenarios where the slave must be kept in sync with the master with little or no delay. Having the capability to detect when a threshold expires ensures the delay is identified before replication is halted on the slave.

You can configure master heartbeat using a parameter in the `CHANGE MASTER` command with the `master_heartbeat_period=<value>` setting (added in MySQL version 5.4.4), where the value is the number of seconds at which you want the heartbeat to occur. You can monitor the status of the heartbeat with the following commands:

```
SHOW STATUS like 'slave_heartbeat period'
SHOW STATUS like 'slave_received_heartbeats'
```

Monitor and Manage Slave Lag

Periods of massive updates, overburdened slaves, or other significant network performance events can cause your slaves to lag behind the master. When this happens, the slaves are not processing the events in their relay logs fast enough to keep up with the changes sent from the master.

As you saw with the SHOW SLAVE STATUS command, Seconds_Behind_Master can show indications that the slave is running behind the master. This field tells you by how many seconds the slave's SQL thread is behind the slave's I/O thread—that is, how far behind the slave is in processing the incoming events from the master. The slave uses the timestamps of the events to calculate this value. When the SQL thread on the slave reads an event from the master, it calculates the difference in the timestamp. The following excerpt shows a condition in which the slave is 146 seconds behind the master. In this case, the slave is more than two minutes behind; this can be a problem if your application is relying on the slaves to provide timely information.

```
mysql> SHOW SLAVE STATUS \G
...
        Seconds_Behind_Master: 146
...
```

The SHOW PROCESSLIST command (run on the slave) can also provide an indication of how far behind the slave is. Here, we see the number of seconds that the SQL thread is behind, measured using the difference between the timestamp of the last replicated event and the real time of the slave. For example, if your slaves have been offline for 30 minutes and have reconnected to the master, you would expect to see a value of approximately 1,800 seconds in the Time field of the SHOW PROCESSLIST results. The excerpt below shows this condition. Large values in this field are indicative of significant delays that can result in stale data on the slaves.

```
mysql> SHOW PROCESSLIST \G
...
   Time: 1814
...
```

Depending on how your replication topology is designed, you may be replicating data for load balancing. In this case, you typically use multiple slaves, directing a portion of the application or users to the slaves for SELECT queries, thereby reducing the burden on the master.

Causes and Cures for Slave Lag

Slave lag can be a nuisance for some replication users. The main reason for lag is the single-threaded nature of the slave (actually, there are two threads, but only one executes events and this is the main culprit in slave lag). For example, a master with a multiple-core CPU can run multiple transactions in parallel and will be faster than a slave that is executing transactions (events from the binary log) in a single thread. We have already discussed some ways to detect slave lag. In this section, we discuss some common causes and solutions for reducing slave lag.

There are several causes for slave lag (e.g., network latency). It is possible the slave I/O thread is delayed in reading events from the logs. The most common reason for slave lag is simply that the slave has a single thread to execute all events, whereas the master has potentially many threads executing in parallel. Some other causes include long-running queries with inefficient joins, I/O-bound reads from disk, lock contention, and InnoDB thread concurrency issues.

Now that you know more about what causes slave lag, let us examine some things you can do to minimize it:

Organize your data

> You can see performance improvements by normalizing your data and by using sharding to distribute your data. This helps eliminate duplication of data, but as you saw in Chapter 8, duplication of some data (such as lookup text) can actually improve performance. The idea here is to use just enough normalization and sharding to improve performance without going too far. This is something only you, the owner of the data, can determine either through experience or experimentation.

Divide and conquer

> We know that adding more slaves to handle the queries (scale-out) is a good way to improve performance, but not scaling out enough could still result in slave lag if the slaves are processing a much greater number of queries. In extreme cases, you can see slave lag on all of the slaves. To combat this, consider segregating your data using replication filtering to replicate different databases among your slaves. You can still use scale-out, but in this case you use an intermediary slave for each group of databases you filter, then scale from there.

Identify long-running queries and refactor them

> If long-running queries are the source of slave lag, consider refactoring the query or the operation or application to issue shorter queries or more compact transactions. However, if you use this technique combined with replication filtering, you must use care when issuing transactions that span the replication filter groups. Once you divide a long-running query that should be an atomic operation (a transaction) across slaves, you run the risk of causing data integrity problems.

Load balancing

> You can also use load balancing to redirect your queries to different slaves. This may reduce the amount of time each slave is spending answering queries, thereby leaving more computational time to process replication events.

Ensure you are using the latest hardware

> Clearly, having the best hardware for the job normally equates to better performance. At the very least, you should ensure your slave servers are configured to their optimal hardware capabilities and are at least as powerful as the master.

Reduce lock contention

> Table locks for MyISAM and row-level locks for InnoDB can cause slave lag. If you have queries that result in a lot of locks on MyISAM or InnoDB tables, consider refactoring the queries to avoid as many locks as possible.

Conclusion

This chapter concludes our discussion of the many ways you can monitor MySQL, and provides a foundation for you to implement your own schedules for monitoring virtually every aspect of the MySQL server.

Now that you know the basics of operating system monitoring, database performance, and MySQL monitoring and benchmarking, you have the tools and knowledge to successfully tune your server for optimal performance.

Joel smiled as he compiled his report about the replication issue. He paused and glanced at his doorway. He could almost sense it coming.

"Joel!"

Joel jumped, unable to believe his prediction. "I've got the replication problem solved, sir," he said quickly.

"Great! Send me the details when you get a moment."

"I also discovered some interesting things about the order processing system." He noticed Mr. Summerson's eyebrow raise slightly in anticipation. Joel continued, "It seems we have sized the buffer pool incorrectly. I think I can make some improvements in that area as well."

Mr. Summerson said, "Monitoring again?"

"Yes, sir. I've got some reports on the InnoDB storage engine. I'll include that in my email, too."

"Good work. Good work indeed."

Joel knew that look. His boss was thinking again, and that always led to more work. Joel was surprised when his boss simply walked away slowly. "Well, it seems I finally stumped him."

Replication Troubleshooting

The message subject was simply "Fix the Seattle server." Joel knew such cryptic subject lines came from only one person. A quick scan of the message header confirmed the email was from Mr. Summerson. Joel opened the message and read the contents.

"The Seattle server is acting up again. I think the replication thingy is hosed. Make this your top priority."

"OK," Joel muttered to himself. Because the monitoring reports he had produced last week showed no anomalies and he was sure the replication setup was correct the last time he checked, Joel wasn't sure how to attack the problem. But he knew where to find the answers. "It looks like I need to read that replication troubleshooting chapter after all."

A familiar head appeared in his doorway. Joel decided to perform a preemptive maneuver by saying, "I'm on it." This resulted in a nod and a casual salute as his boss continued down the hall.

MySQL replication is usually trouble-free and rarely needs tuning or tweaking once the topology is active and properly configured. However, there are times when things can go wrong. Sometimes an error is manifested, and you have clear evidence with which to start your investigations. Other times the condition or problem is easily understood, but the causes of the more difficult problems that can arise are not so obvious. Fortunately, you can resolve these problems if you follow some simple guidelines and practices for troubleshooting replication.

This chapter presents these ideas by focusing on techniques to resolve replication problems. We begin with a description of what can go wrong, then we discuss the basic tools available to help troubleshoot problems, and we conclude with some strategies for solving and preventing replication problems.

Troubleshooting replication problems involving the MySQL Cluster follows the same procedures presented in this chapter. If you are having problems with MySQL Cluster, see Chapter 15 for troubleshooting cluster failures and startup issues.

Seasoned computer users understand that computing systems are prone to occasional failures. Information technology professionals make it part of their creed to prevent failures and ensure reliable access and data to users. However, even properly managed systems can have issues.

MySQL replication is no exception. In particular, the slave state is not crash-safe. This means that if the MySQL instance on the slave crashes, it is possible the slave will stop in an undefined state. In the worst case, the relay log or the *master.info* file could be corrupt.

Indeed, the more complex the topology (including load and database complexity) and the more diverse the roles are among the nodes in the topology, the more likely something will go wrong. That doesn't mean replication cannot scale—on the contrary, you have seen how replication can easily scale to massive replication topologies. What we are saying is that when replication problems occur, they are usually the result of an unexpected action or configuration change.

What Can Go Wrong

There are many things that can go wrong to disrupt replication. MySQL replication is most susceptible to problems with data, be it data corruption or unintended interruptions in the replication stream. System crashes that result in an unsafe and uncontrolled termination of MySQL can also cause replication restarting issues.

You should always prepare a backup of your data before changing anything to fix the problem. In some cases the backup will contain data that is corrupt or missing, but the benefits are still valid, specifically, that no matter what you do, you can at least return the data to the state at the time of the error. You'd be surprised how easy it is to make a bad situation worse.

In this section, we begin exploring replication troubleshooting by describing the most common failures in MySQL replication. These are some of the more frequently encountered replication problems. While the list is not complete in the sense that it includes all possible replication problems, it does give you an idea of the types of things that can go wrong. We include a brief statement of some likely causes for each.

Problems on the Master

While most errors will manifest on the slave, look to this section for potential solutions for problems originating on the master. Administrators sometimes automatically suspect the slave. You should take a look at both the master and the slave when diagnosing replication problems.

Master crashed and memory tables are in use

When the master is restarted, any data for memory tables is purged (as is normal for the memory storage engine). However, if a table that uses the memory storage engine (hence, a memory table) is being replicated, the slave may have outdated data if it wasn't restarted (the server, not the slave).

Fortunately, when the first access to the memory table occurs after a restart, a special delete event is sent to the slaves to signal the slaves to purge the data, thereby synchronizing the data. However, the interval between when the table is referenced and when the replication event is transmitted can result in the slave having outdated data. To avoid this problem, use a script to first purge the data, then repopulate it on the master at startup using the init_file option.

For example, if you have a memory table that stores frequently used data, create a file like the following and reference it with the init_file option:

```
# Force slaves to purge data
DELETE FROM db1.mem_zip;
# Repopulate the data
INSERT INTO ...
```

The first command is a delete query, which will be replicated to the slaves when replication is restarted. Following that are statements to repopulate the data. In this way, you can ensure there is no gap where the slave could have out-of-date information in a memory table.

Master crashed and binary log events are missing

It is possible for the master to fail and not write recent events to the binary log on disk. That is, if the server crashes before MySQL flushes its binary events cache to disk (in the binary log), those cached events can be lost.

This is usually indicated by an error on the slave stating that the binary log offset event is missing or does not exist. In this case, the slave is attempting to reconnect on restart using the last known binlog file and position of the master, and while the binlog file may exist, the offset does not because the events that incremented the offset were not written to disk.

Unfortunately, there is no way to retrieve the lost binlog events. To solve this problem, you must check the current binlog position on the master and use this information to tell the slave to start at the next known event on the master. Be sure to check the data on both your master and slave once the slave is synchronized.

It is also possible that some of the events that were lost on the master were applied to the data prior to the crash. You should always compare the tables in question on the master to determine if there are differences between the master and the slave. This situation is rare, but it can cause problems later on if an update for a row is executed on the master against one of these missing events, which then causes a failure when run on the slave. In this case, the slave is attempting to run an update on rows that do not exist.

For example, consider a scenario of a fictional, simplified database for an auto dealer where information about cars for sale is stored in tables corresponding to new and used cars. The tables are set up with autoincrement keys.

On the master, the following happens:

```
INSERT INTO auto.used_cars VALUES (2004, 'Porsche', 'Cayman', 23100, 'blue');
```

A crash occurs after the following statement is executed but before it is written to the binary log:

```
UPDATE auto.used_cars SET color = 'white' WHERE id = 17;
```

In this case, the update query was lost during the crash on the master. When the slave attempts to restart, an error is generated. You can resolve the problem using the suggestion just shown. A check on the number of rows on the master and slave shows the same row count. Notice the update that corrected the color of the 2004 Porsche to white instead of blue. Now consider what will happen when a salesperson tries to help a customer find the blue Porsche of her dreams by executing this query on the slave:

```
SELECT * FROM auto.used_cars
WHERE make = 'Porsche' AND  model = 'Cayman' AND color = 'blue';
```

Will the salesperson who runs the query discover he has a blue Porsche Cayman for sale? A good auto salesperson always ensures he has the car on the lot by visual inspection, but for argument's sake let us assume he is too busy to do so and tells his customer he has the car of her dreams. Imagine his embarrassment (and loss of a sale) when his customer arrives to test-drive the car only to discover that it is white.

 To prevent loss of data should the master crash, turn on sync_binlog (set to 1) at startup or in your configuration file. This will tell the master to flush an event to the binary log immediately. While this may cause a noticeable performance drop for InnoDB, the protection afforded could be great if you cannot afford to lose any changes to the data (but you may lose the last event, depending on when the crash occurred).

While this academic example may not seem too bad, consider the possibilities of a missing update to a medical database or a database that contains scientific data. Clearly, a missing update, even a seemingly simple one, can cause problems for your users. Indeed, the above scenario can be considered a form of data corruption. Always check the contents of your tables when encountering this problem. In this case, crash recovery ensures the binary log and InnoDB are consistent when `sync_binlog=1`, but it otherwise has no effect for MyISAM tables.

Query runs fine on the master but not on the slave

While not strictly a problem on the master, it is sometimes possible that a query (e.g., an update or insert command) will run properly on the master but not on the slave. There are many causes of this type of error, but most point to a referential integrity issue or a configuration problem on the slave or the database.

The most common cause of this error is a query referencing a table that does not exist on the slave or that has a different signature (different columns or column types). In this case, you must change the slave to match the server in order to properly execute the query.

In some cases, it is possible the query is referencing a table that is not replicated. For example, if you are using any of the replication filtering startup options (a quick check of the master and slave status will confirm this), it is possible that the database the query is referencing is not on the slave. In this situation, you must either adjust your filters accordingly or manually add the missing tables to the missing database on the slave.

In other cases, the cause of a failed query can be more complex, such as character set issues, corrupt tables, or even corrupt data. If you confirm your slave is configured the same as your master, you may need to diagnose the query manually. If you cannot correct the problem on the slave, you may need to perform the update manually and tell the slave to skip the event that contains the failed query.

 To skip an event on a slave, use the `sql_slave_skip_counter` variable and specify the number of events from the master you want to skip. Sometimes this is the fastest way to restart replication.

Table corruption after a crash

If your master or slave crashes and, after restarting them both, you find one or more tables are corrupt or find that they are marked as crashed by MyISAM, you will need to fix these problems before restarting replication.

You can detect which tables are corrupt by examining the server's logfiles, looking for errors like the following:

```
... [ERROR] /usr/bin/mysqld: Table 'db1.t1' is marked
as crashed and should be repaired ...
```

You can use the following command to perform optimization and repair in one step to repair all of the tables for a given database (in this case, *db1*).

```
mysqlcheck -u <user> -p --check --optimize --auto-repair db1
```

For MyISAM tables, you can use the `myisam-recover` option to turn on automatic recovery. There are four modes of recovery. See the online MySQL Reference Manual for more details.

Once you have repaired the affected tables, you must also determine if the tables on the slave have been corrupted. This is necessary if the master and slave share the same data center and the failure was environmental (e.g., they were connected to the same power source).

 Always perform a backup on a table before repairing it. In some cases a repair operation can result in data loss or leave the table in an unknown state.

It is also possible that a repair can leave the master and slave out of sync, especially if there is data loss as a result of the repair. You may need to compare the data in the affected table to ensure the master and slave are synchronized. If they are not, you may need to reload the data for the affected table on the slave if the slave is missing data, or copy data from the slave if the master is missing data.

Binary log is corrupt on the master

If a server crash or disk problem results in a corrupt binary log on the master, you cannot restart replication. There are many causes and types of corruption that can occur in the binary log, but all result in the inability to execute one or more events on the slave, often resulting in errors such as "could not parse relay log event."

In this case, you must carefully examine the binary log for recoverable events and rotate the logs on the master with the `FLUSH LOGS` command. There may be data loss on the slave as a result and the slave will most definitely fail in this scenario. The best recovery method is to resynchronize the slave with the master using a reliable backup and recovery tool. In addition to rotating the logs, you can ensure any data loss is minimized and get replication restarted without errors.

In some cases, if it is easy to determine how many events were corrupted or missing, it may be possible to skip the corrupted events by using the `sql_slave_skip_counter` on the slave. You can determine this by comparing the master's binlog reference on the slave to the current binlog position on the master.

Killing long-running queries for nontransactional tables

If you are forced to terminate a query that is modifying a nontransactional table, it is possible the query has been replicated to and executed on the slave. When this occurs, it is likely the changes on the master will be different than on the slave.

For example, if you terminate a query that updates 400 out of the 600 rows in a table such that only 200 of the 400 changes are complete, it is possible that the slave completed all 400 updates.

Thus, whenever you terminate a query that updates data on the master, you need to confirm the change has not executed on the slave and if it has (or even as a precaution), you should resynchronize the data on the slave once you've corrected the table on the master. Usually in this case, you will fix the master and then make a backup of the data on the master and restore it on the slave.

Problems on the Slave

Most problems you will encounter will be the result of some error on the slave. In some situations, like those described in the previous section, it may be a problem that originated on the master, but it almost always will be seen on the slave in one form or another. The following sections list some of the common problems on the slave.

Use Binary Logging on the Slave

One way to ensure a more robust slave is to turn on binary logging using the `log-slave-updates` option. This will cause the slave to log the events it executes from its relay log, thereby creating a binary log that you can use to replay events on the slave in the event that the relay log (or the data) becomes corrupt.

Slave server crashed and replication won't start

When a slave server crashes, it is usually easy to reestablish replication with the master once you determine the last known good event executed on the slave. You can see this by examining the SHOW SLAVE STATUS output.

However, where there are errors regarding account access, it is possible that replication cannot be restarted. This can be the result of authentication problems (e.g., the slave's replication account was deleted) or corrupted tables on the master or slave(s). In these cases, you are likely to see connection errors in the console and logs for the slave MySQL server.

When this occurs, always check the permissions of the replication user on the master. Ensure the proper privileges are granted to the user defined in either your configuration file or on your CHANGE MASTER command. The privileges should be similar to the following:

```
GRANT REPLICATION SLAVE ON *.*
TO 'rpl_user'@'%' IDENTIFIED BY 'password_here';
```

You can change this command to suit your needs as a means to solve this problem.

Slave connection times out and reconnects frequently

If you have multiple slaves in your topology and have either not set the `server_id` option or have the same value for `server_id` for two or more of your slaves, you may have conflicting server IDs. When this happens, one of the slaves may exhibit frequent time-outs or drop and reconnect sequences.

This problem is simply due to the nonunique IDs among your slaves and can be difficult to diagnose (or, we should say, it's easy to misdiagnose as a connection problem). You should always check the error log of the master and slave for error messages. In this case, it is likely the error will contain the nature of the timeout.

To prevent this type of problem, always ensure that all of your servers have a `server_id` option set either in the configuration file or in the startup command line.

Query results are different on the slave than on the master

One of the more difficult problems to detect occurs when the query results performed on one or more slaves do not match that of the master. It is possible you may never notice the problem. The problem could be as simple or innocuous as sort order issues, or as severe as missing or extra rows in the result set.

The main causes of this type of problem are character set differences between the master and slave. For example, the master can be configured with one character set and collation defaults while one or more slaves are configured with another.

If your users start complaining of extra or missing rows or differing result orders, you should check the character set setting first on both the master and your slaves.

Another possible cause of this problem is using different default storage engines on the master and slave—for example, if you use the MyISAM storage engine on the master and use the InnoDB storage engine on the slave. In this case, it is entirely likely that the query results will be in different orders if you used an `ALTER TABLE` command that changed the storage engine to one that has a different collation than the master.

Perhaps a more subtle cause of this type of problem is when the table definitions differ on the master and slave. It is possible to have differences in which a subset of the columns for a given table is the same and either some initial columns or ending columns (order is important here) are missing on the slave.

There are many potential errors when you use this feature, but it can sometimes result in the expectation that the data for some columns is replicated but the slave doesn't have the columns defined. While having fewer columns on the slave may be desired, a careless user can achieve this accidentally by dropping columns in such a way that replication can still proceed. In some cases, the `SELECT` queries executed on the slave will fail when referencing the missing columns, thereby giving you a clue to the problem. Other times you can simply be missing data in your applications.

A common user error that can result in differences in query results between the master and slave is making other types of changes to the tables or databases executed on the slave but not executed on the master. That is, a user performs some nonreplicated data manipulation on the slave that changes a table signature but does not execute the same on the master. When this occurs, queries can return either the wrong results, wrong columns, wrong order, or extra data, or simply fail due to referencing missing columns. It is always a good precaution to check the layout of a table involved in these types of problems to ensure it is the same on the master and slave. If it is not, resynchronize the table and retry the query.

Slave issues errors when attempting to restart with SSL

Problems related to SSL connections are typically the usual permission issues described previously. In this case, the privileges granted must also include the REQUIRE SSL option as shown below. Be sure to check that the replication user exists and has the correct privileges.

```
GRANT REPLICATION SLAVE ON *.*
TO 'rpl_user'@'%' IDENTIFIED BY 'password_here' REQUIRE SSL;
```

Other issues related to restarting replication when SSL connections are used are missing certificate files or incorrect values for the SSL-related options in the configuration file (e.g., ssl-ca, ssl-cert, and ssl-key) or the related options in the CHANGE MASTER command (e.g., MASTER_SSL_CA, MASTER_SSL_CAPATH, MASTER_SSL_CERT, and MASTER_SSL_KEY). Be sure to check your settings and paths to ensure nothing has changed since the last time replication was started.

Memory table data goes missing

If one or more of your databases uses the memory storage engine, the data contained in these tables will be lost when a slave server is restarted (the server, not the slave threads). This is expected, as data in memory tables does not survive a restart. The table configuration still exists and the table can be accessed, but the data has been purged.

It is possible that when a slave server is restarted, queries directed to the memory table fail (e.g., UPDATE) or query results are inaccurate (e.g., SELECT). Thus, the error may not occur right away and could be as simple as missing rows in a query result.

To avoid this problem, you should carefully consider the use of memory tables in your databases. You should not create memory tables on the master to be updated on the slaves via replication without procedures in place to recover the data for the tables in the event of a crash or planned restart of the server. For example, you can execute a script before you start replication that copies the data for the table from the master. If the data is derived, use a script to repopulate the data on the slave.

Other things to consider are filtering out the table during replication or possibly not using the memory storage engine for any replicated table.

Temporary tables are missing after a slave crash

If your replicated databases and queries make use of temporary tables, you should consider some important facts about temporary tables. When a slave is restarted, its temporary tables are lost. If any temporary tables were replicated from the master and you cannot restart the slave from that point, you may have to manually create the tables or skip the queries that reference the temporary tables.

This scenario often results in the case where a query will not execute on one or more slaves. The resolution to this problem is similar to missing memory tables. Specifically, in order to get the query to execute, you may have to manually re-create the temporary tables or resynchronize the data on the slave with the data on the master and skip the query when restarting the slave.

Slave is slow and is not synced with the master

In slave lag, also called *excessive lag*, the slave cannot process all of the events from the master fast enough to avoid delays in updates of the data. In the most extreme cases, the updates to the data on the slave become out of date and cause incorrect results. For example, if a slave server in a ticketing agency is many minutes behind the master, it is possible the ticketing agency can sell seats that are no longer available (i.e., they have been marked as "sold" on the master but the slave did not get the updates until too late).

We discussed this problem in previous chapters, but a summary of the resolution is still relevant here. To detect the problem, monitor the slave's SHOW SLAVE STATUS output and examine the Seconds_Behind_Master column to ensure the value is within tolerance for your application. To solve the problem, consider moving some of the databases to other slaves, reducing the number of databases being replicated to the slave, improving network delays (if any), and making data storage improvements.

For example, you can relieve the slave of processing extraneous events by using an additional slave for bulk or expensive data updates. You can relieve the replication load by making updates on a separate slave and applying the changes using a reliable backup and restore method on all of the other machines in the topology.

Data loss after a slave crash

It is possible that a slave server may crash and not record the last known master binlog position. This information is saved in the *relay_log.info* file. When this occurs, the slave will attempt to restart at the wrong (older) position and therefore attempt to execute some queries that may have already been executed. This normally results in query errors; you can handle this by skipping the duplicate events.

However, it is also possible these duplicate events can cause the data to be changed (corrupted) so that the slave is no longer in sync with the master. Unfortunately, these types of problems are not that easy to detect. Careful examination of the logfiles may reveal that some events have been executed, but you may need to examine the binlog events and the master's binary log to determine which ones were duplicated.

Table corruption after a crash

When you restart a master following a crash, you may find one or more tables are corrupt or marked as crashed by MyISAM. You need to resolve these issues before restarting replication. Once you have repaired the affected tables, ensure the tables on the slave have not suffered any data loss as a result of the repair. It is very unusual for this to occur, but it is something that you should check. When in doubt, always manually resynchronize these tables with the master using a backup and restore or similar procedure before restarting replication.

 Data loss after a repair operation is a very real possibility for MyISAM when a partial page write occurs during a hardware or server crash. Unfortunately, it is not always easy to determine if the data has been lost.

Relay log is corrupt on the slave

If a server crash or disk problem results in a corrupt relay log on the slave, replication will stop with one of several errors related to the relay log. There are many causes and types of corruption that can occur in the relay log, but all result in the inability to execute one of more events on the slave.

When this occurs, your best choice for recovery is identifying where the last known good event was executed from the master's binary log and restarting replication using the CHANGE MASTER command, providing the master's binlog information. This will force the slave to re-create a new relay log. Unfortunately, this means any recovery from the old relay log can be compromised.

Multiple errors during slave restart

One of the more difficult problems to detect and fix is multiple errors on the slave during initial start or a later restart. There are a variety of errors that occur and sometimes they occur at random or without a clearly identifiable cause.

When this occurs, check the size of the max_allowed_packet on both the master and the slave. If the size is larger on the master than on the slave, it is possible the master has logged an event that exceeds the slave's size. This can cause random and seemingly illogical errors.

Consequences of a failed transaction on the slave

Normally when there is a failed transaction, the changes are rolled back to avoid problems associated with partial updates. However, this is complicated when you mix transactional and nontransactional tables—the transactional changes are rolled back, but the nontransactional changes are not. This can lead to problems such as data loss or duplicated, redundant, or unwanted changes to the nontransactional tables.

The best way to avoid this problem is to avoid mixing transactional and nontransactional table relationships in your database and to always use transactional storage engines.

Advanced Replication Problems

There are some natural complications with some of the more advanced replication topologies. In this section, we examine some of the common problems you might encounter while using an advanced feature of replication.

A change is not replicated among the topology

In some cases, changes to a database object are not replicated. For example, ALTER TABLE may be replicated, while FLUSH, REPAIR TABLE, and similar maintenance commands are not. Whenever this happens, consult the limitations of data manipulation (DML) commands and maintenance commands.

This problem is typically the result of an inexperienced administrator or developer attempting database administration on the master, expecting the changes to replicate to the slaves.

Whenever there are profound changes to a database object that change its structure at a file level or you use a maintenance command, execute the command or procedure on all of the slaves to ensure the changes are propagated throughout your topology.

Savvy administrators often use scripts to accomplish this as routine scheduled maintenance. Typically, the scripts stop replication in an orderly manner, apply the changes, and restart replication automatically.

Circular replication issues

If you are using circular replication and you have recovered from a replication failure whereby one or more servers were taken out of the topology, you can encounter a problem in which an event is executed more than once on some of the servers. This can cause replication to fail if the query fails (e.g., a key violation). This occurs because the originating server was among those servers that were removed from the topology.

When this happens, the server designated as the originating server has failed to terminate the replication of the event. You can solve this problem by using the IGNORE_SERVER_IDS option (available in MySQL versions 5.5.2 and later) with the CHANGE MASTER command, supplying a list of server IDs to ignore for an event. When the missing servers are restored, you must adjust this setting so that events from the replaced servers are not ignored.

Multimaster issues

As with circular replication (which is a specific form of multimaster topology), if you are recovering from a replication failure, you may encounter events that are executed more than once. These events are typically events from a removed server. You can solve this problem the same way as you would with circular replication—by placing the server IDs of the removed servers in the list of the `IGNORE_SERVER_IDS` option with the `CHANGE MASTER` command.

Another possible problem with multimaster replication crops up when changes to the same table occur on both masters and the table has an autoincrement column for the primary key. In this case, you can encounter duplicate key errors. If you must insert new rows on more than one master, use the `auto_increment_increment` and `auto_incre ment_offset` options to stagger the increments. For example, one server can increment only even numbers while the other increments odd numbers. While this solves the immediate problem, it can be complicated to get more than two masters updating the same table with an autoincrement primary key. Not only does it make it more difficult to stagger the increments, it becomes an administrative problem if you need to replace a server in the topology that is updating the table. For instance, you can end up with gaps in your incremented values, which can ultimately lead to exceeding the maximum values of the data type for the key for larger tables.

The HA_ERR_KEY_NOT_FOUND error

This is a familiar error encountered in a row-based replication topology. The most likely cause of this error is a conflict whereby the row to be updated or deleted is not present or has changed, so the storage engine cannot find it. This can be the result of an error during circular replication or changes made directly to a slave on replicated data. When this occurs, you must determine the source of the conflict and repair the data or skip the offending event.

Tools for Troubleshooting Replication

If you have used or set up replication or performed maintenance, many of the tools you need to successfully diagnose and repair replication problems are familiar to you.

In this section, we discuss the tools required to diagnose replication problems along with a few suggestions about how and when to use each:

`SHOW MASTER STATUS` *and* `SHOW SLAVE STATUS`
> These SQL commands are your primary tool for diagnosing replication problems. Along with the `SHOW PROCESSLIST` command, you should execute these commands on the master and then on the slave, then examine the output. The slave command has an extended set of parameters that are invaluable in diagnosing replication problems.

SHOW GRANTS FOR `<replication user>`

Whenever you encounter slave user access problems, you should first examine the grants for the slave user to ensure they have not changed.

CHANGE MASTER

Sometimes the configuration files have been changed either knowingly or accidentally. Use this SQL command to override the last known connection parameters and to diagnose slave connection problems.

STOP/START SLAVE

Use these SQL commands to start and stop replication. It is sometimes a good idea to stop a slave if it is in an error state.

Examine the configuration files

Sometimes the problem occurs as a result of an unsanctioned or forgotten configuration change. Check your configuration files routinely when diagnosing connection problems.

Examine the server logs

You should make this a habit whenever diagnosing problems. Checking the server logs can sometimes reveal errors that are not visible elsewhere. As cryptic as they can sometimes be, the error and warning messages can be helpful.

SHOW SLAVE HOSTS

Use this command to identify the connected slaves on the master if they use the `report-host` option.

SHOW PROCESSLIST

When encountering problems, it is always a good idea to see what else is running. This command will tell you the current state of each of the threads involved in replication. Check here first when examining the problem.

SHOW BINLOG EVENTS

This SQL command displays the events in the binary log. If you use statement-based replication, this command will display the changes using SQL statements.

`mysqlbinlog`

This utility allows you to read events in the binary or relay logs, often indicating when there are corrupt events. Don't hesitate to use this tool frequently when diagnosing problems related to events and the binary log.

PURGE BINARY LOGS

This SQL command allows you to remove certain events from the binary log, such as those that occur after a specific time or after a given event ID. Your routine maintenance plan should include the use of this command for purging older binary logs that are no longer needed.

Now that we have reviewed the problems you can encounter in replication and have seen a list of the tools available in a typical MySQL release, we now turn our attention to strategies for attacking replication problems.

Best Practices

Reviewing the potential problems that can occur in replication and listing the tools available for fixing the problems is only part of the complete solution. There are some proven strategies and best practices for resolving replication problems quickly.

This section describes the strategies and best practices you should cultivate when diagnosing and repairing replication problems. We present these in no particular order—depending on the problem you are trying to solve, one or more may be helpful.

Know Your Topology

If you are using MySQL replication on a small number of servers, it may not be that difficult to commit the topology configuration to memory. It may be as simple as a single master and one or more slaves, or as complex as two servers in a multimaster topology. However, there is a point at which memorizing the topology and all of its configuration parameters becomes impossible.

The more complex the topology and the configuration, the harder it is to determine the cause of a problem and where to begin your repair operations. It would be very easy to forget a lone slave in a topology of hundreds of slave servers.

It is always a good idea to have a map of your topology and the current configuration settings. You should keep a record of your replication setup in a notebook or file and place it where you and your colleagues or subordinates can find it easily. This information will be invaluable to someone who understands replication administration but may have never worked with your installation.

You should include a textual or graphical drawing of your topology and indicate any filters (master and slave), as well as the role of each server in the topology. You should also consider including the CHANGE MASTER command, complete with options, and the contents of the configuration files for all of your servers.

A drawing of your topology need not be sophisticated or an artistic wonder. A simple line drawing will do nicely. Figure 11-1 shows a hybrid topology, complete with notations for filters and roles.

Note that the production relay slave (192.168.1.105) has two masters (192.168.1.100 and 192.168.1.101). This is strange, because no slave can have more than one master. To achieve this level of integration—consuming data from a third party—you would need a second instance of a MySQL server on the production relay slave to replicate the data from the strategic partner (192.168.1.101) and use a script to conduct periodic transfers of the data from the second MySQL instance to the primary MySQL instance on the production relay slave. This would achieve the integration depicted in Figure 11-1 with some manual labor and a time-delayed update of the strategic partner data.

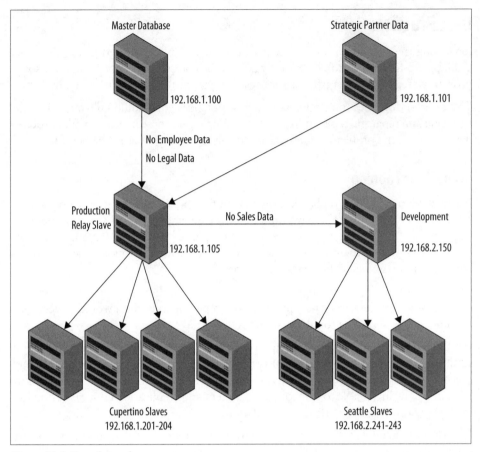

Figure 11-1. Sample topology map

There are certain problems inherent in certain topologies. We have already discussed many of these in this and previous chapters. What follows is a list of the types of topologies, including a short description and some common issues to be aware of concerning known vulnerabilities:

Star (also called single master)
> This is the typical single master, many slaves topology. There are no special limitations or problems other than those that apply to replication as a whole. However, the process of promoting a slave to a master can be complicated in that you must use the slave that is most up-to-date with the master. This can be difficult to determine and may require examination of the state of every slave.

Chain
> In this configuration, a server is a master to one slave, which is in turn a master to another slave, and so on, with the end point being a simple slave. Other than the server ID issue mentioned earlier, there is also the problem of determining which

position an intermediate master/slave was at when it failed. Promoting a new master/slave node can require additional work to ensure consistency.

Circular (also called ring)
This is the same as the chain topology except there is no end point. This topology requires careful setup so that events are terminated at the originating server.

Multimaster
This is similar to a circular topology, but in this case each master is a slave of every other master. This topology has all of the limitations and problems of circular replication as well as being one of the most complex topologies to manage due to the possibility of conflicting changes. To avoid this problem, you must ensure you make changes using only one of the masters. If a conflicting change occurs, say an UPDATE on one master and a DELETE statement on the other master, it is possible the DELETE statement will execute before the UPDATE, which will force the UPDATE to fail.

Hybrid
A hybrid topology uses elements of some or all of the other topologies. You typically see this topology in a large organization that has compartmentalized functions or divisions that require similar but often isolated elements of the infrastructure. Isolation is accomplished using filtering whereby data is divided among several slaves from an original master (sometimes called the *prime* or *master master*) that contains all of the data sent to the slaves, which become masters to their own star topologies. This is by far the most complex topology and requires careful notation and diligence to keep your documentation updated.

Check the Status of All of Your Servers

One the best preventive tasks you can perform is to regularly check the status of all of the servers in your topology. This need not be complicated. For instance, you can set up a scheduled task that launches the MySQL client and issues a SHOW MASTER STATUS or SHOW SLAVE STATUS and prints out or emails the results.

Of course, you have to read these email messages! We suggest setting up the scheduled task to run at a point before you have time to read them. For example, you can set up the tasks to run right before lunch, then read the output during or after lunch.

Keeping a close eye on your server status is a good way to stay informed when there is a potential problem. It also gives you a chance to react more quickly when errors occur.

You should look for errors, monitor the slave lag, check your filters to see that they match your records, and ensure all of your slaves are running and not reporting warnings or connection errors.

Check Your Logs

Along with checking your server status regularly, you should also consider checking the logs of your servers periodically. You can accomplish this easily using the MySQL Administrator graphical user interface to connect to each server in turn and look at the most recent entries in the logs.

If you are diligent in this effort, it will pay dividends in the form of early problem detection. Sometimes errors or warnings that, at the time, do not manifest in anything detectable are written to the log. Catching these telltale signs early can make your repair work much easier.

We recommend examining your logs at the same time you examine the status of your servers.

Check Your Configuration

Along with the servers and logfiles, you should also routinely examine your configuration files to ensure your documentation is up-to-date. This isn't as critical as checking the logs, but it is often overlooked. We recommend checking your configuration files and updating your documentation at least once a week if you have a lot of changes, and at least once a month if you have few changes to the topology or servers. If you have an environment in which there is more than one administrator, you may want to consider doing this more frequently.

Conduct Orderly Shutdowns

Sometimes it is necessary to stop replication while you diagnose and repair a problem. If replication has already stopped, you may not need to do anything, but if you have a complex topology and the error is related to data loss, it may be safer to stop replication across the topology. But you should do so in a controlled and safe manner.

There are several strategies for doing a controlled shutdown of your replication topology. If data loss is an issue and slave lag is not, you may want to lock the tables on your master and flush the binary logs, then wait for all of the (remaining) slaves to catch up and then shut the slaves down. This will ensure all events are replicated and executed on the slaves that are operational.

On the other hand, if the problem is severe, you may want to start with the slaves on the leaves of your topology and work your way up the topology, leaving the master running. However, if you leave the master running (i.e., you don't lock all of the tables) and you have a heavy load of updates running and your diagnostic and repair takes a long time, your slaves will be lagging behind your master when you restart replication. It is better to stop updates on the master if you think your repair will take a long time.

If you are faced with a difficult problem or (worse) a problem that appears randomly or without warning, you may want to consider shutting down replication completely. This is especially true if you have a problem with only one of your slaves. Shutting down replication will allow you to isolate the server while you diagnose the problem.

Conduct Orderly Restarts After a Failure

It is also important to restart replication in an orderly manner. It is often best to restart the replication topology under controlled conditions, such as on only one master and one slave. Even if your topology is more complex, having the most basic building blocks of replication started initially will allow you to test and ensure the problem is fixed before restarting all of your servers.

Isolation is essential when dealing with problems that are confined to a single slave or a set of events. It is also helpful to start with a single master and a single slave so that if you cannot fix the problem, you can get help from MySQL professionals more easily because you have isolated the problem to the smallest set of parameters as possible. See "Reporting Replication Bugs" on page 407 for more details.

Manually Execute Failed Queries

One of the most overlooked ostrategies is examining the queries in the relay log or binary log for clues as to what has gone wrong. It is easy to get stuck on researching the error on the slave and diagnosing all of the many things that can go wrong, but sometimes (especially when there is a query involved) you can gain far more information about the problem by isolating the slave server in question and attempting the query manually.

If you are using statement-based replication, this is an easy task because the query is human-readable in the binary or relay log. If you use row-based replication, you can still execute the query, but you cannot read the query itself. In this case, a malformed query or a query that uses a missing, incorrect, or corrupt reference may not be obvious until you execute the query manually.

Remember, you should always make a backup of your data before attempting diagnostics that could result in changes to the data. Running a broken query is definitely one of those cases. We have seen queries that cause replication errors but sometimes succeed when run manually. When this occurs, it is usually indicative of a slave configuration error or binary or relay log issue rather than a problem with the query itself.

Common Procedures

There are also some common procedures you can use to execute the practices just discussed. These include troubleshooting replication and pausing replication on the master.

Troubleshooting replication failures

The following is a stepwise procedure you can use when attacking replication problems. Most of these steps have been described elsewhere in this book or may already be familiar to you.

 You should write down or electronically record all observations while you conduct this procedure. Seeing the information consolidated in one place can sometimes present a much clearer body of evidence.

1. Check the status on the master. Record any anomalies.
2. Check the status on each slave. Record any anomalies.
3. Read the error logs on all of your servers.
4. Examine the process list on each server. Look for anomalies in status.
5. If no errors are reported, attempt to restart the slave. Record any errors presented.
6. Check the configuration of the server in question to ensure nothing has changed.
7. Examine your notes and form a plan to research and fix the problem.

This procedure is oversimplified, but it should help you diagnose the replication problem more quickly than chasing the errors presented will (if there are any errors to chase).

Pausing replication

To pause replication, execute the following steps on each of your master servers, starting with the prime master (the first master):

On the master:

1. Run the `FLUSH TABLES WITH READ LOCK` command.
2. Run the `SHOW MASTER STATUS` command.
3. Record the master binary log and position.

On the slaves:

4. Run `SELECT MASTER_POS_WAIT` (`binary_log_name, position`).

On each remaining active slave connected to this master, examine the results of `SHOW SLAVE STATUS` until the slave has synchronized with the master. Once the slave reaches this state, it is safe to shut down the slave.

When you restart your replication topology, all slaves will automatically start without any lag. This procedure is useful in cases where there has been a disruption and you want to get things going again to avoid a prolonged slave lag.

Reporting Replication Bugs

Once in a while you may encounter a replication problem that you cannot solve without outside help. Even if you do not have a support agreement in place, you can report a bug for the MySQL release you are using.

The best bug reports are those that describe errors that can be demonstrated or repeated using an isolated test case, for example, a replication problem that can be demonstrated on a test master and slave, and that has a minimal set of data needed for the problem. Often this is nothing more than a complete and accurate report of the configuration and event in question.

To report a bug, visit *http://bugs.mysql.com* and (if you have not done so already) register for an account. When you enter your bug report, be sure to describe the problem as completely as possible. For fastest results and a quick resolution, include as many of the following details as possible:

- Record all error messages verbatim.
- Include the binary log (in full or an excerpt).
- Include the relay log (in full or an excerpt).
- Record the configuration of the master and slave.
- Copy the results of the SHOW MASTER STATUS and SHOW SLAVE STATUS commands.
- Provide copies of all error logs.

 Be sure to exhaust all of the above techniques and explore the problem using all of the available tools.

The MySQL bug tracking tool will keep you apprised of your bug submission by sending you email alerts whenever the bug report is updated.

Conclusion

This chapter includes suggestions for solving some of the common problems that can arise when using replication. We examined some of the ways replication can fail and discussed how to solve the problems and prevent them in the future. We also examined some tools and best practices for troubleshooting MySQL replication.

Joel smiled as he heard his boss coming toward his door. He was ready this time and started speaking as soon as he saw Mr. Summerson's polished wingtips. "I've got the Seattle server back online, sir. It was a problem with a couple of queries that failed because the tables were changed on the slave. I have advised the Seattle office to direct all schema changes and table maintenance to the master here. I will keep a watch on it from now on and let you know if the problem returns."

Mr. Summerson smiled. Joel could feel perspiration beading on his forehead. "Great! Good work."

Joel was relieved. "Thank you, sir."

His boss started to leave, but performed one of his now-routine pause, turn, and task maneuvers. "One more thing."

"Sir?" Joel said a little too quickly.

"It's Bob."

Joel was confused. Mr. Summerson's tasking usually involved a complete sentence. "Sir?" he said hesitantly.

"You can call me Bob. I think we're well past the 'sir' stuff."

Joel sat for a few moments until he realized he was staring into the middle distance of space. He blinked and realized his friend Amy from the development staff was standing in front of his desk.

"Are you OK, Joel?"

"What?"

"You were zoned out there. What were you thinking about?"

Joel smiled and reclined his chair. "I think I finally got to him."

"Who? Mr. Summerson?"

"Yeah, he just told me to call him Bob."

Amy smiled and crossed her arms, then jokingly said, "Well, I suppose we'll be calling you Mr. Joel from now on."

Joel laughed and said, "Have you had lunch yet?"

Protecting Your Investment

Joel pulled open the middle drawer of his desk and was rummaging for a working pen when he heard a familiar staccato rap on his door frame. "Joel, I need you to talk with the information assurance auditors and tell them what our recovery plans are. Oh, and be sure you order your tapes so they'll know we're prepared."

"Auditors? Tapes?" Joel asked as he made eye contact with Mr. Summerson.

"Be sure to start working on whatever disaster recovery planning document they're asking about. And tell the procurement office what kind of media you need to get started with your archives. They will show you what forms to fill out. Get some extras just in case," Joel's manager said as he disappeared from view.

Joel pushed his drawer closed and stood up. The boss must mean media for backups, he thought. But what was all that about auditors and planning? Joel pulled his chair over to his workstation and sat down. "Well, I guess I'll have to figure out what information assurance is and how to do a backup," he mumbled as he opened his browser.

Mr. Summerson popped his head back into the doorway and said, "Oh, and Joel, I'd like to see your recovery plan on my desk by tomorrow morning before the continuity of operations planning session at 1400."

Joel sighed as he realized his manager had asked for far more than he originally thought. Joel reached for his handy MySQL book. "Money well spent," he said as he opened the book to the chapter titled "Protecting Your Investment."

This chapter focuses on protecting data and providing data recovery. Practical topics in the chapter include backup planning, data recovery, and the procedures for backing up and restoring in MySQL. Any discussion of these topics would be incomplete without an introduction to the concepts of information assurance, information integrity, disaster recovery, and related terms. Indeed, once you have read through these sections you will see there is much more to protecting your investment than simply being able to back up and restore data.

What Is Information Assurance?

This section introduces the concept of information assurance, what it means to an organization, and how to get started practicing good information assurance. Although we do not intend to include a full description of all areas, we'll make sure to present the basics so you can begin your study of the subject well prepared. Oh, and so you can explain it to your boss too!

Information assurance (IA) is the management of technologies designed to administer, monitor, ensure the availability of, and control security in information systems. The goals of IA are to ensure the control and protection of the data and systems, the authenticity of access, and the confidentiality and availability of the information. While this book focuses on the database system, IA applies to all aspects of information technology. The following sites include useful background about IA:

- *http://www.nsa.gov/ia/*
- *http://en.wikipedia.org/wiki/Information_assurance*

The Three Practices of Information Assurance

Some researchers break down the field of IA into three related practices:

Information security
> The protection of computing systems from damage by managing the risk of threats, both internal and external

Information integrity
> The assurance of continued availability and continuity of the system and its data (sometimes called *data protection*)

Information significance
> The assessment of the value of the system to the user.

Information security is the most common and most well documented of the three practices. There are countless references on how best to maintain an expected level of protection for computing systems. There are also many references for physical security measures.

Information integrity is, however, the most important but also the most often overlooked practice. This chapter focuses on the importance of best practices for information integrity.

Information significance is the least commonly understood practice. Organizations that practice total quality management and related disciplines are familiar with assessing the value of the system, but generally consider only the financial aspects of the business instead of the value of information to employees in the course of doing their work. While one can argue that what is good for the company is good for the employees, we have encountered policies that seem well intended but may frustrate the employees.

When you consider information integrity and significance, IA comes to include disaster planning and disaster recovery, which otherwise are often left out of the calculations.

Well-planned IA includes both nonphysical (data, access codes, etc.) and physical (computers, access cards, keys, etc.) aspects. This chapter focuses on the physical aspect in some detail because database systems can be one of the most important resources to an organization.

Why Is Information Assurance Important?

With the increasing importance of computing systems to organizations and the rising costs of technology, conserving revenue and planning for the unexpected become priorities. As a result, the field of IA has grown beyond the scope of sequestered researchers and government agencies (two of the most interested groups). As these concepts become more popular, they are finding their way into many corporate auditors' toolboxes.

As an information technology leader, you need to be prepared to address the needs of your business to protect it from the unknown, including physical, nonphysical, and financial threats. One common place to turn is IA. If your organization has or is planning to initiate its own IA program, you owe it to yourself to learn how IA affects you.

Information Integrity, Disaster Recovery, and the Role of Backups

Information integrity is sometimes referred to as *business continuity*. The term underlines the importance of ensuring that an organization can continue its mission without interruption, and that you can carry out a controlled restore in the event of an unexpected catastrophic event. The effects of such an event can range from a minor problem to a devastating loss of operations or data that you cannot solve quickly (e.g., recovering from a power outage) or without considerable expense (e.g., replacing the information technology systems). It is important to acknowledge that there is no single solution that can help you prevent or recover from all events.

 Remember, hardware can and will eventually fail; be prepared.

The areas of responsibility for information integrity include:

Data integrity
    Ensures data will never be lost and that it is up-to-date and not corrupted

Communication integrity

> Ensures that communication links are always available, are recoverable in the case of an outage, and can initiate a trusted connection

System integrity

> Ensures you can restart the system in case of a malfunction, that you can recover the data and server state in case of loss or damage, and that the system maintains a level of continuity

As businesses grow more dependent on their information systems, the systems become more and more critical to business operations. Indeed, most modern businesses that utilize information technology have become so dependent on these systems that the business and its information technology become one. That is, the business cannot exist without it.

When this becomes true, an organization must recognize that it cannot operate effectively (or perhaps at all) if its information technology becomes disabled. Businesses in this situation place a great deal of importance on being able to recover the system as quickly as possible. The ability to recover operational capability or data in the event of a sudden unplanned event is called *disaster recovery*.

Businesses that fall under the scrutiny of regulatory organizations are aware (or soon will be made so) that there are several legal decisions and standards that may require the company to adopt IA and disaster recovery. More importantly, there are efforts underway to ensure the protection of certain forms of data. In the United States, these include the Health Insurance Portability and Accountability Act of 1996 (HIPAA), the Patriot Act, and the Sarbanes-Oxley Act of 2002 (SOX).

 For more information about the Sarbanes-Oxley Act, see *http://www .soxlaw.com/*.

High Availability Versus Disaster Recovery

Most businesses recognize they must invest in technologies that allow their systems to recover quickly from minor to moderate events. Technologies such as replication, redundant array of inexpensive disks (RAID), redundant power supplies, etc., are all solutions to these needs. These are considered high availability options because they are all intended to permit real-time or near real-time recovery without loss of any data (or to minimize the data loss to very small segments, such as the last changed record).

Unfortunately, few businesses take the extra step to ensure their investments are protected from devastating (and expensive) loss. Those that do are protecting their investments with the ultimate form of risk analysis—disaster recovery.

Certainly there is some overlap between the practices of high availability and disaster recovery. High availability solutions can address the minor disasters and even form one layer of defense for major disasters. However, each provides a different type of protection. High availability protects against the known or expected, while disaster recovery allows you to plan for the unexpected.

Disaster Recovery

Disaster recovery involves the process, policies, and planning for the continuation of information integrity after a catastrophic event. The most important aspect is creating and maintaining a document that contains this information: a *disaster recovery plan*.

Entire texts have been devoted to each aspect of disaster recovery. This section presents an overview of each so you can justify the importance of disaster recovery to your management team.

We have already discussed one form of disaster recovery in Chapter 2. These are sometimes the frontline tools that organizations use to recover from small disasters, but what happens if something really bad happens, like a RAID array fails beyond recovery or your server is destroyed by fire?

Before you can plan for the worst, you need to answer a series of questions that will form the premise or goals of the disaster recovery plan. These questions also form the criteria you can use to determine the effectiveness of the plan.

- What are the physical and nonphysical threats to your organization?
- What level of operational capability is needed or desired to maintain your business?
- How long can your business wait until operations are restored?
- What resources are available to plan and execute disaster recovery?

The first step of disaster recovery is acknowledging the worst-case scenario: the loss of the entire data center due to a catastrophic event. This includes not only the loss of the technology (servers, workstations, network equipment, etc.), but also the loss of the computing facility itself—and let's not forget the loss of personnel to operate the systems (this is seldom considered, but should be).

While that may seem like a doomsday story, real events have happened and may happen again that could result in just such a level of disruption. It could be as simple as a widespread power outage or as catastrophic as a hurricane, earthquake, or even war.

Imagine that the building that houses your information technology falls victim to a severe storm that damages the building beyond repair. The roof is torn away and 90 percent of the physical resources are damaged by water and falling debris. Let us also suppose your company is in the middle of a very lucrative and time-sensitive business transaction.

How will your company recover from this disaster? Were there any plans for such an event? How much will a prolonged loss of operations affect the revenue of the company? How quickly can you reestablish operations? This scenario may spur your management to invest in disaster recovery.

As another incentive, consider that if you plan for the worst and have procedures for recovering your systems, mundane outages become that much easier to endure. The planning aspect is the most important part of disaster recovery and offers the assurance of continuity of operations.

No One Is Exempt from Disaster

Disasters such as flood or fire can occur almost anywhere and to any organization. Some areas are more susceptible to natural disasters than others. However, no matter where your organization is located, there exists some element of risk. There is, however, one type of disaster that can strike anywhere and at any time—the man-made kind.

All organizations are responsible for preparing against malicious human activities, including those carried out by internal staff. And even if some parts of your operations are fully protected, some parts are likely to be distributed across less secure sites.

For example, suppose your company is located where natural disasters rarely happen. You are located far from earthquake fault lines and flooding is not a measurable risk. The building has an excellent fire suppression system, is protected physically, and is monitored 24/7 by trained responders. Overall, there is very low risk of physical loss due to natural disasters. Your predecessor had thought of everything, and management is not convinced of the need for a disaster recovery plan.

Now suppose an employee wants to damage the organization from within. When designing a disaster recovery plan, ask yourself, "What damage could an otherwise trusted employee do to the systems, data, or infrastructure?" While it may seem disconcerting and even paranoid to think like this, a glance through the reports of organizations victimized by sabotage from within should make you consider the unthinkable—that one of your employees could be a saboteur.

A good disaster recovery plan will include measures to reduce the risk of sabotage by identifying potential vulnerabilities, such as physical access to the building and equipment, as well as a review of all administrative rights to sensitive systems and data.

The goal of disaster recovery is to reestablish the operational capability of an organization as quickly as possible, which means its information technology must be restored. Best practices of disaster recovery include assessing the risk and planning recovery of all aspects of the information technology—both the physical and electronic. Good disaster planners include provisions for reestablishing a physical location for the organization as well as reconstructing the information technology from scratch. This should include the ability to acquire any equipment needed in an expedient manner by having a standby ready, by replacing a failed site with equipment taken from remaining sites, or by purchasing new equipment.

Rebuilding the network and the data from scratch includes acquiring a minimal set of computing and networking equipment to restore the data and applications to a state where the organization can operate at an acceptable level of reduced operations. Therefore, you need to determine the minimal set of technology that will allow the organization to continue its mission with little or no loss of revenue.

Personnel are also a key asset that your plan must consider. Thus, one recovery procedure is notifying all personnel in the case of an emergency. This may be as simple as a phone tree, where each employee is responsible for calling a set of her peers to pass on critical information. It may also be a sophisticated automated contact system that telephones all employees with a prerecorded message. Most automated systems provide a level of assessment by requiring each employee to acknowledge the message. The best notification systems include multiple point escalation. For example, the home phone numbers of employees are called first, followed by email, mobile, and text messages.

Disaster recovery also has a policy aspect, which includes the assessment of risks during emergencies (what assets are in danger, and how important is each one?) and who is to make decisions in the case of unavailability (or death) of members in the chain of command. For example, if the employee in charge of the networking systems is unavailable, his subordinate is designated to assume his responsibilities (and make any necessary decisions).

Disaster recovery planning

Planning is a much larger area and consists of making contingencies in the case of all known or expected scenarios. For example, a good disaster recovery plan has written procedures for establishing an alternative site and step-by-step instructions on how to build the information systems from scratch.

This is a good time to point out one fatal flaw in some disaster recovery plans. Little can be gained by expending countless hours and resources developing a disaster recovery plan if it is then stored on the hard drives of the systems it is designed to recover. Take the time to secure a copy of your disaster recovery plan in an offsite fireproof safe.

Disaster recovery workflow

You may have several questions by now. How do you get started with disaster recovery? How do you go from surveying your inventory of information technology to handing your boss a disaster recovery plan? It all begins with an examination of your goals. From there, you can proceed to planning and eventually evolve your own disaster recovery plan document.

If this sounds like a lot of work, it is. Most organizations form a team of experts from across the organization. The most successful teams are staffed by individuals who understand what is at stake (the organization could go bankrupt and everyone could lose their jobs), and who understand their areas of expertise well enough to identify critical systems.

It might seem obvious, but you must also plan for the possibility that those who create, test, and author a disaster recovery plan may not be the people who execute it. This consideration underscores the importance of comprehensive and unambiguous documentation, as well as clear assignment of responsibilities with some built-in redundancy.

The following describes the steps in typical disaster recovery planning. These steps provide an overview; later sections offer a more in-depth look:

1. Establish your disaster recovery team. Assuming your organization consists of more than a handful of employees, you should inform your manager now that you need to form a team to accomplish the goal of delivering a disaster recovery plan. Identify key roles you think will be needed to staff the team. Be sure to include personnel from all aspects of the organization and avoid the temptation to staff the group with only technology-savvy people. You need a complete perspective up and down the organization, and the only way to get that is to diversify.

2. Develop a mission statement. Conduct a study of your current state of operations, identify the acceptable minimal level of operations for your organization, and state the goals of your disaster recovery process.

3. Get management buy-in. Unless management initiated the task, it is your responsibility to persuade your management personnel that disaster recovery will require their support in order to succeed. It may be the only way you can get the needed resources (time, budget, personnel) to accomplish your goals.

4. Plan for the worst. This is the part that many people find the most fun. You should start recording scenarios that describe the types of catastrophic events that could occur in your region. Include everything from theft, sabotage, weather events, and fire to disease and even worse. Be sure to start a file for these scenarios, as you will need them later when developing your recovery plans.

5. Assess your inventory and organizational resources. Make a list of all of the information technology in your organization. Be sure to include everything needed for operational success, including employee workstations and network connectivity. You should list things that exist now, not what you deem the minimal set. Reducing the assets to the minimum acceptable set will come later. You should also record the current organizational chart and the chain of command, complete with primary and secondary decision makers. Remember to write all of this down and save it for later.

6. Conduct risk assessment. Determine the effects that the loss of each of your resources could have on your organization. This will form your minimal level of operations. You should establish a priority for each resource and even establish more than one acceptable level of operations. Be sure to include a careful study of the applications and data needed. This will be used to help you decide which procedure to use when responding to events. You may be able to recover from partial losses, for instance, by redeploying your remaining systems instead of bringing up

new systems, at a savings of critical time and money. It may be that you can operate for a short period of time with lower operational capability.

7. Develop contingency plans. Now that you have the disaster scenarios, your assessment of your inventory, and your risk assessment, you can begin writing the first draft of your disaster recovery plan. These contingency plans can take any form you find useful, but most planners start making procedures using lists and narration. Use whatever format makes sense to your team.

8. Create verification procedures. No plan is useful if it falls apart during execution. Now is the time to develop procedures to verify your disaster recovery plan. Start by having mock exercises in which you walk through your list of contingencies and make any adjustments needed. Go back to step 4 and cycle through the steps as you refine your disaster recovery plan.

9. Practice makes perfect. After refining your disaster recovery plan, start real-life exercises to ensure the plan works. The ultimate goal is to demonstrate to management that you can achieve each acceptable level of operations. If you can't, go back to step 6 and cycle through the remaining steps until you reach a complete and repeatable set of procedures.

Your disaster recovery plan should have at least one full operational test yearly or whenever a major element in the organization or information technology changes.

Tools for disaster recovery

Although disaster recovery involves more than just your data and computers, the focus of disaster recovery is always the data and the information technology capabilities. There are numerous tools and strategies that you can use in your disaster recovery plans. The following are a few of the more popular tools and strategies.

Backup power
  Always include some form of uninterruptible power supply. The durability and cost of such equipment are largely dependent on how much downtime your company can permit. If you must have continuous operational capability, you will need a system capable of powering your equipment for extended periods of time.

Network connectivity
  Depending on your need to reach customers and business partners electronically, you may need to consider redundant or alternative network access. This could be as simple as different media (say, an extra fiber trunk line to your access point) or as complex as alternative connection points (like satellite or cellular carriers).

Alternative site
  If your company must have full capability and as little downtime as possible, you may need to ensure rapid recovery with no data or operational loss. The ultimate

strategy is to secure an alternative site to house your information technology or even your entire company. This can take the form of a mobile office (a temporary office trailer or similar platform) that contains a replica of your information technology.

Supplemental personnel

Disaster recovery planners often overlook this component. One possible disaster you must consider is the loss of part or all of your staff in critical roles. This could take the form of infectious disease, a hostile takeover by a rival firm, or even mass loss of life. Whatever the possible cause, you should include an analysis of the critical roles in your organization and have contingencies for filling them in the event of a disaster. One obvious choice is to cross-train personnel. This will increase your talent pool, with the added benefit of making your employees more valuable.

Backup hardware

Perhaps the most obvious aspect of continued operations is the need to have additional hardware. Your high availability technology can partially fulfill this need, but the ultimate strategy is to store replacement hardware off site (or at your alternative site) so that you can place it into service quickly. This hardware must not simply be left to gather dust, but should be up-to-date with your latest software and exercised regularly.

Secure vault

Another aspect that planners often overlook is a secure place to store backups of critical data. You should acquire a storage space at a secure facility (the level of security will depend on the value and sensitivity of your data) that matches your downtime needs. That is, if you have a very low downtime threshold, a bank or similar repository may not be able to retrieve the data fast enough. In contrast, storing backups of critical data in your basement or in a public place may not be safe enough.

High availability

As mentioned earlier, high availability options form the first layer of defense in a disaster recovery plan. The ability to fail over to alternative data repositories can help you to overcome minor events.

 Always keep copies of your data and your disaster recovery plan in a secure offsite location.

One rule of thumb applies to all disaster recovery tools and strategies: the faster you need to recover from a disaster and the greater operational capability you need to restore, the higher the cost will be. This is why it is important to develop several levels of operational capability—so that you can adapt your plan and management will have options for different levels of loss and circumstances. It may be that your company is suffering from a recession or other financial limitation and may have to sacrifice operational capability. The more options you have, the stronger your disaster recovery plan will be.

The Importance of Data Recovery

Since most businesses consider their data their most valuable asset (outside of their personnel, the most difficult asset to replace), the primary focus of most disaster recovery plans is restoring the data and making it accessible. Yes, it *is* all about the data.

Data recovery is defined as the planning, policies, and procedures for restoring the organization's data to an acceptable operating state. The most important part of data recovery is the ability to back up and restore data. The success of a backup and recovery capability is sometimes called *resiliency* or *recoverability*.

The key aspects of data recovery are the ability to plan, execute, and audit data backup and to restore operations. The one aspect that is most often overlooked is auditing. A good backup and restore service should be one that you can rely on. Too often backup systems fail without any indication that the data is absent, is corrupted in the archive, or has been destroyed. This is usually discovered the moment something goes wrong and a restore is attempted. Clearly, learning that data doesn't exist or has been corrupted during the moment of crisis can make data recovery very difficult.

Terminology

Two terms are found in almost all references to data recovery and backup solutions, so it's important to understand them:

Recovery Point Objective (RPO)
> The state of the system that is acceptable for use. Thus, RPO represents the maximum acceptable degradation of services (operational capability) or maximum acceptable data loss. Use these goals for measuring the success of a recovery action.

Recovery Time Objective (RTO)
> The maximum amount of time permitted to endure a loss of capability (also called downtime).

The RTO is affected a great deal by the RPO. If you need to recover all data (or almost all data, such as all transactions that were replicated), you will need work harder to recover it, so achieving a fast recovery—a low RTO—will be more costly. A higher RPO or lower RTO requires a bigger investment in hardware and software as well as training administrators to use systems that guarantee higher RTO and RPO, because they tend to be complex solutions. For example, if your RTO is less than three seconds and your RPO is full capability with no data loss, you must invest in an extensive high availability solution that can tolerate the complete loss of a server, data repository, etc., without loss of data (or time).

Backup and Restore

This section describes the two most important tools in data recovery. It drills down into the concepts of backup and restore, the planning you need to do, and the backup and restore solutions available.

For database systems like MySQL, backup and restore capability means making copies of the data that you can store and later reload so that the state of the data returns to the point at which the backup was made.

The following sections are provided for those who may not be familiar with backup and recovery systems and the available solutions for MySQL. We'll explore the benefits of the various solutions and how to create an archival plan that you can use to recover your data with minimal loss.

Why back up?

Some might think that a backup is not necessary if you use replication or some form of hardware redundancy. While that may be true for recovering data quickly in the event of a mechanical or electronic failure, it will not help you recover from a loss due to a catastrophic event.

Table 12-1 describes some of the most likely ways data can be lost and corresponding ways of recovering. Many of these situations, as you can see, benefit from having backups. In addition to recovery from failures and errors, there are several excellent reasons to integrate backup into your daily data protection plans. These include generating a new slave for a replication topology, using it as a tool for failover, and even using it as a means to transport data from one network to another.

Table 12-1. Common causes of data loss

Type of failure	Description	Recovery method
User error	A user accidentally deletes data or updates it with incorrect values.	Recover deleted data with a restore from backup.
Power outage	One or more systems lose power.	Employ uninterruptible power supplies.
Hardware failures	One or more components or systems fail.	Use redundant systems or replicated data.
Software failure	Data is changed or lost due to transformation.	May be difficult to detect and may require restoring from backup (if there's no way to fix the transformation).
Facility issues	The facility that houses the equipment becomes uninhabitable and connectivity to the data is lost.	You may require a new facility in order to establish an acceptable level of operations.
Network failure	The servers that contain the data are not accessible.	This may require reestablishing connectivity or establishing a new data repository.
Sabotage	Data is stolen or damaged intentionally.	Close the security breach and inspect and sanitize the data.

If you have developed your own routine backup and utilize offsite storage, you may be more prepared for disaster recovery than you think. Consider, for example, what would happen if your database system, its redundant hardware, and even its replicant (the slave in MySQL replication) were to suddenly disappear either through theft or catastrophic failure. Having regular backups available off site will allow you to recover the data and the database system up to the last backup.

Hardware Horrors

Table 12-1 describes some generalized categories of data loss. However, hardware failures are seldom routine and can often be far more serious than Table 12-1 indicates. Here are some real-world hardware failures that you may encounter, along with some tips for how to deal with the recovery:

Losing more than one disk of a hardware array
> If multiple disks of a single hardware RAID fail, it is likely that recovery will fail. If this happens (and it happens more often than you may think), you may have no choice but to restore the data in the array from backups.

Disk failure on both master and slave
> If both your master and slave systems fail (particularly if it's a disk failure), you may be without your hot standby. This can manifest in a variety of ways. For example, it is possible for a particular table (or shard) to become corrupt or for the disk it is stored on to fail on both the master and slave. Again, a restore of the data may be the only solution.

Backup power failure
> This is perhaps one of the most humiliating scenarios. Your high-value power backup system fails the moment you need it—during a power outage. If power outages are a possibility you need to prepare for, consider installing a backup plan in case your primary power backup fails.

Now let's say your database system runs on commodity hardware (MySQL is famous for its hardware independence). Along with your last backup, you can order replacement hardware or repurpose existing hardware and restore your database server to operation quickly (depending, of course, on how much data you need to restore).

The point is that having routine backups of your data is a basic and sound data recovery practice. High availability options such as replication or RAID hardware are clearly a better choice for up-to-the-second recovery, but none of these technologies can help you in the event of a catastrophic loss. You have seen that replication can help prevent data loss, but what happens, for example, if the disaster is such that both your masters and slaves are damaged beyond repair? In this case, only a good and recent backup can save you.

The following sections discuss backup in more detail and show you how you can begin making backups of your MySQL data right away.

Expectations for backups

A backup operation must have the capability to make copies of the data in a form that you can restore later. Furthermore, the backup copy must be consistent. For a transactional database, this means that the backup contains only transactions committed prior to the start of the copy, not partial or uncommitted data. Backups must also support monitoring so that you can validate the performance of the backup and the state of the data.

There are several forms of backup:

Full backup
> Makes a full backup of everything stored by the server. Nothing is omitted. This form requires the most time and storage space.

Differential backup
> Backs up just the data that changed since the last full backup. This typically requires less space than the full backup and is much faster.

Incremental backup
> Backs up only data that has changed since the last incremental or full backup. This normally takes the form of a change log (e.g., the binary log in MySQL). This backup typically takes much less time than a differential or full backup and, depending on the number of changes since the last backup, may require very little space.

When developing your data recovery plan, pick a naming convention for your backup archives (also called a backup image or simply backup file). For example, you might name each file with a date and any other pertinent information such as *full_backup_2009_09_09* or *incr_backup_week_3_september*. There is no right or wrong here, so feel free to use something that makes sense to you and meets your needs.

Expectations for the restore process

A restore operation must have the capability to replace the data on the system with data that is in an archive such that the data replaced is identical to that in the archive. Like backups, the restore process must support monitoring so that you can validate the performance of the restore and the state of the data.

Unfortunately, few backup systems meet all of these criteria for backup and restore. Those that do are often proprietary platforms (installations of customized hardware and software) that are expensive and difficult to maintain. This chapter includes economical options to back up and restore your MySQL data.

Logical versus physical backup

One misunderstood concept of backup is the difference between logical and physical modes; the choice you make can have significant effects on both the efficiency of your backups and options for restoring data.

A *logical backup* is simply a collection of normal SQL **SELECT** queries. The backup is usually built through a table scan, which is a record-by-record traversal of the data.

A *physical backup* is a copy of the original binary data (files) and it often makes a copy of the files at the operating-system level. Any backup method that involves copying the data, index, and buffer memory (files) that does not use record-by-record access is considered a physical backup.

As you might imagine, logical backups can be considerably slower than physical backups. This is because the system must use the normal SQL internal mechanisms to read one record at a time. Physical backups normally use operating system functions and do not have nearly as much overhead. Conversely, physical backups may require locking the tables associated with the binary files until the binary copy is complete, while some forms of logical backups do not lock or block access to the tables while the backup is running.

Deciding which method to use may be harder than you think. For example, if you want to make a copy of a MySQL database server that includes all of its data, you can simply take it offline, shut down the server, and copy the entire *mysql* directory to another computer. You must also include the data directories for the InnoDB files if you have changed their default locations. This will create a second instance of the server identical to the first. This may be a great way to build your replication topology, but it is very inconvenient for backing up a few important databases that cannot be taken offline. In this case, a logical backup may be your best (and only) choice.

Forming an archival plan

Getting what you need from backup and restore tools requires discipline and some thought. The most overlooked step is developing what is called an *archival plan*. This is the analysis that determines how frequently you need to make copies of your data.

The first thing you must ask yourself is, "How much data can I afford to lose in the event that I need to recover from scratch?" In other words, how much data can you afford to skip or perhaps never recover in the event of a total loss of your data? This becomes your RPO, or the level of operational capability that your company must have in order to conduct business.

Clearly, any loss of data is bad. You must consider the value of the data itself when you plan your RPOs. You may find some data is more valuable than other data. Some data may be critical to the well-being and stability of your company while other data may be less valuable. Clearly, if you identify data that is critical to your organization, it must be recovered without loss. Thus, you may come up with a few different RPOs. It is always a good practice to define several levels, then determine which one fits the recovery needs at hand.

This is important because the archival plan determines how often you must perform a backup and at what capacity (how much is backed up). If you cannot tolerate any loss of data whatsoever, you are more than likely going to have to extend your high availability options to include replication of some sort to an offsite location. But even that is not 100 percent foolproof. For instance, corruption or sabotage in the master may propagate to the replicas and go undiscovered for some time.

You are more likely to measure your tolerance for data loss by the maximum amount of time you can allow for the recovery of lost data. That is, how long can you afford to have the data unavailable while it is being recovered? This directly translates to how much money your organization can stand to lose during the downtime. For some organizations, every second that passes without access to the data is very costly. It may also be true that some data is more valuable to the company's income than other data and as such you can afford to spend more time recovering that data.

Again, you should determine several time frames, each of which is acceptable depending on the state of the business at the time. This forms your RTO options and you can match them with your RPO levels to get a picture of how much time each level of recovery requires. Determining your RTO levels can mean reentry of the data into the system or redoing some work to reacquire the data (e.g., performing another download of data or an update from a business partner).

Once you determine the amount of data loss you can tolerate (RPO) and how long you can tolerate for the recovery (RTO), you should examine the capabilities of your backup system and choose the frequency and method that meets your needs. But don't stop there. You should set up automated tasks that perform the backup during times when it is most beneficial (or least disruptive).

Finally, you should test the backups periodically by practicing data recovery (i.e., restoring the data). This will ensure you have good, viable backups free of defects, thereby ensuring safe data recovery with low risk.

Backup Utilities and OS-Level Solutions

Oracle provides the InnoDB Hot Backup solution for backing up InnoDB and MyISAM tables. Additionally, there are several third-party solutions for performing backups on MySQL. You can also perform some unsophisticated but effective backups at the operating system level.

The final section of this chapter briefly discusses the most popular alternatives:

- InnoDB Hot Backup
- Physical file copy
- The `mysqldump` utility
- XtraBackup
- Logical Volume Manager snapshots

There are other options as well, but most are similar in purpose to these.

The InnoDB Hot Backup Application

If you use InnoDB as your only storage engine, or regularly back up InnoDB tables without backing up other types, you can use the InnoDB Hot Backup application from Oracle. InnoDB Hot Backup is a commercial product. Its great advantage is that you can keep databases running for both queries and updates during the backup—you don't have to take the server offline or lock the tables explicitly.

> Hot Backup can also back up MyISAM tables, but it blocks updates for MyISAM tables while the backup is running.

InnoDB Hot Backup creates a consistent copy of all databases without blocking any transactions. You can back up some or all of the databases, compress the output file created by the backup, and perform selective backup (e.g., only specified tables).

InnoDB Hot Backup is available for MySQL version 4.0 and later and is supported on Linux, Unix, and Windows platforms. If you are interested in learning more about InnoDB Hot Backup, visit the Innobase Hot Backup website (*http://www.innodb.com/products/hot-backup/*).

> Oracle announced at the 2010 MySQL Users' Conference that the next release of InnoDB Hot Backup will become MySQL Enterprise Backup. Many new features are planned for the rebranded product.

The InnoDB Hot Backup solution is composed of two files, *ibbackup* and *innobackup*. In the following sections, we explain the details of the InnoDB Hot Backup application and demonstrate how to perform a backup and restore data.

The core backup utility is *ibbackup*. It can perform three main operations: backing up data, applying the log to a backup, and restoring data. A Perl script named *innobackup* provides a higher-level interface to *ibbackup* as well as some extended features.

Performing a backup with ibbackup

Using *ibbackup* is a bit unusual: you must pass the parameters for the backup in two files specified on the command line. The first file, which is typically the standard *my.cnf* configuration file, contains information about the databases you want to back up. The second file contains information about the files you want to create to hold the backup. The directives in each file have the same names, and their values point to information about the files on the filesystem that store the databases. A typical execution of the command looks like this:

```
ibbackup my.cnf backup.cnf
```

The parameters in each file are:

```
datadir = directory
innodb_data_home_dir = directory
innodb_data_file_path = parameter-list
innodb_log_group_home_dir = directory
innodb_log_files_in_group = group_number
innodb_log_file_size = size
```

You can find the definitions for these parameters in the online MySQL Reference Manual. The following shows a configuration file with typical settings for the first file, covering the data you want to back up:

```
[mysqld]
datadir = /usr/local/mysql/data
innodb_data_home_dir = /usr/local/mysql/data
innodb_data_file_path = ibdata1:10M:autoextend
innodb_log_group_home_dir = /usr/local/mysql/data
set-variable innodb_log_files_in_group = 2
set-variable innodb_log_file_size = 20M
```

Now let's suppose you want to write the backup files to a directory named */home/cbell/backup*. The resulting configuration file, which we called *backup.cnf* in our `ibbackup` command, will look like this:

```
datadir = /home/cbell/backup
innodb_data_home_dir = /home/cbell/backup
innodb_data_file_path = ibdata1:10M:autoextend
innodb_log_group_home_dir = /home/cbell/backup
set-variable innodb_log_files_in_group = 2
set-variable innodb_log_file_size = 20M
```

You can also make a compressed backup using the `--compress` option:

```
ibbackup --compress my.cnf backup.cnf
```

Applying the log to a backup

Because the InnoDB databases are still running while the backup operation is running, the data may not correspond to any specific point in time. If you are looking for a consistent backup, you must apply the current log to the backup files to synchronize the data. This is possible because the *ibbackup* tool creates a log called *ibbackup_logfile*, which contains the changes that occurred during the backup. You can apply this log to the backup files and roll them forward to the point in time corresponding to the moment the backup completed.

To perform this operation, you need only the backup configuration file and the `--apply-log` option, as shown here:

```
ibbackup --apply-log /home/cbell/backup.cnf
```

If you use the `compress` option, you need to supply the `--uncompress` option to apply the log to a compressed backup, as shown here:

```
ibbackup --apply-log --uncompress /home/cbell/backup.cnf
```

Restoring data with ibbackup

Restoring data requires applying the log described in the previous section. This operation essentially points the MySQL instance to the backup copies of the database. It does not copy the files to the normal MySQL *datadir* location. If you want to do this, you must copy the files manually or use the *innobackup* script. The reason for this is that the *ibbackup* utility is designed to refuse to overwrite any data. To start a MySQL instance and use a backup of your data, execute a command like the following:

```
mysqld -defaults-file=/home/cbell/backup.cnf
```

The innobackup script

The *innobackup* file is a Perl script designed to automate many of the operations of *ibbackup*. It can create backups; restore data; start a MySQL instance using the data from a backup; or copy data, index, and logfiles from a backup directory back to their original locations.

 The *innobackup* script is currently not available for use on Windows.

Unlike the *ibbackup* utility, you do not need to specify the commands in a separate configuration file for *innobackup*. Rather, you specify the parameters for the backup or restore using command-line options. These options are described in Table 12-2.

Table 12-2. innobackup options

Option	Function
--help	Displays a list of all options.
--version	Displays the version of the script.
--apply-log	Applies the backup log to the backup in preparation for starting a MySQL server with the backup files.
--copy-back	Copies data and index files from the backup location to their original locations.
--use-memory=MB	Passed to ibbackup, this option controls how much memory is used during restoration.
--sleep=MS	Passed to ibbackup, this option causes the utility to pause after every 1 Mb of data is copied.
--compress=LEVEL	Passed to ibbackup, this option provides the compression level to use.
--include=REGEXP	Passed to ibbackup, this option instructs the process to back up only those table files that match the regular expression. This is used for a selective backup.
--uncompress	Passed to ibbackup, this option uncompresses a compressed backup.
--user=NAME	Username to use for connecting to the server.
--password=PWD	Password for the user.
--port=PORT	Port for the server.
--socket=SOCK	Socket of the server.

Performing a backup with innobackup

To create a backup, you need only two options: the configuration file of the server and the location for your backup files:

```
perl innobackup /etc/mysql/my.cnf /home/cbell/backup
```

If you want a consistent backup, specify the `--apply-log` option as well:

```
perl innobackup --apply-log /etc/mysql/my.cnf /home/cbell/backup
```

Restoring data with innobackup

To restore data, apply the log and use the `--copy-back` option to copy the files to the original location. We show a sample of these commands below. You must stop the server before the copy and then restart it afterward.

```
perl innobackup --apply-log /etc/mysql/my.cnf /home/cbell/backup
mysqladmin -uroot shutdown
perl innobackup --copy-file /etc/mysql/my.cnf /home/cbell/backup
/etc/init.d/mysql start
```

Additional features

InnoDB Hot Backup also supports PITR. See the InnoDB Hot Backup documentation (*http://www.innodb.com/doc/hot_backup/manual.html*) for more details about this and other advanced features.

> You can download a trial version of InnoDB Hot Backup for evaluation purposes. This trial is active for 30 days, during which you can use InnoDB Hot Backup without limitations. To sign up for a free trial copy, visit *http://www.innodb.com/products/hot-backup/order/order/*.

Physical File Copy

The easiest and most basic form of backup for MySQL is a simple file copy. Unfortunately, this requires you to stop the server for best results. To perform a file copy, simply stop your server and copy the data directory and any setup files on the server. One common method for this is to use the Unix **tar** command to create an archive. You can then move this archive to another system and restore the data directory.

The following is a typical sequence of **tar** commands that backs up the data from one database server and restores it on another system. Execute the following command on the server you want to back up, where *backup_2009_09_09.tar.gz* is the file you want to create and */usr/loca/mysql/data* is the path for the data directory:

```
tar -czf backup_2009_09_09.tar.gz /usr/loca/mysql/data/*
```

The *backup_2009_09_09.tar.gz* file must reside on a directory shared by the two servers (or you must physically copy it to the new server). Now, on the server where you want to restore the data, change to the root installation of your new installation of MySQL. Delete the existing data directory, if it exists, then execute the following:

```
tar -xvf ../backup_2009_09_09.tar.gz
```

As mentioned earlier, it is always a good idea to use meaningful file-names for your backup images.

As you can see from this example, it is very easy to back up your data at the operating system level. Not only can you get a single compressed archive file that you can move around easily, you also get the benefit of fast file copy. You can even do a selective backup by simply copying individual files or subdirectories from your data directory.

Unfortunately, the `tar` command is available only on Linux and Unix platforms. If you have Cygwin installed on a Windows system and have included its version of the command, you can also use `tar` there.

Other than Cygwin or another Unix-on-Windows package, the closest equivalent to this command on Windows is the handy folder archive feature of the Explorer or an archive program such as WinZip. To do this, open Windows Explorer and navigate to your data directory. But instead of opening the directory, right-click the data directory and choose an option that compresses the data, which will have a label such as Send To→Compressed (zipped) Folder, and then provide a name for the *.zip* file.

While a physical file copy is the quickest and easiest form of backup, it does require that you shut down the server. But that isn't necessary if you are careful to ensure there are no updates occurring during the file copy. To do this, you must lock all tables and perform a `flush tables` command, then take your server offline before making the file copy.

This is similar to the process for cloning a slave. See Chapter 2 for more details and an example of cloning a slave using file copy.

Additionally, depending on the size of the data, your server must be offline not only for the time to copy the files, but also for any additional data loads like cache entries, the use of memory tables for fast lookups, etc. For this reason, physical copy backup may not be feasible for some installations.

Fortunately, there is a Perl script, created by Tim Bunce, to automate this process. The name of the script is *mysqlhotcopy.sh* and it is located in the *./scripts* folder of your MySQL installation. It allows you to make hot copies of databases. However, you can use it only to back up MyISAM or Archive storage engines and it works only on Unix and Netware operating systems.

The *mysqlhotcopy.sh* utility also includes customization features. You can find more information about it at *http://dev.mysql.com/doc/refman/5.4/en/mysqlhotcopy.html*.

The mysqldump Utility

The most popular alternative to the physical file copy feature is the `mysqldump` client application. It has been part of the MySQL installation for some time and was originally donated to MySQL by Igor Romanenko. `mysqldump` creates a set of SQL statements that re-create the databases when you rerun them. For example, when you run a backup, the output contains all of the `CREATE` statements needed to create the databases and the tables they contain, as well as all the `INSERT` statements needed to re-create the data in those tables.

This can be very handy if you need to do a search-and-replace operation in the text of your data. Simply back up your database, edit the resulting file with a text editor, then restore the database to effect the changes. Many MySQL users use this technique to correct all sorts of errors caused by making batch edits to the data. You will find this much easier than writing, say, 1,000 `UPDATE` statements with complicated `WHERE` clauses.

The drawbacks of using `mysqldump` are that it takes a lot more time than the binary copies made by file-level (physical) backups like InnoDB Hot Backup, LVM, or a simple offline file copy, and it requires a lot more storage space. This cost in time can be significant if you make frequent backups, want to restore a database quickly after a system failure, or need to transfer the backup file across a network.

You can use `mysqldump` to back up all your databases, a specific subset of databases, or even particular tables within a given database. The following examples show each of these options:

```
mysqldump -uroot -all-databases
mysqldump -uroot db1, db2
mysqldump -uroot my_db t1
```

You can also use `mysqldump` to do a hot backup of InnoDB tables. The `--single-trans action` option issues a `BEGIN` statement at the start of the backup, which signals the InnoDB storage engine to read the tables as a consistent read. Thus, any changes you make are applied to the tables, but the data is frozen at the time of backup. However, no other connection should use data definition language (DDL) statements like `ALTER TABLE`, `DROP TABLE`, `RENAME TABLE`, `TRUNCATE TABLE`. This is because a consistent read is not isolated from DDL changes.

 The `--single-transaction` option and the `--lock-tables` option are mutually exclusive because `LOCK TABLES` issues an implicit commit.

The utility has several options that control the backup as well as what is included. Table 12-3 describes some of the more important options. See the online MySQL Reference Manual at *http://dev.mysql.com/doc/refman/5.4/en/mysqldump.html* for a complete set of options.

Table 12-3. mysqlbackup options

Option	Function
--add-drop-database	Includes a DROP DATABASE statement before each database.
--add-drop-table	Includes a DROP TABLE statement before each table.
--add-locks	Surrounds each included table with LOCK TABLES and UNLOCK TABLES.
--all-databases	Includes all databases.
--create-options	Includes all MySQL-specific table options in the CREATE TABLE statements.
--databases	Includes a list of databases only.
--delete-master-logs	On a master, deletes the binary logs after performing the backup.
--events	Backs up events from the included databases.
--extended-insert	Uses the alternative INSERT syntax that includes each row as a VALUES clause.
--flush-logs	Flushes the logfiles before starting the backup.
--flush-privileges	Includes a FLUSH PRIVILEGES statement after backing up the *mysql* database.
--ignore-table=db.tbl	Does not back up the specified table.
--lock-all-tables	Locks all tables across all databases during the dump.
--lock-tables	Locks all tables before including them.
--log-error=filename	Appends warnings and errors to the specified file.
--master-data[=value]	Includes the binlog filename and position in the output.
--no-data	Does not write any table row information (only CREATE statements).
--password[=password]	The password to use when connecting to the server.
--port=port_num	The TCP/IP port number to use for the connection.
--result-file=filename	Outputs to a specific file.
--routines	Includes stored routines (procedures and functions).
--single-transaction	Issues a BEGIN SQL statement before dumping data from the server. This allows for a consistent snapshot of the InnoDB tables.
--tables	Overrides the --databases option.
--triggers	Includes triggers.
--where='condition'	Includes only rows selected by the condition.
--xml	Produces XML output.

You can also include these options in a MySQL configuration file under the heading [mysqldump]. In most cases, you can specify the option simply by removing the initial dashes. For example, to always produce XML output, include xml in your configuration file.

One very handy feature of mysqldump is the ability to dump a database schema. You can normally do this using a set of the CREATE commands to re-create all of the objects without the INSERT statements that include the data. This usage can be very useful for keeping a historical record of the changes to your schema. If you use the --no-data option along with the options to include all of the objects (e.g., --routines, --triggers), you can use mysqldump to create a database schema.

Notice the option --master-data. This option can be very helpful for performing PITR because it saves the binary log information like InnoDB Hot Backup does.

There are many more options that allow you to control how the utility works. If creating a backup in the form of SQL statements sounds like the best option for you, feel free to explore the rest of the options for making mysqldump work for you.

XtraBackup

Percona, an independent open source provider and consulting firm specializing in all things MySQL (LAMP, actually), has created a storage engine called XtraDB, which is an open source storage engine based on the InnoDB storage engine. XtraDB has several improvements for better scaling on modern hardware and is backward compatible with InnoDB.

In an effort to create a hot backup solution for XtraDB, Percona has created XtraBackup. This tool is optimized for InnoDB and XtraDB, but can also back up and restore MyISAM tables. It provides many of the features expected of backup solutions, including compression and incremental backup.

You can download and build XtraBackup by getting the source code from Launchpad at *https://launchpad.net/percona-xtrabackup*. You can compile and execute XtraBackup on most platforms. It is compatible with MySQL versions 5.0 and 5.1.

The online manual for XtraBackup is located at *http://www.percona.com/docs/wiki/percona-xtrabackup:xtrabackup_manual*.

Logical Volume Manager Snapshots

Most Linux and some Unix systems provide another powerful method of backing up your MySQL database. It makes use of a technology called the *logical volume manager* (LVM).

Microsoft Windows has a similar technology called *Volume Shadow Copy.* Unfortunately, there are no generic utilities to make a snapshot of a random partition or folder structure as there are for LVM. You can, however, make snapshots of an entire drive, which can be useful if your database directory is the only thing on that drive. See the Microsoft online documentation for more information.

An LVM is a disk subsystem that gives you a lot of administrative power to create, remove, and resize volumes easily and quickly without using the older, often complicated and unforgiving disk tools.

The added benefit for backup is the concept of taking a *snapshot*—that is, a copy of an active volume—without disrupting the applications that access the data on that volume. The idea is to take a snapshot, which is a relatively fast operation, and then back up the snapshot instead of the original volume. Deep inside LVM, a snapshot is managed using a mechanism that keeps track of the changes since you took the snapshot, so that it stores only the disk segments that have changed. Thus, a snapshot takes up less space than a complete copy of the volume and when the backup is made, the LVM copies the files as they existed at the time of the snapshot. Snapshots effectively freeze the data.

Another benefit of using LVM and snapshots for backing up database systems lies in how you use the volumes. The best practice is to use a separate volume for each of your MySQL installations so that all of the data is on the same volume, allowing you to create a backup quickly using a snapshot. Of course, it is also possible to use multiple logical volumes in some situations, such as using one logical volume for each tablespace or even different logical volumes for MyISAM and InnoDB tables.

Getting started with LVM

If your Linux installation does not have LVM installed, you can install it using your package manager. For example, on Ubuntu you can install LVM using the following command:

```
sudo apt-get install lvm2
```

Although not all LVM systems are the same, the following procedure is based on a typical Debian distribution and works well on systems like Ubuntu. We don't mean to write a complete tutorial on LVM but just to give you an idea of the complexity of using LVM for making database backups. Consult your operating system documentation for specifics about the type of LVM your system supports, or simply browse the many how-to documents available on the Web.

Before we get started with the details, let's take a moment to understand the basic concepts of LVM. There is a hierarchy of levels to the LVM implementation. At the lowest level is the disk itself. On top of that are *partitions,* which allow us to communicate with the disk. On top of the partition we create a *physical volume,* which is the control mechanism that the LVM provides. You can add a physical volume to a *volume group* (which can contain multiple physical volumes), and a volume group can contain one or more *logical volumes*. Figure 12-1 depicts the relationship among filesystems, volume groups, physical volumes, and block devices.

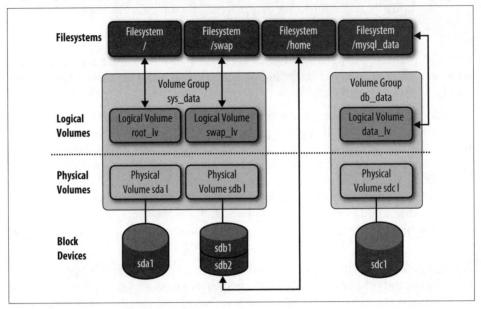

Figure 12-1. Anatomy of LVM

A logical volume can act as either a normal mounted filesystem or a snapshot. The creation of a snapshot logical volume is the key to using snapshots for backup. The following sections describe how you can get started experimenting with LVM and making backups of your data.

There are several useful commands that you should become familiar with. The following list contains the most frequently used commands and their uses. Be sure to consult the documentation for more information about these commands:

pvcreate
:   Creates a physical volume

pvscan
:   Shows details about the physical volumes

vgcreate
:   Creates volume groups

vgscan
:   Shows details about volume groups

lvcreate
:   Creates a logical volume

`lvscan`

Shows details about logical volumes

`lvremove`

Removes a logical volume

`mount`

Mounts a logical volume

`umount`

Unmounts a logical volume

To use LVM, you need to have either a new disk or a disk device that you can logically unmount. The process is as follows (the output here was generated on a laptop running Ubuntu version 9.04):

1. Create a backup of an existing MySQL data directory.

   ```
   tar -czf  ~/my_backups/backup.tar.gz /dev/mysql/datadir
   ```

2. Partition the drive.

   ```
   sudo parted
   select /dev/sdb
   mklabel msdos
   mkpart test
   quit
   ```

3. Create a physical volume for the drive.

   ```
   sudo pvcreate /dev/sdb
   ```

4. Create a volume group.

   ```
   sudo vgcreate /dev/sdb mysql
   ```

5. Create a logical volume for your data. Here we create a 20 GB volume.

   ```
   sudo lvcreate -L20G -ndatadir mysql
   ```

6. Create a filesystem on the logical volume.

   ```
   mke2fs /dev/mysql/datadir
   ```

7. Mount the logical volume.

   ```
   sudo mkdir /mnt
   sudo mount /dev/mysql/datadir /mnt
   ```

8. Copy the archive and restore your data to the logical volume.

   ```
   sudo cp ~/my_backups/backup.tar.gz
   sudo tar -xvf backup.tar.gz
   ```

9. Create an instance of a MySQL server and use `--datadir` to point to the folder on the logical volume.

   ```
   ./mysqld --console -uroot --datadir=/mnt
   ```

If you want to experiment with LVM, we recommend you use a disk whose data you can afford to lose. A good, cheap option is a small USB hard drive.

That's all you need to get started with a logical volume. Take some time to experiment with the LVM tools, until you are certain you can work with them effectively, before you start using them for your production systems.

LVM in a backup and restore

To do your backup, you need to flush and temporarily lock all of the tables, take the snapshot, and then unlock the tables. The lock is necessary to ensure all of your ongoing transactions are finished. The process is shown here along with the shell-level commands that perform the operations:

1. Issue a `FLUSH TABLES WITH READ LOCK` command in a MySQL client.
2. Create a snapshot of your logical volume (the `-s` option specifies a snapshot).

   ```
   sudo lvcreate -L20M -s -n backup /dev/mysql/datadir
   ```
3. Issue an `UNLOCK TABLES` command in a MySQL client (your server can now resume its operations).
4. Mount the snapshot.

   ```
   sudo mkdir /mnts
   sudo mount /dev/mysql/backup /mnts
   ```
5. Perform a backup of the snapshot.

   ```
   tar -[FIXTHIS]f snapshot.tar.gz /mnts
   ```

Of course, the best use of the snapshot is to initiate a copy periodically so that you can do another backup. There are scripts available from volunteers on the Web to automate this process, but the tried and true mechanism is to remove the snapshot and re-create it using the following procedure:

1. Unmount the snapshot.

   ```
   sudo umount /mnts
   ```
2. Remove the snapshot (logical volume).

   ```
   sudo lvremove /dev/mysql/backup
   ```

You can then re-create the snapshot and perform your backup. If you create your own script, we recommend adding the snapshot removal after you have verified the backup archive was created. This will ensure your script performs proper cleanup.

If you need to restore the snapshot, simply restore the data. The real benefit of LVM is that all of the operations for creating the snapshot and the backup using the tar utility allow you to create a customized script that you can run periodically (such as a cron job), which can help you automate your backups.

LVM in ZFS

The procedure for performing a backup using Sun Microsystems' ZFS filesystem (available in Solaris 10) is very similar to the Linux LVM procedure. We describe the differences here for those of you using Solaris.

In ZFS, you store your logical volumes (which Sun calls filesystems for read/write and snapshots for read-only copies) in a pool (similar to the volume group). To make a copy or backup, simply create a snapshot of a filesystem.

Issue the following commands to create a ZFS filesystem that you can manage:

```
zpool create -f mypool c0d0s5
zfs create mypool/mydata
```

Use the following command to make a backup (take a snapshot of the new filesystem):

```
zfs snapshot mypool/mydata@backup_12_Dec_2009
```

Use the following commands to restore the filesystem to a specific backup:

```
cd /mypool/mydata
zfs rollback mypool/mydata@backup_12_Dec_2009
```

ZFS provides not only full volume (filesystem) backups, but also supports selective file restore. For more information about ZFS and performing backup and restore, visit *http://dlc.sun.com/osol/docs/content/ZFSADMIN/gavvx.html.*

Comparison of Backup Methods

InnoDB Hot Backup, mysqldump, and third-party backup options differ along a number of important dimensions, and there is almost no end to the nuances of how each method works. We provide a comparison of backup methods here based on whether they allow for hot backups, their cost, the speed of the backup, the speed of the restore, the type of backup (logical or physical), platform restrictions (operating system), and supported storage engines. Table 12-4 lists each of the backup methods mentioned in this chapter along with a column for each comparison item.

Table 12-4. Comparison of backup methods

	InnoDB Hot Backup	mysqldump	Physical copy	XtraBackup	LVM/ZFS snapshot
Hot backup?	Yes (InnoDB only)	Yes (InnoDB only requires --single-transaction)	No	Yes (InnoDB and XtraDB only)	Yes (requires table flush with lock)
Cost	Paid license	Free	Free	Free	Free
Backup speed	Medium	Slow	Fast	Medium	Fast
Restore speed	Fast	Slow	Fast	Fast	Fast
Type	Physical	Logical	Physical	Physical	Physical

	InnoDB Hot Backup	mysqldump	Physical copy	XtraBackup	LVM/ZFS snapshot
OS	All	All	All	All	LVM supported only
Engines	InnoDB, MyISAM	All	All	InnoDB, XtraDB, MyISAM	All

 InnoDB Hot Backup is not supported fully on Windows. The Perl script does not execute on some Windows configurations. See the online documentation for more details.

Table 12-4 can help you plan your data recovery procedures by allowing you to find the best tool for the job given your needs. For example, if you need a hot backup for your InnoDB database and cost is not a factor, the Innobase InnoDB Hot Backup application is the best choice. On the other hand, if speed is a factor, you need something that can back up all databases (all storage engines), and you work on a Linux system, LVM is a good choice.

Backup and MySQL Replication

There are two ways to use backup with MySQL replication. In previous chapters, you learned about MySQL replication and its many uses for scale-out and high availability. In this chapter, we examine two more common uses for MySQL replication involving backup. These include using replication to create a backup copy of the data and using backups taken previously for PITR.

Backup and recovery
> Keeping an extra server around for creating backups is very common; it allows you to create your backups without disturbing the main server at all, since you can take the backup server offline and do whatever you like with it.

PITR
> Even if you create your backups regularly, you may have to restore the server to an exact point in time. By administering your backups properly, you can actually restore the server to the granularity of a specific second. This can be very useful in recovering from human error—such as mistyping commands or entering incorrect data—or reverting changes that are not needed anymore. The possibilities are endless, but they require the existence of proper backups.

Backup and Recovery with Replication

One shortcoming of backups in general is that they are created at a specific time (usually late at night to avoid disturbing other operations). If there is a problem that requires you to restore the master to some point after you created the backup, you will be out of luck, right? Nope! As it turns out, this is indeed not only possible, but quite easy if you combine the backups with the binary logs.

The binary log records all changes that are made to the database while the database is running, so by restoring the correct backup and playing back the binary log up to the appropriate second, you can actually restore a server to a precise moment in time.

The most important step in a recovery procedure is, of course, recovery. So let's focus on performing recovery before outlining the procedure for performing a backup.

PITR

The most frequent use for backup in replication is PITR, the ability to recover from an error (such as data loss or hardware failure) by restoring the system to a state as close as possible to the most recent correct state, thus minimizing the loss of data. For this to work, you must have performed at least one backup.

Once you repair the server, you can restore the latest backup image and apply the binary log using that binary log name and position as the starting point.

The following describes one procedure you can use to perform PITR using the backup system:

1. Return your server to an operational state after the event.
2. Find the latest backup for the databases you need to restore.
3. Restore the latest backup image.
4. Apply the binary log using the `mysqlbinlog` utility using the starting position (or starting date/time) from the last backup.

At this point, you may be wondering, "Which binary log do I use for PITR after a backup?" The answer depends on how you performed the backup. If you flushed the binary log prior to running the backup, you need to use the name and position of the current log (the newly opened logfile). If you did not flush the binary log prior to running the backup, use the name and position of the previous log.

 For easier PITR, always flush the logs prior to a backup. The starting point is then at the start of the file.

Restoring after an error is replicated

Now let's see how a backup can help you recover unintentional changes in a replication topology. Suppose one of your users has made a catastrophic (yet valid) change that is replicated to all of your slaves. Replication cannot help you here, but the backup system can come to the rescue.

Perform the following steps to recover from unintentional changes to data in a replication topology:

1. Drop the databases on the master.
2. Stop replication.
3. Restore the latest backup image before the event on the master.
4. Record the master's current binlog position.
5. Restore the latest backup image before the event on the slaves.
6. Perform a PITR on the master, as described in the previous section.
7. Restart replication from the recorded position and allow the slaves to sync.

In short, a good backup strategy is not only a necessary protection against data loss, but an important tool in your replication toolbox.

Recovery example

Now, let's look at a concrete example. Assume you're creating backups regularly every morning at 2:00 A.M. and save the backup images away somewhere for later usage. For this example, let's assume all binary logs are available and that none are removed. In reality, you will prune the binlog files regularly to keep the disk space down, but let's consider how to handle that later.

You have been tasked with recovering the database to its state at 2009-12-19 12:54:23, because that's when the manager's favorite pictures were accidentally deleted by his overzealous assistant, who took his "Could you please clean my desk?" request to include the computer desktop as well.

1. Locate the backup image that was taken before 2009-12-19 12:54:23.

   It does not actually make any difference which one you pick, but to save on the recovery time, you should probably pick the one closest, which would then be the backup image dated in the morning of the same day.

2. Restore the backup image on the machine to create an exact copy of the database at 2009-12-19 02:00:00.

3. Locate all the binlog files that include the entire range from 2009-12-19 02:00:00 to 2009-12-19 12:54:23. It does not matter if there are events from before the start time or after the end time, but it is critical that the binlog files cover the entire range you want.

4. Play the binlog files back using the `mysqlbinlog` utility and give a start time of 2009-12-19 02:00:00 and an end time of 2009-12-19 12:54:23.

You can now tell your manager that his favorite pictures are back.

To automate this, it is necessary to do some bookkeeping. This will give you an indication of what you need to save when doing the backup, so let's go through the information that you will require when doing a recovery.

- To use the backup images correctly, it is critical to label each with the start and end time it represents. This will help you determine which image to pick.
- You also need the binlog position of the backup. This is necessary because the time is not sufficiently precise in deciding where to start playing back the binlog files.
- You also need to keep information about what range each binlog file represents. Strictly speaking, this is not required, but it can be quite helpful because it helps you avoid processing all binlog files of a recovery image. This is not something that the MySQL server does automatically, so you have to handle it yourself.
- You cannot keep these files around forever, so it is important to sort all the information, backup images, and binlog files in such a way that you can easily archive them when you need to free up some disk space.

Recovery images

To help you administer all the information about your backups in manageable chunks, we introduce the concept of a *recovery image*. The recovery image is just a virtual container and is not a physical entity: it contains only information about where all the necessary pieces are to be able to perform recovery.

Figure 12-2 shows a sequence of recovery images and the contents of each. The final recovery image in the sequence is special and is called the *open recovery image*. This is the recovery image that you are still adding changes to, hence it does not have an end time yet. The other recovery images are called *closed recovery images* and these have an end time.

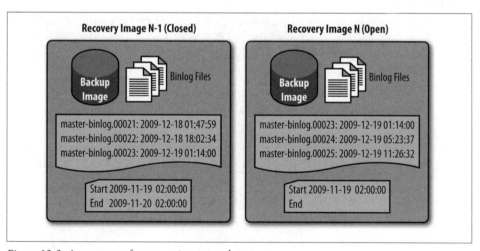

Figure 12-2. A sequence of recovery images and contents

Each recovery image has some pieces of information that are necessary to perform a recovery:

A backup image
> The backup image is required for restoring the database.

A set of binlog files
> Binlog files must cover the entire range for the recovery image.

Start time and an optional end time
> These are the start and end time that the recovery image represents. If this is the open recovery image, it does not have an end time. This recovery image is not practical to archive, so for our purposes, the end time of this recovery image is the current time.

> The binlog files usually contain events outside the range of start and end times, but all events in that range should be in the recovery image.

A list of the name and start time for each binlog file
> To extract the correct binlog files from, say, an archive, you need the names and the start and end times for each file. You can extract the start time for the binlog file using `mysqlbinlog`.

Backup procedure

The backup procedure gathers all the information required and structures it so that we can use it for both archiving and recovery. For this procedure, assume that we are going to create recovery image n and that we have a sequence of recovery images, Image_1 to Image_{n-1}.

1. Create a backup using your favorite method and note the name of the backup image and the binlog position it represents. The binlog position also contains the binlog filename.

   If you used an offline backup tool, the backup time is the time when you locked the tables, and the binlog position is the position given by SHOW MASTER STATUS after you locked the database.

2. Create a new open recovery Image_n with the following parameters:
   - $\text{Backup}(\text{Image}_n)$ is now the backup image from step 1.
   - $\text{Position}(\text{Image}_n)$ is the position from step 1.
   - $\text{BinlogFiles}(\text{Image}_n)$ is unknown, but it starts with the filename from the position from step 1.
   - $\text{StartTime}(\text{Image}_n)$ is the start time of the image, which is taken from the event at the binlog position from step 1.

3. Close Image$_{n-1}$, noting the following:

- BinlogFiles(Image$_{n-1}$) is now the binlog files from Position(Image$_{n-1}$) to Position(Image$_n$).
- EndTime(Image$_{n-1}$) is now the same as StartTime(Image$_n$).

PITR in Python

To manage the various sorts of backup methods in a consistent manner, we've created the class `PhysicalBackup` in Example 12-1. The class holds two methods:

`class PhysicalBackup.PhysicalBackup(image_name)`
> The constructor for the class takes the name of an image that it will use when backing up or restoring a server.

`PhysicalBackup.backup_from(server)`
> This method will create a backup of the server and store it under the image name given to the constructor.

`PhysicalBackup.restore_on(server)`
> This method will use the backup image for the backup and restore it on server.

By using a class to represent a backup method in this manner, it is easy to replace the backup method with any other method as long as it has these methods.

Example 12-1. Class for representing the physical backup method

```
class BackupImage(object):
    "Class for representing a backup image"

    def __init__(self, backup_url):
        self.url = urlparse.urlparse(backup_url)

    def backup_server(self, server, db):
        "Backup databases from a server and add them to the backup image."
        pass

    def restore_server(self, server):
        "Restore the databases in an image on the server"
        pass

class PhysicalBackup(BackupImage):
    "A physical backup of a database"

    def backup_server(self, server, db="*"):
        datadir = server.fetch_config().get('datadir')
        if db == "*":
            db = [d for d in os.listdir(datadir)
                    if os.path.isdir(os.path.join(datadir, d))]
        server.sql("FLUSH TABLES WITH READ LOCK")
        position = replicant.fetch_master_pos(server)
        if server.host != "localhost":
            path = basename(self.url.path)
        else:
```

```
            path = self.url.path
        server.ssh(["tar", "zpscf", path, "-C", datadir] + db)
        if server.host != "localhost":
            subprocess.call(["scp", server.host + ":" + path, self.url.path])
        server.sql("UNLOCK TABLES")
        return position

    def restore_server(self, server):
        if server.host == "localhost":
            path = self.url.path
        else:
            path = basename(self.url.path)

        datadir = server.fetch_config().get('datadir')

        try:
            server.stop()
            if server.host != "localhost":
                call(["scp", self.url.path, server.host + ":" + path])
            server.ssh(["tar", "zxf", path, "-C", datadir])
        finally:
            server.start()
```

The next step is to introduce a representation of the recovery image, as shown in Example 12-2. The recovery image stores the pieces of information as five fields:

`RecoveryImage.backup_image`
    The backup image to use.

`RecoveryImage.start_time`
    The start time of the recovery image.

`RecoveryImage.start_position`
    The binlog position that the backup image represents. Use this instead of the start time as the starting point for playing back the binlog files, since it will be accurate. There can be a lot of transactions executed during a second, and using the start time will fail because it will pick the first event with the start time, while the real start position may be somewhere else.

`RecoveryImage.binlog_files`
    A list of the binlog files that are part of this recovery image.

`RecoveryImage.binlog_datetime`
    A dictionary mapping binlog filenames to date/times, which are the date/time of the first event of the binlog file.

In addition, the recovery image must have the following utility methods:

`RecoveryImage.contains(datetime)`
    Decides whether `datetime` is contained in the recovery image. Since the binlog file may have been rotated mid-second, the `end_time` is inclusive.

`RecoveryImage.backup_from(server)`

Creates a new open recovery image by creating a backup of **server** and collects information about the backup.

`RecoveryImage.restore_to(server, datetime)`

Restores the recovery image on the server so that all changes up to and including `datetime` are applied. This assumes `datetime` is in the range for the recovery image. If `datetime` is before the recovery image's start time, nothing will be applied, and if it is after the recovery image's end time, all will be applied.

Example 12-2. A representation of a recovery image

```python
class RecoveryImage(object):
    def __init__(self, backup_method):
        self.backup_method = backup_method
        self.backup_position = None
        self.start_time = None
        self.end_time = None
        self.binlog_files = []
        self.binlog_datetime = {}

    def backup_from(self, server, datetime):
        self.backup_position = backup_method.backup_from(server)

    def restore_to(self, server):
        backup_method.restore_on(server)

    def contains(self, datetime):
        if self.end_time:
            return self.start_time <= datetime < self.end_time
        else:
            return self.start_time <= datetime
```

Because managing the recovery images requires manipulating several images, we introduce the `RecoveryImageManager` class in Example 12-3. The class contains two methods in addition to the constructor:

`RecoveryImageManager.point_in_time_recovery(server, datetime)`

A method to perform PITR of **server** to `datetime`

`RecoveryImageManager.point_in_time_backup(server)`

A method to perform a backup of the server for PITR

The recovery image manager keeps track of all recovery images and the backup method used. Here we assume that the same backup method is used for all the recovery images, but that is not strictly required.

Example 12-3. RecoveryImageManager class

```python
class RecoveryImageManager(object):
    def __init__(self, backup_method):
        self.__images = []
        self.__backup_method = backup_method
```

```
def point_in_time_recovery(server, datetime):
    from itertools import takewhile
    from subprocess import Popen, PIPE

    for im in images:
        if im.contains(datetime):
            image = im
            break
    image.restore_on(server)

    def before(file):
        return image.binlog_datetime(file) < datetime

    files = takewhile(before, image.binlog_files)
    command = ["mysqlbinlog",
               "--start-position=%s" % (image.backup_position.pos),
               "--stop-datetime=%s" % (datetime)]
    mysqlbinlog_proc = Popen(mysqlbinlog_command + files, stdout=PIPE)

    mysql_command = ["mysql",
                     "--host=%s" % (server.host),
                     "--user=%s" % (server.sql_user.name),
                     "--password=%s" % (server.sql_user.password)]
    mysql_proc = Popen(mysql_command, stdin=mysqlbinlog_proc.stdout)
    output = mysql_proc.communicate()[0]

def point_in_time_backup(self, server):
    new_image = RecoveryImage(self.__backup_method)
    new_image.backup_position = image.backup_from(server)
    new_image.start_time = event_datetime(new_image.backup_position)

    prev_image = self.__images[-1].binlog_files
    prev_image.binlog_files = binlog_range(prev_image.backup_position.file,
                                           new_image.backup_position.file)
    prev_image.end_time = new_image.start_time

    self.__images.append(new_image)
```

Automating Backups

It is fairly easy to automate backups. In the previous section, we demonstrated how to do a backup and recovery with replication. In this section, we generalize the procedure to make it easier to do nonreplication-related backup and restore.

The only issue you may encounter is providing a mechanism to automatically name the backup image file. There are many ways to do this, and Example 12-4 shows a method that names the file using the backup time. You can add this backup method to the Python library to complement your replication methods. This is the same library shown in previous chapters.

Example 12-4. Backup script

```python
#!/usr/bin/python

import MySQLdb, optparse

# --
# Parse arguments and read Configuration
# --
parser = optparse.OptionParser()
parser.add_option("-u", "--user", dest="user",
                  help="User to connect to server with")
parser.add_option("-p", "--password", dest="password",
                  help="Password to use when connecting to server")
parser.add_option("-d", "--database", dest="database",
                  help="Database to connect to")
(opts, args) = parser.parse_args()

if not opts.password or not opts.user or not opts.database:
    parser.error("You have to supply user, password, and database")

try:
    print "Connecting to server..."
    #
    # Connect to server
    #
    dbh = MySQLdb.connect(host="localhost", port=3306,
                          unix_socket="/tmp/mysql.sock",
                          user=opts.user, passwd=opts.password,
                          db=opts.database)

    #
    # Perform the restore
    #
    from datetime import datetime

    filename = datetime.time().strftime("backup_%Y-%m-%d_%H-%M-%S.bak")
    dbh.cursor().execute("[BACKUP COMMAND]%s'" % filename)
    print "\nBACKUP complete."

except MySQLdb.Error, (n, e):
    print 'CRITICAL: Connect failed with reason:', e
```

 Substitute the executable command for your backup solution for [*BACKUP COMMAND*].

Automating restores is a bit easier if you consider that there is no need to create a backup image name. However, depending on your installation, usage, and configuration, you may need to add commands to ensure there is no destructive interaction with activities by other applications or users. Example 12-5 shows a typical restore method that you can add to the Python library to complement your replication methods.

Example 12-5. Restore script

```python
#!/usr/bin/python

import MySQLdb, optparse

# --
# Parse arguments and read Configuration
# --
parser = optparse.OptionParser()
parser.add_option("-u", "--user", dest="user",
                help="User to connect to server with")
parser.add_option("-p", "--password", dest="password",
                help="Password to use when connecting to server")
parser.add_option("-d", "--database", dest="database",
                help="Database to connect to")
(opts, args) = parser.parse_args()

if not opts.password or not opts.user or not opts.database:
    parser.error("You have to supply user, password, and database")

try:
    print "Connecting to server..."
    #
    # Connect to server
    #
    dbh = MySQLdb.connect(host="localhost", port=3306,
                        unix_socket="/tmp/mysql.sock",
                        user=opts.user, passwd=opts.password,
                        db=opts.database)

    #
    # Perform the restore
    #
    from datetime import datetime

    filename = datetime.time().strftime("backup_%Y-%m-%d_%H-%M-%S.bak")
    dbh.cursor().execute("[RESTORE COMMAND]%S'",
                        (database, filename))
    print "\nRestore complete."
except MySQLdb.Error, (n, e):
    print 'CRITICAL: Connect failed with reason:', e
```

 Substitute the executable command for your backup solution for [*RESTORE COMMAND*].

As you can see in Example 12-5, you can automate a restore. However, most people prefer to execute the restore manually. One scenario in which an automated restore might be helpful is in a testing environment where you want to start with a baseline and restore a database to a known state. Another use is in a development system where you want to preserve a certain environment for each project.

Conclusion

In this chapter, we studied IA and drilled down to the aspects that most affect you as an IT professional. We saw the importance of disaster recovery planning and how to make your own disaster recovery plan, and we saw how the database system is an integral part of disaster recovery. Finally, we examined several ways you can protect your MySQL data by making regular backups.

In the next few chapters, we will examine more advanced MySQL topics, including MySQL Enterprise, cloud computing, and MySQL Cluster.

Joel glanced at his terminal window and issued another command to check on his database backups. He had set up a recurring backup script to back up all of his databases and felt confident this simple operation was working. He lamented that it was only a small start toward getting his disaster recovery plan written. He looked forward to experimenting with more scripts and scheduling his first disaster planning meeting. He already had several of his new colleagues in mind for the team. A sharp rap on his door startled him from his thoughts.

"Did you get that media order in yet, Joel? What about that plan thing?" Mr. Summerson asked.

Joel smiled and said, "Yes, and I've determined I can back up the entire database with just a..."

"Hey, that's great, Joel. I don't need the details; just keep us off of the auditor's radar. OK?"

Joel smiled and nodded as his boss disappeared on his way to execute a drive-by tasking on another employee. He wondered if his boss really understood the amount of work it would take to reach that goal. He opened his email application and started composing a message to request more personnel and resources.

MySQL Enterprise

Joel clicked open another terminal window and read the output. He rubbed his eyes until his vision cleared. The numbers were beginning to run together as he tried to keep tabs on all of his servers spread out over three sites. His report was overdue.

He had tried using a spreadsheet to tabulate the data, which had worked when he had only a few servers, but it was getting tedious now that he had more than 30 to monitor. His friends had tried to convince him to buy an enterprise monitoring suite, but his boss had a reputation of vetoing any purchases that didn't immediately contribute to the company's ability to produce revenue.

"Hey, Joel."

Joel looked up to see his friend Doug from customer support standing at his door with a stained coffee cup in hand. "Hey," Joel replied.

"You look like you could use a break."

"No time. I've got to get a report together that shows the status of all of the servers and I can't write it until I finish checking each server."

"Wow, that's a real hands-on approach."

"I know. I've read about these enterprise suites that make this all easier to do, but I don't know which one to buy or even if Mr. Summerson will sign off on it."

"Well, if you could show him how much time it takes you to do all this..." Doug said, with a dangerous wave of his mug.

Joel thought for a moment. "If only I could show him the difference between what I've had to slog through and what it would be like to use a good tool...."

"Good plan. Now how about a cup? My treat."

Joel followed Doug to the break room and chatted with him about a recent Dave Matthews Band concert they'd attended.

When Joel returned to his office, he started reading about the MySQL Enterprise offering from Oracle.

Monitoring a group of servers can be a lot of work. The tools needed to properly monitor a server are numerous and while most are easy to use once you understand what they do, they still require a bit of work to get going. Scripting and even some creative web hosting can help manage the execution of the various tools and the collection of the data, but as the number of servers to monitor grows, the task of collecting and analyzing all of the data can become time-consuming.

The monitoring techniques discussed so far in this book can become unmanageable for installations with more than a few servers. Indeed, manual monitoring and reporting can turn into a full-time job for one or more technicians in an organization with dozens of servers.

 We focus on monitoring in this chapter, but the same can be said about administration. Specifically, administrators often see time savings when they use administration tools that permit automation of common tasks, such as running scripts to populate tables, performing table maintenance, etc.

Fortunately, this problem isn't new, nor is it insurmountable. Indeed, there are several enterprise monitoring suites that can make life in a sea of servers much easier.

One of the most underestimated tools available for monitoring MySQL is the MySQL Enterprise Monitor (MEM), which comes with the MySQL Enterprise subscription. The MEM tools can greatly enhance monitoring and preventive maintenance and can dramatically reduce diagnostic time and downtime. While it is a fee-based tool, the savings of having a well-maintained data center will more than cover the cost.

This chapter introduces the MySQL Enterprise suite of tools and shows you how they will save you time while keeping your MySQL servers running at the highest levels of performance and availability. We also include an example of the monitoring tools running on a complex replication topology.

Getting Started with MySQL Enterprise

MySQL Enterprise was launched in 2006 and comprises the Enterprise MySQL server release, a set of monitoring tools, and product support services. This new packaging is intended for customers who use MySQL for data management. Early on, MySQL recognized the need organizations have for stability and reliability. MySQL Enterprise was the answer to this need.

 If you are not ready to purchase a MySQL Enterprise subscription or you want to try it out for a while before deciding, you can get a trial subscription that will last for 30 days. Apply for a trial subscription at *http://mysql.com/trials/*.

MySQL Enterprise adds the web-based MEM application, along with a separate MySQL server instance to be a repository for the metrics collected by other applications installed on your MySQL servers, called *agents*. MEM combines the metrics into reports that you can enhance with heuristics called *advisors* that help you enforce best practices based on MySQL research and expertise. The reports are displayed on a web page called a *dashboard*. We'll discuss later in this chapter how to install and use these components.

The following sections describe the available options for the MySQL Enterprise subscription service as well as an overview of the installation process. Later sections describe the features and benefits in more detail.

Subscription Levels

You can purchase the MySQL Enterprise Suite at one of four subscription levels, called basic, silver, gold, and platinum. The basic level is the least expensive and offers the fewest tools. The next three levels offer graduated levels of tool support. Thus, you can choose the level that best meets both your budget and needs for improving the availability of your servers:

Basic
> This level includes the Pro version of the MySQL server. It provides basic coverage for the MySQL server, including software updates and two support incidents. Support turnaround and response time is two business days. Also included is access to MySQL's vast knowledge base for researching common problems and solutions. This level does not include the monitoring tools. The basic level is best for organizations that need production-quality software but may not need advanced monitoring or immediate response to support issues.

Silver
> This level includes the options for the basic level along with the monitoring tools with a limited set of advisors for administration and upgrades. A phone support option is included, with unlimited incident reports, and turnaround time is four hours. The silver level is a good start for most organizations that rely on MySQL for their database management solutions and that want to ensure their installations are configured correctly.

Gold
> This level adds the Advanced version of the MySQL server (which includes partitioning) and includes all options for the silver level plus additional advisors for monitoring replication and memory. It also includes the MySQL Query Analyzer option for the monitor. Consultation support is added, covering replication and partitioning. Response times for incident reports are two hours, with an emergency response option. The gold level is an excellent choice for organizations that use replication as part of their MySQL installations.

Platinum

This level includes all of the options from the gold level, plus all advisors, expanded consultation support for all areas, 24/7 phone support, and a one-hour response to incidents, with a 30-minute emergency response time. This level even provides an option for having a custom build of the MySQL server. The platinum level is for organizations that need the highest level of support for their most critical data management needs.

With so many options to choose from, you can add more support as your business grows. You can find specific details about pricing and what is included with each level at *http://mysql.com/products/enterprise/features.html*.

Installation Overview

When you purchase a MySQL Enterprise subscription, you are given a product key and login credentials to the MySQL Enterprise portal. Connection to this portal is necessary to activate the MySQL Enterprise tools. The portal is your one-stop location for downloading updates, checking for upgrades, news, information about your subscription, and access to the knowledge base.

The portal is called the MySQL Enterprise Customer Center and it is located at *https://enterprise.mysql.com/*.

> For offline installations and those without an Internet connection on the server on which you want to install MySQL Enterprise, you can download your product key via a file from the portal and use that during the installation. You will also need your advisory bundle *.jar* file. You can download both of these files from the portal.

Visit the portal first to download the Enterprise tools installation files for your platforms, your production release of the MySQL server, the Getting Started guide, and Enterprise documentation. Be sure to read the Getting Started guide, as it has specific instructions for installing and configuring the Enterprise tools for Mac OS X, Linux, and Windows platforms.

Complete detailed installation instructions are beyond the scope of this book. However, we briefly describe the steps necessary to install and configure the MySQL Enterprise suite. Installation involves the following steps (at a minimum):

1. Install the service manager component, including the metrics repository (a separate installation of MySQL), which is operating system–specific. For example, you would install the file named *mysqlmonitor-2.1.0.1096-osx-installer* on a Mac OS X system.

2. Activate your subscription and enable the Enterprise Dashboard. During this stage, you are required to enter your product key, either via a file or by logging into the MySQL Enterprise portal.

3. Install the monitoring agent on your MySQL servers. This is also operating system–specific. For example, you would install an agent such as *mysqlmonitor-agent-2.1.0.1093-linux-glibc2.3-x86-32bit-installer.bin* on Linux systems.

4. Configure the dashboard to reflect your environment.

While it is possible to install the monitor agent on any server and monitor another, it is best to install the agent on the server you wish to monitor. This permits the agent to send operating system statistics, performance data, and configuration parameters to the Dashboard. If you install the agent on another system, the system section of the Dashboard report for the MySQL server will be blank.

It is possible to configure an agent to report statistics for multiple servers as well as to report to multiple monitors. The former lets a single agent monitor two or more instances of the MySQL server on a single system; the latter allows multiple dashboards to report data from MEM. Both of these scenarios are described in the MEM reference manual.

The installation of the MEM package includes a self-contained web server and MySQL instance that you install on the system where you want to host the Dashboard and metrics collection. This system is the destination for each of the monitoring agents. This process is very easy to perform and does not require any web administration expertise.

During the installation of the monitor package, you will have to make decisions about the names of certain accounts and note the location (e.g., IP address) of your server. You will need this information when installing the monitoring agents. The Getting Started guide notes all of these items. Pay particular attention to the example screens in the guide. It may be helpful to print out the guide and use it to write down the information you supply during the installation for later reference.

Installation of the monitoring agents is also very easy. Once your monitoring server is up and running and the product key has been validated, you can install one agent on each of the MySQL servers in your network. Some systems may require manually starting the agent, which is explained in detail in the guide.

Once at least one agent is installed and started, you can return to the Enterprise Dashboard and start configuring it to fit your needs.

MySQL Enterprise Components

MySQL Enterprise comprises the MySQL server software, the MEM toolset, and production support.

MySQL Enterprise Server

Two versions of the MySQL server are included in the MySQL Enterprise subscription. The Pro version is the production release with the most stable feature set. The Advanced version adds more experimental features—for example, horizontal table and index partitioning, which can improve the performance of very large databases.

MEM

The MEM forms the core of the continuous server monitoring and alerts. The MySQL website states it best: "It's like having a 'Virtual DBA Assistant' at your side to recommend best practices to eliminate security vulnerabilities, improve replication, optimize performance and more." Despite the marketing angle, the MEM gives you professional-level tools to meet the growing needs of your business's data center.

The MEM includes the following key features:

- A single web-based display to monitor the health of all of your servers
- Over 600 metrics, including the MySQL server and its host operating system
- The ability to monitor performance, replication, schema, and security
- Immediate health status via an easy-to-read heat chart
- Notification of metric threshold violations
- Implementation of the best practices ruleset from the creators of MySQL

The MEM is composed of a distributed web-based application that you run on your internal network. A monitoring agent is installed on each MySQL server that sends metrics to the web server component, called the Enterprise Dashboard. It is here that you can see all of the statistics and graphs that depict the status of your servers. There are also advisors that implement the best practices for ensuring your installations are properly configured and running at peak efficiency.

Enterprise Dashboard

The face of the MySQL Enterprise tools is the Enterprise Dashboard, the web application running on your monitoring server. The Enterprise Dashboard provides a single location where you can monitor all of your servers, either individually or in groups. You can see the availability, security, and performance data for all of your servers in one place. You can check the relative health of each, examine graphs of performance and memory use, and see vital operating system statistics for each server.

The Enterprise Dashboard presents monitoring and alert information to you in an easy-to-read format. An example of a simple installation is shown in Figure 13-1.

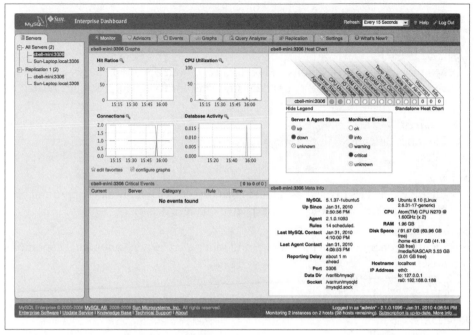

Figure 13-1. The MySQL Enterprise Dashboard

As you can see, the Enterprise Dashboard provides all of the critical information on a single screen. There are tabs for advisors, events, additional performance graphs, the Query Analyzer, replication, and configuration settings. The What's New? tab contains links to news and events concerning the tools and your Enterprise subscriptions.

Monitoring agent

The monitoring agent is a special lightweight application that gathers information about a MySQL server, including statistics about the host operating system. The monitoring agent is therefore the key component in the monitoring tools. Designed to be installed on each server you want to monitor, the agent is not only lightweight, but almost transparent, with no noticeable performance degradation.

Advisors

The MySQL Enterprise tools include one feature that departs from typical enterprise monitoring solutions: a mechanism that monitors specific areas of system performance and configuration and sends alerts when a server diverges from the best practices defined by the designers of MySQL. This means you can get immediate feedback on anything that can cause your system to become suboptimal in configuration, security, or performance. This mechanism is called an advisor, and there are many of them monitoring and reporting on a wide variety of areas. The advisors supplied are:

Administration
> Monitors general database administration and performance.

Upgrade
> Monitors upgrade conditions and sends alerts about potential issues with version-specific bugs. Also suggests upgrade strategies for fixing specific bugs related to upgrade issues.

Performance
> Identifies differences in performance based on MySQL performance best practice rules.

Schema
> Identifies changes to database and schema objects. Can monitor changes and provide alerts when unwanted or unexpected changes occur.

Memory Usage
> Identifies changes in memory usage and sends alerts when suboptimal conditions arise.

Security
> Identifies and sends alerts when potential security vulnerabilities arise.

Replication
> Identifies replication-specific conditions related to configuration, health, synchronization (delays), and performance issues.

Custom
> You can also create custom advisors to support your own best practices or specific needs.

Each advisor provides comprehensive coverage of a specific area of the server using a set of rules based on best practices. The advisors help you identify where your servers need attention and give you advice on how to improve or correct the situation. If the set of advisors isn't broad enough, you can create your own advisors to meet your needs.

Query Analyzer (gold and platinum levels)

Complex databases and the complex applications that they tend to support can result in the execution of complex queries. Given the expressiveness of SQL, queries are often not written to execute as efficiently as possible. Furthermore, poorly written queries can often be the source of poor performance on other levels. Savvy DBAs acknowledge this and often look to the queries first for database performance diagnostics.

You can normally find a poorly performing query by watching the slow query log or the process list (i.e., issuing a `SHOW PROCESSLIST` command). Once you have identified a query that needs your attention, you can use the `EXPLAIN` command to see how MySQL will execute the query. While this process is well known and has been used by DBAs for some time, it is a labor-intensive task that does not easily lend itself to scripting. As the complexity of the database grows, so too does the labor involved in diagnosing poorly performing queries.

You can examine user queries with this method, but what do you do when investigating application performance where the SQL statements are included in the application code itself? This situation is among the hardest to diagnose and repair, as it requires changing the application. Assuming that is possible, how do you advise the developers to improve their queries?

Unfortunately, the SQL statements in the application code are rarely suspected of being the source of performance problems. DBAs and developers are all too quick to blame the server or system instead of application code or embedded SQL queries. Worse still, the MySQL system does not support robust performance metric collection and there is little support for finding troublesome queries.

Wouldn't it be better to see a list of all of the long-running queries on your server and examine the slowest ones? The Query Analyzer component of the Enterprise Monitor tools provides this help.

You can enable the Query Analyzer via the Enterprise Dashboard. Installation and configuration require a little work, so be sure to consult the Getting Started guide for details.

The Query Analyzer provides an aggregate display showing performance statistics for queries in real time. It shows all of your queries from all of your servers in one place so you don't need to go from server to server looking for poorly performing queries. This same list maintains a history of the queries so you don't have to worry about the additional space for logs.

You can get two different views for each query: a canonical view (no numeric data) to see a pictorial version of the query, and a version that shows specific timing and access data for the query. Best of all, the advisor can even alert you when a given query was executed and on which server.

The Query Analyzer allows you to see which queries are performing poorly and to identify a solution by examining the suspected query's execution plan. Clearly, this feature alone can provide huge time savings, especially for situations in which you are developing or tuning an application for deployment or need to optimize your queries for improved performance.

MySQL Production Support

The MySQL Enterprise subscription includes access to support professionals who can help you with development, deployment, and management of your MySQL servers. Support includes problem resolution, consulting, access to an online knowledge base of common solutions, and (with the platinum subscription) a technical account manager who will be your point of contact, helping you with all of your support needs.

Using MySQL Enterprise

Now that we have described the features of MySQL Enterprise and its components, let's take a look at an example of how the tools can truly benefit an organization. In this example we use a hypothetical—albeit not uncommon—information infrastructure for a web-based company. This example is representative of the types of replication models seen in industry. It includes a complex multiple-master replication setup and replication in a series among database systems that replicate some of their databases but not others.

This scenario, shown in Figure 13-2, consists of a data center with two masters set up for high availability and load balancing. These data centers host the company's databases, each associated with a product line. A slave is connected to the main data center for internal production and day-to-day operations. This server also has slaves for various departments, including a slave to a third party, providing independent verification and validation (IVV) services. Connected to the same master server is another slave for the development departments responsible for building and enhancing the product lines.

Each of the slaves beneath the data centers can (and typically does) host additional databases that are not replicated. For example, the production server typically hosts a human resources database that is not replicated to most of its slaves (e.g., it is not replicated to the development center). Similarly, the third-party server hosts its own results database and the development server has various incarnations of the product line databases in various states of development.

Installation

Installing MySQL Enterprise entails setting up your database servers to run the latest Pro or Advanced release. You can use your existing MySQL server installations, but for the best return on your investment, you should be using the versions provided by your MySQL Enterprise subscription. Once your database servers are configured and running properly, you can begin the installation of the Enterprise Monitor and monitoring agents.

You should begin by installing the MEM on a machine on your network that has connectivity to all of the servers you want to monitor (we recommend always using MEM to monitor your MySQL servers). During the installation process, be sure to write down the hostname or IP address of this server and the username and password you specified for the agent access. The installation process is very easy and is well documented on the Enterprise subscription portal.

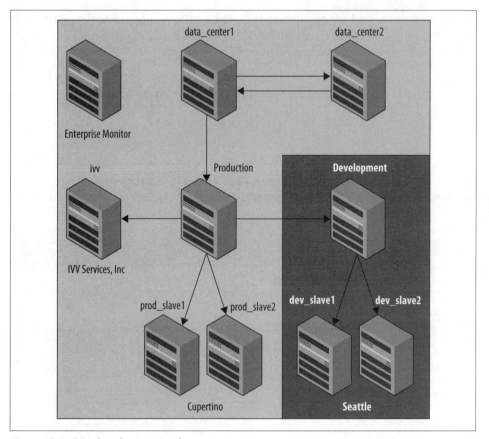

Figure 13-2. Sample information infrastructure

 There are several user accounts involved in the installation of MySQL Enterprise. Besides your Enterprise subscription account, you will also be using a MEM administrator, an agent access account to your MEM server, and an agent access account for the monitoring agent running on each MySQL server. Getting these confused can lead to a failed installation.

Once the MEM is up and running on your monitoring server, you can begin installing the monitoring agent on each of your MySQL servers. When you install the monitoring agent, you will need to provide a user account and password for a connection from the monitoring agent to your MySQL server. It is best to use the same username and password for all of your servers, but remember that these are individual accounts, so you will have to create the account on each server. Grant rights to this user as follows:

```
GRANT SELECT, REPLICATION CLIENT, SHOW DATABASES, SUPER, PROCESS ON *.*
TO 'agent_user'@'localhost' IDENTIFIED BY 'agent_password';
```

Once you have created the account and granted it privileges to access the server, start the monitoring agent and observe the MEM. The server should show up in the MEM within a few moments depending on your refresh settings.

 The installation process for MEM and the monitoring agent differ slightly for each platform. Be sure to refer to the documentation for specific details for your operating system.

Repeat the installation on each of your servers and observe the results in the Enterprise Dashboard. Figure 13-3 shows the Enterprise Dashboard for the example information infrastructure with all monitoring agents reporting.

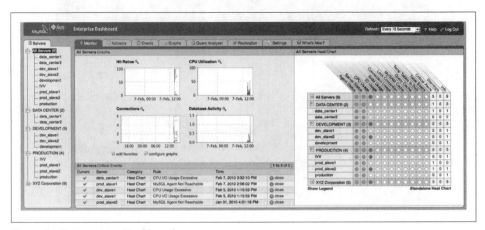

Figure 13-3. Enterprise Dashboard

Each of the servers is reporting its agent and server status in the heat chart on the right as green dots (green is good). There are four charts in the center that depict composite graphs of the query cache hit ratio, CPU utilization, connection information, and database activity for all of your servers. Below that is a list of default critical events reported by the advisors. In this figure, there are alerts for CPU, I/O, and usage.

As you can surmise, this page presents all of the pertinent information about your servers so that you can, at a glance, see the overall health of your information infrastructure. Clearly, monitoring can't get any easier than that!

Fixing Monitoring Agent Problems

While the installation process for the monitoring agent is very streamlined, there are times when things can go wrong. If you are careful to supply the correct information, everything should work correctly.

The following are some basic procedures for diagnosing and correcting problems in getting the monitoring agent to report to the MEM:

- Check the *mysql-monitor-agent.log* file if your monitoring agent starts but the server is not shown on the Enterprise Dashboard, or if the agent or service status indicates an error (a red dot) in the heat chart. This file contains a wealth of information that can help you solve most problems. You can find the logfiles in the following locations:

  Mac OS X
  > */Applications/mysql/enterprise/agent/*

  Linux/Unix
  > */opt/mysql/enterprise/agent on Linux*

  Windows
  > *C:\Program Files\MySQL\Enterprise\Agent*

- Check the user account and permissions specified for the monitoring agent on the MySQL server.
- Check the user account and password in the *agent-instance.ini* file. Be sure they are the same ones used on the MySQL server you are monitoring.
- Verify the port and hostname of your local MySQL server. Be sure the information matches what is in the *agent-instance.ini* file.
- Check the port for the server in the *agent-instance.ini* file. Be sure you can log into the local MySQL server using the port, user, and password specified in this file.
- Check the hostname, user, and password for the MEM server in the *mysql-monitor-agent.ini* file. Be sure you can ping the MEM server.

If you are having trouble getting the Query Analyzer to work, also check the proxy port in the *mysql-monitor-agent.ini* file and be sure you can connect a MySQL client to the proxy using the information specified in that file.

Monitoring

There are several areas in which MySQL Enterprise makes monitoring much easier for the administrators of a complex infrastructure. These areas include:

- Heat chart
- Alert details
- Consolidated server graphs
- Server details
- Replication details
- Advisors

We will examine each of these in greater detail in the following sections.

You can rename the servers using the Manage Servers option on the Settings page. This allows you to use more meaningful names on the Enterprise Dashboard while leaving the actual hostnames of the servers unaltered.

You can also create groups to combine related servers. This can be very handy, because the group is displayed on the various controls, allowing you to collapse the group and alter the display as needed.

Heat chart

As shown earlier, the heat chart to the right of the monitoring page of the Enterprise Dashboard provides an at-a-glance look at the relative health of your servers. The legend (which you can switch on or off) shows a series of colors that indicate states of operation from online and fully operational (green) to offline or not communicating (red). Clearly, your eye can quickly take in the areas that demand further inspection. Figure 13-4 shows an example of the heat chart for the information infrastructure example.

Notice that the heading on the heat chart lists several categories that represent critical monitoring areas. These areas cover the critical aspects of monitoring discussed in Chapter 8 through Chapter 10 (CPU, memory, etc.). Unlike those manual monitoring methods, this chart presents a relative health meter that allows you to read the status quickly.

Along with the general monitoring areas are MySQL-specific areas such as lock contention, MyISAM cache utilization, query cache utilization, and the number of table scans. MySQL Enterprise can and does report on a lot more areas, as you will see, but these are the most-watched areas.

To the right of these categories are columns that keep a count of recent critical events, warnings, and informational messages.

The values in the heat chart are updated periodically, so the counts may rise and fall depending on the recentness and resolution of the problems.

Alert details

The best thing about the heat chart, which may not be obvious, is that you can click on any one of the dots or numbered entries to get more information. For example, if you click the I/O usage dot for a server encountering I/O problems, you will see a list of all of the alerts for that system, as shown in Figure 13-5. You can then click the most recent alert and get a detailed report like the one shown in Figure 13-6.

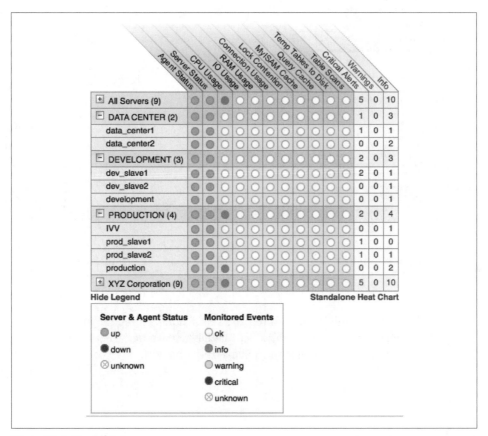

Figure 13-4. Heat chart

All Servers Critical Events					[1 to 5 of 5]
Current	Server	Category	Rule	Time	
✔	data_center1	Heat Chart	CPU I/O Usage Excessive	Feb 7, 2010 3:32:10 PM	⊗ close
✔	prod_slave1	Heat Chart	MySQL Agent Not Reachable	Feb 7, 2010 2:06:02 PM	⊗ close
✔	dev_slave1	Heat Chart	CPU Usage Excessive	Feb 5, 2010 1:15:59 PM	⊗ close
✔	dev_slave1	Heat Chart	CPU I/O Usage Excessive	Feb 5, 2010 1:15:59 PM	⊗ close
✔	prod_slave2	Heat Chart	MySQL Agent Not Reachable	Jan 31, 2010 4:51:19 PM	⊗ close

Figure 13-5. Sample alerts list

This report indicates the server on which the alert occurred, the time it occurred, and advice following the established best practices. There are tabs across the top for closing the alert to clear it from the display (which you can do once you have either fixed or accepted the incident), seeing more details (such as an expanded problem description), and an Advanced tab that shows how the alert was triggered.

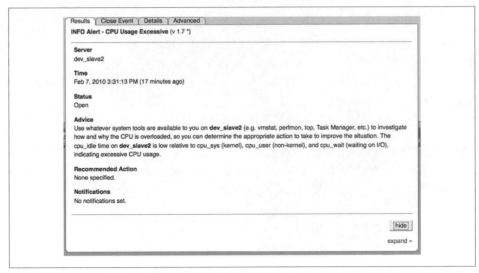

Figure 13-6. Sample alert report

The alert reports make the MySQL Enterprise stand alone among the monitoring options. This is what is meant by having a "virtual DBA assistant." The alerts will make your life much easier by trapping the problems from servers all over your organization and reporting them in a single place. This saves you the time and tedium of costly diagnostic efforts or active monitoring and gives you tips on how to solve problems quickly.

Consolidated server graphs

At the center of the Enterprise Dashboard display is a consolidated set of graphs that show colored lines for each of the servers being monitored (Figure 13-7). The default settings keep these charts very small, but you can change both the size and reporting time scales.

You can use these charts to get another pictorial view of the health of the systems in your organization. Even at the small default size it is easy to spot anomalies. Like with the heat chart, you can click a consolidated server graph to see more details about each event.

Server details

Another nice feature of the Enterprise Dashboard is that it lets you click on a specific server in the list of servers to see more details about the system. The server details report shows the version of the MySQL server; when it was last started (uptime); where the data is located; the host operating system; and CPU, memory size, disk space, and network information.

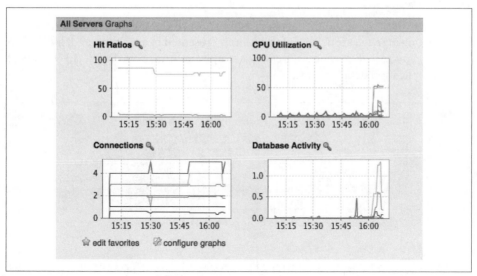

Figure 13-7. Sample consolidated server graphs

You can use this information for inventory purposes (determining what hardware is on your network) as well as for a quick look at what operating system is running to give you a clue about how to fix a problem. For example, you can remotely log into a server to fix something and know its hostname, IP address, MySQL version, and most importantly, the host operating system before you log in—all critical information that most administrators memorize or write down in a notebook. Figure 13-8 shows an example of the server details portion of the Enterprise Dashboard.

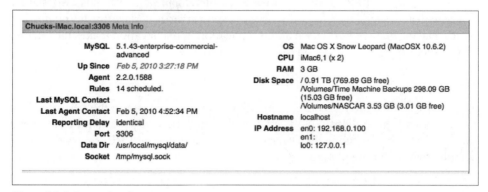

Figure 13-8. Server details

Replication details

The Replication tab of the Enterprise Dashboard includes a list of all of your servers participating in replication. The information is presented in a list form and, like all lists in MEM, you can click on each item to get more information. Figure 13-9 shows a sample replication details report.

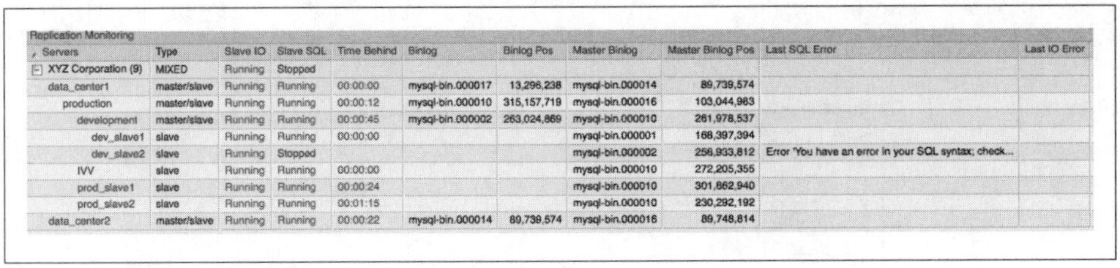

Replication Monitoring

Servers	Type	Slave IO	Slave SQL	Time Behind	Binlog	Binlog Pos	Master Binlog	Master Binlog Pos	Last SQL Error	Last IO Error
XYZ Corporation (9)	MIXED	Running	Stopped							
data_center1	master/slave	Running	Running	00:00:00	mysql-bin.000017	13,296,238	mysql-bin.000014	89,739,574		
production	master/slave	Running	Running	00:00:12	mysql-bin.000010	315,157,719	mysql-bin.000016	103,044,983		
development	master/slave	Running	Running	00:00:45	mysql-bin.000002	263,024,869	mysql-bin.000010	261,978,537		
dev_slave1	slave	Running	Running	00:00:00			mysql-bin.000001	168,397,394		
dev_slave2	slave	Running	Stopped				mysql-bin.000002	256,933,812	Error 'You have an error in your SQL syntax; check...	
IVV	slave	Running	Running	00:00:00			mysql-bin.000010	272,205,355		
prod_slave1	slave	Running	Running	00:00:24			mysql-bin.000010	301,862,940		
prod_slave2	slave	Running	Running	00:01:15			mysql-bin.000010	230,292,192		
data_center2	master/slave	Running	Running	00:00:22	mysql-bin.000014	89,739,574	mysql-bin.000016	89,748,814		

Figure 13-9. Replication details

Notice that items in the list are grouped by topology (e.g., "XYZ Corporation," which you can rename), including the type of topology, what role(s) the server is performing, and critical statistics about replication, including status of the threads, time behind master, current binary log, log position, master log information, and the most recent errors.

In this example, we see there is a problem on *dev_slave2*, where an error occurred on query execution. This is an excellent example of how you can get a quick picture of your replication topology. The list shows the masters and slaves grouped hierarchically. That is, a master is listed at a level directly under the group and its slaves under each master. In Figure 13-9, it is easy to see the *development* server has two slaves, *dev_slave1* and *dev_slave2*, and the *development* server is a slave to the *production* server. Having all the information about replication in one location makes the tedious task of monitoring replication on each server obsolete.

Advisors

What makes all of the alerts and pretty charts so informative are the best practices implemented in the advisors. You can see all of the active advisors (and create your own) on the Advisors tab in the Enterprise Dashboard. Figure 13-10 shows the list of default advisors for the platinum subscription.

Figure 13-10 shows the advisors that are active for a specific server on your network. You can enable, disable, or unschedule any of the advisors (unscheduling removes the data collected).

Perhaps the most useful feature of this page is adding your own advisors. This feature allows you to expand the MEM to meet your specific needs. It also gives you the one thing you need most when migrating from a manual monitoring solution: the ability to preserve your hard work.

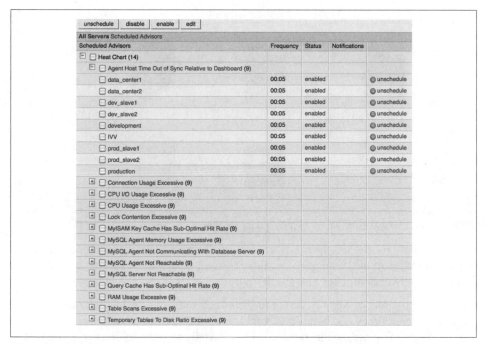

Scheduled Advisors	Frequency	Status	Notifications	
unschedule disable enable edit				
All Servers Scheduled Advisors				
⊟ ☐ Heat Chart (14)				
⊟ ☐ Agent Host Time Out of Sync Relative to Dashboard (9)				
☐ data_center1	00:05	enabled		◉ unschedule
☐ data_center2	00:05	enabled		◉ unschedule
☐ dev_slave1	00:05	enabled		◉ unschedule
☐ dev_slave2	00:05	enabled		◉ unschedule
☐ development	00:05	enabled		◉ unschedule
☐ IVV	00:05	enabled		◉ unschedule
☐ prod_slave1	00:05	enabled		◉ unschedule
☐ prod_slave2	00:05	enabled		◉ unschedule
☐ production	00:05	enabled		◉ unschedule
⊞ ☐ Connection Usage Excessive (9)				
⊞ ☐ CPU I/O Usage Excessive (9)				
⊞ ☐ CPU Usage Excessive (9)				
⊞ ☐ Lock Contention Excessive (9)				
⊞ ☐ MyISAM Key Cache Has Sub-Optimal Hit Rate (9)				
⊞ ☐ MySQL Agent Memory Usage Excessive (9)				
⊞ ☐ MySQL Agent Not Communicating With Database Server (9)				
⊞ ☐ MySQL Agent Not Reachable (9)				
⊞ ☐ MySQL Server Not Reachable (9)				
⊞ ☐ Query Cache Has Sub-Optimal Hit Rate (9)				
⊞ ☐ RAM Usage Excessive (9)				
⊞ ☐ Table Scans Excessive (9)				
⊞ ☐ Temporary Tables To Disk Ratio Excessive (9)				

Figure 13-10. Advisors

For example, if you create a reporting mechanism that monitors a custom application, you can create an advisor for it and add alerts to the Enterprise Dashboard. The specific details of how to add new advisors and alerts are covered in the MySQL Enterprise Monitor manual on the Enterprise subscription portal. This customization feature is one the most powerful and underutilized features of MySQL Enterprise.

Query Analyzer

The newest feature of MySQL Enterprise is the Query Analyzer. Savvy administrators have long known of the standalone Query Analyzer for MySQL, but until recently it was not integrated into the Enterprise tools.

The Query Analyzer works by intercepting SQL commands using MySQL Proxy and processing them, then passing them on to the local server for execution. This allows it to record statistics so that you can view them at any time. The Query Analyzer also supports advisors that fire alerts for slow queries. Figure 13-11 shows a conceptual drawing of how MySQL Proxy intercepts queries and reports the statistics to the MEM.

> The Query Analyzer runs over the user-defined port 6446 (by default) and can introduce some performance delay. Thus, you should enable it only when you are searching for problems.

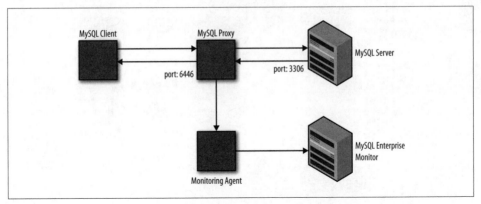

Figure 13-11. Using MySQL Proxy to collect data for Query Analyzer

To collect data for the Query Analyzer, you must direct your client to connect to the MySQL Proxy port and configure the agent to use port 6446. Be sure you can connect to this port if you do not see any queries reported in the Enterprise Dashboard.

While it is possible for MySQL Proxy to introduce some minor delays in query execution throughput times, the benefits of analyzing poorly running queries more than pay for the delays. You may want to use the Query Analyzer only on certain development or experimental machines rather than on your live production servers. One nice thing about the Query Analyzer and the Enterprise Dashboard is the tight integration among the tools. If you have an alert about a slow query or drill down into a CPU utilization report or other MySQL-based statistic, you will see the Query Analyzer page (which you can also access directly by clicking the Query Analyzer tab). Figure 13-12 shows an example of the Query Analyzer page on the Enterprise Dashboard.

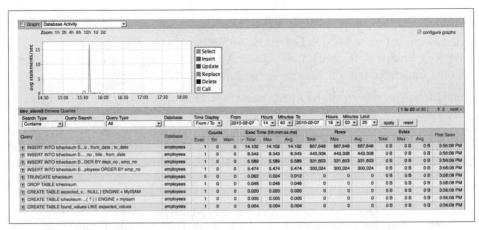

Figure 13-12. Query Analyzer display

The Query Analyzer page displays a list of servers on the left. You can click a specific server to see a list of queries executed on that server, sorted by longest running query. You can also use the chart at the top to narrow the time window to see queries during a specific time period.

You can sort the list on any column by clicking the column heading. This makes it a bit easier to see repetitive queries and diagnostics by sorting the rows with the longest-running queries at the top, showing the query statement, the amount of data manipulated, etc.

You can click any row to get a more detailed report on the query. Figure 13-13 shows a sample canonical query report. As with the other reports, you can get more detailed information, including the actual query on the Example Query tab, the output of the EXPLAIN command on the Explain Query tab (if you enabled that option), and graphs for execution time, number of executions, and number of rows returned on the Graphs tab.

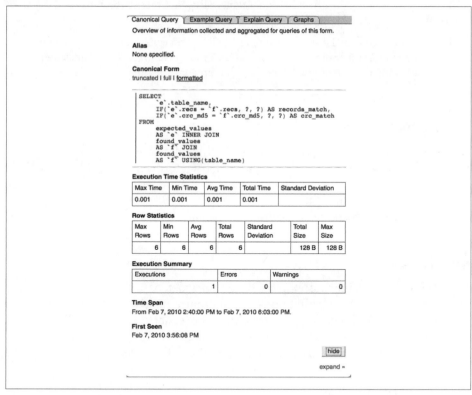

Figure 13-13. Canonical query report

This report presents details of the query captured, including the canonical form of the query (a pictorial representation of the query as it was written), details of its execution including time taken, and rows returned or affected.

Once again, we see a monitoring tool that will save you a considerable amount of time diagnosing problems with MySQL. The Query Analyzer component of the MySQL Enterprise tools is a vital monitoring tool that will help you keep your servers running well and your queries executing efficiently.

MySQL Enterprise and Cloud Computing

The MySQL Enterprise tools can also function well in a cloud computing environment. The same rules apply, however, regarding the persistence of the data and server instances. Just be sure to request a persistent IP address for your MEM server. Repeatedly starting and stopping your instances will cause no ill effects, but changing hostnames and some types of reconfiguration can cause the monitoring agents to stop reporting. Typically, truncating the *mysql.inventory* table solves this, but it is best to use the same hostnames and IP addresses for all of your servers.

There is one excellent benefit of running MySQL Enterprise tools in a commercial provider's cloud: you pay only for computation and storage space. Data transfer within the cloud is usually free or much less than shipping data in and out of the cloud.

Further Information

A complete and thorough description of the MEM and its many features is beyond the scope of this book. However, there is a great deal of information available on the Web. For more information about custom advisors and more, see the MySQL Enterprise Monitoring manual located on your Enterprise subscription portal. Also, check out the knowledge base on the portal for answers to common problems.

Conclusion

The MySQL server is the most popular open source database system for good reason. It is so versatile that any organization can use it, from a single self-contained web server providing content to users to online transaction processing systems (OLTPs) to highly available massively scaled-out data center infrastructures. MySQL can handle all of this and more. The MEM makes it possible to extend MySQL to large installations while preserving peak performance and reliability.

If you need high availability and want to build the best and most reliable data center based on MySQL, you should consider purchasing the MySQL Enterprise platinum-level subscription. Other solutions exist, but none have the depth of expertise for best practices offered by MySQL Enterprise and none give you the sophistication of the advisors and Query Analyzer for a bargain price.

Joel was ready. He had sent his proposal to purchase the much-needed MySQL Enterprise subscription to cover all of the company's servers. Mr. Summerson had a reputation for spending as little as possible, so Joel was ready to defend his proposal and had decided not to give up until Mr. Summerson had at least heard him out.

Each time he heard footsteps approaching, Joel would look up at his doorway. He knew his boss would stop by any moment. Another set of footsteps approached and he steeled himself once more. Mr. Summerson whisked by without a glance. "Wait for it," Joel whispered.

"Joel, I like this MEM thing. I want you to put together a cost estimate and..."

Joel interrupted his boss. "I already have a report for you, Bob."

Mr. Summerson raised his eyebrows and said, "Send it to me, and I'll get the bean counters to see if we can work it into the budget for next year." With that, Mr. Summerson was gone, on his way to his next victim.

Joel eased back in his desk chair and crossed his arms in satisfaction. "I'll take that as an 'attaboy,'" he said.

High Availability Environments

Cloud computing and MySQL Cluster offer new opportunities for meeting your high availability needs. This part of the book introduces these topics.

Cloud Computing Solutions

Joel pushed his office door partially closed while he hung his jacket on the hook on the back of the door. He jumped at the sound of knuckles rapping on his door. "Come in," he said, as he pulled the door open and walked over to his desk. When he turned to face his visitor, he knew who it was. "Mr. Summerson. Good morning, sir."

"Good morning, Joel. Nice work on that report about high availability and scale-out. I especially like your recommendations on how we can improve throughput for some of our products."

"Thanks." Joel held his breath, waiting for the tasking he knew was sure to come.

"Last night the board and I signed a contract to customize one of our products for a new customer. The ink isn't dry on the contract, so I won't go into any details, but suffice it to say we will need a lot of new servers in a high availability setup. Of course, they'll be using MySQL for the database component."

Joel tried to remember all the details he'd read about MySQL high availability, wondering how much money he'd need to set up a host of servers. He snapped out of his thoughts as his boss continued, "... then there's that stuff about load balancing."

After an uncomfortable pause, Joel said, "Yes, sir."

"The problem is we don't have resources to buy a bunch of servers, and the contract is for a six-month period of service. The board will never approve spending a bunch of money on new hardware that we may not need after the contract expires. Not to mention the dent to our profit margin."

Joel didn't know what to say, so he simply waited.

"So, we'd like you to put together a cloud-based solution." With that, Mr. Summerson patted Joel on the shoulder and left. Joel stood for several moments before walking behind his desk and sitting down.

Joel considered himself informed about emerging technologies, but he'd figured the cloud computing stuff was as fluffy as its namesake. He picked up his dog-eared MySQL book and flipped to the next chapter. "Well, look at that," he said, starting to read.

The demands of today's economy present new challenges as well as potentially new solutions for information infrastructure planners. No longer can organizations afford to simply buy more hardware every time they need to add computing power. While the cost of computing hardware has gone down over the last decade, so too have organizations' profit margins, particularly of late.

Thus, organizations must make decisions with a much stronger fiscal burden and look for the most affordable services and tools to increase their customer bases by expanding their product lines while reducing costs and increasing profits. It is all about the money, after all.

This need for affordable computational solutions has led technology providers to create a new way to use computers using a pay-as-you-use philosophy that allows organizations to purchase computational and data usage on an ad hoc basis. This is the essence of what computer scientists describe as *cloud computing*.

What Is Cloud Computing?

Cloud computing is one of those phrases that is often misunderstood and unfortunately has several—and sometimes conflicting—definitions. Some are quick to say it's a buzzword that describes existing technologies, while others would rather debate the finer academic and scientific (and sometimes social) aspects, and still others insist cloud computing is the future of information technology.

Thus, some have flatly stated that cloud computing is nothing more than grid computing, while others suggest cloud computing could represent the entire Internet. Both views are flawed. Others will explain in detail all aspects of "as a service" concepts and use those to define cloud computing. Fortunately, these more nuanced views are much closer to the truth.

Cloud computing is essentially a remix of a group of technologies that include grid computing and virtualization combined with application programming interfaces (APIs) and utilities to supply access to the virtualized environments. In his book *Cloud Computing Architectures* (O'Reilly, *http://oreilly.com/catalog/9780596156374*), George Reese states, "There is nothing fundamentally new in any of the technologies that make up cloud computing." This is a sobering observation that some pundits and marketers would rather not face. However, the advancement comes in the packaging, through which giants like Amazon have made it possible to use existing technologies in a whole new way.

In his treatise "15 Ways to Tell It's Not Cloud Computing," James Governor makes some strong statements concerning what is and what isn't cloud computing. To paraphrase his arguments, Governor makes it clear that cloud computing isn't something that takes a long time to explain, has a complex and steep learning curve, is isolated or requires a dedicated connection to use, or requires you to purchase hardware. Whether you agree with him or not, he forces patrons of companies trying to rebadge their products with the word "cloud" in them to consider their purchases carefully because the cloud isn't what most people think it is.

The term "cloud computing" is derived from the conceptual drawing that depicts resources hosted in a large network (a cloud). We use a cloud symbol because the resource implementation (e.g., the hardware, operating system, etc.) is hidden and has little bearing on what the service is or what it provides—it is simply a service you can use. Thus, instead of seeing gateways, routers, and servers, you see the resources presented as a service. Consumers of the resources don't care how the service is implemented; of overarching importance is for the service to solve the need and be available when required.

Rather than say "cloud computing is many things to many people," the National Institute of Standards and Technology (NIST) defines cloud computing as follows:

> Cloud computing is a model for enabling convenient, on-demand network access to a shared pool of configurable computing resources (e.g., networks, servers, storage, applications, and services) that can be rapidly provisioned and released with minimal management effort or service provider interaction. This cloud model promotes availability and is composed of five essential characteristics, three service models, and four deployment models.

The characteristics that most cloud researchers define as essential to cloud computing include the following:

On-demand self-service
Customers can pick and choose what they need on an ad hoc basis without intervention of the vendor or a third party.

Broad network access
The resources are available through existing networking capabilities.

Resource pooling
Multiple users share the provider's hardware (e.g., a multitenant sharing model).

Rapid elasticity
Customers are able to rapidly scale resources either manually or automatically.

Measured service
Services for resource monitoring and management are provided, either actively or passively (see Chapter 10).

The three service models are:

Infrastructure as a Service (IaaS)
Resources are provided as virtual instances of complete hardware or operating system platforms. The client can add virtualized computational resources on demand (e.g., servers, load balancers). Thus, the components of an information infrastructure are provided as components or middleware. The consumer has access to and control of the resources (e.g., the customer can manage an allocated server).

Platform as a Service (PaaS)
> An API allows clients to create applications designed specifically to run on the provider's hardware (platforms). The vendor provides the hosting environment and programming tools to permit customers to build solutions for the specific environment.

Software as a Service (SaaS)
> Software is provided as a resource in the form of applications that run on the provider's hardware. The consumer sees only the interface to the software, just like with a desktop application. The hardware, operating system, etc., are all hidden and controlled exclusively by the vendor. This is the oldest model currently included in definitions of the cloud, and for many decades it was known as an *Application Service Provider* (ASP).

The deployment models refer to the availability or accessibility of the resulting solutions and include:

Private
> Access to resources is limited to the customer only.

Community
> Access to resources is shared among one or more customers.

Public
> Access to resources is available to the general public.

Hybrid
> This is an infrastructure composed of two or more of the other models. Typically, this results in a division of private and public resources that can communicate.

A document with a complete discussion of the NIST's view of cloud computing is located at *http://csrc.nist.gov/groups/SNS/cloud-computing/*.

Cloud Architectures

In this section, we will briefly examine the underlying technologies commonly used in cloud computing. You will find that most cloud computing solutions employ most if not all of these technologies:

- Virtualization
- Grid computing
- Transactional computing
- Elasticity
- Software libraries

Virtualization

There are many forms of virtualization. If you have ever used Sun's VirtualBox or Microsoft's VirtualPC, you have used a form of virtualization. In essence, this technology creates a pseudoplatform based on a conceptual computing hardware model. For example, it is possible to run an instance of the Microsoft Windows operating system on a Linux machine inside VirtualBox. VirtualBox creates a software-based model of each component in a PC. These form a foundation upon which Windows can boot and run as if it were on real hardware.

This is just one form of virtualization. There are several mechanisms for simulating the hardware, as well as optimizations for launching, execution, and management of instances. The virtualization used in most IaaS solutions requires you to use prepackaged machines (called *images*), where each virtual machine is called an *instance* of an image. For example, the Amazon cloud uses Xen virtualization technology, an open source and common solution that permits scaling of the virtualized hardware (e.g., the number of CPUs), fault tolerance, and other advantages.

Furthermore, some vendors let you modify existing images to customize machines to your needs, using either vendor-specific tools or a machine description in a specific format. This can be an issue if you decide you want to move from one vendor to another: your images may not be portable. You should check the vendor's documentation about images and customizing images before you invest a lot of time and effort in this solution.

Grid computing

In the days when computing power was limited and the need to solve complex analytical or scientific problems was great, a technology that allowed programs to share extra computing power among a community of connected machines was invented and termed *grid computing*. It works by breaking a problem down into smaller computational units that can be shipped to other machines for processing, then retrieving the results and correlating them on one machine.

The key technology that permits these machines to communicate is a sophisticated queuing mechanism. This queuing mechanism is like a workflow and can be demonstrated as follows. A *data manager* machine delegates jobs and their data to slave machines and then reads their results. This involves setting up one or more queuing machines that send the processing job to any connected computers and then return their results to the data manager. When a user wants to participate in a grid computing program, he first connects his donor computer to a queuing machine and issues a pull of the processing package (a job plus data). His machine executes the job and sends the results to the queuing machine. A simplified example of this process is shown in Figure 14-1.

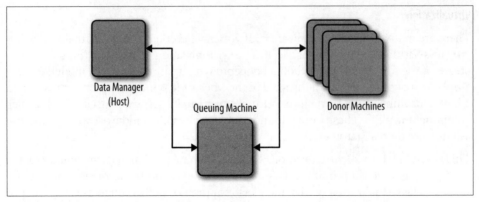

Figure 14-1. Grid computing workflow

Queuing systems are also present in cloud computing. Thus, it is possible to migrate existing grid computing solutions or build new grid computing solutions in cloud computing. This capability is why some insist cloud computing is simply grid computing with virtualization. But as you will see, there is far more to cloud computing than just these two technologies.

Transactional computing

Transactional computing is familiar to database users: multiple segments of data are processed together as a single transaction and correlated with other data. The idea is to define a job to include particular data and perform some action on that data as a single step (transaction). The best grid computing solutions use this concept to ensure proper delivery of the results. However, cloud computing is a bit more complicated. Specifically, large transactional applications are intended to be running for a long period of time, whereas grid solutions have very small execution times.

The good news is that it is possible to build a transactional computing system in the cloud. To do so, we must ensure the longevity of the computing resources and provide mechanisms to allow the data to be segmented and processed in parallel. If you're thinking, "Hey, this sounds like server farms," you are correct. Most cloud computing vendors provide virtualized resources to support a transactional computing solution including load balancers, persistent instances, and permanent assignment of networking resources.

Elasticity

Elasticity is a term we use to describe an abstraction of a networking or system resource that has been made a commodity. For example, Amazon allows you to apply a given IP address to any instance of a server in its cloud. This takes on great importance in transactional systems, where you need a pool of servers that answers to a particular address. While it is fine to virtualize the servers so that they can run anywhere in the cloud, you must have a way to ensure that the IP address remains constant.

In this case, the IP address becomes an elastic resource that you can assign to any instance you want. It isn't tied to a particular machine. Similarly, disk resources can be elastic, so you can store your data on a disk resource and make it accessible to any running instance in the cloud.

Elasticity solves the problem of running virtualized machines in a pooled hardware configuration. The machines become truly plug-and-play and you can easily create and destroy them. For example, you can swap a machine running one operating system for another during development and (perhaps with a few minor changes) still access the same data—no need to build a whole new database.

Software libraries

You may be wondering how all of these technologies tie together and how it is possible to work with resources in a dynamic environment. The answer is that most cloud vendors have a specific set of tools for creating and manipulating resources in the cloud.

For example, Amazon has tools on its APIs for managing your resources, creating instances, creating volumes (disk objects), and much more. These encompass the Amazon EC2 API Tools for working with cloud resources as well as Amazon EC2 AMI (Amazon Machine Image) Tools for creating and modifying machine images.

Similarly, Microsoft Azure has extensions to the .NET development environment to permit you to build your cloud applications and run them in the Azure cloud. The resemblance ends here, though, because the Microsoft Azure environment also requires you to build your applications with these libraries, whereas Amazon does not.

Thus, software libraries form the glue that allows all of these existing technologies to work together and become something greater than their parts—a cloud computing environment.

Is Cloud Computing an Economical Choice?

There are analysts and pundits on both sides of this question. The bottom line is: it depends. That is, it depends on which cloud provider you use, how many servers you need (measured in computation time), how much space you need, and for how long.

One comparative study (*http://www.uptimesoftware.com/uptimeblog/cloud-virtualiza tion/cost-of-cloud-computing-expensive/*) shows that the cost of a cloud solution versus a traditional solution (buying your own hardware) for a typical e-commerce situation over a period of five years comes out only slightly in favor of cloud computing.

You could see this as evidence that cloud computing doesn't offer much of a savings, and on the surface you'd be correct. However, the details of the study show the initial investment for the traditional solution to be very high. While it is true at the end of five years an organization owns its own hardware (or amortizes it to the point of obsolescence), the hardware in the cloud is of no concern because it is not a factor in the cost.

That is, there are no recurring costs for equipment upgrades when using a cloud-based solution. The study does not include this cost in the comparison and if it did, it is likely that the difference in expenditures over five years would be considerably higher for the traditional solution.

In order to answer the question of whether cloud computing is economical, you have to do your homework. The cost factor will be different for each organization and for each project. The best way to analyze this cost is to determine (or estimate) the number of servers, how much data you will need to store, how much data will be moved around in the cloud, and which additional features you need (VPN, load balancing, etc.). Specifically, you need to examine the billable components of the cloud computing vendor and estimate the cost based on those parameters. Once you have that, you can determine the costs for a traditional solution, factoring in maintenance and upgrades, and then make a fair comparison.

Many clients use cloud computing not to save money, but for its flexibility. We'll discuss why it can be a valuable solution in the following section.

However, there are some organizations that view the use of cloud computing as prohibited either by policy or fear. For example, some organizations do not allow storage of their private data on systems that they do not own and that (conceivably) some administrator outside of the organization (i.e., one of the cloud vendor's employees) could use to gain access to the data. If you find yourself facing these demons, you should contact the cloud vendor and discuss your concerns and weigh the risks accordingly. One way to overcome this limitation is to segregate your data and use the cloud for public data only. Also, in the case of Amazon Web Services (AWS), the cloud vendor may have features that permit you to isolate your cloud instances or connect them via a VPN to your own IT infrastructure (see *http://aws.amazon.com/vpc/* for more details on Amazon's VPN Cloud offering).

Cloud Computing Use Cases

Now that you have a good understanding of what cloud computing is, let's examine what you can do with it. All manner of organizations have found new and exciting uses for cloud computing. These include start-up companies looking for an inexpensive entry into the market, researchers who need computational power for a limited time, and information technology managers who feel the budget crunch but must still meet the needs of their users. In this section, we discuss some common use cases for employing cloud computing:

Traditional web services
    Cloud resources supply content or applications to users on the Internet.

Shared services
> One or more applications run in the cloud and are shared by different users. An example is an application that allows partners to collaborate and share data (e.g., a supply chain).

Scale-out from enterprise
> This allows rapid expansion of an application using solutions that run in the cloud and connect to the enterprise.

Cloud bursting
> This allows users to deploy temporary resources quickly to solve immediate, short-term computational tasks.

Research and development
> This allows developers to explore multiple system and application configurations without the need for dedicated hardware.

As you can see, there are many ways to use cloud computing, and more uses are being discovered every day. What we've seen in the field so far is just a start to the possibilities.

Cloud Computing Benefits

The potential benefits of cloud computing include:

Reduced runtime and response time
> By leveraging grid or scale-out techniques, it is possible to reduce the amount of time a task takes to complete and even improve data access time dramatically. You can use hardware-based solutions for similar effects, but at a severe investment cost. Cloud solutions allow you to generate as many machine instances as you need and pay only for what you use.

Minimize infrastructure risk and maintenance
> Hardware failure is no longer your responsibility. The vendor owns and maintains the machines that run the cloud systems, so you do not require a large staff or investment in service providers.

Lower cost of entry
> With the ability to pay for only what you use, you no longer have to budget for a large infrastructure that you may or may not use. Best of all, you can grow your infrastructure on the fly and, better still, reduce it without having to amortize the hardware or declare it surplus.

Increased pace of development
> The lower cost of entry and the ability to pay only for what you need means you can get a new application started with far less investment than in the past (on your own or using a service provider's hardware). This has the side effect of leveling the field for start-up companies, allowing them to compete early in their development.

Of course, for each advantage there is a corresponding drawback. Some of the potential risks of cloud computing are:

Service failure
Service level agreements (SLAs) tend to be poorly defined (or nonexistent) in the cloud computing field, and if your underlying service is unreliable, you have little recourse.

Potential runaway costs
If you experience an unusually heavy load and scale up to meet it, you may succeed in meeting the need, but incur high usage costs in doing so.

Lack of features
You may decide at some point that you need to implement a feature in your architecture or application that the vendor doesn't support.

Security risks
You are sharing machines with other users, and software flaws can allow data to be leaked or stolen.

Cloud Computing Vendors

Whenever there is an emerging technology, there is inevitably an explosion of vendors, products, and services that all claim in one form or another to provide the new technology. Cloud computing is not immune to this phenomenon. There are hundreds of vendors that provide everything from specialized hardware, software services, and platforms to turnkey pick-and-pay portfolios. If you use the NIST definition presented in "What Is Cloud Computing?" on page 478, you'll quickly find that many vendors aren't meeting all of the tenets of the definition.

However, there are a number of vendors that are striving to meet the full definition for cloud computing. The following list names 10 of the top vendors, along with a brief description of the type of solutions each provides:

3Tera (http://www.3tera.com/)
An IaaS provider specializing in rapid scale-out capabilities

Akamai (http://www.akamai.com/)
An IaaS provider specializing in managing data on the Web

Amazon (http://aws.amazon.com/)
A cloud computing vendor offering virtualized SaaS, PaaS, and IaaS solutions along with storage solutions

Enki Consulting (http://www.enkiconsulting.net/)
An IaaS provider specializing in virtual private data center solutions

IBM Blue Cloud (http://www.ibm.com/ibm/cloud/)
A cloud computing vendor offering virtualized SaaS, PaaS, and IaaS solutions

---

Joyent (http://www.joyent.com/)
  An IaaS provider specializing in the needs of large enterprises

Layered Technologies (http://www.layeredtech.com/)
  A PaaS and IaaS provider

Rackspace (http://www.rackspace.com/)
  A PaaS specializing in providing host services for web applications

Salesforce.com (http://www.salesforce.com/)
  An SaaS vendor specializing in shared customer relationship management (CRM) solutions

Terremark (http://www.terremark.com/)
  An IaaS provider

Even Apple has announced plans for expanding its services and products to include Internet-accessible pay-as-you-go solutions. While not expressly defined or presented as a cloud computing solution, it will be a competitor to Google Docs and Microsoft's online Office suite plans. Clearly, the concepts behind cloud computing are having a profound effect on many of the big players in the information technology industry.

Given the popularity, wide variety of services, maturity, and sophistication of the AWS, we have chosen to focus on the Amazon cloud computing products in this chapter. We encourage you to consider and balance your specific needs when choosing a cloud computing vendor. However, you will find the Amazon solutions are rapidly becoming commonplace.

The (Amazon) Cloud: Another Xerox?

Just as many of us refer to any office copier as a "Xerox machine," and use the related verb "xeroxing," many technology pundits describe cloud computing (or simply "the cloud") in terms of what AWS provides. Only time and industry adoption patterns will tell us whether Amazon's solution becomes the standard by which all solutions are judged. However, we often hear cloud computing defined as having elasticity—a term made (more) popular by Amazon's choice to name its IaaS product "Elastic Cloud Computing" (EC2).

AWS

Amazon offers a large portfolio of developer tools and solutions called AWS. While collectively they have become known as the "Amazon cloud," the products and services provided include computational services (cloud), content delivery, database system support, e-commerce solutions, messaging, monitoring, networking, payment and billing solutions for vendors, cloud storage solutions, support services for AWS products, web traffic management, and workforce software solutions. Amazon adds new products regularly, so by the time you read this, the list may have grown considerably.

The Amazon products are fee-based, but are designed to allow users to consume and pay for services as they are needed.

In the next section, we discuss the technologies available in AWS and provide a brief introduction to using cloud computing the Amazon way.

A Brief Overview of Technologies

Since the technologies are numerous and diverse, we will focus only on areas that pertain to building reliable data centers. You will, of course, want to explore the details of all of the AWS products, and you can do so by clicking on the Products tab at the top of the page at *http://aws.amazon.com*.

All of the following technologies are built on simple web services, making it easy to build applications that can communicate with every tool over a RESTful web interface:

Amazon Elastic Compute Cloud (EC2)
　　Along with Amazon Simple Storage Service (S3), makes up the heart of the Amazon cloud. This is the main technology that makes the cloud possible. It manages the virtual computing resources.

Amazon Elastic MapReduce
　　Uses the Hadoop framework to provide an environment for data-intensive tasks.

Auto Scaling
　　Provides the ability to automatically scale your solution based on parameters you define. This is a key feature in building highly available cloud solutions.

Amazon CloudFront
　　A content management service that allows you to provide static and streaming content (sometimes called *active content*) to users in widely different geographic locations.

Amazon SimpleDB
　　Provides very basic nonrelational database storage and retrieval.

Amazon Relational Database Service (RDS)
　　Amazon's offering of the MySQL database system. You can use this service instead of creating and managing your own MySQL installation.

Amazon Fulfillment Web Service (FWS)
　　Provides a bundled set of e-commerce tools—the same tools that the now-famous Amazon merchant website uses.

Amazon Simple Queue Service (SQS)
　　The queuing message service used in grid computing solutions.

Amazon CloudWatch
　　Provides monitoring capabilities for all of your Amazon cloud resources.

Amazon Virtual Private Cloud (VPC)

An exciting recent capability that permits enterprises to extend their infrastructures privately using a VPN into the Amazon cloud. The resources you allocate in the VPC communicate with your internal infrastructure as if they were located on the same internal network. This could become a must-have for organizations that must ramp up their computational resources quickly.

Elastic Load Balancing

Another key component of the cloud services. It provides the ability to balance the load of network traffic across your solution.

Amazon Flexible Payments Service (FPS)

A development library that provides payment processing tools for building charitable foundations and e-commerce sites.

Amazon DevPay

An online billing and accounting service for online retailers.

Amazon S3

Another key component in Amazon's cloud offerings. It provides fast, permanent storage for files up to 5 GB in size.

Amazon Elastic Block Storage (EBS)

The key module that stores your data. It is a block-level device that you can attach to any instance for data storage and retrieval.

AWS Import/Export

Services for importing and exporting large amounts of data into and out of your cloud solutions.

AWS Premium Support

Support services for all of the AWS products, providing one-on-one assistance for building and running applications with the AWS products.

Alexa Web Information Service

A service that gathers metadata about the traffic and structure of websites.

Alexa Top Sites

A service that ranks websites based on traffic and frequency.

Amazon Mechanical Turk

A collaborative solution that supports on-demand workforce solutions. It is specifically designed to integrate human-based tasking into computational systems, such as photography, audio recording, and other human-centric tasks that are common among data providers and consumers.

Now that you have seen a list of the relevant products, we'll focus on the essential technologies you need to know to begin working with your first cloud solution. While this list is short and may seem to be a pittance compared to the long list we just laid out, these are by far the most frequently used technologies in building a cloud solution. Once you master these, you can begin to explore the more advanced services.

Amazon EC2

The Amazon EC2 service was first released in 2006 to beta users and became publicly available in 2008. EC2 is the power behind the dynamic computing capability in the Amazon cloud. It provides virtualized hardware for server instances that you can allocate on the fly and that support a host of available operating systems and environments. EC2 is essentially what makes the cloud tick.

EC2's virtualization uses the open source Xen technology, allowing fine-grained hardware virtualization and customization. The Xen virtualization platform, which was created by XenSource (later purchased by Citrix) allows guest operating systems such as Linux, Windows, or Solaris to run as virtual machines on the same hardware concurrently.

A virtual machine in EC2 is known as an instance, and you can connect to, monitor, and administer it as if it were an operating system running on dedicated hardware.

One of the interesting capabilities of EC2 and Xen virtualization is support for virtual instances of both 32-bit and 64-bit CPUs. A CPU core or processing core is known as a computational unit (CU), which, besides being the governor of processing power, is the unit Amazon uses as a cost multiplier. The more computational units you use, the more it costs to run the instance. Hence, you should choose the smallest computational unit that meets the needs of your task. An instance can be one of several *instance types*, listed in Table 14-1.

Table 14-1. Instance types

Type	CPU	Memory	Local storage	Platform	I/O	Name
Small	1 EC2 CU	1.7 GB	160 GB instance storage (150 GB plus 10 GB root partition)	32-bit	Moderate	m1.small
Large	4 EC2 CU (2 virtual cores with 2 EC2 CU each)	7.5 GB	850 GB instance storage (2 × 420 GB plus 10 GB root partition)	64-bit	High	m1.large
Extra large	8 EC2 CU (4 virtual cores with 2 EC2 CU each)	15 GB	1690 GB instance storage (4 × 420 GB plus 10 GB root partition)	64-bit	High	m1.xlarge
High-CPU medium	5 EC2 CU (2 virtual cores with 2.5 EC2 CU each)	1.7 GB	350 GB instance storage (340 GB plus 10 GB root partition)	32-bit	Moderate	c1.medium
High-CPU extra large	20 EC2 CU (8 virtual cores with 2.5 EC2 CU each)	7 GB	1690 GB instance storage (4 × 420 GB plus 10 GB root partition)	64-bit	High	c1.xlarge
High-memory extra large	6.5 EC2 CU (2 virtual cores with 3.25 EC2 CU each)	17.1 GB	420 GB instance storage (1 × 420 GB)	64-bit	Moderate	m2.xlarge

Type	CPU	Memory	Local storage	Platform	I/O	Name
High-memory double extra large	13 EC2 CU (4 virtual cores with 3.25 EC2 CU each)	34.2 GB	850 GB instance storage (1 × 840 GB plus 10 GB root partition)	64-bit	High	m2.2xlarge
High-memory quadruple extra large	26 EC2 CU (8 virtual cores with 3.25 EC2 CU each)	68.4 GB	1690 GB instance storage (2 × 840 GB plus 10 GB root partition)	64-bit	High	m2.4xlarge

Amazon bills you based on the computational hours during which you've reserved your virtual machine, using the instance type as a cost multiplier. The instances themselves can run in one of several regions (locations around the world that host the hardware). For more information concerning instance pricing and configurations, see *http://aws .amazon.com/ec2/#pricing*.

EC2 instances use an AMI. The AMI is composed of an operating system and any additional software you choose to preload. Amazon has cataloged many prebuilt AMIs, which makes getting started with EC2 that much easier. For instance, you can load up a prebuilt AMI that runs a Linux, Apache, MySQL, PHP/Perl/Python (LAMP) stack.

Amazon S3

Also in 2006, Amazon created S3 as its premier online storage web service. S3 provides developers with easy, secure, persistent online storage offering essentially unlimited capacity. At a high level, S3 is similar (at least in concept) to a storage area network (SAN) in that the resources are available from any connected device. Amazon charges usage fees based on the data stored and the bandwidth consumed in storing and retrieving data.

Unlike a traditional filesystem that uses a directory structure, S3 uses an object store mechanism called *buckets*, which you can define using names that are publicly readable. That is, anyone can store something in your "mycompanyname" bucket, so beware of using common names like "database" or "public" or "documents." Most users use their domain names in the name of their buckets, but even that doesn't prevent others from storing something in the same bucket.

Amazon refers to things stored in the buckets as *objects,* and each object can be as small as a single byte or up to 5 GB. Buckets and the objects they contain physically reside in one of the two regions called *availability zones* (one encompassing a variety of data centers in North America and the other encompassing data centers in Europe), but you can access them from anywhere.

Furthermore, Amazon provides web services that allow you to make use of S3 in almost any web-based application.

The S3 mechanism is not meant to be a fast read/write mechanism and is really best used for archival purposes like storing a customized AMI or a bulk data copy or backup. Thus, you would not want to use it to store your active databases.

Amazon EBS

Amazon released EBS in 2008. It was a giant leap forward for cloud computing. EBS is a virtualized block storage device, like a disk drive. Not only does it have the performance of a typical block device, offering fast read and write capability, but it is also independent of a running instance. This is really important because in the past, users had to rely on bringing their data from S3 or outside the cloud and loading it on the instance. But the instance was volatile, so when it terminated (which could be unexpected and occur without warning), you would lose any changes made on the instance. So before EBS, you had to make your applications back up to S3 frequently or use tools such as a volume manager.

With EBS, users can now create independent devices (called *volumes* or simply *EBS stores*) and attach them to any running instance, not unlike a USB hard drive. EBS volumes appear to developers as standard block devices that range from 1 GB to 1 TB in size. Much like their SAN counterparts, EBS volumes can be resized on the fly using snapshotting. This is very handy, as it allows you to grow your disk usage as your application and data grow.

You can also use multiple EBS volumes for striping to improve throughput and I/O performance. Better still, EBS volumes are replicated among the Amazon EC2 availability zones, which means that even if the zone you're in suffers a disaster, your data is still accessible. EBS is therefore even more reliable than traditional disk storage systems. However, EBS volumes you attach to your EC2 instance must reside in the same availability zone.

EBS also supports backup using point-in-time snapshots to S3. Each backup is a differential snapshot: only the blocks that have changed since the last snapshot are saved. Point-in-time snapshots provide an effective and efficient way to create durable backups, especially for your MySQL databases.

With all the capability of a normal disk and much more, EBS volumes are the perfect solution for storing your MySQL database files. You get snapshotting and similar backup capabilities, and the sustainability is unparalleled.

How Does It All Work?

Before we go into the specifics of setting up an AWS account and running instances of AMIs, it is important for you to understand conceptually how you interact with the Amazon cloud and how your virtualized servers are realized. Figure 14-2 depicts a conceptual model of how the EC2 instances are realized and executed.

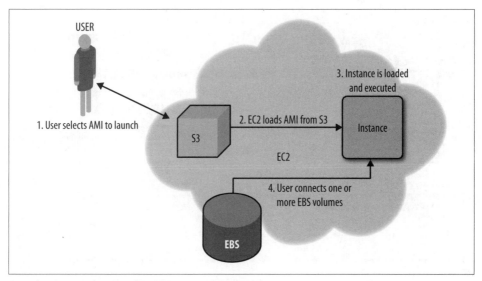

Figure 14-2. How AMIs become server instances in EC2

Amazon Cloud Tools

There are two types of tools available for purchasing services, initiating resources, and managing them: a GUI and a command-line interface. There are actually two types of GUIs. Amazon provides a web-based console to access its services, and there are a number of plug-ins for web browsers that you can use as an alternative. Amazon also provides a set of utilities built on its EC2 API (called EC2 command-line tools).

Amazon console

Amazon provides a web-based interface for interacting with all of its products called the AWS Management Console. You can find it at *https://console.aws.amazon.com/ec2/home*.

You will need an AWS account to launch it; we'll show you how to do that in an upcoming section. We want to introduce the console first to give you a better picture of how to work with AWS and EC2.

You can use the interface to create instances, connect to them, create EBS volumes and connect them to instances, and much more. As you will see, this is the default mechanism for working with EC2 and other AWS products. Figure 14-3 shows the AWS Management Console for a typical user.

 In Figure 14-3 and several others in this chapter, we have masked out specific portions that show user contextual information that is not pertinent to the points discussed.

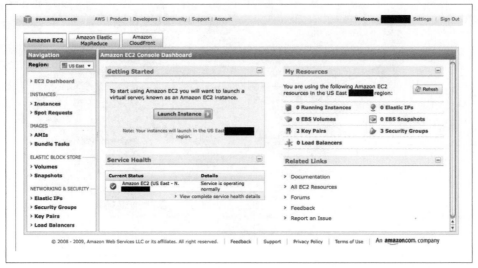

Figure 14-3. AWS Management Console

The left center of the screen shows a button labeled Launch Instance. As you can guess, this is your starting point for creating EC2 instances. On the left of the screen are links for many of the AWS cloud resources, such as volumes (EBS), elastic IPs, load balancers, and more.

Across the top are the three tabs that you use to access the different groupings of cloud services. The default (shown) is the Amazon EC2 tab, followed by the Amazon Elastic MapReduce tab, which allows you to set up and execute grid computing solutions, and Amazon CloudFront, for control of your web content.

We will look at more details and step through creating an EC2 instance in the next sections.

Browser plug-ins

If you want a bit more power on a single web page, you can use a browser plug-in for Mozilla Firefox called Elasticfox. You can download it at *http://developer.amazonweb services.com/connect/entry.jspa?externalID=609*.

Elasticfox is a web-based GUI that executes the complete EC2 tools API, permitting you to control every aspect of your EC2 instances, from creating instances to creating volumes and connecting them to instances and much more. In many ways it is more powerful than the AWS Management Console, in that it puts everything at your fingertips (or mouse pointer). Figure 14-4 shows Elasticfox in action.

Be sure to read the Getting Started documentation located at *http://developer.amazon webservices.com/connect/entry.jspa?externalID=1797* to set up and configure Elasticfox for EC2 access.

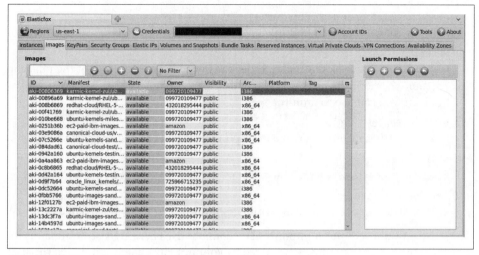

Figure 14-4. Elasticfox Firefox plug-in

Several other vendors and developers are building web-based alternatives to the AWS Management Console. One of the most noteworthy is the shareVM project. You can find more information about this solution at *http://blog.sharevm.com/2009/01/09/web-based-ec2-console-alternative-to-elasticfox/*.

EC2 command-line tools

You can also interact with EC2 using command-line tools. There are two sets: the API and AMI tools. The API tools interact with EC2 and include tools for launching instances, creating and attaching volumes, managing security groups, and more. The AMI tools create and manipulate AMIs.

EC2 API tools. You can download the EC2 API command-line tools from *http://developer.amazonwebservices.com/connect/entry.jspa?externalID=351&categoryID=88*. Follow the instructions for installing and configuring the tools for your host operating system.

The documentation for the EC2 API tools is included in the Getting Started documentation, which you can find at *http://docs.amazonwebservices.com/AWSEC2/latest/CommandLineReference/*. The EC2 user guide also contains documentation on the command-line tools. You can download the user guide from *http://awsdocs.s3.amazonaws.com/EC2/latest/ec2-ug.pdf*.

Take a moment to download and install the EC2 API tools. They contain numerous utilities that allow you to perform a great many things in EC2. The following lists the more commonly used utilities:

`ec2-add-key-pair`
    Creates a new SSH key pair.

`ec2-run-instances`

Launches EC2 instances. You must specify at least the name of the image and your key pair. You can launch multiple instances at the same time.

`ec2-describe-images`

Lists available images. Output includes the image ID, the location of the image in S3, and whether the image is available for launching. There are a number of parameters you can use to limit the search.

`ec2-stop-instances`

Stops or pauses instances. You can stop multiple instances at the same time.

`ec2-start-instances`

Starts or resumes instances. You can start multiple instances at the same time.

`ec2-terminate-instances`

Terminates instances. You can terminate multiple instances at the same time.

These are only a few of the commonly used commands. There are also commands for working with security groups, keys, images, volumes, and much more. See the user guide for more details.

EC2 AMI tools. You can download the EC2 AMI command-line tools from *http://developer .amazonwebservices.com/connect/entry.jspa?externalID=368&categoryID=88*. Follow the instructions for installing the tools for your host operating system.

If you want to work with images and create your own customized images, you may also want to explore the following documentation links:

> *http://docs.amazonwebservices.com/AWSEC2/latest/DeveloperGuide/*
> *http://docs.amazonwebservices.com/AWSEC2/latest/CommandLineReference/*

Getting Started

The Amazon AWS products are fee-based solutions, so you need to set up an account and provide Amazon with a valid payment source. It is very easy to get started using the Amazon cloud, and while you will be paying for your learning curve, if you keep your exercises small (e.g., use small instances and don't leave them running for long periods of time), you can explore and learn how to use the cloud for a very small amount. For example, the research for this chapter was billed for less than a lunch at a popular fast food restaurant. That's way cheaper than buying a small server!

 Amazon charges for many of its products, including computation time and storage. Be sure to terminate your instances when they are not in use and purge temporary storage. While the costs are minimal on a per-hour or per-data-size basis, you will still be billed, even if you are not actively using the resources. Think of it like this: if you leave all the lights on when you go on vacation for two weeks, you shouldn't be surprised when you get the electric bill.

In the next sections, we will show you how to get an AWS account, launch an instance, create a disk volume, and connect it to your running instance. Later in this chapter we will also show you how easy it is to use MySQL in the cloud.

Getting an account

The first thing you need is an Amazon AWS account. To use the basic cloud services, you must create the account, sign up for EC2 access, and sign up for S3 and EBS services. Fortunately, the process is very simple:

1. Go to the AWS website (*http://aws.amazon.com*).
2. Click the Create an AWS Account link.
3. Click the Sign Up Now button.
4. Enter your desired sign-in ID (e.g., your email address) and choose the "I am a new user" option. Click the "Sign in using our secure server" button.

> If you already have an Amazon account for the merchant site, you can use this account instead of creating a new one.

5. Choose a password and verify it by entering it twice. Also supply your email address here. Click the "Create account" button.
6. Enter the full details of your account, including your billing address and contact information. You can optionally supply your own website name and URL. You must accept the AWS customer agreement at the bottom of this page to continue. When you have read and agreed to the customer agreement, click the agreement checkbox, enter the symbols displayed in the security check area, then click the Continue button.
7. Check your email for a confirmation and follow the instructions provided there.
8. Go to your account and supply your billing information on the Account page by clicking on the Payment Method link on the right side of the main page.

> You cannot use AWS EC2 until you have an active payment option.

To sign up for Amazon EC2 (or any service or product), go to the Products page and click the link in the blue box that appears. Then click the "Sign up for" button in the top right of the screen and follow the on-screen instructions. Repeat this process for S3 and any other services or products you want to use.

Getting your credentials

Access to EC2 and other AWS products requires one of several forms of security protocols. These include your AWS sign-in name and password, access keys for accessing the AWS API, X.509 certificates for SOAP protocol access to the AWS API, and key pairs used to access EC2 and CloudFront. Be sure to check the sign-in requirements of the products you want to use to ensure you have the correct credentials.

Amazon recommends creating a folder to store your private keys. Take a moment to create such a folder and protect it from casual discovery before you download your private keys and other security credentials.

Amazon login and password

To use the AWS Management Console and all account actions, you will need the login name and password that you set up when you signed up for AWS.

Access key ID and secret access key

To use the query APIs (e.g., to search for images) and many of the GUI tools (e.g., Elasticfox), you will need an access key ID and a secret access key. These are the most frequently requested credentials. Use the following steps to see and create your access keys:

1. Go to the AWS main page (*http://aws.amazon.com*).
2. Click the Account tab.
3. Click the Security Credentials link.

 You will be asked to sign in if you have not already done so.

4. Locate the Access Credentials section and click the Access Keys tab.
5. If you created access keys when you signed up for AWS, they will be listed here. To see the secret access key, click the Show link next to the desired access key. You can copy this key to a safe (access-protected) file on your system.
6. If there are no access keys or you want to create a new access key, you can click the "Create a new access key" link.

SOAP and EC2 command-line tools

Running the EC2 command-line tools or connecting using the SOAP protocols requires an X.509 certificate and private key. You should rotate your access keys periodically to reduce security risks. Amazon will automatically rotate the keys every 90 days. Use the following steps to see and create your X.509 certificates:

1. Go to the AWS main page (*http://aws.amazon.com*).
2. Click the Account tab.
3. Click the Security Credentials link.

 You will be asked to sign in if you have not already done so.

4. Locate the Access Credentials section and click the X.509 Certificates tab. This will display all of the certificates you have and allow you to activate or deactivate them.
5. To create a new certificate and private key, click the "Create a new certificate" link. This will create a new certificate and start a download of your private key.

 You are allowed to have two certificates. If you already have two, you will need to delete one to create another.

6. When the dialog appears, click the Download Private Key File button and save your private key in the folder you created earlier.
7. Click the Download X.509 Certificate button and save your certificate in the same folder.
8. Click the Close button when you are finished.

You should now have one file that begins with *pk-* and another that begins with *cert-*. These are your private key and certificate files.

Credentials for working with CloudFront

CloudFront requires access via another specific key pair mechanism. These are called simply key pairs and are often confused with the key pairs used with instances. The CloudFront key pairs work like the X.509 certificates in that you must access them on your account's security credentials page and you can have only two active at a time. Use the following steps to see your CloudFront key pairs or to create a new key pair:

1. Go to the AWS main page (*http://aws.amazon.com*).
2. Click the Account tab.
3. Click the Security Credentials link.

 You will be asked to sign in if you have not already done so.

4. Locate the Access Credentials section and click the Key Pairs tab. This will display all of the certificates you have and allow you to activate or deactivate them.

5. To create a new key pair, click the "Create a new key pair" link. This will create a new certificate and start a download of your private key.

You are allowed to have two key pairs. If you already have two, you will need to delete one to create another.

Credentials for working with instances

Instances require access via an SSH key pair. These are created inside the AWS Management Console. You can create as many as you need. The best practice is to create one per instance to reduce risk of accidental or deliberate disclosure.

You will need to do this at least once to get an SSH key pair to launch your first instance.

These keys allow you to access your running instance without the need to remember and manage passwords. This works by embedding one of the keys in the instance and authenticating you when you provide the other key pair on sign-in. You can name the key pairs to help you manage them. You must specify a key pair by name when launching an image.

To create a new SSH key pair, follow the procedure shown here:

1. Go to the AWS Management Console (*https://console.aws.amazon.com/ec2/home*).

You will be asked to sign in if you have not already done so.

2. Click the Key Pairs link on the left side of the page.

3. Click the Create Key Pair button and provide a unique name.

4. Click the Create button. This will create the key pair and begin a download of your private key. Save the key in the folder you created previously.

5. Click the Close button.

Other credentials

Located at the bottom of your accounts security credentials page are your sign-in credentials and your account identifiers. If you want to change your email address or password, you can do so on this page. If you want to collaborate with other AWS accounts, you will need to provide those account holders with your account identifiers and they will need to supply you with theirs. You can find your account identifiers on the bottom of this page.

You can sign up for an optional service called AWS Multi-Factor Authentication, which uses a key generator pad to further increase the security of your account. If security is a high concern when working in AWS, you should consider reading more about what this service can provide. There are buttons and links on this page to assist you in determining whether you should use this service.

Running an instance with the AMS Management Console

Running an instance in EC2 is very easy. It may not seem that way at first, but Amazon has done a great job of making the initial learning curve as gentle as possible.

To run an instance in EC2, go to the *http://aws.amazon.com* page and click the "Sign in to the AWS Management Console" link. You will see a button labeled Launch Instance in the left center of the screen (Figure 14-5).

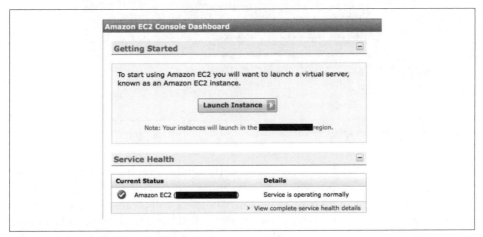

Figure 14-5. Launching an instance in EC2

Next, you will need to choose the image to launch. You will be presented with the Request Instances Wizard, whose first page contains a list of available images provided by Amazon. You will see multiple tabs, allowing you to choose Quick Start (a list of Amazon-provided images preconfigured for common tasks), a MyAMIs tab if you have created any AMIs, and finally the Community AMIs tab with a list of AMIs that developers have created and provided for your use.

Some community AMIs may be fee-based. These are typically AMIs that contain specialized configurations and software. Make sure you're using a free AMI to avoid extra charges, or check the price of the AMI before using it.

Since you are working with MySQL, it is a good idea to choose the image labeled LAMP Web Starter, since it has everything you need to get started using MySQL in the cloud. At this time, the LAMP stack is running on a Fedora host. Figure 14-6 shows the dialog for choosing an image.

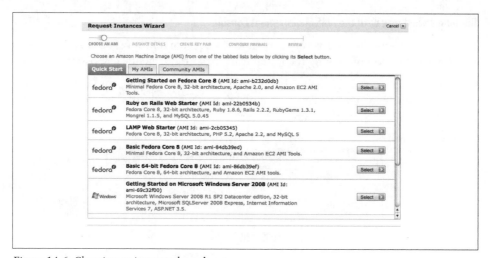

Figure 14-6. Choosing an image to launch

Notice that there is also a Windows server in the Quick Start list. So far, most of the images are Linux-based, but Windows developers are making the Windows images more popular. It remains to be seen whether someone will create a Mac OS X image (perhaps not, given the proprietary nature of the platform). In the case of Windows, you may need to provide your own Windows product keys to use the images.

When you have selected the image you want to launch, click the Select button to the right of its name. On the next page, shown in Figure 14-7, choose the number of instances to launch (yes, you can launch several at once) and the instance type. You can refer back to Table 14-1 to choose the instance type. For most experimentation, the small type is sufficient.

You will also have to choose an availability zone. Choose the one closest to your location. Finally, you must choose between launching an instance and requesting a spot image.

A spot image is an on-demand instance whose usage is charged based on demand (also by the hour). Prices for usage go up as more people bid higher for the instance, and

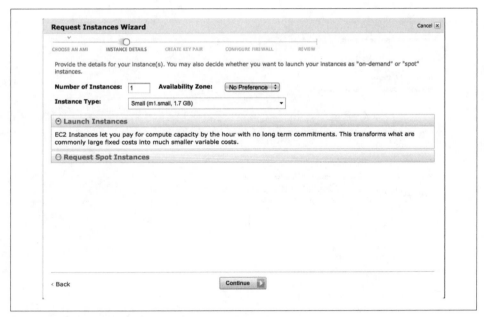

Figure 14-7. Instance details

drop as people bid less, so you can choose how much the instance is worth to you and just wait until there's a lull and the current charges drop below the threshold. This is a great way to run some computations that are not time-sensitive (that is, you can run them anytime during a given period) and do so inexpensively.

When you have selected the number of instances, the instance type, and the availability zone, click the Continue button at the bottom of the dialog.

 The virtual resources you create in AWS have identifiers that start with a short form of the type. For example, instances start with *i-*, volumes with *vol-*, and snapshots with *snap-*. This makes it easy see what you are working with.

On the next screen, shown in Figure 14-8, you specify the kernel ID and RAM disk ID. You should use the default settings for most launches. See the links on this page to learn more about specifying specific kernels and disks. You can also choose to turn on cloud monitoring and record any comments you like about the launch.

Click the Continue button once you have made your selections. On the next screen, shown in Figure 14-9, specify the SSH key pairs you want to use to access this instance. You can use an existing SSH key pair, create a new key pair, or proceed without a key pair (not recommended). Click the "Create a new key pair" button to create a new key pair and give it a name. When you have finished, click the Continue button.

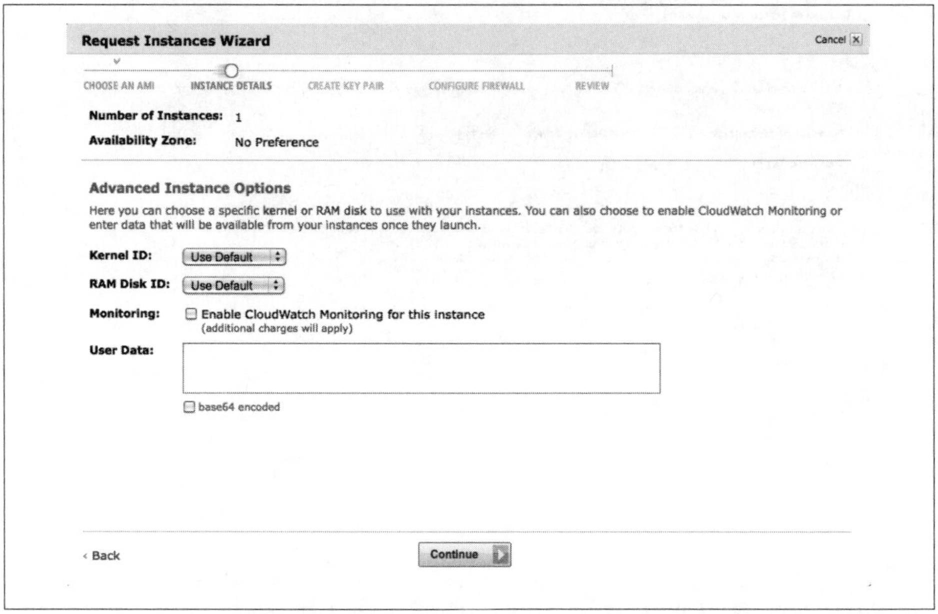

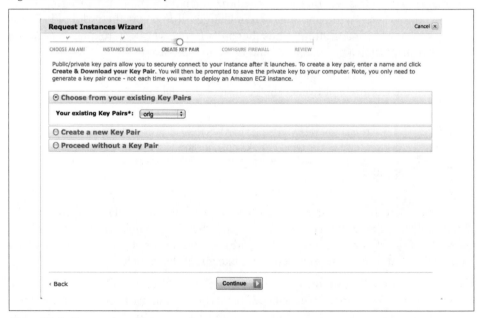

Figure 14-8. Advanced instance options

Figure 14-9. Create a key pair

On the next screen, you must choose a security group or create a new security group to use with this instance. These settings establish the firewall settings for your instance. To get started, click the "Create a new security group" radio selection. Enter a name for the security group followed by a description (be sure to include something meaningful, as shown in Figure 14-10).

Next, define the types of connection allowed. By default, the dialog includes access for SSH TCP port 22 (required to connect using EC2 SSH key pairs) and any other image-specific access. For example, the LAMP image includes HTTP TCP port 80 access and MySQL TCP port 3306. Figure 14-10 shows an example of the default security settings for the LAMP image.

After you have made your selections, click the Continue button.

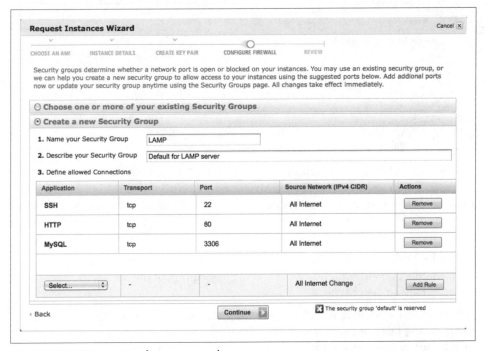

Figure 14-10. Setting network access control

On the next screen, shown in Figure 14-11, you can review your selections and make any necessary changes. When you are ready, click the Launch button to launch your instance.

 You can also use the Back button to return to the previous dialogs.

Request Instances Wizard　　　　　　　　　　　　　　　　　　　　　　　Cancel ✕

CHOOSE AN AMI　　INSTANCE DETAILS　　CREATE KEY PAIR　　CONFIGURE FIREWALL　　REVIEW

Please review the information below, then click **Launch**.

AMI:	🐧 Other Linux AMI ID ami-2cb05345 (i386)	
Name:	LAMP Web Starter	
Description:	Fedora Core 8, 32-bit architecture, PHP 5.2, Apache 2.2, and MySQL 5 Edit AMI	
Number of Instances:	1	
Availability Zone:	No Preference	
Monitoring:	Disabled	
Instance Type:	Small (m1.small)	
Instance Class:	On Demand	Edit Instance Details
Kernel ID:	Use Default	
Ramdisk ID:	Use Default	
User Data:		Edit Advanced Details
Key Pair Name:	orig	Edit Key Pair
Security Group(s):	LAMP	Edit Firewall

‹ Back　　　　　　　　　　　　　　Launch ▶

Figure 14-11. Final launch instance review

A dialog will advise you of your instance status. It informs you that your instance (or instances) will now be shown in the My Instances section of the AWS Management Console. When you return to the console, click on the "running instances" link in the My Resources section. You will see your instance in various stages of launching. When it has launched, you can see its details in the list.

Figure 14-12 shows what images look like when they are running. Notice that you can see the connection information as well as the description of the image, the AMI ID, its status, and its instance type.

You can perform various actions on your instances on this page: start and stop (pause) them, terminate them, and even connect to them. You must first select the checkbox next to one or more instances before performing an action on them.

Let us now connect to the instance. Check the box next to your instance, then use the Instance Actions drop-down list and select Connect. This will display a dialog box like the one shown in Figure 14-13. The dialog will show you the commands you need to use to connect to your instance. Open a terminal or command shell and enter the command as shown. You can click the Close button to dismiss the dialog.

> Be sure to secure your SSH keys properly. For example, issue the CHMOD 0400 <key> command to secure the key.

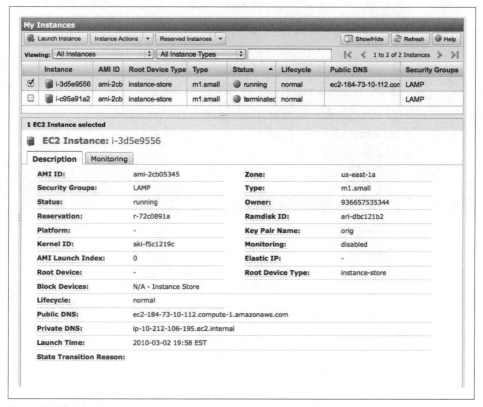

Figure 14-12. My Instances

When you have connected to the instance, you will see a terminal session (SSH) like this:

```
Chucks-MacBook-Pro:~ Chuck$ ssh -i ./ec2_credentials/new_mac.pem
root@ec2-184-73-64-130.compute-1.amazonaws.com

    _|  _|_  )   Fedora 8
    _| (    /    32-bit
  __|\__|__|

Welcome to an EC2 Public Image
              :-)

    Base

--[ see /etc/ec2/release-notes ]--

[root@ip-10-245-114-64 ~]#
```

Since you have root access, you can perform whatever actions you want on your instance. After you have finished experimenting with the instance, you can terminate the instance by returning to the My Instances page in the AWS Management Console,

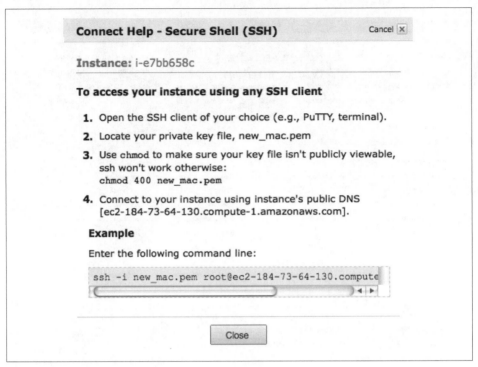

Figure 14-13. Connect Help dialog

checking the box next to the instance, and choosing Terminate in the Instance Actions drop-down list. You will need to confirm the action to continue.

There are many actions available on instances, such as viewing the system log, launching more instances, rebooting an instance, stopping or starting an instance, and enabling or disabling monitoring.

When the instance has terminated, it will be displayed with the terminated status. Before logging out of the AWS Management Console, it is a good idea to make sure you have terminated all of the instances you don't want running. You must terminate the instances because other states may be considered active and may not stop the billing cycle; otherwise, you may be surprised by the bill for the time executed.

Launching an instance with the EC2 API tools

Now that you have seen how easy it is to launch instances from the AWS Management Console, let's look at launching an instance using the EC2 API tools.

Once you have installed the tools, you can follow along as we take a look at launching an image and connecting to it.

The first step is to list the available images. Do this with the `ec2-describe-images` command. In the following example, we use **grep** to search for those images that support MySQL:

```
Chucks-MacBook-Pro:~ Chuck$ ec2-describe-images -o self -o amazon | grep mysql
IMAGE    ami-225fba4b    ec2-public-images/fedora-core4-apache-
    mysql-v1.07.manifest.xml
    amazon    available    public    i386    machine    instance-store
IMAGE    ami-25b6534c    ec2-public-images/fedora-core4-apache-mysql.
    manifest.xmamazon
    available    public    i386    machine    instance-store
IMAGE    ami-255fba4c    ec2-public-images/fedora-core4-mysql-v1.07.
    manifest.xmlamazon
    available    public    i386    machine    instance-store
IMAGE    ami-22b6534b    ec2-public-images/fedora-core4-mysql.
    manifest.xml
    available    public    i386    machine    instance-storee
```

 You can use these commands on Microsoft Windows using Cygwin. Consult the Amazon EC2 user guide for details about setting up the tools on Windows.

Now that we have a list of the available images, we can select the LAMP image and launch it using the `ec2-run-instances` command. Here we supply the image name (AMI ID) from the list we just displayed, as well as our downloaded SSH key file. The following shows the message returned from the command, which displays the instance ID, AMI ID, status (pending), key used, instance type, date/time, region, whether monitoring is enabled, and type of storage:

```
Chucks-MacBook-Pro:~ Chuck$ ec2-run-instances ami-225fba4b -k new_mac
RESERVATION    r-2249194a    936657535344    default
INSTANCE    i-75af711e    ami-225fba4b    pending    new_macm1.small
    2010-03-09T02:13:27+0000    us-east-1d    monitoring-disabled
    instance-store
```

You can check the status of your instances using the `ec2-describe-instances` command. This returns the same information as the previous command, but updated with the latest status.

```
Chucks-MacBook-Pro:~ Chuck$ ec2-describe-instances
RESERVATION    r-2249194a    936657535344    default
INSTANCE    i-75af711e    ami-225fba4b    pending    new_macm1.small
    2010-03-09T02:13:27+0000    us-east-1d    monitoring-disabled
    instance-store
```

Once your instance is running, you will see a display like the following example. Notice that it shows the IP addresses for the instance. You will see two IP addresses. The first is the public IP address of your instance. You can use this or the name of the instance to log in. The second is the private IP address that you can use inside the cloud to communicate among your instances (or another's).

```
Chucks-MacBook-Pro:~ Chuck$ ec2-describe-instances
RESERVATION     r-2249194a     936657535344     default
INSTANCE        i-75af711e     ami-225fba4b     ec2-184-73-9-65.compute-1.
   amazonaws.com
   domU-12-31-39-02-EC-E7.compute-1.internal     running     new_mac     0
   m1.small
   2010-03-09T02:13:27+0000     us-east-1d                  monitoring-disabled
   184.73.9.65     10.248.243.21               instance-store
```

To access your instance, you will need to authorize the security group. We use a short-cut here provided by the `ec2-authorize` command to set the default security group and allow SSH TCP port 22 as shown. See the Amazon EC2 Users Guide for a complete description of the command, and examples of setting custom security groups using the EC2 API tools.

```
Chucks-MacBook-Pro:~ Chuck$ ec2-authorize default -p 22
GROUP        default
PERMISSION       default     ALLOWS     tcp     22     22     FROM     CIDR
   0.0.0.0/0
```

Now we can connect to our instance using SSH.

```
Chucks-MacBook-Pro:~ Chuck$ ssh -i ./ec2_credentials/new_mac.pem
root@ec2-184-73-9-65.compute-1.amazonaws.com

   __| __|_  )  Rev: 2
   _|  (     /
   ___|\___|___|


Welcome to an EC2 Public Image
                 :-)

   Apache2+MySQL4


   __ c __ /etc/ec2/release-notes.txt

[root@domU-12-31-39-02-EC-E7 ~]# exit
logout

Connection to ec2-184-73-9-65.compute-1.amazonaws.com closed.
```

Success! Finally, let's exit the instance and shut it down. To do so, we use the `ec2-terminate-instances` command, supplying the instance ID (from the `describe-instances` results).

```
Chucks-MacBook-Pro:~ Chuck$ ec2-terminate-instances i-75af711e
INSTANCE     i-75af711e     running     shutting-down
Chucks-MacBook-Pro:~ Chuck$ ec2-describe-instances
RESERVATION     r-2249194a     936657535344     default
INSTANCE     i-75af711e     ami-225fba4b     ec2-184-73-9-65.compute-1.amazonaws.com
   domU-12-31-39-02-EC-E7.compute-1.internal     shutting-down     new_macm1.small
   2010-03-09T02:13:27+0000     us-east-1d                  monitoring-disabled
   184.73.9.65     10.248.243.21               instance-store
```

Your instance will now terminate. You can run the `describe-instances` command again (or several times) to verify that the instance has been terminated.

```
Chucks-MacBook-Pro:~ Chuck$ ec2-describe-instances
RESERVATION    r-2249194a    936657535344    default
INSTANCE    i-75af711e    ami-225fba4b                terminated    new_mac    0
        m1.small    2010-03-09T02:13:27+0000    us-east-1d
        monitoring-disabled            instance-store
```

As you can see, all of the functionality to launch an instance in the AWS Management Console is available via the power of the EC2 API tools. Many prefer this form of working with EC2 to the GUI environments. Of course, you can pick and choose what works best for oyou.

Working with Disk

Now that you can launch instances at will, it's time to look at disk storage. In this section, we discuss how disk storage inside the instance (called instance stores or instance volumes) behave, how to back up this data, and how to work with permanent storage by creating an EBS volume and connecting it to a running instance. We conclude with an example of how to perform a snapshot backup of an EBS volume.

 You may want to terminate your running instances while you experiment with creating EBS volumes, but the process is quick and easy so you are unlikely to run up a lot of usage if you leave your instances running.

Using instance storage

Each instance has its own fixed amount of disk storage, which you are free to use for anything you want. However, you must copy this data to a permanent storage area because when the instances are shut down, the data will be lost (and so will any system changes).

This is of particular importance when working with database systems like MySQL. You should not store your data on your instance storage, because if the instance terminates for some reason, you will lose your data.

You can either make regular backups of the data or attach a permanent storage area to your instance. The perfect solution for this, as explained earlier in the chapter, is EBS. With EBS, you can create a volume to hold your data and its storage will survive the instance itself.

The Amazon EC2 user guide has additional information about working with instance storage, including RAID configuration and backing up the data.

Using EBS volumes with the AWS Management Console

Let's create the volume first, then start an instance and connect it. Use the following steps to create a new EBS volume with the AWS Management Console:

1. Go to the AWS Management Console (*https://console.aws.amazon.com/ec2/home*).

 You will be asked to sign in if you have not already done so.

2. Click the Volumes link to the left of the page.
3. Click the Create Volume button and provide the size in gigabytes and the availability zone. Leave the snapshot value as the default.
4. Click the Create button. This will create the volume and return you to the AWS Management Console. You will see the status of your volumes in the EBS Volumes list. Once the volume is ready, you will see the status changed to available.

 You will be charged for EBS storage, including some forms of I/O related to the storage. Be sure to delete any volumes you create that you are not actively using.

Be sure to remember in which zone you created the volume. You can connect volumes only to instances running in the same zone. Figure 14-14 shows what the EBS volume looks like in the list when it is ready.

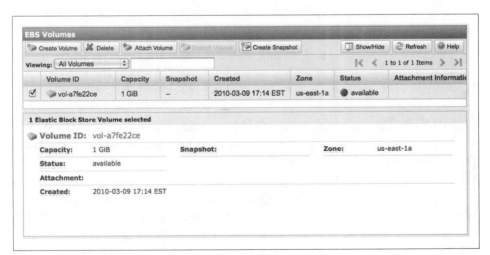

Figure 14-14. EBS Volumes

Note the volume ID of the EBS volume. You can also see additional metadata about the volume in the detail box underneath.

Now you can launch an instance. Once an instance is launched, you can attach the volume to the instance. To do this, return to the EBS Volumes list, select the volume you want to attach to an instance, and click on the Attach Volume button. This opens a dialog like the one shown in Figure 14-15, where you can select the instance to attach and the disk device (e.g., */dev/sdf*). If you use Windows, you will see an appropriate disk name.

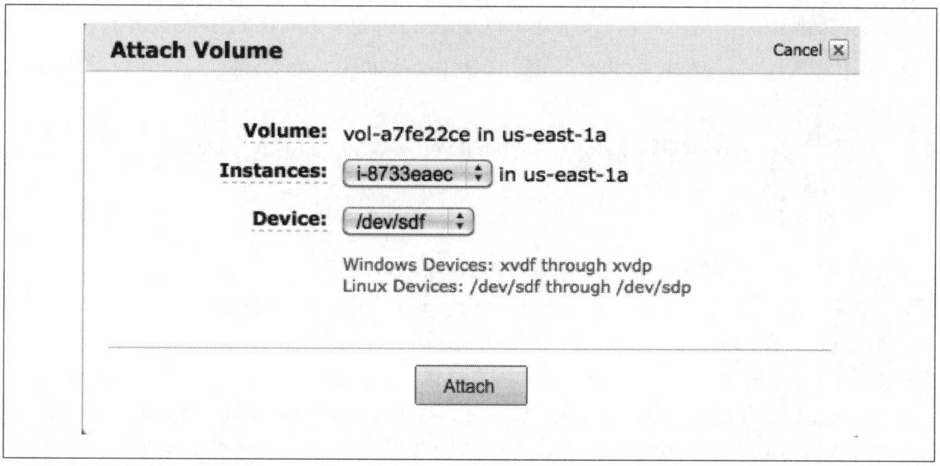

Attach Volume   Cancel ☒

Volume: vol-a7fe22ce in us-east-1a

Instances: [i-8733eaec ⬍] in us-east-1a

Device: [/dev/sdf ⬍]

Windows Devices: xvdf through xvdp
Linux Devices: /dev/sdf through /dev/sdp

[Attach]

Figure 14-15. Choose an instance to attach

You can now log into your instance and begin using the volume. First, make the volume usable. We show a typical Linux procedure below. For Windows, use the *diskmgmt.msc* console to format the drive for use.

1. Create an XFS filesystem.

   ```
   yes | mkfs -t xfs /dev/sdf
   ```

2. Create a mount point.

   ```
   mkdir /mnt/mysql-data
   ```

3. Mount the device.

   ```
   mount /dev/sdf /mnt/mysql-data
   ```

> You may need to install the XFS utilities (e.g., *xfsprogs*) if the image you are using does not have XFS installed.

To disconnect your volume, unmount the device and return to the AWS Management Console, select the volume, and click the Detach Volume button. You will be asked to confirm the operation.

Using EBS snapshots with the AWS Management Console

If you use EBS volumes for storing your data, you can perform a fast backup at any point using EBS snapshots. This creates a new copy of the volume with all of your changes up to the point of the backup.

To create a snapshot of an existing volume, follow the procedure shown here:

1. Issue the command FLUSH TABLES WITH READ LOCK on your database server. This is necessary to ensure all of the data is written to disk and to ensure consistency.

2. Go to the AWS Management Console (*https://console.aws.amazon.com/ec2/home*).

 You will be asked to sign in if you have not already done so.

3. Click the Snapshots link to the left of the page.

4. Click the Create Snapshot button, select the volume to take a snapshot of, and enter a name for the snapshot. Figure 14-16 shows the Create Snapshot dialog.

5. Click the Create button. This will create the snapshot and display the AWS Management Console. You will see the status of your snapshots in the EBS Snapshots list. Once the volume is ready, you will see the status changed to available. Figure 14-17 shows an example of the EBS Snapshots list.

6. Issue the command UNLOCK TABLES on your database server to unlock the tables.

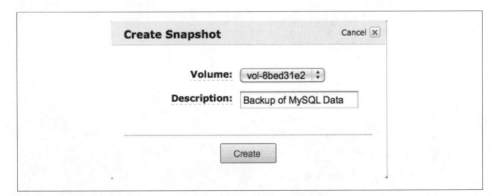

Figure 14-16. Create Snapshot dialog

To delete a snapshot, select the snapshot in the EBS Snapshots list and click the Delete button. You will be asked to confirm the operation.

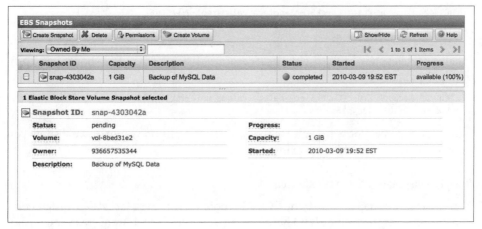

Figure 14-17. EBS Snapshots

Using EBS volumes with the EC2 API tools

You can also create, attach, detach, and delete volumes using the EC2 API tools. To create a volume, use the `ec2-create-volume` command as shown here. Include at least the size of the volume in gigabytes and the zone.

```
Chucks-MacBook-Pro:~ Chuck$ ec2-create-volume -s 1 -z us-east-1a
VOLUME     vol-7fec3016    1        us-east-1a      creating
    2010-03-10T00:28:09+0000
```

You can list all of your volumes by using the `ec2-describe-volumes` command. This provides the same information shown in the EBS Volumes section of the AWS Management Console. The following shows this command in action. Note the volume ID. You will need this to perform operations on the volume.

```
Chucks-MacBook-Pro:~ Chuck$ ec2-describe-volumes
VOLUME     vol-7fec3016    1        us-east-1a      available
    2010-03-10T00:28:09+0000
```

To attach the volume to a running instance, use the `ec2-attach-volume` command as follows, providing the volume ID, the instance ID, and the device name:

```
Chucks-MacBook-Pro:~ Chuck$ ec2-attach-volume vol-7fec3016 -i i-414f962a
 -d /dev/sdf
ATTACHMENT     vol-7fec3016    i-414f962a    /dev/sdf     attaching
    2010-03-10T00:31:06+0000
```

To mount and format the volume for use, follow the procedure described earlier in "Using EBS snapshots with the AWS Management Console" on page 514. Follow the procedure described earlier to unmount the volume from the instance.

To disconnect a volume from an instance, use the `ec2-detach-volume` command as in the following example. You will need to provide the volume ID.

```
Chucks-MacBook-Pro:~ Chuck$ ec2-detach-volume vol-7fec3016
ATTACHMENT    vol-7fec3016    i-414f962a    /dev/sdf    detaching
    2010-03-10T00:31:06+0000
```

Finally, to delete a volume, use the `ec2-delete-volume` command as shown here, providing the volume ID:

```
Chucks-MacBook-Pro:~ Chuck$ ec2-delete-volume vol-7fec3016
VOLUME    vol-7fec3016
```

Now that you know how to perform the basic operations on volumes, we'll show you how to create a snapshot of an existing volume.

Using EBS snapshots with the EC2 API tools

You can create a snapshot with the EC2 API tools using the `ec2-create-snapshot` command, supplying the volume ID. The following example shows how to create a snapshot from the volume we created earlier:

```
Chucks-MacBook-Pro:~ Chuck$ ec2-create-snapshot vol-a7fe22ce
SNAPSHOT    snap-ad5a5dc4    vol-a7fe22ce    pending
    2010-03-09T22:45:22+000936657535344    1
```

It could take a few moments to create the snapshot. You can list your snapshots using the `ec2-describe-snapshots` command:

```
Chucks-MacBook-Pro:~ Chuck$ ec2-describe-snapshots
SNAPSHOT    snap-ad5a5dc4    vol-a7fe22ce    completed
    2010-03-09T22:45:23+0000    100%    936657535344    1
```

Finally, to delete a snapshot, use the `ec2-delete-snapshot` command as follows. This will permanently delete the snapshot, so use it with caution:

```
Chucks-MacBook-Pro:~ Chuck$ ec2-delete-snapshot snap-ad5a5dc4
SNAPSHOT    snap-ad5a5dc4
```

Be sure to check the status of your snapshots to ensure they have been deleted. In this case, the `ec2-describe-snapshots` command should return an empty list.

Where to Go from Here

The Amazon cloud products are very complex and can lead to a steep learning curve. Fortunately, a lot of resources are available on the AWS website. We list a few of the more commonly accessed and must-read links here:

http://aws.amazon.com/documentation/ec2/
http://aws.amazon.com/ec2/
http://aws.amazon.com/autoscaling/
http://aws.amazon.com/s3/
http://aws.amazon.com/ebs/

MySQL in the Cloud

If you are wondering if there is something special about running MySQL in a cloud environment, you can relax. Running MySQL in a cloud is no different from running MySQL on "real" hardware. You can still run replication, set up high availability and scale-out solutions, and use the same tools to monitor and manage those solutions.

What makes using MySQL in the cloud different is the capability to rapidly deploy hundreds of servers whenever you need them. In this section, we will examine some of the solutions presented in previous chapters and how implementation in the cloud affects them. We begin with an example of how you can use MySQL replication in the Amazon cloud.

MySQL Replication and EC2

In this section, we will show you how easy it is to use MySQL replication in EC2. This example launches an instance using the LAMP Web Starter image and connects to it using the EC2 command-line tools. We then modify the instance to act as a master, start a local instance of MySQL, and use it as the slave. The process is identical to setting up replication in a local environment. The only difference is that the master in this example is running in the cloud.

The first step is to launch an instance and connect to it. The following code shows the steps and results of connecting to a running EC2 instance:

```
Chucks-MacBook-Pro:~ Chuck$ ssh -i ./keys/orig.pem
root@ec2-184-73-10-112.compute-1.amazonaws.com
The authenticity of host 'ec2-184-73-10-112.compute-1.amazonaws.com
(184.73.10.112)' can't be established.
RSA key fingerprint is cd:79:eb:e5:e9:2e:d6:a2:9c:79:65:2a:27:c5:1b:ba.
Are you sure you want to continue connecting (yes/no)? yes
Warning: Permanently added 'ec2-184-73-10-112.compute-1.amazonaws.com,
184.73.10.112' (RSA) to the list of known hosts.
Permission denied (publickey,gssapi-with-mic).

      _|  _|_  )   Fedora 8
     _|  (    /      32-bit
    _|\___|__|

  Welcome to an EC2 Public Image
                   :-)

      Base

   --[ see /etc/ec2/release-notes ]--

[root@ip-10-212-106-195 ~]# mysql -uroot
Welcome to the MySQL monitor.  Commands end with ; or \g.
Your MySQL connection id is 2
Server version: 5.0.45 Source distribution
```

```
Type 'help;' or '\h' for help. Type '\c' to clear the buffer.

mysql>
```

The next step is to shut down the remote instance and edit the *my.cnf* file (located in */etc/my.cnf*). At a minimum, set `server-id = 1` and `log-bin = mysql-bin`. Restart the MySQL server and verify it is ready for connections as shown:

```
mysql> SHOW MASTER STATUS;
+------------------+----------+--------------+------------------+
| File             | Position | Binlog_Do_DB | Binlog_Ignore_DB |
+------------------+----------+--------------+------------------+
| mysql-bin.000001 |       98 |              |                  |
+------------------+----------+--------------+------------------+
1 row in set (0.00 sec)
```

You must then issue the `GRANT` statement to permit the slave to connect:

```
mysql> GRANT REPLICATION SLAVE ON *.* TO 'rpl'@'%' IDENTIFIED BY 'rpl';
```

The next step is to configure your slave to connect to the master in EC2. Use the `CHANGE MASTER` command and supply the EC2 instance address and the master's binary log information and the replication user account, as shown in this example:

```
mysql> CHANGE MASTER TO
    MASTER_HOST='ec2-184-73-10-112.compute-1.amazonaws.com',
    MASTER_USER='rpl',
    MASTER_PASSWORD='rpl',
    MASTER_PORT=3306,
    MASTER_LOG_FILE='mysql-bin.000001',
    MASTER_LOG_POS=98;
Query OK, 1 row affected (0.00 sec)
mysql> START SLAVE;
Query OK, 1 row affected (0.00 sec)
```

You can check that replication is working by checking the slave status using the `SHOW SLAVE STATUS` command. The results should show an active slave like that shown here:

```
mysql> SHOW SLAVE STATUS \G
*************************** 1. row ***************************
               Slave_IO_State: Waiting for master to send event
                  Master_Host: ec2-204-236-207-171.compute-1.amazonaws.com
                  Master_User: rpl
                  Master_Port: 3306
                Connect_Retry: 60
              Master_Log_File: mysql-bin.000001
          Read_Master_Log_Pos: 325
               Relay_Log_File: mysqld-relay-bin.000002
                Relay_Log_Pos: 470
        Relay_Master_Log_File: mysql-bin.000001
             Slave_IO_Running: Yes
            Slave_SQL_Running: Yes
              Replicate_Do_DB:
          Replicate_Ignore_DB:
           Replicate_Do_Table:
       Replicate_Ignore_Table:
```

```
            Replicate_Wild_Do_Table:
         Replicate_Wild_Ignore_Table:
                           Last_Errno: 0
                           Last_Error:
                        Skip_Counter: 0
                 Exec_Master_Log_Pos: 325
                     Relay_Log_Space: 626
                     Until_Condition: None
                      Until_Log_File:
                       Until_Log_Pos: 0
                   Master_SSL_Allowed: No
                   Master_SSL_CA_File:
                   Master_SSL_CA_Path:
                     Master_SSL_Cert:
                   Master_SSL_Cipher:
                      Master_SSL_Key:
               Seconds_Behind_Master: 0
    Master_SSL_Verify_Server_Cert: No
                       Last_IO_Errno: 0
                       Last_IO_Error:
                      Last_SQL_Errno: 0
                      Last_SQL_Error:
1 row in set (0.00 sec)
```

Now let's create a database on the master in the EC2 instance and check it on the local slave:

```
mysql> CREATE DATABASE amazon_ec2_test;
Query OK, 1 row affected (0.00 sec)

mysql> SHOW DATABASES;
+--------------------+
| Database           |
+--------------------+
| information_schema |
| amazon_ec2_test    |
| mysql              |
| test               |
+--------------------+
4 rows in set (0.02 sec)
```

When we return to the slave, we see that the database has been created:

```
mysql> SHOW DATABASES;
+--------------------+
| Database           |
+--------------------+
| information_schema |
| amazon_ec2_test    |
| employees          |
| mysql              |
| sakila             |
| test               |
+--------------------+
6 rows in set (0.00 sec)
```

Take some time to try this out and see how easy it is to use MySQL in EC2. Once you complete the steps we've shown, you will have a local slave replicating data from the EC2 master. We leave the reverse experiment for you to set up and evaluate. You should ensure your firewall and router allow incoming traffic on TCP port 3306.

 Remember, your instances in Amazon EC2 are public. Be careful how you set your security access levels and passwords. For example, don't forget to set the root password of your MySQL installation and disable remote logins so that only authorized users can connect to your server. Similarly, open only the ports you need to communicate with your software in the cloud.

Best Practices for Using MySQL in EC2

As mentioned previously, you can do almost anything with MySQL in the cloud that you can on your own physical hardware. We exclude, of course, dedicated hardware clustering solutions and similar hardware-based high availability solutions. But we must remind ourselves that hardware can be virtualized, so even if you have a specific hardware solution that you use today, there is a good possibility it will become a virtualized resource in the cloud tomorrow.

Using MySQL in the Amazon cloud is only slightly different from using MySQL on your own hardware. If you use an AMI with MySQL installed and configured, you can quickly connect your data on your EBS volumes and launch a server. Or you can create your own AMI with a specific MySQL configuration to automate some of the minor setup needed to point the *datadir* to the EBS volumes.

What, then, are the best practices for using MySQL in the cloud? The following lists a few of the more common practices to get the best performance using MySQL in the cloud:

Run only one MySQL server per EC2 instance
> MySQL will run faster with dedicated computational units and memory resources. Given the ease and relative low cost of creating new instances, you will see greater performance by running a single MySQL instance in a smaller instance type than by attempting to run multiple MySQL instances in a larger instance type. Remember, you can add as many instances as you need anytime you need them, allowing you to scale out or scale back at will.

Leverage larger instance types for heavy usage
> Consider using larger instance types for high transactional or heavy read or write databases. The larger instance types not only have more computational units and memory, they also have higher I/O throughput capabilities. In this case, paying a little extra is worth the cost.

Use additional EBS volumes for InnoDB tablespaces

Databases are typically I/O hogs and can become I/O bound. Use multiple EBS volumes to separate your databases and use multiple InnoDB tablespaces (e.g., one per EBS volume) to get better I/O performance.

Warm up data partitions

There is one drawback to using disk I/O in EC2: a "first write" performance hit when initially writing to new partitions. To avoid this penalty, you can "warm up" the partition by executing a sort of throwaway command that accesses it. For example, you can use the Linux **dd** command to write to the disk. While the penalty still occurs and cannot be avoided, at least the first legitimate write to your databases will not suffer the effects.

Configure MySQL properly

Simply running MySQL in EC2 isn't going to make it faster. You cannot skip the configuration and fine-tuning of the MySQL system to meet your specific application needs. Doing so will allow you to better utilize EC2's resources.

Don't forget monitoring

You can and should monitor your MySQL servers running in the cloud, using your choice of the methods discussed in this book. You should also use the Amazon cloud instance monitoring tools to keep tabs on your servers. Just because they're virtualized doesn't make them immune to runaway queries and similar performance problems.

Use MySQL replication

You have seen in previous chapters how important MySQL replication is for scale-out, load balancing, and high availability. The cloud makes these features easier to use because you can create as many MySQL instances as you need to implement almost any MySQL high availability solution.

Use standard AMIs

The capacity to build your own AMIs from scratch allows you to tailor your servers to meet your specific platform needs. Unfortunately, unless you have vast experience in running the host operating system in a virtual environment (or start with a known stable AMI and make only minor changes), the task of building custom AMIs can be time-consuming and error-prone. Whenever possible, use the existing Amazon AMIs or known stable community AMIs.

Use good security practices

The cloud is no different from any other Internet-connected device. Always implement well-documented security protocols for MySQL (e.g., don't leave your root account password blank). You should also restrict access to the EC2 instance such that only authorized users (and systems such as replication slaves) can access your virtual systems. EC2 contains a firewall preconfigured to restrict inbound traffic. Some AMIs have certain ports open, like 3306 for MySQL clients, but you must explicitly open the additional ports you need. Use custom security groups to manage common rules across a group of EC2 instances.

Mount partitions with the `noatime` *and* `nodiratime` *options*

Mounting your partitions with either of these options should yield up to 10 percent faster I/O performance. This is because Linux will not have to perform a write operation after every read access. `noatime` is a superset of `nodiratime`.

Use EBS with MySQL

As mentioned previously, EBS is a block store device with good performance and sustainability from instance failures, as well as elasticity. Not only do you get persistent storage for your data and logfiles, you can also fail over to another server in the event your instance terminates.

Perform snapshotting using S3

You can leverage EC2's capabilities to make a snapshot of your volumes and store it on S3 as part of your backup strategy. Snapshots are an effective and efficient way to create a backup and provide a mechanism for rapid recovery in the event that data becomes corrupt.

Use load balancing

Applications with high loads or a high number of concurrent connections can benefit from load balancing. As described in previous chapters, you can use MySQL replication across multiple MySQL slaves to improve read performance and use sharding to improve write performance. You can use the Amazon Elastic Load Balancing resource or even run your own software load balancer such as HAProxy. For more information about HAProxy, see *http://haproxy.1wt.eu/*.

Open Source Cloud Computing

If you have concerns about spending money on experimenting or learning more about cloud computing, consider an open source solution. The Ubuntu server comes prepackaged with the latest open source cloud system, called Eucalyptus, which is in many ways similar to Amazon EC2 and can help you learn cloud computing without spending any money. For example, if you want to learn how to configure a cloud solution for inhouse experimentation or development, you can load the Ubuntu cloud server and get started right away. The following sequence of commands shows you an example of launching an instance in the Ubuntu cloud using the command-line tools. Notice how similar the commands are to the Amazon commands shown earlier in this chapter:

```
cbell@ubuntu-cloud:~$ euca-describe-images
IMAGE    eri-099C1159    image-store-1266350672/ramdisk.manifest.xml    admin
    available    public    x86_64    ramdisk
IMAGE    emi-DED7106D    image-store-1266350672/image.manifest.xml    admin
    available    public    x86_64    machine
IMAGE    eki-F52D10EB    image-store-1266350672/kernel.manifest.xml    admin
    available    public    x86_64    kernel
```

```
cbell@ubuntu-cloud:~$ euca-describe-volumes
VOLUME     vol-330A04B9    10        cloud9    in-use    2010-02-17T18:54:43.589Z
ATTACHMENT   vol-330A04B9    i-41EE0860    unknown,requested:/dev/sdb
     2010-02-18T17:44:11.561Z
VOLUME     vol-32DC04A3    10        cloud9    in-use    2010-02-17T18:54:41.002Z
ATTACHMENT   vol-32DC04A3    i-4DDB09AC    unknown,requested:/dev/sdb
     2010-02-18T17:44:11.561Z

cbell@ubuntu-cloud:~$ euca-describe-instances
RESERVATION    r-5C060A63    admin    default
INSTANCE    i-41EE0860    emi-DED7106D    172.19.1.3    172.19.1.3
     running    mykey    0    c1.medium    2010-02-18T17:32:12.441Z
     cloud9 eki-F52D10EB    eri-099C1159
RESERVATION    r-4027075E    admin    default
INSTANCE    i-4DDB09AC    emi-DED7106D    172.19.1.2    172.19.1.2
     running    mykey    0    c1.medium    2010-02-18T17:31:55.128Z
     cloud9 eki-F52D10EB    eri-099C1159
```

To learn more about Ubuntu cloud systems and to install your own private cloud computing solutions, see the following links:

http://www.ubuntu.com/cloud
https://help.ubuntu.com/community/UEC

To install an Ubuntu cloud computing environment, you need at least two servers that have virtualization support and multiple core CPUs.

Conclusion

Now that we have taken a look into cloud computing and seen the power of the Amazon cloud solution, it is easy to see how new the old technologies can become when combined in a new way. Cloud computing has made the need for a traditional information infrastructure a thing of the past. With cloud computing you can grow your infrastructure as your business grows and you don't have to hire a squad of technicians to manage it.

In this chapter, we defined cloud computing, examined some of the architectures involved, and took a brief tour of the Amazon EC2, S3, and EBS products. We also presented an example of how you can replicate to and from the Amazon EC2 environment.

Finally, we discussed how you can use MySQL in the cloud, with the good news being that you can do anything in the cloud that you can do on your own physical hardware quicker, faster, and with less investment of resources and money. You can even set up your Amazon cloud solution to automatically scale with your workload. Who wouldn't love that?

"Joel!"

An admonishing audio cue sounded from Joel's speakers as he involuntarily pushed several keys at once. He looked up to see a smiling Mr. Summerson in his office doorway.

Before Joel could say anything, his boss said, "Nice work on that cloud solution proposal. That's just the thing we needed. I'm headed to a board meeting this afternoon." Mr. Summerson made a Frisbee-throwing motion with his arm, tossing a copy of Joel's proposal, which landed with a slap on his desk. "I've made a few notes. I want you to prepare a dozen or so slides and come to the boardroom around 12:30."

Joel looked down at the red ink in dismay. "Um, sir?" he said cautiously.

"Nothing fancy, Joel. Most of the board members were once grunts like us. I hope you like pizza."

Joel thought about that "us" part a moment. He started to ask a question, but Mr. Summerson had already left. Joel sat down and looked at his polo shirt and jeans. He wondered if he had time to go home to change clothes and still get the presentation done in time.

MySQL Cluster

A subdued knock on his door alerted Joel to his visitor. He looked up to see a worried-looking Mr. Summerson.

"I've got to dump on you this time, Joel. We're in a real bind here."

Joel remained silent, wondering what his definition of "dump on you" meant. So far, he had tasked Joel with some pretty intense work.

"We've just learned of a new customer who wants to use our latest database application in a real-time, five-nines environment."

"Always up and no downtime?"

"That's right. Now, I know MySQL is very reliable, but there's no time to change the application to use a fault-tolerant database server."

Joel remembered skimming a chapter on a special version of MySQL and wondered if that would work. He decided to take a chance: "We could use the cluster technology."

"Cluster?"

"Yes, MySQL has a cluster version that is a fault-tolerant database system. It has worked in some pretty demanding environments, like telecom, as I recall...."

Mr. Summerson's eyes brightened and he appeared to stand a little straighter as he delivered his coup de grâce. "Perfect. Give me a report by tomorrow morning. I want cost, hardware requirements, limitations—the works. Don't pull any punches. If we can get this to work I want to do it, but I don't want to risk our reputation on a hunch."

"I'll get right on it," Joel said, wondering what he had gotten himself into this time. After Mr. Summerson left, he sighed and opened his favorite MySQL book. "This may be my greatest challenge yet," he said.

When high performance, high availability, redundancy, and scalability are paramount concerns for database planners, they often seek to improve their replication topologies with commodity high-availability hardware and load-balancing solutions. Although this approach often meets the needs of most organizations, if you need a solution with no single points of failure and extremely high throughput with 99.999% uptime, chances are the MySQL Cluster technology will meet your needs.

In this chapter, we will introduce the concepts of the MySQL Cluster technology; provide you an example of starting and stopping a simple cluster; and discuss the key points of using MySQL Cluster, including high availability, distributed data, and data replication. We begin by describing what MySQL Cluster is and how it differs from a normal MySQL server.

What Is MySQL Cluster?

MySQL Cluster is a shared-nothing, distributed node architecture storage solution designed for fault tolerance and high performance. Data is stored and replicated on individual data nodes (sometimes called *storage nodes*), where each data node executes on a separate server and maintains a copy of the data. Each cluster also contains management nodes. Updates use read-committed isolation to ensure all nodes have consistent data and a two-phased commit to ensure the nodes have the same data (if any one write fails, the update fails).

The original implementation of MySQL Cluster stored all information in main memory with no persistent storage. Later releases of MySQL Cluster permit storage of the data on disk. Perhaps the best quality of MySQL Cluster is that it uses the MySQL server as the query engine via the storage engine layer. Thus, you can migrate applications designed to interact with MySQL to MySQL Cluster transparently.

The shared-nothing, peer node concept permits an update executed on one server to become visible immediately on the other servers. The transmission of the updates uses a sophisticated communication mechanism designed for very high throughput across networks. The goal is to have the highest performance possible by using multiple MySQL servers to distribute the load, and high availability and redundancy by storing data in different locations.

Terminology and Components

Typical installations of the MySQL Cluster involve installing the components of the cluster on different machines on a network. Hence, MySQL Cluster is also known as a network database (NDB). When we use the term "MySQL Cluster," we refer to the MySQL server plus the NDB components. However, when we use "NDB" or "NDB Cluster" we refer specifically to the cluster components.

MySQL Cluster is a database system that uses the MySQL server as the frontend to support standard SQL queries. A storage engine named NDBcluster is the interface that links the MySQL server with the cluster technology. This relationship is often confused. You cannot use the NDBcluster storage engine without the NDB Cluster components.

However, is it is possible to use the NDB Cluster technologies without the MySQL server, but this requires lower-level programming with the NDB API.

The NDB API is object-oriented and implements indexes, scans, transactions, and event handling. This allows you to write applications that retrieve, store, and manipulate data in the cluster. The NDB API also provides object-oriented error-handling facilities to allow orderly shutdown or recovery during failures. If you are a developer and want to learn more about the NDB API, see the MySQL NDB API online documentation (*http://dev.mysql.com/doc/NDBapi/en/index.html*).

How Does MySQL Cluster Differ from MySQL?

You may be wondering, "What is the difference between a cluster and replication?" There are several definitions of clustering, but it can generally be viewed as something that has membership, messaging, redundancy, and automatic failover capabilities. Replication, in contrast, is simply a way to send messages (data) from one server to another. We discuss replication within a cluster (also called *local replication*) and MySQL replication in more detail later in this chapter.

Typical Configuration

You can view the MySQL Cluster as having three layers:

- Applications that communicate with the MySQL server
- The MySQL server that processes the SQL commands and communicates to the NDB storage engine
- The NDB Cluster components (sometimes called *data nodes*) that process the queries and return the results to the MySQL server

 You can scale up each layer independently with more server processes to increase performance.

Figure 15-1 shows a conceptual drawing of a typical cluster installation.

The applications connect to the MySQL server, which accesses the NDB Cluster components via the storage engine layer (specifically, the NDB storage engine). We will discuss the NDB Cluster components in more detail momentarily.

There are many possible configurations. You can use multiple MySQL servers to connect to a single NDB Cluster and even connect multiple NDB Clusters via MySQL replication. We will discuss more of these configurations in later sections.

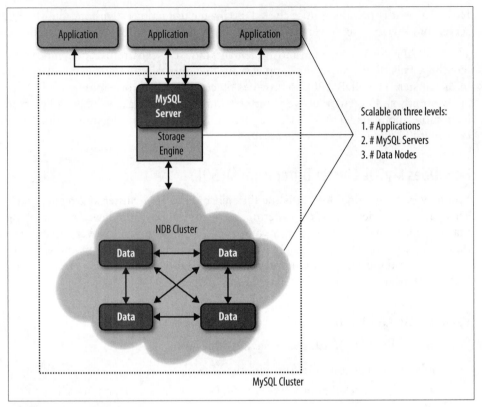

Figure 15-1. MySQL Cluster

Features of MySQL Cluster

To satisfy the goals of having the highest achievable performance, high availability, and redundancy, data is replicated inside the cluster among the peer data nodes. The data is replicated using a synchronous mechanism in which each data node connects to every other data node and data is stored on multiple data nodes.

> It is also possible to replicate data between clusters, but in this case you use MySQL replication, which is *asynchronous* rather than *synchronous*. As we've discussed in previous chapters, asynchronous replication means you must expect a delay in updating the slaves, slaves do not report back the progress in committing changes, and you cannot expect a consistent view across all servers in the replicated architecture like you can expect within a single MySQL cluster.

MySQL Cluster has several specialized features for creating a highly available system. The most significant ones are:

Node recovery

Data node failures can be detected via either communication loss or heartbeat failure, and you can configure the nodes to restart automatically using copies of the data from the remaining nodes. Failure and recovery can comprise single or multiple storage nodes. This is also called *local recovery*.

Logging

During normal data updates, copies of the data change events are written to a log stored on each data node. You can use the logs to restore the data to a point in time.

Checkpointing

The cluster supports two forms of checkpoints, local and global. Local checkpoints remove the tail of the log. Global checkpoints are created when the logs of all data nodes are flushed to disk, creating a transaction-consistent snapshot of all node data to disk. In this way, checkpointing permits a complete system restore of all nodes from a known good synchronization point.

System recovery

In the event the whole system is shut down unexpectedly, you can restore it using checkpoints and change logs. Typically, the data is copied from disk into memory from known good synchronization points.

Hot backup and restore

You can create simultaneous backups of each data node without disturbing executing transactions. The backup includes the metadata about the objects in the database, the data itself, and the current transaction log.

No single point of failure

The architecture is designed so that any node can fail without bringing down the database system.

Failover

To ensure node recovery is possible, all transactions are committed using read commit isolation and two-phase commits. Transactions are then doubly safe; that is, they are stored in two separate locations before the user gets acceptance of the transaction.

Partitioning

Data is automatically partitioned across the data nodes. MySQL version 5.1 Cluster supports user-defined partitioning.

Online operations

You can perform many of the maintenance operations online without the normal interruptions. These are operations that normally require stopping a server or placing locks on data. For example, it is possible to add new data nodes online, alter table structures, and even reorganize the data in the cluster.

For more information about MySQL Cluster, see the online reference manual (*http:// dev.mysql.com/doc/mysql-cluster-excerpt/5.1/en/index.html*).

Local and Global Redundancy

You can create local redundancy (inside a particular cluster) using a two-phase commit protocol. In principle, each node goes through a round in which it agrees to make a change, then undergoes a round in which it commits the transaction. During the agreement phase, each node ensures that there are enough resources to commit the change in the second round. In NDB Cluster, the MySQL server commit protocol changes to allow updates to multiple nodes. NDB Cluster also has an optimized version of two-phase commit that reduces the number of messages sent using synchronous replication. The two-phase protocol ensures the data is redundantly stored on multiple data nodes, a state known as *local redundancy*.

Global redundancy uses MySQL replication between clusters. This establishes two nodes in a replication topology. As discussed previously, MySQL replication is asynchronous because it does not include an acknowledgment or receipt for arrival or execution of the events replicated. Figure 15-2 illustrates the differences.

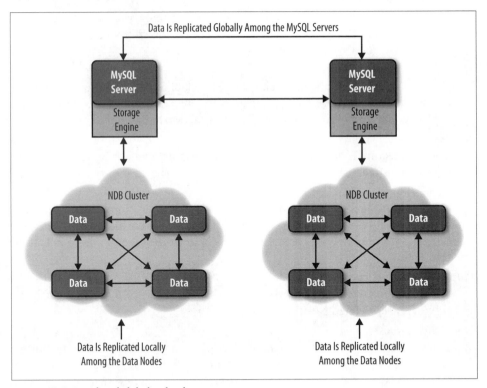

Figure 15-2. Local and global redundancy

Log Handling

MySQL Cluster implements two types of checkpoints: local checkpoints to purge part of the redo log and a global checkpoint that is mainly for synchronizing between the different data nodes. The global checkpoint becomes important for replication because it forms the boundary between sets of transactions known as *epochs*. Each epoch is replicated between clusters as a single unit. In fact, MySQL replication treats the set of transactions between two consecutive global checkpoints as a single transaction.

Redundancy and Distributed Data

Data redundancy uses *replicas*. Each replica has a copy of the data. This allows a cluster to be fault tolerant. If any data node fails, you can still access the data. Naturally, the more replicas you allow in a cluster, the more fault tolerant the cluster will be.

Split-Brain Syndrome

If one or more data nodes fail, it is possible that the remaining data nodes will be unable to communicate. When this happens, the two sets of data nodes are in a split-brain scenario. This type of situation is undesirable, because each set of data nodes could theoretically perform as a separate cluster.

To overcome this, you need a network partitioning algorithm to decide between the competing sets of data nodes. The decision is made in each set independently. The set with the minority of nodes will be restarted and each node of that set will need to join the majority set individually.

If the two sets of nodes are exactly the same size, a theoretical problem still exists. If you split four nodes into two sets with two nodes in each, how do you know which set is a minority? For this purpose, you can define an arbitrator. In the case that the sets are exactly the same size, the set that first succeeds in contacting the arbitrator wins.

You can designate the arbitrator as either a MySQL server (SQL node) or a management node. For best availability, you should locate the arbitrator on a system that does not host a data node.

The network partitioning algorithm with arbitration is fully automatic in MySQL Cluster, and the minority is defined with respect to node groups to make the system even more available than it would be compared to just counting the nodes.

You can specify how many copies of the data (NoOfReplicas) exist in the cluster. You need to set up as many data nodes as you want replicas. You can also distribute the data across the data nodes using partitioning. In this case, each data node has only a portion of the data, making queries faster. But since you have multiple copies of the data, you can still query the data in the event that a node fails, and the recovery of the missing node is assured (because the data exists in the other replicas). To achieve this, you need multiple data nodes for each replica. For example, if you want two replicas and partitioning, you need to have at least four data nodes (two data nodes for each replica).

Architecture of MySQL Cluster

MySQL Cluster is composed of one or more MySQL servers communicating via the NDB storage engine to an NDB cluster. An NDB cluster itself is composed of several components: data or storage nodes that store and retrieve the data and one or more management nodes that coordinate startup, shutdown, and recovery of data nodes. Most of the NDB components are implemented as daemon processes, while MySQL Cluster also offers client utilities to manipulate the daemons' features. A list of the daemons and utilities follows. Figure 15-3 depicts how each of these components communicates.

mysqld
> The MySQL server

NDBd
> A data node

NDBmtd
> A multithreaded data node

NDB_mgmd
> The cluster's management server

NDB_mgm
> The cluster's management client

Each MySQL server with the executable name *mysqld* typically supports one or more applications that issue SQL queries and receive results from the data nodes. When discussing MySQL Cluster, the MySQL servers are sometimes called *SQL nodes*.

The data nodes are NDB daemon processes that store and retrieve the data either in memory or on disk depending on their configuration. Data nodes are installed on each server participating in the cluster. There is also a multithreaded data node daemon named NDBmtd that works on platforms that support multiple CPU cores. You can see improved data node performance if you use the multithreaded data node on dedicated servers with modern multiple-core CPUs.

The management daemon, NDB_mgmd, runs on a server and is responsible for reading a configuration file and distributing the information to all of the nodes in the cluster. NDB_mgm, the NDB management client utility, can check the cluster's status, start backups, and perform other administrative functions. This client runs on a host convenient to the administrator and communicates with the daemon.

There are also a number of utilities that make maintenance easier. A few of the more popular ones follow. Consult the NDB Cluster documentation for a complete list.

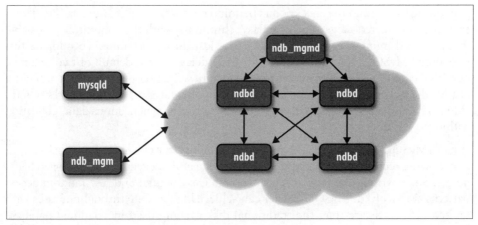

Figure 15-3. The MySQL Cluster components

NDB_config
    Extracts configuration information from existing nodes.

NDB_delete_all
    Deletes all rows from an NDB table.

NDB_desc
    Describes NDB tables (like SHOW CREATE TABLE).

NDB_drop_index
    Drops an index from an NDB table.

NDB_drop_table
    Drops an NDB table.

NDB_error_reporter
    Diagnoses errors and problems in a cluster.

NDB_redo_log_reader
    Checks and prints out a cluster redo log.

NDB_restore
    Performs a restore of a cluster. Backups are made using the NDB management client.

How Data Is Stored

MySQL Cluster keeps all indexed columns in main memory. You can store the remaining nonindexed columns either in memory or on disk with an in-memory page cache. Storing nonindexed columns on disk allows you to store more data than the size of available memory.

When data is changed (via INSERT, UPDATE, DELETE, etc.), MySQL Cluster writes a record of the change to a redo log, checkpointing data to disk regularly. As described previously, the log and the checkpoints permit recovery from disk after a failure. However, because the redo logs are written asynchronously with the commit, it is possible that a limited number of transactions can be lost during a failure. To mitigate this possibility, MySQL Cluster implements a write delay (with a default of two seconds, but this is configurable). This allows the checkpoint write to complete so that if a failure occurs, the last checkpoint is not lost as a result of the failure. Normal failures of individual data nodes do not result in any data loss due to the synchronous data replication within the cluster.

When a MySQL Cluster table is maintained in memory, the cluster accesses disk storage only to write records of the changes to the redo log and to execute the requisite checkpoints. Since writing the logs and checkpoints is sequential and few random access patterns are involved, MySQL Cluster can achieve higher write throughput rates with limited disk hardware than the traditional disk caching used in relational database systems.

You can calculate the size of memory you need for a data node using the following formula. The size of the database is the sum of the size of the rows times the number of rows for each table. Keep in mind that if you use disk storage for nonindexed columns, you should count only the indexed columns in calculating the necessary memory.

$$(SizeofDatabase \times NumberOfReplicas \times 1.1) / NumberOfDataNodes$$

This is a simplified formula for rough calculation. When planning the memory of your cluster, you should consult the online MySQL Cluster Reference Manual for additional details to consider.

You can also use the Perl script *NDB_size.pl* found in most distributions. This script connects to a running MySQL server, traverses all the existing tables in a set of databases, and calculates the memory they would require in a MySQL cluster. This is convenient, because it permits you to create and populate the tables on a normal MySQL server first, then check your memory configuration before you set up, configure, and load data into your cluster. It is also useful to run periodically to keep ahead of schema changes that can result in memory issues and to give you an idea of your memory usage. Example 15-1 depicts a sample report for a simple database with a single table. To find the total size of the database, multiply the size of the data row from the summary by the number of rows. In Example 15-1, we have (for MySQL version 5.1) 84 bytes per row for data and index. If we had 64,000 rows, we would need to have 5,376,000 bytes of memory to store the table.

 If the script generates an error about a missing *Class/Method-Maker.pm* module, you need to install this class on your system. For example, on Ubuntu you can install it with the following command:

```
sudo apt-get install libclass-methodmaker-perl
```

Example 15-1. Checking the size of a database with NDB_size.pl

```
cbell@cbell-mini:~/mysql-cluster-gpl-7.0.13-linux-i686-glibc23/bin$ ./NDB_size.pl \
--database=cluster_test --user=root
NDB_size.pl report for database: 'cluster_test' (1 tables)
-----------------------------------------------------------
Connected to: DBI:mysql:host=localhost

Including information for versions: 4.1, 5.0, 5.1

cluster_test.City
-----------------

DataMemory for Columns (* means varsized DataMemory):
    Column Name  Type    Varsized   Key    4.1    5.0    5.1
       district  char(20)                   20     20     20
     population  int(11)                      4      4      4
          ccode  char(3)                      4      4      4
           name  char(35)                    36     36     36
             id  int(11)    PRI                4      4      4
                                            --     --     --
Fixed Size Columns DM/Row                    68     68     68
 Varsize Columns DM/Row                       0      0      0

DataMemory for Indexes:
    Index Name      Type      4.1    5.0     5.1
       PRIMARY      BTREE     N/A    N/A     N/A
                              --     --      --
    Total Index DM/Row          0      0       0

IndexMemory for Indexes:
           Index Name     4.1     5.0      5.1
              PRIMARY      29      16       16
                          --      --       --
        Indexes IM/Row     29      16       16

Summary (for THIS table):
                            4.1     5.0      5.1
    Fixed Overhead DM/Row    12      12       16
        NULL Bytes/Row        0       0        0
        DataMemory/Row       80      80       84
(Includes overhead, bitmap and indexes)

  Varsize Overhead DM/Row     0       0        8
 Varsize NULL Bytes/Row       0       0        0
     Avg Varside DM/Row       0       0        0

             No. Rows         3       3        3

      Rows/32kb DM Page     408     408      388
Fixedsize DataMemory (KB)    32      32       32

Rows/32kb Varsize DM Page     0       0        0
 Varsize DataMemory (KB)      0       0        0

       Rows/8kb IM Page     282     512      512
```

```
        IndexMemory (KB)        8        8        8

Parameter Minimum Requirements
------------------------------
* indicates greater than default

              Parameter   Default     4.1     5.0     5.1
         DataMemory (KB)     81920      32      32      32
      NoOfOrderedIndexes       128       1       1       1
             NoOfTables       128       1       1       1
        IndexMemory (KB)     18432       8       8       8
     NoOfUniqueHashIndexes      64       0       0       0
          NoOfAttributes      1000       5       5       5
            NoOfTriggers       768       5       5       5
```

Notice that while Example 15-1 uses a very simple table, the output shows not only the row size, but also a host of statistics for the tables in the database. The report also shows the indexing statistics, which are the key mechanism the cluster uses for high performance.

The script displays the different memory requirements across MySQL versions. This allows you to see any differences if you are working with older versions of MySQL Cluster.

Partitioning

One of the most important aspects of MySQL Cluster is data partitioning. MySQL Cluster partitions data horizontally. That is, the rows are automatically divided among the data nodes using a function to distribute the rows. This is based on a hashing algorithm that uses the primary key for the table. In early versions of MySQL, the software uses an internal mechanism for partitioning, but MySQL versions 5.1 and later allow you to provide your own function for partitioning data. If you use your own function for partitioning, you should create a function that ensures the data is distributed evenly among the data nodes.

 If a table does not have a primary key, MySQL Cluster adds a surrogate primary key.

Partitioning allows the MySQL Cluster to achieve higher performance for queries because it supports distribution of queries among the data nodes. Thus, a query will return results much faster when gathering data across several nodes than from a single node. For example, you can execute the following query on each data node, getting the sum of the column on each one and summing those results:

```
SELECT SUM(population) FROM cluster_db.city;
```

Data distributed across the data nodes is protected from failure if you have more than one replica (copy) of the data. If you want to use partitioning to distribute your data across multiple data nodes to achieve parallel queries, you should also ensure you have at least two replicas of each row so that your cluster is fault tolerant.

Transaction Management

Another aspect of MySQL Cluster's behavior that differs from MySQL server concerns transactional data operations. As mentioned previously, MySQL Cluster coordinates transactional changes across the data nodes. This uses two subprocesses called the *transaction coordinator* and the *local query handler*.

The transaction coordinator handles distributed transactions and other data operations on a global level. The local query handler manages data and transactions local to the cluster's data nodes and acts as a coordinator of two-phase commits at the data node.

Each data node can be a transaction coordinator (you can tune this behavior). When an application executes a transaction, the cluster connects to a transaction coordinator on one of the data nodes. The default behavior is to select the closest data node as defined by the networking layer of the cluster. If there are several connections available within the same distance, a round-robin algorithm selects the transaction coordinator.

The selected transaction coordinator then sends the query to each data node and the local query handler executes the query, coordinating the two-phased commit with the transaction coordinator. Once all data nodes verify the transaction, the transaction coordinator validates (commits) the transaction.

MySQL Cluster supports the read-committed transaction isolation level. This means that when there are changes during the execution of the transaction, only committed changes can be read while the transaction is underway. In this way, MySQL Cluster ensures data consistency while transactions are running.

For more information about how transactions work in MySQL Cluster and a list of important limitations on transactions, see the MySQL Cluster chapter in the online MySQL Reference Manual.

Online Operations

In MySQL versions 5.1 and later, you can perform certain operations while a cluster is online, meaning that you do not have to either take the server down or lock portions of the system or database. The following list briefly discusses a few of the online operations available in MySQL Cluster and lists the versions that include each feature:

Backup (versions 5.0 and later)
> You can use the NDB management console to perform a snapshot backup (a non-blocking operation) to create a backup of your data in the cluster. This operation includes a copy of the metadata (names and definitions of all tables), the table data,

and the transaction log (a historical record of changes). It differs from a `mysql`
`dump` backup in that it is nonblocking and does not use a table scan to read the
records. You can restore the data using the special `NDB_restore` utility.

Adding and dropping indexes (versions 5.1 and later)

You can use the `ONLINE` keyword to perform the `CREATE INDEX` or `DROP INDEX` command online. When online operation is requested, the operation is noncopying—
it does not make a copy of the data in order to index it—so indexes do not have to
be re-created afterward. One advantage of this is that transactions can continue
during alter table operations and tables being altered are not locked against access
by other SQL nodes. However, the table is locked against other queries on the SQL
node performing the alter operation.

> In MySQL versions 5.1.7 and later, add and drop index operations
> are performed online when the indexes are on variable-width col-
> umns only.

Alter table (versions 6.2 and later)

You can use the `ONLINE` keyword to execute an `ALTER TABLE` statement online. It is
also noncopying and has the same advantages as adding indexes online. Additionally, in MySQL versions 7.0 and later, you can reorganize the data across partitions
online using the `REORGANIZE PARTITION` command as long as you don't use the `INTO`
`(partition_definitions)` option.

> Changing default column values or data types online is currently
> not supported.

Add data nodes and node groups (versions 7.0 and later)

You can manage the expansion of your data nodes online, either for scale-out or
for node replacement after a failure. The process is described in great detail in the
reference manual. Briefly, it involves changing the configuration file, performing a
rolling restart of the NDB management daemon, performing a rolling restart of the
existing data nodes, starting the new data nodes, and then reorganizing the
partitions.

For more information about MySQL Cluster, its architecture, and its version 7.0 features, see the white paper available at *http://www.mysql.com/why-mysql/white-papers/
mysql_wp_cluster7_architecture.php*.

Example Configuration

In this section, we present a sample configuration of a MySQL Cluster running two data nodes on two systems, with the MySQL server and NDB management node on a third system. We present examples of simplified data node setup. Our example system is shown in Figure 15-4.

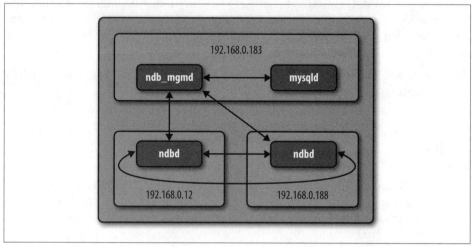

Figure 15-4. Sample cluster configuration

You can see one node that contains both the NDB management daemon and the SQL node (the MySQL server). There are also two data nodes, each on its own system. You need a minimum of three computers to form a basic MySQL Cluster configuration with either increased availability or performance.

This is a minimal configuration for MySQL Cluster and, if the number of replicas is set to two, the minimal configuration for fault tolerance. If the number of replicas is set to one, the configuration will support partitioning for better performance but will not be fault tolerant.

It is generally permissible to run the NDB management daemon on the same node as a MySQL server, but you may want to move this daemon to another system if you are likely to have a high number of data nodes or want to ensure the greatest level of fault tolerance.

Getting Started

You can obtain MySQL Cluster from the MySQL downloads page (*http://www.mysql .com/downloads/cluster/*). It is open source, like the MySQL server. You can download either a binary distribution or an installation file for some of the top platforms. You can also download the source code and build the cluster on your own platform. Be sure to check the platform notes for specific issues for your host operating system.

You should follow the normal installation procedures outlined in the online MySQL Reference Manual. Aside from one special directory, the NDB tools are installed in the same location as the MySQL server binaries.

Before we dive into our example, let us first review some general concepts concerning configuring a MySQL cluster. The cluster configuration is maintained by the NDB management daemon and is read (initially) from a configuration file. There are many parameters that you can use to tune the various parts of the cluster, but we will concentrate on a minimal configuration for now.

There are several sections in the configuration file. At a minimum, you need to include each of the following sections:

mysqld
> The familiar section of the configuration file that applies to the MySQL server, the SQL node.

NDB DEFAULT
> A default section for global settings. Use this section to specify all of the settings you want applied to every node, both data and management. Note that the name of the section contains a space, not an underscore.

NDB_MGMD
> A section for the NDB management daemon.

NDBD
> You must add one section with this name for each data node.

Example 15-2 shows a minimal configuration file that matches the configuration in Figure 15-4.

Example 15-2. Minimal configuration file

```
[NDBD DEFAULT]
NoOfReplicas= 2
DataDir= /var/lib/mysql-cluster

[NDB_MGMD]
Hostname=192.168.0.183
DataDir= /var/lib/mysql-cluster

[NDBD]
Hostname=192.168.0.12

[NDBD]
Hostname=192.168.0.188

[MYSQLD]
Hostname=192.168.0.183
```

This example includes the minimal variables for a simple two data-node cluster with replication. Thus, the `NoOfReplicas` option is set to 2. Notice we have set the `datadir` variable to `/var/lib/mysql-cluster`. You can set it to whatever you want, but most installations of MySQL Cluster use this directory.

Finally, notice we have specified the hostname of each node. This is important, because the NDB management daemon needs to know the location of all of the nodes in the cluster. If you have downloaded and installed MySQL Cluster and want to follow along, make the necessary changes to the hostnames so they match our example.

You should place your cluster configuration file in the */var/lib/mysql-cluster* directory and name it *config.ini* (the standard name and location for this file).

 It is not necessary to install the complete MySQL Cluster binary package on the data nodes. As you will see later, you need only the NDBd daemon on the data nodes.

Starting a MySQL Cluster

Starting MySQL Cluster requires a specific order of commands. We will step through the procedures for this example, but it is good to briefly examine the general process:

1. Start the management node(s).
2. Start the data nodes.
3. Start the MySQL servers (SQL nodes).

For our example, we first start the NDB management node on 192.168.0.183. Then we start each of the data nodes (192.168.0.12 and 192.168.0.188, in either order). Once the data nodes are running, we can start the MySQL server on 192.168.0.183 and, after a brief startup delay, the cluster is ready to use.

Starting the management node

The first node to start is the NDB management daemon named NDB_mgmd. This is located in the *libexec* folder of the MySQL installation. For example, on Ubuntu it is located in */usr/local/mysql/libexec*.

Start the NDB management daemon by issuing a superuser launch and specify the `--initial` and `-f` options. The `--initial` option tells the cluster that this is our first time starting and we want to erase any configurations stored from previous launches. The `-f` option tells the daemon where to find the configuration file. Example 15-3 shows how to start the NDB management daemon for our example.

Example 15-3. Starting the NDB management daemon

```
cbell@mysql-xps-400:/usr/local/mysql/bin$ sudo ../libexec/NDB_mgmd --initial \
-f /var/lib/mysql-cluster/config.ini
```

```
2010-03-25 09:10:28 [MgmtSrvr] INFO
    -- NDB Cluster Management Server. mysql-5.1.44 NDB-7.0.14
2010-03-25 09:10:29 [MgmtSrvr] INFO
    -- Reading cluster configuration from '/var/lib/mysql-cluster/config.ini'
```

It is always a good idea to provide the -f option when you start, because some installations have different default locations for the configuration file search pattern. You
can discover this pattern by issuing the command NDB_mgmd --help and searching for
the phrase "Default options are read from." It is not necessary to specify the -f option
on subsequent starts of the daemon.

Starting the management console

While not absolutely necessary at this point, it is a good idea to now launch the NDB
management console and check that the NDB management daemon has correctly read
the configuration. The name of the NDB management console is NDB_mgm and it is
located in the *bin* directory of the MySQL installation. We can view the configuration
by issuing the SHOW command, as shown in Example 15-4.

Example 15-4. Initial start of the NDB management console

```
cbell@mysql-xps-400:/usr/local/mysql/bin$ ./NDB_mgm
-- NDB Cluster -- Management Client --
NDB_mgm> SHOW
Connected to Management Server at: 192.168.0.183:1186
Cluster Configuration
---------------------
[NDBd(NDB)]    2 node(s)
id=2 (not connected, accepting connect from 192.168.0.188)
id=3 (not connected, accepting connect from 192.168.0.12)

[NDB_mgmd(MGM)]    1 node(s)
id=1    @192.168.0.183  (mysql-5.1.44 NDB-7.0.14)

[mysqld(API)]    1 node(s)
id=4 (not connected, accepting connect from 192.168.0.183)

NDB_mgm>
```

This command displays the data nodes and their IP addresses as well as the NDB management daemon and the SQL node. This is a good time to check that all of our nodes
are configured with the right IP addresses and that all of the appropriate data nodes are
loaded. If you have changed your cluster configuration but see the old values here, it
is likely the NDB management daemon has not read the new configuration file.

This output tells us that the NDB management daemon is loaded and ready. If it were
not, the SHOW command would fail with a communication error. If you see that error,
be sure to check that you are running the NDB management client on the same server
as the NDB management daemon. If you are not, use the --NDB-connectstring option

and provide the IP address or hostname of the machine hosting the NDB management daemon.

Finally, notice the node IDs of your nodes. You will need this information to issue commands to a specific node in the cluster from the NDB management console. Issue the HELP command at any time to see the other commands available. You will also need to know the node ID for your SQL nodes so that they start up correctly.

 You can specify the node IDs for each node in your cluster using the --NDB-nodeid parameter in the *config.ini* file.

We can also use the STATUS command to see the status of our nodes. Issue ALL STATUS to see the status of all nodes or *node-id* STATUS to see the status of a specific node. This command is handy for watching the cluster start up, because the output reports which startup phase the data node is in. Refer to the MySQL Cluster section of the online MySQL Reference Manual for more details about the phases of data node startup.

Starting data nodes

Now that we have started our NDB management daemon, it is time to start the data nodes. However, before we do that, let's examine the minimal setup needed for an NDB data node.

To set up an NDB data node, all you need is the NDB data node daemon (NDBd) compiled for the targeted host operating system. First, create the folder */var/lib/mysql-cluster*, then copy in the NDBd executable, and you're done! Clearly, this makes it very easy to script the creation of data nodes (and many have).

You can start the data nodes (NDBd) using the --initial-start option, which signals that this is the first time the cluster has been started. You also must provide the --NDB-connectstring option, providing the IP address of the NDB management daemon. Example 15-5 shows starting a data node for the first time. Do this on each data node.

Example 15-5. Starting the data node

```
cbell@mysql-mini:~/mysql-cluster-gpl-7.0.13-linux-x86_64-glibc23/bin$
 sudo ./NDBd --initial-start --NDB-connectstring=192.168.0.183
2010-03-25 09:04:18 [NDBd] INFO
    -- Configuration fetched from '192.168.0.183:1186', generation: 1
```

If you are starting a new data node, have reset a data node, or are recovering from a failure, you can specify the --initial option to force the data node to erase any existing configuration and cached data and request a new copy from the NDB management daemon.

Be careful when using the `--initial` options. They really do delete your data!

Return to the management console and check the status (Example 15-6).

Example 15-6. Status of data nodes

```
NDB_mgm> SHOW
Cluster Configuration
---------------------
[NDBd(NDB)]     2 node(s)
id=2    @192.168.0.188  (mysql-5.1.41 NDB-7.0.13, Nodegroup: 0, Master)
id=3    @192.168.0.12  (mysql-5.1.41 NDB-7.0.13, Nodegroup: 0)

[NDB_mgmd(MGM)]     1 node(s)
id=1    @192.168.0.183  (mysql-5.1.44 NDB-7.0.14)

[mysqld(API)]    1 node(s)
id=4 (not connected, accepting connect from 192.168.0.183)
```

You can see that the data nodes started successfully, because information about their daemons is shown. You can also see that one of the nodes has been selected as the master for cluster replication. Since we set the number of replicas to 2 in our configuration file, we have two copies of the data. Don't confuse this notion of master with a master in MySQL replication. We discuss the differences in more detail later in the chapter.

Starting the SQL nodes

Once the data nodes are running, we can connect our SQL node. There are several options we must specify that enable a MySQL server to connect to an NDB cluster. Most people specify these in the *my.cnf* file, but you can also specify them on the startup command line if you start the server in that manner.

NDBcluster
: Tells the server that you want to include the NDB cluster storage engine.

NDB_connectstring
: Tells the server the location of the NDB management daemon.

NDB_nodeid *and* server_id
: Normally set to the node ID. You can find the node ID in the output from the SHOW command in the NDB management console.

Example 15-7 shows a correct startup sequence for the SQL node in our cluster example.

Example 15-7. Starting the SQL node

```
cbell@mysql-xps-400:/usr/local/mysql/bin$ sudo ../libexec/mysqld -NDBcluster \
--console -umysql
100325  9:14:21 [Note] Plugin 'FEDERATED' is disabled.
100325  9:14:21  InnoDB: Started; log sequence number 0 1112278176
100325  9:14:21 [Note] NDB: NodeID is 4, management server '192.168.0.183:1186'
100325  9:14:22 [Note] NDB[0]: NodeID: 4, all storage nodes connected
100325  9:14:22 [Note] Starting Cluster Binlog Thread
100325  9:14:22 [Note] Event Scheduler: Loaded 0 events
100325  9:14:23 [Note] NDB: Creating mysql.NDB_schema
100325  9:14:23 [Note] NDB: Flushing mysql.NDB_schema
100325  9:14:23 [Note] NDB Binlog: CREATE TABLE Event: REPL$mysql/NDB_schema
100325  9:14:23 [Note] NDB Binlog: logging ./mysql/NDB_schema (UPDATED,USE_WRITE)
100325  9:14:23 [Note] NDB: Creating mysql.NDB_apply_status
100325  9:14:23 [Note] NDB: Flushing mysql.NDB_apply_status
100325  9:14:23 [Note] NDB Binlog: CREATE TABLE Event: REPL$mysql/NDB_apply_status
100325  9:14:23 [Note] NDB Binlog: logging ./mysql/NDB_apply_status
(UPDATED,USE_WRITE)
2010-03-25 09:14:23 [NdbApi] INFO     -- Flushing incomplete GCI:s < 65/17
2010-03-25 09:14:23 [NdbApi] INFO     -- Flushing incomplete GCI:s < 65/17
100325  9:14:23 [Note] NDB Binlog: starting log at epoch 65/17
100325  9:14:23 [Note] NDB Binlog: NDB tables writable
100325  9:14:23 [Note] ../libexec/mysqld: ready for connections.
Version: '5.1.44-NDB-7.0.14-debug'  socket: '/var/lib/mysql/mysqld.sock'
port: 3306  Source distribution
```

The output includes extra comments about the NDB cluster connection, logs, and status. If you do not see these or if you see errors, be sure that you started your SQL node with the proper options. Of particular importance is the message stating the node ID and the management server. If you have multiple management servers running, be sure your SQL node is communicating with the correct one.

Once the SQL node starts correctly, return to the management console and check the status of all of your nodes (Example 15-8).

Example 15-8. Example status of a running cluster

```
NDB_mgm> SHOW
Cluster Configuration
---------------------
[NDBd(NDB)]     2 node(s)
id=2    @192.168.0.188  (mysql-5.1.41 NDB-7.0.13, Nodegroup: 0, Master)
id=3    @192.168.0.12   (mysql-5.1.41 NDB-7.0.13, Nodegroup: 0)

[NDB_mgmd(MGM)]    1 node(s)
id=1    @192.168.0.183  (mysql-5.1.44 NDB-7.0.14)

[mysqld(API)]    1 node(s)
id=4    @192.168.0.183  (mysql-5.1.44 NDB-7.0.14)
```

As you can see, all of our nodes are now connected and running. If you see any details other than what is shown here, you have a failure in the startup sequence of your nodes. Be sure to check the logs for each node to determine what went wrong. The most common cause is network connectivity (e.g., firewall issues). The NDB nodes use port 1186 by default.

The logfiles for the data nodes and the NDB management daemon are located in the data directory. The SQL node logs are located in the usual location for a MySQL server.

Testing the Cluster

Now that our example cluster is running, let's perform a simple test (shown in Example 15-9) to ensure we can create a database and tables using the NDBcluster storage engine.

Example 15-9. Testing the cluster

```
mysql> create database cluster_db;
Query OK, 1 row affected (0.06 sec)

mysql> create table cluster_db.t1 (a int) engine=NDBCLUSTER;
Query OK, 0 rows affected (0.31 sec)

mysql> show create table cluster_db.t1 \G
*************************** 1. row ***************************
       Table: t1
Create Table: CREATE TABLE `t1` (
  `a` int(11) DEFAULT NULL
) ENGINE=NDBcluster DEFAULT CHARSET=latin1
1 row in set (0.00 sec)

mysql> insert into cluster_db.t1 VALUES (1), (100), (1000);
Query OK, 3 rows affected (0.00 sec)
Records: 3  Duplicates: 0  Warnings: 0

mysql> select * from cluster_db.t1 \G
*************************** 1. row ***************************
a: 1
*************************** 2. row ***************************
a: 1000
*************************** 3. row ***************************
a: 100
3 rows in set (0.00 sec)
```

Now that you have a running cluster, you can experiment by loading data and running sample queries. We invite you to "fail" one of the data nodes during data updates and restart it to see that the loss of a single data node does not affect accessibility.

Shutting Down the Cluster

Just as there is a specific order for startup, there is a specific order to shutting down your cluster:

1. If you have replication running between clusters, allow the slaves to catch up, then stop replication.
2. Shut down your SQL nodes (mysqld).
3. Issue `SHUTDOWN` in the NDB management console.
4. Exit the NDB management console.

If you have MySQL replication running among two or more clusters, the first step will ensure the replication slaves catch up (synchronize) with the master before you shut the SQL nodes down.

When you issue the `SHUTDOWN` command in the NDB management console, it will shut down all of your data nodes and the NDB management daemon.

Achieving High Availability

The main motivation for using high availability is to keep a service accessible. For database systems, this means we must always be able to access the data. MySQL Cluster is designed to meet this need. MySQL Cluster supports high availability through distribution of data across data nodes (which reduces the risk of data loss from a single node), replication among replicas in the cluster, automatic recovery (failover) of lost data nodes, detection of data node failures using heartbeats, and data consistency using local and global checkpointing.

Let's examine some of the qualities of a high-availability database system. To be considered highly available, a database system (or any system) must meet the following requirements:

- 99.999% uptime
- No single point of failure
- Failover
- Fault tolerance

A 99.999% uptime means the data is, for practical purposes, always available. In other words, the database server is considered a nonstop, continuous service. The assumption is that the server is never offline due to a component failure or maintenance. All operations such as maintenance and recovery are expected to work online, where access is not interrupted, to complete the procedure.

This ideal situation is rarely required and only the most critical industries have a real need for this quality. Additionally, a small period of routine, preventive maintenance is expected (hence the asymptotic percentage rating). Interestingly, there is an accepted granularity of uptime related to the number of 9s in the rating. Table 15-1 shows the acceptable downtime (offline time) per calendar year for each level of the rating.

Table 15-1. Acceptable downtime chart

Uptime	Acceptable downtime
99.000%	3.65 days
99.900%	8.76 hours
99.990%	52.56 minutes
99.999%	5.26 minutes

Notice in this chart that the more nines there are in the rating, the lower the acceptable downtime. For a 99.999% uptime rating, it must be possible to perform all maintenance online without interruption except for a very short period of time in a single year. MySQL Cluster meets this need in a variety of ways, including the capability to perform rolling restarts of data nodes, several online database maintenance operations, and multiple access channels (SQL nodes and applications connecting via NDB API) to the data.

Having no single point of failure means that no single component of the system should determine the accessibility of the service. You can accomplish this with MySQL Cluster by configuring every type of node in the cluster with redundancy. In the small example in the previous section, we had two data nodes. Thus, the data was protected against one data node failing. However, we had only one management node and one SQL node. Ideally, you would also add extra nodes for these functions. MySQL Cluster supports multiple SQL nodes so that if the management node fails, the cluster can still operate.

Failover means that if a component fails, another can replace its functionality. In the case of a MySQL data node, failover occurs automatically if the cluster is configured to contain multiple replicas of the data. If a MySQL data node fails for one replica, access to the data is not interrupted. When you restart the missing data node, it will copy back its data from the other replica. In the case of SQL nodes, since the data is actually stored in the data nodes, any SQL node can substitute for another.

In the case of a failed NDB management node, the cluster can continue to operate without it and you can start a new management node at any time (provided the configuration has not changed).

And you can employ the normal high availability solutions discussed in previous chapters, including replication and automated failover between whole clusters. We discuss cluster replication in more detail later in this chapter.

Fault tolerance is normally associated with hardware such as backup power supplies, redundant network channels, etc. For software systems, fault tolerance is a by-product of how well failover is handled. For MySQL Cluster, this means it can tolerate a certain number of failures and continue to provide access to the data. Much like a hardware RAID system that loses two drives on the same RAID array, loss of multiple data nodes across replicas can result in an unrecoverable failure. However, with careful planning, you can configure MySQL Cluster to reduce this risk. A healthy dose of monitoring and active maintenance can also reduce risk.

MySQL Cluster achieves fault tolerance by actively managing the nodes in the cluster. MySQL Cluster uses a heartbeat to check that services are alive, and when it detects a failed node, it takes action to perform a recovery.

The logging mechanisms in MySQL Cluster also provide a level of recovery for failover and fault tolerance. Local and global checkpointing ensures data is consistent across the cluster. This information is critical for rapid recovery of data node failures. Not only does it allow you to recover the data, but the unique properties of the checkpointing also allow for rapid recovery of nodes. We discuss this feature in more detail later.

Figure 15-5 depicts a MySQL cluster configured for high availability in a web service scenario.

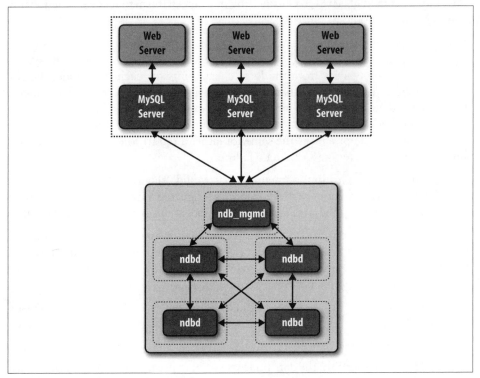

Figure 15-5. A highly available MySQL cluster

The dotted boxes in Figure 15-5 denote system boundaries. These components should reside on separate hardware to ensure redundancy. Also, you should configure the four data nodes as two replicas. Not shown in this drawing are additional components that interact with the application, such as a load balancer to divide the load across the web and MySQL servers.

When configuring a MySQL cluster for high availability, you should consider employing all of the following best practices. We discuss these in more detail later in this chapter when we examine high performance MySQL Cluster techniques.

- Use multiple replicas with data nodes on different hardware.
- Use redundant network links to guard against network failures.
- Use multiple SQL nodes.
- Use multiple data nodes to improve performance and decentralize the data.

System Recovery

There are two types of system recovery. In one type, you shut down the server for maintenance or similar planned events. The other is an unanticipated loss of system capability. Fortunately, MySQL Cluster provides a mechanism to recover functionality even if the worst should occur.

When MySQL Cluster is shut down properly, it restarts from the checkpoints in the logs. This is largely automatic and a normal phase of the startup sequence. The system loads the most recent data from the local checkpoints for each data node, thereby recovering the data to the latest snapshot on restart. Once the data nodes have loaded the data from their local checkpoints, the system executes the redo log up to the most recent global checkpoint, thereby synchronizing the data to the last change made prior to the shutdown. The process is the same for either a restart following an intentional shutdown or a full system restart after a failure.

You may not think a startup is something that would "recover," but remember that MySQL Cluster is an in-memory database and, as such, the data must be reloaded from disk on startup. Loading the data up to the most recent checkpoint accomplishes this.

When recovering a system from a catastrophic failure or as a corrective measure, you can also recover from a backup of the data. As mentioned previously, you can restore data by invoking the NDB_restore utility from the NDB management console and using the output of a recent online backup.

To perform a complete system restore from backup, you should first place the cluster in single-user mode using the following command in the NDB management console:

```
ENTER SINGLE USER MODE node-id
```

The *node-id* is the node ID of the data node you want to use for the NDB_restore utility. See the online MySQL Reference Manual for more details about single-user mode and connecting API-based utilities.

You then run restore on each data node in the cluster. Once you have restored the data on each data node, you can exit single-user mode and the cluster will be ready for use. To exit single-user mode, issue the following command in the NDB management console:

For more information about MySQL Cluster backup and restore, please see the "Using the MySQL Cluster Management Client to Create a Backup" and "Restore a MySQL Cluster Backup" sections of the online MySQL Reference Manual at the following URLs:

http://dev.mysql.com/doc/refman/5.1/en/mysql-cluster-backup-using-management -client.html
http://dev.mysql.com/doc/refman/5.1/en/mysql-cluster-programs-NDB-restore .html

 Do not use the `--initial` option when restarting your server after a failure or scheduled takedown.

Node Recovery

There can be several reasons for a node failure, including network, hardware, memory, or operating system issues or failures. Here, we discuss the most common causes of these failures and how MySQL Cluster handles node recovery. In this section, we concentrate on data nodes, as they are the most important nodes with respect to data accessibility.

Hardware
> In the event the host computer hardware fails, clearly the data node running on that system will fail. In this case, MySQL Cluster will fail over to the other replicas. To recover from this failure, replace the failed hardware and restart the data node.

Network
> If the data node becomes isolated from the network due to some form of network hardware or software failure, the node may continue to execute, but since it cannot contact the other nodes (via heartbeating), MySQL Cluster will mark the node as "down" and fail over to another replica until the node returns and can be recovered. To recover from this failure, replace the failed network hardware and restart the data node.

Memory
> If there is insufficient memory on the host system, the cluster can essentially run out of space for data. This will result in that data node failing. To solve the problem, add more memory or increase the values of the configuration parameters for memory allocation and perform a rolling restart of the data node.

Operating system
> If the operating system configuration interferes with the execution of the data node, resolve the problems and restart the data node.

For more information about database high availability and MySQL high availability, see the following white papers:

> *http://www.mysql.com/why-mysql/white-papers/mysql_db_high_availability.php*
> *http://www.mysql.com/why-mysql/white-papers/mysql_ha_solutions.php*

Replication

We have already briefly discussed how MySQL replication and replication inside the cluster differ. MySQL Cluster replication is sometimes called *internal cluster replication* or simply *internal replication* to clarify that it is not MySQL replication. MySQL replication is sometimes called *external replication*.

In this section, we discuss MySQL Cluster internal replication. We will also look at how MySQL replication (external replication) replicates data between MySQL clusters instead of between individual MySQL servers.

Replication inside the cluster versus MySQL replication

We mentioned earlier that MySQL Cluster uses synchronous replication inside the cluster. This is done to support the two-phase commit protocol for data integrity. Conversely, MySQL replication uses asynchronous replication, which is a one-way transfer of data that relies on the stable delivery and execution of events without verification that the data has been received before the commit.

Replicating inside the cluster

Internal MySQL Cluster replication provides redundancy by storing multiple copies of the data (which are called *replicas*). The process ensures data is written to multiple nodes before the query is acknowledged as complete (committed). This is done using a two-phase commit.

This form of replication is synchronous in that the data is guaranteed to be consistent at the point at which the query is acknowledged or that the commit has completed.

Data is replicated as *fragments*, where a fragment is defined as a subset of rows in a table. Fragments are distributed across the data nodes as a result of partitioning, and a copy of the fragment exists on another data node in each replica. One of the fragments is designated as the primary and is used for query execution. All other copies of the same data are considered secondary fragments. During an update, the primary fragment is updated first.

MySQL replication between clusters

Replication between clusters is very easy to do. If you can set up replication between two MySQL servers, you can set up replication between two MySQL clusters. This is because there are no special configuration steps or extra commands or parameters needed to start replication between clusters. MySQL replication works just as it does between individual servers. It just so happens that in this case the data is stored in NDB clusters. However, there are some limitations to external replication. We list a few here for your consideration when planning external replication. Consult the "MySQL Cluster Replication" section of the online MySQL Reference Manual for the latest details concerning external replication.

- External replication must be row-based.
- External replication cannot be circular.
- External replication does not support the `auto_increment_*` options.
- The size of the binary log may be larger than for normal MySQL replication.

MySQL replication to replicate data from one cluster to another permits you to leverage the advantages of MySQL Cluster at each site and still replicate the data to other sites.

Can MySQL Replication Be Used with MySQL Cluster?

You can replicate from a MySQL Cluster server to a non-MySQL Cluster server (or vice versa). No special configuration is necessary other than to accommodate some potential storage engine conflicts, which is similar to replicating among MySQL servers with different storage engines. In this case, use default storage engine assignment and forgo specifying the storage engine in your `CREATE` statements.

Replicating from a MySQL cluster to a non-MySQL cluster requires creating the special table called *ndb_apply_status* to replicate the epochs committed. If this table is missing on the slave, replication will stop with an error reporting that *ndb_apply_status* does not exist. You can create the table with the following command:

```
CREATE TABLE `mysql`.`ndb_apply_status` (
  `server_id` INT(10) UNSIGNED NOT NULL,
  `epoch` BIGINT(20) UNSIGNED NOT NULL,
  `log_name` VARCHAR(255) CHARACTER SET latin1
    COLLATE latin1_bin NOT NULL,
  `start_pos` BIGINT(20) UNSIGNED NOT NULL,
  `end_pos` BIGINT(20) UNSIGNED NOT NULL,
  PRIMARY KEY (`server_id`) USING HASH
) ENGINE=NDBCLUSTER DEFAULT CHARSET=latin1;
```

Replication of the MySQL cluster using external replication requires row-based MySQL replication, and the master SQL node must be started with `--binlog-format=ROW` or `--binlog-format=MIXED`. All other requirements for MySQL replication also apply (e.g., unique server IDs for all SQL nodes).

External replication also requires some special additions to the replication process, including use of the cluster binary log, the binlog injector thread, and special system tables to support updates between clusters. External replication also handles transactional changes a bit differently. We discuss these concepts in more detail in the next section.

Architecture of MySQL Cluster (external) replication

You can consider the basic concepts of the operations of external replication to be the same as MySQL replication. Specifically, we define the roles of master and slave for certain cluster installations. As such, the master contains the original copy of the data and the slaves receive copies of the data in increments based on the incoming flow of changes to the data.

Replication in MySQL Cluster makes use of a number of dedicated tables in the *mysql* database on each SQL node on the master and the slave (whether the slave is a single server or a cluster). These tables are created during the MySQL installation process. The two tables are *NDB_binlog_index*, which stores index data for the binary log (local to the SQL node), and *NDB_apply_status*, which stores a record of the operations that have been replicated to the slave. The *NDB_apply_status* table is maintained on all SQL nodes and kept in sync so that is the same throughout the cluster. You can use it to execute PITR of a failed replicated slave that is part of a MySQL cluster.

These tables are updated by a new thread called the *binlog injector thread*. This thread keeps the master updated with any changes performed in the NDB cluster storage engine by recording the changes made in the cluster. The binlog injector thread is responsible for capturing all the data events within the cluster as recorded in the binary log and ensures all events that change, insert, or delete data are recorded in the *NDB_binlog_index* table. The master's dump thread sends the events to the slave I/O thread using MySQL replication.

One important difference in external replication involving MySQL Cluster is that each epoch is treated as a transaction. Since an epoch is a span of time between checkpoints, and MySQL Cluster ensures consistency at each checkpoint, epochs are considered atomic and are replicated using the same mechanism as a transaction in MySQL replication. The information about the last applied epoch is stored in the NDB system tables that support external replication between MySQL clusters.

Single-channel and multichannel replication

The MySQL replication connection between a master and slave is called a *channel*. A channel is, in effect, the networking protocol and medium used to connect the master to its slaves. Normally, there is only a single channel, but to ensure maximum availability, you can set up a secondary channel for fault tolerance. This is called *multichannel replication*. Figure 15-6 shows multichannel external replication.

Multichannel replication enhances recovery of a network link failure dramatically. Ideally, you would use active monitoring to trigger a potential failure of the network link to signal when the link is down. This can be accomplished in a variety of ways, from scripts that use simple heartbeat mechanisms to alerts and advisors such as those available in the MySQL Enterprise Monitor.

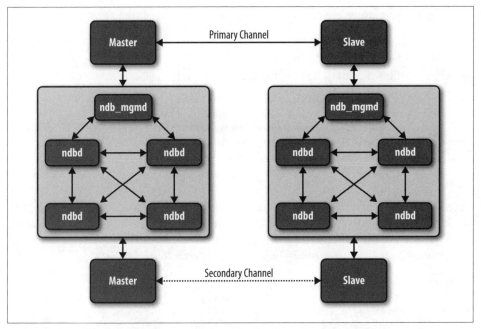

Figure 15-6. Multichannel external replication

Notice that the setup in Figure 15-6 has a total of four SQL nodes. The cluster acting as the master has two nodes acting as masters, one primary and one secondary. Likewise, the cluster acting as a slave has a primary slave and secondary slave. The primary master/slave pair communicates over one network connection, and the secondary master/slave pair communicates over a different network connection.

 Don't take your networking components for granted. Even a switch can fail. Using different cabling on the same switched network gains very little. It is best to use a completely separate set of redundant connections and intermediary networking components to achieve true network redundancy.

Setup of multichannel replication does not differ much from single-channel (normal) MySQL replication. However, the replication failover is a little different. The idea is that you do not start the slave on the secondary channel. Failover to the secondary channel requires some special steps.

Use the following procedure to start multichannel external replication with the primary channel active and the second channel in standby mode. We assume the redundant networking communication and hardware is in place and working properly.

1. Start the primary master.
2. Start the secondary master.
3. Connect the primary slave to the primary master.
4. Connect the secondary slave to the secondary master.
5. Start the primary slave.

Do not start the secondary slave. If you do, you risk primary key conflicts and duplicate data issues. You should, however, connect the secondary slave to the secondary master so the secondary channel can be started quickly if the primary channel fails.

Failover to the secondary channel requires a different procedure. It is not enough to just start the secondary slave. To avoid having the same data replicated twice, you must first establish the last replicated epoch and use it to start replication. The procedure is as follows (notice that we use variables to store intermediate results):

It is a good idea to ensure the primary channel is indeed offline. You may want to consider stopping the primary slave just in case.

1. Find the time of the most recent global checkpoint the slave received. This requires finding the most recent epoch from the *ndb_apply_status* table on the primary slave.

    ```
    SELECT @latest := MAX(epoch) FROM mysql.ndb_apply_status;
    ```
2. Get the rows that appear in the *ndb_binlog_index* table on the primary master following the failure. You can find these rows from the primary master with the following query:

    ```
    SELECT @file := SUBSTRING_INDEX(File, '/', -1), @pos := Position
    FROM mysql.ndb_binlog_index
    WHERE epoch > @latest ORDER BY ASC LIMIT 1;
    ```
3. Synchronize the secondary channel. Run this command on the secondary slave, where **file** is the actual filename and **pos** is the position:

    ```
    CHANGE MASTER TO MASTER_LOG_FILE = 'file', MASTER_LOG_POS = pos;
    ```
4. Start replication on the secondary channel by running this command on the secondary slave:

    ```
    START SLAVE;
    ```

This failover procedure will fail over to the replication channel. If you have failures of any of the SQL nodes, you must deal with those issues and repair them before executing this procedure.

Achieving High Performance

MySQL Cluster is designed not only for high availability, but also for high performance. We have already reviewed many of these features, as they are often beneficial for high availability. In this section, we examine a few features that provide high performance. We conclude with a list of best practices for tuning your system for high performance.

The following features support high performance in MySQL Cluster; we have examined many of these in previous sections:

Replication between clusters (global redundancy)
: All data is replicated to a remote site that can be used to offload the primary site.

Replication inside a cluster (local redundancy)
: Multiple data nodes can be used to read data in parallel.

Main memory storage
: Not needing to wait for disk writes ensures quick processing of updates to data.

Considerations for High Performance

There are three main considerations when tuning your system to support high performance.

- Ensure your applications are as efficient as they can be. Sometimes this requires modification of your database servers (e.g., optimizing the configuration of the servers or modifying the database schema), but often the application itself can be designed or refactored for higher performance.

 Queries with joins can often be very time-consuming.

- Maximize access to your databases. This includes having enough MySQL servers for the number of connections (scale-out) and distributing the data for availability, such as through replication.
- Consider making performance enhancements to your MySQL Cluster, for instance, by adding more data nodes.

You may need to make certain trade offs between the level of high availability you desire and high performance. For example, adding more replicas increases availability. However, while more replicas protect against loss of data nodes, they require more processing power and you may see lower performance during updates. The reads are still quick, since multiple replicas do not need to be read for the same data. Having a greater number of data nodes (scale out) while keeping the number of replicas low leads to higher write performance.

Another primary consideration is the distributed nature of MySQL Cluster. Because each node performs best when run on a separate server, the performance of each server is critical, but so are the networking components. Since coordination commands and data are being transported from node to node, the performance of the networking interconnect must be tuned for high performance. You should also consider parameters such as selection of transport (e.g., TCP/IP, SHM, and SCI), latency, bandwidth, and geographic proximity.

 You can set up and run MySQL Cluster in a cloud environment. One advantage of doing so is that the network interconnections are very fast and optimized. Since the data nodes require mainly a fast processor, adequate memory, and a fast network, virtual server technology is more than adequate for using MySQL Cluster in the cloud.

You can find a complete list of all of the considerations for high performance in the "MySQL Cluster" section of the online MySQL Reference Manual. For general MySQL performance improvements, see *High Performance MySQL* (*http://oreilly.com/catalog/9780596101718/*) by Baron Schwartz et al. (O'Reilly).

High Performance Best Practices

There are a number of things you can do to ensure your MySQL Cluster is running at peak performance. We list a few of the top performance enhancement practices here, along with a brief discussion of each. Some of these are more general in nature, but we do not want to overlook these in our quest for the highest performance possible.

Tune for access patterns
> Consider the methods your applications use to access data. Since MySQL Cluster stores indexed columns in memory, accesses referencing these columns show an even greater speed-up over nonindexed columns than you get on single MySQL servers. MySQL Cluster requires a primary key in every table, so applications that retrieve data by primary key are almost guaranteed to be fast.

Make your applications distribution-aware
> The best-case scenario for accessing data on a partitioned data store is to isolate a query to a single node in the cluster. By default, MySQL Cluster uses the primary key for hashing the rows across the partitions. Unfortunately, this isn't always optimal if you consider the behavior of master/detail queries (common applications that consult a master table followed by details in other tables that refer back to the master table). In this case, you should alter the hashing function to ensure the master row and the detail rows are on the same node. One way to accomplish this is *partition pruning*, whereby you drop the secondary field used in the detail table partition hash and partition the detail rows with only the master's primary

key (which is the foreign key in the detail table). This allows both the master and detail rows to be allocated to the same node in the partition tree.

Use batch operations

Each round trip of a query has significant overhead. For certain operations like inserts, you can save some of that overhead by using a multiple insert query (an `INSERT` statement that inserts multiple rows). You can also batch operations by turning on the `transaction_allow_batching` parameter and including multiple operations within a transaction (within the `BEGIN` and `END` blocks). This lets you list multiple data manipulation queries (`INSERT`, `UPDATE`, etc.) and reduce overhead.

 The `transaction_allow_batching` option does not work with `SELECT` statements or `UPDATE` statements that include variables.

Optimize schemas

Optimizing your database schemas has the same effect for MySQL Cluster as it does for normal database systems. For MySQL Cluster, consider using efficient data types (e.g., the minimum size needed to save memory; 30 bytes per row in a million-row table can save you a significant amount of memory). You should also consider denormalization for certain schemas to take advantage of MySQL Cluster's parallel data access methods (partitioning).

Optimize queries

Clearly, the more optimized the query, the faster the query performance. This is a practice common to all databases and should be one of the first things you do to improve the performance of your application. For MySQL Cluster, consider query optimization from the standpoint of how the data is retrieved. Specifically, joins are particularly sensitive to performance in MySQL Cluster. Poorly performing queries can sometimes cause anomalies that are easily mistaken for inefficiencies in other parts of your system.

Optimize server parameters

Optimize your cluster configuration to ensure it is running as efficiently as possible. This may mean spending some time to understand the many configuration options as well as securing the correct hardware to exploit. There is no magic potion for this task—each installation becomes more and more unique as you change more parameters. Use this practice with care, tune one parameter at a time, and always compare the results to known baselines before instituting a change.

Use connection pools

By default, SQL nodes use only a single thread to connect to the NDB cluster. With more threads to connect, the SQL nodes can execute several queries at once. To use connection pooling for your SQL nodes, add the `NDB-cluster-connection-pool` option in your configuration file. Set the value to be greater than 1 (say, 4) and place it in the [mysqld] section. You should experiment with this setting because it is frequently too high for the application or hardware.

Use multithreaded data nodes

If your data node has multiple CPU cores or multiple CPUs, you will gain additional performance by running the multithreaded data node daemon named NDBmtd. This daemon can make use of up to eight CPU cores or threads. Using multiple threads allows the data node to run many operations in parallel, such as the local query handler (LQH) and communication processes, to achieve even higher throughput.

Use the NDB API for custom applications

While the MySQL server (the SQL node) offers a fast query processor frontend, MySQL has built a direct-access C++ mechanism called the NDB API. For some operations, such as interfacing MySQL Cluster with LDAP, this may be the only way to connect the MySQL cluster (in this case just the NDB cluster) to your application. If performance is critical to your application and you have the necessary development resources to devote to a custom NDB API solution, you can see significant improvements in performance.

Use the right hardware

Naturally, faster hardware results in faster performance (generally speaking). However, you should consider every aspect of the cluster configuration. Consider not only faster CPUs and more and faster memory, but also high-speed interconnect solutions such as SCI and high-speed, hardware-redundant network connections. In many cases, these hardware solutions are built as turnkey commodities and do not require reconfiguring the cluster.

Turn off the query cache

Because MySQL Cluster does not use the MyISAM storage engine, there is nothing to gain from using the query cache. You can turn it off.

Do not use swap space

Make sure your data nodes are using real memory and not swap space. You will notice a dramatic performance drop when the data nodes start using swap space. This affects not only performance, but also possibly the stability of the cluster.

Use processor affinity for data nodes

In multiple-CPU machines, lock your data node processes to CPUs that are not involved in network communications. You can do this on some platforms (e.g., Sun CMT processor systems) using the LockExecuteThreadToCPU and LockMaint ThreadsToCPU parameters in the [NDBd] section of the configuration file.

If you follow these best practices, you will be well on your way to making MySQL Cluster the best high-performance, high-availability solution for your organization. For more information about optimizing MySQL Cluster, see the white paper "Optimizing Performance of the MySQL Cluster Database" at *http://www.mysql.com/why-mysql/white-papers/mysql_wp_cluster_perfomance.php*.

Conclusion

In this chapter, we discussed the unique high availability solution for MySQL using MySQL Cluster. The strengths of MySQL Cluster include partitioning tables and distributing them across separate nodes and the parallel architecture of MySQL Cluster as a multimaster database. This allows the system to execute high volumes of both read and write operations concurrently. All updates are instantly available to all application nodes (via SQL commands or the NDB API) accessing data stored in the data nodes.

Because write loads are distributed across all of the data nodes, you can achieve very high levels of write throughput and scalability for transactional workloads. Finally, with the implementation of multiple MySQL server nodes (SQL nodes) running in parallel, where each server shares the load with multiple connections, and the use of MySQL replication to ensure data shipping among geographic sites, you can build highly efficient, high-concurrency transactional applications.

Although few applications may have such stringent needs, MySQL Cluster is a great solution for those applications that demand the ultimate form of MySQL high availability.

"Joel!"

Joel smiled as his boss backtracked to stand in his doorway.

"Yes, Bob?" Joel asked.

Mr. Summerson stepped into the office and closed the door, then pulled up a chair and sat down directly across from Joel.

Momentarily taken off-guard, Joel merely smiled and said, "What can I do for you, Bob?"

"It's what you have done for me, Joel. You've come up to speed on this MySQL stuff very quickly. You have kept pace with our ramp-up and recent acquisitions. And now you've helped make us a lot of money on this last deal. I know I've thrown a lot at you and you deserve something in return." After an uncomfortable pause, he asked, "Do you play golf, Joel?"

Joel shrugged. "I haven't played since college, and I was never very good at it."

"That won't be a problem. I love the game, but the feeling isn't mutual. I lose half a box of balls every time I play. Are you free Saturday for a game of nine holes?"

Joel wasn't sure where this was going, but something told him he should accept. "Sure, I'm free."

"Good. Meet me at the Fair Oaks course at 1000 hours. We'll play nine holes, then discuss your future over lunch."

"OK. See you there, Bob."

Mr. Summerson stood, opened the door, and paused. "I've told the accounting office to create a budget for you to manage, including enough to cover the cost of the MySQL Enterprise subscription and funding for two full-time assistants."

"Thanks," Joel said, stunned. He wasn't prepared for outright acceptance of his proposal, much less more responsibility.

As Mr. Summerson disappeared down the hall, Joel's friend Amy came in and stood next to him. "Are you OK?" she asked with concern.

"Yeah, why?"

"I've never seen him close the door to talk to someone. If you don't mind me asking, what was that all about?"

With a wave of his hand over the documentation on his desk, Joel said, "He asked me to play golf and then said I had my own budget and could buy the MySQL Enterprise subscription."

Amy smiled and touched his arm. "That's good, Joel—really good."

Joel was confused. He didn't think the responsibility of managing money or the approval for a purchase order was worthy of such a reaction. "What?"

"The last person who played golf with Mr. Summerson got a promotion and a raise. Mr. Summerson may be tough on the outside, but he rewards loyalty and determination."

"Really?" Joel stared at the papers on his desk. He told himself not to get his hopes up.

"Are you free for lunch?" Amy asked with a light squeeze of his arm.

Joel looked at her hand on his arm and smiled. "Sure. Let's go somewhere nice." But in accepting her offer, Joel knew he would be up late working on a plan for their next date.

Replication Tips and Tricks

The following is a collection of useful tips and tricks for running, diagnosing, repairing, and improving MySQL replication.

The tips in this chapter are intended to be supplemental material and, as such, may not contain all of the details needed for a full tutorial. Consult the online MySQL Reference Manual at *http://dev.mysql.com/doc/refman/5.4/en/index.html* for more details about MySQL replication.

You can also find the latest information and cutting-edge techniques at the replication development zone at *http://dev.mysql.com/replication/*.

The last few sections of this appendix describe features that will be offered by MySQL soon, but are not officially available at the time of this writing.

My Slave Stopped. Now What?

If your slave stops without warning and there is an error message, consult the documentation about the likely causes of the error and perform any repairs necessary.

Once you have corrected the error, follow this procedure to determine where to restart the slave after the event that caused the error:

1. Check the position it stopped on using the following command:

    ```
    SHOW SLAVE STATUS
    ```

2. Use `Master_Log_File` and `Read_Master_Log_Pos` to determine the next event to transfer from the master.

3. Use `Relay_Master_Log_File` and `Exec_Master_Log_Pos` to determine the next event to apply for the master log.

4. Use `Relay_Log_File` and `Relay_Log_Pos` to determine the next event to apply for the relay log.

5. Use `mysqlbinlog` to read the contents:

```
mysqlbinlog master-log.000001
mysqlbinlog relay-log.000001
```

6. Investigate the problem and, if required, remove rows in database:

```
SET SQL_SLAVE_SKIP_COUNTER=1; START SLAVE
```

Examining the Binary Log with Verbose

If you are using row-based logging, you can use the `--verbose` option to see a recon-struction of the queries in the event. The following shows what this looks like when run on a binary log with row-based logging:

```
$ mysqlbinlog --verbose master-bin.000001
BINLOG '
qZnvSRMBAAAAKQAAAAYCAAAAABAAAAAAAAABHRlc3QQAAnQxAAEDAAE=
qZnvSRcBAAAAJwAAACoCAAAQABAAAAAAAAEAAf/+AwAAAP4EAAAA '/*!*/;
### INSERT INTO test.t1
### SET
### @1=3
### INSERT INTO test.t1
### SET
### @1=4
```

Notice that the values are given using @n-style names for the columns. This is because row-based replication is transferring the record and applying it by column position, but ignores the names of the columns.

Using Replication to Repopulate a Table

If a table on your slave becomes corrupt either through error or accident (e.g., a user deletes the data), you can use replication to recover the data. Do so by creating a tem-porary table on the master that is a copy of the original table, dropping the original table, and then re-creating it from the copy. This works very well as long as you do not have any column data types that this could affect (e.g., `autoincrement`). You are using the power of replication to reproduce the table on the slaves. There are two forms of this process, based on which form of logging you are using.

Statement-Based Logging

If you are using statement-based logging, run the following for each table:

```
SELECT * INTO OUTFILE 't1.txt' FROM t1;
DROP TABLE IF EXISTS t1;
CREATE TABLE t1 ...;
LOAD DATA INFILE 't1.txt' INTO TABLE t1;
```

Row-Based Logging

If you are using row-based logging, the temporary table is not transferred to the slave. Therefore, send only the data that is necessary to bootstrap the table using the INSERT INTO command as follows:

```
CREATE TEMPORARY TABLE t1_tmp LIKE t1;
INSERT INTO t1_tmp SELECT * FROM t1;
DROP TABLE IF EXISTS t1;
CREATE TABLE t1 SELECT * FROM t1_tmp;
```

Using MySQL Proxy to Perform Multimaster Replication

No slave can have more than one master, but a master can have many slaves. This isn't an issue for most installations, but what if you need to combine data from two different masters and replicate the combined data to your slaves?

One way to do this is to use MySQL Proxy as an intermediate slave. Figure A-1 shows a conceptual drawing of this configuration.

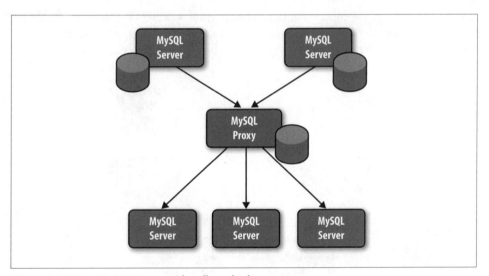

Figure A-1. Using MySQL Proxy to handle multiple masters

MySQL Proxy will receive changes (events) from both masters and write a new binary log without saving the data (writing it to a database). Your slaves use MySQL Proxy as a master. This has the effect of combining data from two masters and replicating to a set of slaves. This effectively implements multimaster replication.

For more information about MySQL Proxy, see the section on MySQL Proxy in the online MySQL Reference Manual at *http://dev.mysql.com/doc/refman/5.4/en/*.

Using a Default Storage Engine

If you use a default storage engine on your master by issuing the SET GLOBAL STORAGE ENGINE command, this command is not replicated. Therefore, any CREATE statement that does not specify a storage engine will get the default storage engine as it was set on the slaves. Thus, it is possible that your InnoDB tables will be replicated to MyISAM tables. If you ignore the warnings when this occurs, you can encounter a scenario in which replication stops due to some incompatibility.

One solution is to ensure the global storage engine is set on each slave by including the default-storage-engine option in the configuration file. However, the best practice is to specify the storage engine on the CREATE statement.

This does not prevent issues in which a storage engine used on the master does not exist on the slave. In this case, you may encounter problems that can be solved only by installing the missing storage engine on the slave.

MySQL Cluster Multisource Replication

You can set up multisource replication using MySQL Cluster (Figure A-2). To do so, set up the masters to replicate different data. By keeping the data on different masters, you avoid cross-contamination of keys and similar context-dependent values.

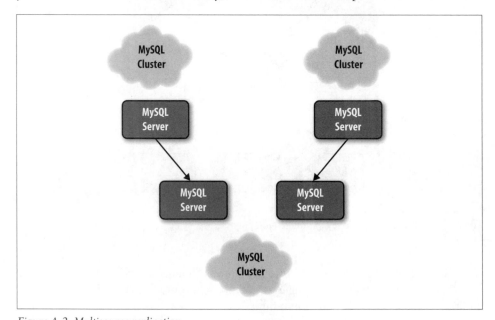

Figure A-2. Multisource replication

Multichannel Replication with Failover

For greater reliability and rapid recovery, you can use a dual replication setup (Figure A-3), in which two sets of replication topologies replicate from one cluster to another. If one stream goes down, you can fail over to the other stream quickly.

Notice that server names are of the form *mysql.X* and saved positions are of the form *mysql.X.savepos*.

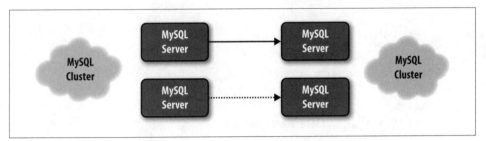

Figure A-3. Multichannel replication

Using the Current Database to Filter

The binlog filters can be quite convenient for eliminating statements for particular purposes.

For example, some statements may be meant only for the server, such as setting the engine of a table where you want the engines to be different on the master and the slave. There are many reasons to use a different engine on the slave, including the following:

- MyISAM is more suitable for reporting, and since the binary log contains complete transactions, you can use InnoDB on the master for transactional processing and MyISAM on slaves for reporting and analytical processing.

- To save memory, you can eliminate some tables on a slave used for analytical processing by replacing the engine with Blackhole.

You can suspend writing to the binary log by setting the `SQL_LOG_BIN` server variable to 0. For instance Example A-1 turns off logging (`SQL_LOG_BIN = 0`) before changing a table to the MyISAM engine, so that it takes place only on the master, then turns logging back on (`SQL_LOG_BIN = 1`). However, setting `SQL_LOG_BIN` requires `SUPER` privileges, which you probably don't want to grant to regular database users. Therefore, Example 5-4 shows an alternative way to change an engine on the master without logging it. (In the example, it is assumed that the table `my_table` resides in a database `my_db`.) Create a dedicated database (in this case, we use the name `no_write_db`). Then, any user who wants to execute a statement that should not be replicated can `USE` the `no_write_db` database, and the statement will be filtered out. Since using a database requires access privileges, you can control who has the privileges to hide statements without providing the SUPER privilege to an untrusted user.

Example A-1. Two different ways to filter a statement from the binary log

```
master> SET SQL_LOG_BIN = 0;
Query OK, 0 rows affected (0.00 sec)

master> ALTER TABLE my_table ENGINE=MyISAM;
Query OK, 92 row affected (0.90 sec)
Records: 92  Duplicates: 0  Warnings: 0

master> SET SQL_LOG_BIN = 1;
Query OK, 0 rows affected (0.00 sec)

master> USE no_write_db;
Reading table information for completion of table and column names
You can turn off this feature to get a quicker startup with -A

Database changed
master> ALTER TABLE my_db.my_table ENGINE=MyISAM;
Query OK, 92 row affected (0.90 sec)
Records: 92  Duplicates: 0  Warnings: 0
```

More Columns on Slave Than Master

If you need to include additional columns on the slave that the master doesn't have—for example, to record timestamps or add routing or other localized data—you can add columns to a table on a slave without having to add the columns on the master. MySQL replication supports this scenario by ignoring the additional columns. To actually insert data into the extra columns on the slave, define them to accept default values (an easy way to insert timestamps, for instance) or use a trigger defined on the slave to provide the values.

For statement-based logging, you can create the columns as follows:

1. Create the table on the master:

    ```
    CREATE TABLE t1 (a INT, b INT);
    ```

2. Alter the table on the slave:

    ```
    ALTER TABLE t1 ADD ts TIMESTAMP;
    ```

3. Sample insert on the master:

    ```
    INSERT INTO t1(a,b) VALUES (10,20);
    ```

For row-based logging, you must make the new columns appear at the end of the row and have default values. Row-based replication will fail if you add columns in the middle or at the front of the row. As long as you add columns at the end of the table and give them default values, no special consideration needs to be taken regarding which statements to use when replicating, since row-based replication will extract the columns directly from the row being updated, inserted, or deleted.

Fewer Columns on Slave Than Master

If you need to have fewer columns on the slave than the master—for example, to protect sensitive data or to reduce the amount of data replicated—you can remove columns from a table on a slave without having to remove the columns on the master. MySQL row-based replication supports this scenario by ignoring the missing columns. However, the missing columns on the slave must be from the end of the master's row.

For row-based replication, you can drop the columns as follows:

1. Create the table on the master:

   ```
   CREATE TABLE t1 (a INT, b INT, comments TEXT);
   ```

2. Alter the table on the slave:

   ```
   ALTER TABLE t1 DROP comments;
   ```

3. Sample insert on the master:

   ```
   INSERT INTO t1 VALUES (1,2,"Do not store this on slave");
   ```

For row-based replication, you can replicate an arbitrary set of columns of a table without regard to whether they are at the end or not by using a trigger on the master to update the table from a base table in a separate database so that the table in the replicated database with fewer columns is replicated instead of the base table. Figure A-4 shows a conceptual drawing of this solution. Here, a table with three columns is transformed using a trigger to a table in the replicated database.

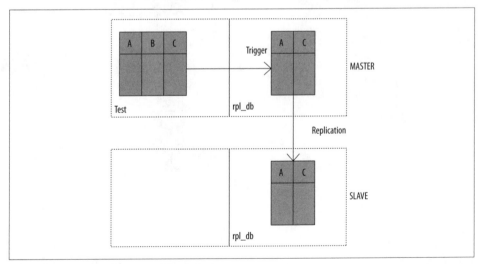

Figure A-4. Replicating a subset of columns

An example follows of how you can use a trigger to update the table in the replicated database. On the master, execute the following:

```
CREATE DATABASE rpl_db;
USE test;
CREATE TABLE t1 (a INT, b BLOB, c INT);
CREATE TRIGGER tr_t1 AFTER INSERT ON test.t1 FOR EACH ROW
INSERT INTO rpl_db.t1_v(a,c) VALUES(NEW.a,NEW.c);
USE rpl_db;
CREATE TABLE t1_v (a INT, c INT);
```

When executing a normal insert, the trigger will extract a subset of the columns and write it to the table in the *rpl_db* database. This database will then be replicated, but the original table will not.

```
USE test;
SET @blob = REPEAT('beef',100);
INSERT INTO t1 VALUES (1,@blob,3), (2,@blob,9);
```

Replicate Selected Rows to Slave

You can also segment replication so that only rows satisfying a certain condition are replicated. This technique uses a special database that is replicated from the master to the slave (this is accomplished by setting up a filter) and a trigger to determine which rows are to be replicated. The trigger determines which rows are to be replicated by inserting them into the replicated table (Figure A-5).

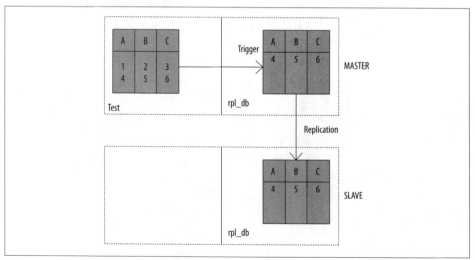

Figure A-5. Replicating a subset of rows

An example follows of how you can use a trigger to update the table in the replicated database with only rows having an odd value in column **a** inserted:

```
# Just replicate rows that has odd numbers in first column.
USE rpl_db;
CREATE TABLE t1_h (a INT, b BLOB, c INT);
--delimiter //
CREATE TRIGGER slice_t1_horiz AFTER INSERT ON test.t1
FOR EACH ROW
BEGIN
  IF NEW.a MOD 2 = 1 THEN INSERT
    INTO rpl_db.t1_h VALUES (NEW.a, NEW.b, NEW.c);
  END IF;
END//
--delimiter ;
```

Replication Heartbeat

It is possible to improve the reliability of replication and improve failover using the replication heartbeat mechanism. When the heartbeat is turned on, the slave will periodically challenge the master. As long as the slave gets a response, it will continue as usual and challenge the master again at the next interval. The server maintains statistics of the number of heartbeats received, which can help to determine whether the master is offline or not responding. Figure A-6 shows a conceptual drawing of the heartbeat mechanism.

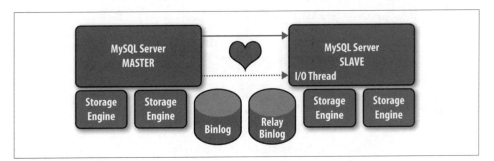

Figure A-6. Heartbeat during replication

The heartbeat mechanism allows the slave to detect when the master is still responding, and has the following advantages and capabilities:

- Automatic checking of connection status
- No more relay log rotates when the master is idle
- Detection of master/slave disconnect configurable in milliseconds

Thus, you can use the heartbeat mechanism to perform automatic failover and similar high availability operations. Use the following command to set the heartbeat interval on the slave:

```
CHANGE MASTER SET master_heartbeat_period= val;
```

The following commands allow you to check the settings and statistics of the heartbeat mechanism:

```
SHOW STATUS like 'slave_heartbeat period';
SHOW STATUS like 'slave_received_heartbeats';
```

 This feature is relatively new. It was introduced in MySQL version 5.4.4.

Ignoring Servers in Circular Replication

If you have a circular replication topology and one of the servers fails, you must change the topology to exclude the failed server. In Figure A-7, server A has failed and you must remove it from the circle. In this case, you can set server B to terminate server A's events in the new circle.

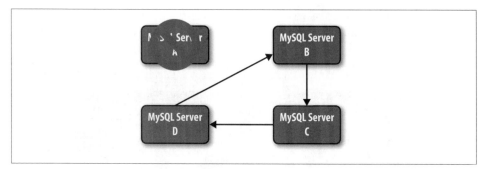

Figure A-7. Replacing a server in circular replication

You can do this by issuing the following command on server B:

```
CHANGE MASTER TO MASTER_HOST=C ... IGNORE_SERVER_IDS=(A)
```

This feature was introduced in MySQL version 5.5.

Feature Preview: Time-Delayed Replication

There is sometimes a need to delay replication, for example, to ensure slaves are not overloaded with changes. This feature provides the ability to execute replication events on a slave so that it is *n* seconds behind the master at all times. You can set this parameter as shown:

```
CHANGE MASTER TO MASTER_DELAY= n
```

n is a nonnegative integer less than `MAX_ULONG` number of seconds for the slave to wait (attempts to set the number higher will be rejected with an error).

You can verify the delayed setup by running the SHOW SLAVE STATUS command and examining the Seconds_behind_master column of the output.

You can read more about time-delayed replication at *http://forge.mysql.com/wiki/Rep licationFeatures/DelayedReplication*.

Feature Preview: Scriptable Replication

If you need to perform transformations, specific low-level filtering, or similar operations on the replication stream, write scripts to operate at one of four times:

- As the event is written to the binary log on the master
- As the event is written to the dump thread on the master
- After the I/O thread reads the event, but before it is written to the relay log on the slave
- As the event is read from the relay log on the slave

Depending on your needs, you may want to use one or more of these points to perform operations on the events. Figure A-8 shows the locations of the scriptable points. This feature allows you to execute scripts using the Lua language.

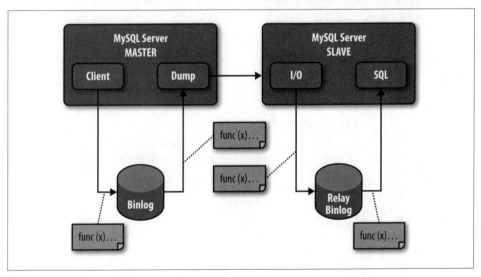

Figure A-8. Points at which you can insert scripts

You can read more about scriptable replication at *http://forge.mysql.com/wiki/Replica tionFeatures/ScriptableReplication*.

Feature Preview: The Oracle Algorithm

As part of the scriptable replication solution, you can use the "oracle" algorithm developed by Paul Tuckfield (Google/YouTube) to filter events (Figure A-9).

```
module(..., package.seeall); require "luasql.mysql"
pattern = {
        [ "UPDATE%s+(%w+) . *%s(WHERE.*)"] = "SELECT * FROM %1 %2",
        ["DELETE%s+FROM%s+(%w+) .*%s(WHERE.*)"] = "SELECT * FROM %1 %2",
}
env = luasql.mysql ()
con = env:connect("test", "root", "", "localhost", mysql.port)

function before_write(event)
        local line = event.query
        if not line then return end
        for pat,repl in pairs(pattern) do
                local str = string.gsub(line, pat, repl)
                if str then con:execute(str) ; break; end
        end
end
```

Figure A-9. Paul Tuckfield's oracle algorithm

Interestingly, the algorithm got its name from the concept that it lets the replication thread "see" into future events and prime its cache accordingly. It has nothing to do with Oracle Corporation or the Oracle text-scoring algorithm.

 If you use Maatkit, you can use mk-slave-prefetch to perform the same function using SQL commands. Find out more at *http://www.maatkit .org/doc/mk-slave-prefetch.html*.

Index

We'd like to hear your suggestions for improving our indexes. Send email to *index@oreilly.com*.

external replication, 552

F

Faroult, Stephane, 320
fdisk command, 264
Federated storage engine, 335
fetch_global_trans_id function, 140
fetch_master_pos function, 35, 186, 191
fetch_relay_chain function, 191
fetch_remote_binlog function, 40, 138
fetch_slave_pos function, 35
fetch_trans_id function, 190
file IDs, 57
filesystem
    coordinating synchronization, 83
    disk usage and, 250
    logging changes, 51, 76
    logical volumes and, 434
    memory considerations, 250
    object definitions and, 180
    reading remote files, 93
    snapshot support, 108
filtering
    current database, 567
    partitioning events to slaves, 165
    replication events, 163–164
    row-based replication, 240
    scaling out and, 149
    skipping events, 221–222
    SQL threads and, 217
filtering, binary log filters and, 59–61
Final role, 29
find_datetime_position function, 40
FLUSH LOGS command
    binlog file support, 47
    functionality, 18, 84
    monitoring master servers, 374
    privilege considerations, 16
    troubleshooting binary log, 392
FLUSH QUERY CACHE command, 300
FLUSH STATUS command, 307
FLUSH TABLES command, 429
FLUSH TABLES WITH READ LOCK
        command
    cloning the master, 31
    EBS snapshots and, 514
    InnoDB cautions, 34
    LVM support, 436
    pausing replication, 406

releasing locks, 27
foreign keys, 338
format description events
    binlog event structure, 47, 48–50
    functionality, 19, 20
    header restrictions, 97
    I/O threads and, 216
    in binary log, 20, 84
    interpreting, 97
    printing, 89
    XA and, 81
fragments, defined, 552
free command, 253, 259
fsync call, 223, 224

G

general query logs, 314
getArticlesForUser function, 177, 182
getCommentsForArticle function, 178
getServerConnection function (PHP), 157
global redundancy, 530, 557
global transaction IDs
    circular replication, 144, 145
    data consistency example, 188, 191
    defined, 130
    slave promotion and, 130–135, 137, 139
GNOME desktop project, 264
Gnome System Monitor, 252
Governor, James, 478
GRANT OPTION privilege, 16
graphical user interfaces (GUIs), 268, 302
grep command, 258, 509
grid computing, 481
groups, defined, 48
group_by_event function, 138
group_by_trans function, 138
GUIs (graphical user interfaces), 268, 302

H

hardware
    data loss and, 421
    node recovery and, 551
hash mark (#), 90
HA_ERR_KEY_NOT_FOUND error, 399
Health Insurance Portability and
        Accountability Act (HIPAA), 412
heartbeats, 383, 551, 571
heat charts, 464

master heartbeats, 383
master log information file
  flushing, 224
  functionality, 198
  manipulating slave threads, 201
  replication status information, 212
Master role
  defined, 29
  replicate_from function and, 35
master servers
  checking status, 403
  circular replication, 142–146
  cloning, 30, 31
  configuring, 13
  connecting to slaves, 14, 15
  creating, 7
  creating replication users, 14
  delayed slaves, 5
  dual-master setup, 6, 23, 115–124
  handling failures, 106, 109
  hierarchal replication, 159
  monitoring, 372–376
  monitoring thread status, 371
  multimaster issues, 399
  replication overview, 5
  scripting the clone operation, 35
  server roles, 28–30
  status variables and, 376
  switching, 109, 112–114
  tips and tricks, 568–570
  troubleshooting, 388–393
  two-phase commit and, 150
  upgrading, 110
master-connect-retry option, 215
master-retry-count option, 215
MASTER_POS_WAIT function
  data consistency example, 185, 187
  functionality, 40, 172
  relay log processing and, 213
max-allowed-packet option, 58, 397
max-binlog-cache-size option, 100
max-binlog-size option, 100
Maxia, Giuseppe, 155
MD5 function, 220
MEM (see MySQL Enterprise Monitor)
memcached technique, 156, 171
memory
  cautions when tweaking, 250
  Mac OS X environment, 274

monitoring, 247, 249, 259–261
  node recovery and, 551
  troubleshooting, 389, 395
Memory storage engine, 335
memory-bound processes, 249
Merge storage engine, 335
MERGE view, 122
Microsoft Azure, 483
Microsoft Management Console snap-ins, 42
mission statements, 416
mixed-mode replication, 231
Mollinaro, Anthony, 320
monitoring, 292
  (see also performance considerations)
  automated, 268
  benefits of, 247
  buffer pools, 360–363
  categories of, 246
  defined, 246
  disk usage, 247, 250, 261–264, 274
  general system statistics, 266
  InnoDB storage engine, 352–365
  key cache, 348
  Linux environment, 246, 253–268
  logfiles, 359
  Mac OS X environment, 246, 268–276
  master servers, 372–376
  memory, 247, 249, 259–261, 274
  MyISAM storage engine, 344–352
  MySQL Administrator and, 381
  MySQL Enterprise, 463–469
  MySQL servers, 292–319
  network activity, 248, 251, 265, 275
  as preventive maintenance, 288
  process activity, 253–258
  processor, 247, 248
  replication, 367–386
  semisynchronous replication, 127
  slave lag, 383
  slave servers, 376
  tablespaces, 363
  tools for, 252
  Unix environment, 246, 253–268
  usage examples, 7
  Windows environment, 246, 276–288
monitoring agents, 457, 462
MONyog tool, 317
mount command, 435
mpstat command, 253, 255, 257

multichannel replication, 554, 567
multimaster topology, 399, 403
multisource replication, 226–228, 566
Musumeci, Gian-Paolo D., 262
mutex, 356
myisam ftdump utility, 345
MyISAM storage engine
    compressing tables, 347
    consistency considerations, 82
    defragmenting tables, 348
    dual-master setup and, 118
    functionality, 334
    handling row locks, 183
    high availability and, 352
    improving performance, 344
    monitoring key cache, 348
    nontransactional changes and, 73, 75, 225
    OPTIMIZE TABLE command, 330
    optimizing disk storage, 344
    parameters supported, 351
    preloading key cache, 349
    query cache and, 298, 307
    recovery considerations, 119
    slave promotion and, 131
    tables in index order, 347
    troubleshooting tables, 397
    tuning tables, 345–346
myisam-recover option, 392
myisamchk utility
    defragmenting tables, 348
    functionality, 345–346
    tables in index order, 347
myisamlog utility, 345
myisampack utility, 345, 347
MySAR system activity report, 316
MySQL
    additional information, 8
    version considerations, 24
MySQL Administrator
    Connection Health tab, 303
    functionality, 302
    Key Efficiency graph, 307
    Memory Health tab, 306
    page tool, 311
    Query Cache Hitrate graph, 307
    replication monitoring, 381
    Server Variables tab, 309
    Status Variables tab, 310
    Traffic graph, 304

MySQL Cluster
    architecture basics, 532–538, 554
    commit support, 151
    data nodes, 543
    data storage, 533–536
    example configuration, 539–547
    features, 528–529
    functionality, 526
    getting started, 539–541
    high availability and, 547–556
    high performance and, 557–560
    log handling, 531
    management node, 541
    NDB management console, 542
    online operations, 537
    partitioning and, 536
    redundancy and, 530, 531, 557
    reload event, 86
    replication, 566
    replication and, 553
    shutting down clusters, 546
    SQL nodes, 544
    starting, 541–546
    terminology and components, 526
    testing clusters, 546
    transaction management, 537
    typical configuration, 527
mysql database
    logging transactions, 76
    object definitions and, 180
MySQL Enterprise
    alert details, 464
    background information, 452
    clouding computing and, 472
    components, 456–460
    fixing monitoring agents, 462
    installing, 454–455, 460–462
    monitoring, 463–469
    production support, 459
    Query Analyzer, 469–472
    subscription levels, 453
    usage considerations, 460
MySQL Enterprise Backup, 425
MySQL Enterprise Monitor
    additional information, 252
    advisors, 457
    background information, 453
    Enterprise Dashboard, 456
    functionality, 452, 456

replication and, 369
restoring after replicated error, 439
Platform as a Service (PaaS), 480
pmap command, 253, 259
point-in-time recovery (see PITR)
polling, 189
pool_add function, 158
pool_del function, 158
pool_set function, 158
Position class, 25
post headers, 48–50, 98
primary keys, 338
primary servers, 116, 117
private keys, 203
privileges
    configuring replication, 14, 16
    reading remote files, 93
    security and binary log, 64
    setting thread IDs, 57
    stored functions and, 70
proactive monitoring, 247
procedures (high availability)
    best practices, 406
    circular replication, 142–146
    considerations for, 108–110
    defined, 104
    dual-master setup, 6, 23, 115–124
    hot standby, 11, 111–114
    semisynchronous replication, 116, 124–127
    slave promotion and, 109, 127–141
process IDs
    identifying, 258
    temporary tables and, 56
    TLS support, 220
processes
    assigning priorities, 249, 255
    CPU-bound, 249
    defined, 248
    disk-bound, 250
    I/O-bound, 251
    I/O-starved, 251
    killing runaway, 248
    memory-bound, 249
    monitoring activity, 253–258
    network-bound, 251
    processor-bound, 249
    removing unnecessary, 248
    rescheduling, 249

solutions to overloading, 248
processlist command, 301
processor, monitoring, 247, 248
processor-bound processes, 249
Promotable class, 136
promote_slave function, 140
proxy
    defined, 153
    distributing queries, 154
ps command, 253, 257
pseudothread ID, 221
pseudo_thread_id server variable, 57
public certificates, 203
PURGE BINARY LOGS command, 47, 86, 400
purge index file, 85
pvcreate command, 434
pvscan command, 434
Python (see MySQL Python)

Q

queries
    analyzing, 153
    best practices, 559
    data sharding and, 171
    data-mining, 37
    distributing, 153, 154
    EXPLAIN command and, 458
    improving performance, 340
    manually executing, 405
    slave lag and, 385
    troubleshooting, 391, 392, 394
Query Analyzer
    functionality, 458, 469–472
    troubleshooting, 463
query cache
    best practices, 336, 560
    functionality, 298
    MySQL Administrator and, 306
    server variables, 299
query events
    binlog event structure, 48
    context events and, 217
    current database and, 97
    execution contexts, 51, 53–54
    functionality, 19
    interpreting, 94–97
    logging, 51–57
    mysqlbinlog example, 91

W

wait_for_pos function, 186, 191
wait_for_trans_id function, 190
WHERE clause
    DELETE statement and, 46
    EXPLAIN command and, 322
    SELECT statement and, 336
    UPDATE statement and, 46, 50
wildcards
    mysqlbinlog support, 92
    slave filters and, 164
Windows environment
    Cygwin and, 429
    Event Viewer, 281–283
    InnoDB Hot Backup application, 425
    managing replication, 24
    monitoring, 246, 276–288
    Performance Monitor, 285–288
    Reliability Monitor, 283
    System Health Report, 277, 278–280, 285
    Task Manager, 285
    virtualization and, 481
    Volume Shadow Copy, 432
    Windows Experience report, 277
Windows Experience report, 277
Windows Vista environment
    monitoring, 276–288
    scheduling tasks, 42
worst case scenario, 413, 416
Write_rows events, 232, 237
writing data
    data sharding and, 149
    load balancing and, 148
    scaling out and, 149
    thread-local objects, 220

X

X.509 certificates, 498
X/Open Distributed Transaction Processing
        model XA, 79–81
XA protocol, 79–81, 83
Xid event, 81, 91
XtraBackup, 432, 437
XtraDB, 432

Z

Zawodny, Jeremy D., 316

ZFS (Zettabyte File System), 34, 437

About the Authors

Dr. Charles Bell is a senior software engineer at Oracle. He is currently the lead developer for backup and a member of the MySQL Backup and Replication team. He lives in a small town in rural Virginia with his loving wife. He received his Doctor of Philosophy in Engineering from Virginia Commonwealth University in 2005. His research interests include database systems, versioning systems, semantic web, and agile software development.

Dr. Mats Kindahl is a senior software developer working on the MySQL server. He is the main architect and implementor of MySQL's row-based replication and is responsible for strategic development of replication, reengineering, and the plug-in architecture. Before starting at MySQL, he did research in formal methods, program analysis, and distributed systems, the area where he earned his doctoral degree in computer science. He has also spent many years developing C/C++ compilers and knows more programming languages than he has fingers.

Dr. Lars Thalmann is the development manager for MySQL replication and backup. He is responsible for the strategy and development of these features and leads the corresponding engineering teams. Thalmann has worked with MySQL development since 2001, when he was a software developer working on MySQL Cluster. More recently, he has driven the creation and development of the MySQL Enterprise Backup feature, has guided the evolution of MySQL replication since 2004, and has been a key player in the development of MySQL Cluster replication. Thalmann holds a doctorate in Computer Science from Uppsala University, Sweden.

Colophon

The animal on the cover of *MySQL High Availability* is an American robin (*Turdus migratorius*). Instantly recognizable by its distinctive appearance—dark head, reddish-orange breast, and brown back—this member of the thrush family is among the most common American birds. (Though it shares its name with the European robin, which also has a reddish breast, the two species are not closely related.)

The American robin inhabits a range of six million square miles in North America and is resident year-round through much of the United States. Commonly considered a harbinger of spring, robins are early to sing in the morning and among the last birds singing at night. Their diets consist of invertebrates (often earthworms) and fruit and berries. Robins favor open ground and short grass, so they are frequent backyard visitors, and they are often found in parks, in gardens, and on lawns.

The cover image is from *Johnson's Natural History*, Volume II. The cover font is Adobe ITC Garamond. The text font is Linotype Birka; the heading font is Adobe Myriad Condensed; and the code font is LucasFont's TheSansMonoCondensed.

Get even more for your money.

Join the O'Reilly Community, and register the O'Reilly books you own. It's free, and you'll get:

- 40% upgrade offer on O'Reilly books
- Membership discounts on books and events
- Free lifetime updates to electronic formats of books
- Multiple ebook formats, DRM FREE
- Participation in the O'Reilly community
- Newsletters
- Account management
- 100% Satisfaction Guarantee

Signing up is easy:

1. **Go to: oreilly.com/go/register**
2. **Create an O'Reilly login.**
3. **Provide your address.**
4. **Register your books.**

Note: English-language books only

To order books online:

oreilly.com/order_new

For questions about products or an order:

orders@oreilly.com

To sign up to get topic-specific email announcements and/or news about upcoming books, conferences, special offers, and new technologies:

elists@oreilly.com

For technical questions about book content:

booktech@oreilly.com

To submit new book proposals to our editors:

proposals@oreilly.com

Many O'Reilly books are available in PDF and several ebook formats. For more information:

oreilly.com/ebooks

Spreading the knowledge of innovators   www.oreilly.com

Buy this book and get access to the online edition for 45 days—for free!

MySQL High Availability
By Charles Bell, Mats Kindahl & Lars Thalmann
June 2010, $49.99
ISBN 9780596807306

With Safari Books Online, you can:

Access the contents of thousands of technology and business books

- Quickly search over 7000 books and certification guides
- Download whole books or chapters in PDF format, at no extra cost, to print or read on the go
- Copy and paste code
- Save up to 35% on O'Reilly print books
- **New!** Access mobile-friendly books directly from cell phones and mobile devices

Stay up-to-date on emerging topics before the books are published

- Get on-demand access to evolving manuscripts.
- Interact directly with authors of upcoming books

Explore thousands of hours of video on technology and design topics

- Learn from expert video tutorials
- Watch and replay recorded conference sessions

To try out Safari and the online edition of this book FREE for 45 days,
go to ***www.oreilly.com/go/safarienabled*** and enter the coupon code FYIIPXA.
To see the complete Safari Library, visit safari.oreilly.com.

Spreading the knowledge of innovators

safari.oreilly.com